UNDISCOVERED AMERICA

The 201 great places you may have missed

By Don & Betty Martin

DISCOVERGUIDES • Henderson, Nevada

UNDISCOVERED AMERICA
The 201 great places you may have missed

ꟼ

Library of Congress Cataloging-in-Publication Data
Martin, Don and Betty —
Undiscovered America
1. United States—description and travel

ISBN: 0-942053-46-X

ILLUSTRATIONS: **Bob Shockley,** Mariposa, Calif.

BOOK DESIGN: **Dave Bonnot**, Columbine Type & Design, Sonora, Calif.; and **Judith Stoltenberg**, Blue J Graphics, Twain Harte, Calif.

FRONT COVER: One of America's least visited national parks is among its most beautiful. This undiscovered gem is Great Basin National Park in remote eastern Nevada. *— Don W. Martin*

BACK COVER: A tropical sunset on a solitary beach signals the end of a perfect getaway vacation day. This one could be in Flordia, Lousiana's Gulf Coast, southern California or Hawaii. *— Betty Woo Martin*

The traveler sees what he sees;
the tourist sees what he has come to see.
— Gilbert K. Chesterson

WE'VE BEEN EVERYWHERE, MAN!
Those intriguing places in between

Every time I hear a recording of Johnny Cash singing *I've Been Every-where* (now a TV commercial), I think of our many years on the road. The song, written by Geoff Mack, lists ninety-two different places in North America and we've been to nearly all of them!

The more we travel, the more we realize that it's not the destination that's important, but the journey. It's the opportunity to make new discoveries, to find interesting places that many travelers overlook. When people pick a vacation destination and draw a straight line between departure and arrival points, they miss a lot of intriguing places in between.

In researching nearly two dozen guidebooks and writing hundreds of travel articles, Betty and I have visited every section of our great nation. In our travels, we've encountered scores of lesser-known yet fascinating places. And that's what this book is about. We've selected the 201 best places that you might have missed. They're a mix of interesting old towns, little-visited national parks and monuments, vacation regions and scenic driving tours. They can be the main focus of your next vacation, a fun side trip or just a cause to pause while you're headed somewhere else. Many of our choices are well known regionally but little known nationally.

Are you ready to be surprised? Did you know that the world's oldest Shakespeare festival is not in England but in a small Oregon town? Or that you can experience the great folk music of Appalachia by following a crooked road? Do you know where to find our country's best island vacation hideaways and its most interesting art towns?

We do! Let's go discover Undiscovered America.

Don & Betty Martin

CONTENTS

CHAPTER ONE: THE NORTHWEST & BEYOND

CHAPTER TWO: THE SOUTHWEST

CHAPTER THREE: THE ROCKY MOUNTAIN WEST

CHAPTER FOUR: THE NORTHERN HEARTLAND

CHAPTER FIVE: THE SOUTHERN HEARTLAND

CHAPTER NINE: THE MID-SOUTH

CHAPTER TEN: THE DEEP SOUTH

CHAPTER ELEVEN: THE VERY BEST OF AMERICA — 434

BOOKS BY DON & BETTY MARTIN

Adventure Cruising • 1996
Arizona Discovery Guide • 1990, 1996
Arizona in Your Future • 1991, 1997, 2003
The Best of Denver & the Rockies • 2001
The Best of Phoenix & Tucson • 2001
The Best of San Francisco • 1986, 1990, 1994, 1997, 2002, 2005
The Best of the Gold Country • 1987, 1992
The Best of the Wine Country • 1991, 1995, 2001, 2005
California-Nevada Roads Less Traveled • 1999
Hawai'i: The Best of Paradise • 2003
Inside San Francisco • 1991
Las Vegas: The Best of Glitter City • 1998, 2001, 2003, 2006
Nevada Discovery Guide • 1992, 1997
Nevada in Your Future • 2000, 2004
New Mexico Discovery Guide • 1998
Northern California Discovery Guide • 1993
Oregon Discovery Guide • 1993, 1999
San Diego: The Best of Sunshine City • 1999, 2002
San Francisco's Ultimate Dining Guide • 1988
Seattle: The Best of Emerald City • 2000
The Toll-free Traveler • 1997
The Ultimate Wine Book • 1993, 2000
Undiscovered America • 2006
Utah Discovery Guide • 1995
Washington Discovery Guide • 1994, 2000

Undisco

1
NORTH WEST & BEYOND

Alaska

Hawaii

Washington

Oregon

Montana **3**

Idaho

Wyoming

ROCKY MOUNTAIN WEST

Utah

Colorado

North Dak

NOR HEA

South Dako

Nebraska

Kans

2

Nevada

California

SOUTHWEST

Arizona

New Mexico

5

SOUTH HEARTL

Texas

vered America

Minnesota

...ERN
...ND

Iowa

Missouri

...ma

...N
...D

Wisconsin

Michigan

Illinois | Indiana

Ohio

GREAT
LAKES

6

New York

Pennsylvania

NJ

MD

DE

7

8

Maine

VT

NH

MA

CT

RI

NEW
ENGLAND

MID
ATLANTIC

9

West
Virginia

Kentucky

Tennessee

Virginia

MID SOUTH

North Carolina

South
Carolina

Arkansas

DEEP SOUTH

Mississippi

Louisiana

Alabama

Georgia

10

Florida

ASTORIA WATERFRONT, OR.

Chapter One

The Northwest and Beyond

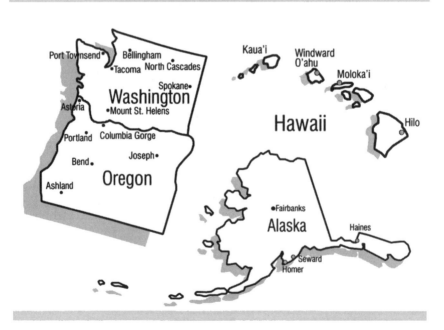

FROM HALIBUT TO HULAS TO HAMLET

We start our journey through Undiscovered America with a very diversified chapter, simply because we have to put our two outlying states somewhere. Hawaii and Alaska present America's two geographic and climatic extremes, from tropic to arctic. The northwestern corner of our nation is home to the country's greatest forest lands and some of its finest alpine scenery.

ALASKA is our last undiscovered place, and we help you find it by providing a sampler of our forty-ninth and largest state. We found Alaska in the halibut-rich waters off the Kenai Peninsula, along the Inside Passage and out on that vast interior that really defines The Great Land.

Where to learn more: Alaska Travel Industry Association, 2600 Cordova St., Suite 201, Anchorage, AK 99501; (907) 929-2200; *www.travel alaska.com.*

HAWAI'I calls us to America's paradise. And you'll know there's more to hula land than Waikiki when we direct you to O'ahu's other side. We also fly you to a soggy town draped with orchids, to the "Garden Isle" with its awesome canyon, and to the most Hawaiian of all the islands.

Where to learn more: Hawai'i Visitors & Convention Bureau, 2270 Kalakaua Ave., #801, Honolulu, HI 96815; (800) GO-HAWAII or (808) 923-1811; *www.gohawaii.com.*

OREGON is the reward that lies at the end of its namesake trail. It offers the diversity of a beautiful coastline, a famous river gorge, America's oldest Shakespeare festival, a region named for a great native peoples' hero, a volcanic vacationland and a really cool city.

Where to learn more: Oregon Tourism Commission, 775 Summer St. NE, Salem, OR 97301; (800) 547-7832; *www.traveloregon.com.*

WASHINGTON is real George. In the only state named for a U.S. President, we explore a headline-making volcano, two waterfront Victorian towns, the Northwest's largest inland city, a little-visited mountain wilderness and Seattle's surprising stepsister.

Where to learn more: Travel Development Division, Department of Commerce & Economic Development, Box 42500, Olympia, WA 98504; (800) 544-1800 or (360) 725-4028; *www.experiencewashington.com.*

Fairbanks
Mini-city in the middle of the Great Land

O̲ur list of the 201 best undiscovered places in America begins with a town and a region that define the term, "The Great Land." Sitting near the state's geographic center, Fairbanks is Alaska's second largest city, although that's not really large. Its population is about 35,000.

Most Alaska-bound visitors head for the Inside Passage or for Anchorage and the adjacent Kenai Peninsula. However, we've always felt that the vast interior represents the true Alaska, with its endless tundra, meandering glacial-fed rivers and great mountain ranges. It's the Alaska of the midnight sun and the *aurora borealis*, of long and surprisingly warm summer days, of tundra marbled with fall color, and of winter sled dog and snowmobile races.

One of our earliest Alaskan memories is of a summer stroll along Fairbanks' Chena River. It was warm and sunny, yet it was nearly midnight! An odd thing about interior Alaskan summers is that visitors experience a sort of reverse jet lag. Since the sun is still shining, they're often wide awake and eager to continue exploring, even though the clock says it's way past their bedtime.

Fairbanks sits in the broad Tanana Valley between the Brooks and Alaska mountain ranges, 358 miles north of Anchorage. It was established in 1901 at the end of navigation on the Chena River. And we mean literally at the end; a riverboat carrying supplies for a trading post ran aground on a mudflat, and that's where the settlement began. It was fortuitous because several gold strikes were made in the area a year later. Then the 1968 discovery of black gold in Prudhoe Bay about 450 miles north kick-started the town's contemporary economy.

Tours to the **North Slope** up the Dalton Highway that parallels the Trans-Alaska Pipeline are popular with visitors. Most groups pause at a rest stop where the road crosses the Arctic Circle, and guests usually are presented with "Midnight Sun" certificates. They continue through the arctic alpine splendor of the Brooks Range and skim the edge of the much-discussed **Arctic National Wildlife Refuge**, then head into the broad North Slope tundra. The highway, hacked out in a hurry after the oil discovery and still mostly gravel, was opened to the public in 1995.

Considerably more popular are tours to nearby **Denali National Park**, offered by several firms. Our favorite is the Denali Star Train of the **Alaska**

Railroad, whose domeliners pass through the park en route to Anchorage. Running daily from mid-May to mid-September, the trips offer several options, including park stopovers, and floating, fishing and flightseeing combinations; (800) 544-0552; *www.alaska railroad.com.*

Don't just leave

But wait! Fairbanks is certainly more than a jumping off place for exploring Alaska's interior. It's a destination in its own right—the northernmost mini-city in America, with the modern amenities to prove it. Yet, it still has a kind of frontier look and attitude, with good-old-boy pickups and even a couple of topless joints. However, it also boasts museums, a few art galleries and a large campus of the University of Alaska.

The Fairbanks campus is home to the **Alaska Museum of the North**, with exhibits on the flora, fauna and history of the area, and an interesting "Dynamic Aurora" multi-media show about the Northern Lights; (907) 474-7505; *www.uaf.edu/museum.* The university also operates the **Large Animal Research Station** on Yankovitch Road just south of town, where visitors can get close to critters of the north; (907) 474-7207; *www.uaf.edu.*

Pioneer Park, a history-based theme attraction on the Chena River, is home to the **Alaska Salmon Bake** cookout and an old fashioned revue at the **Palace Theatre**, (800) 354-7274; *www.akvisit.com.* Other Fairbanks lures include the **Ice Museum**, displaying ice sculptures in an old theater at 500 Second Avenue, (907) 451-8222, *www.icemuseum.com*; *Riverboat Discovery* paddlewheeler cruises, (866) 479-6673, *www.riverboatdiscovery.com;* and **Gold Dredge Number 8**, a survivor from Fairbanks' mining days, a few miles north of town, (907) 457-6058, *www.golddredge8.com.*

Fairbanks is a fine place to witness the *aurora borealis* because the night skies are usually clear and the area is within the *auroral oval.* That's the donut-shaped ring around the North Pole, where most auroras occur. Peak viewing time is late August through April. Aurora-watchers can book dogsled or sleigh rides, snowcat trips and heated wilderness cabins. Also, desk clerks will awaken guests on request, if an aurora display begins.

"We can't make them appear at the flick of a switch," said Roger Smith, director of the university's Geophysical Institute, "but we can provide one of the best places on earth to see them."

Where to learn more

Fairbanks Convention & Visitors Bureau, 550 First Ave., Fairbanks, AK 99701; (800) 327-5774 or (907) 456-5774; *www.explorefairbanks.com.*

Haines

The weather outside is frightful, but the view!

$\mathbb{P}$

A hamlet of about 2,000 contented souls, Haines is one of the smallest, funkiest and least visited places on Alaska's famous Inside Passage. And therein lies much of its appeal. With only a few shops, art galleries and restaurants, it's mercifully spared the cruise ship hoards that swarm ashore in Juneau, Skagway and Ketchikan. Haines gets daily Alaska Ferry service from Juneau, although only a few cruise ships call.

The town occupies a stunning setting, on a tilted coastal shelf of the Chilkat Peninsula, with the snowcapped and glacier-streaked Takshanuk Mountains and the Chilkat Range as dramatic backdrops. In spring and summer, snowmelt waterfalls spill from the heights into foothill forests.

If Haines has a downside, it's the soggy weather. Although it's not as frigid as Alaskan towns farther north, it gets nearly 44 inches of precipitation a year, much of it falling as winter snow. October is the wettest month, although rainfall isn't unusual in summer.

Haines was established as a missionary outpost in 1879 at the request of local Tlingit Indians. None other than John Muir accompanied missionary S. Hall Young up the Inside Passage in a native dugout canoe. Young wrote in his diary that "we were greeted by what seemed to be rather too warm of a reception: a shower of bullets falling unpleasantly about us."

However, Muir's Indian guide Stickeen John shouted that "a great preaching chief and a great ice chief are come to bring you a good message," so the party was allowed to land. A trading post soon was set up and some of Alaska's first canneries were built here, fed by the fish-rich waters of the Inside passage.

Most of the canneries have moved elsewhere and Haines now dozes peacefully in its splendid setting. The Chilkat Peninsula offers some of the best of outdoor Alaska, from fishing and hiking to camping and wildlife viewing. Its most famous wildlife area is the 48,000-acre **Alaska Chilkat Bald Eagle Preserve** in the Chilkat River Valley. From late October through December, thousands of bald eagles converge here to feed on spawning salmon. Indeed, the area is known as the Valley of the Eagles. Two thickly wooded state parks, **Chilkoot Lake** and **Chilkat**, reached by short drives north and south of town, offer wildlife viewing, hiking trails, camping and RV sites.

Haines is a rather serious art and cultural colony, with several galleries and artists-in-residence. The **Chilkat Center** is a venue for a variety of performing arts, and the **Chilkat Dancers** stage "story dances" in their tribal house in summer; (907) 766-2540; *www.tresham.com.*

Haines' cultural focal point is the former **Fort William Seward**, occupying an upslope at the base of grand snowcapped peaks. It was established in 1903 to provide a military presence during a border dispute with Canada. Although it was Alaska's first military installation, it was declared surplus property after World War II. Five former GIs and their families scraped together funds for a down payment and the bought the fort's 400 acres and eighty-five buildings sight unseen. They weren't Alaskan residents; they were *cheechakos* (newcomers) who'd heard that the installation was for sale. Four of the five stuck it out, establishing the community of Port Chilkoot, which later became part of Haines.

Through the decades, they and their descendants have worked to create a community of galleries, restaurants and lodgings at the old fort. **Alaska Indian Arts** has several galleries, workshops and residence artists; (907) 766-2160; *www.alaskaindianarts.com.* Some area artists conduct classes for summer visitors, including **Tresham Gregg**, a descendant of one of the fort buyers; (907) 766-2540; *www.tresham.com.*

Haines' rustic downtown area is compact and walkable, with a trio of museums and half a dozen art galleries. The **Sheldon Museum** at Main and Front Streets is a nicely done archive with exhibits on the flora, fauna, history and native culture of the area; (907) *766-2366; www.sheldonmuseum. org.* Also check out the **American Bald Eagle Foundation Museum** at Second Avenue and Haines Highway, a fine nature center with a large diorama of Alaskan wildlife; (907) 766-3094; *www.baldeagles.org.* The **Hammer Museum** at 108 Main Street is more interesting than it sounds, with a collection of more than 1,400 different hammers; (907) 766-2374.

With its laid-back lifestyle and relatively inexpensive restaurants and lodgings (at least by Alaskan standards), consider Haines as your home base for a summer of exploring the Inside Passage. Camp out, hook up at an RV park or check into one of the town's lodgings. Or you can fly into Haines from Juneau. Small commuter airlines have several flights daily, and the view of glacier-streaked mountains en route is spectacular.

Where to learn more

Haines Convention & Visitors Bureau, P.O. Box 530 (122 Second Ave.), Haines, AK 99827; (800) 458-3579; *www. haines.ak.us.*

Alaska Marine Highway, 6858 Glacier Hwy., Juneau, AK 99801; (800) 526-6731 or (800) 642-0066; *www.akferry.org.*

Homer
Catching the big ones that don't get away

W hile Haines is rustic and charming, Homer is rather homely. However, it also occupies a striking setting, on the edge of Kachemak Bay, with the jagged, snowcapped Kenai Mountains as an imposing backdrop.

Located near the tip of the Kenai Peninsula, this community of about 4,000 is the southernmost town served by highway on the Alaskan mainland. It's 227 miles south of Anchorage, the state's capital and largest city.

Homer was seriously damaged during the 1964 Alaska earthquake, when the community shook, rattled, rolled and dropped six feet. It was rebuilt with little thought for esthetics. Apparently, the rugged Alaskan individualism that resists government authority includes planning commissions.

The main business district is a mismatched scatter along Highway 1, just up from the shore of Kachemak Bay. Most visitor facilities and a large marina occupy the 4.5-mile-long Homer Spit that reaches into the bay like a skinny, crooked finger.

Homer may not be pretty but people aren't drawn here for its civic planning. Many come for its fine salmon and halibut fishing. Freshwater-fed Kachemak Bay and the Gulf of Alaska merge to create one of the world's finest sportfishing grounds. Indeed, Homer is known as the "Halibut Fishing Capital of the World," and it hosts a couple of annual fishing derbies. More than 700 charter and commercial fishing boats operate out of the marina, and that number doubles during the summer.

Folks can fish from shore or from rental boats available at the marina, and several companies offer charter trips. The waters and mudflats also abound with mussels, clams and oysters. Betty, a rank amateur as a fisherperson, came back with two huge salmon after going fishing with a well-run outfit called **Winter King Charters**, (907) 235-9113; *www.winterking.com.* (We enjoyed salmon filets from our freezer for months afterward.)

Homer also is a good base for flightseeing, since it sits on the edge of some of Alaska's most scenic wilderness. **Homer Air** flies over the craggy peaks and icefields of the Kenai Mountains and nearby Kenai Fjords National Park; (907) 235-8591; *www.homerair.com.*

Closer to the ground, the 250,000-acre **Kachemak Bay State Park** directly opposite Homer is popular for wildlife watching, with island bird rookeries, wooded inlets and tidepools. A particularly appealing enclave within the bay is rock-ribbed and tree-clad **Halibut Cove**, where boardwalks link hideaway homes, restaurants, art galleries and rustic resorts. The wooded shoreline of this isolated community is so steep that its homes and shops can be reached only by boat; no road serves the cove.

Three firms offering Kachemak Bay trips are the non-profit **Center for Alaskan Coastal Studies**, (907) 235-6667, *www.akcoastalstudies.org*; **Bay Excursions**, (907) 235-7525; *www.bayexcursions.com*; and **St. Augustine's Kayak & Tours**, (907) 299-1894; *www.homerkayaking.com*.

Back in town, landlubbers can walk or bike a trail that follows the length of Homer Spit. A second walking/biking trail stretches for seven miles along the edge of Kachemak Bay. Birdwatching also is a popular pastime and the **Kachemak Bay Shorebird Festival** is held in early May, with workshops, guided birding tours and an art fair; *www.homeralaska.org/shorebird.htm*.

Visitors can even sip locally-made wines here. **Bear Creek Winery** produces wines from local fruits and imported grapes, with a tasting room on Bear Creek Drive off East End Road; (907) 2]35-3491; *www.bearcreekwineryalaska.com*.

Like Haines, Homer is something of an art town, with several galleries and resident artists. The art community sponsors the "Artrageous Weekend" in early November with gallery open houses, art lectures, demonstrations and tours. Galleries also host art walks the first Friday of each month. These activities are coordinated by the **Homer Council on the Arts**, with a gallery at 355 W. Pioneer Avenue; (907) 235-4288; *www.homerart.org*.

The town also has a couple of fine museums. The Alaska Maritime National Wildlife Refuge, which covers much of the state's coastline, operates the excellent **Alaska Islands & Oceans Visitor Center** at 95 Sterling Hwy.; (907) 226-4619; *www.islandsandocean.org*. The **Pratt Museum** at 3779 Bartlett Street is one of Alaska's best small town archives, focusing on the history and environment of Homer and the Kenai Peninsula; (907) 235-8635; *www.prattmuseum.org*.

Although Homer is famous for its fishing, it was mining that lured its first non-native residents. Homer Pennock set up camp on the spit in 1896, planning to mine shoreline gravels for gold. He didn't find much, although he gave the town his name. Cook Inlet Coal Fields Company arrived three years later and built Homer's first permanent structures. Coal was mined in this area until World War I.

Where to learn more

Homer Chamber of Commerce, P.O. Box 541 (201 Sterling Hwy.), Homer, AK 99603; (907) 235-7740; *www.homeralaska.org*.

Seward
A funky old town with fjords and fishing

Seward happened in 1903 because early railroad builders needed an ice-free port to haul ship cargo into Alaska's interior. And it happened in a very attractive setting. This rustic old town occupies a low coastal flat at the head of Resurrection Bay, across the Kenai Peninsula from Homer.

About 135 miles south of Anchorage, Seward is easily approachable, served by scenic Highway 9, the Alaska Railway, the Alaska Marine Highway ferry system and by occasional cruise ships.

Its rustic downtown area is busy with cafés, tourist shops, art galleries and restaurants. Seward becomes awash with visitors when cruise ships land, although it's rather uncrowded and calm the rest of the time. The small boat harbor about a mile from downtown bustles in summer, mostly with commercial fishing boats, tour charters and bait shops.

Mount Marathon, towering 3,022 feet above Seward, shields two of the reasons many visitors come to town—**Kenai Fjords National Park** and the huge **Harding Icefield**, a 300-square-mile mass left over from the last Ice Age. Several tour operators offer flights over the icefield and cruises into the park's many fjords, where some of the glaciers calve into the sea. Lists of operators and other details are available at the **National Park Visitor Center** at the small boat harbor at 1212 Fourth Avenue.

Visitors can reach the edge of the national park by driving nine miles west to **Exit Glacier**, one of the few drive-up glaciers in America. However, this is but a tiny sample of what can be seen from a coastal cruise or sightseeing flight into the park. Two outfits that we like are **Kenai Fjord Tours**, (877) 777-2805; *www.kenaifjords.com*; and **Major Marine Tours** which are accompanied by park rangers, (800) 764-7300; *www.majormarine.com*. **Sunny Cove Sea Kayaking** offers paddling in the park's fjords; the trips are linked to Kenai Fjord Tours, plus Resurrection Bay paddle trips; (800) 770-9119; *www.sunnycove.com*.

Renown Charters & Tours offers four-hour whale watching trips from the Seward Small Boat Harbor and the firm also has tours to Kenai Fjords; (800) 655-3806 or (907) 224-3806. To see the area from aloft, book a sightseeing flight with **Scenic Mountain Air**, which operates wheeled planes out of Seward Airport and float planes from Trail Lake; (907) 288-3646.

Fishing is excellent in Resurrection Bay. More than thirty operators offer charter trips, and visitors can rent boats and tackle at the harbor. With luck and good gear, even amateur anglers can haul in their share of flippers.

Seward's best attraction is the waterfront **Alaska Sealife Center**, with fine exhibits of marine life above and below the water; (800) 224-2525; *www.alaskasealife.org*. Visitors can visit with Stellar sea lions, harbor seals and seabirds that dive for their dinner in the habitat display. The center has several interactive exhibits and a Discovery Pool where folks can examine tidal creatures. The small **Seward Museum** at 336 Third Avenue offers the usual historical and cultural relics and a nice native basket and ivory collection; (907) 224-3902.

Local operators operate summer dogsledding, both on ice and dry land. For the real thing, book an outing with **Godwin Glacier Dog Sled Tours**; (888) 989-8239 or (907) 234-823; *www.alaskadogsled.com*. Participants are helicoptered to Godwin Glacier, where they learn to mush across icefields. **Ididaride Sled Dog Tours** run wheeled sleds on a two-mile trip through scenic Box Canyon; (800) 478-3139 or (907) 224-8607; *www.ididaride.com*.

Hikers and walkers can follow a 4.5-mile coastal trail to **Caines Head State Recreation Area**, with beaches, meadows, forests, and picnic and camping areas, plus the ruins of a World War II fort; (907) 262-5581. If you're a really serious hiker, you can grunt to the top of Mount Marathon for an absolutely awesome view of Seward and Resurrection Bay. It's about a four-hour trudge.

If this works up an appetite, wrap yourselves around hefty meals at the **Exit Glacier Salmon Bake** restaurant on Exit Glacier Road; (907) 224-2204; *www.sewardalaskacabins.com*.

You've probably guessed this: The town was named for U.S. Secretary of State William Henry Steward, who negotiated the purchase of Alaska from the Czar of Russia in 1867 for $7.2 million. Although that came to about two cents an acre, many naysayers called the deal "Seward's Folly." Folly, indeed! His namesake Alaskan town earns more than that each year, just from tourism. And then there's that oil business on Alaska's North Slope that generates billions in revenue.

Appropriately, the local transit system that links downtown with the harbor is called Seward's Trolley.

Where to learn more

Seward Chamber of Commerce, P.O. Box 749 (Mile 2, Seward Highway), (907) 224-8051; *www.seward.com*.

Kenai Fjords National Park, P.O. Box 1727, Seward, AK 99664; (907) 224-2132 (recorded message) or (907) 224-7500; *www.nps.gov/kefj*.

Alaska Marine Highway, 6858 Glacier Hwy., Juneau, AK 99801; (800) 526-6731 or (800) 642-0066; *www.akferry.org*.

Hilo and about
Paradise with a price: It rains a lot

M̲ost Big Island visitors head for the western shore, seeking the sun-drenched resorts of the Kona and Kohala coasts. So do we, although we also like the Hilo area on the eastern side. It's a virtual tropical paradise with un-crowded and palm-shaded beaches, bayfront parklands, waterfall canyons, orchid farms and quiet neighborhoods shaded by flowering trees.

With all of this appeal, why do most visitors prefer the island's western shore? Because Hilo is the wettest city in America, with an annual rainfall of 130 to 200 inches. Look at the bright side, however. Most of the rain falls at night and without it, this wouldn't be a tropical paradise. In fact, this is the island's tropic agricultural belt.

Hilo, the Big Island's county seat, is a charming old town of about 45,000 residents. Several of its brick and woodframe buildings have a New England or Victorian look, a legacy of its days as a missionary settlement. The low rise, well-tended downtown area is set back from the attractive bay-front, which is lined with parks, gardens and walkways. This appealing look came at a tragic price, however. In 1946 and again in 1960, Hilo was hit by devastating tidal waves that claimed scores of lives and destroyed its rustic waterfront area. After the 1960 *tsunami,* officials decided to build a protec-tive seawall and turn most of the waterfront into parklands.

Lush green residential areas rise steeply from the downtown area, crawl-ing into foothills that present another potential danger. The world's most ac-tive volcanic area is just a few miles southwest of Hilo, much of it within the boundaries of **Hawai'i Volcanoes National Park.** Lava flows have en-gulfed homes and small villages in the region, and one crept within eight miles of Hilo in 1984.

This pleasant town is an easy reach, since Island Air, Aloha and Hawai-ian airlines offer service from Honolulu. Once there, you'll find a good choice of lodgings in town and on its edges, although there are no opulent beach resorts. We like the old but well-kept **Hilo Hawaiian Hotel** just off Hilo Bay at 71 Banyan Drive; (800) 367-5004; *www.castleresorts. com/hhh.* The lushly landscaped Banyan Drive wraps around Hilo's bayfront.

Hilo's most interesting attraction is the **Pacific Tsunami Museum** at 130 Kalakaua Avenue, with high-tech *tsunami* exhibits and displays about the town's two disastrous tidal waves; (808) 935-0926, *www.tsunami.org.*

The **Lyman Museum** occupies an old mission house at 276 Haili Street with exhibits about the old community's early days, (808) 935-5021; *www.lymanmuseum.org*. A short drive inland will take you through green-clad residential areas and to **Wailuku River State Park** and **Rainbow Falls**, which cascades down a 200-foot lava cliff.

Side trips: Lava flows and a paradise coast

Vents from Kilauea Caldera at **Hawai'i Volcanoes National Park** have been erupting continuously since 1983. You may be able to catch some of the action on a flightseeing trip from Hilo or by driving out the park's Chain of Craters Road. The park is less than an hour from Hilo. Once there, take the eleven-mile **Crater Rim Drive** that loops around Kilauea. Learn about volcanic geology at informational signs and pause at turnouts to peer down into that gaping black basin. Trails lead down into the caldera.

The **Chain of Craters Road** tilts 4,000 feet down to the sea, passing through an outerworldly region of craters and glossy black lava fields. Although the road once continued out of the park, it now simply disappears under a lava flow as if it had somehow managed to crawl beneath it. During our last visit, molten magma from one of Kilauea's vents was hissing into the sea and rangers were posted to keep people at a safe distance. We stood in awe, watching great steam clouds rising from the surf.

Back in Hilo, head northwest along the **Hamaka Coast**, a gorgeous mix of rainforests, green-clad canyons spilling with waterfalls, and taro, papaya and macadamia farms. Pretty, uncrowded beach parks line the shoreline and rainforest trees sometimes form canopies over the highway.

About eight miles from Hilo, check out the flora of **Hawai'i Tropical Botanical Gardens**, (808) 964-5233; *www.hawaiigarden.com*. Three miles beyond is **Akaka Falls State Park**, where two cataracts spill down from the slopes of Mauna Kea. The route continues along wooded bluffs cut by sheer-walled canyons. In *Umauma*, head inland for more tropical flora at **World Botanical Gardens** near *Honomu*, (808) 963-5427.

Just beyond are two old plantation towns dozing in the sun, **Pa'auilo** and **Honoka'a.** The route swings inland at Honoka'a, taking you through **Parker Ranch** and ultimately to the Big Island's western side.

Where to learn more

Big Island Visitors Bureau, 250 Keawe St., Hilo, HI 96720; (800) 648-2441 or (808) 961-5797; *www.bigisland.org*.

Hawai'i Volcanoes National Park, P.O. Box 52, Hawai'i Volcanoes National Park, HI 96718-0052; (808) 985-6000; *www.nps.gov/havo*.

Kaua'i
Discoveries on a treasured island

This undiscovered treasure is not a town or a region; it's an entire island. And what an island! If you want to see all of Hawai'i but have time for only one isle, it should be Kaua'i. This is a true Hawaiian sampler, with awesome cliffs and chasms, tropical lowlands, rainforests, waterfalls cascading into hidden grottoes, beautiful beaches and a few luxurious resorts.

All Kaua'i lacks is crowds, traffic congestion and mega-malls. Why more people don't visit this treasured island is a mystery, although most of its 58,000 residents probably prefer it that way.

There are essentially three resort areas on the island—**Po'ipu** on Kaua'i's southern tip, with several upscale resorts; the **Coconut Coast** just north of Lihu'e, with a few mid-range resorts; and verdant **Princeville** on the island's northern end, which shelters some quite opulent getaways.

The oldest of Hawai'i's islands, Kaua'i emerged from the sea as a single shield volcano about five to six million years ago. Centuries of pummeling by wind, rain and sea have shaped two dramatic landforms—imposing Waimea Canyon and the fluted, impossibly sheer seacliffs of Na Pali Coast.

The best way to see these attractions is by air and water. **Air Kaua'i** has helicopter flights into Waimea Canyon and along Na Pali Coast, (800) 972-4666, *www.airkaui.com*; and **Liko Kaua'i** offers snorkel/sightseeing cruises beneath the Na Pali cliffs; (888) SEA-LIKO; *www.liko-kauai.com.*

The island also is easy to explore on land since it has just two main roads. They lead in opposite directions from the airport at *Lihu'e*, near the island's southeastern corner. (Can a round island have corners?) Lihu'e is the county seat and the only town of any size, which isn't much; population is less than 6,000. It's also the least attractive area of an otherwise beautiful island, but some place has to serve the mundane role of commercial center.

Two scenic drives, each easily done within a day, will take you to Kaua'i's most popular destinations—Waimea Canyon west and then north of Lihu'e, and the Na Pali Coast, reached by going north from the airport.

First, check out a pair of Lihu'e lures. The **Kaua'i Museum** at 4428 Rice Street is one of Hawai'i's better small-town archives, with a time line theme and a collection of Polynesian artifacts; (808) 245-6931; *www.kauaimuseum.org*. **Grove Farm Homestead**, west of town at 4050 Nawiliwili Street, is a preserved 1864 sugar plantation with tours of the elaborate mansion and the surrounding farmyard; (808) 245-3202.

West of Lihu'e, you can either take Highway 520 down to the *Po'ipu* resort area, or follow Highway 50 to *Hanapepe*, a former sugar town that has become a mini-art center. Just beyond, the **Gay & Robinson Sugar Plantation** and factory offers interesting public tours; (808) 335-2824.

Waimea, another old sugar town, is the gateway to **Waimea Canyon**. This spectacular chasm is carved into the slopes **Mount Wai'ale'ale**, the wettest place on earth, with an annual rainfall of 428 inches. Visitor facilities are pleasantly rustic, consisting of a museum/interpretive center, store and basic lodgings. Trails lead into the Wai'ale'ale wilds; (808) 335-9975.

If you head north from Lihu'e on Highway 56, you'll pass a string of resorts and small towns along the **Coconut Coast**, one of the few areas of the island that's relatively level. Silky green mountains form a dramatic backdrop to this region of resorts, golf courses and palm groves.

You'll shortly encounter **Smith's Tropical Paradise**, a *faux* Polynesian village with attractive botanical gardens. This is the launch point for boat rides on the Wailua River to the **Fern Grotto**, the island's most popular tourist gimmick; (808) 821-6895; *www.smithskauai.com.* Above Smith's, follow Highway 380 inland to **Opaeka'a Falls**, set in a box canyon. Nearby is one of Hawai'i's undiscovered gems, **Kamokila Hawaiian Village**; (808) 822-4826. It's a living history replica of a early day settlement.

Several miles beyond the scattered town of **Kapa'a**, watch on your right for the turnoff to **Kilauea Lighthouse and National Wildlife Refuge**, a bird-busy promontory with a visitor center and fine bird-viewing sites; (808) 828-1413. Five miles further is the planned community of *Princeville* with several upscale resorts. The highway then drops down into *Hanalei*, a funky old town that's become gentrified in the name of tourism.

West of Hanalei, the highway twists along the edge of palm-draped **Hanalei Bay**, one of the most idyllic settings in all Hawai'i. A sign marks pristine **Lumahai Beach**, where Mitzi Gaynor tried to wash Rossano Brazzi out of her hair in *South Pacific*. A bit farther along is **Ha'ena Beach Park** with picnic and swimming areas. Nearby **Limahuli Garden** has one of the state's best collections of tropical flora; (808) 826-1053; *www.ntbg.org.*

You'll hit road's end at **Ha'ena State Park** beside the spectacular **Na Pali cliffs**. You can explore a couple of huge lava caves and relax at **Ke'e Beach**. If you've come prepared to hike, follow the **Kalalau Trail** two miles along the cliffs to hidden Hanakapiai Beach.

Where to learn more

Kaua'i Visitors Bureau, 4334 Rice St., Suite 101, Lihu'e, HI 96766; (800) 262-2400; *www.kauaidiscovery.com.*

Moloka'i
Hawai'i, the way it was

ᛈ

It is perhaps unfortunate that Moloka'i is famous mostly for its Kalaupapa leper colony. It has given the pretty isle an undeserved reputation for sorrow and suffering. The island is even shunned by other travel guides. The thick *Rough Guide to USA* and *Let's Go Travel Guide USA* both have Hawai'i sections but they don't even mention Moloka'i.

That's a pity because this is a very appealing place, with uncrowded white sand beaches, lush forests, dramatic seacliffs and funky old towns. No buildings are taller than a palm tree and the island has not a single traffic light. Still, the island provides the comfort of modern resorts. Moloka'i has the true flavor of old Hawai'i. Sixty percent of its 7,000 residents have mostly Hawaiian genes. Life moves at a leisurely pace here. A sign at the airport advises arriving passengers: *Aloha! This is Moloka'i. Slow down!*

Ironically, the Kalaupapa leper colony is no longer a place to be shunned. Now a national historic park, it's one of the island's most popular tourist attractions. Although leprosy is completely curable, many of its former victims choose to remain at the colony, which occupies a lava peninsula at the base of a steep, brushy seacliff.

A fun way to get there is aboard one of the **"Moloka'i Mules"** that plod down a cliff-edge switchback trail from **Pal'au State Park**. Once at the bottom, one is struck by the peninsula's beauty. It's lushly vegetated, with a rough, lava-ridged shoreline. Rainforests reach inland to the base of towering cliffs. After visitors climb stiffly from their mules, they board a tour bus that's usually driven by a former leper. The tour includes the old village, an historic lighthouse, the prim white St. Francis Church with an adjacent museum, and the original leper colony site, where grassy lawns surround two old churches. One is dedicated to Father Damien, who treated the lepers here for sixteen years until he died of the disease in 1889 at the age of 49.

Mule rides and tours are popular and must be booked well in advance. For the mules—**Moloka'i Mule Rides,** (800) 567-7550, *www.muleride.com;* and for colony tours—**Damien Tours,** (808) 567-6171.

For an island measuring only ten by thirty-eight miles, Moloka'i is rather diverse. The western half varies from cactus to dry grasslands, with a few abandoned cane and pineapple fields and sparkling white sand beaches. The eastern half is mountainous and lush, topped by 4,970-foot Mount Kamakou, and it boasts the world's highest seacliffs, rising 3,000 feet from the surf.

When you fly into Moloka'i, you'll land near tiny *Ho'olehua* on the island's western side. The rolling sprawl of **Moloka'i Ranch** is just to the west, with the tidy ranch town of *Maunaloa* as its retail center. The island's most upscale digs are here: the full-service **Sheraton Moloka'i Lodge** and **Kaupoa Beach Village** (877) 726-4656, *www.molokai-ranch com*; and **Kaluakoi Villas**, (800) 367 5004; *www.castleresorts.com.*

Go east briefly from Maunaloa, turn northwest onto Kaluakoi Road and follow it four miles through dry scrubland to **Kepuhi Bay**. You'll pass through a resort area that stalled out during an economic slump, although there are a few lodgings here. Go south from Kepuhi Bay to **Papohaku Beach Park**, a three mile stretch of dazzling white sand. You can see **O'ahu** from here, across the Kaiwi Channel.

Most of Moloka'i's attractions are on the island's other end. Take Highway 460 east to the village of *Kualapu'u* and visit the **Moloka'i Coffee Company**, (800) 709-BEAN, *www.molokaicoffee.com.* From here, Highway 470 climbs steeply into **Pala'au State Park**, the gateway to the mule rides and the Kalaupapa leper colony. You can pause at a Kalaupapa overlook, and hike some of the park's trails into lush tropical forest.

Return to Kualapu'u and follow Highway 450 west to funky old *Kaunakakai*, the only Moloka'i town of any size, and that's not much. Its weathered main street has a few curio shops, galleries and small cafés. Pressing westward, you'll soon encounter our favorite place to stay on the island, the Polynesian style beachside resort of **Hotel Moloka'i**, (800) 535-0085; *www.hotelmolokai.com.*

Just beyond the hotel, you'll slip into some of the most beautiful coastal scenery in the islands. Its vistas surpass the more famous drive to Hana on Maui which, incidentally, is visible just across the Lahaina Roadstead. The route rarely leaves the coast as it travels past palm-lined beaches, ancient lava-walled fish ponds, verdant pasturelands and forests. Worth a pause is the restored **Church of St. Joseph's**, built by Father Damien in 1876.

After twisting for several more miles along this unspoiled coast, the road ends in the **Halawa Valley**. It's an awesome setting, right out of a Hollywood movie. The valley is cradled by steep seacliffs and two waterfalls spill from their heights. A river winds lazily into a small crescent bay with an inviting beach of sand, cobbled lava stones and beach grass.

It's the sort of place you really won't want to leave.

Where to learn more

Moloka'i Visitors Association, P.O. Box 960, Kaunakakai, HI 96748; (800) 800-6367; *www.molokai-hawaii.com.*

Windward Oʻahu
The quiet side of a busy island

⌘

While not the largest of Hawaiʻi's islands, Oʻahu is certainly the most popular. More than half of the state's seven million visitors spend their vacations there and the vast majority—ninety percent—focus on Honolulu's famous Waikiki Beach area. The only real metropolis in the state, Honolulu is one of our favorite big cities. And Waikiki, although crowded and commercialized, still seems like some idyllic haven out of an Elvis Presley movie.

When we want to escape from those crowds, we head for the windward side of the island. The scenery's grand, some of the towns are charming, the beaches are pretty and the farther you go, the thinner the crowds, except for a few popular attractions along the way.

Escaping from Waikiki is easy, but take a good map because there isn't space here for detailed directions of our drive. Follow Kalakaua Avenue east and just keep going. The route travels along the foothills of **Diamond Head** above Maunalua Bay, with beach parks, picnic areas and elegant homes. You'll soon encounter **Hanauma Bay Nature Preserve**, which is definitely not uncrowded, since it's a popular snorkeling area; (808) 396-4229.

The highway continues along a wind and wave sculpted coast, then drops onto a coastal plain at **Sandy Beach Park**, which is rarely crowded. Just beyond is the popular **Sea Life Park** with performing sea critters and aquariums; (808) 259-7933; *www.dolphindiscovery.com/hawaii*.

From here, the terrain changes from the low semi-arid slopes of the southeast coast to the dramatically fluted and green-clad cliffs of the Koʻolau Range. You'll pass through the pleasantly scruffy beach town of *Waimanalo*, then skim the western edges of *Kailua* and *Kaneʻohe*, ordinary towns in a splendid setting at the base of those accordion-creased cliffs. Using your map—you did bring it, didn't you?—drive out to **Kailua Beach Park** with its rolling lawn areas, shade trees and beaches of tawny sand.

From the park, use your map to stay close to the edges of **Kailua Bay** and then **Kaneʻohe Bay**. The town of *Kaneʻohe* is the largest community on Oʻahu's windward side, a good place for provisions, food and fuel. Follow your map to **Hoʻomaluhia Botanic Garden**, (808) 233-7323, *www. co.honolulu.ci.us/parks*; and then to the pretty **Valley of the Temples** memorial park, with its ornate **Byodo-In Buddhist Temple**; (808) 239-8811.

Pick up the Kamehameha Highway, which will be your main route for most of the rest of the drive. It passes three parks along the bayfront, then enters rather unpopulated coastal countryside. After passing through a scattering of small towns, it skims **Kahana Valley State Park** and **Sacred Falls State Park**. (Sacred Falls was closed when we last passed.) Three miles beyond is the state's most visited attraction, the **Polynesian Cultural Center**, with mockup villages and shows representing various South Pacific societies; (808) 293-3333; *www.polynesia.com.*

Pressing onward, you'll encounter the large **Malaehana State Recreation Area** and then rustic and rusting **Kahuku Sugar Mill**, with a shopping complex nearby. The mill was closed to visitors for safety reasons in 2001, so the adjacent businesses are drying up. Have lunch at the **"Famous Kahuku Shrimp Truck"** if it's still there. It occupies an old delivery van that now delivers tasty fried shrimp and calamari through a takeout window. Picnic tables are adjacent. A couple of miles past the sugar mill is the oceanfront **Turtle Bay Resort**, the most elaborate retreat on O'ahu's windward side; (800) 203-3650; *www.turtlebayresort.com.*

You're now on O'ahu's **North Shore**, home to world surfing championships and the infamous Banzai Pipeline, the wildest surf on the planet. Before visiting Hawai'i's hottest surfing area, pause at quiet and gorgeous little **Kawela Beach** about a mile past Turtle Bay. No sign marks it; just pull off the highway at the first beach park you see. Beyond here, **Sunset Beach** of surfing fame stretches for two miles. Again, there's no sign; it starts near a traffic light in the surfer-bum hamlet of **Kahikilani**. About five miles beyond the Sunset Beach area is beautiful **Waimea Falls Park**, with elaborate botanical gardens; (808) 638-8511; *www.hawaiiweb.com.*

Pressing onward, pass large **Hale'iwa Beach Park** and fork to the right onto Highway 830 for funkily historic *Hale'iwa*. This former sugar town is now a popular visitor stop, with shops, boutiques and galleries occupying old false front buildings. Hale'iwa's lures include the **North Shore Surfing Museum** in the North Shore Marketplace (808) 637-8888; the restored 1832 **Lili'uokalani Church**; and **M. Matsumoto Grocery Store**, famous for shave ice. (Think of shave ice as a snow cone, Hawaiian style.)

Beyond Hale'iwa at **Dillingham Field**, you can take a glider ride above the scenic north coast with **Honolulu Soaring**; (808) 637-0207; *www.honolulusoaring.com.* Continue to road's end at **Ka'ena Point State Park**. There are nice views from here, but no facilities. A jeep road used as a hiking trail leads four miles out to Ka'ena Point, O'ahu's northwestern tip.

Where to learn more

O'ahu Visitors Bureau, 735 Bishop St., Suite 35, Honolulu, HI 96813; (877) 525-OAHU; *www.visit-oahu.com.*

Ashland
Brush up your Shakespeare

Nay, good fellow. 'Tis not Stratford-Upon-Avon or London's Old Vic that boasts the world's oldest Shakespeare festival. 'Tis a small former lumber town called Ashland. The annual celebration of the Bard is the centerpiece of this tree-clad community in the Siskiyou Mountain foothills of southwestern Oregon.

Ashland is a handsome little town with a neat-as-a-pin business district, an active university campus and one of America's prettiest public parks. Its **Oregon Shakespeare Festival** is the world's longest-lived celebration of the Bard, and one of America's oldest and largest professional repertory theater companies. Each year, it lures more than 100,000 visitors, who buy more than 350,000 tickets. That a town of about 21,000 people can support such a venture is surprising. That it's nearly 300 miles from the nearest large city—Portland—is amazing.

Despite the festival's name, it isn't all about the Bard. A large troupe of theater professionals presents a mix of Elizabethan and contemporary classics and occasional new dramas in three venues—the outdoor Elizabethan Theatre (summers only), the modern Angus Bowmer Theatre and the intimate New Theatre. The season extends from February through October, featuring nearly eight hundred performances of eleven different plays. In the summer, all Ashland becomes an Elizabethan festival, with entertainment, foods, tours, classes and workshops.

Adjacent to the Shakespeare complex, **Lithia Park** decorates the banks of cascading Ashland Creek for more than a mile. It was named for a spritzy mineral water that contains lithium salts. The town was popular as a health spa during the first third of the last century. For a sip of Lithia water—it's an acquired taste—there's a public fountain on the Plaza, a small wedge formed by Main Street and Winburn Way near the entrance to the park.

Shakespeare came to town in 1935 when Angus L. Bowmer, a drama teacher from Ashland State Normal School (now Southern Oregon University) asked the city to underwrite the production *Twelfth Night* as part of its annual Fourth of July Celebration. Officials agreed to advance him a sum "not to exceed $400," but only if he would permit boxing matches as a financial backup. The pugilists lost money and Shakespeare won, earning enough to offset the boxing matches' deficit. Bowmer remained the festival's driving force until his retirement in 1971, producing, directing and often acting in the shows. He died in 1979.

The Oregon Shakespeare Festival fertilizes a cultural garden that has made this region one of the most artistically rich in America. Ashland is home four other theater groups, and it has an active arts scene, with more than two dozen galleries and several artists in residence. The Ashland Gallery Association sponsors **Friday Art Walks** the first Friday of each month.

The restored former mining town of *Jacksonville*, twelve miles northwest of Ashland, hosts the **Peter Britt Festivals** from June through September. They offer a musical mix ranging from jazz and folk to classic and pops, drawing top national performers. The festivals were named in honor of Peter Britt, a pioneer Oregon photographer and horticulturist. They're held on the elaborate grounds of his former estate; (800) 882-7488; *www.brittfest.org.*

Even folks with tin ears will enjoy a visit to Jacksonville, with its brick-front national historic district busy with shops and restaurants, its courthouse museum and other historic sites. Dating from 1852, Jacksonville was the site of the Pacific Northwest's first gold discovery.

A dozen miles up Interstate 5 from Ashland, *Medford* is the region's commercial center and the Jackson County seat. It's home to the **Ginger Rogers Craterian Theater**, a refurbished movie house that books top performers. It's also the home stage for the Rogue Valley Symphony, Ballet Rogue Company and Rogue Opera; (541) 779 3000; *www.craterian.org.*

This area offers lures outdoors as well. **Bear Creek Greenway**, a walking-biking path, extends for twenty-one miles along Bear Creek between Ashland and Central Point just north of Medford. **Emigrant Lake** six miles east of Ashland provides swimming, fishing, boating and a water slide.

Mount Ashland Ski Resort, run by the City of Ashland, is about a dozen miles south in the Siskiyou Mountains off I-15; (541) 482-2897; ski report (541) 482-2754; *www.mtashland.com.*

Where to learn more

Ashland Chamber of Commerce, P.O. Box 1360 (110 E. Main St.), Ashland, OR 97520; 482-3486; *www.ashlandchamber.com.*

Jacksonville Chamber of Commerce, P.O. Box 33 (185 N. Oregon St.), Jacksonville, OR 97530; (541) 899-8118; *www.jacksonvilleoregon.org.*

Medford Visitors & Convention Bureau, 101 E. Eighth St., Medford, OR 97501; (541) 779-4847; *www.visitmedford.org.*

Oregon Shakespeare Festival, 15 S. Pioneer St., Ashland, OR 97520; (541) 482-4331; *www.orshakes.org.*

Astoria

Discoveries at the end of the Lewis & Clark trail

🏳

Most of the commotion concerning the bicentennial of Lewis & Clark's trek across the continent has died down. However, the town that was born at the end of their trail still thrives as a popular visitor destination.

When Captain Meriwether Lewis and William Clark reached the mouth of the Columbia River in 1805, they needed a place to hang out for the winter. They built a crude log settlement they called Fort Clatsop, named for local Indians. Later, Boston fur baron John Jacob Aster sent agents to establish a site for shipping furs to Asia.

His Fort Astoria was built in 1811, a few miles from the Lewis & Clark encampment. Local chamber of commerce folks proudly insist that it's the oldest American settlement west of the Mississippi. Well sort of, although the British chased Astor's men out in 1812 and the area wasn't reoccupied for another thirty years.

But never mind that. Astoria is an appealing old town of about 10,000 citizens, with Victorian homes tucked among hillside trees, several historic sites and a rustic waterfront that suggests a setting for Rogers & Hammerstein's *Carousel*. In fact, the town has been the setting for several films, including such forgettable epics as *Kindergarten Cop* and *The Goonies*.

However, the waterfront is hardly a movie prop. Strung along Marine Drive, it's a busy working area of tugs, commercial fishing boats and charters. Piers Six and Eleven offer an assortment of curio shops and restaurants.

Although Astoria is inland, the mouth of the Columbia is so wide here that early navigators thought it was a large inlet. The opposite bank, in Washington state, is so distant that it looks like an offshore island. The two shores are linked by the imposing four-mile-long high-arched **Astoria Bridge.** It's worth crossing just to enjoy the views and watch cargo ships navigate the river's tricky sandbars and shoals below. As American sea captain Robert Gray learned when he sailed into the river's mouth in 1792, this is a very dangerous channel. He realized that he'd discovered a great river and he named it for his ship, the *Columbia Rediviva*.

The mighty Pacific is just around the corner, marking the beginning of the **Oregon Coast Highway** that passes some of the finest seastack scenery on the planet. Astoria is worth a few days' pause before heading down that legendary road. Expect to get wet, since the town receives more than sixty-five inches of rainfall a year. However, July and August are fairly dry, and all of that rain produces the lush forests that bedeck the hills above town.

The area's most popular attraction is **Lewis and Clark National Historical Park** near Astoria's neighboring town of *Warrenton*. It's a faithful reconstruction of Lewis & Clark's log fort, down to the last wooden peg and squared nail. Rangers in period costume demonstrate musketry, candle-making and other skills of the time. A six-mile **Fort to Sea Trail** was completed in 2006, re tracing a footpath that Lewis & Clark's crew blazed to reach the ocean; (503) *861- 2471; www.nps.gov/focl.*

Another interesting stop is **Fort Stevens State Park** on Oregon's northwesternmost tip, where the Columbia meets the Pacific. It was built during the Civil War to protect the area from invasion by sea and it remained on duty until the end of World War II. The only enemy who ever fired on it was the impudent crew of a Japanese submarine in 1942. The men on watch were so startled that they forgot to shoot back. The fort's visitor offerings include hiking trails, a war games museum, campsites and old coastal artillery batteries; (503) 861-2000; *www.oregonstateparks.gov.*

Back in Astoria, the **Columbia River Maritime Museum** at the riverfront on Marine Drive is one of the Northwest's finest archive; (503) 325-2323; *www.crmm.org.* Excellent exhibits, from shipwrecks to ships models, trace the story seafaring, with a special focus on the Columbia River and the maritime heritage of the Northwest. **Flavel House Museum** features regional history exhibits and several handsomely furnished rooms, in a restored 1885 Victorian at 441 Eighth Street (503) 325-2203. More of Astoria's yesterdays are on display in a neoclassical building at the **Heritage Museum**, 1618 Exchange St.; (503) 325-2203.

A requisite stop is **Astoria Column**, a 125-foot barber pole that overlooks the city from Coxcomb Hill. It was erected in 1926, with a spiral frieze depicting the westward movement. If you climb the 164-step spiral stairway inside the column's gloomy interior, you'll be rewarded with a splendid view of the surrounding countryside.

After your climb, you should have an appetite for a seafood lunch or dinner. Since we're plebeians, we like the old fashioned **Ship Inn** which has been serving great fish and chips at Second Street and Marine Drive for decades; (503) 325-0033. Also popular is the funky **Columbian Café** at 1114 Marine Drive; (503) 325-2233. For seafood to go, stop by the legendary **Josephson's Smokehouse**, which has been producing tasty smoked fish since 1920. It's at 106 Marine Dr.; (503) 325-2190; *www.josephsons.com.*

Where to learn more

Astoria-Warrenton Area Chamber of Commerce, P.O. Box 176 (111 W. Marine Dr.), Astoria, OR 97103; (800) 875-6807; *www.oldoregon.com.*

Bend and beyond
Central Oregon's vast vacationland

꒰

Oregonians know that the central part of their state is a grand outdoor playground, and they come by the tens of thousands to do so, both in summer and winter.

Described variously as Oregon's High Desert, Lava Lands or just central Oregon, the area is a mix of rushing rivers, quiet fishing lakes, tortured volcanic areas, forests and ski slopes. And it's backdropped by the dramatic spires of the Cascade Range. About all Oregon's High Desert lacks is desert, although that's the term climatologists use. It receives only about twelve inches of precipitation a year—much of it as snow—because it lies in the rainshadow of the Cascades.

However, the mountains' eastern watershed feeds the region's pine forests, lakes and streams. The area's largest river, the northward-flowing Deschutes, is a serious whitewater stream and several local outfitters offer an assortment of soggy trips.

Although the region is relatively level—we like to use the term "tree plain"—it tilts up toward the Cascades and parts of the region have been wrinkled by thousands of years of volcanic activity.

A town with a dull name but a strong vacation reputation, **Bend** is the center of all this. With a population of about 55,000, it's large enough to provide all the essential services. Although this region is far from any major city, it's so popular that **Redmond Airport** just north of Bend has scheduled air service, with several flights daily; (541) 548-0646; *www.flyrdm.com.*

Bend has an abundance of lodgings, and several resorts and dude ranches are in the surrounding area. The largest resort, eighteen miles below Bend, is actually a community. The large, thickly wooded *Sunriver* complex has three golf courses, its own airport, a meandering stream and several small lakes, plus a shopping center and a mix of lodge rooms, condos and vacation homes; (800) 801-8765; *www.sunriver-resort.com.*

Newberry National Volcanic Monument covers 50,000 acres of old lava flows, lakes and cindercones southeast of Bend. The U.S. Forest Service calls the region Lava Lands because of its broad mix of volcanic features. The Lava Lands Visitor Center is off Highway 97, eleven miles south of Bend at the base of **Lava Butte**, a 500-foot cindercone. A lookout at the top provides fine view of this vast tree plain and many of the more than 400 other cindercones that break its surface. **Lava River Cave** is a mile-long lava tube that would make a great wine cellar; bring a jacket.

The other major Lava Lands lure is **Newberry Crater,** farther south on Highway 97 and then east on paved Forest Road 21. It's a massive caldera with two lakes, and a scenic drive to the summit of Paulina Peak. There are several hiking trails, including one to an area of glittering obsidian. If you'd like to spend the night in a caldera, **Paulina Resort** offers rustic cabin lodgings, plus a restaurant, general store and boat rentals; (541) 536-2240.

Don't miss the **High Desert Museum** on 150 wooded acres just south of Bend on U.S. 97; (541) 382-4754; *www.highdesertmuseum.org.* It's one of the finest indoor-outdoor history and nature centers in America. Exhibits cover the geology, geography, flora, fauna and human history of the region. They range from realistic historical dioramas to fenceless animal grottos.

The scenic 87-mile **Cascade Lakes Drive** starts in Bend and winds through the Cascade foothills, offering views of the area's signature volcanic peaks, the **Three Sisters** and **Broken Top.** Another notable peak, standing off from his "sisters," is **Mount Bachelor,** a major ski resort that also has a summer program; (800) 829-2442; *www.mtbachelor.com.* The scenic drive passes a parade of good fishing lakes, then hits Highway 97 at Sunriver.

If you'd like to get closer to the volcanic peaks that tower over this area, take the **Cascade Loop Drive.** It starts at the deliberately rustic-chic wannabe cowboy town of *Sisters* twenty-one miles northwest of Bend. You'll want to browse about this "cowpoke Carmel" before heading into the hills.

Drive west on State Route 242 and climb a steep fifteen miles up to **McKenzie Pass,** surrounded by a massive field of rough lava. The area looks like a coal mine that exploded. Should you care to hike north to Canada or south to Mexico, the **Pacific Crest Scenic Trail** passes through here. A less ambitious hike south will take you into the gorgeous alpine foothills of the **Three Sisters Wilderness.** Six mostly uphill miles gets you to Collier Glacier, Oregon's largest icefield.

Back behind the wheel, spiral downhill through the heavily wooded western slope of the Cascades to *Belknap Springs.* Turn north onto State Route 126 and follow the McKenzie River along the lower edge of the **Mount Washington Wilderness.** After twenty miles, turn east on U.S. 20 and cross over **Santiam Pass** to get you back to Bend and its neighbors.

Where to learn more

Central Oregon Visitors Association, 661 SW Powerhouse Dr., Suite 1301, Bend, OR 97702; (800) 800-8334; *www.covisitors.com.*

Newberry National Volcanic Monument, Lava Lands Visitor Center, 58201 S. Highway 97, Bend, OR 97707; (541) 593-2421; *www.fs.fed.us/r6/centraloregon.*

Columbia River Gorge
America's parade of waterfalls

⚑

The Columbia is one of the nation's great rivers, draining eighty-five percent of the Northwest's land area. Of all the streams in North America, only the Mississippi, St. Lawrence and Mackenzie have a greater water volume. Starting high in the Canadian Rockies, the Columbia carries more water to the Pacific than any other stream.

Its most spectacular feature is the Columbia Gorge east of Portland, where the mighty river carved a swath through the Cascade Range. Within the last 100,000 years, Ice Age glaciers in present-day Montana and Idaho alternately dammed upstream rivers and then broke loose. Great walls of water called the "Missoula Floods" thundered across the Northwest. They carved deep gorges in eastern Washington's landscape and ripped away the Oregon side of the Cascades to create 1,000-foot basaltic cliffs. Creeks that once meandered down to the Columbia River were left hanging in midair, creating the gorge's famous parade of waterfalls.

Idealistic highway builders

Enter Samuel Hill, an idealistic pacifist and entrepreneur. Early in the last century, he built a mansion and started a utopian Quaker farm community in Maryhill, Washington, across the Columbia from Briggs, Oregon. To reach his utopia, he convinced Portland businessmen and state officials to help him build a road along the Oregon side of the Columbia. With engineer and landscape architect Samuel C. Lancaster in charge, they created America's first scenic highway.

Construction began in 1913 and was completed nine years later. The first paved road in the Northwest, this was no mere highway, but a work of engineering art in the classic European style. Lancaster incorporated into his design Florentine viaducts and handsome mortar-free stonework in bridge railings, arches and retaining walls.

The Columbia River Highway later became part cross-country U.S. Highway 30. After the completion of a water-level route in 1954 (now Interstate 84), the surviving section of the road was designated as the **Historic Columbia River Highway**.

To travel this scenic road, one must be in no hurry, since Lancaster cantilevered it high into the basaltic cliffs, with many curves and frequent turnouts to enjoy the views. And he designed it to pass close to the Columbia Gorge's many waterfalls.

Although much of the original 74-mile-long highway has been abandoned or buried under new road construction, about fourteen miles remain relatively untouched. This portion can be reached via I-84 exit 22 on the western end near *Corbett*, or exit 35 on the east side near *Dodson*. The meandering route passes eight waterfalls that can be reached either from turnouts or short hikes. The most famous is 620-foot **Multnomah Falls**, the fourth highest in cataract America. Near its base, the bold stone Normandy style 1925 **Multnomah Falls Lodge** has a restaurant, gift and souvenir shop, snack bar and a U.S. Forest Service information center; (503) 695-2376; *www.multnomahfallslodge.com.*

Our personal waterfall favorite is **Upper Horsetail Falls**, accessible via a half-mile switchback trail from the **Horsetail Falls** parking area. The views of the Columbia River Gorge are awesome from up here, and what's really neat is that the trail leads behind the falls. It's like looking at the world through marbled glass.

Near the scenic drive's midpoint is **Crown Point Vista House**, which has been drawing in Model-T's and tour buses since 1917. Perched 725 feet above the river, this circular pre-art deco stone structure has a gift shop, Forest Service interpretive center and lots of big windows for Columbia Gorge viewing; (503) 695-2230.

Only Multnomah Falls Lodge and Crown Point offer visitor facilities on the historic route, although they're abundant in the towns of *Cascade Locks, Hood River* and *The Dalles* to the east. Also worth a look in the region are Hill's **Maryhill Mansion**, now an art museum; and a replica of **Stonehenge** that Hill had constructed as a monument to fallen heroes of World War I. They're both just across the river from *Biggs*, via I-84 exit 104. Also, **Bonneville Dam** near Cascade Locks and **McNary Dam** just beyond Biggs have tour facilities. If you'd like to bike or hike a section of the former scenic highway that's now closed to vehicle traffic, check out the **Historic Columbia River Highway State Trail.** It runs between I-84 exits 64 near Hood River and exit 69; *www.oregonstateparks.org.*

Where to learn more

Columbia River Gorge Visitor's Association, 2149 W. Cascade, #106-A, Hood River, OR 97031; (800) 98-GORGE; *www.crvga.org.*

Other useful websites are *www.columbiariverhighway.com* and the Oregon Department of Transportation's *www.odot.state.or.us/hcrh*. Also, go to the National Park Service's *www.cr.nps.gov*, then type "Historic Columbia River Highway" in the search box.

Joseph and Hells Canyon
History, scenery and art at the end of a road

꒥

One of the intrigues of wandering America's highways is reaching the end of a road and finding something fascinating there.

At the end of State Route 82 in northeastern Oregon is the picturesque hamlet of Joseph. It occupies a splendid setting, surrounded by grasslands and woodlands of the Wallowa Valley, with the 9,000-foot snowcapped Wallowa Mountains rising above and the oval jewel of Wallowa Lake tucked in between.

Joseph is a charming town in an area once known for its sadness. It was in the Wallowa Valley that the great Chief Joseph of the Nez Percé band made an heroic stand against white man's intrusion. Finally forced to flee in 1877, he led his people on an epic 1,700-mile journey across Idaho and Montana, seeking sanctuary in Canada. Trapped just fifty miles short of the border, he and his people were forced to surrender. There, he made one of history's most poignant speeches, ending with:

Hear me, my chiefs. I am tired. My heart is sick and sad. From where the sun now stands, I will fight no more forever.

It seems cruel irony that the settlement established on lands stolen from Chief Joseph's band was named in his honor.

When we first visited the town many decades ago, it was a rustic ranching center. While still somewhat bucolic, it's now a serious art town, known particularly for its Western-theme bronzes. Each of seven local artists has contributed a piece to form the **Bronze Artwalk** along Main Street.

It must be said that Joseph works at being rustic, with peeled and polished logs popular as a building material. Both new and old log and wood-frame structures house galleries, shops and restaurants. Joseph also has a few motels, and several rental cabins and small resorts are in the area.

The town's memories are preserved in the **Wallowa County Museum** in an 1888 bank building at 110 S. Main St.; (541) 432-6095. In the works but not open at this writing is a **Nez Percé Trail Interpretive Center**; (541) 886-3101; *www.wallowanezperce.org.* To see the town's bronze casters at work, visit **Valley Bronze of Oregon** at 18 S. Main St.; (541) 432-7445; *www.valleybronze.com.* Or stop by Kelly's Gallery on Main Street to arrange for a tour of **Joseph Bronze**; (541) 432-3116; *www.josephbronze.net.*

Joseph is a staging and provisioning center for treks into the **Eagle Cap Wilderness** of the Wallowa Mountains, and to **Hells Canyon National Recreation Area**.

The region's most popular attraction is **Wallowa Lake**, a six-mile-long oval gem at the base of those mountains. It is not, however, a wilderness area. **Wallowa Lake State Park** on the lake's southern edge might more accurately be called Wallowa Lake Amusement Park. Its amusements include an aerial tram ride, bumper boats, miniature golf and horseback riding; (541) 432-4185; *www.oregonstateparks.org.*

Rustic **Wallowa Lake Lodge**, dating from 1923, has twenty-two rooms, eight cabins and a dining room; (541) 432-9821; *www.wallowalake.com.*

Hells Canyon National Recreation Area

One of America's most remote preserves, Hells Canyon National Recreation Area sprawls over 652,488 acres of mountains, high desert and gorges on the Oregon and Idaho sides of the Snake River. Its centerpiece is **Hells Canyon**, said to be North America's deepest gorge, at 8,043 feet. But that's cheating because it's measured from the highest peaks of the Seven Devils Mountains. From ground level, the Grand Canyon is still the champ.

Most of the area is accessible only by foot or by taking commercial whitewater trips down the Snake from **Hells Canyon Dam** on the Oregon-Idaho border, or jet-boat trips upriver from *Lewiston, Idaho.*

However, if you're willing to take a few bumps, you can reach a Hells Canyon overlook from Joseph, but don't try it in winter. Load up on fuel and grub and take Little Sheep Creek Highway east from town. Drive twenty-eight miles to *Imnaha*, a tiny town in a striking high mountain setting. From here, follow Forestry Road 4240 twenty-four miles to **Hat Point**. Hells Canyon falls away at your feet, with the Snake River a thin blue line far below.

To see the canyon without such vehicular abuse, drive to *Baker City* on I-84. While you're there, visit the outstanding **National Historic Oregon Trail Interpretive Center** at Flagstaff Hill, 22267 Highway 85; (541) 523-1843; *www.nps.gov/oreg,* then type "Baker City."

Continue east on Route 86 about sixty-five miles to *Copperfield.* Cross to the Idaho side of the Snake River and follow a paved road through an extremely scenic area of the canyon to **Hells Canyon Dam**. There's a seasonal ranger station here, plus the Idaho Power Company's **Hells Canyon Park** with tent and trailer sites and picnic tables.

Where to learn more

Hells Canyon National Recreation Area, c/o Wallowa Mountains Visitor Center, 88401 Highway 82, Enterprise, OR 97828; (541) 426-4978; *www.fs.fed.us.hellscanyon.*

Joseph Chamber of Commerce, P.O. Box 13, Joseph, OR 97846; (541) 431-1015; *www.josephoregon.com.*

Portland
Raindrops and roses and being green

If there's a cloud hanging over Portland—and there often is—it has a silver lining and it's probably wearing a grin. Why? Because it's looking down onto one of the cleanest, safest and most appealing metropolitan centers in America.

Portland is what a city should be but rarely is—vibrant, attractive, culturally alive and ethnically diverse. It's carefully maintained, from its jade green parklands to its revitalized waterfront and clean-swept streets.

Those of us who live in the West have long known that Portland is a major vacation destination. If folks from the rest of the country aren't aware of that fact, it's high time they learned. With its 37,000 acres of parks, fifty galleries and museums, more than twenty theater companies, an historic old town and a grand riverfront park, it could keep a visitor busy for weeks.

If you like an urban vacation without the urban sprawl, this is your place. The city is comfortably sized, with fewer than 600,000 residents. It has an excellent public transit system, including a downtown "Fareless Square" where public buses and streetcars are free. Parking isn't a serious problem and there are several hotels in the heart of town, from which many of the city's attractions are walkable.

It has been rated as America's top urban travel destination by *Travel & Leisure* and *"Best Big City" by Money* magazine. *Reader's Digest* called it "America's cleanest city," *Bicycle* magazine named it the nation's best cycling city and *Runner's World* picked it as the best city for the fleet of foot.

Portland has been known for decades as the "City of Roses" because of its many rose gardens and its annual Rose Festival. It's also known as the "Green City," and not because it gets thirty-six inches of rainfall a year. Officials and residents have made it one of the world's most environmentally correct communities. It's a leader in everything from recycling to cycling. Five thousand commuters bike to work and the city has 431 miles of bike trails or dedicated bicycle lanes.

It's also green literally, with 278 public parks and gardens, including 5,000-acre **Forest Park**, one the nation's largest urban woodlands. The city's focal point is **Tom McCall Waterfront Park**, a two-mile greenbelt along the Willamette River at the foot of downtown. During the 1970s, when most cities were building more freeways and expressways, Portland officials demolished one. They ripped out an ugly expressway to create this park, and named it for a former governor who was a leader in the environmental movement. It's great for strollers, office workers on lunch breaks and even for kayakers, since rentals are available. The park is the scene of frequent public concerts and the focal point of many civic celebrations.

Portland is arrayed along both banks of the Willamette River, linked together by a network of eleven bridges. Many of the city's major museums are near the waterway, reachable by foot or public transit. The noted **Oregon Museum of Science and Industry** sits right on the river's east bank, across from Tom McCall Park. And the river itself is an attraction. One can watch a parade of cargo ships, pleasure boats, kayaks, cruise boats and even Chinese "Dragon Boats" that stage frequent rowing competitions. Several local firms offer river trips, including jetboats, sternwheelers and dining cruises.

Downtown Portland is fairly compact. Its tight cluster of high rises and many public parks and squares are within a fourteen-by-fourteen block area. The centerpiece is **Pioneer Courthouse Square** at SW Sixth and Morrison, home to the **Portland Oregon Information Center**, (503) 275-8355. A walking tour map available here will guide you to downtown's many lures, including the **Portland Art Museum, Portland Center for the Performing Arts** and the **Oregon History Center.**

Immediately north of downtown are **Old Town** and **Chinatown**, neighborhoods of old brick and masonry where the city began in 1845. According to legend, town founders Amos Lovejoy of Portland, Maine, and Francis Pettygrove of Boston, Massachusetts, flipped a penny to see who got to name the new settlement for their hometown.

Their original townsite is now a vibrant center of ethnic cafés and stores, specialty shops, nightclubs, art galleries and brewpubs. Check out **Powell's City of Books** at Eleventh Avenue and Couch Street, the world's largest independent book store with more than 1.5 million volumes; (503) 228-0540. The **Portland Saturday Market** at 108 Burnside (held both Saturday and Sunday despite the name) is one of America's largest open air markets. It has more than 350 booths with international foods, crafts and live entertainment; (503) 222-6702; *www.portlandsaturdaymarket.com.*

And if all of this isn't enough to entice you, Portland is regarded as the "Beer capital of the world," with thirty-two breweries inside its city limits. Per capita beer consumption is three times the national average, apparently because quaffing suds is a nice way to pass a rainy day.

Where to learn more

Portland Oregon Visitors Association, 1000 SW Broadway, Suite 2300, Portland, OR 97205; (800) 962-3700; *www.travelportland.com.*

Bellingham and beyond
More than just an Alaskan gateway

Charming in a funky sort of way and occupying a woodsy bay on Puget Sound just below Canada, Bellingham is the southern terminus for the Alaska Marine Highway.

However, one shouldn't pause there just to ask for directions to the ferry terminal. There's much to see and do in this old fashioned but well-kept town of about 68,000. Since it sits on Puget Sound, it offers a variety of charter fishing trips, boat rentals and sightseeing cruises. Bellingham has some surprisingly interesting museums and fine old neighborhoods of Victorian and Craftsman homes. Parks laced with hiking trails are tucked into wooded hills above.

The town sits in the middle of serious outdoor country, with Puget Sound at its feet and the Cascade Range at its back. *National Geographic Adventure* magazine placed it on its ten best "Adventure Towns" list and *Outside* magazine said it was among the top ten "Dream towns" in America.

Finding one's way around Bellingham can be an interesting challenge since four already-established communities were merged in 1903 to create a single town. Further, it's built along the curving shoreline of Bellingham Bay. Streets approach on another at curious angles and they tend to change names with no compelling reason.

Bellingham's largest archive is the **Whatcom Museum of History and Art,** occupying four fine old brick buildings along Prospect Street, including the ornate former city hall; (360) 676-6981; *www.whatcommuseum.org.* A museum of quite a different sort is **Mindport** at 210 W. Holly Street, offering an beguiling blend of fine art and interactive art, (360) 647-5614; *www.mindport.org.* The **American Museum of Radio and Electricity** at 1312 Bay Street traces society's entry into the electronic age; (360) 738-3886; *www.americanradiomuseum.org.* The **Maritime Heritage Center** at 1600 C Street is a public park and fish hatchery on the site of an old sawmill, with an interpretive path and native plant garden; (360) 676-6806.

The most appealing of Bellingham's four merged communities is *Fairhaven.* Despite its picturesque name, it once was a raunchy waterfront town of bordellos and Shanghai saloons. It has since become quite gentrified; its renovated old brick buildings house trendy shops, restaurants and galleries. After exploring Fairhaven, head south on Twelfth Street, following signs to **Chuckanut Drive**. It's one of the state's most popular scenic routes, winding cliffside along the edge of Puget Sound and up into the Chuckanut Mountains. It was completed in 1896 to provide a road link between this isolated region and the rest of the world.

The **Bellingham Cruise Terminal** at the foot of C Street in Fairhaven is the southern terminus for the **Alaska Marine Highway**; (800) 642-0066; *www.akferry.org*. Several private companies offer sailings from Bellingham. **Island Mariner Cruises** has whale-watching trips, Bellingham Harbor cruises and multi-day Inside Passage voyages; (360) 734-8867; *www.orcawatch.com*. **Victoria San Juan Cruises** offers harbor and whale watching trips and voyages to the San Juan Islands and Victoria, B.C.; (800) 443-4552; *www.whales.com*.

Back on land, our favorite side trips out of Bellingham are to Mount Baker and Point Roberts, two quite diverse destinations.

A great snowcapped sentinel standing watch over Bellingham, 10,775-foot **Mount Baker** is the photographic focal point of a vast recreation area. It's reached by State Route 542, the scenic Mount Baker Byway. The road climbs gradually and then more steeply onto the mountain's flanks, ending dramatically at a viewpoint where the sawtoothed majesty of the **North Cascades** unfolds. To learn more about this region, contact the **Mount Baker Foothills Chamber of Commerce,** P.O. Box 866, Maple Falls, WA 98266; (360) 599-1518; *www.mtbakerchamber.org*.

Point Roberts is a silly geographic anomaly, a tiny nub of American soil surrounded by Canada. When the U.S.-Canadian border was settled at the 49th parallel, that straight line nipped off a small peninsula extending into Puget Sound. It would have been logical to assign this little nub to Canada since Puget Sound's shoreline isolated it from the U.S. Somehow that never happened, so it remains a piece of Washington State's Whatcom County, with U.S. currency and even a customs gate.

To get there, take Interstate 5 north and enter Canada at *Blaine*; the **International Peace Arch** here is worth a look. Follow signs to *Tsawwassen* and thence to Point Roberts. There's not much to see; it draws tourists mostly for its curiosity value, and it even has its own **chamber of commerce**; (360) 945-2315; *www.pointrobertschamber.com*. You can explore this pleasant little community in an hour or so, since it covers only five square miles. Uh, excuse us, Canadians, that's thirteen square kilometers.

Where to learn more

Bellingham/Whatcom County Visitors Bureau, 904 Potter St., Bellingham, WA 98229; (800) 487-2032; *www.bellingham.org*.

Mount St. Helens
America's fascinating volcanic museum

⚑

If it's gonna take me, let it come and get me. If it takes my goddamned mountain, let it take Truman with it.

Harry Truman, not the late president but the late owner of a lodge on Mount St. Helens, died with his mountain on the morning of March 18, 1980. He and fifty-six other people perished in the largest American volcanic explosion in recorded history.

The irascible whiskey-sipping 83-year-old owner of Spirit Lake Lodge refused to leave his mountain, despite warnings that an eruption was imminent. When the mountain blew, it came down on top of Harry. It also razed 230 square miles of timberland, destroyed four billion board feet of lumber and 220 buildings, and damaged or buried dozens of miles of roads and rails.

After officials of the area's Gifford Pinchot National Forest recovered from shock and awe, they saw a fine opportunity to study a landscape recovering from a volcanic blast. To keep the hand of man out of the picture, they urge Congress to set aside much of the devastated area as a preserve. Mount St. Helens National Volcanic Monument was created in 1982, and it's one of the few federal reserves administered by the Forest Service instead of the National Park Service.

We have visited Mount St. Helens repeatedly through the years and each time we're surprised at how quickly the area's plant life is recovering. Our first visit revealed a colorless moonscape; the only living things were bright purple fireweed, poking timidly through thick layers of ash. All the trees were dead; some blasted to the ground and some still standing, with limbs and bark ripped away.

Now, thick green forests pepper the slopes and seasons of rain and snowfall have turned the ash layers into fertile soil. Returning to the mountain is like making repeated trips to an outdoor natural history museum, whose exhibits continue to evolve. Only the tilted, steep-walled crater reminds visitors that all hell broke loose here less than three decades ago. And St. Helens apparently hasn't gone back to sleep. Occasional seismic activity and ominous puffs of steam from a lava dome within the crater suggest that this very unsaintly mountain may yet again raise a lot of hell. As this book went to press, several of the park's trails had been closed.

Despite its fame and fascination, Mount St. Helens doesn't draw as many tourists as most of the other national parks and monuments in the Northwest.

However, its visitors centers do get busy on sunny summer weekends. The monument has no overnight lodgings and public facilities are minimal, to avoid disturbing the natural cycles of this ever-changing outdoor museum.

U.S. Forest Service campgrounds rim the monument, and restaurants, motels, small resorts and RV parks are available in nearby towns of *Cougar* to the south and *Randle* in the north. Flightseeing tours are offered out of several nearby communities; see chamber of commerce listings below.

Mount St. Helens' visitor facilities can be reached from Interstate 5 between *Woodland* and *Castle Rock*. This should be a spring through fall trip, since many of the roads and tourist centers are closed by winter snow.

To tour the southeastern edge of the monument, take State Route 503 east from *Woodland* to *Cougar*, then continue on a series of forestry roads that will deliver you to **Windy Ridge**. It's within five miles of the crater and just above **Spirit Lake,** which is still strewn with dead trees blown in by the blast. Rangers give periodic talks in an informal amphitheater at the ridge, with that ominous looking crater at their backs.

Further up I-5, head east from *Castle Rock* on State Route 504, and you'll encounter six official and unofficial visitor facilities. All but two are outside the monument. The largest is **Coldwater Ridge Visitor Center**, providing imposing views of the crater and the upper Toutle River Valley; (360) 274-2114. The facility has several fine interactive exhibits and a multi-media presentation concerning the explosion. A few miles beyond is the high tech **Johnston Ridge Observatory,** (360) 274-2140. It was named in honor of geologist Dr. David Johnston, who died when his observation station was blown away in the eruption. Visitors view a multi-media show about the volcano, then the screen lifts and curtains part to reveal the crater, just five miles away. The effect is absolutely smashing.

Where to learn more

Mount St. Helens National Volcanic Monument, 42218 NE Yale Bridge, Amboy, WA 98601; (360) 449-7800; *www.fs.fed.us/gpnf/mshnvm.*

Castle Rock Chamber of Commerce, 147 Front St. NW, Castle Rock, WA 98611; (360) 274-6603; *www.castlerockchamber.com.*

Cowlitz County Department of Tourism, 207 Fourth Ave. N., Kelso, WA 98626; (360) 577-3137; *www.co.cowlitz.wa.us/tourism.*

Woodland Chamber of Commerce, 900 Goerig St., Woodland, WA 98674; (360) 225-9552; *www.lewisriver.com/woodlandchamber.*

Two websites, ***www.mountsthelens-awesome.com*** and ***www.mountsthelens.com***, offer material on Mount St. Helens and nearby communities.

The North Cascades
Wilderness peaks, reservoirs and art towns

ꝏ

*N*owhere do the mountain masses and peaks present such strange, fantastic, dauntless and startling outlines. — **From the journal of Henry Custer, 1859**

Washington state's most magnificent mountain wilderness lies just east
of its busiest population corridor. Each year, hundreds of thousands of mo-
torist whiz along Interstate 5, hurrying between Seattle and the Canadian
border. Only a handful turn inland to visit the North Cascades, so jagged and
glacier-streaked that they're called the American Alps.

Half a million acres of this wilderness was set aside in 1968 as North
Cascades National Park. Slicing through the heart of the park is Ross Lake
National Recreation Area, offering water play on a chain of reservoirs in the
Skagit River Gorge. The national park is primarily a backpackers' haven.
Hundreds of miles of trails reach into the half-million-acre wilderness area,
whose lofty peaks are chilled by more than 300 glaciers. Only the tantalizing
edges of these wilds are visible from the scenic highway.

However, even if you aren't a hiker, this route offers several lures. It
travels through the rugged river gorge, climbs a high mountain pass and
drops down into the Methow Valley to a pair of arty rural towns, Winthrop
and Twisp. You can take a lake cruise and dam tour sponsored by Seattle
City Light; enjoy dramatic views of river, reservoir and mountains; and
check out rustic saloons, art galleries and shops in the Methow Valley.

Reservations are suggested for Seattle City Light's lake cruises, tours of
its Skagit hydroelectric facility and the "Diablo Dam Good Dinner Tour."
Call (206) 684-2020; or e-mail *www.skagittours.reservations@seattle.gov.*

Despite its closeness to Washington's main population corridor, the
North Cascades area remained virtually unknown until recent history. One
of the first outsiders to visit the area was Henry Custer, exploring the region
in 1859 as an agent of the International Boundary Commission.

Because of its ruggedness, the region remained isolated. Place names
speak of the difficulties of early exploration: Mount Despair, Forbidden
Peak and Mount Torment. Then a wagon road was hacked part way into the
region in the late 1800s, following the Skagit River. Seattle City Light began
building dams in the 1920s. However, a highway all the way through the
North Cascades into eastern Washington wasn't completed until 1972.

North Cascades National Park and Ross Lake National Recreation Area
are spring through fall places. The North Cascades Scenic Highway is usu-

ally closed by snow from November to April, and the Skagit tours operate only from June through September.

Facilities are limited in the park and the recreation area. Several campgrounds are available, although the only lodging is at **Ross Lake Resort**. Sitting on the opposite shore and reached by ferry, it offers charming floating cabins, dining and boat rentals. It also provides water taxi and portage service for hikers and boaters; (206) 386-4437; *www.rosslakeresort.com*.

To begin your tour of the region, head east from I-5 on State Route 20 at the small town of *Burlington*. The highway follows the delta-like Skagit River Valley, passing the hamlets of *Sedro Woolley, Concrete, Rockport* and *Marblemount*. You'll enter the Ross Lake National Recreation Area at the tiny town of *Nehalem*. It consists of a North Cascades visitor center and museum, a campground and the Skagit General Store, which sells limited provisions. Pressing onward, you'll travel alongside the foaming, cascading river. Then a series of dams stops the stream in its tracks, forming a chain of skinny reservoirs. Beyond **Ross Dam**, the highway leaves the waterway and begins a wildly scenic climb into the North Cascades.

Pause for a look at the **Liberty Bell**, a 7,808-foot cluster of granite peaks just short of mile-high **Washington Pass**. From here, you'll spiral quickly down into the wide **Methow Valley** and its two "cowboy art" towns.

Despite its wimpy name, *Winthrop* is a former mining and ranching center. It has been duded up with boardwalks, false front stores, Western shops and saloons with names like Three-Finger Jack and Grubsteak & Co. It offers lodging ranging from log cabin motels to posh resorts. It's also home to several galleries and working artists, and the town hosts an annual rhythm and blues festival. Winthrop's **Shafer Historical Museum** preserves the area's yesterdays in a collection of old buildings; (509) 996-7200.

Eleven miles south is another arty town with a funny name, and without Winthrop's funky Western look. *Twisp* (a native word for yellowjacket) has a few art galleries and a professional summer drama program at the **Merc Playhouse**, which occupies a 1924 mercantile. The town also is home to the Cascadia Music Association, sponsors of the Methow Music Festival.

Where to learn more

North Cascades National Park, 820 Highway 20, Sedro-Woolley, WA 98274; (360) 856-5700; *www.nps.gov/noca*.

Winthrop Chamber of Commerce, P.O. Box 39, Winthrop, WA 98862; (888) 463-8469 or (509) 996-2125; *www.winthropwashington.com*.

Twisp Chamber of Commerce, P.O. Box 666 (201 S. Methow Valley Hwy.), Twisp, WA 98856; (509) 997-2926; *www.twispinfo.com*.

Port Townsend
The Olympic Peninsula's Victorian gem

Perched on the scenic northeastern tip of the Olympic Peninsula, gracefully aging Port Townsend is one of the most appealing communities in Washington. It's a virtual outdoor museum of Victorian and early American architecture. Preening contentedly with its yesterday look, this small town of about 9,000 has more than seventy historic buildings and much of the downtown and nearby residential areas are in protected historical districts.

Port Townsend's downtown area, occupying a low coastal shelf, has one of Western America's largest collections of 19th century brick, cut stone and false front buildings. They house boutiques, galleries, antique shops, coffee houses and restaurants. Cluster-globe street lamps add a final touch to this Gay Nineties setting. Elegant Victorian homes stand in neighborhoods on the bluffs above.

This architectural treasure trove resulted from the town's brief and prosperous tenure as a key Puget Sound shipping point. Port Townsend was established in 1851 as a lumber cargo center and within three years, the U.S. Customs House was shifted here from Olympia. Now the official port of entry for Puget Sound, and with a safe harbor to shelter cargo ships, the new town prospered. It even hosted consulates from several nations. By the late 19th century, it boasted a population of 7,000, making it the largest town on the Olympic Peninsula and one of the largest in the state.

However, plans for a Northern Pacific rail line failed in 1895. Cargo ships began bypassing the town, continuing on to new transcontinental railheads in Tacoma and Seattle. Port Townsend soon went to sleep. And as Rip Van Winkle discovered, in hibernation there is preservation.

The town slumbered for decades, then it began awakening as shopkeepers and tourists were drawn to its yesterday charms. Several old Victorian houses were gussied up as bed & breakfast inns, and local groups worked to set aside much of the town as an historic district.

The preservation movement began just in time. If you approach Port Townsend along the waterfront on State Route 20, you'll see an unfortunate mistake by planners—an incongruously modern strip mall. The historically protected downtown area begins just beyond.

A non-profit body called **Port Townsend Main Street** coordinates and sponsors activities to support downtown's historic image, and the city's **Port Townsend Arts Commission** promotes visual and performing arts. The town has several small drama and musical groups.

Much of Port Townsend's history is preserved in the **Jefferson County Historical Society Museum** in the 1891 former city hall at Madison and Water streets. Three floors of the old structure practically sag with pleasantly cluttered exhibits; (360) 385-1003; *www.jchsmuseum.org*.

Also worth a pause is the splendidly restored 1868 Greek Revival **Rothschild House** at Jefferson and Taylor streets, with original furnishings and elaborate gardens; (360) 379-8076; *www.jchsmuseum.org/rothschild/house.html*. Other buildings of historic note are the 1892 Romanesque-Gothic **Jefferson County Courthouse** at Jefferson and Walker, which can be toured during weekday business hours; the 1893 **Customs House** at Washington near Van Buren, now the U.S. Post Office, with historic exhibits in the lobby; and the 1865 **St. Paul's Church** at Taylor and Jefferson, one of the oldest Episcopal churches in the state.

Several of the area's visitor lures are on the grounds of **Fort Worden State Park and Conference Center** is about a mile north of town. The fort was established in the 1890s as part of the "Triangle of Death" to guard the entrances to Puget Sound. Its Victorian style Officers Row has been restored and now houses a conference center, vacation rentals and other facilities. The fort also has campsites and miles of hiking trails; (360) 344-4400; *www.fortworden.org*.

Among Fort Worden's many attractions are the **Coast Artillery Museum,** exhibiting heavy metal of the late 19th century, (360) 385-0373; the restored 1904 **Commanding Officer's Quarters**, with splendid Victorian furnishings, (360) 344-4400; and the **Marine Science Center** with exhibits of Puget Sound marine life, (360) 385-5582, *www.ptmsc.org*.

With several motels and quaint B&Bs, Port Townsend is a handy base for exploring the rest of the Olympic Peninsula and Puget Sound. A short drive will deliver you to **Olympic National Park** with its rainforests, snowy peaks and wilderness coastline. If you head northwest from Port Townsend, you'll reach the absolute northwestern tip of mainland America at rugged and windswept **Cape Flattery** on the Makah Indian Reservation.

Washington State ferries offer auto and passenger service to several other Puget Sound ports from Port Townsend; (206) 464-6400; *www.wsdot.wa.gov/ferries*. The **Puget Sound Express** offers tours to the nearby **San Juan Islands**; (360) 385-5288; *www.pugetsoundexpress.com*.

Where to learn more

Port Townsend Chamber of Commerce Visitor Information Center, 2437 E. Sims Way, Port Townsend, WA 98368; (888) ENJOY-PT or (360) 385-2722; *www.ptchamber.org*.

Spokane
The good life in the Inland Empire

One of the best balanced mini-cities in the Northwest, Spokane is the economic, recreational and cultural hub of a vast swatch of prairie called the Inland Empire. This region of undulating plains, river canyons, wheat fields and vineyards occupies the eastern two-thirds of Washington and the western edge of Idaho.

With a population pushing 200,000, Spokane is Washington's second largest city, yet one of its most remote. It's a community alive with old West spirit, although it's contemporary and cultural, with fine shopping and dining, several performing arts groups and art galleries. Visitor accommodations are abundant, ranging from luxury hotels to modest motels.

Within the city limits are enough attractions, parks, special events and shopping facilities to occupy visitors for several days. Just beyond, one can hike the surrounding hills and enjoy water sports in rivers and lakes. Although Spokane is a prairie city, mountains are nearby. A short drive east will deliver travelers to the lake and mountain resort areas of *Coeur d' Alene* and *Sandpoint* in the Idaho Panhandle; see page 120.

By stretching an historical point, Spokane can claim to be the Northwest's oldest settlement. In 1810, a year before Astoria, Oregon, was founded, David Thompson of England's Northwest Fur Company started a trading post on the Little Spokane River. His Spokane House thrived until 1826. Then later settlers established a permanent town nine miles southeast above Spokane River Falls in 1872. With fast-flowing water to power its mills, Spokane became an important lumbering and flour milling center. By century's end, it had more than 20,000 residents, a number still not approached by any other eastern Washington town.

Never known for modesty, Spokane earned world attention in 1974 when it became the smallest city ever to stage an international exposition. Its Expo '74 was the first such worldwide affair with an environmental theme. Appropriately, officials cleaned up a rundown, polluted industrial area on Havermale Island near Spokane Falls to become the fair's center stage. It is today Riverfront Park, an active cultural and entertainment center within steps of the downtown area.

The city also is noted for a resident who left to croon his way to stardom. Harry Lillis "Bing" Crosby was born in Tacoma, grew up in Spokane and attended Gonzaga University. His career is enshrined in the **Bing Crosby Collection** in the university's Crosby Student Center; (509) 328-4420.

Downtown Spokane is a sturdy mix of old brick and new glass and steel. It's a likable area, slow-paced yet thriving, historic yet modern. While looking properly metropolitan, it's small enough to be explored on foot. Unlike many cities, Spokane has kept most of its shopping downtown, and elevated skywalks link many of its large stores—handy for cold winter days. And it does get chilly in Spokane, although spring through falls days are generally sunny and warm. Annual precipitation is only 16.5 inches, with most of it coming as winter snow.

The 100-acre **Riverfront Park** beside the Spokane River is the city's premiere visitor attraction. It has several leftover world's fair structures and a fun zone with a carousel, roller coaster, Ferris wheel and gondola rides over the river. An IMAX theater shows wide-screen films and the **Opera House** hosts several local performing arts groups and traveling shows; (800) 336-PARK or (509) 625-6600; *www.spokaneriverfrontpark.com.*

The **Northwest Museum of Arts & Culture** has both fine art galleries and historical exhibits. It's in one of the town's fine old neighborhoods at 2316 W. First Ave.; (509) 456-3931, *www.northwestmuseum.org.* Expansive **Manito Park** on Grand Boulevard between 17th and 25th avenues has several formal gardens and a conservatory, (509) 625-6622.

The city's visual arts and performing arts scene includes several galleries, a professional ballet company, a professional theater and several other drama groups. For details, contact the **Spokane Arts Commission** at (509) 625-6050; *www.spokanearts.org.* The **Spokane Symphony** presents more than sixty performances a year, mostly at the Opera House; (509) 326-3136; *www.spokanesymphony.org.*

A couple of nearby attractions are definitely worth a pause. **Spokane House Interpretive Center** occupies the original settlement site, with graphics, photos and historic artifacts. It's in **Riverside State Park**, nine miles northwest of the city; (509) 466-4747; *www.riversidestatepark.org/ spokane_house.* **Mount Spokane** is a popular outdoor recreation area thirty miles northeast, in Mount Spokane State Park. It has more than 100 miles of hiking and biking trails, plus camping and picnicking areas. The Vista House on the mountain's 5,878-foot crest offers a panorama of the surrounding countryside; (509) 238-4258; *www.parks.wa.gov.*

Where to learn more

Spokane Regional Convention & Visitors Bureau, 801 W. Riverside, Suite 301, Spokane, WA 99201; (800) 662-0084 or (509) 624-1341; *www. visitspokane.com.* The *Spokane Area Information Center* is at 201 Main Ave.; (888) SPOKANE or (509) 747-3230.

Tacoma
Washington's city of surprises

ᛒ

Anyone who regards Tacoma as Seattle's poor little sister hasn't been there—at least not lately. This former blue collar town has become a thriving, vibrant and culturally rich community.

Born a lumbering town in 1852, Tacoma is Washington's third largest city after Spokane, with just under 200,000 residents. This thriving town may soon occupy the second spot. For the past two decades, it has reinvented itself as an appealing visitor destination and a fine place to live and work. The downtown area has been spruced up and revitalized, a modernized container port has stolen cargo trade from Seattle and Olympia, and the city boasts some of the finest museums in the state.

Tacoma's vitality is reflected in the many new businesses in the historic downtown area, which is perched above Commencement Bay off Puget Sound. New landscaping, green zones and pedestrian overcrossings add to the area's appeal. The vision is enhanced by the broad-shouldered mass of Mount Rainier, which can be as vivid as a painted backdrop on clear days.

Tacoma's most dramatic renaissance is in its Museum District, a former industrial area surrounding the old beehive-domed Union Station. The district has been shaped to a great degree by the influence of Tacoma-born Dale Chihuly, the world's most famous glass sculptor, although his studios are now in Seattle. The stunning **Museum of Glass** just below Union Station exhibits outstanding glass sculptures and constructions from around the world. Visitors can watch glass artists at work in Jane's Hot Shop; (253) 284-4750; *www.museumofglass.org*.

Sitting across from the glass museum is the **Washington State Museum**, one of the most imposing archives in the Northwest, both inside and out. It's busy with pioneer relics and modern interactive exhibits; (253) 272-3500; *www.wshs.org*. The two museums are linked by the **Chihuly Bridge of Glass** pedestrian way, lined with his dazzling creations. The handsomely renovated **Union Station** next door to the state museum is now a federal courthouse. Its imposing high-domed rotunda has several Chihuly glass exhibits that are free to the public. The dramatic steel and glass **Tacoma Art Museum**, a block from the state museum, has works by Northwest and international artists, and again including many of Chihuly's creations; (253) 272-4258; *www.tacomaartmuseum.org*.

Some warehouses in the adjacent waterfront area have been converted into artists' lofts and a once-deteriorating railway cargo shed is now the

Freighthouse Public Square and Market, busy with stores, boutiques and cafes. Just beyond is the almost excessively imposing **Tacoma Dome,** which hosts a variety of sports events, shows, conventions and concerts.

Tacoma is rich in performing arts as well as museums. Its Theater District downtown is home to the **Broadway Center for the Performing Arts.** The complex includes the restored Greco-Roman Pantages and art deco Rialto theaters, both built in 1918, and the Tacoma Actors Guild's Theatre on the Square; (253) 591-5890; *www. broadwaycenter.org.*

One of our favorite Tacoma haunts is the **Thea Foss Waterway,** a waterfront inlet with a pedestrian path leading northwest from the Museum District into downtown. Along the way, you'll encounter the **Working Water front Maritime Museum** at 705 Dock Street, with exhibits focusing on Tacoma's nautical history; (253) 272-2750; *www.wwfrontmuseum.org.*

If you drive northwest from downtown, you'll reach **Rustin Way** on the edge of Commencement Bay, with pleasing views of Puget Sound and distant mountains. Several popular restaurants sit on piers along this route. At the end of Rustin Way is the weathered old town of *Rustin,* with several restaurants and antique shops occupying 19th century buildings.

Pressing onward, you'll wind up in huge **Point Defiance Park,** with grassy lawns, botanical gardens, picnic areas, miles of walking and biking trails and scenic drives; (253) 305-1000; *www.metroparkstacoma.org.*

Among the park's numerous lures are **Point Defiance Zoo and Aquarium,** (253) 591-5337, *pdza.org*; **Fort Nisqually Living History Museum,** a reconstructed 1833 Hudsons Bay Company fur trading post, (253) 591-5339; *www.fortnisqually.org;* and **Camp Six Logging Exhibit** with displays of old lumbering equipment, (253) 752-0047, *www.camp-6-museum.org.*

Brief drives in two directions from Tacoma will deliver you to a pair of other interesting towns. West across the sleek **Tacoma Narrows Bridge** is the charming village of *Gig Harbor* with a Mystic Seaport look and an abundance of shops, boutiques and seafood restaurants. Ten miles southeast of Tacoma is the suburban town of *Puyallup* which is emerging as an art and antique center, with several galleries and antique dealers. Its new **Arts Downtown Outdoor Gallery** displays more than fifty sculptures. In September, the town hosts the Puyallup Fair, the largest in Washington.

Where to learn more

Tacoma Regional Convention & Visitor Bureau, 1119 Pacific Ave., Tacoma, WA 98402; (800) 272-2662 or (253) 627-2836; *www.traveltacoma. com.* The CVB's **Visitor Information Center** is inside the Courtyard by Marriott at 1516 Commerce Street (at South Fifteenth Street).

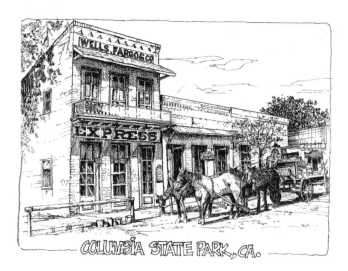

COLUMBIA STATE PARK, CA.

Chapter Two

The
Southwest

THE SUNBELT AND WELL BEYOND

When folks think of the American Southwest, they think of warm winter vacations, canyon lands, Navajo lands and probably Las Vegas. They don't normally think of California's lofty Sierra Nevada range, its stately redwoods or scenically rugged and rainy coastlines. However, unless we're willing to chop the state in half somewhere below San Francisco—which has been suggested by some northern Californians—we must include these non-Sunbelt areas in our Southwestern chapter.

ARIZONA is the most typical of the Southwestern states, without the distraction of redwoods and rainy coastlines. Included in our sampler is the least-visited side of the Grand Canyon, the site of America's most famous gunfight, the Navajo-Hopi Reservation and the West's only National Heritage Area.

Where to learn more: Arizona Office of Tourism, 1110 W. Washington St., Suite 155, Phoenix, AZ 85007; (888) 520-3434 or (602) 364-3700; *arizonaguide.com.*

CALIFORNIA, here we come, with more listings than any other state. We had to, and not because we live here part time. It's the most diverse state in the Union, so we must include a restored Gold Rush town, the beautiful North Coast, the awesome Eastern Sierra, the California Mission Trail, a southern coastal county and of course, a less trammeled area of the Wine Country.

Where to learn more: California Travel and Tourism Commission, P.O. Box 1499, Sacramento, CA 95812-1499; (877) CALIFORNIA; *www.gocalif.ca.gov.*

NEVADA beyond Las Vegas is amazing, and it's surprisingly diverse. For our Silver State discoveries, we traveled to the eastern edge of the vast and lonely Great Basin, to a tough old town where cowboys recite poetry without blushing, and to a lively place that's still the "Biggest Little City in the World."

Where to learn more: Nevada Commission on Tourism, 401 N. Carson St., Carson City, NV 89701; (800) NEVADA-8; *www.travelnevada.com.*

NEW MEXICO is a true Land of Enchantment, unlike any other state. A high mountainous plateau, it has a special quality of light that has lured hundreds of artists. New Mexico gave us Southwestern architecture and cuisine, Smoky Bear, Billy the Kid, the a-bomb and maybe aliens.

Where to learn more: New Mexico Department of Tourism, Lamy Building, 491 Old Santa Fe Trail, Santa Fe, NM 87501; (800) 733-6396, ext. 063 or (505) 827-7400; *www.newmexico.org.*

The Arizona Strip and North Rim
A grand approach to the Grand Canyon

Arizona's Grand Canyon is hardly undiscovered and of itself is not an appropriate subject for this book. However, the canyon's North Rim is little-visited, at least compared with the South Rim, which draws more than five million tourists a year. The North Rim receives one tenth that number.

Further, the North Rim is adjacent to one of Arizona's most remote and intriguing regions. The Arizona Strip is a semi-arid land of rolling prairies cut off from the rest of the state by the Grand Canyon. This Arizona-Utah borderland is a vast space of red rock cliffs and high blue skies, where cattle roam free and ranch houses huddle in the shade of cottonwoods. Settlements are few and small and mostly Mormon, for this marks the southernmost reach of Brigham Young's former empire of Deseret.

Ironically, this remote land is an easy reach from the most visited place on earth. If you're among the 37 million annual travelers to Las Vegas and need a solitude fix, the Arizona Strip and North Rim offer an appealing side trip. To get there, head northeast on Interstate 15 to the Arizona-Nevada border town of *Mesquite*, then continue through the scenic and steep-walled **Virgin River Gorge**. The freeway nips the northwestern corner of Arizona and soon passes through *St. George, Utah*. Ten miles north, fork right onto State Route 9 and take it to the small town of *Hurricane*.

Go right again, following the twisting route of State Highway 59 up to the **Colorado Plateau**. Upon this vast plateau, Mom Nature has shaped dramatic canyons, buttes and red wall escarpments, including the Grand Canyon and Utah's Bryce Canyon and Zion national parks. It's also the platform for the Arizona Strip. You'll enter Arizona and the Strip at *Colorado City*, a fundamentalist Mormon settlement where gossips say some folks on the fringes still practice polygamy.

The highway becomes Route 389 in Arizona and soon reaches **Pipe Spring National Monument** on the Kaibab Indian Reservation. Pipe Spring is a nicely preserved early Mormon ranch settlement and it's definitely worth a browse; (928) 643-7105; *www.nps.gov/pisp*.

Fourteen miles beyond is the hamlet of *Fredonia*, which offers little cause to pause. From here, head southeast on Highway 89-A and begin a long, gentle climb up to the Kaibab Plateau. As you enter Kaibab National Forest, prairie grasses give way to piñon and Ponderosa pines. You'll shortly enter *Jacob Lake*, a woodsy settlement that serves as the northern gateway to Grand Canyon National Park, with a store, dining, lodging and camping. However, the North Rim is still forty miles away, reached by a long, sloping and pleasant climb through pine forests.

Facilities at the **North Rim** are pleasantly limited compared with those at the crowded South Rim. They're focused around the rustically elegant Grand Canyon Lodge, with a visitor center, dining, lodging, a gift shop and saloon. A service station, grocery store and campground are nearby.

Because the Kiabab Plateau—through which the Grand Canyon is carved—slopes from north to south, the North Rim is as much as 2,000 feet higher than the South Rim. Elevations reach 8,800 feet at the North Rim and it's closed in winter. Another major difference is that the North Rim consists of narrow peninsulas that thrust out into the main chasm, while the South Rim is more of an irregular proscenium. These peninsulas provide some of the national park's grandest viewpoints.

Doing the North Rim is relatively simple, although one could spend days here, hiking and relaxing and enjoying the world's grandest canyon scenery. Basically, the park has just one paved road, which travels northeast to the **Point Imperial** viewpoint, with a much longer branch that follows a peninsula south to **Cape Royal.** An unpaved road reaches west to **Point Sublime** and indeed this uncrowded vista point is that.

From the North Rim, return to Jacob Lake, then go east on Highway 89 for a scenic downhill return to the Arizona Strip. As you descend, views of the distant **Vermilion Cliffs** are quite awesome. Back down on the prairie, you'll pass tiny towns that are essentially motel-restaurant-service station clusters—*Cliff Dwellers, Vermilion Cliffs* and *Marble Canyon*.

The lonely drive across the Arizona Strip ends rather dramatically at the Colorado River's Marble Canyon, which marks the upstream beginning of the Grand Canyon. This steep-walled chasm was named by explorer John Wesley Powell, who mistook its glossy granite walls for marble. The preserved remnants of **Lees Ferry**, an early Mormon outpost, is just upstream, with a campground and a seasonal ranger station. It's the launch point for many whitewater raft trips through the Grand Canyon. The lofty Navajo Bridge spans the river here, and you can continue north to *Page* and **Glen Canyon National Recreation Area** that rims Lake Powell, or return to your starting point.

Where to learn more

Grand Canyon National Park, P.O. Box 129, Grand Canyon, AZ 86023; (928) 638-7888; *www.nps.gov/grca*.

Flagstaff
High country haven on historic Route 66

ꔛ

Scattered along the base of the often snowcapped San Francisco Peaks, Flagstaff would seem to belong in Oregon or Washington instead of the sunbelt state of Arizona. It has the mountain scenery and pine forests of the Northwest, yet little of the daily drizzle. Annual rainfall is only twenty-three inches and sunshine is the norm, even in winter.

If location is everything, as Realtors like to say, then Flagstaff offers everything and more. One of Arizona's highest towns at nearly 7,000 feet, it has an abundance of four season recreational opportunities. It's home to one of America's finest small universities, it supports an active arts scene and it has several interesting museums. Within short drives are the Grand Canyon and several other national parks and monuments, including several prehistoric native peoples' villages.

With a population around 60,000, Flagstaff is large enough to provide ample shopping and services, and small enough to have a folksy hometown feel. Although this is a fine community, it is something of a flawed beauty, a direct result of its heritage. Because it developed as a railroading center and a supply stop along historic Highway 66, the town has a rather scattered look. Three miles of budget motels, service stations and businesses line one side of the highway while trains rumble, chug and blat along the other.

The old downtown area, adjacent to a classic Santa Fe railroad station, fell to hard times in recent decades, the victim of suburban business flight. However, it is now enjoying a renaissance. Planners wisely kept out glass and steel office buildings and restored most of the town's fine old brick and masonry structures. The revitalized downtown offers a walkable mix of boutiques, specialty shops, restaurants, art galleries and outdoor stores. Most of modern Flagstaff is found in pockets of businesses and strip malls in its scattered suburbs.

Although Historic Route 66 isn't pretty, lift thine eyes unto the hills— the San Francisco Peaks in this case. Their presence lures thousands of visitors and hundreds of new residents every year. One of Flagstaff's great appeals is that people can reach this outdoor playground within minutes. The **Arizona Snowbowl**, the state's largest ski area, provides winter sports, and folks can hike, camp, fish, hunt and talk to the trees up there the rest of the year; (928) 779-1951; *www.arizonasnowbowl.com.*

Flagstaff's academic and cultural focal point is the 750-acre campus of **Northern Arizona University**. It was rated by *Money* magazine as one of the ten top university values in the nation, because of its high quality of education and relatively low tuition. The university's galleries and performance halls generate an aura of artistic diversity that seeps into the rest of the community. NAU's **Audrey Auditorium** is home to the **Flagstaff Symphony and Flagstaff Light Opera** and it hosts scores of other performing arts events; (928) 523-4120; *www.nau.edu/auditoria.* Off campus, the classic art deco **Orpheum Theater** at 15 W. Aspen Avenue downtown is now a performing arts center; (928) 556-1580; *www.orpheumpresents.com.*

After all this waving of Flagstaff's flag, one might wonder how the town got its odd name. There are several stories afloat. The most popular yarn is that early settlers shucked the limbs from a tall ponderosa and raised a flag on July 4, 1876, to honor America's centennial. Later, on a chilly winter's day, the tree was chopped down to provide firewood for Sandy Donahue's saloon. So much for historic preservation.

Fortunately, the town is now more preservation-minded. It has an abundance of visitor lures, including fine museums and historic sites.

The outstanding **Museum of Northern Arizona** at 3101 N. Fort Valley Road focuses on the geology, natural science, native culture and contemporary history of northern Arizona; (928) 774-5213; *www.musnaz.org.* The nearby **Pioneer Historical Museum** at 2340 Fort Valley Road is busy with Flagstaff's yesterday relics and memories; (928) 774-6272; *www.arizonahistoricalsociety.org.* **Riordan State Historic Park** at 409 W. Riordan Road is an unusual forty-room "double cabin" built in 1904 for two brothers and their families and restored to that era; (928) 779-4395; *www.pr.state.az.us.*

The Arboretum at 4001 Woody Mountain Road contains one of America's largest selections of high altitude plants; (928) 774-1442; *www.thearb. org.* **Lowell Observatory** at 1400 W. Mars Hill Road offers interactive exhibits, astronomy displays and tours; (928) 774-2096; *www.lowell.edu.* Pluto was discovered from here in 1930. No, not Mickey Mouse's dog.

And finally, don't leave town without stopping at the **Museum Club** at 3404 E. Historic Route 66; (928) 526-9434; *www.museumclub.com.* This grand old log cabin saloon dates from 1931 and it's cluttered with so many stuffed critters that aficionados simply call it "The Zoo."

Where to learn more

This town is so full of itself that it has two visitor centers:

Flagstaff Chamber of Commerce, 101 W. Route 66, Flagstaff, AZ 86001; (928) 774-4505; *www.flagstaffchamber.com.*

Flagstaff Visitor Center, One W. Route 66, Flagstaff, AZ 86001; (800) 842-7293 or (928) 774-9541; *www.flagstaffarizona.org.*

Nava-Hopi land
Surprising discoveries in Four Corners country

⚑

The large Navajo and Hopi reservations in northeastern Arizona encompass some of the state's most interesting terrain, from starkly beautiful canyons to netherworld sandstone spires.

The combined reservations cover about 29,000 square miles, encompassing all of northeastern Arizona and spilling over into Colorado, Utah and New Mexico. That's nearly as big as New England. By an unfortunate whim of the federal government, Hopi lands are surrounded by the much larger Navajo Nation. However, the Hopi Reservation includes some of the tribe's ancestral lands. One pueblo, Old Oraibi, dates from 1150 A.D. It may be the oldest continually occupied settlement in America.

Both the Hopi and Navajo are known for their fine silver and turquoise jewelry and the Navajo are excellent wool rug weavers. The Navajo Reservation is busy with gift shops and roadside crafts stands.

Much of Nava-Hopi Land is rolling grassland, punctuated by startling scenery. Canyon de Chelly (pronounced *shay*) is one of the most incredible chasms we've ever seen. Monument Valley looks even more dramatic than it appears in photos. After you've driven for hours across the reservation, seeing nothing but prairie and an occasional farmhouse, a great red butte may appear on the horizon or a cathedral-like spire may crop up in a pasture.

To explore Nava-Hopi lands, we'll use Page as a starting point. Drive south on U.S. 89, then turn east on U.S. 160. You'll soon enter *Tuba City*, the largest town on the Navajo reservation. Follow Highway 264 south from here into the **Hopi Nation**. Most of their celebrated pueblos occupy three mesas, simply called First, Second and Third. Some are true cliff dwellings, perched on shelves and niches high above the valley floor.

While intriguing, the pueblo villages are not models of neatness. The earthy style of these ancient dwellings does not blend well with non-biodegradable objects such as rusting cars and tin cans. The gentle Hopi are more into spiritual things than landscaping. Among the more interesting pueblos you'll encounter on this drive are *Old Oraibi* (*oh-RYE-bee*), *Kykotsmovi* (*Kee-KOTS-mo-vee*), *Shungopovi* (*Shung-O-PO-vee*), *Shipaulovi* (*Shih-PAW-lo-vee*) and *Mishongnovi* (*Mih-SHONG-no-vee*).

To learn more about these people and their ancient pueblos, visit the **Hopi Cultural Center** complex on Second Mesa. This pueblo style facility includes a museum, gift shops, restaurant and a motel; (928) 734-2401; *www.psv.com/hopi.html*. The Hopi still perform centuries-old ceremonial dances in traditional dress. Check with the cultural center to see if a dance is planned in the area. Photography and recording aren't allowed at the dances.

Leaving Hopi land, follow Highway 264 east to **Hubbell Trading Post National Historic Site** near the Navajo village of *Ganado.* Dating from 1876, it's both an historic landmark and a working trading post; (928) 755-3475; *www.nps.gov/hutr.* East of Ganado, you'll reach *Window Rock,* the Navajo administrative center. The fine **Navajo Nation Museum** at Highway 64 and Loop Road traces native history in the region from the basketmakers of 50 A.D. to the present; (928) 871-4090; *www.discovernavajo.com.*

From the tribal museum, head north briefly on Highway 12. After half a mile, watch on the right for a sign pointing to the community's namesake, **Window Rock.** A few blocks off the highway, it's a natural arch sculpted by wind and rain, and surrounded by a small park.

Press northward on Route 12, which takes you in and back out of New Mexico while passing imposing beige and red rock formations. At the hamlet of *Tsaile,*follow Highway 64 west to **Canyon de Chelly National Monument**, which preserves two unexpectedly beautiful sheer-walled canyons; (928) 674-5500; *www.nps.gov/cach.* From here, drop down into the small town of *Chinle* and head north, following Highway 191 past several free-standing red rock mesas. At U.S. 160, go east through *Mexican Water,* following signs to **Four Corners** where the borders of Arizona, New Mexico, Colorado and Utah merge. It's interesting mostly for its geographic novelty. A flat concrete monument with the four states' seals marks the spot. Four Corners is a Navajo tribal park, with several craft and food stalls.

Retrace your route on U.S. 160 past more imposing red rock formations, following the highway to the town of *Kayenta.* Turn north for a visit to the Navajo Nation's most famous attraction, **Monument Valley Tribal Park** on the Arizona-Utah border; (435) 727-5870; *www.navajonationparks.org.* It exhibits an amazing collection of sandstone buttes, fins, spires and ridges. You've often seen these incredible shapes in TV commercials.

Return to Kayenta and continue west on U.S. 160 to **Navajo National Monument**, which offers an excellent small museum and some of America's finest Anasazi ruins; (928) 672-2700; *www.nps.gov/nava.* Betatakin ruin can be visited on ranger tours, although advance reservations are needed to hike out to the incredibly well-preserved Keet Seel ruin.

From the monument, you can take Highway 98 back to Page.

Where to learn more

Navajoland Tourism, P.O. Box 663, Window Rock, AZ 86515; (928) 871-7371; *www.discovernavajo.com.*

Prescott
Mid-America charm and Western art

ꀊ

Prescott isn't your typical Arizona sunbelt city. It's not typically Arizonan at all, except for a rich cowboy culture. You won't find cactus, kokopelli bolo ties or sleek winter resorts here, because the town isn't the sunbelt. It's nestled in the cool cottonwood foothills of the Bradshaw Mountains of central Arizona. Just over a mile above sea level, it offers four relatively mild seasons.

With its brick downtown, Victorian style homes and fall color, the look is more New England or the Midwest. The town supports an active cultural scene, although most gallery art is more cowboy than contemporary. Western lore is embedded in Prescott's history. It's home to the world's oldest rodeo, now called Frontier Days. It started in 1888 when, for the first time anywhere, wranglers competed for prize money in a "cowboy tournament."

One of the first thing visitors must learn is how to pronounce the town's name. It's *PRESS-cut,* with the last syllable bitten off rather crisply.

PRESS-cut could have been the Arizona capital instead of a quiet community far from the beaten political path. When Congress sliced the Arizona territory from New Mexico in 1863, a temporary capital was set up in the Chino Valley, where the Army had established Fort Whipple to keep an eye on the native people. Then both the government and the fort moved fifteen miles south to Prescott's present location alongside Granite Creek.

However, older and better-established Tucson lured the capital away in 1867. Then Prescott took it back ten years later, buoyed by gold strikes and a growing timber industry. In 1889, it lost out to newly booming Phoenix, America's first true sunbelt city. Many local folks decided that was just fine. Who needed all that political ruckus anyhow? Without the capital, they still had a thriving community in a scenic basin, surrounded by thousands of square miles of ponderosas.

Prescott wears its heritage proudly; the low-rise downtown area and several neighborhoods have been designated as historic districts. About 800 buildings are listed on the National Register of Historic Places, more than any other town of its size in Arizona. Bronze plaques identify many old buildings and historic sites.

Downtown is built around an old fashioned square called **Courthouse Plaza** with the Grecian style Yavapai County Courthouse as its centerpiece. The plaza is the venue for arts and crafts fairs, concerts and other public events. Once notorious Whiskey Row occupies a block-long section of Montezuma Street opposite the plaza. Benches in the plaza and elsewhere downtown invite lingering, suggesting that life here moves at a leisurely pace.

Although Prescott cherishes its history, it's hardly stuck in a time warp. Many old storefronts house boutiques, specialty shops, bookstores, galleries and restaurants, along with a few surviving saloons and a couple of western wear shops. This business mix has allowed downtown to thrive, while modern shopping centers emerge in the suburbs.

Prescott is remarkably versatile for a mini-city of about 40,000. It has a strong artistic and cultural base, the academic lures of three colleges, several interesting museums, some good restaurants, ample shopping, and the recreational potential of 1.5 million acres of surrounding national forest. The town even has a couple of casinos, operated by the Yavapai tribe. An estimated 100,000 Yavapai once thrived in these central Arizona highlands. Only about 150 remain, occupying a small reservation on the edge of town.

The outstanding **Sharlot Hall Museum** at 415 Gurley Street is a large complex with a main exhibit center and several historic buildings, with the original wood frame territorial governor's mansion as its centerpiece; (928) 445-3122; *www.sharlot.org.* The **Smoki Museum** at 147 N. Arizona Street has a fine collection of native peoples' lore, housed in a couple of fieldstone structures; (928) 445-1230; *www.smoke-eye.com.* Seven miles north of town at 4701 Highway 89 is the **Phippen Museum of Western Art**. It has an excellent collection of works by the likes of Charles Russell and Frederick Remington, plus the noted local painter and sculptor George Phippen; (928) 778-1385; *www.phippenmuseum.org.*

Several art galleries are in Prescott's downtown area, mostly along Gurley and Montezuma streets. A brochure called *Art: Prescott's 4th Dimension* lists the town's twenty or more art spaces. Performing arts are focused in three areas—the **Prescott Fine Arts Center** in a former church at 208 N. Marina Street, (928) 445-3286, *www.pfaa.net*; the classic 1905 **Elks Opera House** on Gurley between Cortez and Marina streets, (928) 777-1100, *www.cityofprescott.net*; and **Yavapai College Performance Hall** at 1100 E. Sheldon Street, (928) 776-2000; *www.2yc.edu.* The Fine Arts Center and Yavapai College also have galleries.

Strolling along a downtown street one afternoon, we caught a vignette that typified today's Prescott—a group of bearded and Stetson-topped cowboys sipping lattes at a coffee house.

Where to learn more

Prescott Chamber of Commerce, P.O. Box 1147 (117 W. Goodwin St.), Prescott, AZ 86302; (800) 266-7534 or (928) 445-2000; *www.prescott.org.*

Tombstone and the cowboy corner
Tough towns, historic sites and Apache lore

Ⴒ

The Cowboy Corner is a history-laden rectangle in southeastern Arizona that's overlooked by the vast majority of the state's visitors. 'Tis pity, since this region is busy with attractions, from tough old cowboy and mining towns to a trio of national preserves. This corner of Arizona was witness to the famous shootout at the O.K. Corral and the nobly futile resistance battles of Cochise and his Chiricahua Apaches.

Begin your exploration by heading southeast from *Tucson* on Interstate 10 to *Benson*, then go south on State Route 90 to **Kartchner Caverns State Park**. These caverns are among the world's best-preserved "wet" limestone cave complexes, only recently opened to the public. Advance reservations are required for a tour; (520) 586-CAVE; *www.pr.state.az.us/parks*.

From here, continue south on Highway 90, then go east on State Route 82 to *Tombstone*, the "town too tough to die." It can't die, for Hollywood would never permit it. Here, on October 26, 1881, the Earp brothers and Doc Holliday shot it out with the Clantons and McLaurys near the O.K. Corral. Thanks to moviemakers, they've been shooting it out ever since.

Today's Tombstone is a semi-tacky living history museum with both authentic and contrived exhibits about the old mining town's wild and wicked days. It's busy with restored saloons and curio shops disguised as museums. The main attractions are **Boothill Cemetery** with a gift shop up front, (520) 457-9344; and **Tombstone Courthouse State Historic Park** with the town's best history exhibits; (520) 457-3311; *www.pr.state.az.us/parks*. Re-enactments of "The Shootout" are performed for tourists beside the O.K. Corral.

Having had your Hollywood history fix, backtrack to Route 90 and continue south, passing through *Huachuca City* to *Sierra Vista*, a growing retirement community. It offers little of travelers' interest, although adjacent **Fort Huachuca**, an historic and still-active army post, is worth a look. It's home to the excellent **Fort Huachuca Museum** with exhibits on the military's role in the Southwest; (520) 533-5736. Continue south from Sierra Vista on State Route 92. If birdwatching interests you, watch for signs to the Nature Conservancy's **Ramsey Canyon Preserve**, a wooded gorge that's a favorite hummingbird hangout; (520) 378-2785; *www.nature.org*.

Pressing southward on Highway 92, follow signs to **Coronado National Memorial** with exhibits concerning Francisco Vásquez de Coronado's legendary trek in search of the fictional cities of Cibola in 1540; (520) 366-

5515; *www.nps.gov/coro*. He passed through present-day Arizona although he didn't come this way. "We put the memorial here because the land was available to us," a ranger told us with a perfectly straight face.

Follow Highway 92 east to State Route 80 and go north briefly to *Bisbee*, a sturdy old former copper mining town cantilevered into the steep slopes of Mule Pass Gulch. At the edge of town is the **Lavender Pit**, once one of the world's largest open pit copper mines. Rough-shod Bisbee has a pair of interesting lures. **Queen Mine Tours** take visitors into an underground copper mine; (877) 432-2071 or (520) 432-2071, *www.cityofbisbee.com/queenminetours.html*. The **Bisbee Mining and Historical Museum** preserves the town's memories in a bold brick building that served as a mining company's headquarters, (520) 432-7071, *www.bisbeemuseum.org*.

Travel southeast on Highway 80, then go north on U.S. 191 about forty miles to State Route 181. Follow it east and north to **Chiricahua National Monument** where rhyolite formations have been eroded into fantastic shapes; (520) 824-3560; *www.nps.gov/chir*. This wild landscape was a hideout for Cochise's Chiricahua Apache warriors during their battles with intruding settlers. A museum covers the area's geology and native history.

The last stop on this meandering tour is Willcox and if you don't mind a few dusty bumps, you can visit the ruins of an old army fort en route. Head northwest from Chiricahua on State Route 186 then follow a dirt but navigable road eight miles north. At a parking lot, you'll have to hike 1.5 miles to **Fort Bowie National Historic Site**. It has a small visitor center and several crumbling adobe and stone walls; (520) 847-2500; *www.nps.gov/fobo*.

From the fort, return to Highway 186 and follow it to *Willcox* on Interstate 10. This small ranching and railroad town offers two visitor attractions. **Chiricahua Regional Museum** at 127 E. Maley Street features exhibits of the area's settlement history and the Chiricahua wars; (520) 384-3971. The **Rex Allen Arizona Cowboy Museum** at 150 N. Railroad Avenue focuses on the cowboy film star's life, and cowboying in general, (877) 234-4111 or (520) 384-4583; *www.rexallenmuseum.org*. A real cowboy, Rex Allen grew up on a homestead ranch near Willcox.

Where to learn more

Greater Bisbee Chamber of Commerce, P.O. Box BA (31 Subway St.), Bisbee, AZ 85603; (520) 432-5421; *www.bisbeearizona.com*.

Tombstone Office of Tourism, P.O. Box 248, Tombstone, AZ 85638; (800) 457-3423 or (520) 457-3929; *www.cityoftombstone.com*.

Willcox Regional Visitor Center, 11500 N. Circle I Rd., Willcox, AZ 85643; (800) 200-2272 or (520) 384-2272; *www.willcoxchamber.org*.

Yuma and surrounds
A famous crossing, Snowbirds and cactus

⚐

After decades of dozing in the sun, Yuma has awakened in recent years to become an interesting travel destination and a major retirement community. *Money Magazine* recently called it one of the best places to live in America, and it's our sunniest city, with 339 days of sunshine a year.

A key to Yuma's renaissance was the restoration of the its historic river crossing site. The Colorado River had long been an impediment to westward movement. Then Father Eusebio Kino found a place to ford the stream at a shallow bend near present-day Yuma. It was Kino who named the river *Rio Colorado* for its reddish, silt-laden waters.

In the decades that followed, this Yuma crossing became the primary route to southern California. Father Francisco Tomas Garcés built two missions here in 1779. Explorer Stephen Watts Kearny and his frontier scout Kitt Carson forded the stream on their way west in 1846. Colonel Philip Cooke's Mormon Battalion soon followed, carving the first crude wagon road into the Golden State. During the California Gold Rush, many argonauts took this southern route to avoid the hike over the northern mountains. So did the Butterfield Overland Stage, which provided America's first cross-country mail and passenger service from 1858 until 1861.

The U.S. Army operated the Yuma Crossing Quartermaster Depot here from 1864 until 1883, bringing cargo by river steamers to supply its Southwestern forts. In the years that followed, Yuma chugged along as a farming and punishment center. The infamous Yuma Territorial Prison, built during the 1870s, was the stuff of Western legend and many a Hollywood film.

Then, late in the last century, the deteriorating quartermaster depot was restored and is now Yuma Crossing State Historic Park. It's one of only twenty-three National Heritage Areas in the country and the only one in the West. Downtown Yuma also is undergoing a renaissance. Several historic buildings have been restored, and a new art center was established in 2004.

The community continues its role as a supply center, luring travelers off Interstate 8 with a good selection of lodgings and restaurants. Many of those travelers are choosing to linger awhile, discovering that the old town has its fair share of attractions. Many come for months; every winter, about 50,000 Snowbirds flock to mobile home parks on both sides of the Colorado River.

If you approach from the west, watch for signs to the former **Fort Yuma** near the California hamlet of *Winterhaven*. The fort has a small museum and a handsome Spanish mission style church; (619) 572-0661. Fort Yuma was built on the site of one of the Father Garcés missions in 1849. It's now part of the Quechan Nation Indian Reservation.

Shortly after crossing the river into Arizona, you'll encounter **Yuma Crossing State Historic Park** with its restored quartermaster depot and other exhibits; (928) 329-0471; *www.pr.state.az.us/parks*. On a hill overlooking the river and town is the area's other major attraction, **Yuma Territorial Prison State Park**, with most of its sturdy stone and adobe buildings still intact; (928) 783-4771; *www.pr.state.az.us/parks.*Despite its reputation as the "hell hole of Arizona," museum exhibits suggest that it was actually a model prison for its day—but without air conditioning.

Three other Yuma area attractions are worthy of pause. The **Sanguinetti House Museum** at 240 Madison Avenue is a restored 19th century home with a large garden and aviary; (928) 782-1841, *www. yumalibrary.org/ahs*. About two miles east of town at 868 Avenue B and Eighth Street is **Erlich's Date Garden,** where you can sample and buy a variety of locally-grown dates; (800) 301-9349; *www.nvo.com/imperialdate*. At the **Peanut Patch** at 4322 E. County Thirteenth Street (not far from the Yuma County Fairgrounds and the Marine Corps Air Station), you can watch the fall harvest, tour the processing plant and buy peanutty things; (800) USA-PNUT or (928) 726-6292; *www.thepeanutpatch.com*.

Beyond Yuma

If you'd like to sample a bit of old Mexico that isn't excessively touristy, head south from Yuma on U.S. 95 to *San Luis*. The weathered business district in this town of about 50,000 has a few shops and cafés within two blocks of the border. To avoid the need for Mexican auto insurance (most U.S. insurance isn't recognized in Mexico), you can park in the Friendship Lot in San Luis, Arizona, and walk over.

Organ Pipe Cactus National Monument, little visited yet intriguing, is less than three hours' drive from Yuma; (520) 387-6849; *www.nps.gov/orpi*. Take I-8 115 miles east to *Gila Bend*, then go south fifty miles on State Route 85. Arizona's largest and most remote national monument preserves a desert landscape of incredible beauty, with cactus gardens set among rock-strewn hills. It's named for the multi-stemmed organ pipe cactus that grows in profusion here but in few other places on earth. Worth a look as you leave or enter the monument is the old company mining town of *Ajo*, with an overlook to a huge copper pit and a neat Spanish style downtown.

Where to learn more

Yuma Convention & Visitors Bureau, 277 S. Main St., Yuma, AZ 85364; (800) 293-0071 or (928) 783-0071; *www.visityuma.com*.

Columbia and Sonora
Gold rush lore and the great outdoors

Ⴗ

Selecting our part-time home town for this book has nothing to do with excess community pride. Located in the heart of the California Gold Country, Columbia is the state's oldest historic park and the most-visited attraction in the region. Nearby Sonora, another former Gold Rush town, is the area's commercial center and a major cultural haven.

The two towns are in the foothills of the Sierra Nevada, the craggy mountain range that separates California and Nevada. The region offers a rich mix for visitors—historic sites, museums, a lively arts scene, interesting shopping and dining and outdoor lures in the mountains and foothills.

Sonora is the seat of Tuolumne County and a sizable chunk of that county is occupied by Yosemite National Park. Much of the rest is thatched by national forests, and these woods are busy with hiking trails and campgrounds. Lakes and rivers lure boaters, anglers and whitewater rafters. Reservoirs, which provide vital water for much of northern California, provide water sports for Tuolumne County and its visitors. Two ski resorts—one within the national park—attract winter sports enthusiasts.

And finally, for wine lovers, several premium winery tasting rooms are just north of Columbia in next-door Calaveras County.

Columbia and Sonora, six miles apart, have taken quite different paths since the wild days of their youth. "Sonorian Camp" was established in 1848 by Mexican miners, who were later pushed off their claims by greedy Gringos. Columbia was born two years later. A party of prospectors, pausing in a wooded basin to dry their gear after a rainstorm, did some panning just to kill time and made a major strike.

A fiery comet of a town, Columbia rose and fell quickly. The "Gem of the Mother Lode" was California's fourth largest city by the late 1850s. Then the gold ran out and it became a near ghost town. The mining lasted longer in Sonora, then lumbering and railroading kept the town going. It's now the marketing center for Tuolumne and two adjacent counties. However, it's not a *big* commercial center; its population is less than 6,000.

Much of sleepy Columbia was purchased by the state in 1945, and its surviving brick buildings—with their distinctive iron doors and shutters—have been restored. They now house curio shops, restaurants and historic displays. Columbia's 600,000 annual visitors can ride stagecoaches, pan for gold and follow costumed docents on historic tours. And they can sleep in Victorian finery in the City and Fallon hotels.

Although the state owns most of the townsite, there are some private in-holdings, allowing a few of us call Columbia home. We go to the post office for mail and town gossip, and we buy groceries at Columbia Mercantile, where tourists buy licorice whips and sarsaparilla.

Although Sonora is now a modern community, it has preserved many historic buildings in the downtown area. They house specialty shops, art galleries and restaurants. Contemporary Sonora thrives in its hilly suburbs, with shopping centers, a new regional hospital and homes shaded by foothill trees. Small **Columbia College**, occupying a pretty wooded campus between Columbia and Sonora, provides an academic climate for the county; (209) 588-5100; *www.columbia.yosemite.cc.ca.us.*

Both towns are active in the performing arts, thanks primarily to **Sierra Repertory Theatre**, a professional drama group with a national reputation; (209) 532-3120; *www.sierrarep.com.* SRT presents several musicals, comedies and dramas each year in a 200-seat theater in East Sonora and in the handsome 1886 Fallon Theatre in Columbia, one of the oldest in the West.

Just uphill, the nationally ranked **Strawberry Music Festival** is held over Memorial Day and Labor Day weekends at Camp Mather outside Yosemite National Park; (209) 532-3120; *www.sierrarep.com.* International folk, country and bluegrass groups perform on an outdoor stage.

Fine arts also thrive in the county. Both Columbia and Sonora sponsor arts and crafts fairs and several working artists live in the area.

The county's memories are preserved in the **Columbia Museum** on Main Street, (209) 532-3184; and the **Tuolumne County Museum** at 158 W. Bradford Avenue in Sonora, (209) 532-1317, *www.tchistory.org.*

Another former mining town worth a look is *Jamestown*, just south of Sonora. Curio shops and restaurants occupy old fashioned false front buildings on its Main Street. Just above town is **Railtown 1897 State Historic Park**, where visitors can view rolling stock of the old Sierra Railroad, tour a roundhouse and take train rides; (209) 984-3953; *www.railtown1897.com.* Railtown's trains have been featured in more than 200 movies.

Where to learn more

Columbia State Historic Park, P.O. Box 151, Columbia, CA 95310; (209) 532-0150; *www.parks.ca.gov*; or *www.columbiacalifornia.com.*

Tuolumne County Visitors Bureau, P.O. Box 4020 (542 Stockton Street), Sonora, CA 95370; (800) 446-1333 or (209) 533-4420; *www.the-greatunfenced.com.*

Eureka and Arcata
Cultural cool on the Redwood Coast

ꔪ

At first look, Eureka and Arcata on California's far north coast would seem an odd pair. Eureka is a sturdy blue collar town sprawled along the mudflat shores of huge Humboldt Bay. Across that bay, Arcata is liberal cool—a small town shaped by the presence of Humboldt State University.

At second look, these two towns have much in common. Both are culturally alive, thanks mostly to HSU's presence. Both have well-preserved old downtown areas worth a look, and either would be a good base for exploring California's Redwood Empire. With a population of about 27,000—10,000 more than Arcata—Eureka offers a much better selection of lodgings.

California's splendid redwood preserves are but a short drive from the two Humboldt Bay communities. **Redwood National Park**, mixed with a string of redwood-busy state parks, is just to the north. To the south lies the large **Humboldt Redwood State Park** with its famous scenic drive, the **Avenue of the Giants**.

Years ago, visitors were drawn to *Eureka* mostly for its sportfishing and for clamming in its mudflats, and these are still popular lures. However, the old town has become much more diversified and it's seriously into preservation. Its downtown area has two designated historic districts. **Historic Downtown** inland from U.S. 101 is the main commercial area with a fine collection of century-old stone and masonry buildings. Many are dressed with whimsical murals.

Across the highway along the waterfront is **Historic Old Town** with art galleries, specialty shops and restaurants in vintage buildings with ornate and brightly painted façades. Stroll along Old Town's **Eureka Boardwalk**, a concrete promenade on the bayfront with historical markers, exhibits and benches for sitting and gazing across Humboldt Bay. This is a focal point of waterfront development and plans are afoot for new retail facilities and hotels. Make it a point to see the **Carson Mansion** near old town at Second and M streets, an incredibly ornate Victorian built by a lumber baron in 1866. It's a private club and can be admired only from the outside.

Eureka offers an interesting assortment of other visitor attractions. **Clarke Memorial Museum** at Third and F streets preserves the area's yesterday memories; (707) 443-1947; *www.clarkemuseum.org*. **Humboldt Bay Maritime Museum** in Old Town at 423 First Street displays nautical memorabilia of California's North Coast; (707) 444-9440. **Blue Ox Millworks and Historical Park** near the bayfront at First and X streets is a Victorian carpentry shop where visitors can learn about the finer arts of woodworking; (800) 248-4259 or (707) 444-3437; *www.blueoxmill.com.*

Fort Humboldt State Park & Logging Museum south of town is a former army post with both early day military and logging displays; (707) 445-6567; *www.parks.ca.gov.* A young Lieutenant Ulysses S. Grant was posted here in 1854 and he apparently didn't care much for the place. Lonely and taken to drink, he resigned his commission and returned to his family farm in Missouri.

A required stop for area visitors is the 1893 **Samoa Cookhouse** on the Samoa Peninsula. This cavernous former lumberjack dining hall now feeds monstrous meals to the public at long family-style tables; (707) 442-1659.

Arcata is built around old fashioned **Arcata Plaza**, which is the venue for a festive Saturday Market and other community events. It's rimmed by specialty shops, art galleries, book stores and restaurants. Particularly interesting is the barn-like brick and stone 1857 **Jacoby Storehouse**, a former mercantile that has been converted into a mall. The small **Arcata Railroad Museum** is on the ground floor; *www.jacobystorehouse.com.*

The lushly landscaped **Humboldt State University** campus occupies the high ground—figuratively and literally—above Arcata. With old and new brick buildings, plazas and botanical gardens, it's worth a stroll. For more strolling, the town has its own personal woodland, **Arcata Community Forest**, with 575 acres of second growth redwoods and ten miles of hiking trails. For even more walking, adjourn to the **Arcata Marsh and Wildlife Sanctuary** with an trail network along the marshy mudflats south of town on the edge of Humboldt Bay.

Both Eureka and Arcata support lively cultural scenes. They're nurtured by Humboldt State and by the Humboldt Arts Council, based in the **Morris Graves Museum of Art** at 636 F Street in Eureka; (707) 442-0278; *www. humboldtarts.org.* Humboldt State's **CenterArts** complex hosts all genres of the performing arts, from local and national theater and dance to top-rated stars; (707) 826-3928; *www.humboldt.edu/~carts.*

The two towns began life in the mid-1800s as lumbering and fishing communities. Then in 1913, Arcata was granted a state college, which has evolved into one of the West's most respected universities.

Where to learn more

Arcata Chamber of Commerce, 1635 Heindon Rd., Arcata, CA 95521; (707) 822-3619; *www.arcatachamber.com.*

Greater Eureka Chamber of Commerce, 2112 Broadway, Eureka, CA 95501; (707) 442-3738; *www.eurekachamber.com.*

The Eastern Sierra
California's high lonesome

The Sierra Nevada, Spanish for "snowy peaks," is one of the highest and most rugged mountain ranges in America. It stretches for 450 miles between California and Nevada, although most of the range lies within the Golden State. During the great westward migration of the mid-1800s, the mountains were a serious impediment. Historian Oscar Lewis called the Sierra Nevada a "bulky, awkward and inconveniently high barrier."

Once that barrier was breached, settlers flowed into California and they're still flowing, making it the most populous state in America. However, few people live in the eastern foothills of the Sierra. This is a rather arid region of mile-high desert and pasturelands, with cold winters and strong winds that often sweep down from the mountains.

Yet, it's strikingly beautiful.

When the Sierra Nevada range was uplifted eons ago, the push came from the west, causing a west-to-east tilt, like a gigantic chunk of broken sidewalk. The western slope is marked by a wide band of undulating foothills while the eastern face is dramatically steep, dropping more than two vertical miles into the Owens Valley and Great Basin Desert. Jagged granite peaks rise from the foothills like giant petrified waves. This is one of the world's most imposing escarpments.

The trek down U.S. Highway 395 through the Eastern Sierra foothills is one of our favorite scenic drives. It begins in Nevada, in the twin farming towns of *Minden* and *Gardnerville*, just south of Lake Tahoe and Carson City. Fifteen miles further south, you'll enter California at **Topaz Lake**, a blue desert pond with a small casino and mini-mart. The highway travels along a gently rolling alluvial plain with the grand Sierra escarpment filling the western horizon. After passing through several nondescript towns, the highway spirals down into the weathered old hamlet of *Bridgeport*. Pause for a peek at the 1880 Greco-Roman **Mono County Courthouse** and the **Mono County Museum** behind the courthouse on Emigrant Street.

Below Bridgeport, a side trip east will take you to **Bodie State Historic Park**, an old mining town that's being preserved in a state of "arrested decay." There are no services; only a ranger station; (760) 647-6445. Back on Highway 395, you'll drop dizzily down to *Lee Vining*, the eastern gateway to Yosemite National Park. To the east is the pallid blue oval of **Mono Lake**, famous for its strange tufa formations. You can learn about them at the **Mono Lake Tufa State Reserve Visitor Center**; (760) 647-3044.

Below Lee Vining, you can take the **June Lake Loop** up into wooded foothills, passing four alpine lakes and the village of *June Lake*. Just down the highway, a second loop leads to the large **Mammoth Lakes** ski area and village. With more than 5,000 residents, the town of *Mammoth Lakes* is the largest community along this route. It's also the gateway to **Devil's Postpile National Monument**, which preserves an intriguing collection of cliff-face basaltic columns; (760) 934-2289; *www.nps.gov/depo*.

Below Mammoth, you'll drop down into the **Owens Valley**, scene of California's most violent water war early in the last century. The town of *Bishop*, occupying a stunning setting between the Sierra Nevada and White Mountains, has a trio of lures: **Laws Railroad Museum**, five miles east on U.S. Highway 6, (760) 873-5950; the **Owens Valley Paiute-Shoshone Indian Cultural Center** at 2300 W. Line Street, (760) 873-4478; and **Schat's Bakkery** at 763 N. Main Street, which has been serving tasty and rich European-style pastries and light meals since 1907; (760) 873-7156.

Your next encounter along this route is the hamlet of *Independence* in the heart of the Owens Valley. Check out the **Eastern California Museum** three blocks east of the Federalist style Inyo County Courthouse; it's at 155 N. Grant Street, (760) 878-0258. Also, visit the 1927 **Winnedumah Hotel** at 211 N. Highway 395, now a B&B; (760) 878-2040; *www.winnedumah.com*.

Five miles south is **Manzanar National Historic Site**, a former relocation camp where Japanese-American citizens were imprisoned during World War II. Little remains of the original camp, although the old auditorium has a fine interpretive center; (760) 878-2194; *www.nps.gov/manz*.

The final stop in our trek is *Lone Pine*, which sits between the highest and lowest elevations on the American mainland—Mount Whitney and Death Valley. Remarkably, they're just fifty miles apart. For information on both, stop at the **Mount Whitney-Death Valley Interagency Visitor Center** south of town at Highway 395 and State Route 136; (760) 876-4252.

From Lone Pine, head uphill toward **Whitney Portal**. En route, you'll pass through the rock-jumbled **Alabama Hills** where more than 300 Western movies and TV shows have been filmed. At road's end, look up to the grand cathedral of granite peaks and down to the vast Owens Valley. You'll agree that the Eastern Sierra is one of America's best undiscovered places.

Where to learn more

Bishop Area Chamber of Commerce, 690 N. Main St., Bishop, CA 93514; (888) 395-3952 or (760) 873-8405; *www.bishopvisitor.com*

Lone Pine Chamber of Commerce, Box 749 (120 S. Main), Lone Pine, CA 93545; (877) 253-8981 or (760) 876-4444; *www.lonepinechamber.org*

Mendocino and Fort Bragg
Coastal habitats for art and nature

ⴼ

A charming New England style village on California's north coast, Mendocino has been a famous art colony for more than half a century. Much lesser known yet coming into its own is Fort Bragg, ten miles north.

While Mendocino flourished as an art colony and pricey coastal retreat, the old lumbering and fishing town of Fort Bragg served as the area's commercial center. Then its largest employer, a Georgia-Pacific lumber mill, closed in 2002 and the town went into a skid. Now it's rebounding as a second art colony, and a more affordable place to stay, dine an play. With galleries, coffee houses, cafés and boutiques occupying many of its old fashioned downtown storefronts, it's quickly shedding its blue collar label.

Both communities are in the heart of the Mendocino Coast, a spectacular 115-mile stretch of seascapes midway between San Francisco and the Oregon Border. It's an idyllic haven of wooded headlands, Kelly green moors, sea stacks, hidden coves and redwood groves. The area offers refuge for artists, storm watchers and folks who like to scuff along lonely beaches or stroll in the solitude of redwoods.

The Mendocino Coast is isolated from the rest of California, reached only by narrow, scenically twisting roads. Because of its remoteness, the area's total population is only about 25,000, not enough to fill a baseball park. Fort Bragg, the largest and only incorporated town in the area, is home to fewer than 8,000 and Mendocino has only a thousand residents.

Several state parks have the two towns in an environmental squeeze, protecting the area's beauty and limiting development. **Van Damme State Park** is south of Mendocino, while **Mendocino Headlands State Park** rims the town and **Russian Gulch State Park** is just to the north. **Caspar Headlands State Beach Reserve** and **Jug Handle State Reserve** are south of Fort Bragg and **Mackerricher State Park** occupies its northern border.

Mendocino's setting is more appealing than Fort Bragg's. The town occupies a small peninsula and its main street stands alongside a fifty-foot sea cliff above a driftwood-littered cove. Old woodframe storefronts are busy with art galleries, boutiques and restaurants. With a New England look brought by nor'eastern settlers in the 1850s, it has been used as the setting for dozens of movies and TV shows.

The town will remain charmingly unchanged, for it's protected by an historic district and the peninsula is hemmed in by all those state parks. To learn about its charms, stop by the **Ford House Museum** in an old Victorian house on Main Street. It's a combined state park visitor center and local history museum; (707) 937-5397; *www.parks.ca.gov.* **Kelley House Museum** at 45007 Albion Street preserves more of the region's history; (707) 937-5791; *www.mendocinohistory.org.* The rustic and rambling **Mendocino Art Center** at 45200 Little Lake Street is the focal point of the local cultural scene, with several galleries and a performing arts center; (707) 937-5818; *www. mendocinoartcenter.org.*

The impeccably restored 1878 **Mendocino Hotel** at 45080 Main Street offers luxury lodging and dining; (800) 548-0513 or (707) 937-0511; *www. mendocinohotel.com.* Several Victorian style bed & breakfast inns and woodsy resorts are in Mendocino and the neighboring coastal hamlets of *Little River* and *Albion* to the south.

Fort Bragg has its own appeal. Although the old Georgia-Pacific millsite stands between downtown and the ocean, the town is rustically attractive, with a mix of old fashioned brick and woodframe buildings. Plans are afoot to develop the millsite, with a seaside park, a new town square and a nautical theme shopping and lodging complex. A seacliff easement rimming the site has been donated to a conservation group to develop a coastal trail.

Just south of town, **Noyo Harbor** seems transplanted from the seacoast of Maine. Tucked into a narrow estuary below steep cliffs, it's home to a commercial fishing fleet, sportfishing and whale-watching charters and a few seafood restaurants and fish markets.

Fort Bragg's best-known attraction is the **"Skunk Train"** which hauls visitors along a former logging route through redwood forests to the inland town of *Willets*; (800) 866-1690; *www.skunktrain.com.* Officially the California Western Railway, the line earned the Skunk Train moniker because it once used smelly gasoline powered railcars. It now employs old steam engines, diesel locomotives and diesel-powered railcars.

The **Guest House Museum** at 343 North Main Street is Fort Bragg's history center, occupying a mansion that once served as a guest house to lumber officials; (707) 964-4251. South of town, **Mendocino Coast Botanical Gardens** has forty-seven acres of blooming plants and native woodlands on a bluff above the Pacific; (707) 964-4352; *www.gardensbythesea.org.*

Where to learn more

Mendocino Coast Chamber of Commerce, P.O. Box 1141 (332 N. Main St.), Fort Bragg, CA 95437; (707) 961-6300; *www.mendocinocoast.com.*

Mendocino County Alliance is a trade group promoting the county's visitor lures; at 525 S. Main St., Suite E, Ukiah, CA 95482; (866) 466-3636; *www.gomendo.com.*

Lava Beds and birds
Moonscapes, wildlife and Captain Jack

⚑

In California, Lava Beds National Monument is about as far from no-where as one can get. It occupies a high, lonely prairie called the Modoc Plateau, so far north that it's practically out of the state. The nearest town of significance is *Klamath Falls, Oregon*, nearly fifty miles northwest.

So, why go there? Because it's a very intriguing yet little-visited element of the National Parks system—a mean sprawl of lava fields, cindercones and lava tubes. Further, it's adjacent to Klamath Basin National Wildlife Ref-uges, among the best bird watching regions in the entire country. It's also the site of one of the nation's last Indian wars.

The look of Lava Beds is stark. It's Marlboro Country with cinder-cones—a great sprawl of sagebrush and gray-green juniper, with the snow-capped Cascade Range on the far horizon. North of Lava Beds, the wildlife refuges occupy a mix of marshlands, farmlands and reservoirs made square to increase their irrigation efficiency.

There are no services within Lava Beds or the wildlife refuges, other than a campground in the monument and a couple more outside. Limited services and a few modest cafés and motels are available in *Tulelake*, with a population of about a thousand and shrinking. The old town looks so dusty and tired, we half expect return one day and find it blown away by a high desert wind.

To reach **Lava Beds National Monument**, head south from *Klamath Falls* on State Route 39, past elements of the wildlife refuge. The California approach is north on Interstate 5 to *Weed*, northeast on U.S. 97 and then west cross the top of the state on Route 161. Between *Tulelake* and *Newell*, follow signs into the national monument. You'll enter an area so outer-worldly with its craters and broken lava fields that you might expect a lunar rover to pop over yonder ridge.

At monument headquarters, you can check out a small interpretive center and explore a couple of nearby lava tubes, either on ranger tours or on your own. The visitor center has maps to other lava tubes, cindercones and hiking trails, and you can borrow, buy or rent flashlights and "bump hats." There are 335 known lava caves within the monument. Also, plan an after hours walk, when jackrabbits and kangaroo rats with silly looking pom-pom tails dance in the beam of your flashlight. They have little fear of humans.

The most-visited site in Lava Beds is **Captain Jack's Stronghold**, a se-ries of rough lava corridors where a band of Modoc Indians held off a U.S.

Army force ten times their size for five months. This was the main battle-ground of the Modoc War of 1872-73. It was the only major Indian war in California and one of the last such conflicts in America. It also was one of the few wars in which a general was killed in battle.

After suffering the humiliation of several broken treaties, about fifty Modocs led by *Kientpoos*—known to whites as Captain Jack—fled the Klamath Indian Reservation and holed up in the Lava Beds. Later, during an unsuccessful peace negotiation, a frustrated Captain Jack drew a pistol and shot the chief negotiator, Brigadier General E.R.S. Canby. Jack and his band retreated to their stronghold and weren't rooted out until hunger and thirst forced them to surrender. Captain Jack fled, but he was later captured and hanged. Markers and signs point out the various Modoc War sites. Details are available at the visitor center.

The **Klamath Basin National Wildlife Refuges** consist of six sanctuaries around Tule Lake just north of Lava Beds, and on Lower Klamath Lake in Oregon. Six million waterfowl once paused in this complex of lakes and marshes during their migrations. Then a federal reclamation project in 1905 reduced the wetlands by seventy-five percent. The wildlife refuges were formed to preserve the remaining bird habitats, and they still play host to as many as a million waterfowl a year. It's estimated that up to seventy percent of the birds on the Pacific Flyway make a pit stop here. Also, about 500 bald eagles hang out in the area during January and February.

Best bird-viewing times are during the spring and fall migrations, and particularly in the fall. Several bird blinds and viewing platforms are set up in the refuges although—unfortunately—hunting is permitted and the critters are rather skittish.

Start your visit by following signs to refuge headquarters at 4009 Hill Road, south of State Route 161. It has several interesting exhibits, including stuffed waterfowl and interactive conservation displays. You can pick up driving maps to various birdwatching areas.

Viewing areas and hunting blinds on the wildlife refuge are separate, although someone needs to tell that to the poor birds.

Where to learn more

Klamath Basin National Wildlife Refuges, 4009 Hill Rd., Tulelake, CA 96134; (530) 667-2231; *www.fws.gov/klamathbasinrefuges*.

Lava Beds National Monument, 1 Indian Well, Tulelake, CA 96134; (530) 667-8100; *www.nps.gov/labe*.

The Mission Trail
In search of California's romantic past

ᛒ

The California that most of us know, sometimes love and often complain about came as a direct rush of the great 1849 Gold Rush. The discovery of all that glitter led to the area's settlement by gringos, and this huge migration soon spread into the rest of the state.

However, the state's first settlements were of a more romantic and less frenzied era. Friar Junipero Serra was sent forth by officials of New Spain (Mexico) to colonize what is now California. The purpose was two-fold—to discourage encroachment by Russians and English and to convert native Californians "into a society that is human, Christian, civil and industrious."

Between 1769 and 1823, twenty-one missions were established between San Diego and Sonoma northeast of San Francisco. These weren't just missionary churches; they were vast agricultural empires with outbuildings, pasturelands, gardens and vineyards. After Mexico won its independence from Spain in the early 1800s, the missions were secularized and turned into parish churches. Their landholdings were parceled out to favored government officials and military heroes. This led to the era of the great *rancheros* which lasted until the United States snatched California from Mexico in 1848.

In picturing early California, it's easy to image humble and industrious padres, and *ranchos* with *vaqueros* in sombreros and pretty señoritas in flaring skirts. It wasn't all that innocent. This was an era of subjugation of the natives, of forcing upon them a strange religion, of making them do most of the work, including the building of the missions themselves.

Although time and neglect have damaged most of the missions, elements of all of them survive or have been reconstructed. A tour of these sites can provide an historical, scenic and cultural vision of early California. Visiting all of them on a single trek can be an ambitious and fascinating undertaking. Our you can tour just a favored few. Wherever you travel in southern and central California, there's a mission not far away. Indeed, most were spaced to be a day's march apart, linked by a roadway called El Camino Real.

Some years ago, we toured all twenty-one to do a series of articles for several newspapers. These were our favorites, working south to north:

San Diego de Alcala, 10818 Mission Rd., San Diego; (619) 281-8449. California's mission movement began when Father Serra erected a crude brush hut and simple cross on a hill overlooking San Diego Bay on July 16, 1769. It evolved into an extensive complex, although only a church, garden and classic three-tiered *campanile* or bell wall survive.

Santa Barbara, 2201 Laguna St., Santa Barbara; (805) 682-4712. Founded in 1786, the *Queen of Missions* is gorgeous, with a restored church, extensive grounds and fountains, and an outstanding museum.

La Purisima Conception, 2295 Purisima Rd., Lompoc; (805) 733-3713. Established in 1787, it's the most authentically restored of all the missions, since the work was done by the Civilian Conservation Corps during the Depression. Workers used period tools to create a virtual replica of the original.

San Carlos Borromeo de Carmelo, 3080 Rio Rd., Carmel; (831) 624-3600. Started the year after San Diego, this was mission headquarters and it's among the most elaborate and well-kept. Father Serra is buried here.

San Francisco de Asis, 3321 Sixteenth St., San Francisco; (415) 621-8203. Standing in the shadow of the newer Basilica of San Francisco, the humble 1776 "Mission Dolores" offers sanctuary from the bustle of the surrounding city. Much of the interior, including the artwork, is original.

San Francisco Solano at 20 E. Spain St., Sonoma; (707) 938-1519. Established in 1823 as the last of the missions, it's now a state park and the original church has been faithfully restored. Nearby are several other preserved buildings, part of Sonoma State Historic Park.

Missions impossible?

Most of California's missions are in serious trouble. All but two are part of Catholic churches and often the local parishes lack the funds to preserve and protect them. San Miguel Archangel in the small farm town of San Miguel is so fragile that it has been fenced off from visitors. In 2005, Congress passed a bill introduced by California Senator Barbara Boxer to provide $10 million in matching funds to help restore the missions. However, it was blocked by a lawsuit filed by a group called Americans United for Separation of Church and State.

On the positive side, an organization called the California Missions Foundation is working hard to raise funds for the salvation of these important landmarks. The group needs all the help it can get: 4129 Main St., Suite 207, Riverside, CA 92501; (951) 369-0440; *www.missionsofcalifornia.org.*

Where to learn more

The website of the *California Missions Foundation* (above) contains details of all the missions, including locations and visitor information.

Other informative sites are *www.californiamissions.com* and *www.missiontrailtoday.com*, with photos and historical backgrounds. The website of California's Department of Parks and Recreation has a very informative link called "The Mission Trail" that includes "quick studies" and addresses of each mission: *www.parks.ca.gov/default.asp?page_id=22722.*

Northern Sonoma winelands
Napa who?

Ꝑ

All right class, where is the largest premium wine producing area in California? No, it's not the legendary Napa Valley, nor the Sonoma Valley. Northern Sonoma County has more acres of premium wine grapes under cultivation than any other area in the United States.

Further, northern Sonoma has more than sixty tasting rooms, ranging from family funky to high end elegant. Some of the region's more opulent wine *châteaux* rival many of those in the Napa Valley.

The Napa and Sonoma valleys are beautiful and the wineries are fun to visit, but good grief, the crowds! The winelands of northern Sonoma County are equally attractive, set in rolling hills and often framed in gnarled oaks. The wines are fine and the tasting rooms aren't nearly as busy. On weekdays, they aren't busy at all. The vinelands begin north of *Santa Rosa* and they're concentrated in three major areas—the Alexander Valley northeast of Healdsburg, the Dry Creek Valley west of Geyserville, and the Russian River Valley that surrounds the old resort town of Guerneville

For us, sipping good wine is reason enough to go touring, although northern Sonoma offers other lures as well. En route to the wine country, pause in Santa Rosa for two attractions. The **Charles M. Schulz Museum** at 2301 Hardies Lane preserves memories of our beloved Snoopie and friends, (707) 579-4452, *www.schulzmuseum.org.* The **Luther Burbank Home & Gardens** at Santa Rosa and Sonoma avenues preserves the botanical estate of America's plant wizard, (707) 524-5445; *www.lutherburbank.org.*

Healdsburg, an old style town built around a public square, has become gentrified of late, with boutiques, fine dining and—oh yes—winery tasting rooms. The **Healdsburg Museum** offers historical exhibits in a classic Andrew Carnegie library building at 221 Matheson Street; (707) 431-3325. Northwest of Healdsburg, boaters head for **Lake Sonoma**, a reservoir above the Dry Creek Valley. The **Russian River Valley** is noted for its funky old time resorts, and the river is popular for swimming and canoeing. **Armstrong Redwoods State Reserve** and **Austin Creek State Recreation Area** offer fine stands of redwoods that shade picnic areas and hiking trails.

The northern Sonoma coast is gorgeous, a rival to the fabled Mendocino Coast above. If you follow the Russian River to its mouth at the cute hamlet of *Jenner* and head south, you'll soon reach *Bodega* and *Bodega Bay*, forever etched in our nightmares as the locales for Alfred Hitchcock's thriller, *The Birds.* Much of the coastline here is preserved in **Sonoma Coast State**

Beach. Traveling north from Jenner, you'll encounter **Fort Ross State Historic Park**, a replica of an early Russian fur trading post. Beyond Fort Ross are **Salt Point State Park** and **Kruse Rhododendron State Reserve**, which exhibits a stunning display of springtime blooms.

However, we came to northern Sonoma County to taste wine, and these are our favorite places to do so:

Ferrari-Carano Winery is an elegant blend of manor house, castle and modern winery, with elaborate gardens, in the Dry Creek Valley at 8761 Dry Creek Road; (707) 433-6700; *www.ferrari-carano.com.*

Hop Kiln Winery occupies an impressive triple-towered 1903 hop-drying barn in the Russian River Valley at 6050 Westside Road; (707) 433-6491; *www.hopkilnwinery.com.*

J. Pedroncelli Winery is a family-owned operation noted for good zinfandel and other fine wines at modest prices. It's in the Dry Creek Valley at 1220 Canyon Road; (707) 857-3531; *www.pedroncelli.com.*

Korbel Champagne Cellars is a handsome vine-covered facility that could have been transplanted from the Rhine Valley. It specializes in champagne and it offers interesting tours. It's on the Russian River near Guerneville, 13250 River Road.; (707) 887-2294; *www.korbel.com.*

Roshambo Winery & Gallery is a stunningly modern complex of glass and curved laminate, with modern art gracing the tasting room walls. It's also in the Russian River Valley at 3000 Westside Road; (888) 525-WINE or (707) 411-2051; *www.roshambowinery.com.*

Where to learn more

The Best of the Wine Country guidebook has complete details on the area's wineries; it's available at book stores or from *www.amazon.com.*

Alexander Valley Winegrowers, P.O. Box 248, Healdsburg, CA 95448; (888) 289-4637; *www.alexandervalley.org.*

Healdsburg Chamber of Commerce, 217 Healdsburg Ave., Healdsburg, CA 95448; (707) 433-6935; *www.healdsburg.org.*

Russian River Chamber of Commerce, P.O. Box 331 (16209 First St.), Guerneville, CA 95446; (707) 869-9000; *www.russianriver.com.*

Russian River Wine Road is a guide map available from area wineries or from P.O. Box 46, Healdsburg, CA 95448; (800) 723-6336 or (707) 433-4335; *www.wineroad.com.*

Santa Rosa Convention & Visitors Bureau, 9 Fourth St., Santa Rosa, CA 95404; (800) 404-7673 or (707) 577-8674; *www.visitsantarosa.com.*

Santa Ynez Valley
Danish delights, wineries and Michael

Ⅎ

What do Michael Jackson's Neverland Valley Ranch, Kentucky Derby winner Charismatic, a winery belonging to television's Davey Crockett, an old Spanish mission and America's largest Danish village have in common? They're all in the Santa Ynez Valley, a pretty rural haven forty-five miles above Santa Barbara. It's a region of vineyards and wineries, high end horse farms, extravagant country estates and a curious mix of Danish and Spanish architecture.

Although U.S. Highway 101 skims the western edge of the valley, the most interesting approach is via State Route 154, traveling northwest from Santa Barbara through the Santa Ynez Mountains. The highway climbs quickly, offering pretty vistas back to the scenic Santa Barbara coastline. The route crests 2,225-foot **San Marcos Pass** then crosses the lofty Cold Spring Arch bridge that spans a steep-walled, thickly wooded ravine. Dropping down toward the valley, it passes **Cachuma Lake Recreation Area**, encompassing a large reservoir with water sports, camping, picnicking, hiking trails and a store; (805) 686-5054.

From there, the highway spirals down into the Santa Ynez Valley. A left turn onto State Route 246 will take you through and to its three primary attractions—the Santa Ynez Valley wine country, Old Mission Santa Inéz and the excessively charming Danish shopping village of Solvang.

Navigational note: If you're approaching from the north on Highway 101, you can reach Solvang by turning east onto Route 246 at *Buellton*.

Solvang is one of California's unexpected delights—a cute and festive Danish village set among the valley's vineyards and pasturelands. Danish immigrants settled here in 1911 to establish a farming community and school. Through the years, it has evolved into a tourist-oriented Scandinavian village, complete with cross-timbered houses and inns, gift shops and enough *smörgasbord* to feed the Danish navy.

This is a serious shopping village, with more than 300 shops offering imports from Denmark and other European countries. Several bakeries issue tasty Danish pastries. Restaurants specialize in *smörgasbord* and other hearty Scandinavian fare. Particularly tasty is a breakfast treat called *aebleskivers,* waffle-like but cone-shaped, stuffed with apple slices and served with powdered sugar and raspberry jam.

The town has two small museums. Exhibits at the **Elverhoj Museum** at 1624 Elverhoj Way focus on Solvang's Danish heritage; (805) 686-1211;

www.elverhoj.org. The **Hans Christian Andersen Museum** above the Book Loft and Coffee House at 1680 Mission Drive chronicles the life and writings of Denmark's legendary storyteller; (805) 688-2052.

Solvang hosts a Danish Days celebration the third weekend of September and a summer-long outdoor drama festival, the Pacific Conservatory for the Performing Arts' Theaterfest; (805) 922-8313; *www.pcpa.org.*

Next door to Solvang and from quite another cultural world is **Mission Santa Ínes** at 1760 Mission Drive, established in 1804; (805) 688-4815. Its museum displays a nice collection of Spanish and Chumash Indian artifacts.

One can gallop off in several directions to explore the Santa Ynez Valley wine country, since vineyards nearly surround Solvang. Most are in the heart of the Santa Ynez Valley, fanning out east, north and south of town. Still more are along scenic, oak-shrouded Foxen Canyon Road northeast of *Los Olivos.* If you head for *Buellton,* you'll encounter several winery tasting rooms along Santa Rosa Road west of town. Both Solvang and Los Olivos have clusters of tasting rooms detached from their wineries.

Here are some of our favorites places to visit and sip good wine:

Bridlewood Winery at 3555 Roblar Avenue is an opulent California mission style complex; (800) 467-4100 or (707) 688-9000; *www.bridlewoodwinery.com.*

Fess Parker Winery at 6200 Foxen Canyon Road, styled like an elegant hunting lodge, is owned by television's former Daniel Boone and Davey Crockett; (805) 688-1545; *www.fessparker.com.*

Firestone Winery at 5000 Zaca Station Road was one of the valley's first major operations, established in 1972 by tire and rubber company heirs Leonard Firestone and his son Brooks. It offers guided tours; (805) 688-3940; *www.firestonewine.com.*

The Gainey Vineyard at 3950 E. Highway 246 is a stylish facility described as "one of the most beautiful wineries in the world" by wine columnist Robert Lawrence Balzer. It also has guided tours; (805) 688-0558; *www.gaineyvineyard.com.*

Where to learn more

The Best of the Wine Country guidebook has complete details on the valley's wineries; it's available at book stores or from *www.amazon.com.*

Solvang Conference & Visitors Bureau, P.O. Box 70 (1511 Mission Dr.), Solvang, CA 93463; (805) 688-6144; *www.solvangusa.com.*

Wineries of Santa Barbara County map is available from tasting rooms or from the Santa Barbara County Vintners' Association, P.O. Box 1558, Santa Ynez, CA 93460-1558; (805) 688-0881; *www.sbcountywines.com.*

Ventura County
Three towns, two marinas and lots of beach

⚑

A thick wedge of beaches, orange groves and mountains tucked between Los Angeles and Santa Barbara, Ventura County is little known outside of California. However, it is certainly familiar to Los Angelenos. Every weekend, tens of thousands of them pour into the county to escape the congestion and smog of their great urban sprawl.

What attracts these folks is numerous public beaches, two marinas, an offshore national park, an old Spanish mission, several museums, a famous art colony and health spa, and a mountain wilderness.

The area's largest community is the oddly named *Oxnard*, with a population of more than 170,000. Occupying a broad coastal flood plain, it was named for Henry T. Oxnard, who brought a sugar beet factory and thus prosperity to the area in the late 1800s. The town has several lures, including the **Carnegie Art Museum** at 424 S. C Street, (805) 385-8179; the **Murphy Auto Museum** at 2230 Statham Boulevard, (805) 487-4333, *www.murphy automuseum.com*; and **Herzog Wine Cellars**, a kosher winery at 3201 Camino del Sol; (805) 983-1560; *www.herzogwinecellars.com*.

Most visitors to Oxnard head for the water. **Channel Islands Harbor** is a busy marina with boat rentals, lodging, restaurants and a Fisherman's Wharf shopping area; (805) 985-4852; *www.channelislandsharbor.org*. The nearby **Ventura County Maritime Museum** at 2731 S. Victoria Avenue displays assorted things nautical; (805) 984-6260.

Two beach communities, *Hollywood Beach* and *Silver Strand*, both dating from the 1920s, flank either side of Channel Islands Harbor. They're fronted by wide public beaches. State and county beach parks run almost continuously along low-lying coastal flats between Oxnard and Ventura. By consulting a local map and driving close to the shoreline, you'll encounter the county's second marina, **Ventura Harbor**. It offers boat rentals, dining, lodging and the Spanish seacoast style Ventura Harbor Village; (877) 89-HARBOR or (805) 642-8538; *www.venturaharbor.com* and *www.ventura-harborvillage.com*.

The county's oldest community, *Ventura* dates from 1782 with the founding of San Buenaventura Mission. It's a more attractive city than Oxnard, sitting on a coastal shelf with wooded hills rising steeply behind. **San Buenaventura** near downtown at 225 East Main Street is one of the best-preserved of the California missions; (805) 648-4496. Other Ventura lures include the **Ventura County Museum of Art** at 100 E. Main Street; (805)

653-0323, *www.venturamuseum.org*; and the Victorian style **Dudley House Museum** with historic exhibits at Ashwood and Loma Vista streets, (805) 642-3345, *www.dudleyhouse.org*.

Both Ventura and Oxnard are gateways to **Channel Islands National Park**, via their respective harbors. The park occupies five of the eight off-shore Channel Islands, with camping, trails and beaches. To preserve the islands' pristine look, there are no facilities other than campsites. The islands are home to 2,000 species of plants and animals and 145 are endemic. Transport to the islands is offered by **Island Packers** with boat slips at both Ventura and Channel Islands harbors; (805) 642-1393; *www.islandpackers.com*. Park headquarters is at Ventura Harbor; (805) 658-5730; *www.nps.gov/chis*.

Inland from Ventura is the famed art and cultural colony of *Ojai* (pronounced *O-high*), in a lush green mountain-cradled valley. The setting is so idyllic that it was used as the establishing shot for Frank Capra's 1937 film, "Lost Horizon." Dressed in orange groves and gnarled oak woodlands, the Ojai Valley is noted for health spas, private schools, horse farms and spiritual retreats such as the Krishnamurti Foundation. The neat Spanish style downtown area is busy with art galleries, book stores and boutiques.

The town's memories are preserved in the **Ojai Valley Museum** in the former St. Thomas of Aquinas Church building at 130 W. Ojai Avenue; (805) 640-1390; *www.ojaivalleymuseum.org*. The **Ojai Center for the Arts** at 113 S. Montgomery Street is the town's cultural focal point, with galleries, performance venues and art classes; (805) 646-0117; *www.ojaiartcenter.org*. This culturally inclined haven sponsors the **Ojai Music Festival** in early June, (805) 646-2094, *www.ojaifestival.org*; the **Ojai Shakespeare Festival** from mid-August to early September, (805) 646-9455, *www.ojaishakespeare.org*; and the **Ojai Film Festival** in mid-October, (805) 640-1947, *www.ojaifilmfestival.com*.

North of town, State Route 33 winds through the thickly wooded **Los Padres National Forest**, with campgrounds, hot springs, fishing streams and trailheads for the Sespe and Matilija wilderness areas. For details, check with the Ojai Ranger Station in town at 1190 E. Ojai Ave.; (805) 646-4348.

Where to learn more

Ojai Valley Chamber of Commerce, 150 W. Ojai Ave. (P.O. Box 1134), Ojai, CA 93024-1134; (805) 646-8126; *www.ojaichamber.org*.

Oxnard Convention & Visitors Bureau, 200 W. Seventh St., Oxnard, CA 9330; (800) 2-OXNARD or (805) 385-7545; *www.oxnardtourism.com*.

Ventura Convention & Visitors Bureau, 89 S. California St., Ventura, CA 93001; (800) 483-6214 or (805) 648-2075; *www.ventura-usa.com*.

The eastern edge
Discoveries along lonely Highway 93

Although Nevada is our seventh largest state, with about 110,000 square miles of land area, it ranks only thirty-fifth in population, with nineteen people per square mile. Further, that population is badly distributed, with more than sixty percent in Clark County, home to the state's two largest cities, Las Vegas and Henderson.

Thus, the rest of Nevada is even more thinly settled than statistics indicate. Remove Clark County, the Reno-Tahoe and Carson City areas, and the state's population would be only about 100,000, or less than one lonely person per square mile!

Thus, it's easy to escape the crowds by exploring the Silver State's lonely and often fascinating interior. Our Nevada home is in Henderson and when we need a wide open spaces fix, we head north on U.S. Highway 93. In less than an hour, we're driving through Nevada's high lonesome.

Known here as the Great Basin Highway, U.S. 93 separates from Interstate 15 about twenty-one miles northeast of Las Vegas. It takes travelers into one of America's most intriguing topographical features. The Great Basin is a mile-high landlocked and arid desert-prairie corrugated with north-south mountain ranges. It's a massive region, covering more than eighty percent of Nevada and ten percent of the contiguous United States. Highway 93 travels along the basin's eastern edge.

The first civilization you'll encounter on this route is tiny *Alamo*, nearly a hundred miles from Las Vegas. A dozen miles north, Highway 93 makes an abrupt left turn and heads for *Caliente*, a hamlet that has something in common with Las Vegas. Both were born in 1905 as railroad division points. Check out the California mission style **Caliente Railroad Station**, now housing city offices and the Lincoln County Chamber of Commerce.

Just east of town, take a twenty-one-mile side trip through the floor of **Rainbow Canyon**, a handsome chasm carved by Clover Creek. Montana's Senator William Clark, founder of Caliente and Las Vegas, routed his railroad through here and nearly went broke when a flood washed out his tracks in 1910. The rails have since been elevated.

Above Caliente, pause to explore the geological wonderland of **Cathedral Gorge State Park**; (775) 728-4460; *www.parks.nv.gov/cg.htm*. More of a shallow basin than a gorge, it's busy with fantastically shaped pinnacles, spires, columns, fins and narrow serpentine ravines. Several other state parks are in this area and you can learn about them at a regional information center near the park's entrance.

Next stop on Highway 93 is funkily charming old *Pioche (pee-OACH)*, a former mining town with many of its 19th century buildings intact. Visit its **Million Dollar Courthouse**, so named because its construction in 1871 went way over budget; and the **Lincoln County Historical Museum**; (775) 962-5207. Also worth a look is the still-intact **Pioche Tramway** that hauled silver ore from the mines to a smelter. Above Pioche, you'll begin a ninety-one-mile stretch of lonely highway through broad Lake Valley, with lofty peaks forming the eastern horizon.

At a pit stop called *Majors Junction*, head east on Highway 6/50 to **Great Basin National Park**; (775) 234-7331; *www.nps.gov/grba.* More mountain than basin, this little-visited park encompasses Wheeler Peak— Nevada's second highest—and the former Lehman Caves National Monument. A small café and gift shop are the park's only facilities, although there are cafés and motels in nearby *Baker*. Follow winding Wheeler Peak Scenic Drive to its terminus at Wheeler Peak Campgrounds. It offers splendid views of the mountain and Great Basin far below. If you hike up the Bristlecone Pine Grove Trail from here in the fall, you'll see this book's cover.

Retreat from the park and head for *Ely*, the final stop in our eastern Nevada trek. This old mining town is home to the **Nevada Northern Railway Museum** at 1100 Avenue A, a former railyard where you can view and ride vintage rolling stock; (866) 40-STEAM or (775) 289-2085; *www.nevada northernrailway.net.* The area's archives are preserved in the **White Pine Public Museum** at 2000 Aultman Street; (775) 289-4710.

Just west of Ely off U.S. Highway 50, pause to explore the **Ruth Mining District**, a manmade badlands of green, yellow and rust colored tailing dumps, mining terraces and open pit mines. Follow signs to the Copper Pit, one of America's largest manmade holes in the ground. This old mining district yielded copper, gold and silver around the turn of the last century. Mining had resumed when we last visited, spurred by rising metal prices.

Where to learn more

Lincoln County Chamber of Commerce, P.O. Box 553 (in the train depot), Caliente, NV 89008; (775) 726-3129; *www.lincolncountynevada.com.*

Pioche Chamber of Commerce, P.O. Box 127, Pioche, NV 89043; (775) 962-5544; *www.piochenevada.com.*

White Pine County Tourism & Recreation Board, 150 Sixth St., Ely, NV 89301; (800) 496-9350 or (775) 289-3720; *www.elynevada.org.*

Elko
Cowboy cool and wide open spaces

⚐

*A*nd still amongst the workin' hands
The words come now and then,
To write a livin' history
Of the stock, and earth and men.

— © J.B. Allen, *The Medicine Keepers*

Laconic cowboys—most of them real—stroll onstage at Elko's Western Folklife Center to recite poetry, "slinging lingo" about their lives on the range, the traditions of ranching, their favorite horse or bits of humor, some of it rather bawdy.

Cowboys reciting poetry? And without blushing?

The annual National Cowboy Poetry Gathering in late January personifies the character of Elko, an old ranching and mining town in northeastern Nevada. Its citizens, wanting to preserve their old West heritage, established the Western Folklife Center in 1980. Five years later, they started the annual poetry gathering, inviting cowboy poets, singers and musicians to perform.

The town of about 17,000, Elko has no great claim to fame other than two nationally recognized annual events—the cowboy poets' gathering and the National Basque Festival in early July. It isn't a serious art colony and it has no trendy shops. It sits in the middle of a high desert, miles from anywhere. Yet it's a fairly popular tourist stop, and it ranks high on several rosters of the nation's most livable communities.

Your first impression of Elko may be of a tough old Humphrey Bogart of a town—solid, a bit homely and unpretentious. Since its citizens weren't into historic preservation until recently, its century old storefronts are an eclectic mix of weathered brick, wooden false front and 1960s masonry.

The old fashioned downtown area is walkable, for it covers only a few blocks. Short strolls will take you to a pair of century-old hotel-casinos—the **Commercial** and **Stockmen's**. The Commercial has an interesting claim to fame. It was here, not in Las Vegas or Reno, that the first big-name entertainers were hired to lure gamblers. Owner Milton Crumbly, Jr., booked nightclub entertainer Ted Lewis and bandleader Paul Whiteman in 1941.

Near the casinos is the outstanding **Western Folklife Center**, in the old brick former Pioneer Hotel at 501 Railroad St.; (888) 880-5885 or (775) 738-7508; *www. westernfolklife.org*. It features Western arts, crafts, historic displays and videos, plus a gift shop and an old Western bar. Nearby, at

Fifth and Commercial, is the penultimate saddle shop and cowboy store, **J.M. Capriola**; (775) 738-5816; *www.capriolas.com.*

Elko's two other major lures are northeast along Idaho Street. **Sherman Station**, half a mile from downtown at 1405 Idaho, consists of a collection of old log buildings moved here from other areas. They house several historical exhibits and the **Elko Chamber of Commerce**; (775) 738-7135; *elkonevada.com.* Just beyond at 1515 Idaho is the excellent **Northeastern Nevada Museum**; (775) 738-3418; *www.nenv-museum.org.* It offers professionally-done exhibits on the history and geology of the area, plus extensive wildlife and gun collections and an art gallery.

A popular pastime for both visitors and locals is to pig out at one of Elko's Basque restaurants, where huge meals are served family style at long tables. Our favorite and the most authentic is the **Star Bar & Hotel**, a former bachelors' boarding hotel at 495 Silver St.; (775) 738-9925. The others are **Bil Tóki Basque-American Dinner House** at 405 Silver St., (775) 738-9691; **Nevada Dinner House** at 351 Silver St., (775) 738-8485; and **Tóki Ona** at 1550 Idaho St., (775) 738-32114.

Elko began life in 1869 as a stop on the transcontinental railroad. Entrepreurs set up tents to provide food and lodging to travelers, local miners, ranchers and railroad crews, and a wild frontier town soon blossomed.

Getting out there

For outdoor types, Elko is an ideal base, since it sits in the heart of the Great Basin. The **Ruby Mountains**, scenically jagged peaks twenty miles southeast of town, lure hikers, backpackers, fisherpersons, hunters and mountain bikers. Outfitters offer backpacking and horsepacking trips to remote alpine lakes and glacial-carved basins. **Lamoille Canyon Recreation Area** on the mountains' south flank has campgrounds, scenic viewpoints and trailheads into the Rubies. En route to the canyon, visit the charming old country town of *Lamoille*, with a couple of art galleries and a popular Western style restaurant, **Pine Lodge Dinner House**; (775) 753-6363.

Another fascinating outdoor area is the **Jarbidge Wilderness**, up north near the Idaho border and reached by State Route 225. It's a remote land of rock-ribbed canyons, high peaks and brushy woodlands. The area is popular with four-wheelers, although many of the roads are navigable by family sedans. On the edges of the wilderness, explore the tiny old towns of *Jarbidge*, *Mountain City* and *Tuscarora*.

Where to learn more

Elko Convention & Visitors Authority, 700 Moran Way, Elko, NV 89801; (800) 248-3556 or (775) 738-4091; *www.elkocva.com.*

Reno
Still the biggest little city

₧

When you think of Reno, you probably think of glittering casinos and you may think it's Nevada's second largest city. If you haven't been there lately—or if you've never been there—much of what you think about "The Biggest Little City in the World" may be outdated.

Reno's gaming activity has slumped because of competition from Indian casinos in California and mega-resorts in Las Vegas. Several small casinos have closed in recent years. Further, it's no longer Nevada's second largest city; it now ranks third behind Henderson, a sprawling Las Vegas suburb.

However, to paraphrase Mark Twain's quote about his premature obituary, the demise of Reno has been greatly exaggerated. It's doing just fine, thank you. Civic leaders are diversifying their town, attracting new light industry and huge distribution centers to provide jobs for its residents, and new recreational and cultural lures for visitors. The result is a nicely balanced, thriving mini-city of about 225,000 residents. We think it's more appealing than ever.

Since Reno sits at the foot of the Sierra Nevada range, not far from **Lake Tahoe**, the region is noted for its outdoor lures. Those mountains shelter the world's largest concentration of ski resorts, and Lake Tahoe is a serious summer playground. State parks on both the Nevada and California shores offer water sports, camping and hiking. Rand McNally recently rated Reno-Tahoe as best region in the nation for outdoor recreation.

However, one doesn't have to trek to Tahoe to enjoy of the outdoor life. A recreational trail follows the shoreline of the Truckee River as it meanders through the heart of Reno. This **Truckee River Walk** is lined with parklands and picnic areas and it's a good birdwatching area. Folks can fish within view of high rise casinos, and a section of the river has been shaped into a kayaking course. The city also has miles of bike routes and several large parks with multi-use trails.

For a town of its size, Reno offers a surprising variety of visitor lures. Its most famous is the **National Automobile Museum** on the river at 10 Lake St.; (775) 333-9300; *www.automuseum.org*. It exhibits a fine assortment of vehicles, ranging from steam carriages to Stutz Bearcats. Another popular attraction is the **Fleischmann Planetarium** on the campus of the University of Nevada Reno at 1600 Virginia St.; (775) 784-4812; *www.planetarium. unr.nevada.edu*. It's a combined planetarium, science museum and widescreen movie theater.

The **Wilbur D. May Museum** north of town in Rancho San Rafael Park exhibits artifacts and hunting trophies from the May Company scion's worldwide travels. The **Great Basin Adventure,** a playground and theme park, is part of the complex; (775) 785-5961; *www.maycenter.com.* Among Reno's other lures are the **Nevada Historical Society Museum** at 1650 N. Virginia St., (775) 668-1190; the **Nevada Museum of Art** at 160 W. Liberty St.; (775) 329-3333, *www.nevada art.org*; and the **Keck Mineral Museum** on the University of Nevada campus; (775) 784-4528; *www.unr.edu.*

Reno has become a major arts and cultural venue, once ranked as America's number one literary city by the National Endowment for the Arts. Several old buildings have been recycled into cultural centers. The **Riverside Hotel** at 17 Virginia Street, once Reno's oldest casino, is now a complex of artists' lofts and galleries, and it's the home of Sierra Arts; (775) 329-ARTS; *www.sierra-arts.org.* The Theater Coalition's **Lear Theater** occupies an historic church building at 528 W. First Street; (775) 786-2278; *www.theater coalition.org.* An old grade school complex at 925 Riverside Drive serves as the **McKinley Art and Cultural Center**; (775) 334-2417.

A downtown section of the River Walk and adjacent streets have been designated as the **Truckee River Arts District.** The area is busy with galleries, public art, shops, restaurants and coffee houses. During July, Reno becomes **ARTown**, with more than 200 cultural events. Locals say it's the largest visual and performing arts festival in America.

Reno began life as a distribution center for the transcontinental railroad in the 1860s. When Nevada legalized gambling in 1931, it was Reno—not Las Vegas—that became the first major gaming center. Nevada's largest city for many decades, Reno thrived while Las Vegas remained a dusty desert town. It wasn't until the development of the Las Vegas Strip in the 1940s and 1950s that Glitter City zoomed past its northern neighbor.

However, lest we've misled you, Reno still offers plenty of gaming action. No major casino hotels have closed during the gambling downturn. Four of them—Circus Circus, Silver Legacy, Reno Hilton and John Ascuaga's Nugget in *Sparks*—match the room count and amenities of many Las Vegas resorts. Downtown Reno is still mostly glitter and casinos, with some of them linked by elaborate skybridges. Thus, even with the Biggest Little City's new diversification, it is still northern Nevada's Party Central.

Where to learn more

Reno-Sparks Convention & Visitors Authority, 4001 S. Virginia St. (P.O. Box 837), Reno, NV 89504; (800) FOR-RENO or (775) 827-RENO; *www.renolaketahoe.com.*

Albuquerque to Gallup
Meeting the native folk, from Acoma to Zuñi

⚑

West central New Mexico is one of the least visited areas in the Land of Enchantment. Travelers whizzing along Interstate 40 between Albuquerque and Gallup find nothing enchanting about billboards and rest stops.

However, there are several attractions in this area if you shed the freeway. One of New Mexico's great intrigues is its pueblo villages that have been continuously inhabited for hundreds of years. Three are in this region, along with two national monuments, El Malpais and El Morro. And finally, Gallup is an interesting old town worth a day or so of exploration.

Head west from Albuquerque on I-40 and take exit 114 to *Laguna Pueblo*, terraced into a low slope within sight of the freeway. Little remains of the pueblo itself, although its **St. Joseph's Mission** is one of the prettiest Catholic churches in New Mexico; (505) 552-9330. The pueblo's more contemporary community is *Cresta Blanca*, just beyond at exit 108, with native jewelry shops and the **Dancing Eagle Casino**; (877) 440-9966.

Opposite Cresta Blanca, follow Road 23 south into the Acoma Reservation to the amazing *Acoma Sky City*, perched atop a 350-foot mesa. This pueblo dates from 1150, and its imposing yet simple San Esteban del Rey Church was added in 1629 after the Spanish conquest. Visiting Sky City can be a mystical, spiritual experience, a journey into the native peoples' past. It has changed little through the centuries and only a handful of traditionalists now live up there. Most of the Acoma folks occupy the village below. To tour the pueblo, one must check in at a visitor center at the base, then take a shuttle up to the mesa; (800) 747-0181 or (505) 469-1052.

Follow Road 38 back to I-40 and go west to *Grants*, a rather nondescript town that prospered briefly as the "Uranium capital of the world." From the 1950s to the 1970s, more than half the nation's uranium came from nearby mines. The **New Mexico Mining Museum** at Santa Fe and Iron avenues tells the story of that era and a mock-up mine has been tunneled into the basement; (800) 748-2142 or (505) 287-4802; *www.grants.org*.

From Grants, go south on State Route 53 to **El Malpais National Monument and Conservation Area**. It encloses a vast sprawl of contorted lava flows, lava tubes, cinder cones, sculpted sandstone shapes and traces of pueblo ruins. The visitor center is on Route 53 twenty-three miles south of Grants; (505) 783-4774; *www.nps.gov/elma*. Nearby is the privately-operated **Bandera Volcano and Ice Cave**. Trails lead to the top of the extinct volcano and down to the cave, with a small pond of algae-stained ice; (888) ICE-CAVE or (505) 783-4303; *www.icecaves.com.*

Following Route 53 west of Bandera, you'll cross the Continental Divide, although it's little more than a bulge in this rough terrain. **El Morro National Monument** is just ahead; (505) 783-4226; *www.nps.gov/elmo.* Here, travelers have been leaving their graffiti on a 400-foot butte for centuries. A trail leads to the top, which once was occupied by pueblo villages.

Continuing westward on Route 53, you'll encounter the sprawling *Zuñi Pueblo*, New Mexico's largest native settlement. Once regarded as one of the fabled seven cities of Cibola (*SEE-bola*), it's now a scattered village of woodframe homes and businesses. However, a small section of the original adobe pueblo remains, with the humble **Old Zuñi Mission** (Our Lady of Guadalupe Church) as its centerpiece. Isolated from other Pueblo tribes, the fierce Zuñi were the first to be encountered by Spanish *conquistadores* and the last to be conquered. Considerably more friendly these days, they are excellent artisans. Their silver and turquoise jewelry, needlework and carved animal fetishes are available at several local shops. **A:Shiwi A:wan Museum and Heritage Center** tells the Zuñi story; (505) 782-4403. The contact for Zuñi tourism is (505) 782-7238; *www.experiencezuni.com.*

Backtrack on Highway 53 to Route 602 and follow it north to *Gallup.* It's a tough old town on historic 66, surrounded by red rock formations. A major rest stop on I-40, Gallup is noted for its native arts centers and jewelry stores, along with tourist shops selling rubber tomahawks. Local history and Southwest native culture is the focus of the **Gallup Cultural Center** at 201 Highway 66; (505) 863-4131. Nearby **Red Rock State Park** at the base of imposing redwall cliffs has an amphitheater, a fine native cultural museum and hiking trails; (505) 722-3839. It's the site of the **Gallup Inter-Tribal Indian Ceremonial** in August, America's oldest and largest native peoples' gathering; (888) 685-2564; *www.indianceremonial.com.*

The **Navajo Nation** is just northwest of Gallup, and U.S. 491 leads north into the New Mexico portion of this huge reservation. If you're headed that way, drive to 1,700-foot **Ship Rock** of U.S. 666, one of the most imposing promontories in the Southwest. This dramatically eroded volcanic plug figures prominently in Navajo folklore.

Where to learn more

Gallup Convention & Visitors Bureau, P.O. Box 600 (701 E. Montoya Blvd.), Gallup, NM 87305; (800) 242-4282 or (505) 863-3841; *www.gallup-chamber.com.*

O'Keeffe country
Pueblos, red rocks and a scenic train ride

Ꝺ

When hen I got to New Mexico, that was mine. As soon as I saw it, that was my country.
— **Georgia O'Keeffe**

Georgia O'Keeffe's love affair with New Mexico lasted for nearly seventy years. She passed through the state in 1917 during a trip to Colorado. Starting in 1929, she became a frequent visitor to the Taos art colony, moving within a cultural circle that included D.H. Lawrence and Ansel Adams. She spent several summers at a dude ranch in the Río Chama Valley, then she bought a rustic adobe in Abiquiu and became a full-time resident. Failing health forced her to move to Santa Fe in 1984. She died there two years later at the age of ninety-eight.

If you're planning a vacation in Santa Fe, you can sample an interesting slice of New Mexico by heading north through the red rock country where the famous artist lived and painted. You might start with a visit to the **Georgia O'Keeffe Museum** in a handsomely restored adobe at 217 Johnson Street in Santa Fe; (505) 946-1000; *www.okeeffemuseum.org*. You can view a video about her life and see a fine retrospective of her works, ranging from early surrealistic charcoals to those familiar stark desert scenes.

Head north from Santa Fe on U.S. 84/285 into a region busy with ancient and still-active pueblos villages. The first is the well-kept *Tesuque Pueblo*, built around a plaza with a traditional Spanish church. Farther along, you'll encounter the large *Pojoaque Pueblo* complex with a tourist information center, large native crafts shop, the excellent Poeh Museum and Cities of Gold Casino; (505) 455-3460; *www.citiesofgold.com*. At the tourist center or museum, you can pick up a travel guide to several other pueblo villages in the region. Or contact the **Eight Northern Indian Pueblos Council**; (800) 793-4955 or (505) 852-4256.

Continue north on highways 84/285 to *Española*, the commercial hub of the Española Valley. About ten miles beyond, the highways separate. Stay with U.S. 84, following the Río Chama into the red rock formations of "O'Keeffe Country." Many of these sandstone shapes were inspirations for her paintings. About twenty-five miles north of Española, watch on your left for a sign to **Poshouinge**, an un-excavated village of the Anasazi, New Mexico's first residents. It's closed to the public, although you can take a short path to an overlook, where a display shows how the village may have looked. You'll get a fine view of the Río Chama Valley from here.

Just beyond is *Abiquiu*, where O'Keeffe lived for nearly forty years. The old adobe village has the look of a native pueblo, although it was settled by the Spanish in 1776. The **O'Keeffe home** is hidden behind adobe walls; any local can point it out. It recently was acquired by the Georgia O'Keeffe Museum; for details about tours, call (505) 946-1000.

A bit further north is **Ghost Ranch** where she spent many summers. Set against gorgeous red rock cliffs, it's now a retreat, also owned by the Georgia O'Keeffe Museum. Visitors can view cultural and historical exhibits about the area and see reproductions of some of the artist's works. To schedule a tour of the ranch and other O'Keeffe sites, call (877) 804-4678.

If you'd like to visit a hidden religious retreat backdropped by red rock cliffs, turn right onto Road 151 several miles above Ghost Ranch. Follow it a bumpy thirteen miles to the **Monastery of Christ in the Desert**; *www. christdesert.org*. Back on Highway 84, you'll soon encounter **Echo Canyon Amphitheater**, a huge natural coliseum carved into a 300-foot cliff. It has picnic areas, campsites and hiking trails.

North of the amphitheater, you'll begin spiraling high into a piñon-juniper zone of the upper Río Chama Valley. This could be a scene from Monument Valley or Utah's Canyonlands, with its vibrant colors and sculpted sandstone shapes. It's a Georgia O'Keeffe landscape in three dimension.

By the time you reach the scattered ranch town of *Tierra Amarilla*, you're in New Mexico's high country. It's a splendid landscape of evergreens and aspens, with the Sangre de Cristo mountains to the east and the Rockies to the west. At 11,268 feet, Brazos Peak dominates the northeastern horizon. You may catch glimpses of the Brazos Cliffs, rising 2,000 feet from the valley floor. Two state parks west of Tierra Amarilla offer camping, fishing and water play—**El Vado Lake State Park** on State Route 112, (505) 588-7247; and **Heron Lake State Park** on U.S. 95, (505) 588-7470.

The old railroading town of *Chama* marks the end of your trip and, for many, the beginning of a train ride. Steam trains of the narrow gauge **Cumbres & Toltec Scenic Railroad** take passengers on a specular run into the Sangre de Cristo and San Juan mountains to the isolated Colorado town of Osier. Advance reservations are essential, particularly in summer; (888) 286-2737 or (505) 756-2151; *www.cumbrestoltec.com*.

Where to learn more

Chama Valley Chamber of Commerce, P.O. Box 306-RB, Chama, NM 87520; (800) 477-0149 or (505) 756-2306; *www.chamavalley.com*.

Santa Fe Convention & Visitors Bureau, P.O. Box 909, Santa Fe, NM 87504; (800) 777-2489 or (505) 955-6200; *www.santafe.org*.

Roswell to White Sands
Aliens, A-bombs and sand dunes

⌐⌐

*W*e were buck naked...havin' a good old time...when all hell broke loose. There was a big explosion...and this thing came plowing through the trees, sheared off the tops and then stopped between two big rocks.

Thus began one of history's great mysteries. Jim Ragsdale, now departed, insisted that he and his girlfriend, makin' whoopee in the bed of his pickup, had witnessed the crash of a "flying dish" near Roswell on the night of July 4, 1947. Others said they saw it, too, and newspapers reported that debris had been found by the U.S. Army and locked away in a warehouse.

Fact or fiction? Government cover-up or somebody's idea of a joke? Many people in this southeastern New Mexico town are convinced that spaceships crashed nearby and that the evidence—including bodies of little oval-eyed aliens—later disappeared. They are so convinced that the town sponsors a UFO museum and an annual UFO convention. Alien dolls, T-shirts, bumper stickers, coffee mugs and "Alien Glow Pop" lollipops are hot sellers at the UFO museum gift shop and local souvenir stores.

This tour starts where space vehicles may be a fantasy and ends in Alamogordo and White Sands, where's they're an established fact.

Roswell's **International UFO Museum and Research Center** is at Second and Main streets; (505) 625-9495; *www.iufomrc.org*. After seeing its exhibits of alien models, photos, newspaper clippings and films about UFO sightings, you may or may not be convinced that something strange interrupted Jim Ragsdale's night of passion.

For you unbelievers, the town offers other archives. The fine **Roswell Museum and Arts Center** has exhibits of regional art and culture, a planetarium and a mockup of the laboratory of Robert H. Goddard, at 100 W. Eleventh St.; (505) 624-6744; *www.roswellmuseum.org*. Goddard, the "father of modern rocketry," conducted many of his experiments near here. The **Historical Center for Southwest New Mexico** occupies an early American mansion at 200 N. Lea Ave., (505) 6222-8333. The **General Douglas L. McBride Military Museum** focuses on New Mexico's role in America's wars. It's at the New Mexico Military Institute, 101 W. College Blvd.; (505) 624-8220; *www.nmmi.cc.nm.us/ museum*.

After doing Roswell, head west on U.S. 70, passing the edge of *Ruidoso*, which we'll visit in the next listing. The highway climbs from the prairie into the wooded Capitan and Sacramento Mountains, passing through the

Mescalero Apache Indian Reservation. It's home to one of the West's most luxurious native-run resorts, the $200 million **Inn of the Mountain Gods**; (800) 595-9011 or (505) 464-7777; *www. innofthemountaingods.com.* Casino Apache part of the complex and the **Ski Apache** winter sports area is nearby; (505) 336-4356; *www.skiapache.com.*

Beyond Mescalero, pick U.S. 54 and head south into an agricultural valley and *Alamogordo*, where space is a definite reality. Rocket research is conducted at Holliman Air Force Base and in the vast deserts of the nearby White Sands Missile Range. Lunar module engines that returned our moon-walking astronauts to their mother ships were tested here in the 1960s.

Before you reach Alamogordo, you'll encounter the **New Mexico Museum of Space History**; (877) 333-6589 or (505) 437-2840; *www.space-fame.org.* It's an extensive complex that includes the International Space Hall of Fame, Snapp Air and Space Park that bristles with spacecraft and launch vehicles, the Astronaut Memorial Garden, and an IMAX theater.

An Alamogordo attraction of quite a different sort is the **Toy Train Depot** at 1991 White Sands Blvd.; (888) 207-3564 or (505) 437-2855. Housed in an 1898 train depot, it displays hundreds of model trains and offers narrow gauge train rides through adjacent Alameda Park.

The Alamogordo area is perhaps best known for **Trinity Site**, where the first atomic bomb—developed at New Mexico's Los Alamos Laboratory—was tested on July 16, 1945. Tours of the site, which is now part of the missile range, are allowed twice a year, on the first Saturday in April and October; (800) 826-0294 or (505) 437-6120.

Drive fifteen miles southwest of Alamogordo to the rolling dunes of **White Sands National Monument**; (505) 479-6124; *www.nps.gov/whsa.* Stop at the visitor center and then take a sixteen-mile round trip on Dune Drive past great mounds of pure white gypsum sand. This is a mystical and sensual place of soft, feminine curves, like a great sea of sugar. Best times to enjoy and photograph the dunes are at sunup and sundown, when slanting sunlight and shadows highlight the shapes. Get away from the other visitors and find a place alone in the dunes. It is said that you can hear the whisper of sand spilling over the ridges, like the sigh of a woman.

Where to learn more

Alamogordo Chamber of Commerce, 1301 N. White Sands Blvd., Alamogordo, NM 88310; (800) 826-0294 or (505) 437-6120; *www. alamogordo.com.*

Roswell Convention & Visitors Bureau, P.O. Drawer 70 (131 W. Second St.), Roswell, NM 88202; (505) 623-5695; *www.roswellcvb.com*

Ruidoso and Billy
Cowboy culture and a legendary outlaw

Ⴙ

Ruidoso is an attractive Western style town in the heart of New Mexico's "equestrian culture," where fine horses are bred and raced. It also once was a haunt of Billy the Kid, America's most famous outlaw.

The town was born in the 1870s when a grist mill and trading post were built on Río Ruidoso, a small stream spilling down from the mountains. (*Río Ruidoso* is Spanish for "noisy river.") Ruidoso and next-door Ruidoso Downs are the heart of an appealing vacation area, noted for art galleries, a major performing arts complex, an outstanding museum of Western culture and a nationally famous race track.

Billy the Kid spent the last years of his short life in this part of south central New Mexico, first as a hired gunman during the Lincoln County War, then as a common criminal. Most of the fighting was centered around Lincoln, about twenty miles northeast. However, the Kid passed through Ruidoso a few times, and he once was cornered at the mill by another gunman. The brave young Billy escaped detection by hiding in a flour barrel.

Visitor are drawn to Ruidoso not for Billy, but for the many cultural offerings and the outdoor lures of surrounding Lincoln National Forest. *U.S. News & World Report* once picked this as one of the top seven vacation and second home sites in America. Sitting more than 6,000 feet above sea level, the region has four relatively mild seasons. The **Inn of the Mountain Gods** and **Ski Apache**, a luxury resort and ski area, are a short drive away; see the previous page.

The two Ruidosos have a kind of cowboy alpine look. Ruidoso's downtown low-rises house art galleries, boutiques, curio shops and some very good restaurants, and it's free of neon. Its cultural centerpiece is the imposing **Spencer Theater for the Performing Arts** north of town; (888) 818-7872 or (505) 336-4800; *www.spencertheater.com*. It offers a year-around season of classics, pops and jazz concerts, theater, ballet and dance.

The rather upscale village of Ruidoso Downs occupies the horsy end of the valley. Its **Ruidoso Downs** is the one of the top quarterhorse and Thoroughbred tracks in the country, with a May to September season; (505) 378-4431. The adjacent Western-theme **Billy the Kid Casino** sponsors a summer concert series of popular and country music.

The **Hubbard Museum of the American West** is a mile east of the race track; (505) 378-4142; *www.hubbardmuseum.com*. It's an outstanding archive of Western culture and equestrian lore. Its extensive offerings include exhibits of cowboy regalia, Western art, wagons and carriages, historic Lincoln and a Kids' Corner equestrian section. The Ruidoso Downs Hall of Fame focuses on the accomplishments of the Western-bred quarterhorse.

Chasing Billy

The odyssey of Henry McCarty, DBA Billy the Kid, is mostly fiction, the subject of more than eight hundred books and forty movies. After exploring Ruidoso, you can learn his true story by following the **Billy the Kid National Scenic Byway**. It links the area's assorted historic sites, some involving Billy, some not. Begin at the **Billy the Kid Visitors Center** adjacent to the Hubbard Museum; (505) 378-4142; *www.billybyway.com.*

From there, head west on U.S. 70 to *San Patricio*, once a Billy the Kid hangout and now a lively art colony. The **Hurd-La Rinconada Gallery** exhibits the works of Peter and Henriette Wyeth Hurd; (800) 658-6912 or (505) 653-4331; *www.wyethartists.com.* Continue east to *Hondo*, a small ranching and farming town, then head northwest on U.S. 380.

You'll shortly encounter the restored Western town of *Lincoln*, flashpoint of the Lincoln County War and now a state historic monument; (505) 653-4372. You can walk in Billy's footsteps as you visit the former courthouse where he was jailed, and several other restored buildings. Many have exhibits about the town's history, the young outlaw and the Lincoln County War. A well-done video recounts his life, from his birth as a New York slum kid, to his wanderings in the west and finally to his death by the hand of Sheriff Pat Garrett on July 14, 1881.

Continue west briefly on Highway 380, then go south on State Route 220 to **Fort Stanton**. It was a U.S. Army base from 1855 until 1896, then it served variously as a tubercular hospital, a camp for German prisoners and Japanese-Americans during World War II and a facility for the disabled. It's now an historic site run by a state-appointed commission. Facilities include a visitor center and museum; (505) 354-0341; *www.fortstanton.com.*

Return to Highway 380 and continue west to the hamlet of *Capitan*, which has a curious little claim to fame. During a 1950 wildfire in the Capitan Mountains, firefighters found a badly singed bear cub and named him "Smokey." He was nursed back to health and became the national symbol for forest fire safety. Exhibits at **Smokey Bear Historical Park** tell his story and an adjacent museum focuses on forest fire prevention; (505) 354-2748. Everybody's favorite bear died in 1976 and is buried on the grounds.

Where to learn more

Ruidoso Valley Chamber of Commerce, 720 Sudderth Dr., Ruidoso, NM 88355; (877) RUIDOSO or (505) 257-7395; *www.ruidosonow.com.*

Taos
A trio of cultures in an ancient city

ⴽ

Sitting on a high plateau at the base of the Sangre de Cristo Mountains, Taos is our favorite New Mexico town, and one of our favorite towns anywhere. This charming place is a mellow blend of three separate yet compatible cultures—the native people who still occupy the Taos Pueblo, the Hispanics who represent a large part of the area's population and the Anglos who have made it a major art colony.

Taos itself is a triplet—the pueblo that's more than a thousand years old; a "new" Spanish town built around a traditional plaza in the 1600s; and Ranchos de Taos, founded a century later when pueblo residents sought new farmlands. Contemporary buildings and a few Victorians are now mixed with old adobes in the two newer communities. However, Taos Pueblo is little changed, except that art galleries occupy some of its ancient buildings.

Like Santa Fe to the south, Taos offers that appealing New Mexican mix of galleries, native crafts shops, restaurants serving Southwest cuisine and that sensuously rounded look of adobe architecture. We prefer Taos because it's more affordable and much smaller, with a population of about 4,700. Santa Fe is twelve times that size.

Approaching from the south on State Route 68, you'll first encounter Ranchos de Taos, then the central town and, three miles beyond, the pueblo. In Ranchos de Taos, watch for the handsome adobe **San Francisco de Asis Church** on the main road, here called Paseo del Pueblo Sur. Because area streets are rather a tangle, stop at the **Taos Chamber of Commerce** just beyond and pick up a map; (505) 758-3873. A couple of miles further is the main crossroad of Paseo del Pueblo Sur and Kit Carson Road, an intersection that, unfortunately, is often choked with traffic. The town plaza is just to the left on Kit Carson and many art galleries are to the right.

Where to begin? The community offers more than a dozen museums and historic adobes. Here are our favorites:

The **Ernest L. Blumenschein Home** is a furnished adobe mansion and art gallery at 222 Ledeux St.; (505) 758-0505. The **Millicent Rogers Museum** is a rambling adobe displaying the arts and culture of the Southwest, on Millicent Rogers Road off U.S. 64; (505) 758-2462. The **Martinez Hacienda** is the mansion of a former Taos *alcalde* (mayor), and it's one of the few remaining fortified adobe homes in America, at 708 Ranchitos Rd.; (505) 758-1000. The **Kit Carson Home & Museum** displays a few items belonging to the frontier scout, plus lots of other Western and Spanish regalia, on Kit Carson Road just east of the main crossroad; (505) 758-0505. (The famous frontier scout, who rarely stayed in one place, owned this adobe from 1843 until his death in 1868. He returned home often enough to father eight children.)

Save most of a day for the *Taos Pueblo*, the only Native American venue that's a World Heritage Site; (505) 758-1028; *www.taospueblo.com*. Set beside a sparkling stream, it's an elegantly weathered complex of ancient adobes, some as high as five stories. It has become a major native arts center, with more that a dozen galleries occupying its mud buildings. You can watch artisans at work and often see native tribal dances.

The arts are definitely alive in Taos. "We put more oil on canvas than on our salads," reads a chamber of commerce news release. According to the Taos Art Dealers Association, this small town has nearly 1,500 working artists and more than a hundred galleries. The community sponsors the **Taos Spring Art Festival** in May and the **Taos Fall Art Festival** from late September through early October. They feature public art displays all over town, studio tours and art lectures, plus music, drama and dance performances.

The art movement started in 1898 when Eastern painters Bert Phillips and Ernest Blumenschein, headed for red rock country, stopped here to have a wagon wheel repaired. Phillips was so enchanted with Taos that he decided to stay. Blumenschein returned every summer until 1919, then he also became a permanent resident. In 1912, they helped establish the Taos Society of Artists. As word spread, cultural luminaries from around the globe spent time here, including Georgia O'Keeffe, Ansel Adams and D.H. Lawrence, freshly expelled from England for exhibiting "obscene" paintings.

The area also offers outdoor lures. The **Río Grande** has carved a deep and narrow chasm into this flat sagebrush plateau. **The Río Grande Gorge Rim Trail** follows the edge for several miles, and local outfitters offer whitewater trips through the rapids below. The **Río Grande Gorge Bridge** on the Highway 64 seven miles west of town was the world's second highest suspension bridge when it was completed in 1964.

For more of the outdoors, head north into the Sangre de Cristo Mountains to **Taos Ski Valley**, regarded as one of the country's top ski resorts; (800) 517-9816 or (505) 776-2291; *www.taosskivalley.com*. It also has an active summer program of scenic lift rides, high country hiking, concerts, barn dances, fishing and horse and llama trekking.

Where to learn more

Taos County Chamber of Commerce, P.O. Drawer I, Taos, NM 87572; (800) 732-TAOS or (505) 758-3873; *www.taoschamber.com*.

KETCHUM, IDAHO

Chapter Three

The
Rocky Mountain
West

Montana
- Flathead Valley
- Great Falls
- Helena
- Montana's Outback
- Butte
- Bozeman
- West Yellowstone

The Panhandle

Idaho
- Valley County
- Boise
- Ketchum
- Sun Valley

Wyoming
- Cody
- Jackson Hole
- Rawlins
- Laramie
- Cheyenne

Utah
- Logan
- Ogden
- Dinosaur Corner
- Southwest Corner
- Capitol Reef

Colorado
- Steamboat Springs
- Boulder
- Breckenridge
- Glenwood Springs
- Ouray
- Leadville
- Black Canyon Byway

IT'S ALL ABOUT GETTING HIGH

The Rocky Mountains are America's scenic backbone, a summer-winter playground stretching from Montana through Colorado. Satellite ranges reach into Idaho and Utah. The Rockies form the Continental Divide that sends raindrops and occasional acrophobic travelers either east or west. However, the region isn't all mountainous. The eastern two-thirds of Montana, Colorado and Wyoming flatten into the Great Plains, and these areas have their attractions as well.

COLORADO occupies the heart of the Rockies, with the highest mean elevation of any state. In sampling its heights, we take you along the little-visited Black Canyon Corridor, to the state's hippest community, to a pair of its highest towns and to ski resorts that offer summer fun.

Where to learn more: Colorado Tourism Office, 1625 Broadway, Suite 1700, Denver, CO 80202; (800) COLORADO; *www.colorado.com.*

IDAHO is a surprise, with more millionaires per capita than any other state. We take you to affordable places such as a fine mini-city and two of its largest freshwater lakes. We also visit a summer and winter vacationland that few folks know about, and a town full of those millionaires.

Where to learn more: Tourism Division, Idaho Commerce and Labor Department, P.O. Box 83720 (700 W. State St.), Boise, ID 83720-0065; (800) VISIT-ID or (208) 334-2470; *www.visitid.org.*

MONTANA is Big Sky Country and other clichés. It's a vast space of mountain-rimmed valleys and endless prairies where the dinosaurs and buffalo once roamed. Our Montana sampler includes tough old mining towns, little art towns, and—yep—a trek into the prairie country.

Where to learn more: Travel Montana, P.O. Box 200533 (301 S. Park Ave.), Helena, MT 59620-0533; (800) VISIT-MT or (406) 841-2870; *www.visitmt.com.*

UTAH isn't just about Mormons, although my ancestors were among them. It's about geographic and cultural diversity, from salt flats to ski resorts, from fine historical museums to Shakespeare festivals. It's also about the fascinating canyons, buttes and spires of the Colorado Plateau.

Where to learn more: Utah Travel Council, 300 N. State St., Salt Lake City, UT 84114; (800) 200-1160 or (801) 538-1030; *www.utah.com.*

WYOMING is mostly prairie country, although the Rockies meander along its western reaches. Much of the state is serious cowboy country, and we take you to a town founded by Buffalo Bill, and to the home of one of America's grandest rodeos.

Where to learn more: Wyoming Travel and Tourism, I-25 at College Drive, Cheyenne, WY 82002; (800) 225-5996 or (307) 777-7777; *www.wyomingtourism.org.*

Black Canyon byway
A grand chasm in the southwest corner

The Black Canyon of the Gunnison River is one of America's steepest chasms, providing a geological exclamation point to the dry, rough-hewn plateau country of southwestern Colorado.

This is not the Colorado of Rocky Mountain highs or aprés ski parties. It's a little-visited region of agricultural valleys edged by distant mountains, of rolling hills and sturdy old towns. The Gunnison River has cut a fifty-three-mile-long gorge through here, although much of it has been flooded by dams. However, a fourteen mile stretch within Black Canyon of the Gunnison National Park remains just as nature carved it—narrow, deep and with walls so sheer that just thinking about them makes one dizzy. In some areas, the canyon is nearly three thousand feet deep—and straight down.

This is one of the most amazing natural formations in America. It's not as deep as the Grand Canyon, but it's very narrow and sheer for its depth. It's just over a thousand feet wide in some places, narrowing to as little as forty feet at the river bed. Quoth geologist Wallace Hanson, who surveyed it in the 1950s: "No other canyon in North America combines the depth, narrowness, sheerness and somber countenance of the Black Canyon."

The chasm gets its name from dark Proterozoic gneiss and schist. Some of the oldest rocks on the planet have been exposed here, thanks to the persistence of the Gunnison River, which is still carving the canyon at the rate of about a millimeter a year,

No freeway provides quick access to this overlooked corner of Colorado. The nearest is Interstate 70, which passes through **Grand Junction** as it crosses the Intermountain West's heartland. From here, take U.S. 50 southeast about forty-five miles to **Delta**, a town of 6,000 in the heart of southwestern Colorado's farm country. While not a tourist town, this handsome old hamlet is decorated with several murals along Main Street. The **Delta County Museum** in an old firehouse at 251 Meeker Street preserves the area's past; (970) 874-8721. Just north of town in Confluence Park is the re-created **Fort Uncompahgre** where costumed docents discuss its founding by French fur traders in 1826; (970) 874-8349; *www.deltafort.org.*

From Delta, continue southeast on Highway 50 to **Montrose**, the largest town in the area, with a population of about 12,000. Worth a look are the **Montrose County Historical Museum** at Main Street and Rio Grande Avenue, with several furnished historical buildings, (970) 249-2085; and the **Ute Indian Museum** three miles south on Highway 50; (970) 249-3098.

Eight miles east of Montrose, State Route 347 takes you north for your first startling look down into the **Black Canyon of the Gunnison**. Begin your visit at the interpretive center, where interactive displays teach you about the area's geology; (970) 641-2337. Take the seven-mile **South Rim Drive**, with ten dizzying overlooks into the canyon. The foaming river far below is reachable, but only by skilled and seasoned hikers. Several outfitters offer whitewater trips on the Gunnison; you can get details at the visitor center. This center and a couple campgrounds are the park's only facilities.

The **North Rim Drive** has even more spectacular vista points than the South Rim, although it's difficult to reach and it's closed in winter. To get there, go east on U.S. 50, cross the gorge near *Sapinero* and follow scenically twisting State Route 92 to *Crawford*. Head south from **Crawford Lake State Park** for eleven miles on a dirt but well-maintained road.

Back on eastbound Highway 50, you'll enter **Cureconti National Recreation Area**, wrapped around the dammed-up part of the Gunnison River. Three reservoirs provide the usual water play and excellent fishing. You can get details at Elk Creek Marina, (970) 641-0707; and Elk Creek Visitor Center, (970) 641-2337. Both are on the twenty-mile-long Blue Mesa Reservoir. The Cimarron Visitor Center, twenty miles east of Montrose, displays rolling stock from the old Denver & Rio Grande Railroad.

The final stop on our Black Canyon Byway is *Gunnison* which, like Delta, occupies a broad agricultural valley. It's a favorite launch point for outdoor activities in the surrounding mountains, lakes and streams. Of course it has the requisite small-town archive. **Gunnison Pioneer Museum** at South Adams Street and Tomichi Avenue has exhibits in several early-day buildings; (970) 641-4530.

Where to learn more

Black Canyon of the Gunnison National Park and *Cureconti National Recreation Area*, 102 Elk Creek, Gunnison, CO 81230; (970) 641-2337; *www.nps.gov/blca and www.nps.gov.cure.*

Delta Area Chamber of Commerce, 301 Main St., Delta, CO 81416; (970) 874-8616; *www.deltacolorado.org.*

Gunnison Chamber of Commerce, P.O. Box 36 (500 E. Tomichi Ave.), Gunnison, CO 81230; (800) 274-7580 or (970) 641-1501; *www.gunnisonco.com.*

Montrose Chamber of Commerce, 1519 E. Main St., Montrose, CO 81401; (800) 923-5515 or (970) 249-5000; *www.montrosechamber.com.*

Boulder
A hip Rocky Mountain high

꒤

When we first visited Boulder, we happened to arrive on a summer's eve and we happened upon the Pearl Street Mall, a four-block pedestrian promenade in the heart of town.

We were greeted by a frolicsome street festival of musicians, wanna-be hippies, pretty university lasses in hip-huggers, fortune tellers, magicians, acrobats and pushcart vendors. The shops along Pearl Street fit the scene—Narayan's Gateway to Nepal, El Loro Jewelry and Clog Company, Ecology House and the Trident Coffee House and Bookstore.

Happily caught between the Rocky Mountains and the University of Colorado, Boulder is the most hip, liberal and outdoor oriented community in the state. The *Denver Post* once described it as "the little town caught between the mountains and reality."

Unhappily, Boulder isn't a little town anymore. With a population pushing 100,000, it's one of the fastest growing communities in the state, with the attendant traffic snarls and suburban sprawl. Those who live here and those who come to the university would like to see the door shut now that they've arrived. Local agencies are looking for ways to slow its growth.

It's still grand place to visit, particularly if you're the fresh air type. Boulder once was rated as America's best outdoor city by *Outside* magazine. Its residents and university students—who resemble healthy young models for a Coors beer ad—hike Boulder's slopes, walk its parklands, pedal its 100 miles of bike paths and even kayak in the middle of town.

Boulder Creek cascades merrily through the city and a section of it is marked off as a competition kayak course. It's also popular for tubing and fishing. The **Boulder Creek Greenway** flanks its banks and a recreational trail runs alongside the stream for sixteen miles. Benches and picnic areas along the route invite lingering, and graphics discuss the creek's riparian flora and fauna. It's estimated that seventy percent of Boulder's residents own bikes and many of them use Boulder Creek Path on the Greenway to commute to work or to class, since the creek runs through the campus.

Boulder has two cultural cores. The first, of course, is the 600-acre campus of the **University of Colorado;** (303) 492-1411; *www.colorado.edu.* The **University of Colorado Museum of Natural History** focuses on the geology and anthropology of the Southwest; (303) 492-6892; *www.cumuseum.colorado.edu.* Stately **Old Main**, built in 1874 as the university's first structure, houses the **Heritage Center**, with exhibits on CU's history and some of its famous graduates, including bandleader Glenn Miller and Robert Redford. The **Boulder History Museum** borders the campus at 1206 Euclid Ave.; (303) 449-3464; *www.boulderhistorymuseum.org*. It's housed in an 1899 mansion, with an extensive array of early day artifacts.

The town's other cultural center is **Chautauqua Park** in the foothills at 900 Baseline Rd.; (303) 442-3282; *www.chautauqua.com*. The Chautauqua group was formed more than a century ago in New York state to create cultural retreats in rural America, and this is one of the surviving few. Its facilities are used for concerts, dramas and workshops. Old cottages provide inexpensive lodging and hiking trails lead into the Rockies' higher reaches.

Another foothill lure is the **National Center for Atmospheric Research** at 1850 Table Mesa Dr.; (303) 497-1174; *www.ncar.ucar.edu*. The world's leading weather research center, it's housed in a kind of high-rise pueblo designed by architect I.M. Pei. Corridors on its second and third floors are lined with dramatic weather photos and hands-on science exhibits.

Back down in the flatlands, an attraction of quite a different cut is the **Leanin' Tree Museum of Western Art** at 6055 Longbow Dr.; (303) 530-1442; *www.leanintree.com/museum*. Operated by the folksy greeting card company, it contains America's largest privately held Western art collection.

Although Boulder begins in the flatlands, its outdoor lures are mostly in the foothills and mountains. **Boulder Mountain Park**, reached by continuing uphill from Chautauqua Park, is a great sprawl of forests, meadowlands and canyons laced with hiking trails. The road switchbacks steeply into the Rockies, providing grand views of the town and the Great Plains beyond. Hiking maps and other park brochures are available at a seasonal ranger station at **Flagstaff Summit**. It has picnic areas and an amphitheater.

Another major outdoor recreation area is **Boulder Canyon**, reached by heading uphill on Canyon Boulevard from downtown. Cascading Boulder Creek is rarely out of sight as you drive this gently twisting highway. Six miles from town, a short and steep trail leads to **Boulder Falls**, tumbling down a sheer rock face.

The Boulder Canyon route ends at *Nederland*, a scruffy former silver mining town on the shores of a pretty reservoir. From here, the Peak to Peak Highway travels north and south along the lofty ramparts of the Rockies. If you head north, you'll soon reach *Estes Park* and **Rocky Mountain National Park**, the ultimate Colorado high.

Where to learn more

Boulder Convention & Visitors Bureau, 2440 Pearl St., Boulder, CO 80302; (800) 444-0447 or (303) 442-2911; *www.bouldercoloradousa.com*.

Breckenridge
The tough old town that became a resort

⚐

Some of the world's most famous ski resorts occupy high Rocky Mountain slopes west of Denver—places like Vail and Beaver Creek. Most were designed as resorts from the get-go, with deliberately charming Bavarian architecture, posh hotels, luxury condos and high end restaurants.

However, one resort has a history that goes beyond an architect's drawing board. Breckenridge—even the name has a tough old Colorado ring to it—began as a wild mining town. A gold strike seventy miles west of Denver in 1859 spurred the usual rush of fortune hunters, rascals and fallen angels. Dozens of tent towns sprung up overnight. When the gold faded after a few decades, so did most of the towns. Breckenridge survived.

Established in 1859 by twenty-nine men and a woman—who must have had her hands full—Breckenridge is the oldest Colorado town west of the Rockies. Further, it's one of the oldest continually inhabited mining towns in western America. Mining near Breckenridge extended well into the last century, and the town was built to last, with sturdy brick and masonry businesses downtown and fine Victorian style homes in its neighborhoods.

Although condos crowd the town's edges, the small, tidy central core retains much of its late 19th century look. It's one of Colorado's largest national historic districts, with 175 buildings on the historic register. Many of those fine old structures now house specialty shops, restaurants, coffee houses, book stores and outdoor outfitters.

Skiing also is a part of the town's history. The Breckenridge Ski Area, established in the nearby Blue Mountains in 1962, is one of the oldest west of the Rockies. It has since become one of the largest, with runs spread over three mountains.

However, this book is not a skiers' guide and Breckenridge is not just a winter destination. With fine shops, restaurants and lodgings and the great Colorado outdoors all around, it's as much a summer place as a ski resort. It occupies the heart of Summit County, one of Colorado's most popular mountain recreation areas. Several outfitters in town can set you up for hiking, biking, fishing and floating.

Before you head out, stop by the **Breckenridge Activities Center** in Blue River Plaza at 137 S. Main Street; (877) 864-0868. You learn about this old town and pick up a self-guiding historical tour map.

Three nearby ski areas run their chairlifts in summer, providing dazzling aerial views, lunch at the top and the opportunity to hike back down. Chairlift rides are available at the **Breckenridge Ski Area**, (970) 453-5000, *www. breckenridge.com*; **Copper Mountain Resort**, (800) 458-8386 or (970) 968-2992, *www.coppercolorado.com*; and **Keystone Resort**, (970) 468-2316; *www. keystone.snow.com*. Keystone also offers summer gondola rides.

Flatlanders soon discover that uphill hiking—not just Summit County scenery—takes one's breath away. The altitude here is over nine thousand feet and hiking trails reach more than two miles above sea level.

If you prefer flatland walking and cycling to hiking and mountain biking, a riverside walk begins at a small park in downtown Breckenridge. It merges with the **Blue River Bikeway**, which follows the stream north for nine miles alongside State Route 9, ending at the old town of *Frisco*.

Finally, if you'd rather enjoy all this alpine beauty from the comfort of your Belchfire Six, we'll recommend a couple of scenic drives. Both cross the Continental Divide at more than 11,000 feet and shouldn't be taken if you have a medical problem with heights. The 11,992-foot **Loveland Pass** was central Colorado's main highway route over the Rockies until the completion of the Eisenhower Tunnel and Interstate 70. Views from up here are splendid; you can park your car at the summit and stroll through arctic tundra high above the tree line. To reach Loveland Pass, pick up Highway 6 in *Keystone* and just start climbing. You can return via the faster Eisenhower Tunnel or keep going east on I-70 if your next destination lies that way.

The 11,541-foot **Hoosier Pass** also provides that alpine lift and it takes you into the little-visited and beautiful **South Park** mountain area. Head south on State Route 9, crest the pass and spiral down to tiny *Fairplay*, sitting at 10,000 feet in the heart of South Park. All that survives from its heyday as an 1860s mining camp are a few old log buildings. It has a couple of restaurants and lodgings, including the funky Fairplay Hotel; (719) 836-2565. Fairplay's **South Park City Museum** complex is a reconstructed 19th century mining town, with about thirty old buildings dragged in from other areas of Colorado; (719) 836-2387; *www.southparkcity.org*.

From here, you can scope out more alpine scenery by following Highway 285 northeast over another pair of lofty divides—9,993-foot **Redhill Pass** and 10,000-foot **Kenosha Pass**. You'll travel through several charming old mountain towns en route, and wind up south of Denver.

Where to learn more

Breckenridge Resort Chamber, P.O. Box 1909 (311 S. Ridge), Breckenridge, CO 80424; (970) 453-2913; *www.gobreck.com*.

South Park Area Chamber of Commerce, P.O. Box 312, Fairplay, CO 80440; (877) 864-0868 or (719) 836-34110.

Glenwood Springs
The place of curative waters

Ӄ

Glenwood Springs has been a popular Colorado tourist destination for more than a century, yet this hot springs spa is little known outside the inter-mountain region. This small town in the western foothills of the Rockies has several serious visitor lures, including one of the world's largest hot springs pool, a limestone cavern complex and an aerial tramway to the top of a lofty lookout peak.

All three are privately owned and thus subject to a certain amount of gimmickry. For instance, Glenwood Caverns is an "adventure park" with thrill rides in addition to cave tours. Further, the town is busy with hotels, motels and—ah yes—timeshares.

However, Glenwood Springs is no Orlando of the Rockies. The old town still has a yesterday charm and its citizens are more into preservation than exploitation. In fact, it was selected in 2004 by the National Trust for His-toric Preservation as one of its "Dozen Distinctive Destinations."

Commented National Trust president Richard Moe: "I don't know of many other places that offer such a wide variety of ways to have fun in a beautiful setting steeped in Rocky Mountain history."

The downtown area is busy with old stone and brick buildings dating from its earliest days. Notable among these are two resorts, the cut stone **Hot Springs Lodge and Pool**, (800) 537-SWIM, *www.hotspringspool.com;* and the castle-like Hotel Colorado that has hosted the likes of Teddy Roosevelt and Molly Brown, (800) 544-3998, *www.hotelcolorado.com.*

Because Glenwood Springs is in the foothills at 5,763 feet—low for a Rocky Mountain town—the climate is relatively mild. Its mineral springs and other attractions are open the year around. The town is an easy reach, since it sits beside Interstate 70, which follows the Colorado River through rugged, sheer-walled Glenwood Canyon.

Ute Indians had probably soaked contentedly in the mineral waters here for centuries. It was a well-established native spa when the first outsider, Captain Richard Sopris, happened across the hot springs in 1860.

The unfortunate Utes eventually were driven out and an engineer named Walter Devereux, newly rich from a nearby silver strike, began developing a spa in 1885. Glenwood Springs soon became a popular resort town, attract-ing folks such as John Henry "Doc" Holliday. He arrived in 1887, hoping the curative waters would help his tuberculosis. It didn't; he died within six months at age thirty-five and is buried in the local Linwood Cemetery.

The mineral waters are still Glenwood's biggest draw. The huge brick-lined **Hot Springs Pool** at Hot Springs Lodge (above), completed in 1888 by convict labor, is one of the world's largest, stretching for two blocks alongside the river. Another popular health lure is **Yampah Spa and Vapor Caves**, where mineral-laden vapors percolate into caverns to create natural steam baths. Once buried under train tracks, the caves have been restored as part of a full-service health spa; (970) 945-0667; *www.yampahspa.com.*

Glenwood Caverns Adventure Park is a mix of the natural and the contrived, with tours through limestone caves and thrill rides such as the Alpine Coaster, Zip Line and a climbing wall called Doc's Rock. The adjacent **Iron Mountain Tramway** hauls visitors to a lookout point 4,300 feet above the town. For information on both: (800) 530-1635 or (970) 945-4228; *www. glenwoodcaverns.com.*

Another attraction that's a mix of nature's work and man's hand is 1,800-foot-high **Glenwood Canyon**, carved by the Colorado River through a high ridge of the Rockies. Man got involved when the canyon was picked as the route for I-70, and it took thirteen years of work to blast it through. Tree-huggers insisted that ripped-away sections of the walls be shaped and re-vegetated, so the canyon looks more or less natural. This narrow corridor carries the freeway, a railway and a twenty-mile-long recreation path that's popular with cyclists, rollerskaters and determined walkers.

Local outfitters book whitewater rafting and float trips down the Colorado River and the Roaring Fork River which—despite its name—is rather tame. Glenwood's environs are popular for mountain biking, hiking, fishing and horseback riding, and there are several golf courses in the area.

You can learn about the town's yesterdays at the small **Frontier Historical Museum** at 1001 Colorado Ave.; (970) 945-4448.

Glenwood Springs' more famous neighbor, *Aspen* is popular as a side trip for visitors. It's reached by a scenic forty-five mile drive southeast and mostly uphill on State Route 82. The ski resort is two thousand feet higher than Glenwood. Like most Colorado winter resorts, it has an active summer program of hiking, mountain biking and a chairlift ride. Also, there are several ghost towns in the area. Contact the Aspen Chamber Resort Association; (800) 670-0792; *www.aspenchamber.org.* Its **Aspen Music Festival** is one of the country's finest; (970) 925-3254; *www.aspenmusicfestival.com.*

Where to learn more

Glenwood Springs Chamber Resort Association, 1102 Grand Ave., Glenwood Springs, CO 81601; (888) 4-GLENWOOD or (970) 945-6589; *www.glenwoodchamber.com.*

Leadville
Colorado's unsinkable tourist town

T here are a few places in America that began as wild boom towns, nearly faded away and then were reborn as tourist destinations. In many cases, colorful characters helped them regain their fame.

There's Tombstone, Arizona, with the famous Earp brothers; and Virginia City, Nevada, touted by the writings of Mark Twain. And then there's the Colorado town made famous by "Leadville Johnny" and Molly Brown. However, their lives were ridiculously distorted in that silly Broadway musical and film, Meredith Willson's *The Unsinkable Molly Brown*. (Molly was more accurately portrayed in the later film, *Titanic*.)

To set the record straight, James Joseph Brown was a mining engineer and mine company manager, not a wild young prospector. He made his fortune in 1890 when he used his engineering skills to sink a deep shaft that struck a rich gold vein. He was rewarded with stock options by his company. Margaret Tobin, while certainly high-spirited, was a simple working girl, not a wild young thing who wrestled in the hay with her brothers. She met J.J. Brown at a Catholic church picnic, not in a saloon. And finally, "Leadville Johnny" and "Molly" weren't their nicknames; these were given to them in the Broadway musical.

You'll find little mention of the Browns in Leadville. The *real* hometown heroes were Horace Austin Warner Tabor and his pretty second wife Elizabeth McCourt Doe. Tabor made a fortune bankrolling silver mines and he became a major political figure, spending his later years in Denver. When the federal government decided in 1893 to back its currency with gold instead of silver, the price crashed and Tabor lost his fortune. Then, on his death bed in 1899, he told Baby Doe to "hang on to the Matchless Mine," one of their few remaining possessions. She returned to Leadville and lived out her days as a poverty-stricken recluse in a rude cabin next to the mine. She was found frozen to death after a cold winter night in 1935.

Many other intriguing characters spent time in Leadville, including Susan B. Anthony, Doc Holliday and Oscar Wilde. Meyer Guggenheim and Marshall Field started their fortunes here.

Leadville exploded onto the scene when gold was discovered in 1860, followed by silver strikes in later years, and then gold again when J.J. engineered his deep mining shaft. During its peak in the 1880s, Leadville was the largest town in Colorado, with a population estimated as high as 30,000. A good number of them were thieves, gamblers and "fallen angels." The town's name is misleading, for the area produced very little lead. The name comes from carbonate of lead, which clogged gold miners' sluices. They cast it aside in frustration until someone realized that it was laden with silver.

Leadville is the highest incorporated town in America, tucked into an alpine valley at a dizzying 10,152 feet above sea level. It's near Colorado's geographic center and the easiest access is south from I-70 on U.S. 24. The route crests a couple of 11,000-foot passes. Because of its elevation and the likelihood of snow in the passes, this is best as a spring through fall destination. Hikers will find most of the area's trails closed until mid-summer.

Although all of Leadville's mines are closed, tourism has kept the town alive. And while it's fun to explore, parts of it are about as authentic as *The Unsinkable Molly Brown*. Many of its fine old brick and woodframe buildings contain T-shirt shops, tacky souvenir stores and quickie cafés.

However, it also has many museums and historic displays, plus some great good old boy saloons. Several blocks have been designated as a National Historic Landmark District. Further, it's in a grand alpine region that offers hiking, fishing, whitewater rafting and other outdoor lures.

Before you begin exploring, stop by the **Leadville Visitor Center** at 809 Harrison Street and view a half-hour slide show about the area's lively mining history, *The Earth Runs Silver*. Then start exploring.

The Victorian style **Healy House** has elegant period furnishings, with a rustic but nicely appointed cabin adjacent, at 912 Harrison St.; (719) 486-0487. The **Heritage Museum** offers a good portrayal of Leadville's wild and raucous history, at Ninth Street and Harrison Avenue; (719) 486-1878. **The Matchless Mine Cabin**, where Baby Doe Tabor spent her last days, is on east Seventh Street; (719) 486-4918.

The excellent **National Mining Hall of Fame and Museum** has a reconstructed underground mine, fine exhibits on the development of mining and a large mineral collection, at 120 W. Ninth St; (719) 486-1229; *www.leadville.com/miningmuseum*. The **Tabor Opera House** still wears the Victorian finery that H.A.W. Tabor bestowed upon it in when he had it built in 1879. Its at 308 Harrison Ave.; (719) 486-8409.

Before you leave town, take a ride on the **Leadville, Colorado & Southern Railroad** that offers narrated trips through the mining region to the nearby town of *Climax*. The depot is on Seventh Street; (719) 486-3936; *www.leadville-train.com*.

Where to learn more

Leadville/Lake County Chamber of Commerce and Visitor Center, 809 Harrison St.; (800) 933-3901 or (719) 486-3900; *www.leadvilleusa.com*.

Ouray & surrounds
Switzerland comes to Colorado?

卫

If you can picture a Victorian style mining town dropped into the Swiss Alps, you can picture Ouray. Indeed, the town (pronounced *yoo-RAY*) is known as "The Switzerland of America."

With its Victorian and early American architecture, Ouray doesn't look Swiss, although the spectacular setting certainly does. The town occupies an alpine bowl nearly 9,000 feet above sea level, with 13,000-foot peaks towering over it like protective giants.

Named for a Ute chief who was friendly to settlers, Ouray has fewer than a thousand residents. However, the population multiplies in summer when thousands more come to marvel at the awesome setting, visit its historic sites and play in its great outdoors. This picturesque town is in southwestern Colorado, in the heart of the San Juan Mountains, a sprawling extension of the Rockies.

Born of a silver strike, Ouray was incorporated in 1876. The town prospered until the silver crash of 1893 sent it into a spin. Three years later, Tom Walsh, a carpenter-turned-prospector found gold in discarded ore from silver mines and bought up several claims. After earning $24 million, he moved to a fancy home in Washington, D.C., and bought his daughter Evalyn an interesting bauble, the Hope Diamond.

Although mining gave Ouray its start, the setting was so stunning than tourism soon followed. A writer for *Harper's Weekly* gushed in 1889:

Ouray is asserted to be the handsomest town in Colorado and I am not inclined to dispute this. As the departing stranger rides slowly up the southern wall of the mountains...on the wonderful toll-road that Otto Mears built...he can only look back at the mighty bowl and its town in the centre, and regret that a beautiful incident in his life has come to an end.

The town is home to several artists and some of their studios welcome visitors. You can watch them work their skills with oils, wood, silver and stained glass. Several galleries, outdoor stores and specialty shops occupy Ouray's old downtown buildings. The town measures only four by six blocks so it's quite walkable. A tour map available at the chamber of commerce and the county museum describes its historic buildings.

Displays at the **Ouray County Museum** ramble through twenty-seven rooms of a former hospital at 420 Sixth Ave.; (970) 325-4576; *www.ouray-countyhistoricalsociety.com*. Visitors can learn about the region's mining lore at the **Bachelor-Syracuse Mine** northeast of town; (970) 325-0220; *www.bachelorsyracuse.com*. Mine trains transport folks along a 3,350-foot horizontal shaft, where fortunes were made in gold and silver.

Silvery cascades spill down sheer granite walls at **Box Cañon Falls and Park** just south of town; (970) 325-7080. Interpretive trails lead through this narrow chasm, which in places is just twenty feet wide and 300 feet high. Another popular pause is the nearby **Natural Hot Springs Pool**, built in 1927 and recently renovated; (970) 325-7073. This huge public pool contains a million gallons of mineral water.

Several other hot spring resorts are in the area, and some offer lodgings. Visitors also can find rooms at a couple of historic hotels, several B&Bs, guest ranches and motels. They fill up quickly in summer, so check with the chamber and make early reservations.

Otto Mears' cliff-hanging toll road over 11,018-foot Red Mountain Pass is now U.S. 550, sometimes called "Million Dollar Highway." There are several legends concerning the source of that name. A popular theory is that, unbeknownst to road-builders, the gravel they used was rich with gold. We like to think it was named for the million-dollar view when you crest the pass and look down to that "mighty bowl and its town in the centre."

The road over the pass is part of the 236-mile-long San Juan Skyway, often described as the most scenic drive in America. It has been designated as a National Scenic & Historic Byway. The route links Ouray with two other towns in impressive settings, *Silverton* and *Durango*. Steam trains of the famous **Durango & Silverton Narrow-gauge Railroad** haul happy tourists from one town to the other; (970) 247-2733; *www.durangotrain. com*. The route passes through forty-five miles of spectacular scenery.

Going north from Ouray, U.S. 550 follows the pretty Uncompahgre River to tiny *Ridgeway*. It's a staging area for outdoor recreation and it was the setting for the 1969 movie *True Grit*, with John Wayne and Glen Campbell. Nearby **Ridgeway State Park** rims a reservoir and offers the usual water play, plus camping, hiking and picnicking; (970) 626-3737. If you continue north on Highway 550, you'll reach *Montrose*, the gateway to **Black Canyon of the Gunnison National Park** (above, on page 104). A turn west from Ridgeway onto State Route 62 will point you toward *Telluride*, a popular ski area and summer playground.

Where to learn more

Ouray Chamber Resort Association, Box 145 (1230 N. Main), Ouray, CO 81427; (800) 228-1876 or (970) 325-4746; *www.ouraycolorado.com*.

Steamboat Springs
Stetson skiing and summer culture

⚐

Skiing in a cowboy hat may be tricky, although that's the winter theme of this resort town in northwestern Colorado. In summer, residents' thoughts turn to music, the arts and warm weather play.

Steamboat Springs calls itself "Ski Town, USA," and posters portray good guys in white hats schussing down its slopes. Its lively February Winter Carnival also carries a Western theme, which makes sense because this was cattle country before it was a ski resort. Settlers came to the surrounding Yampa River Valley in the late 1800s to homestead ranches and farms, after running off the unfortunate Utes.

Skiing goes back to 1913 when the "Flying Norseman," Norwegian ski jumping and cross-country champion Carl Howelsen, came to town and introduced folks to these sports. He started the winter carnival the next year.

Downhill skiing took off much later, when the **Steamboat Ski Area** opened in 1963, three miles south of town; (877) 237-2628 or (970) 879-6111; *www.steamboat.com*. It's now one of the ten top-rated ski resorts in the country. "Ski Town, USA" has produced more Olympic champions than any other community. They include the legendary 1964 and 1970 Winter Olympics champion Billy Kidd, now director of skiing at Steamboat.

In both its location and its laid-back Western lifestyle, Steamboat is far removed from Colorado's trendier ski resorts in the heart of the Rockies. And it's much more than a ski town. Sitting in a wooded river valley, 160 miles northwest of Denver on U.S. Highway 40, it's also an active summer haven. Folks put away their skis and snowshoes and pursue a variety of other activities.

Steamboat has one of the most active fine arts and cultural arts programs in Colorado. The summer-long **Strings in the Mountains Music Festival** draws more than 170 top artists; (970) 879-5056; *www.stringsinthemountains.org*. They perform everything from classics and jazz to bluegrass and international folk music. In addition to its paid performances, the festival presents free Music on the Green concerts in Yampa Botanical Park.

With fewer than 10,000 residents, this town also manages to support opera and ballet companies, a chamber orchestra, a dance theater and a community players group. Several artists live in the region and both Steamboat Springs and the ski village have a selection of galleries. Check out the **Steamboat Springs Arts Depot** in the old train station downtown at 1001 Thirteenth St.; (970) 879-9008; *www.steamboatspringsarts.com*. The **Arti-**

sans' **Market of Steamboat** at 626 Lincoln is a co-op exhibiting the works of local artists; (970) 879-7512; *www.rockymountainfun.com/artisans.html.*

If you're outdoor-inclined instead of culturally-inclined, Steamboat won't disappoint. Surrounding valleys and mountains offer hiking, camping, flatland and mountain biking, river rafting and kayaking, fishing, hot air ballooning and horseback riding. Cyclists and walkers can follow the extensive **Town Trail System** in old Steamboat and the three-mile **Yampa River Core Trail** with parks, fishing spots and launch points for floaters.

Two nearby state facilities, **Stagecoach State Recreation Area** and **Steamboat Lake State Park**, offer camping, picnicking, boating and hiking, plus winter snowmobiling, cross-country skiing and snowshoeing; *www.coloradoparks.org.*

If you'd rather just sit and soak your bones, dip into one of the area's many hot springs. Two of the largest are the **Steamboat Health and Resort Association** spa at 136 Lincoln St., (970) 879-1828; and **Strawberry Park Hot Springs**, seven miles north of town on Strawberry Park Road, (970) 879-0342, *www.strawberryhotsprings.com.* Strawberry is popular with Nordic skiers and snowshoers seeking a soothing winter soak.

Back in town, discover Steamboat's yesterdays at the **Tread of Pioneers Museum**, occupying a 1908 Victorian home at 800 Oak St.; (970) 879-2214. A mile south of town at 100 Pamela Lane is the **Yampa River Botanic Park** with plants native to the area and several theme gardens; (970) 879-4300.

Steamboat Springs has an abundance of lodgings, ranging from luxury condos and hotels at the ski resort to smaller hotels, motels and B&Bs in the downtown area. You can find rather good off-season rates, particularly at the ski resort, since its largest crowds arrive in winter.

Coming or going, try to work southeast-bound Highway 40 into your travel plans. This extremely scenic route crosses the Continental Divide at 9,426-foot Rabbit Ears Pass a few miles south of Steamboat. Then it dips into wooded valleys and tops other passes along the ramparts of the Rockies. It joins Interstate 70 at *Georgetown*, a former mining center. From there, I-70 passes *Idaho Springs*, another rustic mining town, then it drifts down the Rockies' Front Range into Denver. Consider a brief side trip to *Golden* for a tour and a free sip of Coors Light at the world's largest brewery.

Where to learn more

Steamboat Springs Chamber Resort Association, P.O. Box 774408 (1255 S. Lincoln Ave.), Steamboat Springs, CO 80477; (970) 879-0880; *www.steamboat-chamber.com.*

Boise
The great urban outdoors

Boise is one of the nation's most isolated urban centers, more than three hundred miles from any other metropolitan area. Like a ranch family far from its nearest neighbors, this city of nearly 200,000 looks mostly inward for its resources. In doing so, it has become one of the most self-contained, self-sufficient and versatile small cities in America.

It's the *compleat* mini-city, with fine parks, cultural offerings, a large university, a dynamic downtown core and a greenbelt that runs through its heart. Mountain recreation areas and the **Bogus Basin** ski resort are just minutes away. Boise is an urban center with one foot in the great outdoors.

This obviously is a fine place to do business as well, since it's home to six major corporations. In 2005, it topped *Forbes Magazine's* list as the "Best place for business and careers."

It's certainly a great place to visit, particularly for outdoor types. *Sports Illustrated* called it "Idaho's Sportstown USA" and *Bike* magazine says it's America's number one mountain biking town. It's a great place to take it easy as well, called the "Oasis for retirees" by the *Wall Street Journal*.

If you've come for outdoor fun, start with the **Boise River Greenbelt**, where you can fish, float, swim, bike, jog, stroll and picnic right in the middle of town. Boise also offers interesting shopping areas, historic districts and restaurants within walking distance of one another, plus more than a dozen museums. Further, it's affordable. The city's relatively low cost of living is reflected in lodging and restaurant prices.

A really neat way to approach the downtown area is via a river float, assuming it's warm and you're properly attired. Tubes and rafts can be rented at **Barber Park** on the Greenbelt and shuttle service is available; (208) 343-6564. Guided float trips along the Greenbelt are offered by **Boise River Tours**; (208) 333-0003; *www.boiserivertours.com*.

Whether or not you arrive by raft, you can walk to the main business district, which is just east of the riverside **Julia Davis Park**. Many of the city's attractions and cultural facilities are nearby, including the Boise Art Museum, Boise Library, Zoo Boise, and the Idaho state capitol.

Particularly interesting is the **Basque Block** at Capitol Boulevard and Grove Street, with ethnic cafés and markets. Idaho has the largest Basque population per capita in America, and Boise celebrates this heritage with the nation's largest Basque festival every five years; the next one is due in 2010. You can learn all about Basque culture and history at the **Basque Museum and Culture Center** at 611 Grove Street; (208) 343-2671; *www. basquemuseum.com* and *www.boisebasques.com.*

The city's other major attractions include the **Boise Art Museum** at 670 Julia Davis Dr., (208) 345-8330, *www.boiseartmuseum.org*; **Idaho Historical Museum** at 610 Julia Davis Drive, (208) 334-2120, *www.idahohistory. net/museum.html*; **Old Idaho State Penitentiary State Historic Site** on Old Penitentiary Road, with several historical exhibits, (208) 334-2844, *www. idahohistory.net/oldpen.html*; and the **World Center for Birds of Prey** where you can see raptors from around the globe, six miles south of town off I-84; (208) 362-8687; *www.peregrinfund.org.*

Boise's citizens seem particularly sensitive to the need for tolerance, although the city has never been regarded as racially troubled. Three exhibit centers focus on the subject: The **Idaho Black History Museum** at 508 Julia Davis Drive, (208) 433-0017, *www.ibhm.org*; the **World Sports Humanitarian Hall of Fame** at 855 Broad Street, (208) 343-7224; *www.sportshumanitarian.com*; and the very moving **Idaho Anne Frank Human Rights Memorial** in a riverside park near the Boise Library, (208) 345-0304, *www.idaho-humanrights.org.*

Sitting in a seam between desert and mountains, Boise is a good base of operations for exploring other areas of Idaho. There's not much to the west except the state's busiest population corridor and the subsistence farm near the tiny town of *Wilder*, where I grew up. However, the Snake River with its Oregon Trail sites and water recreation lies to the southeast and numerous mountain vacation areas are within short drives north and northeast.

Boise was established in 1863 as a trading center along a river that had been named by French-Canadian trappers. After trekking across Idaho's arid southern plains, they saw a stream lined with cottonwoods and exclaimed: *"Les bois, les bois, voyes les bois"* which roughly translates as: "Well dang my britches, look at all them trees!"

Early settlers planted even more and today, Boise is nicknamed "The City of Trees." It became the state capital when Idaho was admitted to the Union in 1890. It's now the cornerstone of the state's only urban area, which includes *Nampa* and *Caldwell.* Home to more than half of Idaho's 1.3 million citizens, this is one of the fastest growing metro regions in America.

Where to learn more

Boise Convention & Visitors Bureau, P.O. Box 2106 (312 Ninth, Suite 100), Boise, ID 83702; (800) 635-5240 or (208) 344-7777; *www.boise.org.*

Ketchum and Sun Valley
Summary fun in a famous winter resort

ᛒ

Locals claim that if Bruce Willis dropped in at Ketchum's Java Coffee & Café, folks wouldn't put down their cappuccinos and stare at him. Maybe they'd smile and say howdy, but they wouldn't ask him to autograph their paper napkins.

Ketchum is a curious kind of town. It's a mix of trendy boutiques, art galleries, pricey restaurants and good-old-boy saloons. Further, it's a place where a startling number of celebrities live more or less in public anonymity. It is considered cool not to fawn over Bruce, or Demi Moore, Governator Arnold Schwarzenegger, Tom Hanks, Clint Eastwood, Maria Shriver, Mariel Hemingway, Jamie Lee Curtis or Chris Berman when they stroll down Main Street. Not that anyone would fawn over Chris Berman. However, it is significant that all of these folks and many other luminaries spend at least part of their lives in the Ketchum area. And this was the final retreat for Ernest Hemingway, who ended his life here.

How did a former old smeltering and sheep town become Hollywood of the Idaho woods? It started in 1936 when Union Pacific CEO Averell Harriman opened America's first destination ski resort, which he called Sun Valley. As it was being built, he asked engineer James Curran to come up with a way of getting his guests up the mountain, so they could ski back down. Curran recalled seeing a cable system in Honduras used for loading banana boats, so he applied this concept to create the world's first ski lift.

Soon, Hollywood's top bananas were being hauled up the slopes and luxuriating at Harriman's resort. And they're still coming, so this area is hardly undiscovered. Indeed, the ski resort is world-famous. However, many vacation-seekers may not realize that this area has a very active summer program. In fact, it receives more visitors in summer than in winter. **Sun Valley Resort** is particularly busy in summer, with tennis, golf, a year-around ice skating rink, three swimming pools, horseback riding and water sports on Sun Valley Lake; (800) 786-8259; *www.sunvalley.com.*

Sun Valley isn't a town, but a privately-owned resort complex, even though it has its own ZIP code. It wraps around Ketchum, and its main ski hill, Bald Mountain, looms above the town. It isn't bald, but so many ski runs have been cut through its forest that it appears to have a bad haircut.

Ketchum occupies an awesome setting, at the base of that mountain in the heart of the Wood River Valley. And even if the town sat in the middle of an Iowa cornfield, it would be appealing—a pleasing study in old brick and false front stores. Some of the downtown area suffered modernization, although its current residents have enough sense to try to preserve its past.

Ketchum has a good selection of restaurants, shops and book stores. A dozen more shops—mostly upscale—occupy **Sun Valley Village**. The area is serious about art and culture. Ketchum and Sun Valley have more than a dozen galleries and the **Sun Valley Center for the Arts** displays works of local artists at 190 Fifth St. E; (208) 726-9491; *www.sunvalleycenter.org.* The region also offers a variety of cultural activities, with a symphony orchestra, opera and an annual film festival and writers' conference.

Although it's long on culture, it's short on museums. The only local archive is the **Heritage & Ski Museum** at 180 First Street, focusing on area history and the development of skiing; (208) 726-8118. For a taste of old Ketchum, stop by one of its saloons and slam back a beer or two with the locals. Most are within a two-block stroll along Main Street. The lineup includes the **Roosevelt, The Casino, Pioneer Saloon** and the **Sawtooth Club**.

As further evidence that Ketchum isn't entirely given over to Gore-tex and fancy restaurants, sheepherders drive their flocks right through the middle of town every October. They're herding them down to winter pastures. Watch where you step.

Ketchum-Sun Valley is laced with several miles of biking and walking trails. The Wood River Valley is one of Idaho's finest outdoor recreation areas, with more miles of hiking trails, great trout streams and runnable rivers. And the beautiful **Sawtooth National Recreation Area** is just to the north.

So, what's not to like?

Although this is a fine area to visit, not many people can afford to live here. Its appeal to the wealthy and the famous—usually the same folks—has driven up prices. Ketchum has the highest median home price in the state, and lodging and restaurants are rather expensive. However, there are more affordable lodgings in the towns of *Hailey* and *Bellevue*, a few miles south.

Despite its good-old-boy saloons and friendly atmosphere, outsiders won't blend easily into Ketchum's inner circle. So don't ask Bruce Willis to autograph your napkin.

Ironically, it was Hemingway who once wrote, in *The Snows of Kilimanjaro*: "The rich are different from you and me," although he borrowed that line from F. Scott Fitzgerald.

Where to learn more

Sun Valley/Ketchum Chamber & Visitors Bureau, P.O. Box 2420, Sun Valley, ID 83353; (800) 634-3347 or (208) 726-3423; *www.visitsunvalley.com* and *www.visitketchum.com.*

The Panhandle
A tale of two towns in a land of lakes

Idaho is shaped like a fat foot with a skinny ankle, called the Panhandle. This is the state's favorite water play area, with at least fifty-five lakes, more than in any other area of the American West. Left behind when the last Ice Age retreated to the Arctic, they're glacial-carved ponds resting in shallow basins of the thickly wooded Bitterroot and Selkirk Mountains.

The region's primary towns are anchored to a pair of these glacial lakes. *Couer d'Alene*, on the northern tip of its 25-mile-long namesake lake, is the area's largest community, with a population of about 36,000. Smaller *Sandpoint* to the north, with just 7,000 folks, sits on the northwestern edge of an even larger pond, 43-mile-long **Pend Oreille Lake**. It's Idaho's biggest, and one of the largest freshwater lakes in America.

Although both towns are tourism-based, they have different personalities. Couer d'Alene is more commercialized and, well, more touristy. Its downtown is dominated by one of the most upscale resorts in the Northwest. Smaller Sandpoint is more down home and laid back and it's a serious art community. Cross-country Interstate 90 brings more outsiders and their influence to Couer d'Alene, and the mini-city of *Spokane, Washington*, is just forty-six miles west (page 50). Sandpoint, about forty-five miles north of Coeur d'Alene, is more isolated, linked only by two-lane U.S. Highway 95.

If you like big lakes and even fewer people, continue north on Highway 95 to 25-mile long **Priest Lake** up near the Canadian border. It's lakeshore resort town of *Coolin* has just a handful of residents.

Coeur d'Alene

A *Los Angeles Times* writer recently called Coeur d'Alene "one of the best spots for a well-rounded summer of outdoor fun in the Pacific Northwest." Indeed, this town brims with tourist lures—lots of water play on its lake, boat rentals and fishing charters, sightseeing helicopter and seaplane flights, water slides and even a nearby theme park and a native American casino. Although some locals fuss that it's too much, the town has become one of Idaho's most popular vacation destinations.

Worth a look even if you can't afford its rates is the AAA Four Diamond **Coeur d'Alene Resort**, considered one of America's top golfing destinations. It even has an offshore green, so we assume the lake bottom has a good collection of lost balls. For more information on this full-service resort: (800) 688-5253; *www.cdaresort.com*.

The resort rises eighteen stories from the lakefront, either as an imposing presence or a sore thumb, depending on one's point of view. Its adjacent marina and the nearby **City Park** offer all sorts of water activities, including **Lake Coeur d'Alene Cruises**; (800) 365-8338, *www.cdaresort.com.*

The nicely-done **Museum of North Idaho** has the usual history exhibits about the town and the area, plus displays on logging and firefighting, at 115 Northwest Blvd.; (208) 664-3448; *www.museumni.org.*

Silverwood Theme Park offers kids' play fifteen minutes north in *Athol*, (208) 683-3400, *www.silverwoodthemepark.com*. To explore the wilds of the adjacent Bitterroot Mountains, sigh on with **Black Rhino** jeep treks (208) 765-TOUR, *www.blackrhinotours.com*;

Sandpoint

Although Couer d'Alene is more visible as a tourist destination, little Sandpoint is getting most of the press these days. A recent *USA Today* article touted it as a "Norman Rockwell-meets-Ansel Adams" kind of place. *Sunset* magazine called it "the best small town in the west," *National Geographic Adventure* rated it among the nation's top ten adventure towns and it's featured in the book, *The 100 Best Small Art Towns in America.*

Boosted by the **Pend Oreille Arts Council** (208-263-6139; *www.artsin-sandpoint.org*), Sandpoint has more than a dozen galleries, several annual arts and crafts events, art walks and a summer theater. The small downtown area has that funky look suitable for an art colony, with the requisite small book stores and designer coffee galleries. If you don't dig art, there's that big lake. **City Beach** is a large city park with a marina and several water-oriented concessions. **Lake Pend Oreille Cruises** launches its trips from here; (208) 255-5233; *www.lakependoreillelakecruises.com.*

The U.S. Forest Service and Army Corps of engineers operate several other recreation areas around the lake, with docks, launching ramps, camping and picnicking areas and lakeside trails.

Although Sandpoint is still relatively uncrowded, all of the media attention may soon change that. We feel a little guilty writing about it.

Where to learn more

Coeur d'Alene Area Chamber of Commerce, Box 850 (1621 N. Third St.), Coeur d'Alene, ID 83816; (877) 782-9232; *www.coeurdalene.org.*

Greater Sandpoint Chamber of Commerce, P.O. Box 928 (900 N. Fifth Ave.), Sandpoint, ID 83864; (800) 800-2106 or (208) 263-0887; *www.sandpointchamber.com* and *www.sandpointonline.com.*

Priest Lake Chamber of Commerce, P.O. Box 174, Coolin, ID 83821; (888) 774-3785; *www.priestlake.org.*

Valley County
The good life in Idaho's Heartland

꒰

We're going to guess that, unless you're from Idaho, you've never heard of Valley County. However, President George W. Bush has. After he and his wife Laura spent a brief summer vacation at the area's Tamarack Resort in 2005, he described the region as "a spectacular part of the world."

The *Washington Post* agreed with George for a change, saying: "The area is an outdoor enthusiast's dream."

The county, or more specifically the Payette River area, is a wonderland of cascading rivers, steep canyons, lakes, ski resorts and pine-clad mountains. Local folks, particularly tourism promoters, call it "The Idaho Heartland." The region is about 100 miles north of Boise, and to use the old cliché, getting there is at least half the fun. The approach is via the **Payette River Scenic Byway** (State Highway 55) which curls through gorgeous Payette River Canyon. Although not as famous as the Salmon or Snake rivers, it's one of the top whitewater streams in Idaho.

The county was named for Long Valley, just north of Payette River Canyon. The river slows its flow through here, widening into Cascade Lake and Payette Lake. This scenic mountain area was overlooked by most travelers until a few years ago. Its largest town of McCall on the southern shoreline of Payette Lake has been a regionally popular resort for decades, but it was little known outside the state.

Now, as prices rise in other resort areas such as Couer d'Alene and Ketchum/Sun Valley, Long Valley has become one of Idaho's fastest growing recreational areas. Folks in the booming Boise-Nampa-Caldwell population corridor are starting to realized that it's a lot closer than the other two. Still, the area is uncrowded and thinly populated. The entire county has fewer than 9,000 residents.

The fuse that ignited Valley County's rush was **Tamarack Resort** which, after a couple of false starts, began developing in earnest a few years ago. It's the first major winter-summer resort to be built in a quarter of a century. Standing off the shoreline of large Cascade Lake, Tamarack occupies several thousand acres of wooded slopes. The resort offers several ski runs and cross-country ski trails, hiking, biking, boating on Cascade Lake and a golf course; plus private homesites, a retail village and a variety of lodgings; (877) TAM-RESORT, *www.tamarackidaho.com.*

The scenic byway that links this region to the rest of the world begins above ***Horseshoe Bend***, where it joins the cascading Payette River. After twisting through ruggedly handsome Payette River Canyon, it enters the broad, mountain-rimmed Long Valley, skirting the edge of Cascade Lake.

Cascade, an old lumber town at the bottom of the valley, is recovering from the recent closure of the its Boise-Cascade mill by gearing up for tourism. Although it's half the size of McCall, with a population of about a thousand, it's the Valley County seat. Worth a pause here is the handsome, opulent and vaguely Colonial style **Ashley Inn** on Cascade's Main Street; (866) 382-5621; *www.theashleyinn.com.*

Continuing through the valley, you'll encounter *Donnelly*, a literal wide spot in the road with fewer than 200 inhabitants. However, it will grow, since it sits at the junction of a highway leading to Tamarack Resort.

McCall has about 2,500 year-around residents—and growing. This charming community is featured in National Geographic's *Guide to Small Town Escapes.* Luxury homes, marinas and public beaches rim **Payette Lake**, which nudges up to the edge of town. The old downtown area has a mix of modern and rustic buildings, with shops, cafés and a few galleries.

It even has a year-around skating rink, **Manchester Ice and Event Centre** at 200 E. Lake St., (208) 634-3570; *www.manchester-icecentre.com.* The town's memories are preserved in the **Central Idaho Historical Museum**, a complex of eight structures on Highway 55; (208) 634-4497.

Several local operators offer whitewater rafting trips on the Payette River, plus pack trips and hunting and fishing expeditions. Boat rentals are available from marinas on Payette Lake. Cross-country and downhill skiing and snowmobiling are popular in winter, and the week-long **McCall Winter Carnival** is held from late January to early February.

Although Tamarack is getting most of the press, smaller **Brundage Mountain Resort** off Highway 55 above McCall is a popular family-oriented facility. It offers several ski runs, plus a summer season of mountain biking, scenic lift rides, whitewater rafting and outdoor concerts; (800) 888-7544; *www.brundage.com.*

McCall's most opulent lodging is the **Whitetail Inn**, a clubby full-service resort on Payette Lake; (800) 657-6464; *www. whitetailclub.com.* More affordable is the charmingly rustic century old **Hotel McCall** in the historic downtown area; (866) 800-1183.

Where to learn more

Cascade Chamber of Commerce, P.O. Box 571 (500 N. Main St.), Cascade, ID 83611; (208) 382-3833; *www.extremecascade.com.*

McCall Chamber of Commerce, P.O. Box 350 (102 N. Third St.), McCall, ID 83638; (800) 260-5130; *www.mccall-idchamber.org.*

Bozeman and West Yellowstone
A cool university town and a park gateway

ֆ

I grew up hearing my dad say that the only one in our family who ever amounted to a hill of beans was his great uncle, Brooks Martin, who was a successful merchant in Bozeman. Since my parents started out as migrant farm workers who met in a strawberry patch, that probably was an accurate statement.

Having an ancestor in Bozeman is not the reason it's included in this book. When we visited—mostly to check on my uncle's pedigree—we realized that it was a worthy choice without any family ties.

This handsome old town with an ugly name boasts a lively art scene, a rich cultural overlay from Montana State University and the outdoor lures of Montana's Big Sky Country. Further, it's but a short drive to Yellowstone National Park, through its Montana gateway of West Yellowstone.

If you picture small Montana towns as places where dusty cowboys wear dustier boots and slam back Coors in smoky barrooms, you're not in Bozeman. Its cowboys probably drive SUVs and they may look more like Robert Redford than trail hands. In fact, one of them might have been Redford, since he directed *A River Runs Through It* in this area several years ago. Bozeman is an interesting mix of traditional and contemporary, conservative and liberal. It even has an alternative newspaper called *Tributary* that fusses about the lack of recycling and lax anti-smoking laws. The town has several book stores and art galleries, good restaurants and a trio of museums.

Moon Handbook's 'Montana says it's the state's "most beguiling urban experience, though it's not to be mistaken for the real Montana."

Mountain man John Bozeman blazed a path north from the Oregon Trail in 1864, leading a wagon train of settlers into the mountain-rimmed Gallatin Valley. He was killed three years later in Livingston, Montana, and when a town was platted in this scenic basin, it was named in his honor.

A small city of about 28,000, Bozeman retains much of its yesterday look downtown, with many fine old brick buildings. These aren't just historic showplaces; this is still the town's business and retail core. The Downtown Bozeman Association works to preserve the area's old look while encouraging new business; (406) 586-4008; *www.historicbozeman.com.*

The region's history is displayed in the **Gallatin Pioneers' Museum** occupying a 1911 jail building at 317 W. Main St.; (406) 522-8122; *www. pio-*

neermuseum.org. The outstanding **Museum of the Rockies** is on the Montana State University campus at 600 W. Kagy Blvd.; (406) 994-22511; *www. montana.edu/wwwmor.* Its has the largest collection of dinosaur fossils in America, plus exhibits ranging from history to astronomy; see page 130.

Bozeman's third archive—and this is somehow typical of the town—is the **American Computer Museum** in Bridger Park Mall at 2404 N. Seventh Ave.; (406) 582-1288; *www.compustory.com.* It traces the development of the computer from the Univac to the laptop. Bozeman's cultural lures are focused in the **Emerson Center for the Arts** at 111 S. Grand, with galleries and theaters; (406) 587-9797; *www.theemerson.org.*

West Yellowstone

A short drive south from Bozeman on U.S. 191 through a pretty wooded canyon delivers you the western gateway to Yellowstone National Park. You're still in Montana, only just barely. Ninety-nine percent of the park is in Wyoming, and the west entrance is just a few feet from town.

West Yellowstone is a tree-clad village designed to be deliberately rustic, with false front stores and log buildings. However, the look is marred by the presence of chain hamburger joints and motel signs. Still, the town provides places to eat and sleep within a stone's throw—literally—of the park. During Yellowstone's peak summer season, it's easier to find lodgings here than in the park, and they're often less expensive.

Further, the town has a few attractions of its own. Our favorite is the **Grizzly & Wolf Discovery Center**, where various critters found injured or orphaned in the wild are nurtured and displayed in open compounds; (800) 257-2570 or (406) 646-7001; *www.grizzlydiscoveryctr.org.* The **Yellowstone Historic Center**, housed in a 1909 Union Pacific depot, traces the area's history, focusing primarily on the national park. It's open May to October; (406) 646-1100. The **Yellowstone IMAX Theatre** shows big-screen flicks, including a gorgeously scenic film about the park; (888) 854-5862 or (406) 646-4100; *www.yellowstoneimax.com.* If you prefer live amusements, **Playmill Theatre** produces musicals, comedies and dramas between Memorial Day and Labor Day weekends; (406) 646-7757; *www.playmill.com.*

Where to learn more

Bozeman Convention & Visitors Bureau, 2000 Commerce Way, Bozeman, MT 59715; (406) 586-5421; *www.bozemancvb.visitmt.com.*

West Yellowstone Chamber of Commerce, P.O. Box 458, West Yellowstone, MT 59758, *www.westyellowstonechamber.com;* and *Yellowstone National Park,* P.O. Box 168, Yellowstone, WY 82190, (307) 344-7381; *www.nps.gov/yell.*

Butte
"She's a mile high and a mile deep"

ᛒ

A town whose visitor lures include what once was America's longest operating brothel and the childhood home of a nun nominated for sainthood has *got* to be a fascinating place to visit.

Tough old Butte, more than a mile above sea level and with mining shafts burrowed a mile into the earth, is Montana's most intriguing town. And it once was the richest, as America's largest source of silver and copper. Its historic characters include Senator William Andrews Clark, the copper king who later founded Las Vegas; and Mother Celestine Bottego, who grew up here and later established the Xaverian Missionaries of Mary. Butte's many historic sites include her former home and the Dumas building, which operated as a cat house from 1890 until 1982.

For a town of 35,000, Butte has a surprising number of attractions, including eight museums, dozens of historic buildings and some great old saloons and restaurants. It contains one of America's largest National Historic Landmark districts, with more than 4,000 structures. Butte's original district is called Uptown and it's compact enough to be walkable. Or for a good historic overview, catch the **Old Number One Trolley Tour** for a two-hour narrated trip through the business core and Victorian neighborhoods. It departs from the Chamber of Commerce at 1000 George Street and reservations are required; (800) 735-6814 or (460) 723-3177.

Of Butte's many lures, these should rise to the top of your hit list: The **World Museum of Mining** on West Park Street near Montana Tech; (406) 723-7211; *www.miningmuseum.org*. It covers both the history and politics of mining, and a reconstructed 1900-era mining camp called **Hell Roarin' Gulch** is nearby. The smaller **Mineral Museum** on the campus has a large mineral and gem collection; (406) 496-4414. **Copper King Mansion**, the former home of William A. Clark at 219 W. Granite Street is open for public tours; (406) 782-7580; *www.thecopperkingmansion.com*. The **Mai Wah** is an Asian style building with several Chinese businesses and a small museum about the role of the Chinese in early Butte, at 17 W. Mercury St.; (406) 723-3231; *www.maiwah.org*. The **Piccadilly Museum of Transportation** is a kind of "road trip America" archive with everything from antique cars to vintage gas pumps, at 20 W. Broadway; (406) 723-3034.

Also worth a look are the elaborate **Arts Chateau**, an 1898 French style mansion built by Clark's son and now the community arts center, at 321 W. Broadway, (406) 723-7600; the **Mother Bottego House**, being restored as a museum and retreat, at 505 S. Montana St., (406) 723-1275, *www.mother-bottegohouse.org;* and the long-running **Dumas Brothel** at 45 E. Mercury Street; (406) 494-6908, *www.thedumasbrothel.com.* The **Butte-Silver Bow Courthouse** at 115 W. Granite Street, with a stained glass dome over a four-story rotunda, is one of the state's most handsome public buildings.

A short drive from Uptown will take you to the **Berkeley Pit,** a massive open copper mine with a viewing platform on Shields Street. Also visit **Our Lady of the Rockies,** a 90-foot statue of the Virgin Mary on the Continental Divide above Butte, with panoramic views of the surrounding countryside.

Headframes, mining pits and tailing dumps scattered over the rough hills tell of Butte's early days as Montana's largest mining center. The town began in 1864 with a gold strike, followed by a much larger silver strike a decade later. This lured a pair of opportunists who would become the most powerful men in Montana—scheming entrepreneurs William Clark and Marcus Daly. When vast copper deposits were discovered, the two men fought for control of the mines, the town and the state. Clark eventually owned most of Butte's mines and its infrastructure and Daly founded the still-active Anaconda Copper Company. Butte soon became known as "the richest hill on earth." During its peak at the turn of the last century, it boasted a population of nearly 100,000.

The mines gradually played out during the first half of that century. The Anaconda company began digging the Berkeley Pit in 1955 to get at the last of the copper ore. However, pieces of the town began falling into the pit and it was closed in 1983. In addition to this massive hole in the ground, it's estimated that 2,000 miles of mining tunnels were burrowed beneath Butte.

Although this was once the richest town in the state and it's now a popular tourist stop, Butte still hasn't fully recovered from the loss of its mines. Several historic buildings stand vacant and some shops are boarded up. It's a bit surprising that Butte hasn't rebounded more quickly, since it occupies the pivotal transportation point in Montana; it's in the cross-hairs of interstates 15 and 90.

Incidentally, the town has another famous citizen, although he gained his fame elsewhere. Butte is the birthplace of Evel Knievel.

Where to learn more

Butte Chamber of Commerce, 1000 George St., Butte, MT 89701; (800) 735-6814 or (406) 723-3177; *www.butteinfo.org.*

Main Street Uptown Butte, P.O. Box 696 (66 W. Park St., Suite 200), Butte, MT 59703; (406) 497-6464; *www.mainstreetbutte.org.*

The Dinosaur Trail
Exploring Montana's "Cretaceous Park"

Ⱶ

Can you picture a tyrant reptile king galloping through a Montana marshland, in pursuit of a hapless *maiasaura* for lunch? You can if you send your imagination back eighty million years, and go on a dinosaur hunt.

Several dig sites in Montana have yielded some of the world's finest dinosaur fossils. The very first remains of a *tyrannosaurus rex* ("tyrant reptile king") were unearthed here in 1902. Fossils of huge herds of the plant-eating, duck-billed *maiasaura* have been found in several areas of the state. "Leonardo," a mummified *brachylophosaur* found near Malta in 2000, was so intact that the *Guinness Book of World Records* lists it as "the world's best preserved dinosaur."

During the Jurassic and Cretaceous periods, from 65 to 150 million years ago, this area was a lush flood plain, ideal for supporting a large dinosaur population.

The state is so dinosaur-rich that tourism officials have created the **Montana Dinosaur Trail**, with a map and brochure pinpointing fourteen dig sites and museums. Following T-rex and his buddies through Montana can be a fascinating vacation theme. Copies of the brochure are available from Travel Montana; see below.

Most major dinosaur sites are in the prairies of northern and eastern Montana, those vast flood plains of the Jurassic and Cretaceous eras. Through the millennia, this region was folded and warped into mountains and then eroded back into prairies, exposing strata from nearly every geologic era. This action brought many long-buried dinosaur sites to the surface. Since the area is thinly populated, there has been very little disturbance of the land surface, so dinosaur sites have been left intact. Some bones are so exposed that accidental discoveries have been made when farmers, cowboys or hikers practically tripped over fossils poking out of the ground.

Some sites on the Montana Dinosaur Trail are museums, while others are active digs or combinations. A few sites allow the public to participate in digs, with advance arrangements, and under strict supervision.

A good starting point for your quest of T-rex and friends is not in dino country, but at the **Museum of the Rockies** in Bozeman. Its excellent Siebel Dinosaur Complex, opened in 2005, has America's largest display of dinosaur fossils. It was designed by noted paleontologist Dr. Jack Horner, who was the advisor for the Jurassic Park movies. However, Montana is more of a "Cretaceous Park," since most of its dinosaurs lived during the upper Cretaceous Period. The museum is on the Montana State University campus at 600 W. Kagy Blvd.; (406) 994-22511; *www.montana.edu/wwwmor/*.

Your next two stops might be the **Old Trail Museum** in *Choteau* and the **Two Medicine Dinosaur Center** just north, in *Bynum*. To reach them, head west from Bozeman on Interstate 90, go north on I-15 at *Butte*, then northwest from *Great Falls* on U.S. 89. Both sites are combined museums and digs that permit supervised public participation. The **Old Trail Museum** displays many fine specimens from this dinosaur-rich region; (406) 466-5332; *www.oldtrailmuseum.org*. The **Two Medicine** site exhibits the world's largest *seismosaurus halli* ("earth-shaker lizard"); (800) 238-6873, *www.tmdinosaur.org*. Also in this region is the Egg Mountain Paleontology site, operated by the Museum of the Rockies.

Several other digs and museums are scattered across the top of the state on or near Highway 2. You'll first encounter the **H. Earl Clark Memorial Museum** in *Havre*, with displays of rare dinosaur eggs, (406) 265-4000. A recent addition to the Montana Dinosaur Trail is the **Blaine County Museum** in *Chinook*, just beyond Havre. It has a fine dinosaur exhibit along with area history displays; (406) 357-2590; *www.chinookmontana.com*. Just to the south is the site of **Bear Paw Battlefield** of the **Nez Percé National Historic Park**, where Chief Joseph and his tribe were captured, ending their epic flight from northeastern Oregon; see pages 38 and 138.

The **Phillips County Museum** and **Dinosaur Field Station** are both in *Malta*, about seventy miles east of Chinook. The star of the field station is "Leonardo," the world's best preserved dinosaur; (406) 654-5300; *www.montanadinosaurdigs.com*. In 2005, the Montana legislature approved seed money to help fund a more elaborate facility for this rare find. The nearby museum displays several other fossil specimens unearthed in the area; (406) 654-1037; *www.maltachamber.com/museum*.

Fort Peck, just off Highway 2 in Montana's northeast corner, is the site of several major dinosaur discoveries. The **Fort Peck Dinosaur Field Station** is a working dig operated by the State of Montana; (406) 526-3539. The nearby **Fort Peck Interpretive Center and Museum**, opened in 2004, is home to another dinosaur star. "Peck's Rex," discovered in 1997, is one of the most complete *tyrannosaurus rex* fossils ever found; (406) 526-3493. The website for both is *www.pecksrex.com*.

Where to learn more

Travel Montana can send you a copy of the **Montana Dinosaur Trail** brochure-map; P.O. Box 200533, Helena, MT 59620-0533; (800) VISITMT. Or you can download one from *www.mtdinotrail.org*.

The Flathead Valley

A trio of art towns in the great outdoors

⚐

Glance at a Montana map and you'll see an oval swatch of blue in the northwestern sector. That's Flathead Lake, the largest natural body of fresh water west of the Mississippi. Extending beyond the 28-mile-long lake, pointed toward Canada, is the Flathead Valley.

This wooded, mountain-rimmed basin offers three good reasons to head for this far corner of Montana—Kalispell, Whitefish and Bigfork. Each is a serious cultural colony and they're gateways to one of the state's finest outdoor recreation regions. Further, they're within a short drive of Montana's most famous outdoor attraction, **Glacier National Park**.

The Flathead Valley is has that Montana Big Sky look. The basin is so wide and shallow that the mountains seem distant, although that's an illusion. This great bowl, with its huge lake and its mountain fringes, offers every conceivable kind of outdoor recreation, in summer and winter. It lures bikers and hikers, fishing and boating fans, downhill and cross country skiers and snowshoers. The elevation is low by Montana standards, averaging less than 3,000 feet, so the climate is mild for a region this far north.

There's little need to go indoors, except to enjoy the area's surprising array of cultural activities. The Flathead Valley's three communities are featured in John Villani's book, *The 100 Best Small Art Towns in America*. The author writes: "What's truly unusual is that each (of these small towns) has its own community arts center."

Kalispell

With a population of about 15,000, Kalispell is the largest town in this corner of Montana and thus the region's commercial center. Although its fringes suffer strip malls and motel strings, its downtown area is an appealing mix of modern and historic buildings. Many are graced with murals, with art galleries and specialty shops tucked into their storefronts.

The town's cultural focal point is the **Hockaday Museum of Art** in a brick Carnegie library building at 302 Second Ave.; (406) 755-5268; *www.hockadayartmuseum.org*. Six galleries display regional and national art.

The modestly named but excellent **Museum at Central School** occupies an imposing four-story 1894 school building at 124 Second Ave.; (406) 756-8381; *www.yourmuseum.org*. It's the town's historical archive, with a special exhibit about cowboy, legislator, sculptor and writer Frank Bird Linderman who documented the Northwest's native culture.

Bigfork

A prosperous and upscale pine-clad village of about 1,500, Bigfork is prettily situated at the mouth of the Swan River on Flathead Lake. Nice homes and resorts line the lakeshore and forested mountains rise behind. The town is busy with galleries, shops and some remarkably good restaurants. Bigfork is featured in David Vokac's *"The Great Towns of America,"* described as "one of the hidden treasures of the Rocky Mountains."

Its artistic focal point is the **Bigfork Art & Cultural Center** in the town library at 525 Electric Ave.; (406) 837-6927. The adjacent **Bigfork Summer Playhouse** offers a season of Broadway musicals; 526 Electric Ave.; (406) 837-4886; *www.bigforksummerplayhouse.com.*

Whitefish

The northernmost of the trio, pine-clad Whitefish sits on the shore of its own personal lake. The local chamber of commerce describes it well: "Whitefish is an island of culture in an ocean of mountain recreation."

With this town of 6,000 residents as a base, folks can hike in the woods, enjoy water sports on Whitefish Lake, go fishing on the lake or in nearby streams or just bask in the sand at the City Beach. During snow season, people flock here for downhill and cross-country skiing at **Big Mountain**; (800) 858-4157 or (406) 862-2900; *www.big-mountain.com.* It's one of Montana's largest winter resorts.

The **Whitefish Theatre Company** performs at the O'Shaughnessy Cultural Arts Center, which also hosts other community events; (406) 862-5371; *www.whitefishtheatreco.org.* **Stumptown Art Studio** exhibits works of local and regional artists and conducts classes and seminars, 145 Central Ave.; (406) 862-5929; *www.stumptownartstudio.org.* Whitefish has nineteen designated "Art Spots" around town, including galleries, retail shops and restaurants that display art. The town's memories are preserved in the **Stumptown Historical Society Museum** in the Whitefish Railroad Depot at 500 Depot St.; (406) 862-0067.

Whitefish earned the name "Stumptown" after it was selected as a division point for the Great Northern Railroad in 1901. The town grew so fast that new residents didn't bother to dig out the stumps after clearing the land.

Where to learn more

Flathead Convention & Visitors Bureau, 15 Depot Park, Kalispell, MT 59901-4008; (800) 543-3105 or (406) 756-9091; *www.fcvb.org.*

Bigfork Area Chamber, P.O. Box 237, Bigfork, MT 59911; (406) 837-5888; *www.bigfork.org.* **Whitefish Chamber,** 520 E. Second St., Whitefish, MT 59937; (877) 362-3458; *www.whitefishchamber.org*

Great Falls
Discoveries in Charlie Russell country

One can easily get the impression from reading our first three Montana listings that the state is mostly mountainous. Indeed, *montaña* means mountain in Spanish. However, the eastern two-thirds of the state is mostly rolling prairie country. And since this is America's third largest state, that's a lot of prairie!

This is the *real* big sky country of far horizons, the land of Plains Indians, of vast cattle spreads, of the Marlboro Man and Charles M. Russell. The great artist spent most of his life painting the cowboys and Indians and their horses in this vast rolling plains, and he lived in Great Falls, the only town of any size hereabouts.

With a population of 57,000, Great Falls is the state's third largest city and the provisioning center for the handful of folks spread over those thousands of square miles of prairie. It is not a major tourist center, although the city and its surrounds offer several serious attractions. Great Falls should be worth a detour from wherever else you're headed in Montana. And it's an easy detour, since the city sits astraddle Interstate 15, which dissects the state from south to north.

Your first look at this little city on the Missouri River may be disappointing. Its old downtown area has seen its best days, although renovation plans are in the works. It lacks the vitality of downtown Butte, for much of the business has fled to suburban malls. However, many of those century-old brick and sandstone buildings are worth a look, and once you've visited a couple or three fine museums, you'll be glad you came. To get your bearings, book the two-hour tour on the **Great Falls Historic Trolley**; (406) 771-1100. It leaves from the High Plains Heritage Center; see below.

After you've trollied Great Falls, check out its several fine museums. If you like Western art, you're likely to lose most of a day in the outstanding **Charles M. Russell Museum** at 400 Thirteenth St. N.; (406) 727-8787; *www.cmrussel.org*. In addition to its fine collection of Russell art, it displays works of other Western artists who "depict and focus on the culture, life and country of Russell's West," says the museum's mission statement.

Charlie Russell lived in Great Falls from 1903 until his death in 1926, although he traveled into the Great Plains to paint, spent time in New York after he gained fame, and later began wintering in Pasadena, California. His log cabin studio and early American style home are both on the museum grounds and open to visitors.

The **Paris Gibson Square Museum of Art** displays contemporary art in a handsome 1896 sandstone Norman style building that once served as a school. It's at 1400 First Ave. N.; (406) 727-8255; *www.the-square.org*. The area's history is preserved in the **High Plains Heritage Center** at 422 Second St. S.; (406) 452-3462; *www.highplainsheritage.org*. If you have kids in tow, you might pause at the **Children's Museum of Montana** at 22 Railroad Square; (406) 452-6661; *www.childrensmuseumofmt.org*.

Great Falls enjoys a fairly active cultural and festival scene, including several annual art shows and sales. The **C.M. Russell Auction of Original Western Art** in March draws bidders from afar; (406) 727-8787. The **Great Falls Symphony** has been entertaining music lovers with classics-to-pops concerts for half a century; (406) 453-4102; *www.gfsymphony.org*. The city also hosts two of Montana's largest annual events. The **Lewis & Clark Festival** features a living history encampment at Giant Springs State Park in early Summer; (406) 452-5661. The **Montana State Fair** begins in late July at Montana ExpoPark just west of downtown; (406) 727-1481.

Several intriguing lures are nearby. The new $6 million **Lewis & Clark National Historic Trail Interpretive Center** overlooks the Missouri River a few miles northeast of town at 4201 Giant Springs Rd.; (406) 727-8733; *www.fs.fed.us/r1/lewisclark*. High tech exhibits and realistic dioramas focus on the epic trek of the Corps of Discovery, which followed the Missouri River through Montana. Portaging around the cliff-lined Great Falls—now buried under dams—was one of Lewis & Clark's toughest challenges.

A bit farther down Giant Springs Road, **Giant Springs Heritage Park** operated by the Department of Fish and Wildlife preserves one of the world's largest freshwater springs. Lewis & Clark noted the springs in their passing. The facility has scenic overlooks, a pretty spring-side picnic area, a wildlife interpretive center and a fish hatchery; (406) 452-5734.

Ulm Pishkun State Monument fifteen miles north of town off I-15 preserves a site where native people hunted buffalo in a rather brutal manner, by stampeding them over cliffs. Displays in a nicely done interpretive center focus on buffalo jumps and the lifestyles of these early plains dwellers; (406) 866-2217; *http://fwp.mt.ml.gov/lands*.The **Mehmke Steam Museum** in the town of *Fife*, ten miles east on U.S. 87/89, exhibits antique steam traction engines, early tractors and other farm equipment; (406) 452-6571.

Where to learn more

Great Falls Convention & Visitors Bureau, 100 First Ave. N., Great Falls, MT 59403; (800) 735-8535 or (406) 761-4434; *www.greatfallscvb. visitmt.com* or *www.greatfallschamber.org*

Helena

A capital place for history, attractions and culture

⚑

State capitals often are interesting visitor destinations because of their imposing government buildings and because they're usually entrusted with the state's better museums.

Thus, we'd be tempted to send you to Helena and back even if it sat in the middle of a remote empty prairie, somewhere beyond Great Falls. However, it's in the heart of the Rocky Mountains, with their attendant recreational lures. Add to this a lively arts scene and many splendidly restored early day buildings, and Helena ranks high on our "A" list.

The first thing you must learn about Montana's state capital is how to pronounce it. The rugged prospectors who founded the town felt that *hel-LEE-na* sounded too feminine, so it became *HELL-e-na* with the second "e" almost silent. It was named after St. Helena, Minnesota, the hometown of one of the early miners. Fortunately, two other suggestions—Squashtown and Pumpkinville—were discarded.

Helena happened in 1864. Four prospectors, about to give up their search in the area, found gold in a small creek just below the Continental Divide. The elated men called the creek Last Chance Gulch and the rush was on. The area yielded gold, silver and lead, and the town prospered. However, wise residents knew that the ore eventually would give out, so they shifted their town's emphasis to commerce. Helena was on a main stage line and the railroad arrived in 1883, further ensuring the town's role as a trading center.

When Montana became a state in 1889, those two titans of Butte, Marcus Daly and William Clark (page 128), battled for the state capital. Daly wanted it in his company town of Anaconda, and Clark wanted it in Helena, where he had extensive holdings. After a vicious political battle, fought mostly with slanderous newspaper articles, voters gave the nod to Helena.

Last Chance Gulch is still there, now a curving *shoppingstrausse* in the heart of downtown, lined with galleries, cafés and coffee houses. With its many restored brick and sandstone buildings and splendid mansions in the neighborhoods, Helena is the most handsome town in Montana. For an overview, climb aboard an open air tram of **Last Chance Tours**, which passes most of the town's historic sites; (406) 442-1023; *www.lctours.com*.

After your tour, head for the copper-domed Greek Renaissance **Montana State Capitol** at 1301 Sixth Avenue, with historic exhibits, and paintings by Charlie Russell and other Western artists. For hourly guided tours, call (406) 444-2694. The 1888 **Original Governor's Mansion**, home to ten state leaders, has been restored to its Queen Anne finery, at 304 N. Ewing St.; (406) 444-4789; *www.montanahistoricalsociety.org.*

The **Montana Historical Society Museum** in a restored 1865 building has an outstanding collection of Russell paintings and a fine exhibit on the state's history, called Montana Homeland; 225 N. Roberts St.; (406) 444-2694; *www.montanahistoricalsociety.org.* The **Holter Museum of Art** has rotating exhibits of regional arts and crafts, at 12 E. Lawrence St.; (406) 442-6400; *www.holtermuseum.org.*

If you're architecturally inclined, check out the **Cathedral of St. Helena** at Lawrence and Warren Streets, modeled after the magnificent Votive Church in Vienna. Then take a gandering wander past the dozens of opulent Victorian mansions in the hills of Helena's west side residential area.

The arts are quite alive in this fine old town. The **Helena Symphony & Corale** performs in the distinctive Moorish style Civic Center downtown; (406) 442-1860; *www.helenasymphony.org.* The **Myrna Loy Center for the Performing Arts**, in an 1888 county jail building, hosts everything from jazz and modern dance to classic films, at 15 N. Ewing St.; (406) 443-0287; *www.myrnaloycenter.com.* (The beautiful "Queen of hollywood" from the 1930s through the 1950s, Myrna Loy spent her childhood in Helena and on a nearby ranch. The theater was named in her honor.)

The **Montana Shakespeare Company** presents a summer season of the Bard under the stars in Performance Square near the downtown mall; (406) 449-4466; *www.montanashakespeare.org.* The **Grandstreet Theater**, Helena's community player group, offers classic and contemporary plays at 325 N. Park Ave.; (406) 447-1574.

If you're ready to go outside and play, you don't even have to leave town. Within the city limits is **Mount Helena**, both a park and a thousand-foot peak. It's laced with hiking and biking trails, and views of the town and its historic gulches are impressive.

Several nearby lakes offer fishing and water sports. A popular water play area is in a steep canyon of the Missouri River that Lewis & Clark named "Gates of the Mountains." Although dams have turned the stream into Canyon Ferry Lake and Upper Holter Lake, the chasm is still impressive. **Gates of the Mountain Boat Tours** offers cruises up the canyon; (406) 458-5241; *www.gatesofthemountains.com.*

Where to learn more

Helena Convention & Visitors Bureau/Chamber of Commerce, 225 Cruse Ave., Suite A, Helena, MT 59601; (800) 743-5362 or (406) 447-1530; *www.helenacvb.visitmt.com* and *www.helenachamber.com.*

Montana's "Outback"
Losing yourself in Missouri River Country

Ꝑ

Our Montana visit ends with a long trek across the top of the state's Great Plains. If you *really* like wide open spaces, northeastern Montana is your place.

Travel Montana calls this region "Missouri River Country" and *Moon Handbook's Montana* defines it as "The Big Open." We like to think of it as Montana's Outback. No freeways pass through this far corner of the state, and we don't recall seeing many four-lane streets or highways. It's a set-your-own-pace kind of place, and it's ideal for exploring in an RV or with camping gear stuffed into the trunk of your car.

Begin in *Great Falls* where Interstate 15 veers sharply to the northwest, as if wanting to avoid this lonely land. Then follow U.S. 87 northeast, heading into the **Missouri Breaks**, where the great river has carved deeply into the Montana prairies.

Your first stop is one of the state's oldest towns, *Fort Benton*, established in 1846 at the head of navigation on the Missouri River. This town of about 1,600 folks has lots of history and thus two museums. The **Museum of the Northern Great Plains** focuses on the settlement of this agricultural area, at 1205 20th St.; (406) 622-5316; *www.fortbenton.com/museums*. The **Museum of the Upper Missouri River** in Old Fort Park marks the site of the fur trading post that gave the town its start; (406) 622-5316; *www.fort-benton.com/museums*. Lewis & Clark took a break near here and a memorial overlooking the river marks their stay.

Northeast of town, **Upper Missouri River Breaks National Monument** and **Charles M. Russell National Wildlife Refuge** rim the river's steep canyon walls for more than 150 miles. You can learn about both at the **Upper Missouri National Wild & Scenic River Center** in Fort Benton at 1718 Front St.; (406) 622-5185; *www.mt.blm.gov/ido/um*. About the only access to the monument is by dirt roads, or on float trips. Ask at the river center about commercial operators.

Pressing northward from Fort Benton, you'll pick up U.S. Highway 2 at *Havre* (*HAV-er*), one of the larger towns hereabouts, with about 10,000 residents. Tucked between the high plains and Bear Paw Mountains, it's the trading center for area ranches and farms. Havre was established in 1910 as a Great Northern Railway division point, and the rustic old downtown is worth a look. Much of it is underground. Cathouses, opium dens and legitimate businesses operated in tunnels beneath the streets around the turn of the last century. Some tunnels have been restored and can be explored on **Havre Beneath the Streets** tours; (406) 265-888; *www.havremt.com/attractions*. The **H. Earl Clack Museum and Gallery** at 306 Third Avenue preserves the area's past; (406) 265-4000; *www.havremt.com/attractions*.

Incidentally, Havre and several other towns and sites along Highway 2 are on the **Montana Dinosaur Trail**; see pages 130-131.

East of Havre is *Chinook*, home to the **Blaine County Museum** at 501 Indiana St.; (406) 357-2590. The **Bear Paw Battlefield** section of the **Nez Percé National Historic Park** is south of town on State Route 240; (406) 357-3130; *www.nps.gov/nepe*. It was here that Chief Joseph's band was finally captured while trying to reach sanctuary in Canada. Fleeing their northeastern Oregon reservation, they had outmaneuvered the U.S. Army for 1,700 miles, and were stopped just fifty miles short of the border.

Pressing eastward across the prairie, you'll reach *Malta*, an old cattle town and home to the **Phillips County Museum** at 431 U.S. 2E; (406) 654-1037. Another long drive delivers you to and through the town of *Glasgow* to northeastern Montana's major visitor attractions, **Fort Peck Lake** and the **Charles M. Russell National Wildlife Refuge**. Folks come from miles around for water play in the meandering river canyon.

The Big Dry Arm of the reservoir is known as "Baja Montana" because of its sandy beaches and hot summer days. **Fort Peck Dam** is one of the world's largest earth-fill structures, and one of FDR's most ambitious Depression era projects. Tours can be arranged at the new **Fort Peck Museum and Interpretive Center**; (406) 526-3421; *www.fortpeckdam.com*.

Tiny *Fort Peck*, the dam's old construction town, offers a summer drama program at the 1933 **Fort Peck Theater**. For dining or lodging, head for the National Historic Landmark **Fort Peck Hotel**; (800) 560-4931 or (406) 526-3266; *www.www.fortpeckdam.com*.

Where to learn more

Chinook Chamber of Commerce, P.O. Box 744, Chinook, MT 523; (406) 357-3160; *www.chinookmontana.com*.

Fort Benton Chamber of Commerce, P.O. Box 12 (421 Front St.), Fort Benton, MT 59442; (406) 622-3864; *www.fortbenton.com*.

Glasgow/Fort Peck Area Chamber of Commerce, P.O. Box 832 (23 U.S. 2E), Glasgow, MT 59230; (406) 228-2222.

Havre Area Chamber of Commerce, P.O. Box 308 (518 First St.), Havre, MT 59501; (406) 265-4383; *www.havremt.com*.

Malta Area Chamber of Commerce, P.O. Box 1420 (10 S. Fourth St.), Malta, MT 59538; (406) 654-1776; *www.maltachamber.com*.

Capitol Reef and Escalante
Overlooked wonders in Canyon Country

ね

The earth's crust has been uplifted, folded, carved and eroded into more fantastic shapes in southern Utah than any other place on the planet.

Most of the region is part of the Colorado Plateau, which slowly uplifted through the millennia, allowing its rivers to carve downward and create dramatic, steep-walled canyons. Arizona's Grand Canyon is of course the grandest of these chasms. Collectively, however, the canyonlands of southern Utah are equally impressive.

"Maybe all of southern Utah should be a national park," a ranger once told us during a rock talk.

It practically is. The region is home to Zion, Bryce, Capitol Reef, Canyonlands and Arches national parks, plus Cedar Breaks, Grand Staircase-Escalante and Natural Bridges national monuments.

Most of these names are familiar to travelers, although many tend to overlook two of our favorites, Capitol Reef and Grand Staircase-Escalante. We've designed a driving tour through these natural wonders. It's not a loop trip, but ends at the northeastern Arizona border, near **Monument Valley** and the **Four Corners** Area.

This can be a side trip from **Bryce Canyon National Park** because that's where our journey begins. Follow State Route 12 east through the upper edge of the 1.9 million acre wilderness of **Grand Staircase-Escalante National Monument.** Chief architect of this remote region was the twisting Escalante River that left a maze of canyons, buttes and ridges as it carved its way downward. This was the last river system in America to be discovered and mapped, done by a member of John Wesley Powell's party in 1872.

Highway 12 keeps mostly to the ridges, providing great panoramas of this wildly carved countryside. About midway through the drive is the hamlet of *Escalante*, with a few motels, cafés, stores and the Escalante Interagency Visitor Center; (435) 826-5499. Check out nearby **Escalante Petrified Forest State Park**, with a small reservoir and trails leading to some petrified trees; (435) 826-4466. Farther along, near the town of *Boulder* is **Anasazi State Park Museum**, where nearly a hundred rooms of an ancient native village have been excavated; (435) 335-7308.

Head north from Boulder through a wooded upland to the small towns of *Torrey* and *Teasdale*. These are gateways to our favorite outdoor Utah place, **Capitol Reef National Park**; (435) 425-3791; *www.nps.gov/care*. This long and slender park encloses an amazing geological shape called the Waterpocket Fold, a 100-mile-long ridge that nearly folded over onto itself, like a breaking wave. Geologists call this formation a *monocline*, a ridge with the strata tilted in one direction. The "waterpocket" name comes from water trapped in pockets of the fold. "Capitol Reef" refers to its top layer of sandstone, with several rounded promontories suggesting capitol domes.

Highway 24 passes crosses the upper third of the park, following a canyon carved through the ridge by the Fremont River. The **Capitol Reef Scenic Drive** offers a grand geological parade of slickrock slopes, sheer cliff walls, buttes, domes, fins and slot canyons. Colors range from orange-red through pea soup green and magenta to Hershey bar brown and off-white.

Beyond the park, Highway 24 passes through a continuing parade of multicolored cliffs and ridges. At *Hanksville*, head south on State Route 95 and then Route 276 to **Bullfrog Basin Marina** on Lake Powell in **Glen Canyon National Recreation Area**. It has a lodge, cafés, boat rentals and a visitor center; (435) 684-7400. From here, take a car ferry across the lake and continue east on Highway 276 to **Natural Bridges National Monument**, which shelters three water-carved arches; (435) 692-1234; *www.nps. gov/nabr*. The nine-mile Bridge View Drive leads to arch overlooks.

Follow Highway 95 east briefly and then head south on State Route 261 to view the squiggly canyons of the **San Juan River**. Be warned that you must spiral down an equally squiggly and very steep gravel road. If you're faint of heart, you can avoid the grade by taking a longer route.

At the top of the grade, just before the pavement ends, watch for a dirt road to your right. It travels four miles across a flat desert plateau and ends suddenly at the San Juan Canyon's **Muley Point** overlook. (We had visions of that dramatic closing scene in the film *Thelma and Louise*.)

From there, take the above-mentioned squiggly gravel road to the bottom of the steep grade, where you'll regain pavement. Follow Route 261 to **Goosenecks State Park** with another overlook to San Juan Canyon a thousand feet below. Here, the river curves through the chasm like Christmas ribbon candy. Called "entrenched meanders," these curves are so coiled that five miles of river travel covers only a mile as the canyon raven flies.

To do the chicken route, stay with Route 95, go south on U.S. 191 and west on U.S. 163. Then go north on Route 316 just above *Mexican Hat*.

Where to learn more

Capitol Reef Country, P.O. Box 7, Teasdale, UT 84773; (800) 858-7951 or (435) 425-3365; *www.capitolreef.org*.

The Dinosaur Corner
The real Jurassic Park and a fiery chasm

⚑

Once in a lifetime, if one is lucky, one so merges with sunlight and air and running water that whole eons, the eons that mountains and deserts know, might pass in a single afternoon without discomfort.
— **Loren Eisley,** *The Immense Journey,* © 1957

Rafting the Yampa River through Dinosaur National Monument several years ago, we could appreciate author-naturalist Loren Eisley's poignant response to this land of narrow gorges, sandstone cliffs and roiling water. However, we certainly could not have expressed it in his words.

His comments were inspired by Echo Park, where the Yampa and Green Rivers merge, their waters echoing off the towering cliffs. Some miles away, in a place we knew to be fascinating but not peaceful, tourists were visiting the world's largest Jurassic dinosaur dig, pointing to this bone and that.

Dinosaur National Monument is one of two serious reasons to journey to this far northeastern corner of Utah. The other is Flaming Gorge National Recreation Area, where waters of the Green River are becalmed by a huge dam. Both of these attractions spill into neighboring states. The monument reaches east into Colorado and Flaming Gorge extends north into Wyoming.

Although **Dinosaur National Monument** covers 200,000 acres of desert canyonlands, its centerpiece is the quarry. This is one of the world's richest fossil finds, and digging has continued since 1909. However, fossils are no longer removed. Paleontologists clear just enough rock from the bones to create a *bas relief,* so folks in the adjacent gallery can define their shapes. The nearby visitor center has displays on the geology, flora and fauna of the area. A larger interpretive center is twenty miles east, outside the monument in *Dinosaur, Colorado*; (970) 374-3000; *www.nps.gov/dino*.

Flaming Gorge National Recreation Area to the north is a place that Loren Eisley would not like, since a reservoir has flooded a vast network of red rock canyons. Water sports enthusiasts love it of course. The 90-mile-long Lake Flaming Gorge is a huge aquatic playground with marinas in Utah and Wyoming. The main visitor center is at **Flaming Gorge Dam**, where one can view natural history exhibits and arrange for tours; (435) 885-3135.

Most visitors to the national monument and recreation area approach through *Vernal, Utah*, a town's that's ditzy about dinosaurs. A giant pink critter named "Dinah" greets visitors as they enter town. This tree-shaded oasis in the Ashley Valley also is home to T-Rex Taxi, Fossil Valley RV

Park, Dinaville Motel, Dinosaur Inn and Campground Dina. The agency promoting local tourism is the Dinosaurland Travel Board.

The many motels, cafés and gas stations strung out from Vernal's outskirts suggest that this is serious tourist country. The look of downtown is much more appealing. It's neat and well-tended, with flowers spilling from concrete planters. Many of its buildings are a century old, although 1950s trim covers some of the old brick façades.

Speaking of brick, every scribe who writes about Vernal has to tell this story: When the town was established as a farm settlement in 1876, it was one of the most remote outposts in the Mormon empire. It was still remote in 1919, when a local banker wanted a new brick façade on his building. He winced when learned that the freight cost to far-out Vernal was $1.70 a pound. However, the parcel post rate was just $1.05 per pound, so he had his bricks mailed from Salt Lake City.

Today's Vernal, easily reached by highway and scheduled air service, is more than just a gateway to the national monument and Flaming Gorge. It has a few attractions of its own. The best is the **Utah Field House of Natural History State Park Museum** at 235 E. Main St.; (435) 789-3799; *www.utah.com/state parks.* Philantrophist Andrew Carnegie brought fame to Vernal when he financed the first dig in the present-day national monument. He had casts made from fossils and gave them to various cities, including Vernal. As you enter the museum, you'll be greeted by "Dippy," Carnegie's long-necked *diplodocous.* The busy museum has lots of other fossils, plus artifacts of the early Fremont people and exhibits on area flora and fauna.

Other town lures are the **Daughters of Utah Pioneers Museum** at the corner of 200 South and 500 west, (435) 789-0085; and the **Western Heritage Museum** in Heritage Park at 328 E. 200 South; (435) 789-7399. Its startling clutter of exhibits includes pioneer and native peoples artifacts, stuffed critters and a Model-T school bus. If you like cute, the **Ladies of the White House Doll Collection** exhibits sculpted figures representing thirty-eight of America's first ladies in their inaugural ball gowns. It's at the Uintah County Library at 155 East Main; (435) 789-0091.

Whitewater rafting trips through Dinosaur National Monument on the Yampa River can be booked through **OARS**, a leading rafting and outdoor adventure company, at P.O. Box 67, Angels Camp, CA 95222; (800) 346-6277; *www.oars.com.*

Where to learn more

Dinosaurland Travel Board, 55 E. Main St., Vernal, UT 84078; (800) 477-5558 or (435) 789-6932; *www.dinoland.com.*

Logan and surrounds
Of mountain men and Mormons

Hd

Handsome old Logan occupies the lush green Cache Valley north of Salt Lake City. It's cradled by the Wasatch and Bear River mountains, and in autumn, their foothills are painted in fall colors. This could be the prettiest townsite in the state. Equally attractive is Logan Canyon, a popular recreation area just north of town.

Mormons were the first outsiders to arrive in most regions of Utah, although the Cache Valley is a rare exception. Mountain men came here in the 1820s to trap beaver on the Logan River. For several years, the valley was the site of their annual rendezvous, basically a mountain man swap meet and drinking party. The valley's name comes from the French word *cache,* which rhymes with stash and means just that—a place to hide valuables for later retrieval. It was pelts in this case.

The trappers left when the beaver ran out and the comely valley lay undisturbed until the Mormons arrived in the 1850s, drawn by the area's agricultural potential.

Logan has a prosperous yesterday look, with a mix of old brick and contemporary buildings. The area has two modest claims to fame. It's home to Utah State University with an attractive beige brick campus. And the region is noted for its exceptionally rich Cache Valley cheese, produced from contented cows munching on the lush grass hereabouts.

Getting to Logan is about as interesting as being there. If you're coming up from *Ogden* (just two pages ahead), leave Interstate 15 at *Brigham City*, a stately old town named for you-know-who. Its **Box Elder Temple** at Main and 300 South, the **Brigham City Tabernacle** at 251 S. Main Street and the **Brigham City Museum and Gallery** at 24 N. 300 West Street are worth a pause each. If you're a birder, check out the nearby **Bear River Migratory Bird Refuge**, where the Bear River empties into the Great Salt Lake; (435) 723-5887. Then, follow U.S. 89/91 to and through the hamlet of *Mantua*, crest a mile-high pass and drop into the **Cache Valley**.

Near *Wellsville*, you'll encounter the valley's most interesting attraction, the **American West Heritage Center**; (800) 225-FEST or (435) 245-6050; *www.awhc.org*. It's a 160-acre living history site where costumed docents portray life at a native village, a mountain men's camp, a pioneer settlement and a 1917 Mormon farm. Activities include covered wagon rides, shootouts, a barbecue cookout, cowboy music and poetry and native dancing. The center sponsors the **Festival of the American West** in early August. This is an upbeat presentation of Western heritage, with music, dancing, parades and historical re-enactments.

When you reach *Logan*, start with a visit to the **Daughters of Utah Pioneers Museum** in an ancient red brick building at 160 N. Main St.; (435) 752-5139. It shares space with the **Cache Chamber of Commerce** and you can pick up a downtown walking tour map, *Logan's Historic Main Street.* The map will guide you to fine old structures such as the Greek-Federalist style 1883 **Cache County Courthouse**, the imposing 1884 **Logan Temple** perched atop a nearby hill at 100 North, and the brick **Logan Tabernacle** at Main and Center streets, with an elaborate 1908 pipe organ.

The campus of **Utah State University** is worth a stroll, with its beige brick buildings set against a backdrop of the Bear Mountains; (435) 797-1129; *www.usu.edu.* Pick up a campus map at the information center near a parking terrace. Prowl the hallways of the stately 1889 Old Main building and get a scoop of rich Aggie Ice Cream at the Taggart Student Center. The **Nora Eccles Harrison Museum of Art** on campus has one of the Intermountain West's largest collections of ceramics, sculptures and paintings, (435) 797-0163. The university's **Museum of Anthropology** focuses on present and past cultures from around the globe, (435) 797-7545.

An instant canyon

North of town, **Logan Canyon National Scenic Byway** (U.S. 89) curls through a steep-walled chasm in Wasatch-Cache National Forest. It's instant canyon; dramatic ramparts and terraced cliffs appear almost immediately after you leave Logan. Stop at the **U.S. Forest Service Information Center** at the mouth of Logan Canyon for a tour map and other information on the area; (435) 753-2772.

There are a few summer homesites in the canyon, although most of the area is unpopulated. The scenery's just grand, with sheer walls, wooded side canyons and glimpses of distant snowcapped peaks. Logan Canyon is splashed with fall color from late September into mid-October.

At the top of the canyon, **Bear Lake State Recreation Area** offers camping, fishing, a marina and water sports; (435) 946-3343. Your turnaround point is the lakeside village of *Garden City*, since the twenty-mile-long lake extends into Idaho from here. However, if you remembered to check out of your Logan motel room, you can extend yourselves all the way to **Grand Teton** and **Yellowstone** national parks.

Where to learn more

Cache Chamber of Commerce, 195 N. Main St., Logan, UT 84321; (800) 882-4433; *www.tourcachevalley.com.*

Ogden and The Spike
Utah's diverse mini-city and the great railway

⚐

Although not normally regarded as a tourist destination, Ogden offers many surprises. This mini-city of about 78,000 is busy with museums and other attractions and its old downtown area is being redeveloped into one of the West's largest urban historic districts.

The city occupies a fine setting between the Wasatch Range and the Great Salt Lake, with easy access to summer and winter recreation activities. *Sunset* magazine once called Ogden "the best city in the West for access to the outdoors." Established in 1847 as one of Brigham Young's first settlements outside Salt Lake City, it has an interesting dual heritage—weapons and rails.

A gunsmith named Jonathan Browning opened a small gun shop here in 1851. Later his son John, who was literally raised on guns, became the greatest small arms inventor of all time. This Thomas Edison of killing machines invented or perfected the repeating rifle, machine gun and revolver. The "guns that won the west" were all of his design because he licensed many of his patents to Colt and Winchester.

Ogden's train heritage is tied to the transcontinental railroad, which was completed in 1869, about fifty miles away at Promontory Summit. Since that was way out on a sagebrush prairie, Ogden was chosen as the main transfer point. It's still a major rail center.

These dual legacies and others are preserved in the 1924 **Union Station**, downtown at Wall Avenue and 25th street; (801) 393-9886; *www.unionstation.org*. Restored as a history and cultural center, it contains the **Utah State Rail Museum, Browning Firearms Museum, Browning-Kimball Car Museum** and the **Natural History Museum**. Union Station also has two art galleries, plus shops and cafés.

While you're in the neighborhood, check out **Temple Square** at Washington Boulevard and 22nd streets. It contains the dramatically modern **Ogden Temple** with rounded glass corners and a tall golden spire, and the more traditional masonry **Ogden Tabernacle**. The temple is open only to Mormons, although the rest of us can view the ornate polished woodwork inside the tabernacle and join free tours of the landscaped grounds.

Downtown's **Historic 25th Street** is a fun attraction, busy with shops, restaurants, art galleries and a weekend farmers' market. In the works as part of a major redevelopment project is an **Arts District** with an open air theater and a gallery complex.

Ogden has a very active cultural scene, with two major performing arts centers. The wonderfully ornate **Peery's Egyptian Theater**, a restored 1923 movie house, presents live concerts and classic films, at 2415 Washington Blvd.; (801) 395-3227; *www.peeryegyptiantheater.com*. The **Val Browning Center for the Performing Arts** on the campus of Weber State University, books a variety of plays, concerts, dance programs and such; (801) 626-7000. The **Ogden Symphony Ballet Association** imports a variety of performance groups, including the Utah Symphony and Utah Ballet from Salt Lake City; (801) 399-9214; *www.symphonyballet.org*.

This mini-city has several other interesting lures, including the usual **Daughters of Utah Pioneers Museum** at 2148 Grant Ave.; (801) 621-5224. Next door is the furnished **Miles Goodyear Cabin**, built in 1845 by an early mountain man. Ogden is a long way from dinosaur country although the **George S. Eccles Dinosaur Park** features replicas of these creatures, and an exhibit hall displays other prehistoric stuff, at 1544 Park Blvd.; (801) 393-3466; *www.dinosaurpark.org*.

Off to Promontory

Since Ogden had close ties to the transcontinental railroad, a side trip to Promontory seems appropriate. Every school kid and most of their parents know that a ceremonial golden spike was driven to mark its completion. (Actually, several commemorative spikes were driven.) However, the two railroad companies, the Central Pacific and Union Pacific, couldn't agree on a final connecting point. Their crews built 225 miles of useless parallel track before agreeing to link up at Promontory Summit. Folks also may not know that Central Pacific president Leland Stanford was so sloshed from celebrating that he missed his first swing at the famous spike.

You'll learn all of this and more fun stuff at the **Golden Spike National Historic Site**; (435) 471-2209; *www.nps.gov/gosp*. To get there, drive north from Ogden on Interstate 15, then follow signs west from *Brigham City*. Although the rails were later re-routed, a stretch of the original line has been restored, and replicas of the two trains that touched cowcatchers at the ceremony are on display. Even shantytowns that housed the workers have been replicated. A fine visitor center provides all the historic details of the event.

A fun time to visit is on May 10, the anniversary date of the joining of the rails. You can watch a re-enactment of the event, right down to a telegraph operator clicking out a message flashed coast to coast: "Done!"

Where to learn more

Ogden Convention & Visitors Bureau, 2501 Wall Ave., Ogden, UT 84401; (866) 867-8823 or (801) 627-8288; *www.ogdencvb.org*.

The southwest corner
A tale of two Cedars, and Utah's Dixie

Zion National Park isn't the only attraction in southwestern Utah. Just to the north are Cedar City, home to the Utah Shakespearean Festival, and Cedar Breaks National Monument, with an natural amphitheater of vividly colored limestone shapes. To the south is St. George, a sturdy old pioneer town that's enjoying a growth surge. They all share southern Utah's classic signature of awesome and multicolored geological formations.

The area is an easy reach, for Cedar City and St. George are on Interstate 15 that links Salt Lake City to San Diego. Cedar Breaks is just uphill from Cedar City. Both are misnamed, for there's nary a cedar in sight. Mormon pioneers who settled this area in the mid-1800s mistook the region's junipers for cedars.

Southwestern Utah was one of the first areas occupied by the Mormons after Brigham Young set up shop in Salt Lake City in 1847. Cedar City was established in 1850 as the "Iron Mission" to develop iron resources in the area. St. George was settled in 1861 because the Mormons felt they could grow cotton in the toasty climate. This is the lowest and warmest area of the state, often called "Utah's Dixie."

Cedar City is considerably higher and cooler than St. George, occupying a juniper-trimmed basin nearly 6,000 feet above sea level. The town, strung out for several miles alongside I-15, is a bit short on charm, although it's long on culture.

The Tony Award winning **Utah Shakespearean Festival**, held on the campus of Southern Utah University, draws thousands of patrons each year; (800) 752-9849 or (435) 586-7878; *www.bard.org*. The works of Shakespeare and other playwrights are presented in an Elizabethan style outdoor theater and a modern indoor playhouse. The season runs from late June through October. Also on the campus is the excellent **Braithwaite Fine Arts Gallery**, with changing and permanent exhibits, mostly of contemporary American art; (435) 586-5432; *www.suu.edu/pva/gallery*.

Cedar City's story is told at **Iron Mission State Park** at 635 Main St.; (435) 586-9290; *www.stateparks.utah.gov*. It marks the site of the first iron foundry west of the Mississippi. However, it didn't do well because of a lack of skilled ironworkers.

Cedar Breaks National Monument is steeply uphill from Cedar City, near the junctions of state highways 14 and 148; (435) 586-9451; *www.nps.gov/cebr*. Sitting at a chilly 10,350 feet above sea level, this small monument shelters a spectacular amphitheater of eroded and multicolored limestone shapes. It's for eyes only, since no trails lead down into this stone forest, although there are rim trails. A five-mile road runs the length of this grand proscenium, with several viewpoints along the way. The only facilities at Cedar Breaks are a small visitor center and a campground.

Just north of here on Route 148 is **Brian Head,** a Bavarian style ski resort tucked into a shallow wooded canyon. In addition to winter sports, the resort offers a summer program of hiking, biking, horseback riding and scenic chairlift rides; (435) 677-2035; *www.brianhead.com.*

It's quite a drop to our next stop. At 2,840 feet, *St. George* has a climate more akin to Las Vegas, which isn't that far away. With a population pushing 60,000, it's one of Utah's fastest growing cities. Although rather a sprawl, it occupies a pleasing desert oasis along the Virgin River, with red rock cliffs rising all about. It's a popular winter resort area and one of Utah's most historic cities. For those who want to gamble, it's a short drive through scenic **Virgin River Gorge** to the casinos of *Mesquite* on the Nevada border. (Utah is one of only two states with no legalized gaming.)

Like many visitors today, old Brig often wintered in St. George. The restored 1873 **Brigham Young Winter Home** is open to tours, at 67 W. 200 North St.; (435) 673-2517. Other Mormon historic sites are the red sandstone 1863 **St. George Tabernacle** at Main and Tabernacle streets, where church volunteers conduct tours, (435) 628-7274; and the majestic white **St. George Temple**, filling an entire city block at 400 East and 200 South. It's the oldest still-active Mormon temple in the world. Non-Mormons can't enter, although they can see exhibits and watch a video about the Mormon faith in an adjacent visitor center; (435) 673-5181.

The **Daughters of Pioneers Museum** exhibits artifacts from St. George's early days, at 145 N. 100 East Street; (435) 628-7274. The **Rosenbruch Wildlife Museum** features realistic-looking dioramas of world animal habitats, at 1835 Convention Center Dr.; (435) 656-0033.

Before leaving the area, drive eleven miles northwest on State Route 18 to **Snow Canyon State Park**. It offers a fascinating mix of black lava and red rock formations; (435) 628-2255; *www.stateparks.utah.gov.* The canyon wasn't named for the white stuff, but for two pioneer Mormon brothers.

Where to learn more

Cedar City-Brian Head Tourism & Convention Bureau, 581 Main St., Cedar City, UT 84720; (800) 254-4848; *www.scenicsouthernutah.com.*

St. George Area Chamber of Commerce, 97 E. St. George Blvd., St. George, UT 84770; (435) 628-1658; *www.stgeorgechamber.com.*

Cheyenne
A mini-city of cowboys and railroads

Ⴒ

One would have thought that the capital of Wyoming would be in the middle of the state instead of the middle of nowhere. Well, maybe not nowhere, but way out on the Great Plains, where the countryside is as flat as a cowboy's wallet. And it's just barely in Wyoming, in the state's southeastern corner, ten miles from Colorado and forty miles from Nebraska.

However, if you suffer from flatland phobia as we do, you needn't avoid Cheyenne. The Rockies are visible to the west and there's even a ski resort a hundred miles away, just beyond next-door Laramie. (Out on the Great Plains, "next door" is about fifty miles.)

Wyoming is mostly cattle country and Cheyenne was a cowtown. Actually it was a cowtown with rails. It was established in 1867 as a provisioning stop on the transcontinental railroad. With easy transportation available, it became the haven of wealthy ranchers, who lived in grand Victorian mansions on "Cattle Baron's Row." For entertainment, they went to the Cheyenne Opera House to see Sarah Bernhardt, Lily Langtry and—yep—Buffalo Bill. Their wealth bought political power, so this far-away town became the territorial and then the state capital. By the time Wyoming achieved statehood in 1890, Cheyenne was a bustling city of nearly 15,000.

Cheyenne is Wyoming's largest city, although it's still a mini-city, with a population of only about 55,000. However, being the capital gives this little city more than its share of attractions. And it's easy to reach, since it sits astraddle coast-to-coast Interstate 80. Imagine waking up in New York one morning and saying: "I think I'll mosey on over to Cheyenne."

When you get here, head for the old fashioned and well-tended downtown area. You know you're in a cowtown because streets and plazas are decorated with eight foot tall cowboy boots. The little city's centerpiece is **Depot Square** at the base of Capitol Avenue, in front of the steel lacework of the large Cheyenne railyard. The town's railroading history is preserved at the **Cheyenne Depot Museum**, newly installed in the splendid sandstone and brick Italianate 1886 Union Pacific Depot; (307) 632-3905; *www.cheyennedepotmuseum.org*.

The **Cheyenne Area Convention & Visitors Bureau** also occupies the depot complex and you can pick up an historic walking tour map, or book a ride on the **Cheyenne Street Railway Trolley**; (307) 778-3133.

Just up Capitol Avenue, the elaborate, slender-domed State Capitol has free guided tours on weekdays; (307) 777-7220. The nearby 1904 **Historic Governors' Mansion** was re-opened in mid-2006 after a major renovation. It's at 300 E. 21st St.; (307) 777-7878; *www.wyoparks.state.wy.us/*.

Relive Cheyenne's golden era—at least in your imagination—by admiring the grand mansions of **Cattle Baron's Row** along Seventeenth Street. Most are privately owned, although you can bunk in at the **Nagle Warren Mansion**, now a B&B at 222 E. Seventeenth, (800) 811-2610 or (307) 637-3333; *www.naglewarrenmansion.com*. Can't afford the rates? Make a reservation for Victorian style high tea, served on Fridays and Saturdays.

The town's best attraction is the **Cheyenne Frontier Days Old West Museum**. It's next to the rodeo grounds in Frontier Park at the top end of town; (307) 778-7290; *www.oldwestmuseum.org*. Exhibits include Western art, cowboy regalia, native artifact and a large collection of horse-drawn vehicles. There's more cowboy lore at the **Nelson Museum of the West**, including artifacts from Western-theme movies and TV shows. It's at 1714 Carey Ave.; (307) 635-7670; *www.nelsonmuseum.com*.

The **Wyoming State Museum** exhibits still more cowboy regalia, plus other state historical items, military gear, fossils and fine art. It's near the capitol at 2301 Central Ave.; (307) 777-7022; *www.wyomuseum.state.wy.us*. And for yet another sampling of the Old West, a group of friendly rowdies called the **Cheyenne Gunslingers** shoot it out Monday through Saturday during June and July; (307) 653-1028; *www.cheyennegunslingers.org*.

The **Warren ICBM & Heritage Museum** is inside nearby **F.E. Warren Air Force Base,** once a U.S. Army fort that protected the town. Since security is tight these days, call to see if you can get aboard; (307) 773-3381.

If you'd like to see the buffalo roam, mosey on out to the **Terry Bison Ranch** on Terry Ranch Road south of town; take exit 2 from I-25. More than 3,000 bison mill about, and the ranch offers horseback rides and other amusements; (800) 319-4171 or (307) 634-4171.

If you *really* want to feel the pulse of this old cowtown, come for **Cheyenne Frontier Days** the last full week of July. Promoters say it's the world's largest outdoor rodeo, with chuck wagon and wild horse rides, a Native American encampment, parades and entertainment. Get your tickets and room reservations at least six months in advance, since the whole danged town sells out; (800) 227-6336 or (307) 778-7222; *www.cfdrodeo.com*.

Where to learn more

Cheyenne Convention & Visitors Bureau, One Depot Square, Cheyenne, WY 82001; (800) 426-5009 or (307) 778-3133; *www.cheyenne.org*.

Cody
Buffalo Bill: the man and his town

If ever there was a town preoccupied with one man, it's Cody, Wyoming. It has a right to be, because William Frederick "Buffalo Bill" Cody established it. And it's okay that Cody is the most unabashed tourist town in Wyoming, because that's what Buffalo Bill had in mind.

In 1895, he and two partners set up a land and irrigation company in the Bighorn Basin, just fifty-four miles east of Yellowstone National Park. With all those tourists headed for Yellowstone, Cody figured a town would prosper here. Never modest, he named it for himself.

It's really more interesting to talk about the man than the town because Cody practically invented the Wild West. Nearly a century after his death, he is still America's most recognized Western character, more than Wyatt Earp or Billy the Kid. Type "Buffalo Bill" into Google's search engine and you'll get about 11,900,000 references.

The man

Born on an Iowa farm in 1846, Willie Cody was an adventurer almost from the start. His father died when he was eleven and he took a job running dispatches between Army supply wagons. He was a Pony Express rider at age fifteen, then he spent the next several years as a scout and as a buffalo hunter to feed railroad crews. He was so skilled at killing buffalo that the crewmen gave him his famous nickname of "Buffalo Bill."

During the Plains Indian Wars, he became chief scout for the U.S. Cavalry, gaining a reputation for his skills as a tracker and Indian fighter. Dime novelist Ned Buntline heard of his exploits and began writing fanciful tales about him. In 1872, Cody traveled to New York, where Buntline convinced him to perform in a play he had written called *Scouts of the Plains*. His career as an entertainer had begun, even though the play was so awful that "no ordinary intellect is capable of comprehending it," wrote a critic.

Then the Sioux staged a major uprising and the Army called Buffalo Bill back to the plains. In his final battle, he killed and scalped a chief named Yellow Hand, bringing him more national fame. He returned to show biz and eventually created his fanciful Wild West Show that traveled throughout America and Europe. While making him rich and world-famous, it gave mankind a distorted picture of the West that still lingers in some minds. Ironically, also Cody became a supporter of native peoples' rights and a conservationist, speaking out against the slaughter of buffalo.

A great entertainer but a bad businessman, he eventually lost the show and went to work for a competitor. He died in 1917 while visiting his sister in Denver and he's buried on a hill overlooking the Colorado plains.

The town

Cody's preoccupation with tourism isn't subtle. This town of about 8,000 presumed fans of Buffalo Bill has five museums, several art galleries and two old West villages—one full size and another in miniature. Motels, cafés and souvenir shops dot the downtown area. However, most of this is done with a certain level of restraint. Cody isn't as gaudy and gimmicky as some other historic Western towns that have become tourist attractions.

The hub of it all, the **Buffalo Bill Historical Center**, is easily the best Western archive west of the Mississippi, and probably west of the Volga. It's a vast complex with four museums and a Western art gallery spread over 300,000 square feet of display space; (800) 227-8483 or (307) 587-4771; *www.bbhc.org.*

The **Buffalo Bill Museum** spills over with memorabilia about this amazing character, and the **Plains Indian Museum** tells the story of the people he once hunted and later hired for his Wild West Show. The **Draper Museum** focuses on the region's natural history, and the **Cody Firearms Museum** displays more than 5,000 weapons, from crossbows to modern semi-automatics. The **Whitney Gallery of Western Art** is one of the best of its kind, displaying works by George Catlin, Frederic Remington, Charles Russell and N.C. Wyeth.

But wait! There's more! Outside the complex, you'll encounter the **Harry Jackson Museum** with works by the noted artist-in-residence, at 602 Blackburn Ave.; (307) 587-5508; *www.harryjackson.com.* **The Old West Miniature Village and Museum** is housed in Tecumseh's Trading Post at 143 W. Yellowstone Avenue, with a large diorama of hand-carved figures and miniature villages, plus Old West artifacts; (307) 587-5362.

Three miles west of Cody on the highway to Yellowstone, **Trail Town** is an assemblage of twenty-six old buildings dragged here from other places in Wyoming and filled with displays and period furnishings; (307) 587-5302. Its **Museum of the Old West** is busy with Western regalia.

And if all of the above isn't enough for fans of cowboy culture, Cody calls itself the "Rodeo Capital of the World" because it stages a rodeo every single night from June through August; (800) 207-0744.

Where to learn more

Cody Chamber of Commerce, 836 Sheridan Ave., Cody, WY 82414; (307) 587-2297; *www.codychamber.org.*

Jackson's Hole
An old Western town with cowboy *chic*

⚐

My grandaddy Walter C. Dallas, who cowboyed around Jackson's Hole, and also did a little poaching and made moonshine, wouldn't recognize the place today. Being a renaissance man of the American West, he wouldn't like what's happened to his old stomping grounds, particularly the town of Jackson. Not with its trendy shops, Starbucks and *nouveau* cuisine.

We use the original name of *Jackson's* Hole instead of Jackson Hole, in homage to Grandad. This beautiful basin and its Western style town are hardly undiscovered, since about three million people manage to find it each year. Further, it's the gateway to Grand Teton National Park. So why is it in this book? We selected it because many folks may not be aware that Jackson's Hole would be a great vacation destination even without a famous national park practically sitting on top of it.

The town is in a splendid setting. Jackson's Hole is a broad sagebrush prairie with the Snake River running through it and rugged mountains rising on three sides. The incredibly craggy Grand Tetons, among the world's most photographed peaks, dominate the northwestern skyline. The Tetons were named by French trappers too long without the company of women. *Les grande tetons* means—uh—the big boobs.

Within this mountain cradle, folks are at one with the great outdoors, floating the Snake River, fishing crystalline creeks, hiking the heights, cycling in the broad valley and renting nags from dude ranches.

The valley offers an abundance of wintertime frolic. **Jackson Hole Mountain Resort** twelve miles northwest of town is one of the world's top ski areas, with America's highest vertical drop; (888) 333-7766; *www.jacksonhole.com*. The smaller **Snow King Resort** is just seven blocks from downtown; (800) 522-5464; *www.snowking.com*. Skiers can have their morning coffee at Starbucks and walk to the lift. Flatland skiers are offered a choice of three cross country areas: **Jackson Hole Nordic Center**, (307) 733-2291; **Spring Creek Ranch Nordic Center**, (800) 443-6139; and **Teton Pines Cross-Country Ski Center**, (800) 238-2223 .

Downtown Jackson manages to embrace tourism without completely sacrificing its funky Western charm. Visitors can clunk along boardwalks, walk under elk antler arches and poke into art galleries and boutiques housed in chink-log cabins and false front stores. They can drink in tough old saloons and dine on platter-smothering steaks—or sushi. And they can sleep in log cabins or be spoiled silly at luxury resorts.

Grandad, who couldn't carry a tune in a washtub, would be amazed to learn that his old hangout hosts the **Grand Teton Music Festival**, with more than sixty concerts and 200 performers; (307) 733-3050; *www.gtmf.org*. It runs from mid-June through August at the high end resort of Teton Village, at the base of Jackson Hole Mountain Resort.

Jackson also is a serious art center, with four annual art festivals and more than thirty galleries downtown. The outstanding **National Museum of Wildlife Art** occupies a rough-hewn sandstone building two miles north of town; (307) 733-5771; *wildlifeart.org*. Works by America's top wildlife artists are displayed in 51,000 square feet of exhibit space.

Two downtown museums recall the region's earlier days—the **Jackson Hole Museum** at Glenwood and Deloney streets, (307) 733-2414; and the **Jackson Hole Historical Society Museum** at Glenwood Street and Mercill Avenue; (307) 733-9605; *www.jacksonholehistory.org*.

The **National Elk Refuge**, a mile east of town, is the winter home to one of America's largest herds; (307) 733-9212; *www.fws.gov/nationalelkrefuge*. It's the main source for the hundreds of antlers that form those distinctive elk arches downtown. No, people don't shoot the poor critters; elk shed their racks every year.

Jackson's Hole reaches far back into Wyoming history. It had been a hangout for trappers since John Colter, a former Lewis & Clark scout, wintered there in 1807-1808. The Snake River and its tributaries were thick with beaver. Mountain men worked the region and held *rendesvoux* there until the 1840s, when the creatures were pretty much trapped out. The first settlers arrived in the 1880s and began running cattle over the broad basin. When Grand Teton National Park was established in 1929, the log cabin town of Jackson became its southern gateway. Tourism had come to stay.

Although downtown Jackson has more or less preserved its historical look, things have gotten out of hand around the edges. Developers have chopped up old ranches to build shopping malls, supermarkets and so-called "ranchettes." Good grief, there's even a Ripley's Believe It or Don't Museum on the edge of town! The area's population has tripled within the last two decades and is now pushing 10,000.

An anti-growth movement is underway, but it's too late for the grazing lands and elk meadows already lost to suburban sprawl. And there's not a dang thing anybody can do about a museum that exhibits shrunken heads.

Where to learn more

Jackson Hole Chamber of Commerce, P.O. Box 550 (990 W. Broadway), WY 83001; (307) 733-3316; *www.jacksonholechamber.com*.

Laramie to Rawlins
Discoveries in Medicine Bow Country

⚑

Medicine Bow Country is classic Wyoming—sagebrush prairies and grasslands rimmed by wooded mountains. If this were Montana, folks would call it Big Sky Country. Or maybe Big Sky High Country, since even the prairies here are more than 7,000 feet above sea level.

We've designed a driving trip through the region that's anchored by towns with different personalities. Laramie offers a mix of cowboy lore and culture, since it's home to Wyoming's only public university. Rawlins is an oil town that went bust when the wells dried up, and is slowly recovering.

The name Medicine Bow is of native origin, having to do with cedar wood used for their bows and the spiritual values of the mountains, which whites interpreted as "medicine." The high prairies supported nomadic bands of Plains Indians and great herds of buffalo. Then ranchers began settling the region in the 1860s, running their livestock over the plains and eventually killing off the buffalo and forcing the native people out.

Cattle and sheep still munch their way through these short grass prairies, although oil, coal and tourism also help support this thinly populated region. Since Interstate 80 runs through this high prairie country, it's an easy reach for visitors. The loftiest point on the coast-to-coast freeway—8,640 feet—is just east of Laramie. It's near exit 323, marked by a huge bust of Abraham Lincoln at a rest stop. Why Abe? Because the freeway follows the route of U.S. 30, the old Lincoln Highway. There's also a visitor center here.

The third largest city in Wyoming with about 27,500 citizens, *Laramie* is sort of cowboy Berkeley. Coffee houses, vegetarian restaurants and boutiques occupy its old fashioned storefronts, obvious influences from the **University of Wyoming**; (307) 766-4075; *www.uwyo.edu*. On campus is the **American Heritage Museum**, with Western art and historical manuscripts, (307) 766-2570; the **Anthropology Museum**, whose exhibits focus on the Plains Indians, (307) 766-5136; the **Geological Museum** with gems, minerals and fossils of the area, (307) 766-4218; and the **Art Museum** with a mixed collection of American and international works, (307) 766-6622.

Back in town, the **Laramie Plains Museum**, in a huge 1892 Victorian mansion, has period furnished rooms and a grand clutter of historical items, at 603 Ivinson Ave.; (307) 742-4448; *www.laramiemuseum.org*. On the western edge of town, **Wyoming Territorial Park** is a reconstructed pioneer village built around the restored former Wyoming Territorial Prison; (307) 745-6161; *www.wyoprisonpark.org*. It's a lively place with pretend lawmen, bad guys and saloon girls. There are jail breaks and shootouts, and the Horse Barn Dinner Theatre offers grub and cowboy music.

From Laramie, you have three ways to go west. Obviously, I-80 will deliver you to Rawlins quickly. The most scenic route is south of the freeway through the Medicine Bow Mountains, a popular outdoor recreation area. However, it involves a climb over a 10,847-foot pass. If heights are a problem, take the chicken route north of the freeway, along a segment of old Highway 30. It passes through the tiny town of *Medicine Bow*. There's not much to it, except for the **Medicine Bow Museum** in the old railroad depot (307-379-2581) and a bit of fictitious history. It was the site of a shootout in Owen Wister's classic 1902 novel, *The Virginian*. During a poker game, one of the players calls the Virginian an SOB. Our hero draws his weapon and utters that immortal line: "When you call me that, smile!"

The southern route, State Highway 130, has been designated a **National Scenic Byway**, traveling twistily through some of Wyoming's finest alpine landscapes. Because of its heights, it's usually closed from late fall until early spring. As you climb into the Medicine Bow Mountains, you'll pass the **Snowy Range Ski Area**; (800) 462-7669; *www.snowyrange.com*. Beyond here, the highway skirts several alpine lakes and trailheads as it labors upward. At **Sugarloaf Recreation Area**, trails lead to high alpine lakes, mountain meadows and glacier-sculpted peaks. Just over **Snowy Pass**, two observation points offer stellar views of the area.

Down the other side, the highway crosses the North Platte River and follows it up to *Saratoga*. It's a popular local tourist stop with a public hot spring and the **Saratoga Museum**; (307) 326-5511. The highway reaches I-80 just east of *Sinclair*, a tidy little Spanish mission style town once owned by the Sinclair Oil Company. Just short of the town is **Fort Fred Steele**, built in 1868. It's now a state historic park with a visitor center and a few surviving buildings; (307) 320-3013; *www.wyoparks.state.wy.us*.

The somewhat weathered old oil town of *Rawlins* offers a pair of attractions. The **Carbon County Museum** at Ninth and Walnut streets displays the usual frontier artifacts; (307) 328-2740. The 1901 **Wyoming Frontier Prison** at 500 W. Walnut has a small museum and it offers guided tours of the former lockup; (307) 324-4422.

Where to learn more

Carbon County Visitor Information, P.O. Box 856, Saratoga, WY 82331; (800) 228-3547 or (307) 327-5600; *wyomingcarboncounty.com*.

Laramie Area Chamber of Commerce, 800 S. Third St., Laramie, WY 82070; (866) 876-1012; *www.laramie.org*.

VOYAGEURS NATIONAL PARK, MIN.

Chapter Four

The Northern Heartland

North Dakota
• Theodore Roosevelt
National Park

• Bismark

Boundary Waters
Grand Marais •

Minnesota

South Dakota
• Spearfish
• Black Hills

Sioux Falls •

Redwing •
Amish Country •

Nebraska

North Platte Byway

The Heritage Trail

Sioux City

Mason City
Clearlake

Amana Colonies •

Omaha •

Iowa

Brownville •

RIVERS, LAKES, PRAIRIES & HOMEFOLK

To our way of thinking, Heartland has two meanings. It's the middle of our nation and it's a region of good-hearted souls who embody solid middle America values. The Northern Heartland is much more than prairie country. The terrain varies from river valleys to thick forests to ice age lakes. It offers many undiscovered treasures, from the Boundary Waters of Minnesota to Iowa's Loess Hills to the Dakota Badlands.

IOWA is more than cornfields. It's a graceful region of rolling hills, sweeping grasslands and historic towns. It is literally embraced by those two great rivers, the Missouri and the Mississippi, and we found many discoveries between them.

Where to learn more: Iowa Tourism Office, 200 E. Grand Ave., Des Moines, IA 50309; (888) 472-6035; *www.traveliowa.com.*

MINNESOTA is full of holes, and they're all filled with water and rimmed by forests and farmlands. Among our discoveries in the "Land of Lakes" are a lake-based national park, a town made famous by shoes and an industrial city that's also an *Outside* magazine "Dream Town."

Where to learn more: Explore Minnesota Tourism, 100 Metro Square Building, 121 Seventh Place E., St. Paul, MN 55101; (800) 657-3700 or (651) 296-5029; *www.explore minnesota.com.*

NEBRASKA is the land crossed by Westward pioneer trails and we followed two of them across the state's endless grasslands. We also discovered a tiny yet lively art town, and we found many surprising things about Nebraska's largest city.

Where to learn more: Nebraska Division of Travel and Tourism, P.O. Box 98907, Lincoln, NE 68509-8907; (877) NEBRASKA or (402) 471-3796; *www.visitnebraska.org.*

NORTH DAKOTA is a land of vast prairies where the buffalo still roam, and a badlands area where Theodore Roosevelt once roamed. It's so far north that you can see the *aurora borealis* in summer. And in the middle of all this, we found the state's surprisingly cosmopolitan capital.

Where to learn more: North Dakota Tourism Department, 1600 E. Century Ave., Suite 2, Bismark, ND 58503; (800) 435-5663; *www.ndtourism.com.*

SOUTH DAKOTA is famous for the multiple attractions in its Black Hills region, such as Mount Rushmore. However, we found lures here that others may have overlooked, such as a wild horse refuge, a great mini-city and a really "corny" attraction.

Where to learn more: South Dakota Department of Tourism, 711 E. Wells Ave., Pierre, SD 57501-3369; (800) 732-5682; *www.travelsd.com.*

The Amana Colonies
Quaint German communes—with refrigerators?

Often, when I open our refrigerator door, I think of our visit to the Amana Colonies in east central Iowa. I can't help grinning at the irony of it—a peaceful German-American religious colony that's also home to a major appliance maker.

The Amana Colonies are seven quaint yet modern villages set among low hills in the Ohio River Valley. They're laid out in a rural European style. Homes, stores and crafts shops in sturdy brick, sandstone and cedar buildings occupy a central area. Old fashioned barns, vineyards, orchards and gardens are on the periphery.

The colonies were established by a religious sect that fled persecution in Germany in 1842. Its members first settled in Buffalo, New York, then— seeking more space and a peaceful setting—they came to Iowa in 1855. They pooled their resources and eventually bought 26,000 acres of farmland and woods. Later, colony member George Foerstner opened a shop to make beverage coolers, which eventually led to the start of Amana Refrigeration, Inc. The firm later developed the world's first microwave oven.

Despite their high tech achievements, or perhaps because of them, colony members have preserved much of their original lifestyle. And in doing so, they have embraced tourism with gusto. Many of the shops sell hand-crafted furniture, homespun woolens, smoked meats and local wines. There are several German restaurants and bakeries in the villages, along with dozens of shops and import boutiques. A few bed & breakfast inns occupy restored 19th century country homes.

Begin your visit in *Amana*, the most tourist-oriented of the villages. You can pick up a walking tour map at the **Visitor Center** in a restored 1943 corn crib at 622-46th Ave.; (319) 622-7622. The **Amana Heritage Museum** complex on State Route 220 has an 1864 home, a schoolhouse and a wash house; (319) 622-3567; *www.amanaheritage.org*. Exhibits and a fine audio-video show tell the story of this utopian colony. The **Amana Furniture Shop** offers tours of its Old World style facility at 724-48th Ave.; (319) 622-3291. Tours of the **Amana Woolen Mill** are self-guiding, and you can buy its products in the sales room, at 800 48th Ave.; (319) 622-3432.

Three of the other villages also have historic exhibits, many operated by the heritage museum. The **Homestead Store Museum** at 4430 V Street in

Homestead is a mock-up of a community general store, with Amana historical exhibits. Homestead's **Amana Community Church Museum** at 4210 V Street offers insight into the colony's Community of True Inspiration Church. The **Communal Kitchen Museum** at 1003-26th Avenue in *Middle Amana* preserves the colony's early communal life. Exhibits in *South Amana* are the **Mid-America Barn Museum** just off U.S. 6, where a woodworker has crafted more than 200 miniature buildings; and the **Communal Agricultural Museum** in an 1860-era barn at 505 P Street.

Several wineries in the area offer sips of their products, which are usually rather sweet, and the **Millstream Brewing Company** opposite the Woolen Mill sales room produces German style beers.

Two trails invite strolling or cycling in this rural countryside. The 3.1-mile **Kolonieweg Recreational Trail** circles pretty Lily Lake and links Amana and Middle Amana. Signs along the 3.2-mile **Amana Colonies Nature Trail** describe wildlife, geological features and ancient burial mounds in the area.

The colonies even offer theatrical amusements for their visitors. A professional troupe at the **Old Creamery Theatre Company** in Amana presents farce comedies and other light fare from April through December; (800) 352-6262 or (319) 622-6194. The colonies also sponsor an authentic German *Oktoberfest* in late September, plus a *Maifest* in May and a **Winterfest** in late January; (800) 579-2294; *www.festivalsinamana.com.*

When Amana was first established, its colonies were communal, like early Mormon settlements. The houses didn't even have kitchens or dining areas; everyone ate in a communal kitchen. Then in 1932, suffering from the effects of the Depression, its members voted to "separate church and state," creating the Amana Church Society for their religious and social lives and a profit-sharing Amana Society to handle farming and business activities.

Still, the communities remained very close-knit and Germanic. Church services weren't conducted in English until the 1960s. The colonies are sometimes compared with the German Amish communities, although there are major differences. These folks don't chug around in buggies and dress funny, except during their festivals. They drive cars and pickups, and their houses have modern appliances, most likely of the Amana brand—even though the corporation is now owned by Maytag.

Where to learn more

Amana Colonies Convention & Visitors Bureau, P.O. Box 310 (622-46th Ave.), Amana, IA 52203; (800) 579-2294 or (319) 622-7622; *www. amanacolonies.org.*

Mason City & Clear Lake
Two prairie towns and their music heroes

♭

Folks in Mason City can still hear the echo of seventy-six trombonists marching down their main street. Meredith Willson was born and raised here, and he used this classic middle America town as the model for his fictitious River City in *The Music Man.*

Just to the west, the old fashioned and well-kept resort town of Clear Lake sits on the shore of its namesake pond. One of Iowa's most poplar vacation areas, it also has a musical heritage, although a sad one. Buddy Holly, Richie Valens and J.P. Richardson were killed in a plane crash shortly after performing at Clear Lake's Surf Ballroom in 1959.

Both of these north central Iowa towns have visitor appeal. If you're blasting across the state on Interstate 80, a turn north onto I-35 will get you to the area nonstop.

Mason City

Meredith Willson's birthplace was settled as a farming community in the 1850s by followers of the Masonic Order. Originally, it was called *Shibboleth,* which non-Masons couldn't spell or pronounce, so it was changed to Masonic Grove and finally to Mason City.

Most visitors start with **The Music Man Square** at 308 S. Pennsylvania Ave.; (641) 424-2852; *www.themusicmansquare.org*. The complex contains Willson's boyhood home, a museum busy with his memorabilia and a replica of a River City street scene from the 1962 film.

This town of about 30,000 *Music Man* fans has several other attractions, including one of the largest collections of Prairie School style homes on the prairie. That's the bold, angular architectural style developed by Frank Lloyd Wright. Eight of them are in the **Glenn-Rock Crest National Historic District** just north of U.S. 18. Seven were designed by Wright students and one, **Stockman House**, was done by the man himself. Decorated with Arts and Crafts style furnishings, it's open for public tours; 530 First St. NE; (641) 421-3666; *www.stockmanhouse.org*.

The **Charles H. MacNider Museum** displays a large collection of puppets donated by noted movie and TV puppeteer Bil Baird, another Mason City native. It also exhibits American art, from Thomas Hart Benton to Alexander Calder. The museum occupies a Tudor mansion on a bluff overlooking Willow Creek, at 303 Second St. SE; (641) 421-3666; *www. macniderart.org*. Mason City's memories are preserved at the **Kinney Pio-**

neer **Museum**, just east of town at the entrance to the municipal airport; (641) 423-1258. The complex includes an old fashioned school house and a pioneer log cabin.

You can learn about Iowa's flora and fauna at the **Lime Creek Nature Center**. This 400-acre complex has several miles of interpretive trails through woodlands and prairie. It's a mile north of U.S. 65 at 3501 Lime Creek Rd.; (641) 423-5309; *www.limecreeknature.org*.

Clear Lake

This resort town of about 8,000 folks is ten miles west of Mason City, off U.S. 18. The best way to see Clear Lake is from the lake itself. Book passage on the *Lady of the Lake* paddlewheeler, which offers 90-minute evening sightseeing excursions; (641) 357-2243; *www.cruiseclearlake.com*.

The 3,600-acre lake provides every conceivable kind of water play, from water skiing and fishing to swimming and sunning at Clear Lake City Beach. Boat rentals are available at the town's marina. The popular lake has fifteen public access sites around its shoreline, most with docks.

The lakeside **Surf Ballroom** is little changed from that fateful day in early February of 1959, when Buddy Holly and his group performed before a packed house, then boarded a plane for their fatal flight. A monument outside the ballroom marks the sad event. The crash inspired Don McLean to write *American Pie,* with that fateful line: "The day the music died." The ballroom, which dates from the big band era, still books a variety of musical groups, from rock to jazz; (641) 357-6151; *www.surfballroom.com*.

The resort area has two dryland attractions and four golf courses. The Western theme **Fort Custer Maze** challenges folks to find their way through two miles of scrambled corridors, off I-35 exit 193; (641) 357-6102. The **Clear Lake Fire Museum** is a re-creation of an early 1900s firehouse, at 112 N. Sixth St.; (641) 357-4823.

If you're here in winter—and we can't imagine why you'd want to be— you can try your hand at ice fishing on the lake. Or go snowmobiling or cross-country skiing. One reason for coming in winter is for the **50's in February Festival** of Buddy Holly era music, held at the Surf.

Where to learn more

Clear Lake Area Chamber of Commerce, P.O. Box 188 (205 Main Ave.), Clear Lake, IA 59428; (800) 285-5338 or (641) 357-2159; *www. clearlakeiowa.com.*

Mason City Convention & Visitors Bureau, P.O. Box 1128 (25 W. State St.), Mason City, IA 50402; (800) 423-5724 or (641) 422-1663; *www.masoncitytourism.com.*

Sioux City & the Loess Hills
Discoveries along Iowa's western edge

⚐

Three cities Sioux are clustered together on the Missouri River, where the borders of Iowa, Nebraska and North Dakota meet. Our choice is the one in Iowa, with a population of about 85,000. Extending north and south from Sioux City is a long, rugged ridgeline formed by windblown soil called the Loess Hills. They're traversed by the Loess Hills National Scenic Byway.

Lewis & Clark made camp near Sioux City in 1804. It was here that the expedition suffered its only loss. Sgt. Charles Floyd, Jr., died from appendicitis, and a monument marks his burial site. It's on a bluff above U.S. 755, offering a grand view of the river, farms and prairies.

Floyd is further honored at the **Sergeant Floyd Riverboat Welcome Center**. It's a drydocked former Army Corps of Engineers inspection vessel with exhibits about the Lewis & Clark expedition, at 1000 Larson Park Rd.; (712) 279-0198; *www.lewisandclarktrail.com.*

Sioux City emerged in the 1850s as a major supply and meat packing center, served by steamboats chugging upriver from St. Louis. Its industries have declined in recent decades, although town officials have done a fine job of restoring its riverfront and 19th century downtown area.

An extensive network of walking and cycling trails and parks have replaced old packing houses and stockyards along the river. Downtown **Fourth Street** is now a trendy shopping area with boutiques, restaurants, pubs and coffee houses. The meticulously restored 1927 **Orpheum Theatre** is now a major performing arts center, drawing top artists and Broadway shows, at Sixth and Pierce streets; (712) 279-4850; *www.orpheumlive.com.*

The city's archive is the **Sioux City Public Museum** in an elaborate 1890 Romanesque style mansion at 2901 Jackson St.; (712) 279-6174; *www.siouxcitymuseum.org.* The large and very contemporary **Sioux City Art Center** focuses on the works of Northern Heartland artists, at 225 Nebraska St.; (712) 279-6272; *www.siouxcityartcenter.org.* A religious theme attraction called **Trinity Heights** features a life-size wood carving of the Last Supper, meditation gardens and an outdoor cathedral. It's off I-29 exit 147A; (712) 239-8670; *www.sctrinityheights.org.*

The Loess Hills

A geological rarity, the Loess Hills were formed thousands of years ago. Strong winds piled yellow-brown loess silt into ridges, in much the same manner that sand dunes are formed. Through the centuries, they weathered into their present rough shapes and obtained a green mantle of prairie grasses and plants. These formations exist only here and in China's Kansu Province.

The 220-mile-long **Loess Hills National Scenic Byway** extends north along the Missouri River to *Akron* and south to the Missouri border, roughly paralleling I-29. It's not a single highway, but a series of highways and roads linked by Scenic Byway signs. Loop roads lead to turnouts for views of these rough, rolling green-clad hills and Missouri River.

For a quick sampler of the Loess Hills, go north from Sioux City, following Scenic Byway signs. At the upper end of the byway, you can head inland for an ice cream treat. Your first two stops are just north of Sioux City:

Stone State Park encloses a section of these prairie hills, with hiking trails winding among them and overlooks of the Missouri River. Other facilities include picnic areas, a day use lodge and a campground; 5001 Talbot Rd.; (712) 255-4698; *iowadnr.com/parks*.

The **Dorothy Pecaut Nature Center** provides an excellent study of the Loess Hills' natural history. Indoor displays include a look at life beneath the hills and exhibits concerning their flora and fauna. Outside, you can follow a network of nature trails through the hills themselves; 4500 Sioux River Rd.; (712) 258-0838; *www.woodburyparks.com*.

Pressing northward on the scenic byway, you'll encounter the **Five Ridge Prairie** area. There are no facilities here, although you can prowl about the prairie, hike among the Loess Hills and explore forested ravines between their ridges. Farther along is **Broken Kettle Grasslands**, the largest swatch of native prairie left in Iowa, with sections of the Loess Hills passing through it. Strolling about the grasslands, you can imagine yourself in a time and place when early explorers, trappers and settlers passed this way.

At the small prairie town of *Akron*, follow State Route 3 about fifteen miles east to *Le Mars*, the self-proclaimed "Ice Cream Capital of the World." The local Wells Dairy is the planet's largest ice cream producer. You can learn all about their products—and sample some—at the **Ice Cream Capital of the World Visitor Center** at Highways 3 and 75; (712) 546-4090; *www.lemarsioa.com*.

Where to learn more

Sioux City Convention & Visitors Bureau, P.O. Box 3183 (801 Fourth St.), Sioux City, IA 51102; (800) 593-2228 or (712) 279-4800; *www.siouxcitytourism.com*.

Loess Hills National Scenic Byway information is available from the Federal Highway Administration's website, *www.byways.org* or *Loess Hills Scenic Byway Council*, (712) 482-3029.

The Amish and Spam
Scouting woodlands and towns in Bluff Country

⚐

The Amish have nothing to do with Spam. However, the southeastern corner of Minnesota held two surprises for us: It has several Amish settlements, and one of the towns in the area is the world headquarters for the producers of Spam—no, not the stuff that bugs you on the internet.

Minnesota's southeastern corner is called Bluff Country, named for the Mississippi River bluffs on its squiggly northeastern border. This is a quiet, rural region of woodlands, trout streams, neat farms and small towns—a world apart from the bustle of Minnesota's larger cities.

An even greater world apart is the region's Amish culture. Their conservative faith forbids lighting their homes with electricity or owning cars, so they live by kerosene lamp and drive horse-drawn buggies along Bluff Country roads. Women in sun bonnets and bearded Amish men often shop in Harmony, and stores there sell their hand-crafted products, such as furniture, quilts and canned goods. Their old fashioned farms are tucked among the valleys and can be visited on guided tours out of Harmony and Lanesboro. About 135 Amish families live in southeastern Minnesota.

We'll explore the Amish countryside by following the Bluff Country Minnesota Scenic Byway. But first, how about a Spamwitch? The town of *Austin* on Interstate 90 is home to **Hormel Foods**, whose roots go back to George A. Hormel's 1887 butcher shop. George always told his employees: "Originate, don't imitate." So in 1937, the food products company originated Spam. Learn all about it at the **Spam Museum**, off I-90 exit 178B at 1937 Spam Blvd.; (800) 588-7726 or (507) 437-5100; *www.spam.com.*

From here, follow I-90 northeast to *Dexter*, pick up the **Bluff Country Scenic Drive** (State Route 16) and head into the rural countryside. Charming old *Spring Valley* is the largest town in Bluff Country, although it's home to only about 2,500 souls. It also was home to the in-laws of author Laura Ingalls Wilder. Richard Sears, founder of Sears, Roebuck & Co., was born in nearby Stewartville. The **Methodist Church Museum** has small collections of Wilder and Sears photos and memorabilia, as well as the usual clutter of early day artifacts, at 221 W. Courtland St., (507) 346-7659.

Just beyond is the combined **Forestville and Mystery Cave State Park**; (507) 765-2785 for Forestville and (507) 937-3251 for the cave; *www.dnr.state.mn.us.* Forestville is a restored farm village dating from the

1850s. Costumed docents cashier in the general store, work the gardens and put up canned goods. Visitors are invited to pitch in. Five miles away near Preston is **Mystery Cave**, Minnesota's longest cavern, with thirteen miles of passages. Ranger-led tours cover only a small part of this labyrinth.

From here, you'll enter the beautiful **Root River Valley,** with jagged limestone outcroppings, hardwood forests and gently undulating farmlands. Several Amish settlements are in this region and you'll likely see their wagons rolling leisurely along quiet rural lanes. Follow Highway 52 south to the village of *Harmony*, where the Amish often come to trade. Their handcrafted furniture and other products are sold in shops here.

Just southwest of Harmony is **Niagara Cave**, a privately owned limestone cavern with guided tours; (800) 837-6606; *www.niagaracave.com*. Its most impressive feature is a 60-foot underground waterfall.

Back on Highway 16, you'll shortly encounter *Lanesboro*. It's a handsome old town set against limestone bluffs, with the Root River meandering past. The downtown area is a National Historic District. Not a quaint country village, Lanesboro was founded in 1868 as a summer resort. As such, it's the most tourist-oriented community in the area, with a professional drama group, Amish country tours, concerts, art exhibits and bed & breakfast inns.

Learn all about it at the **Lanesboro Historical Museum** at 105 Parkway Ave. S.; (507) 467-2177. The **Commonweal Theatre Company** produces assorted dramas and comedies in the St. Mane Theatre, 206 Parkway Ave. N.; (800) 657-7025 or (507) 467-2525; *www.commonwealtheatre.org*. Two miles west of town off County Road 21 is the **Eagle Bluff Environmental Learning Center**; (888) 800-9558 or (507) 467-2437; *www.eagle-bluff.org*. It has a small natural history museum, hiking trails and an overlook with a splendid view of the Root River Valley

The scenic byway continues through several other small towns and ends at *La Crescent* on the Mississippi River. It's Minnesota's apple capital and the nineteen-mile **Apple Blossom Scenic Drive** meanders past orchards and alongside Bluff Country's namesake riverbanks.

Incidentally, if you've brought bikes or at least good walking shoes to Bluff Country, you can explore two popular recreational trails. The **Root River State Trail** runs for forty-two miles between Houston and Fountain and the eighteen-mile **Harmony-Preston Valley State Trail** starts in Harmony and links up with the Root River Trail.

Where to learn more

Historic Bluff Country, P.O. Box 609, Harmony, MN 55939; (800) 428-2030; *www.bluffcountry.com*.

The Boundary Waters region
Northern Minnesota's wet wonderland

Much of the Minnesota-Canadian border area is defined by water—a wet wonderland of ten thousand lakes. It's paradise for boaters and fisherpersons, and Valhalla for canoeists and kayakers. This wooded region suggests wrinkled velvet, dappled with blue jewels. The area is thinly populated and much of it is little changed since the French-Canadian *voyageurs* paddled their canoes through these waters more than two hundred years ago.

The region's distinctive look was created by Ice Age glaciers that scraped away surface soil to expose the Canadian Shield's 2.7 billion year old Precambrian rock. Left in the glaciers' wake were thousands of gouged-out basins that filled with meltwater. This land of thick forests, ice blue lakes and exposed bedrock is protected in two preserves—Voyageurs National Park and Boundary Waters Canoe Area Wilderness. The areas are rich in wildlife, from bald eagles and loons to black bears, moose and even the rare timber wolf.

Although the two sanctuaries are best explored by boat, drylanders can find much of interest around their edges. Also, outfitters and rental firms can provide access for the boatless. Summer is high season in this area, although winter visitors can indulge in cross-country skiing, dog sledding, ice fishing and other cold weather lures, either in the preserves or adjacent towns.

International Falls and Voyageurs National Park

Voyageurs National Park's main gateway, *International Falls* is the largest town in these parts, home to about 6,700 souls. Sitting on the shores of Rainy Lake, it's popular for fishing and boating. It also offers a few visitor lures. The **Koochiching County Historical Museum** preserves the region's history and culture, in Smokey Bear Park at Sixth Avenue and Third Street; (218) 283-4316. The park's namesake is a 26-foot statue of that gentle preventer of forest fires. The huge **Boise Paper Solutions** plant at Second Street and Fourth Avenue offers public tours; (218) 285-5011. It's among the world's largest and fastest paper-producing operations.

Next-door **Voyageurs National Park** enfolds 218,054 acres of woodlands, lakes and rocky outcroppings. It preserves a large swatch of the historic water route that French-Canadian trappers followed on their way west. The park is forty percent water, providing a recreation haven for fishing, boating and even houseboating vacations. There are no roads into the park; it can be explored only by boat or afoot.

Although the park itself has no facilities, four access points have small resorts, cafés, fishing guides, outfitters and water taxi service. For information on the park, including boat tours and canoe and sea kayak rentals, stop by the **Rainy Lakes Visitor Center** in International Falls, at the junction of highways 53 and 11; (218) 286-5258.

Boundary Waters Canoe Area Wilderness

With 5,000 miles of liquid trails, Boundary Waters is paradise for paddlers. Motorboats are restricted to just a few lakes around the edges. The rest of the wilderness is paddle only. This wild region extends for 150 miles, with more than a thousand lakes dotted over 1.1 million acres. It's perhaps the world's greatest area for canoeing and calm-water kayaking, and it's also noted for its outstanding fishing; (877) 550-6777; *www.bwcaw.org*.

Portage trails link many of these lakes, providing a myriad of routes through this vast, wet landscape. Short hiking trails probe its edges, while the 38-mile Kekekabic Trail and the 24-mile Snowbank Trail provide challenges for the sturdy and the wilderness-savvy.

The major gateway to Boundary Waters is the town of *Ely*, the self-proclaimed "Canoe capital of the world." It's home to several outfitters and canoe rental firms and it offers some dryland attractions.

The **International Wolf Center** is an educational facility with a small resident wolf pack, at 1396 Highway 69; (800) 359-9653 or (218) 365-4695; *www.wolf.org*. The **Dorothy Molter Museum** consists of two cabins once occupied by a legendary woman of the wilderness, at 2002 E. Sheridan St.; (218) 365-4451; *www.canoecountry.com/dorothy*. They were moved here from Knife Lake in the Boundary Waters region. The **Ely-Winton History Museum** preserves the area's legacy, at 1900 E. Camp St.; (218) 365-3226.

Before leaving the area, travel the **Waters of the Dancing Sky Scenic Byway** (Highway 11) from International Falls to Lake of the Woods. Following the Rainy River, it's one of Minnesota's prettiest drives, passing riverside parks, beaches and small towns; *watersofthedancingsky.org*. **Lake of the Woods** is a popular resort area, noted for its boating and fishing.

Where to learn more

Ely Chamber of Commerce, 1600 E. Sheridan St., Ely, MN 55731; (800) 777-7281 or (218) 365-6123; *www.ely.org*.

International Falls-Rainy Lake Convention & Visitors Bureau, 301 Second Ave., International Falls, MN 56649; (800) 325-5766 or (218) 283-9400; *www.rainylake.org*.

Voyageurs National Park, 3131 Highway 53, International Falls, MN 56649-8904; (218) 283-9821; *www.nps.gov/voya*.

Grand Marais & surrounds
Culture, canoeing, scenery: What's not to like?

꿔

If we didn't have to travel about the country to write this book, we'd be tempted to hole up in Grand Marais. We'd settle into a lakeside cottage, peck away at the computer, sip caffé latte and watch the seasons pass.

Grand Marais (*ma-RAY*) is a pleasant little art colony of about 1,400 residents, occupying a natural harbor on the north shore of Lake Superior. It offers something for all the senses—an active art and theater arts scene, cute shops, lonely shorelines, moonrises over Lake Superior, fall color and Christmas card winters, good fishing and birdwatching, and great kayaking.

Just inland is the eastern end of the place we just left, **Boundary Waters Canoe Area Wilderness**. More than a dozen outfitters in town offer guided canoe treks into that wilderness and sea kayaking trips on Lake Superior, the world's largest freshwater pond. (If you like statistics, the lake is about the size of South Carolina, 350 miles long and 160 miles wide, with 2,726 miles of shoreline. It holds one-eighth of the world's fresh water.)

Downtown *Grand Marais* is busy with art galleries, boutiques and cafés. Sailboats bask in their slips at the marina, their rigging clinking to gentle offshore breezes. Short walks lead to the 1922 **Grand Marais Lighthouse**, and up to **Artists Point** for fine views of the countryside.

The local art scene revolves around the **Grand Marais Art Colony**, with a gallery, workshops and classes for artists and writers. Its **Arrowhead Center for the Arts** hosts a mix of plays, films and concerts, at 11 W. Fifth St.; (800) 385-9585 or (218) 387-1284; *www.grandmaraisartcolony.org*. You can hone country skills such as maple syrup making and quilting by signing up for a class at the **North House Folk School** on the harbor at 500 W. Hwy 61; (888) 387-9762 or (218) 387-9762; *www.northhousefolkschool.com*.

Grand Marais, which unfortunately translates as "great swamp" in the native Ojibwe tongue, was established on the site of former fur trading posts in 1871. It prospered modestly on fishing and logging. You can discover the town's past at the **Cook County Historical Museum**, occupying a former lighkeeper's house at 4 S. Broadway; (218) 387-2883.

Two side trips will provide more intimate glimpses of the grand northern Minnesota countryside that surrounds Grand Marais.

The **Gunflint Trail Scenic Byway** (County Road 12) leads sixty-three miles northwest through subtly contoured **Superior National Forest** to Saganaga Lake. It's on the edge of the Boundary Waters Canoe Area Wilderness. You won't encounter any towns en route, although you'll skim past several woodsy resorts, campgrounds and trailheads. As you drive, keep your peepers peeled for bald eagles, deer, moose and maybe even a black bear. At night in one of those resorts, listen for the lonely wail of wolves.

If you have a canoe or kayak aboard, you can find access points for the adjacent Boundary Waters. Or book yourselves into one of the lodges along the way; most offer canoe rentals. Dozens of miles of trails lead into the canoe wilderness and to hike-in campsites of Superior National Forest. Many become cross-country ski trails in winter. For information, contact the **Gunflint Trail Association** at (800) 338-6932; *www.gunflint-trail.com.*

Running northwest from Grand Marais, State Route 61 hugs the edge of Lake Superior all the way to the Canadian border. The highway is busy with timber-sheltered beaches, campsites and the occasional small town. Fourteen miles north of Grand Marais is **Judge C.R. Magney State Park**; (218) 387-3039; *www.dnr.state.mn.us.* Here, the Brule River thrashes its way through a rough lava field on its way to Lake Superior. A short hiking trail leads to **Kettle Falls**, a thunderous fifty-foot cataract.

Just beyond the river's mouth, drop into **Naniboujou Lodge**, a grand lakeside retreat built in 1929 to lure the rich and famous. Among members of its holding company were Babe Ruth, Jack Dempsey and legendary newspaperman Ring Lardner. Today, us ordinary folks can book a room, or take a peek into in the lavish dining room, with its Technicolor splash of native designs; (218) 387-2688; *www.naniboujou.com.*

Further north is the tiny village of *Grand Portage,* established as a fur trading post in 1784 by the North West Company. It's now part of the Grand Portage Indian Reservation and thus has a small casino, plus a few services. The area's lively history is told at **Grand Portage National Monument**, where a spiked-log stockade and several buildings have been reconstructed; (218) 387-2788; *www.nos.gov.* Rangers in period costume conduct living history demonstrations in summer. From Grand Portage village, you can catch passenger launch service to **Isle Royal National Park**, a wilderness preserve in next-door Michigan; (888) 746-2305 or (715) 392-2100.

The end of your trail, unless you're continuing into Canada, is **Grand Portage State Park**. Its scenic exclamation point is the spectacular High Falls, crashing 120 feet into a narrow gorge of the Pigeon River. Short paved trails lead to overlooks; (218) 475-2360; *www.dnr.state.mn.us.*

Where to learn more

Greater Grand Marais Chamber of Commerce, P.O. Box 1048 (13 N. Broadway), Grand Marais, MN 55604; (888) 922-5000 or (218) 387-2524; *www.grandmaraismn.com.*

Redwing

Sensible shoes, pottery and preservation

⚑

A brand of shoes called *Whoo-pa-to-do* wouldn't be taken very seriously. Mention Red Wing, however, and you get instant brand recognition.

The southeastern Minnesota town of Red Wing is one of the world's leading producers of sensible shoes. Millions of pairs of Red Wing work boots and shoes emerge from two factories here each year. What's that got to do with *Whoo-pa-to-do*? The term translates as "Wing of Scarlet," referring to a dyed swan's wing that local Dakota chiefs once carried as a symbol of their authority.

We aren't suggesting that you visit Red Wing just because it's Shoe Town, USA. It's also the most handsome town in Minnesota, with an elegant downtown core of stately red brick mercantile blocks. Old fashioned lamp posts are hung with flower baskets, and grand Victorian and Tudor style mansions bask beneath ancient trees in the neighborhood. Further, the town occupies a splendid setting, at the base of steep, wooded bluffs on a sweeping bend in the Mississippi River.

Most of Red Wing's imposing business district was built or remodeled during a nationwide "Beautiful City" movement near the turn of the last century. It was inspired by a model city built for Chicago's 1893 Columbia Exposition. Red Wing merchants fashioned their buildings in the Classic Revival style, while officials in the prosperous town built beautiful parks and cobbled carriage roads that led to Mississippi River overlooks.

That look of civic elegance remains. Those sturdy mercantile blocks now contain boutiques, antique shops, coffee houses and cafés. And there are several pottery outlets, since the town also is the home of Red Wing Pottery.

The original Red Wing Pottery factory closed in 1967, although a smaller firm continues the tradition. The **Redwing Stoneware Company** offers guided tours of its pottery-making operation at 4909 Moundsview Dr.; (800) 352-4877 or (651) 388-4610; *www.redwingstoneware.com.* The historic 1901 Red Wing factory at 2000 West Main Street has been converted into the attractive **Historic Pottery Place Mall** with a pottery museum, plus specialty and antique shops; (651) 388-1428; *www.potteryplace.com.* The **Red Wing Pottery Salesroom** is nearby at 1920 W. Main St.; (800) 288-0174 or (651) 388-3562.

The local shoe biz is enshrined at the small **Red Wing Shoe Museum,** downstairs from the company offices at 314 Main St.; (651) 388-8211. Other elements of the town's history are displayed at the nicely-done **Good-**

hue County Historical Museum on a bluff above town at 1166 Oak St.;
(651) 388-6024; *wwwgoodhuehistory.mus.mn.us.*

Pick up a copy of the *Footsteps Through Redwing* brochure at the museum or visitor center. It outlines three walking tours past historic buildings
downtown and in nearby neighborhoods. During your strolls, check out the
gorgeous gold-leaf interior of the Beaux-Arts style **Sheldon Theatre** at 433
W. Third St.; (800) 899-5759 or (651) 385-3667; *www.sheldontheatre.org.*
Built in 1904 as the nation's first municipally owned and operated theater,
it's now an active performing arts center.

For nice overviews of the region, climb a stairway to the top of steep-
walled **Barn Bluff** that rises abruptly from the downtown area. Then fetch
your car and follow Scenic Skyline Drive to **Sorin Bluff**.

Redwing began as a Protestant missionary outpost in 1837 to minister to
the Mdewakanton Dakota band, those of the scarlet swan wings. Later, as
homesteaders sowed wheat and plowed their fields on the adjacent prairies,
it grew into a major supply center, served by river steamers. By the 1870s, it
was the world's largest wheat port and a major flour milling center. Red
Wing Stoneware Company was established in 1878, and Red Wing Shoes
made its first pair of sensible work boots in 1905; they sold for $1.75

A drive south from town on U.S. 63 will take you into the Minnesota
Bluff Country, with its scenic riverbanks and hardwood forests. Backed up
by a side stream delta, the Mississippi widens in this region to form Lake
Pepin, a popular water sports area. Ten miles below town, **Frontenac State
Park** preserves a swatch of riverbank and adjacent prairies and oak thickets;
(651) 345-3401. The park has campsites and picnic areas and it's entwined
with hiking trails, some leading to scenic river overlooks. **Mount Frontenac**
ski and summer resort is across the highway; (800) 488-5826 or (651) 388-
5826; *www.mountfrontenac.* Its golf course offers fine views of Lake Pepin.

Below the Frontenacs is the resort town of *Lake City*, famous as the
home of Ralph Samuelson, who—as a reckless teenager—invented water
skiing in 1922. Why reckless? He was towed by an airplane, not a speed-
boat. Fourteen miles farther along is *Wabasha*, one of the state's oldest
towns, dating from the 1830s. This venerable river hamlet's historic district
has a fine collection of late 19th century buildings.

Below Wabasha, a four-lane highway follows the scenery-laden Mississippi River bluffs south to Interstate 90.

Where to learn more

Red Wing Visitors & Convention Bureau, 420 Levee St., Red Wing,
MN 55066; (800) 498-3444 or (651) 385-5934; *www.redwing.org.*

The Heritage Trail
Brownville and a prairie road less traveled

⚑

Let's say you have to get across Nebraska, because it's between where you are and where you need to be. Most folks follow the Platte River route, which travelers have been using since the days of the Oregon Trail. We'll follow that historic byway later. First, we'll suggest a road less traveled, which state tourism promoters call the Heritage Trail.

It crosses the bottom of Nebraska, following U.S. Highway 136 and then U.S. 6. The route offers a mix of lures, starting with a remarkable little art town. *Brownville*, tucked against the Missouri River in the state's southeastern corner, is home to about 150 souls. Yet, it has several museums, historic sites, art galleries and boutiques. One of Nebraska's oldest towns, it's a charming slice of the 19th century, built on seven wooded hills.

Start your visit at the **Captain Bailey House Museum** in a Victorian at 402 Main Street. You'll learn that Brownville dates from 1854, once was a major river port and even vied for the state capital. Another mansion open to the public is the 1860 Italianate **Carson House** at 231 Main Street, built by town founder Richard Brown. Both are operated by the Brownville Historical Society; (877) 559-6005 or (402) 825-6001; *www.brownville-ne.com.*

Culture thrives in this tiny town. Several artists live in the area and galleries display their works. Nebraska's oldest repertory group, the **Brownville Village Theater**, performs in a former church near College and Main; (402) 825-4121. Check out **The Lyceum**, a used book store at 228 Main St.; (402) 825-6441. It has such a huge selection of books that it earned tiny Brownville the title of "Booktown USA," one of only three in America.

Just east of town on Highway 136 is the **Brownville State Recreation Area,** a riverside park that's home to the **Meriwether Lewis Dredge & Missouri River History Museum**, with exhibits aboard a drydocked river dredge; (402) 825-3341. If you prefer a boat that goes somewhere, book a sightseeing, lunch or dinner cruise aboard the riverboat *Spirit of Brownville*; (402) 825-6441; *www.spiritofbrownville.com.*

Westward ho on the Heritage Trail

Highway 136 takes you west into prairies and farmlands, passing through a string of old fashioned Main Street USA towns. *Auburn* is noted for its many antique shops, and *Tecumseh* is noted only as the location site for *Amerika*, a popular and off-beat 1980s television series.

In *Beatrice*, the **Gage County Historical Museum** occupies a brick railroad depot at Second and Court streets; (402) 228-1679. The huge Beatrice Foods conglomerate started in this prairie town. About four miles west on State Route 4 is **Homestead National Monument of America**; (402) 223-3514; *www.nps.gov/home*. It preserves the site of one of the first claims granted under the 1862 Homestead Act. Facilities include a visitor center with exhibits about homesteading, an original cabin and a one-room school.

Rock Creek Station State Historical Park near *Fairbury* marks the site of a stagecoach stop and Oregon Trail crossing, with exhibits on both; (402) 729-5777. It's also the place where James Butler "Wild Bill" Hickok started his murderous reputation, killing Rock Creek Station's owner in cold blood. Twenty miles west, *Hebron* is home to the world's largest porch swing, hanging in the city park. Several **Oregon Trail sites** are in the area.

Red Cloud was the childhood home of Pulitzer Prize winning author Willa Cather, and the locale for six of her twelve novels. Her home is preserved in **Willa Cather State Historical Site** at 413 N. Webster St.; (866) 731-7304 or (402) 746-2653; *www.willacather.org*. You'll discover other Willa Cather lore at the **Webster County Historical Museum** at 721 W. Fourth Ave.; (402) 746-2444; *www.redcloudnebraska.com*.

Continuing west, you'll encounter **Harlan County Lake Recreation Area**, with a large reservoir and an oddly-named museum. The **Lighthouse Antique Museum** displays memorabilia from the first half of the last century, including a fine collection of Depression era glassware; (888) 243-0333 or (308) 799-2033. In the hamlet of *Naponee*, the **Naponee Museum** occupies an unusual octagonal church building; (308) 269-2791.

Above tiny *Edison*, Highway 134 dissolves into U.S. 6, which you'll follow for the rest of the trip. Many prairie miles later, you'll reach *McCook* and the **Senator George Norris State Historical Site**; (308) 345-8484; *www.visitnebraska. org*. It preserves the home of the legislator who helped create the Tennessee Valley Authority and the Rural Electric Administration during the Depression. He was named by the U.S. Senate as one of the five greatest senators in American history.

The final stop of interest along the bottom of Nebraska is **Champion Mill State Historical Park** just below *Imperial*. It contains an 1889 flour mill on Frenchman River; (308) 882-5860; *www.visitnebraska.org*.

Where to learn more

Brownville Historical Society Tourist Center, P.O. Box 1 (131 Main St.), Brownville, NE 68321; (877) 559-6005, (402) 825-6001 or (402) 825-6637; *www.brownville-ne.com*.

The North Platte byway
Following wagon trails across Nebraska

⚑

During the great western migration, most of the pioneer trails passed through Nebraska, following the Platte and North Platte rivers. This was the chosen path of the Oregon Trail, the Mormon Trail and the California Trail, plus sections of the Pony Express route and transcontinental railroad.

The western part of this route, following the North Platte and U.S. Highway 26, has been designated as the **Western Trails Scenic and Historic Byway**; *www.byways.org*. Three pioneer paths overlap here—the Oregon, California and Mormon trails. Some historians simply call it the Emigrant Trail. The highway is busy with markers, monuments and museums that tell the tale of the great westward movement.

We'll run the route in reverse, since we just took you west from Omaha in the previous listing. The byway enters (or leaves) Nebraska just west of *Scottsbluff*. The town was named for an 800-foot cliff rising above this fertile farm valley. It was an important landmark for pioneer travelers. Scottsbluff is the commercial center for farmers and ranchers of the surrounding Nebraska and Wyoming prairies. Oddly, its only tourist attraction is a zoo, not a museum about the westward movement. The very attractive **Riverside Park and Zoo**, a mile west of town on State Route 71, has nice collection of critters from around the world; (308) 630-6236; *www.riversidezoo.org*.

Five miles southwest of town, **Scotts Bluff National Monument** surrounds the famous pioneer landmark; (308) 436-4340; *www.nps.gov/scbl*. An excellent interpretive center tells the story of the trail west, and some wagon ruts are still visible nearby. A winding road leads to the top of Scotts Bluff for a panoramic view of the valley.

Just south of the monument, the midsize town of *Gering* has three visitor lures. The **North Platte Valley Museum and History Archive** is a surprise, containing one of America's largest collections of Emigrant Trail lore. It's at 900 Overland Trails Rd.; (308) 436-5411; *www.npvm.org*. **Wildlife World** has a collection of about 300 stuffed critters from various areas of the globe, set in realistic-looking painted dioramas. It's in a former railroad depot at 950 U St.; (308) 436-7104. The **Farm and Ranch Museum** exhibits just what its name implies, antique farm and ranch equipment. It's at 2390 M. St.; (308) 436-1989; *www.farmandranch museum.com*.

From Gering, take State Route 92 southwest. It blends into U.S. 26, which leads to the most significant landmark on the pioneer trail, at **Chimney Rock National Historic Site**; (308) 586-2581; *www.nebraskahis-*

tory.org/sites/rock. This impossibly slender 300-foot spire could be seen for miles—still can, for that matter—telling the pioneers that they would soon enter the hills of Wyoming. A small visitor center at the base talks about the rock and the Emigrant Trail.

Traveling eastward from Chimney Rock is like reading from an immigrant's diary. You'll see several landmarks that were noted in their journals, such as Jail Rock, Courthouse Rock and Sandpit Lakes. The latter is in the **Bridgeport State Recreation Area**, near the small town of *Bridgeport*. Its **Pioneer Trails Museum** on North Main Street displays an eclectic mix of immigrant memorabilia and early-day odds and ends; (308) 262-0108.

Forty-four miles down highway in the tiny hamlet of *Oshkosh*, more pioneer exhibits and a large stuffed bird collection are on display at the **Garden County Museum** on First Avenue; (308) 772-3115.

Highway 26 joins with historic U.S. 30 and Interstate 80 at the once rowdy cowboy town of *Ogallala*. The whole place could be the setting for a B-western, with plenty of plots to go around. Cowpokes drove their herds to a railhead here, got their pay, got a bath, got drunk and got into trouble.

The former "Gomorrah of the Plains" still has that cowtown look, particularly at an attraction called **Front Street**, at 519 E. First; (308) 284-6000; *www.megavision.net/frontstreet*. Behind mockup store fronts are a cafe, saloon, small museum and a theater that presents a corny revue. The show is considerably cleaner than the bawdy burlesques of yesteryear.

Also worth a look is the **Petrified Wood Gallery**, exhibiting tiny pictures and music boxes made from pieces of petrified wood, at 525 E. First St.; (800) 658-4390 or (308) 284-9996. The **Mansion on the Hill** is a handsomely restored 1880s-era brick Victorian with period furnishings, at West Tenth and Spruce streets; (800) 658-4390 or (308) 284-4066.

Just above town are **Lake McConaughy**, the state's largest reservoir, measuring twenty-two by four miles, and smaller **Lake Ogallala**. Both offer camping, fishing, lakeside resorts and marinas. Tours of the Kingsley Dam are conducted in summer; (308) 284-8800.

From Ogallala, either I-80 or Highway 30 will get you to Omaha, passing Emigrant Trail and other historic sites along the way. Near *Grand Island*, U.S. 30 swings northward to stay with the Platte River Valley.

Where to learn more

Ogallala/Keith County Chamber of Commerce, 204 E. A St., Ogallala, NE 69153; (800) 658-4390 or (308) 284-4066; *www.visitogalalla.com*.

Scottsbluff/Gering Chamber of Commerce, 1517 Broadway, Suite 104, Scottsbluff, NE 69391; (308) 632-2133; *www.scottsbluffgering.net*.

Omaha
The grand city of America's Heartland

⚐

Most of the "undiscovered" places in this book are small towns, interesting byways or overlooked resort areas. So why Omaha, a city of nearly 400,000? Because it's a great old town, well worth the investment of your next vacation. Since it isn't San Francisco or New York or Chicago, it's overlooked by most travelers and is thus very affordable. The cost of dining and reclining is nearly half what it is in those more popular cities.

Downtown Omaha is undergoing a $2 billion renaissance, with several new high rises, a convention center, arena and the new **Lewis & Clark Landing** on the Missouri River. It features an indoor-outdoor restaurant, boardwalk, plaza and walking and biking paths along the riverfront.

Old Omaha is thriving as well. In the **Old Market** area bounded by Tenth, Thirteenth, Jackson and Harney streets, venerable brick warehouses shelter artists lofts, galleries, boutiques, coffee houses, intimate theaters and book stores. With its brick streets, window boxes and sidewalk planters, it could be in Europe instead of middle America.

The arts are alive and thriving here. The splendidly restored **Orpheum Theater** at 409 Sixteenth Street South and the new **Holland Performing Arts Center** at 1200 Douglas-on-the-Mall are the venues for the Omaha Symphony and Ballet Omaha. They also host American and international artists imported by the **Omaha Performing Arts Society**; (402) 345-0202; *www.omahaperformingarts.org.*

The **Omaha Community Playhouse**, where Marlon Brando got his start, is the largest in the country. It's at 6915 Cass St.; (888) 782-4338 or (402) 533-0800; *www.omahaplayhouse.com.* The city also has several art galleries. The **Joslyn Art Museum** at 2200 Dodge Street has an outstanding collection of Western art; (402) 342-3300; *www.joslyn.org.*

The city's visitor attractions are too numerous to list, so we'll offer our favorites. Start with an overview of the area's history at the large **Durham Western Heritage Museum** in the art deco Union Station at 801 Tenth St.; (402) 444-5071; *www.dwhm.org.* Omaha was the transcontinental railroad's eastern gateway, and exhibits focus railroading the opening of the West.

You'll also want to visit the village of **Boys Town** at 13628 Flanagan Blvd.; (800) 625-1400 or (402) 498-1140; *www.visitboystown.org.* This refuge for boys, started by Father Flanagan in 1917, is now a National Historic Landmark, with a museum, shrines and gardens. The organization, now called Girls and Boys Town, is still helping troubled kids.

A rainforest and desert thrive indoors at the **Henry Doorly Zoo** at 3701 S. 10th St.; (402) 733-8400; *www.omahazoo.org.* They are among the world's largest indoor climate zone exhibits. The adjacent **Scott Aquarium** puts visitors beneath the sea, with a glass tunnel running through its large exhibit tanks. More of mother nature is on display at the excellent **Lauritzen Gardens** at First and Bancroft; (402) 346-4002; *omahabotanicalgardens.org.* Plants from around the world thrive in thirteen different theme gardens. The complex also includes **Kenefick Park,** with huge steam locomotives on display and exhibits concerning early Western railroading.

The **Mormon Trail Center** at 3215 State Street preserves the site of Winter Quarters, where a band of 4,000 Utah-bound Mormons wintered in 1846-47. Exhibits include handcarts that the Mormons pulled across the plains, pioneer artifacts and a furnished log cabin. A Mormon temple and pioneer cemetery are adjacent; (402) 453-9372; *www.omaha.org/trails.*

If you just want to have fun in Omaha, head for **Heartland of America Park,** where you can ride a gondola, watch a water fountain show or enjoy an outdoor concert. It's on Douglas Street between Eighth and Ninth; (402) 884-5677; *www.heartlandgondolas.com.* Or catch a riverboat cruise aboard the *River City Star;* (866) 227-STAR; *www.rivercitystar.com.*

The way west

Omaha has been a gateway to the West ever since Lewis & Clark passed through in 1804. The Mormons, evicted from Nauvoo, Illinois, established their Winter Quarters settlement in 1846 and used it for years as a way station. In 1854, U.S. Congress passed the Kansas-Nebraska Act, which essentially evicted the Plains Indians and opened the vast prairie lands for settlement. It also established the Nebraska Territory, which initially stretched north to Canada and west to the Rocky Mountains.

A group from Council Bluffs, just across the Missouri River in Iowa, wanted the capital of the new territory to be on their doorstep, so they platted the townsite of Omaha. The promoters hoped that the coming transcontinental railroad would be routed through the new territorial capital, and thus through their own community as well.

Omaha lost the capital to Lincoln when Nebraska became a state in 1867, but never mind that. It got the railroad and thus became—and continues to be—one of middle America's major transportation and trade centers.

Where to learn more

Greater Omaha Convention & Visitors Bureau, 1001 Farnam on the Mall, Suite 200, Omaha, NE 68102; (866) 937-6624 or (402) 444-4660; *www.visitomaha.com.*

Bismark and Mandan
Urban lures in prairie country

꙾

*B*ismark-Mandan *is transitioning from a big town to a small city,* states the local chamber of commerce. That sums up in a sentence North Dakota's second largest urban area, which has a population pushing 100,000. One publication rated Bismark number one in the country for its quality of life and another called it the "Least stressful city in America."

We aren't necessarily urging that you *move* to the Bismark-Mandan area, unless you dig frigid winters. However, it's worth a visit, with a good balance of attractions, historic sites, cultural lures and outdoor activities.

North Dakota is mostly prairie country, a vast expanse of far horizons, of spacious skies and amber waves of grain; where cattle and cowmen roam free. And there's certainly plenty of room to roam. In a special U.S. census in 2002, it ranked forty-eighth in population, with just 642,000 residents, and it ranked dead last in population growth, actually losing 1.3 percent.

However, the capital city of Bismark and next-door Mandan are both thriving. Sitting opposite one another on the Missouri River, they offer the sorts of things that attract both new residents and visitors, such as art galleries, museums, a ballet and symphony. They have miles of walking and biking trails, and the river offers water play. The area is rich in history as well. Lewis & Clark paused here on their way west, and General George Armstrong Custer launched his fatal pursuit of the warring Sioux from here.

A full-scale replica of a typical keelboat used by Lewis & Clark is in **Keelboat Park** beside the river in Bismark. A paddlewheeler called the *Lewis & Clark* takes visitors on river cruises, departing from the old Port of Bismark; (701) 255-4233; *www.lewisandclarkriverboat.com.*

The **State History Museum** has exhibits about the two explorers and General Custer, as well as displays concerning North Dakota from primordial times to the present. It's part of the North Dakota Heritage Center on the state capitol campus at 612 E. Boulevard Ave.; (701) 328-2666; *www.state. nd/hist.* Nearby is a statue of **Sakakawea,** the legendary "Bird Woman" who accompanied Lewis & Clark's Corps of Discovery.

The **North Dakota State Capitol** is one of the most unusual in the nation—a square nineteen-story art deco structure towering high above this prairie town. Visitors can explore its Roughrider Gallery with portraits of famous North Dakotans and enjoy a prairie panorama from an eighteenth floor observation gallery; (701) 328-248. Just to the south, visitors can tour the former **Governor's Mansion** at 320 E. Avenue B; (701) 328-2666. This opulent Victorian home was in use from 1893 until 1960.

Next-door Mandan also has its share of visitor lures, notably **Fort Abraham Lincoln State Park**; (701) 667-6340; *www.state.nd.us/ndparks*. It has several reconstructed buildings, including the commanding officer's house where General Custer lived. It was from this fort that he and his Seventh Cavalry departed for their date with destiny at the Little Big Horn in Montana in 1876. Also on the state park grounds is the ruins of **On-a-Slant Village**, where a Mandan band lived until smallpox decimated them in 1781. In their diaries, Lewis & Clark noted the abandoned village, which consisted of earthen mounds, structures very untypical of Plains Indians.

The native peoples' history and arts are well represented at the **Five Nations Arts Museum** in Mandan's 1929 train depot at 401 Main St.; (701) 663-4663. It has an excellent selection arts and crafts, representing about 200 artisans from five area tribes. The building itself is worth a look, with its Colonial Revival architecture, stone floors and elaborate wood trim. The **North Dakota State Railroad Museum** in Mandan exhibits early day rolling stock, railroading artifacts and model trains, at 37th Street and Old Red Trail Road; (701) 663-9322.

Incidentally, *this* Mandan isn't where Lewis & Clark spent the winter of 1804-05. After passing through this area, they continued upriver for another thirty miles or so, then constructed **Fort Mandan** near the site of the present town of *Washburn*. You can reach it on Route 25 from Mandan or U.S. 83 from Bismark. The reconstructed fort is part of the **North Dakota Lewis & Clark Interpretive Center**, one of the top Corps of Discovery history sites in the country; (701) 462-8535; *www.fortmandan.com*. In addition to a full-scale replica of the fort, the complex includes an excellent museum, exhibits about an 1830 U.S. Army fort in the area, and a gallery of Western art.

Despite their rich histories, Bismark and Mandan had rather ordinary beginnings. They were both established in 1873, as Northern Pacific Railroad crews pushed their lines through the area. Served by trains and riverboats, their futures were assured. Rail officials named Bismark in honor of the legendary chancellor, in hopes of luring German investment money. Our historical research didn't don't reveal whether or not the ploy worked.

Where to learn more

Bismark-Mandan Convention & Visitors Bureau, 1600 Burnt Boat Rd., Bismark, ND 58503; (800) 767-3555 or (701) 222-4308; *www.bismarkmandancvb.com*.

Theodore Roosevelt National Park
A tribute to our Rough Rider President

Teddy Roosevelt was raised among the elite of New York Society. Yet when first arrived in the North Dakota Badlands in 1883 at the age of 24, the only civilization was the shoddy town of Little Missouri with a saloon called Big-Mouth Bob's Bug-Juice Dispensary. However, Teddy hadn't come to socialize with Big-Mouth Bob; he'd come to shoot buffalo.

He was immediately smitten by this rough-hewn wilderness. Within two weeks, he'd shot his buffalo and bought into a local ranch, which he called the Maltese Cross. A year later, after his wife and mother had died on the same day, he returned to seek solitude and solace in the Dakota wilds. He bought Elkhorn Ranch thirty-five miles farther north, and during the next several years, he returned frequently to live the rough life of a cowboy. Asthmatic as a youth, he credited his years in North Dakota for building the stamina and gusto that became his trademark.

He also became an active environmentalist, after witnessing the slaughter of wildlife and depletion of grasslands by livestock overgrazing. So it was fitting that the preserve set aside to protect the Badlands be named in his honor. Theodore Roosevelt National Memorial Park was established in 1947, then the word "Memorial" was dropped in 1978.

The park embraces not only the Badlands, but 70,400 acres of grasslands, woodlands, and canyons of the cottonwood-lined Little Missouri River. The region again teems with the wildlife that had fascinated Teddy, such as bison, deer, elk, desert pronghorns and prairie dogs. Our twenty-sixth president would feel right at home here today.

"The Bad Lands grade all the way from those that are almost rolling in character to those that are so fantastically broken in form and so bizarre in color as to seem hardly properly to belong to this earth," wrote Roosevelt.

The national park comes in three pieces, ribboned together by the meandering Little Missouri. The **South Unit** is immediately above the town of *Medora*, itself a major tourist draw; see below. The park's main visitor center is at the Medora entrance. A museum presents the geology, wildlife and history of the area, including material relating to Roosevelt and his ranches. A thirty-six-mile scenic drive loops past the South Unit's Badlands.

If you're approaching the park from the east on I-94, stop at the **Painted Canyon Overlook** at exit 32. It provides a splendid view of this multi-shaped, multi-colored Little Missouri River chasm. There's a small visitor center and picnic shelters at the turnout.

The smaller **North Unit** of the park is off U.S 85, about fifty miles north of I-90 and fifteen miles south of *Watford City*. It encloses another geologically grand section of the Little Missouri River, and a fourteen-mile drive leads to the Oxbow Overlook, with views into a curving river canyon. There's a small visitor center at the North Unit entrance.

Between the two sections is the **Elkhorn Ranch** site, reached only by a rough dirt road off Highway 85. Nothing of the original ranch remains, although interpretive signs identify locations of Roosevelt's house and various ranch outbuildings.

All elements of Theodore Roosevelt National Park are enclosed within the one million acre **Little Missouri National Grassland**, administered by the U.S. Forest Service. Check area visitor centers for a driving tour map.

By coincidence, Teddy Roosevelt and a French aristocrat named Antoine de Vallombrosa arrived in this region in the same year. While Teddy had decided to go into ranching on impulse, the Marquis de Mores had come with plans to create a giant cattle empire. He built a large slaughterhouse and the town of *Medora*, which he named for his wife. It was a complete community, with shops, a newspaper and a church. Teddy was a frequent visitor to his twenty-four room hilltop ranch house. However, the marquis was more idealistic than practical, and his ranching empire and town soon went bust.

Medora languished in the Dakota dust for decades. Then wealthy North Dakota businessman Harold Schafer and his wife began buying up parcels and restoring the town's surviving buildings. The family later turned their holdings over to the non-profit Theodore Roosevelt Medora Foundation.

Today, this charming Western style town is one of North Dakota's most popular visitor destinations. And it serves as the park's gateway, providing dining, reclining and shopping.

Medora's 1884 **Rough Riders Hotel**, built by a friend of Roosevelt's, is now a nine-room B&B. Other lures include the **Harold Schafer Heritage Center**, the **Sheila Schafer Gallery** with changing art exhibits, and the **Medora Doll House**, an antique doll museum in one the town's early homes. The **Medora Musical**, a fun variety show about area history, is presented in summers at the Burning Hills Amphitheater. Contact information for all of the above is (800) MEDORA-1; (701) 623-4444; *www.medora.org.*

Where to learn more

Medora Chamber of Commerce, P.O. Box 186, Medora, ND 58645; (701) 623-4910; *www.medora.com.*

Theodore Roosevelt National Park, P.O. Box 7, Medora, ND 58645; (701) 623-4466; *www.nps.gov/thro.*

"Hidden" Black Hills
What to do after you've done Mt. Rushmore

The Black Hills is not an undiscovered area, since it attracts about three million visitors each year. So, what do you do after you've seen Mount Rushmore, admired the Chief Crazy Horse Memorial and done Deadwood?

Some of the attractions in this southwestern corner of South Dakota are overlooked by many visitors. If you're planning a vacation in the Black Hills region, the four places we describe below should be added to your list. They're south, southeast and northwest of *Rapid City*, the commercial and visitor hub of this region.

Picture wild horses galloping across the Dakota prairie, manes and tails flying. Or imagine them standing in high silhouette on a rocky ridge, or splashing through a shallow stream. Seeing these horses running wild and free against a backdrop of splendid scenery was much more fascinating to us than staring at Mount Rushmore's stoic faces.

You can share this experience at the **Black Hills Wild Horse Sanctuary**, sixty miles south of Rapid City near *Hot Springs*. A non-profit group has purchased 11,000 acres of rangeland along the Cheyenne River to create America's first protected haven for wild horses.

More than 300 mustangs and their foals run free on this pristine ponderosa and sagebrush rangeland. From May through September, two-hour bus tours take visitors along the rim of a river canyon, across the prairies and down to the riverbottom to see and sometimes even mingle with one of the herds. For information on bus tours and the wild horse sanctuary's longer Adventure Tours, contact the Institute of Range Management at P.O. Box 998, Hot Springs, SD 57747; (800) 252-6652; *www.wildmustangs.com*.

Since you're in the neighborhood, nearby *Hot Springs* is worth a pause. **Evans Plunge**, created in 1890, is a large indoor public hot spring with a water slide, at 1145 N. River St.; (605) 745-5265; *www.evansplunge.com*. **Fall River County Historical Pioneer Museum** occupies an old red brick schoolhouse at 300 N. Chicago St.; (605) 745-5147; *www.pioneer-museum. com*. A mile southwest of town on U.S. 18 Bypass is the 26,000-year-old **Mammoth Site** with one of the world's largest collections of fossilized bones; (605) 745-6017; *www.mammothsite.com*. Visitors can watch teams uncovering fossils of mammoths, short-faced bears and such. Once uncovered, they're left in place. A visitor center and museum are adjacent.

If you're heading for **Badlands National Park**, take a side trip south into the **Pine Ridge Indian Reservation**. It is a place that anyone who shares our great sadness about the treatment of our native people should visit. America's last major Indian battle—actually a massacre—occurred here on December 29, 1890, when a peaceful band of Ogalala Sioux resisted attempts by Seventh Cavalry troops to disarm them. A skirmish ensued, then the cavalry blasted the encampment with a battery of light artillery pieces. Nearly half the band of 350 warriors, women and children were killed.

A simple monument marks the site of the massacre in the small village of *Wounded Knee*. Tribal leaders and many others are working to create America's first tribal memorial park here. The **Red Cloud Heritage Center** in nearby *Pine Ridge* village has an excellent selection of native peoples art, with many items for sale; (605) 867-5491; *www.redcloudschool.org.*

North of the reservation in the small town of *Wall* just off I-90, visit **Wounded Knee: The Museum**. This modern archive tells the tragic story of the massacre; (605) 279-2573; *www.woundedkneemuseum.org.* The town is also home to the huge, cluttered **Wall Drug** tourist stop; (605) 279-2175.

High in the northeastern corner of the Black Hills, the historic mining town of *Lead* (pronounced *Leed*) is cantilevered into ponderosa slopes. We think it's more appealing than better-known *Deadwood* next door because it's less commercial. This town of about 3,000 folks was born after a major gold strike in 1876. Its Homestake Mine still produces much of the famous Black Hills gold sold in the region's many jewelry, gift and curio shops.

Downtown Lead has none of the glitz and glitter of gambling-rich Deadwood. It retains its gold rush charm, and several Victorian mansions cling to its steep hillsides. You can learn about old and new mining technology at the **Homestake Gold Mine Visitors Center** and arrange for a tour of the Homestake's huge open pit gold mine; 160 Main St.; (605) 584-3110; *www.homestaketours.com.* More mining lore is exhibited at the **Black Hills Mining Museum**, and you can try your hand at gold panning; 323 Main St.; (605) 584-1605; *www.mining-museum.blackhills.com.*

Where to learn more

Hot Springs Area Chamber of Commerce, 801 S. Sixth St., Hot Springs, SD 57747; (800) 325-6991 or (605) 745-4140; *www.hotsprings-sd.com.*

Lead Area Chamber of Commerce, 309 W. Main St., Lead, SD 57754; (888) 701-0164 or (605) 584-1605; *www.leadmethere.org.*

Rapid City Area Convention & Visitors Bureau, P.O. Box 747 (444 Mt. Rushmore Rd.), Rapid City, SD 57709; (800) 487-3223 or (605) 343-1744; *www. rapidcitycvb.com.*

Sioux Falls & Mitchell
A great little city and a great big corn crib

អ

We can think of at least two good reasons to explore South Dakota's southeastern corner—a remarkably interesting and diverse mini-city and a delightfully silly structure coated with corn.

Sioux Falls, the largest city in South Dakota with a population of about 125,000, also is its most appealing. It brims with cultural offerings, visitor attractions, parklands and excellent shopping. Many people call it the most urban small city in the Heartland, and publications often rank it high on their "best places" lists.

The old downtown area has suffered the usual loss of businesses to suburban malls but in a sense, the city is better for it. Officials have worked hard to make it a center for specialty shops, book stores, art galleries and some remarkably good restaurants. Add to this mix a performing arts and visual arts center and you've got a vibrant downtown core.

The **Washington Pavilion of Arts and Sciences** is home to the Husby Performing Arts Center with two theaters, the Kirby Science Discovery Center, Visual Arts Center with six galleries, and the Wells Fargo CineDome Theater with a giant sixty-foot screen. The pavilion is at 301 S. Main Ave.; (877) WASH-PAV or (605) 367-7379; *www.washingtonpavilion.org.*

What makes Sioux Falls really work for us is the sixteen-mile-long **Big Sioux River Recreation Trail**. It's an emerald ribbon that follows the twisting Big Sioux River through town, with parklands and walking-cycling paths. It begins at **Falls Park,** where the Big Sioux River thunders over the city's namesake cataract. Attractions include fall-view walkways, the ruins of an old flour mill and the Horse Barn Art Center. The **Falls Park Visitor Information Center** has a five-story observation tower. Sound and light shows are presented in Falls Park during the summer; (605) 367-7430.

Sioux Falls is a lot about parks, since there are eighty of them within the city limits. **Sherman Park** between 12th and 25th streets hosts three attractions. The **U.S.S South Dakota Memorial** is a full-sized concrete mock-up of the most decorated battleship of World War II, with a museum adjacent. The **Delbridge Museum of Natural History** has one of the world's largest collections of mounted critters. The next-door **Great Plains Zoo** exhibits wildlife on believable facsimiles of the Australian Outback, African savanna and the Great Plains; (605) 367-7059; *www.gpzoo.org.*

Another attraction under the Dakota skies is the **Outdoor Campus,** an education facility with a life science center, riverside aquarium, butterfly garden, a "sample" of a tall-grass prairie with hiking trails. It's off I-229 exit 1 on 57th St.; (605) 362-2777; *www.outdoorcampus.org*. Head indoors to check out the **Center for Western Studies**, with a focus on the study and preservation of Northern Heartland culture. It's on the campus of Augustus College at 2201 S. Summit Ave.; (605) 274-4007; *www.augie.edu/gws*.

The Lakota Sioux called the Big Sioux River the "Laughing Waters," and that's an apt description for this contented, thriving mini-city.

Mitchell

And if you really want a chuckle, or perhaps just stare in amused amazement, head west on I-90 about seventy miles to the prairie farm town of *Mitchell*. Its incredible Corn Palace draws oglers from all over the world. So many folks hop off the freeway to see the thing that this town of about 15,000 has become something of a tourist center.

The **Mitchell Corn Palace** is an elaborate entertainment and exhibition hall topped with multi-colored turrets and spired Moorish domes. It dates from 1892 and the current rendition was built in 1937. Every August, workers hammer, glue and staple hundreds of thousands of ears of corn of varying shades to its outside walls to create decorative murals. It takes about 3,000 bushels to create these surprisingly detailed scenes. Their completion marks the beginning of the annual Corn Palace Festival in August. Guided tours of the palace are offered during the summer; (866) 273-2676 or (605) 996-5567; *www.cornpalace.org*.

Across from the corny castle is the **Enchanted Doll Museum** with a collection of nearly 5,000 antique and contemporary dolls; (605) 996-9896. On the campus of Dakota Wesleyan University, the **Dakota Discovery Museum** is a large complex with art and history galleries and several historic buildings. It's at 1300 E. University Blvd.; (605) 996-2122; *www.dakotadiscovery.com*. An attraction spelled out in its long name, the **Mitchell Prehistoric Indian Village Museum and Archeological Research Center** is on the site of a thousand-year-old fortified village. It has a museum, research archive and a full-size replica of an earthen lodge; 3200 Indian Village Rd.; (605) 996-5473; *www.mitchellindianvillage.org*.

Where to learn more

Corn Palace Convention & Visitors Bureau, P.O. Box 1026 (601 N. Main St.), Mitchell, SD 57301; (866) 273-2676 or (605) 996-5567; *www. cornpalace.org*.

Sioux Falls Convention & Visitors Bureau, P.O. Box 1425 (200 N. Phillips Ave.), Sioux Falls, SD 57104; (605) 336-1620; *www.siouxfalls cvb.com*.

Spearfish
A jewel among Black Hills baubles

❧

Sitting prettily at the mouth of a scenic canyon on the northern edge of the Black Hills, Spearfish is as refreshing as a mountain breeze.

When Gutzon Borglum carved the Mount Rushmore Memorial sixty miles south of here, he created not only the world's largest sculpture but—unintentionally—one large tourist trap. Although the Black Hills are beautiful, they are riddled with gimmicks such as Reptile Gardens, Flying W Chuckwagon Dinners, Flintstones Bedrock City and the National Presidential Wax Museum. The tough old mining town of Deadwood glitters and jangles with slot machines.

The northern gateway to the Black Hills, Spearfish stands above all of this, and not just geographically. Although it does have its Black Hills gold jewelry shops, it has avoided much of the tourist silliness that pervades most of the communities to the south. It's a pleasant little town of old brick, nestled in a green valley with the wooded Black Hills rising above.

Spearfish is famous for the **Black Hills Passion Play**, one of the longest-running outdoor pageants in America. It was started in Germany as the Leuten Passion Play, then the company brought it to the U.S. in 1932 and settled permanently in Spearfish in 1939. This pageant about Christ's last seven days is presented three nights a week in a 6,000-seat amphitheater. With more than 250 performers and even live animals, it's rather a spectacular production. The season runs from June through August, and backstage tours are available; P.O. Box 489, Spearfish, SD 57783; (800) 457-0160 or (605) 642-2646; *www. blackhills.com/bhpp.*

Another cultural lure is the handsomely restored 1906 **Matthews Opera House** at 614 Main Street; (605) 642-7973; *www.moh-scah.com.* Once a vaudevillian palace, it offers drama productions in conjunction with Black Hills State University, plus foreign films, "brown bag lectures" and art exhibits. The cute **Dolls at Home Museum** presents dolls in miniature domestic settings, complete with tiny furniture and little gardens. It's at 236 W. Jackson Boulevard (605) 642-2648.

The **High Plains Heritage Center** features art and artifacts from the Great Plains, and a log cabin and schoolhouse. A theater offers cowboy music and poetry, while cattle and buffalo roam about a small animal farm; 825 Heritage Dr.; (605) 642-9378; *www.westernheritagecenter.com.* The **Spirit of the Hills Wildlife Sanctuary** provides haven for animals, plus wagon rides and other activities for visitors; at 499 Tinton Rd.; (605) 642-2907.

Fish hatcheries normally aren't regarded as history sites, although the **D.C. Booth Historic National Fish Hatchery** is more than just a minnow nursery. It dates from 1896 and the original building contains a museum about fish-raising. The complex also includes the period furnished 1905 home of the first hatchery superintendent, the National Fish Culture Hall of Fame (famous fingerlings?) and viewing windows where trout wriggle past. The facility is off I-90 exit 12 at 434 Hatchery Circle; (605) 642-7730.

The closest thing to a tourist gimmick in Spearfish is **Langers Factory Outlet,** a series of souvenir shops, including some that sell locally-made Black Hills gold jewelry. It's at 603 Main St.; (800) 526-4377 or (605) 642-2383; *www.blackhillsgoldjewelry.com.* Artist Dick Termes sells his unusual rotating globular paintings at the **Termesphere Gallery** at 1920 Christensen Dr.; (605) 642-4805; *www.termespheres.com.*

Spearfish residents and visitors relate to the surrounding outdoor beauty. A walking path follows the course of Spearfish Creek as it burbles through town. Several other trails and bike paths are in the area. *Sports Afield* called this region a "mountain biking mecca."

Spearfish Canyon National Scenic Highway, following the creek into the Black Hills, is one of South Dakota's prettiest drives. Limestone cliffs rise sheer from spruce and pine forests, and occasional waterfalls spill from the heights. Flowers bloom along the creek in spring and summer, and aspen and birch put on a fine color show in October. Trailheads invite hiking into the surrounding Black Hills National Forest.

The first outsiders to enter this region may have been a group prospecting for gold in 1833. A rock inscription found near Spearfish in 1887 supposedly was etched by one of its members, stating that he was the lone survivor of an Indian attack. The stone is on display at the Adams Memorial Museum in Deadwood, although its authenticity has never been verified.

The first confirmed settlers arrived in Spearfish Valley in 1876, attracted by the rich soil and the flow of the creek. The name comes from the Sioux and Cheyenne practice of spearing fish in the clear water. Two years earlier, a scouting party led by none other than George Armstrong Custer had discovered gold in the Black Hills. This led to a land rush and the ousting of the native people, who had regarded this region as sacred. No gold was ever found around Spearfish, and the town is probably the better for it.

Where to learn more

Spearfish Convention & Visitors Bureau, P.O. Box 550 (106 W. Kansas St.), Spearfish, SD 57783-0550; (800) 626-8013 or (605) 642-2626; *www. spearfish.sd.us.*

MARK TWAIN RIVERBOAT, MO.

Chapter Five

The
Southern Heartland

PRAIRIES, COWBOYS & — ALLIGATORS?

America's southern heartland is surprisingly diverse. The Great Plains sweep down through Kansas, Oklahoma, the western edge of Missouri and into Texas. There, the pattern changes. Much of Missouri and most of central Texas are hill country. Finally, although few outsiders associate the Lone Star State with alligators, its southeastern area has several bayous as well as sunny beaches, since it borders on the Gulf of Mexico.

KANSAS is pure prairie country and—a surprise to some—it's also a part of the wild West. That prairie once supported great cattle herds, and Dodge City and Abilene were rowdy cowtowns. The state's mix of famous citizens ranges from Wyatt Earp to Dwight Eisenhower.

Where to learn more: Department of Commerce Travel and Tourism, 1000 SW Jackson St., Suite 100, Topeka, KS 66612-1354; (800) 252-6727 or (785) 296-2009; *www.travelks.com.*

MISSOURI hatched one of America's most celebrated authors and we visit his hometown. We also check out an historic French settlement along the Great River Road, the Missouri Wine Country and the home of "Give 'em hell Harry."

Where to learn more: Missouri Division of Tourism, P.O. Box 1055, Jefferson City, MO 65102; (800) 519-2300 or (573) 751-4113; *www.missouritourism.org.*

OKLAHOMA is certainly okay and we explore a pair of interesting towns in this prairie state—the place where our greatest humorist grew up and the historic site of the Great Oklahoma Land Rush. They're near the state's two largest cities, handy for side-tripping.

Where to learn more: Oklahoma Tourism & Recreation Department, P.O. Box 52002, Oklahoma City, OK 73146-0789; (800) 652-6552; *www.travelok.com.*

TEXAS is so large that it would take nearly 227 Rhode Islands to fill it. Within this vast expanse, we discover a former cowtown all grown up, a large national park that few people visit, a Teutonic town in the Hill Country and alligator bayous on the Gulf Coast.

Where to learn more: Travel Division, Department of Transportation, P.O. Box 149248, Austin, TX 78714-9248; (800) 452-9292 or (512) 486-5800; *traveltex.com.*

Abilene
From herding cattle to liking Ike

*N*ow come along boys and listen to my tale,
And I'll tell you my troubles on the old Chisholm Trail.
— Old trail herding song

Abilene was brought to life in 1867 when Joseph G. McCoy got the idea of using the new Union Pacific Railroad to ship beef east. During the town's peak, millions of longhorns were driven up the Chisholm Trail from Texas, held in McCoy's stockyards, then loaded onto cattle cars.

America's first cattle boomtown, Abilene also was one of the wildest. Thirsty and randy cowmen, paid off at the end of the drive, headed for the saloons and brothels to raise a little hell. In 1871, James Butler "Wild Bill" Hickok was hired to keep the peace. Then in 1872, the rails were shifted closer to Texas and the town's interests shifted to farming and wheat.

Although the Abilene cattle drives lasted only five years, they have provided fodder for dozens of Western movies and the long-running *Rawhide* television series. The bawling of steers, the cranky chuckwagon cook and drovers singing cowboy songs provide enduring images of the great American West.

The stockyards are gone and juiced-up cowpokes no longer slap leather on Texas Street. Old Abilene exists only in memory, the movies and the fine Dickinson County Heritage Center. Now a town of about 7,000 peaceful citizens, it's is an appealing community with a well-kept downtown and fine tree-shaded neighborhoods. And its most famous citizen isn't "Wild Bill." It's Dwight David Eisenhower, supreme allied commander of the European theater during World War II and one of our most popular presidents.

If you like Ike, you'll like Abilene. He lived here from age eight until he left for West Point, and his life story is told at the twenty-two acre **Eisenhower Center** at 200 SE Fourth St.; (877) 746-4453 or (785) 263-6700; *www.eisenhower.archives.gov*. The complex includes his simple wood frame childhood home and the **Eisenhower Museum** that traces his life from boyhood to the Presidency. Also part of the center are the **Eisenhower Presidential Library** with an extensive collection of his White House papers and mementos; and the **Place of Meditation**, where Ike and his wife Mamie Doud Eisenhower are buried.

The **Dickinson County Heritage Center** focuses on the history of Abilene from its cowtown days through its farming era to the present. Exhibits include a pioneer cabin and a still-functioning antique carousel. Within the complex is the **Museum of Independent Telephony**, honoring the small firms that brought phone service to much of rural America. Abilene's Clayson Brown started a phone company here that eventually evolved into Sprint. The Heritage Center is at 412 S. Campbell St.; (785) 263-2681; *www.heritagecenterdk.com*.

Old Abilene Town, a touristy version of "the first cowtown of America," is being built near the Eisenhower Center and adjacent to the 1887 Rock Island Railroad Depot; (785) 263-1868; *www.oldabilenetownks.com*. It opened in 2004 with a few restored or rebuilt structures representing early Abilene, and others will be added. Offerings as we went to press included stagecoach rides, a saloon shootout, Western crafts and souvenirs shops and—unfortunately—the World War II Generals Wax Museum.

The **Abilene & Smoky Valley Railroad** offers excursion rides from the depot; (888) 426-6687 or (785) 263-0118; *www.asvrr.org*. It runs twelve miles across the prairie to nearby *Enterprise*, using a mix of rolling stock that includes a 1945 diesel-electric locomotive, a 1900 dining car and an open gondola car. Another Abilene attraction is the **Greyhound Hall of Fame** at 407 S. Buckeye Ave.; (785) 263-3000; *www.greyhoundhalloffame. com*. No, it's not about heroic bus drivers; it's supposedly the only museum in the world focusing on just one type of dog.

Several historic homes occupy Abilene's handsome old neighborhoods, and you can pick up a walking tour map at the downtown visitors bureau. The 1905 Georgian style **Seelye Mansion** exhibits period furnishings and a Patent Medicine Museum since its builder, Dr. A.B. Seelye, made his fortune selling assorted elixirs. The huge twenty-five-room house is at 1105 Buckeye Ave.; (785) 263-1084. The town's most photogenic historic structure is the elaborate 1880 Italianate **LeBold Mansion** at 106 N. Vine; (785) 263-4356; *www.lebold-mansion.com*. Both are open for public tours.

On the cultural scene, the **Tietjens Center for the Performing Arts** occupies a renovated 1880s-era church at 300 N. Mulberry St.; (888) 222-4574 or (785) 263-4574; *www.greatplainstheatre.com*. Its highly regarded professional troupe presents a variety of plays in an intimate 200-seat theater. Both "Wild Bill" and Dwight Eisenhower worshiped here when it was a church.

Where to learn more

Abilene Convention & Visitors Bureau, 201 NW Second St., Abilene, KS 67410; (800) 569-5915 or (785) 263-2231; *www.abilenekansas.org*.

Dodge City and neighbors
A classic Western town with a wicked past

ⵎ

M ister, I want you out of Dodge by sundown!
— **Marshal Matt Dillon in** *Gunsmoke*

Abilene may have been the nation's first wild cowtown, but folks from Dodge like to boast that their community was the "Wickedest Little City in America."

Both had similar beginnings, as prairie towns at the end of Texas cattle trails. The Cimarron Trail linked with the Santa Fe Trail at Dodge City. Like Abilene, it became a major cattle shipping center, with the attendant wild cowboys, saloons and fallen angels. A virtual honor roll of famous Western characters were drawn to Dodge, including Wyatt Earp, Bat Masterson, Doc Holliday and Luke Short.

Dodge City seems more preoccupied on its colorful history than Abilene, and it encourages visitors to have fun with it. The main street is called Wyatt Earp Boulevard and the Dodge City Trail of Fame is marked with sidewalk medallions honoring characters from the town's past. The former Boot Hill cemetery is a pretend Western town and—good grief!—downtown Dodge is home to the Gunfighter's Wax Museum.

Perhaps some of this preoccupation with the past is more harmless fantasy than reality. Dodge City was the supposed setting of *Gunsmoke*, the longest running show in television history. From 1955 until 1975, steely-eyed Matt Dillon (aka James Arness) battled the bad guys on Front Street. Fact and fantasy are so intermingled that *Gunsmoke* characters are enshrined in the wax museum. Arness and other cast members were added to the Trail of Fame in 2005 to mark the TV show's fiftieth anniversary.

To get a sense of old Dodge City—both real and imagined—head for the **Boot Hill Museum** on Front Street; (620) 227-8188; *www.boothill.org*. This "Western history village" is a full-scale mock-up of Dodge, with false front stores, the Fort Dodge Jail, a one-room school, assorted frontier exhibits and audio-visual programs. Marshals and bad guys shoot it out on Front Street, and saucy ladies perform onstage at the Long Branch Saloon.

The **Gunfighter's Wax Museum** at 603 Fifth Avenue exhibits life-sized images of Earp, Masterson, Belle Starr, Billy the Kid and—oh yes—Doc, Festus and Miss Kitty. In the same building is a museum of quite a different sort, the **Kansas Teacher's Hall of Fame**. It honors outstanding teachers of yesterday and today, with plaques, early classroom materials and photos. Both museums have the same phone number: (620) 225-7311.

The imposing limestone 1881 **Ford Home and Museum** exhibits period furniture and Western regalia, at 112 E. Vine St.; (620) 227-6791. For a guided tour of old downtown and nearby Fort Dodge, hop aboard the **Dodge City Trolley**. It departs from the Convention and Visitors Bureau on one-hour tours; at 400 W. Wyatt Earp Blvd.; (620) 225- 8186.

Not all things in Dodge have Western themes. The **Depot Theater Company** presents dinner theater entertainment in the converted Santa Fe Depot at 201 E. Wyatt Earp Blvd.; (620) 225-1001; *www.depottheaterco.com*. The **Carnegie Center for the Arts** exhibits the works of local and regional artists. It occupies the unusual round brick Carnegie library building at 701 N. Second Ave.; (620) 225-6388; *www.dodgecityarts.org*.

Although Dodge City dates from 1872 when rails reached the area, the **Santa Fe Trail** was blazed through here back in 1821. Surviving ruts are visible nine miles west of Dodge off U.S. 50; watch for "Historic Marker" signs. **Fort Dodge** was established in 1865 to protect wagon trains on the trail, then it was abandoned in 1882. It has been the Kansas Soldiers Home since 1889, and several original sandstone buildings survive. Sixty cottages and other structures have been added to accommodate its resident veterans. A small museum and library are open to the public; (620) 227-2121.

The Daltons and Dorothy

For another taste of Western history, head south nineteen miles on U.S. 283, then southwest on U.S. 54 to the tree-shaded hamlet of *Mead*. The **Dalton Gang Hideout** at 502 S. Pearlette Street is a simple wood frame house where the notorious bunch holed up. A still- intact 95-foot-tunnel leads to a barn where the gang kept their getaway horses. The Dalton Museum in the barn's loft is busy with pioneer relics; (800) 354-2743 or (620) 873-2731. More early day artifacts are displayed at the cluttered **Meade County Historical Society Museum** at 200 E. Carthage; (620) 873-2359.

Forty miles southwest, the town of *Liberal* is home to the fine **Mid America Air Museum**, with a large collection of military aircraft; at 2000 W. Second St.; (620) 624-5263; *www.liberalairmuseum.com*. Since we're in Kansas, Toto, we should call on Dorothy at the **Land of Oz Museum**, reached by the Yellow Brick Road. It contains memorabilia from the classic 1939 film, and the adjacent **Coronado Museum** focuses on area history. They're at 567 E. Cedar St; (620) 624-7624.

Where to learn more

Dodge City Convention & Visitors Bureau, P.O. Box 1474 (400 W. Wyatt Earp Blvd.), Dodge City, KS 67801; (800) OLD-WEST or (620) 225-8186; *www.visitdodgecity.org*.

Lawrence
The best little city in Kansas

Cradled between the Kansas and Wakarusa rivers and rimmed by wooded hills, thriving and culturally-rich Lawrence is the state's most appealing mini-city. It would hardly be regarded as the end of the world.

Yet, the world did end here—and elsewhere—in the starkly realistic television movie, *The Day After*. When it was aired in 1983, it was the most-watched TV show up to that time. The film, mostly shot on location here, portrayed a community dying from nuclear war fallout. Producers picked Lawrence because they felt it was a typical middle America town.

Fortunately, it was fiction, and most people in this progressive community appreciated its strong anti-war message. However, Lawrence did suffer its moment of real violence. During the Civil War, Kansas was torn between northern and southern sympathizers. Lawrence had been settled in 1854 by New England abolitionists. In 1863, renegade Confederate guerrilla William Quantrill, wanting to punish it for its northern sympathies, brutally attacked the town, killing 200 people and burning scores of buildings. It was the Civil War's bloodiest attack outside a combat zone.

Lawrence survived, rebuilt and slowly grew into the handsome, vibrant and diverse community that it is today. Its 80,000 residents appreciate the good life that their small city offers. Visitors will enjoy this good life as well. The mini-city is home to three universities, two performing arts centers, fifty public parks and several museums.

The well-preserved downtown area and several surrounding neighborhoods occupy one of the Midwest's largest historic districts. The National Trust for Historic Preservation lists Lawrence among its "Dozen Most Distinctive Destinations" and the community is included in John Villani's *The 100 Best Small Art Towns in America.*

Influenced by the liberal diversity of three universities, the well-groomed downtown offers a rich mix of dining, shopping and cultural experiences. This is where you come for traditional Midwest beef or sushi; where you can sip local microbrews or imported wine. You can buy everything from handmade quilts to original art to exotic imports, and you can listen to good jazz or get a tattoo. Most of this shopping, dining and entertainment abundance is along Massachusetts Street. To learn more, contact Downtown Lawrence; (785) 842-3883; *http://downtownlawrence.com.*

The **University of Kansas** brims with cultural lures and you can arrange a campus tour by calling (785) 864-2341; *www.ku.edu.* Exhibits at the fine

KU Natural History Museum focus on the flora, fauna and geology of the Midwest, and they reach well beyond, with wildlife scenes from Alaska to Mexico. The museum is in Dyche Hall; (785) 864-4450; *www.nmh.ku.edu.* The **Dole Institute of Politics** on Petefish Drive is both a political think tank, and an archive about Kansas history and the life of native-born Senator Bob Dole, who attended the university; (785) 864-4900; *doleinstitute.org.* The **Spencer Museum of Art** is regarded as one of America's top university art archives, with collections ranging from baroque paintings to decorative arts; at 1301 Mississippi St.; (785) 864-4710; *www.ku.edu/~sma.*

The university also is a serious center for the performing arts. The stunning new $14.3 million **Lied Center of Kansas** hosts concerts, Broadway productions, dance recitals and other entertainments; (785) 864-ARTS; *www.leid.ku.edu.* Student thespians at the **University Theatre** present a variety of dramas, musicals and comedies in Murphy Hall; (785) 864-3982; *www.kutheatre.com.*

Off campus, the **Lawrence Art Center** has two galleries exhibiting local and international art, and a 300-seat theater where local drama and dance groups perform. It's at 940 New Hampshire St.; (785) 843-6629; *www.lawrenceartcenter.com.* The **Lawrence Community Theatre** presents musicals and dramas in a former church at 1501 New Hampshire St.; (785) 843-7469; *www.community/lawrence.com/communitytheatre.* Regional history is on display at the **Watkins Community Museum of History** at 1047 Massachusetts St.; (785) 841-4109; *www.watkinsmuseum.org.*

Two blocks west of downtown, **Old West Lawrence** is a splendid neighborhood of fine Victorian and early American homes. Most of the area's earlier homes were burned during the Quantrill raid. The neighborhood is listed on the National Register of Historic Places, and tour maps are available at the Lawrence Visitors Bureau. Across town in **Old East Lawrence** is the **Hobbs Park Memorial**, a home that was rebuilt after the Quantrill raid. The memorial honors Lawrence's role as an anti-slave community. It's at Eleventh and Delaware streets; (785) 749-7394; *www.hobbsparkmemorial.org.*

If you'd like to chug through the attractive surrounding countryside, book a ride on the **Midland Railway**. Its vintage trains offer twenty-mile round trips over a line built in 1867, departing from a depot on High Street in nearby *Baldwin City*; (800) 6511-0388; *www.midland-ry.org.*

Where to learn more

Lawrence Convention & Visitors Bureau, P.O. Box 586 (734 Vermont St.), Lawrence, KS 66044; (888) 529-5267 or (785) 865-4411; *www.visitlawrence.com.*

Hannibal & beyond
The Unsinkable Mark Twain?

✄

*O*n *the whole, it is better to deserve honors and not have them than to have them and not deserve them.* — **Mark Twain's Notebook, 1902-03**

Charming old Hannibal is mostly a one-industry town and that industry is Samuel Langhorne Clemens. We wonder, if he were alive today, what he would think of all the fuss and bother. In his writings, Mark Twain jokingly feigned humility, although he was at heart something of an egotist.

The *AAA TourBook* lists five Hannibal attractions using Mark Twain's name. Half a dozen old buildings are considered "Mark Twain sites" and a local sightseeing company is called the Twainland Express. Each year, more than half a million visitors come to this Mississippi River town in northeastern Missouri to absorb Mark Twain lore.

However, the great humorist wasn't the only famous person who hailed from Hannibal. This also was Margaret Tobin's home town, and it was Twain who encouraged her to seek her fortunes in the Colorado mining camps. When she got there, this simple small town girl met and married a mining engineer named James Joseph Brown. When writers got through with the tale, she was the "Unsinkable Molly Brown."

Samuel Clemens was born in Florida, Missouri, in 1835, then his family moved to Hannibal when he was four. The quiet little town and its people provided substance for many of his writings, and the community won't let present-day visitors forget that.

Begin with the new **Mark Twain Interpretive Center** with exhibits about his childhood in Hannibal, at 415 N. Main St.; (573) 221-9010; *www. marktwainmuseum.org*. There, you can pick up material on the other Twain sites. The most popular stop is his **Boyhood Home** at 208 Hill Street, built by his father and restored to its original look. The **Mark Twain Museum** is adjacent. Other sites are the **John M. Clemens Justice of the Peace Office** where his father served as the town JP; the **Becky Thatcher House**, the real life home of Laura Hawkins, Mark Twain's model for Miss Becky; and the **Pilaster House**, where the Clemens family lived briefly.

But wait! There's more! The **Mark Twain Riverboat** offers sightseeing and dinner cruises from a dock at the foot of Center Street; (573) 221-3222; *www.marktwainriverboat.com*. The **Mark Twain Outdoor Theater**, four miles south of town at Clemens Landing, presents a play about Tom Sawyer and Huck Finn; (573) 221-2945; *www.clemenslanding.com*. **Mark Twain Cave**, two miles southeast of town on State Route 79, was used as the writer's model for the cave where Tom and Becky got lost in *The Adventures of Tom Sawyer;* (573) 221-1656; *www.marktwaincave.com*.

However, Hannibal isn't only about Mark Twain. The 1898 **Rockcliffe Mansion** overlooking the Mississippi has been restored to its *art nouveau* elegance; at 1000 Bird St.; (573) 221-4140. The downtown **Optical Science Center and Museum** features a large collection of antique eyewear and other things optical; at 214 N. Main St.; (573) 221-2020. The **Molly Brown Birthplace & Museum** at Sixth and Butler has been restored and is open to visitors; (573) 221-2100; *www.mollybrownmuseum.com*. The lush 400-acre **Riverview Park** has walking trails and picnic areas and—oh, yes—a statue of Mark Twain at Inspiration Point; (573) 221-0154.

Hannibal also is an active arts community, with several galleries, crafts shops and working artists. The **Hannibal Arts Council** promotes and coordinates the local cultural scene, including visual and performing arts; at 1221 Market St.; (573) 221-6545; *www.hannibalarts.com*.

A corridor of arts and crafts

Artists are so prevalent in the region that Highway 79, which links three communities on the banks of the Mississippi, has been designated as **"50 Miles of Art."** If you're headed for or coming from St. Louis, this is *the* way to go. The highway travels from Hannibal to Louisiana and Clarksville, tiny 19th century towns that are busy with working artists, sculptors, crafts people, galleries and antique stores. This also is an exceptionally scenic route, with views of the river's steep bluffs and rolling green hills. Several cozy bed & breakfast inns and charming cafés are in the region. You can download a route map and list of galleries at *www.50milesofart.com*.

Folks in charming little *Louisiana* have worked so diligently to preserve their 19th century buildings that all of its small business district is listed on the National Register of Historic Places. Its tidy neighborhoods boast one of the finest collections of Victorian homes in the state.

Clarksville, with a population of fewer than 500, occupies a high bluff, commanding a grand view of the Mississippi River and a nearby lock and dam complex. It's a fine place for watching the passing river traffic. Like Louisiana, it has many restored historic buildings, thanks to a major preservation effort launched late in the last century.

Where to learn more

Hannibal Convention & Visitors Bureau, 505 N. Third St., Hannibal, MO 63401; (800) AND-HUCK or (573) 221-2477; *www.visithannibal.com*.

Independence
Too wild about Harry?

Independence wears its memories of Harry S Truman like a comfortable old overcoat. This attractive and historic community of 114,000 on the eastern edge of Kansas City is as preoccupied with Harry as Hannibal is with Mark Twain.

You've got your Truman Presidential Library, Truman Home, Truman Courthouse, Truman Memorial Building, Truman Depot, Truman Farm and Truman Road. And here's an irony for you. Harry's first job was at Clinton's Soda Fountain, still functioning and filled with Truman memorabilia. Harry, meet Bill. They did, at least in spirit, because the former President Clinton stopped at the soda fountain during a campaign swing.

At the risk of ruffling local folks' feathers, we'll talk less about Harry and more about something of greater significance here. Face it folks, Harry ordered the end of a war—the hard way. However, the town of Independence opened up the West.

During the great westward movement of the mid-1800s, Independence was starting point for the Oregon and California trails, and the Santa Fe Trail passed through here. It's the only city in America that sits at the crossroad of three major pioneer routes. It also was chosen as Zion, God's city on earth, by Mormon Church leader Joseph Smith. He established a large colony here in the early 1850s, but they were driven out by locals who didn't care for their practice of plural marriage. So much for heaven on earth.

Independence was established as the Jackson County seat in 1827 in an area the native people called Big Springs. As usual, those folks were driven off by the incoming settlers. The Santa Fe Trail was already in place, so the new town became an active trading center. It was thus logical that Oregon and California bound migrants would use this already established town as their jumping-off point. During the Civil War, Independence was caught in the struggle between abolitionists and slave holders. It was captured by Confederate troops, them re-captured by the Federals. At war's end, it slowly regained its prosperity.

The town's most famous citizen wasn't born here. Harry S Truman first saw daylight on May 8, 1884 in a farmhouse near *Lamar*, a small town in southwestern Missouri. That house is now the **Harry S Truman Birthplace State Historic Site**; (417) 682-2279; *www.mostateparks.com/trumansite. htm*. However, the family soon moved and Harry spent his most of his childhood in Independence.

Harry's town is rich with historic sites. Begin where the pioneers began, at **Independence Square** and the stately Jackson County Courthouse. It's in the heart of old town, bounded by Liberty, Maple, Main and Lexington streets. This was the actual starting point of the California-Oregon Trail, where pioneers stocked up on supplies before heading into the unknown. The square is now rimmed by boutiques, antique stores, galleries, cozy cafés and curio shops; (816) 252-0608; *www.independencesquare.biz.*

Several attractions are just off the square and more are within walking distance. A good starting point is five blocks south at the **National Frontier Trails Museum** at 318 W. Pacific St.; (816) 325-7575; *www.frontiertrails-museum.org.* Artifacts, videos and an excellent film tell the story of the westward movement. The complex includes two other historic buildings. The **Bingham-Waggoner Estate** across the street was built in 1855 alongside the Santa Fe Trail; (816) 461-3491; *www.bwestate.org.* Grooves along the south side of the estate are thought to be from trail caravans. And interpretive path loops around the site. Another element of the museum complex is the wood frame 1879 **Chicago and Alton Depot**, moved here and restored in 1996; (816) 325-7955; *www.pagehost.com.*

The **1859 Jail, Marshall's Home and Museum** is just off the square at 217 N. Main St.; (816) 262-1892; *www.jchs.org.* Exhibits include weapons confiscated from the bad guys. Jesse James' brother Frank once was an unwilling guest here. Across Main Street is the old fashioned **Clinton's Soda Fountain & Gifts** where Harry Truman once worked and where Bill Clinton stopped by, wearing a campaign sweatshirt; (816) 833-2046.

The town's Mormon memories are preserved at the **Mormon Visitors Center** at 837 W. Walnut St.; (816) 836-3466. Artifacts, artwork and videos focus on the Mormon faith and the group's movement west. One of our favorite Independence attractions is the **Pioneer Trails Nature Center**, marking a site where all three trails passed through. Visitors can choose their "trail" and learn about its history through audio boxes. The center also has a museum with exhibits, films and pioneer journals that folks can read. It's located at 318 W. Pacific St.; (816) 325-7575; *www.independence.mo.com.*

Independence has several other interesting sites, so it's obvious that you'll need more than a brief visit. For instance, did we mention the Truman Presidential Library, Truman Home, Truman Courthouse, Truman Memorial Building, Truman Depot, Truman...?

Where to learn more

Independence Department of Tourism, 111 E. Maple St., Independence, MO 64050; (816) 748-7323; *www.ci.independence.mo.us/tourism.*

The Missouri Rhineland
The state's scenic valley of the grape

Although Missouri produces only a tiny fraction of America's wine, it has a long winemaking tradition. It began in the early 1800s when German families settled in the Missouri River Valley west of St. Louis. That even predates California's legendary Napa Valley.

The state now has about fifty wineries and most of them are still in this region. Many are small family operations and some are still owned by German-Americans. Most have tasting rooms and some offer tours. Local aficionados insist that Missouri wines rival those in California and Europe. However, as fans of lusty California reds, we won't enter that argument.

Our wine route follows State Highway 100, which meanders through a scenic Missouri River region of woodlands, farmlands and vineyards. Even if you're not into wine, you'll enjoy the fine scenery and charming old riverside towns along the route.

To begin, go about forty miles southwest from St. Louis on Interstate 44, take exit 251 and follow Route 100 to *Washington*. This attractive old tree-shaded town of about 13,000 is noted not only for nearby wineries but for corncob pipes. It was settled primarily by German families in the 1830s. In 1869, one of them started the **Missouri Meerschaum Company**, now the world's oldest and largest maker of these rustic pipes. A small "nostalgia room" at the factory focuses on the history of meerschaums, at 400 W. Front St.; (636) 239-2109; *www.corncobpipe.com*.

The nearby **Washington Visitor Center** at 301 W. Front Street can point you in the direction of several area winery tasting rooms. First, check out the museums, art galleries, gift shops and antique stores the handsome brick downtown area. The two-story **Washington Historical Society Museum** has exhibits on area history, at Fourth and Market; (636) 239-0280; *www.washingtonhistorical.org*. The small **Firehouse Museum** displays old firefighting equipment and vintage autos, at Fifth and Stafford streets; (636) 239-0280. The new **Missouri Photojournalist Hall of Fame** honors the state's outstanding media photographers at 8 W. Second St.; (636) 239-7575. It may be the first of its kind in the nation.

Continuing your riverside amble, you'll shortly encounter *New Haven*, a rustic old Teutonic settlement with steepled churches and square-shouldered brick buildings downtown. A new Levee Walk with antique lamp posts is popular for evening strolling, and a one-block section of Front Street has a restored art deco theatre, cafés and specialty shops.

The combined **John Colter Memorial Museum & Visitor Center** at Main and Miller streets honors a member of the Lewis & Clark expedition that camped near here. Colter went on to become a legendary mountain man in the west, then he returned to this area to retire. Several wineries are in the region between New Haven and our final stop at Hermann. Get a copy of the *Hermann Wine Trail* at the New Haven visitor center; (573) 237-3830.

The village of *Hermann* is the most popular stop along this route, as evidenced by the area's thirty bed & breakfast inns. It was settled in 1836 by German families from Philadelphia who were concerned that they were losing their traditional customs and identity. They obviously succeeded in preserving their heritage, for this is the most Teutonic town in Missouri. Folks come to admire its fine Old World architecture, sip wine and perhaps take part in the annual *Oktoberfest*. Several art galleries, craft shops and antique shops are in the old fashioned downtown area.

The **Deutschheim State Historic Site** preserves several of the town's classic structures; at 109 W. Second St.; (573) 486-2200; *www.mostateparks.com/deutschheim*. Two imposing brick homes have been restored and fitted with period furnishings—the four-gabled 1840 Pommer-Gentner house and the three-story 1842 Strehly house with a classic vernacular front. The complex also includes a half-timbered barn, an 1830s style garden, an early-day winery and a gift shop. Several traditional festivals are held here, including *Weihnachfest*, an old style German Christmas celebration.

The town's other archive is the **Historic Hermann Museum**, housed in the 1871 German School Building. It offers exhibits on Germanic arts and crafts and the town's history; (573) 486-2017; *www.historichermann.com*.

Two wineries are close by. The imposing 1847 **Stone Hill Winery** occupies a high point above town just off Twelfth Street. It has a restaurant and it offers tours and tasting; (800) 909-WINE or (573) 486-2129; *www.stonehillswinery.com*. You can sip assorted reds and whites at the brick **Hermannhof Winery** at 330 E. First St.; (800) 393-0100; *www.hermannhoff.com*.

Where to learn more

Hermann Area Chamber of Commerce, 207-A Schiller St., Hermann, MO 65041; (573) 486-2313; *www.hermannmo.info*.

Missouri Wine & Grape Board, P.O. Box 630, Jefferson City MO 65102; (800) 392-WINE; *www.missouriwine.org*.

New Haven Chamber of Commerce, 415 Charles Cook Plaza, New Haven, MO 65068; (573) 237-3830; *www.newhavenmo.com*.

Washington Area Chamber of Commerce, 323 W. Main St., Washington, MO 63090; (636) 239-2715; *www.washmo.org*.

Ste. Genevieve

An old French village in "Upper Louisiana"

⚑

Sitting comfortably near the banks of the Mississippi River, charming Ste. Genevieve is oldest city in the state and one of the oldest west of that great stream. It's in southeastern Missouri, in a region so history-rich that it's called the River Heritage Area.

The town's name is frankly French, and the chamber of commerce boasts that it's the only original French Colonial village left in the country. It is indeed an intriguing place, although later German and American settlers have given it an architectural mix. National Geographic's *Guide to Small Town Escapes* called it "one of the most fascinating small towns in America."

St. Genevieve was established somewhere around 1750 when this region was still part of France, called Upper Louisiana. French trappers likely had sought beaver in the area as early as the 1730s. The 1750s group came to stay, selecting a clear area in the riverside woods where they could set up a trading post, plow and plant. Initially, Ste. Genevieve was right on the edge of the Mississippi, then frequent flooding forced occupants to move their homes and shops inland.

Naming their town for the patron saint of Paris, the settlers built sturdy French-Creole style homes from logs and local stone. Their fields were fertile, river traffic encouraged trade and the town prospered, once rivaling St. Louis in size. Today, its 5,000 or so citizens are so proud of their town's heritage that they celebrate Bastille Day and other French holidays.

Although the usual motels and service stations are on the fringes of Ste. Genevieve, the downtown area is one of the nation's best preserved historic districts. Shops along its narrow streets sell imported giftwares, embroidery, candles, old fashioned candies, antiques and local wines. Nearly a dozen bed & breakfast inns and two venerable hotels offer lodgings.

The village is on the Great River Road, a scenic-historic highway that follows the Mississippi River from New Orleans to the Canadian border. The local **Great River Road Interpretive Center** on Main Street performs double duty as the town's visitor facility. Exhibits and videos tell Ste. Genevieve's story. Folks here will provide a walking tour map and point you in proper historic directions. Ask about candlelight tours of some of the old homes, which will really send you back to the town's earliest days.

Most of the visitor lures are authentically restored and furnished homes. From the center, walk two blocks to the 1770 **Bolduc House** at 125 S. Main Street, regarded as the finest restored French Colonial home in America.

With a stone foundation and walls and a steeply-pitched truss roof, it employs architecture that dates back to the medieval Normans. Next door, the 1820 **Bolduc-LeMeilleur House** exhibits a blend of French and American architecture; (573) 883-3105.

The **Felix Vallé House State Historic Site** at Second and Merchant streets preserves an 1818 Federalist style structure built of sturdy stone. The Vallés were among the town's leading citizens. The 1792 **St. Gemme Beauvais-Amoureux House,** overlooking the first settlers' fields, is a vertical log structure built something like a palisade. The technique is called *poteaux-en-terre* or post-in-ground. Only five of homes of this style survive in the U.S. and three are in Ste. Genevieve. The St. Gemme house is part of the state historic site; (573) 883-7102; *www.mostateparks.com/felixvalle.htm.*

Another *poteaux-en-terre* structure is the 1784 **Maison de Guilbourd-Vallé** at Fourth and Merchant streets, with classic French furniture and European and Asian antiques; (573) 883-7544. While you're here, check out the imposing 1876 Gothic Revival style **Church of Ste. Genevieve** on De-Bourge Place; (573) 883-2731.

The small **Ste. Genevieve Museum** at Merchant and Third streets displays the usual early-day artifacts, plus some bird specimens mounted by John James Audubon during a brief stay in the village; (573) 883-3461. Follow Merchant Street to the **Memorial Cemetery**, where you'll find French-engraved headstones dating back more than two centuries.

If you'd like to see what the area was like even before the first French settlers came, check out a couple of nearby nature preserves. **Hawn State Park** covers nearly 5,000 acres of woodlands, sandstone bluffs and waterways. It's twenty miles southwest of Ste. Genevieve off State Route 32. A ten-mile hiking trail leads to a region so quiet and remote that it's called the Whispering Pines Wild Area. Park facilities include a ranger office, campsites and picnic areas; (573) 883-360 3; *www.mostateparks.com/hawn.htm.*

Just to the west is **Pickle Springs Natural Area**, an imposing region of carved sandstone shapes, canyons, creeks and waterfalls. A two-mile trail winds through the area's natural wonders. There are no services, so bring water and snacks.

Where to learn more

Great River Road Interpretive Center, 66 S. Main St., Ste. Genevieve, MO 63670; (800) 373-7007 or (573) 883-7097; *www.ste-genevieve.com.*

Ste. Genevieve Chamber of Commerce, 251 Market St., Ste. Genevieve, MO 63670; (573) 883-3686; *www.saintegenevieve.org.*

Claremore
Remembering the Cherokee Kid

ᛈ

I think the time will come when everybody will be made to stop off at Claremore on their way to any place they may be going. — Will Rogers

America's greatest humorist and Oklahoma's most famous son is enshrined in this prairie town northeast of Tulsa. Like Independence, Missouri, and Harry Truman, Claremore is absorbed with the memories of one man.

William Penn Adair Rogers was born on a nearby cattle ranch in 1879 when this was still the Indian Territory. Not much for schooling, he grew up just wanting to be a cowboy. Then a former slave who worked on the ranch taught him his first roping tricks and he was hooked. He dropped out of school and, at age seventeen, joined a South America-bound wild west show as the Cherokee Kid.

His trick roping skills soon carried him to the *Ziegfeld Follies* in New York. A born entertainer with dry wit and a shy grin, he began adding humorous comments to his act. Will's fame spread and his talents broadened. Before he died in a plane crash in Alaska in 1933, he was famous as a vaudeville and Hollywood star, an author, a syndicated columnist, a radio commentator and the world's foremost political humorist.

"I am not a member of any organized party," he once quipped. "I am a Democrat."

The story of Will Rogers is told at two historic sites in the area, the Will Rogers Memorial Museum in Claremore and the Will Rogers Birthplace Ranch near Oologah, an old cowtown a few miles north.

The **Will Rogers Memorial Museum** is a large sandstone complex on a hill overlooking Claremore, with nine galleries, three theaters and the Rogers' family tomb; 1720 W. Will Rogers Blvd.; (800) 324-9455 or (918) 341-0719; *www.willrogers.com*. Visitors can spend a couple of hours or a couple of days here. The museum is busy with Rogers memorabilia including artifacts, photos and manuscripts, a saddle collection and Western art. Rogers enthusiasts can watch some of the seventy-one movies he made, including *The Ropin' Fool*, a 1922 silent film about his rope tricks, which he produced.

Rogers was born on the 60,000-acre Dog Iron Ranch, where his father Clem Rogers ran 10,000 head of Texas longhorns. The **Will Rogers Birthplace Ranch** two miles northeast of Oologah has shrunk to 400 acres, although it's still a working cattle spread; (918) 341-0719 *www.willrogers. com/ranch*. The large two-story log ranch house has rustic period furnishings and it contains assorted family memorabilia. Videos about Rogers' career are shown in a replicated 19th century barn. A few Texas longhorns and other critters wander about to lend the ranch authenticity. The complex also has an RV park, a lake and even a grass landing strip.

Tiny *Oologah*, with fewer than a thousand folks, honors Will with a statue of the Cherokee Kid on the town square. The **Oologah Historical Museum** at Maple and Cooweescoowee streets contains more Rogers memorabilia; (918) 443-2934. The 1906 **Bank of Oologah**, closed during the Depression, exhibits period bank furnishings and tellers' cages.

Meanwhile, back in Claremore, there's more to this community of 16,000 citizens than Will Rogers memories. Well, a little more. It's a pleasant, well-tended old cowtown where stores sell saddles, bridles, Western wear and feed. It's also a serious antiquing center, with more than 450 dealers, plus a few specialty shops and boutiques.

If you like weaponry, head for the **J.M. Davis Arms & Historical Museum** at 333 N. Lynn Riggs Blvd.; (918) 341-5707; *www.thegunmuseum. com*. It exhibits what is claimed to be the world's largest private gun collection, with more than 20,000 items. They range from blunder busses to antique machine guns. The collection includes several weapons used by famous outlaws, plus thousands of other bits of Western memorabilia.

Incidentally, Will wasn't Claremore's only famous person. The main drag (Highway 66) was named in honor of Lynn Riggs. Lynn who? She was the author of "Green Grow the Lilacs." The play was used as the basis for that fancifully silly Rogers and Hammerstein musical, *Oklahoma!*.

Even with its Western wear stores, antique malls and huge gun museum, it's difficult to avoid Will in this town. He once said "All I know is what I read in the newspapers" and his face adorns the masthead of the *Claremore Daily Progress*. There's a bronze of him in front of the newspaper office at 3515 W. Will Rogers Boulevard. He's sitting on a bench and reading a copy of the *Progress*. Today's society certainly could use his wry wit and wisdom, which is as timely now as it was in his day:

You can't say civilization isn't advancing: in every war, they kill you in a new way.

Where to learn more

Claremore Convention & Visitors Bureau, 419 W. Will Rogers Blvd., Claremore, OK 74017; (877) 341-9688 or (918) 341-8688; *www.visitclaremore.org*.

Guthrie
A fine old town that history left behind

⚑

Few people outside the Southern Heartland have heard of Guthrie, although it was in its day one of the most famous towns in these parts. Further, it has what may be America's largest National Historic District.

Sitting smack dab in the middle of Oklahoma, Guthrie was born overnight or, more accurately, during one wild and crazy afternoon. At high noon, there was no town and no residents. By sundown, Guthrie was born, with a population of about ten thousand.

You've likely guessed that we're talking about the Great Oklahoma Land Rush, or President Harrison's Hoss Race. In the early 1800s, land here was designated as the Indian Territory. Five Eastern tribes were forcibly relocated, including the Cherokees on their tragic "Trail of Tears." Then in 1889, Congress declared that all "unused" land—two million acres of native hunting grounds on the Cherokee Strip—would be opened for settlers.

Precisely at noon, April 22, 1889, cannons were fired and tens of thousands of people raced hell-bent-for-leather across the prairie—on horseback, in surreys and afoot. However, thousands more had jumped the gun, staking out their claims before the others arrived. This earned Oklahoma its nickname of the "Sooner State."

The site of Guthrie had been pre-selected for the new territorial capital, and it was center stage for the land rush. Thousands of tents went up overnight, and within a few months, sturdy brick buildings were rising. Better Sooner than late, these folks had come to stay. Their town became the capital of the new state in 1907. However, the state government was shifted south to Oklahoma City in 1910, and Guthrie went into a slump.

Today, Oklahoma City thrives and Guthrie preserves its past. Ironically, its population is about the same as it was on Day One. However, with 2,169 buildings in its historic district, it has become popular with visitors. In 2002, the town was named one of a "Dozen Distinctive Destinations" by the National Trust for Historic Preservation. Guthrie's handsome town center of red brick buildings is busy with boutiques, antique shops, art galleries, cafés and museums. Some of the first business blocks were designed by Belgian architect Joseph Pierre Foucart, who was here the day the cannons roared. He gave Guthrie its distinctive European look with brick cobbled streets, arched stained glass windows and intricate bas relief façades.

Historic sites abound in this town where history suddenly started and then suddenly stopped. Exhibits at the **Oklahoma Territorial Museum** focus mostly on the land rush. It's at 406 E. Oklahoma Ave.; (405) 282-1889. Within the complex is a 1903 Carnegie Library building where the first state governor was sworn in. The **State Capital Publishing Museum** occupies a grand old brick building that housed the territory's first newspaper at 301 N. Harrison St.; (405) 282-4123. It's now a museum with a dual role, telling the story of early publishing and of the settlement of Oklahoma.

Check out the imposing 1929 **Guthrie Scottish Rite Temple** at 900 E. Oklahoma Avenue. Occupying the site originally set aside for the state capitol, this massive structure is one of the world's largest Masonic centers. The architecture is eclectic to say the least—Greek Revival, Victorian, Gothic, Egyptian and a little native American. Call for tour times; (405) 282-1281; *www.guthriescottishrite.org.*

The **Oklahoma Frontier Pharmacy Museum** is a turn-of-the-last-century drug store operated by the state pharmacists association, at 214 W. Oklahoma Ave.; (405) 282-1895. It has an old fashioned soda fountain, early-day potions and a large collection of apothecary bottles. It's on the site of the Lillie Drug Store, the territory's first pharmacy. If you like pickin' and strummin', head for the **National Four-String Banjo Hall of Fame** at 116 E. Oklahoma Ave.; (405) 260-1323; *www.banjomuseum.org.* This small museum exhibits antique banjos and it has a performance hall for concerts.

The **Oklahoma Sports Museum** honors the state's college, Olympic and professional athletic heroes, at 315 W. Oklahoma Ave.; (405) 260-1342; *www.oklahomasportsmuseum.com.* Its inductees include Jim Thorpe, Steve Largent and five Oklahoma Heisman Trophy winners.

The classic red brick **Old Santa Fe Depot** at 409 W. Oklahoma Avenue is an active Amtrak station. It also houses the **International Model Train & Automobile Museum** with elaborate track layouts and hundreds of miniature die-cast antique and modern cars; (405) 260-0707. And it's home to the old fashioned **Harvey House Bakery-Café- Pizzeria**; (405) 260-0723.

If you're a fan of country music, stop at the **Double Stop Fiddle Shop and Music Hall** at 121 E. Oklahoma Ave.; (405) 282-6646; *www.doublestop.com.* You can browse among fiddles and guitars by day, then have a barbecue dinner and listen to amazing fiddle playing at night. The professional **Pollard Theatre** offers a season of comedies and dramas at 120 W. Harrison St.; (405) 282-2800; *www.thepollard.org.*

Where to learn more

Guthrie Convention & Visitors Bureau, P.O. Box 995 (212 W. Oklahoma Ave.), Guthrie, OK 73044; (800) 299-1889 or (405) 282-1947; *www.guthrieok.com.*

El Paso
From cowtown to metropolis

> *Out in the west Texas town of El Paso*
> *I fell in love with a Mexican girl.*
> *Night time would find me in Rosa's cantina*
> *Music would play and Feleena would whirl.*
> **— El Paso by Marty Robbins**

If you visit El Paso, you'll find it difficult to picture the dusty cowtown in Marty Robbins' beautifully lyrical song about tragic love between a cowboy and a wicked señorita.

Call it a cowtown and a friendly local might offer an indulgent grin. Then he'll point out that El Paso has more than fifteen museums, an opera company, a symphony orchestra, a chamber music group and several theater companies. Toss in a performing arts center, historic sites, the flavor of Old Mexico, America's largest urban wilderness park and a sunny climate, and you've got one of the most underrated tourist destinations in the country.

With more than half a million people, this "cowtown" is the fourth largest city in Texas and America's largest border town. Across the Río Grande is Mexico's Ciudad Juárez, an city of two million, which contributes to El Paso's rich Tex-Mex atmosphere.

To be sure, El Paso hasn't shaken off all its trail dust. Yesterday lingers in some weathered old neighborhoods, and the occasional good old boy saloon. Historic sites and museum exhibits speak of the town's raucous past, when señoritas as "wild as the west Texas wind" danced in Mexican cantinas. This is no trendy Santa Fe style resort town, and it's not in a pretty setting. It's in desert country, and the steep surrounding hills are dry and rocky, stubbled with cactus. However, it's a fascinating old town with attractions as diverse as its population. Also, consider it as a base for visiting **Guadalupe Mountains** and **Carlsbad Caverns** national parks and **White Sands National Monument**, just short drives away.

Downtown is a mix of modern and rustic and, for a city of its size, it's surprisingly compact—if rather tilted. El Paso is built between two mountain ranges, and it's on an upslope from the Río Grande. For a quick introduction to this old bordertown, stop by the **Convention & Visitors Bureau** in the El Paso Convention & Performing Arts Center. You can pick up a walking map that directs you to twenty-two historic sites.

Also, you can get border crossing information here, should you want to check out the shops, cafés and nightclubs of *Ciudad Juárez*. You can take an **El Paso-Juárez Trolley** from the visitors bureau (915/544-0062) or park on the American side of the border and walk across the **Santa Fe Street Bridge** to Juárez Avenue, the main tourist area. Passports aren't required for short visits. Crime is probably no worse in Ciudad Juárez than any large American city, although tourists who wander off might be mugging targets.

Driving El Paso can be frustrating if you're navigationally challenged, since it's warped between the meandering Río Grande and the foothills of the Franklin Mountains. Streets tend to gallop off in all directions.

This street pattern does offer some scenic drives, notably into 24,300-acre **Franklin Mountain State Park**, which rises above town. Views of the great sprawl of El Paso and Ciudad Juárez and the curving Río Grande are grand from here. Trails lead to higher peaks, or you can take the **Wyler Aerial Tramway** to Ranger Peak; (800) 792-1112 or (915) 566-6622.

While you're at the visitor center, pick up an **El Paso Mission Trail** driving map that leads to three nearby Spanish missions, which will give you insight into the town's earliest days.

El Paso is the oldest settlement in Texas and one of the oldest in America, an outgrowth of the 1682 Mission Nuestra Señora del Carmen. Its full Spanish name is *El Paso del Río del Norte,* the pass through the river of the north. It occupies a critical point between the river and mountains on *El Camino Real,* the King's Road that linked the early mission settlements.

After Texas won its independence from Mexico in 1836, El Paso continued to thrive as a stopover on the old mission trail, served by the Butterfield Overland Mail. With the arrival of the rails in 1881, it became an important shipping center and a wild cowtown. The legendary Texas Rangers were formed to keep order. Today it thrives on agriculture, manufacturing, international trade and—of course—tourism.

We've talked so enthusiastically about the city that we left little room for specifics. Your "A" list should include the **Chamizal National Memorial**, (915) 532-7273; **El Paso Centennial Museum** at the University of Texas, (915) 747-5565; **Insights—El Paso Science Center**, (915) 534-0000; the desert-based **El Paso Museum of Archaeology**, (915) 775-4332; the **El Paso Museum of Art**, (915) 532-1707; and—appropriate to this area—the **National Border Patrol Museum**, (915) 759-6060.

Where to learn more

El Paso Convention & Visitors Bureau, One Civic Center Plaza, El Paso, TX 79901; (800) 351-6024 or (915) 534-0600; *www.elpasocvb.com.*

Fort Davis to Big Bend
An historic desert town and a Texas wilderness

卪

$\mathbf{A}$t Fort Davis National Historic site, it's easy to picture John Wayne squinting into the Texas sun in the Western epic, *She Wore a Yellow Ribbon*. This is the Texas you may have pictured as a kid—dusty wide open spaces and rocky slopes where the bad guys hid from the posse, or the Apaches waited to ambush the cavalry.

Then as you travel south through the Chihuahuan Desert to Big Bend National Park, your early Texas visions are further confirmed. The region's arid mountain ranges and strange desert plants and animals are suggestive of northern Mexico. In those old Western movies, the bad guys often tried to cross the Río Grande to seek sanctuary south of the border.

Fort Davis is both a desert town and an early Army post, one beside the other. Both were named for Jefferson Davis, who was secretary of war when the fort was established in 1854. *Fort Davis*, the town, is a tiny high desert village with barely a thousand residents. It occupies an imposing setting among the rugged, brushy palisades of the Black Mountains. The town developed as a ranching and provisioning center on the Butterfield Overland Mail route, which cut through nearby Limpia Creek Canyon.

The old Western style town is a popular tourist retreat for folks who come to play in the surrounding Davis Mountains. It's busy with specialty shops and bed & breakfast inns. Since it's nearly a mile above sea level, weather extremes are rare. The downtown area is a National Historic District and the **Overland Trail Museum** at Third and Fort streets recalls the region's early days; (432) 426-3904. Among the more interesting buildings around the old fashioned town square are the 1906 Union Mercantile which now houses the Jeff Davis County Library, the 1911 Jeff Davis County Courthouse and the 1913 Fort Davis State Bank with old fashioned teller's cages. The sturdy stone 1913 **Hotel Limpia** still takes guests; (800) 662-5517 or (432) 426-3237; *www.hotellimpia.com*.

Fort Davis, the fort, was established to protect travelers and ranchers along the early stage route. It was abandoned during the Civil War, then it was later rebuilt and reoccupied to curb continuing "Indian troubles" in the area. The legendary African-American Buffalo Solders were stationed here, and they led the fight to quell the last of the uprisings. Ten buildings of the second fort have been restored. Exhibits recall the days when one oppressed minority group chased another across the desert and into the rugged mountains; (432) 426-3224; *www.nps.gov/foda*.

Just four miles away is **Davis Mountains State Park** with hiking trails, picnic areas and campsites among foothill grasslands and volcanic dikes; (432) 426-2227. Watch for Texas high desert critters such as the javalina (wild boar), desert pronghorns and horny toads. A seventy-four mile scenic loop twists through the gnarled ramparts of the Davis Mountains, passing **McDonald Observatory**, one of the world's top astronomical research institutes; (432) 426-3640; *www.mcdonaldobservatory.org*. It has a visitor center with astronomy exhibits and it sponsors "star parties" three nights a week, when folks can scope out the heavens.

Heading southeast from Fort Davis on State Route 118, you'll soon encounter *Alpine*, in a popular outdoor region called the Texas Alps, which is an exaggeration. It's considered a gateway to Big Bend National Park, although it's nearly a hundred miles north of there. However, with 6,000 residents, it's the only town of any size in this high desert region and it has several places to dine and recline. The **Museum of the Big Bend** on the campus of Sul Ross State University does a fine job with its area history and natural science exhibits; (432) 837-8143; *www.sulross.edu/~museum*.

Big Bend National Park is of course named for the great sweeping curve in the Río Grande that creates a fat peninsula between Texas and Mexico. This is the state's only true wilderness, a vast expanse of rocky Chihuahuan desert, eroded volcanic plugs, piñon pine-clad peaks and steep river canyons. Wildlife ranges from javalinas to cougars and bears, and the park is an excellent bird-watching area. This is a grand place for getting away from crowds, since Big Bend gets only about 300,000 visitors a year.

Coming from Alpine, you'll reach the park at the hamlet of *Sturdy Butte*. From there, U.S. 385 leads east to the visitor center at **Panther Junction**. This 801,163-acre park is mostly the domain of hikers and floaters on the relatively calm Río Grande. However, it also offers a variety of ranger programs and guided walks. Two twisting scenic routes, Rio Grande Village Drive and Ross Maxwell Drive, penetrate the wilderness to the river.

Rooms are available at the historic **Chisos Mountains Lodge** built by the Depression-era Civilian Conservation Corps; (432) 477-2291; *www.chisosmountainlodge.com*. Reservations should be made well in advance.

Where to learn more

Big Bend National Park, P.O. Box 129, Big Bend National Park, TX 79834; (432) 477-2251; *www.nps.gov/bibe*; and *Big Bend Area Travel Association*; (877) 244-2363; *www.visitbigbend.com*.

Fort Davis Chamber of Commerce, P.O. Box 378 (4 Memorial Square), Fort Davis, TX 79734; (800) 524-3015; *www.fortdavis.com*.

Fredericksburg and LBJ
Apple strudel and politics in Texas Hill Country

⚑

The great heartland of Texas is called the Hill Country, a lumpy region of wooded hills, bluffs, streams and lakes spreading outward from San Antonio and Austin like rippled water rings on a pond.

The area is dotted with old German towns built around traditional market squares, with steepled community *kirches* that served as places of worship and social centers. The towns were established when thousands of Germans fled their homeland during a period of religious and economic troubles in the mid-1800s. Through the decades, the émigrés adopted the ways of Texas farmers and cowmen, and words like *schuetzenfest* (shooting contest) and *saengerfest* (community sing) became part of their language.

Most of the state's fifty or so wineries are located in the Texas Hill Country. Visitors can sip the essence of the grape out among the vineyards or in tasting rooms in many of the communities.

The region also is the ancestral home of former President Lyndon Baines Johnson. And by ancestral, we mean that the Johnson family settled in the region more than 150 years ago. The small ranch town of Johnson City was founded by a distant LBJ cousin, James Polk Johnson.

LBJ aside—for the moment, at least—the most appealing town in these parts is *Fredericksburg*. Its citizens have worked to preserve its Germanic-Texan charm with half-timbered (*fachwerk*) buildings and covered sidewalks. Aside from occasional *fachwerk* examples, the town looks more Texan than Teutonic, although its heritage survives in place names and German bakeries, brewpubs, sausage-makers and cafés.

Fredericksburg's charm has generated considerable visitor interest, which in turn has generated more than a hundred boutiques, specialty shops and antique stores around **Market Square**. Artists also have been drawn to the region, and downtown has a good number of galleries, many featuring Western art. Fredericksburg and nearby Kerrville have earned a shared spot in John Villani's *The 100 Best Small Art Towns in America*.

The town's dual heritage is evident in its many stores and galleries, and folks from San Antonio, Austin and well beyond come to shop. A favorite stop for urban cowboys, including several Western TV and movie stars, is **Texas Jacks**, which sells fancy duds for dudes. It's at 117 N. Adams St.; (800) 839-5225; *www.texasjacks.com*. The three-story **Homestead** focuses on high end European and contemporary American furniture and decorator items, at 230 E. Main St.; (830) 997-5551; *www.homesteadstores.com*.

Visitors are drawn by the town's museums as well. To explore its Teutonic heritage, head for the octagonal *Vereins Kirche*, the former Society Church on Market Square; (830) 997-2835. Nearby is the **Pioneer Museum** at 309 W. Main St.; (830) 990-8441; *www.pioneermuseum.com*. It's an extensive complex with a combined home and general mercantile in an 1849 stone building, plus two historic homes, a barn, smokehouse, a one-room school and a "Sunday house." These were tiny cottages used by farming and ranching families from distant rural areas when they came to town for Saturday shopping and Sunday church.

An archive of quite a different sort is the **National Museum of the Pacific War**. It occupies the 1852 Steamboat Hotel building and focuses on the Pacific theater of World War II. Why so far from the ocean? Admiral Chester W. Nimitz, commander of the Pacific theater, was born in Fredericksburg and his German grandfather built the unusual steamboat-shaped hotel. It's at 340 E. Main St.; (830) 997-4379; *www.nimitz-museum.org*. A large display of military equipment is nearby.

LBJ country

Johnson City is thirty miles east of Fredericksburg on U.S. 290. About halfway there, near the hamlet of *Stonewall*, you'll encounter **Lyndon B. Johnson National Historical Park**; (830) 868- 7128; *www.nps.gov/lyjo*. This is the LBJ Ranch, which served as the "Texas White House" during Johnson's presidency. Access is by shuttle bus from the visitor center near the highway. Facilities include the original ranch buildings, a reconstruction of the house where LBJ was born, and the Johnson family plot where he and Lady Bird are buried. It's also a working cattle ranch, reflecting the 1960s when Johnson brought the White House to Texas.

The adjacent **Lyndon B. Johnson State Park and Historic Site** features exhibits on the Texas Hill Country and the Johnson family, plus the excellent **Sauer-Beckman Living History Farm**; (830) 644-2252; *www.tpwd .state.tx.us/park/lbj*. Here, costumed docents recreate life on a late 19th century Texas-German farm.

Continuing into the small farm and ranching town of *Johnson City*, you'll encounter **Johnson's Boyhood Home** on Lady Bird Lane, another element of the LBJ National Historical Park; (830) 868-7128. It contains the small white clapboard house where the former president grew up.

Where to learn more

Fredericksburg Convention & Visitors Bureau, 302 E. Austin St., Fredericksburg, TX 78624; (888) 997-3600 or (830) 997-5623; *www.fredericksburg-texas.com*.

Grapevine
Vintage buildings and a vintage train

ꔷ

Despite its name, Grapevine isn't the Napa Valley of Texas. One of the oldest towns in the northern part of the state, it's named for the tart mustang grape that once grew wild in the region. With a nicely preserved 19th century downtown and several historic sites, it has become a popular visitor destination.

This town of about 42,000 isn't way out there on the prairie somewhere among the wild grape vines. It's sandwiched between big and busy Dallas and Fort Worth, one of the state's largest metropolitan areas. Getting there is at least half the fun, because a vintage steam train provides service from Fort Worth.

Settlement began in the area in the 1840s, then a post office was opened in 1854, initially called Grape Vine. As Dallas and Fort Worth mushroomed around it, the old town began to shrivel. Between 1914 and 1925, its population dropped from 1,200 to 821. Then the Dallas-Fort Worth International Airport opened on Grapevine's southern edge in 1974 and the opposite happened. Its population zoomed and concerned citizens wanted to preserved its historic elements. Much of this has been the work of the **Grapevine Heritage Foundation** which raises funds to purchase and restore historic sites; (817) 410-3126; *www.grapevineheritagefoundation.com.*

Today, thanks to the work of the foundation and others, seventy-five buildings in the Main Street Historic District are listed on the National Register of Historic Places. During the early 1990s, a heritage center and a country music organization called the Grapevine Opry were established, and the Grapevine Vintage Railroad began running its steam trains between the here and Fort Worth.

Perhaps inspired by the town's name, seven Texas wineries have opened tasting rooms in Grapevine, even though the area isn't busy with vineyards. Further, it's home to the Texas Wine and Grape Growers Association; (817) 424-0570; *www.twgga.org.*

With this assortment of lures, plus several art galleries, boutiques and antique shops, the town has become a full-fledged—if small—tourist destination. Consider it as a side trip if you're visiting in the *Dallas-Fort Worth* area, or perhaps use it has your base of operations. Grapevine has an abundance of lodgings, since it's adjacent to the international airport.

If it's practical, come to town aboard one of the elegant old passenger cars of the **Grapevine Vintage Railroad**, pulled by "Puffy," an 1896 locomotive; (817) 625-3185; *grapevinevintagerailroad.com*. The only operating 19th century steam train in Texas, it runs from Fort Worth's Stockyard Station to the Cotton Belt Depot in Grapevine. Another run follows the route of the old Chisholm Trail through the southwestern area of Fort Worth. If you're already in Grapevine, a round trip excursion to Fort Worth includes a three-hour layover in the historic stockyards district.

Grapevine's historic area is easily walkable since it occupies only a few square blocks. It has been dressed up with several bronze artworks, including "The Nightwatchman" who stands atop the Grapevine City Hall. It honors the men who patrolled the town every night until the 1950s, checking for unlocked doors and even rounding up stray dogs.

The town's best attraction is the **Grapevine Heritage Center**, a complex that includes the 1901 Cotton Belt Depot, which houses the Grapevine Historical Museum. The Heritage Center, part of the Cotton Belt Railroad Historic District, also has the Grapevine Visitor Information Center, a restored pioneer home, a blacksmith shop, and glass-blowing and bronze foundries where visitors can watch artists at work. The complex is at 701 S. Main St.; (817) 481-0516; *www.grapevineheritagefoundation.com*.

The **Palace Arts Center** hosts plays, concerts and films, and it exhibits the works of local and regional artists, at 300 S. Main St.; (817) 410-3100; *www.palace-theatre.com*. A former theater and then a grocery store, it was converted into a performing and visual arts center by the heritage foundation. The **Grapevine Opry** offers Western variety shows on Saturday nights at the Palace and it often books top country entertainers; (817) 481-8733; *www.gvopry.com*.

If you're in a shopping mood, head for **Grapevine Mills** mall, with fifteen "anchor stores" and more than 200 stores, specialty shops and restaurants at 3000 Grapevine Mills Pkwy.; (972) 724-4900; *www.grapevinemills. com*. It's the largest outlet mall in the Southwest. And if you're in a fishing or boating mood, head for **Grapevine Lake** just outside of town. It's a reservoir on the Elm Fork of the Trinity River; (817) 481-4541.

By the time you reach Grapevine, the **Nash Farm** on the edge of town may be functioning as a living history center, with demonstrations of early-day farming activities. One of the few small farms left in the region, it's another project of the Grapevine Heritage Foundation; (817) 410-3126.

Where to learn more

Grapevine Convention & Visitors Bureau, One Liberty Park Plaza, Grapevine, TX 76051; (800) 457-6338 or (817) 410-3185; *www.grapevinetexasusa.com*.

The Gulf Coast
Charming old beach towns and wildlife retreats

Most folks heading for the beach in Texas head either for Corpus Christi or Galveston. They're the two largest resort towns and the only cities of size along the Texas Gulf Coast. We prefer the smaller beach towns in between. Many are charming or cozy, sometimes both, and they lack the traffic and crowds of the two larger communities.

November through April is the best time to play along the Texas shoreline, since summer days often are muggy. The topography of the Gulf Coast is absolutely flat. Only the thin line of the surf seems to separate water from land. Although Houston is fifty miles inland, it's just thirty-eight feet above sea level. Despite its flatness, the terrain presents a very dimensional picture, from huge chemical plants to cotton fields to bird-busy wetlands to boat-busy marinas.

And there's plenty to do. You can camp in state parks, book charter fishing boats in the small towns, swim, snorkel or scuba, or just lie in the sand. Low barrier islands extend along most of the gulf shore, creating the sheltered Intracoastal Waterway that's a natural aquatic playground. If you're a birder, you'll be in bird heaven here, for this is a terminal point for the Central Flyway and one of the best bird-watching areas in the country.

Begin by heading south from *Galveston* to **Galveston Island State Park**, which offers camping, hiking and water sports; (409) 737-1222; *www.tpwd.state.tx.us.* Just below is the private resort community of *Jamaica Beach*. Pressing southward, you'll re-join the mainland at *Brazosport*, which isn't a town but a collection of small communities. The Brazos and San Bernard rivers empty into the gulf here, forming a delta lacework of marshes, bayous and beaches. Three National Wildlife Refuges, **Brazoria, San Bernard** and **Big Boggy**, are busy with critters ranging from great flocks of snow geese to armadillos to grinning 'gators; (409) 849-6062; *www.fws.gov/southwest/refuges/texas*

Three attractions in the area are worth a pause. The excellent **Center for the Arts and Sciences** is a combined science museum, performing arts and visual arts center, at 300 College Drive in *Clute*; (979) 265-7661; *www.bcfas.org*. The **Brazos County Historical Museum** preserves the area's memories in the century-old former Brazoria County Courthouse, at 100 E. Cedar Street in *Angelton*; (979) 864-1208; *www.bchm.org*. Gulf Coast aquatic life is the focus of the **Sea Center Texas** aquarium, which also has a large fish hatchery, at 300 Medical Drive in *Lake Jackson*; (979) 299-1808.

Continue southwest, and at *Port Lavaca*, follow State Route 35 to the 115,000-acre **Aransas National Wildlife Refuge**; (361) 286-3559; *www. fws.gov/southwest/refuges/aransas*. It's the winter home for the world's largest flock of the endangered whooping crane, America's biggest bird. A sixteen-mile scenic drive passes through the refuge's diverse habitats.

And now, hurry on down to *Rockport*, the most charming town on the Texas Gulf Coast. Here, you can book a wildlife-watching boat tour into the Aransas refuge, which is the best way to see the whooping cranes. They're in the refuge from fall through spring, then they head north to Canada.

It seems that lots of folks love charming old Rockport, including editors of National Geographic's *Guide to Small Town Escapes* and John Villani's *The 100 Best Small Art Towns in America*. It is at once a beguiling old resort village and a working town. You'll see tractors tending cotton fields inland, and commercial fishermen working on their boats in the harbor.

Rockport and next-door *Fulton* share a population of about 8,000, although they're growing—and changing. Old shoreside motor courts are being replaced by marina-condo developments and big box stores are sprouting between Rockport and Fulton. Still, the area retains much of its charm, from fishing boats in the harbor to gnarled live oaks to the old palm-shaded, low-rise downtown area.

Artists and photographers are drawn here to capture the seacoast flavor of Rockport and images of wildlife in the Aransas Refuge. Several galleries share old storefronts with antique stores, boutiques and quaint cafés, and the town hosts the annual Rockport Art Festival in early July. The **Rockport Center for the Arts** is the major force in the region's cultural movement, with galleries, workshops and classes. It occupies a restored Victorian house at 902 Navigation Circle; (361) 729-5519; *www.rockportartcenter.org*.

If you can lure yourself from the town's mile-long public beach, visit the **Texas Maritime Museum** at 202 Navigation Circle; (361) 729-1271.It covers the state's nautical history from early French mariners to offshore oil rigs. A mockup of a ship's bridge provides a fine view of the harbor and Aransas Bay. In next-door Fulton, the extravagant 1877 home of a Texas cattle baron is the centerpiece of **Fulton Mansion State Historic Site**, at 316 S. Fulton Beach Rd.; (361) 729-0386; *www.tpwd.state.tx.us/spdest*.

Where to learn more

Rockport-Fulton Area Chamber of Commerce, 404 Broadway, Rockport, TX 78382; (800) 242-0071; *www.rockport-fulton.org*.

Brazosport Area Chamber of Commerce, 420 Highway 332 West, Brazosport, TX 77531; (979) 265-2506; *www.brazosport.org*.

LINCOLN LIBRARY, ILL.

Chapter Six

The
Great Lakes

A GREAT LAND DEFINED BY WATER

America's five Great Lakes comprise the world's largest inland water complex, covering more than 95,000 square miles. Linked to the Atlantic by the St. Lawrence Seaway, they provide water navigation nearly halfway across the country. Five states hang beneath the lakes, like leaves from a cluster of elongated grapes. They're part of the sturdy American midland and they offer a wide range of lures, from island resorts to Victorian villages and art colonies.

ILLINOIS is home to the great city of Chicago, where we picked up the Mother Road and followed it to the Land of Lincoln. We also explored the town where Frank Lloyd Wright created his distinctive architectural style, and a tiny Mississippi River town with nearly as many historic sites as citizens.

Where to learn more: Illinois Bureau of Tourism, 100 W. Randolph St., Ste. 3-400, Chicago, IL 6060; (800) 226-6632; *www.enjoyillinois.com.*

INDIANA is the "back home again" state, with little rural towns and covered bridges, which we discovered west of Indianapolis. We also found a lakeshore preserve in the midst of urban Indiana, and a small city that's big on leading-edge architecture.

Where to learn more: Indiana Department of Commerce & Tourism, One N. Capitol, Suite 700, Indianapolis, IN 46204-2288; (888) ENJOY-IN or (317) 2322-8860; *www.enjoyindiana.com.*

MICHIGAN is practically entangled in the Great Lakes, with four of these inland seas touching its borders. Three of our choices are on lake shorelines, peninsulas or islands. However, we started in Michigan's heartland to see if there really was a place called Kalamazoo.

Where to learn more: Travel Michigan, P.O. Box 30226, Lansing, MI 48909; (888) 78-GREAT; *www.michigan.org.*

OHIO is tucked up against Lake Erie and we explored its shoreline towns and island resorts. We found other discoveries in an historic "Riverboat Town" and in a small city noted for pottery and a famous author of Western novels.

Where to learn more: Ohio Division of Travel and Tourism, P.O. Box 1001, Columbus, OH 43216; (800) BUCKEYE; *www.discoverohio.com.*

WISCONSIN is America's Dairyland, although we didn't go there to smile and say "Cheese!" We headed for a peninsula famous for football and lakeshore resorts. We also visited one of America's most appealing capital cities, and an island preserve in Wisconsin's far north.

Where to learn more: Wisconsin Department of Tourism, P.O. Box 8690, Madison, WI 53708-8690; (800) 432-TRIP or (608) 266-2161; *www.travelwisconsin.com.*

Historic Highway 66
Getting your kicks through the Illinois heartland

It wasn't the longest highway completed during the road-building frenzy of the 1920s and 1930s. Route 66 reached from Chicago to L.A., while both U.S. 50 and U.S. 40 stretched from coast to coast.

However, no other highway in America has so captured the motoring public's hearts and fancies. Of course, old Highway 66 is the beneficiary of much publicity. In was the "Mother Road" in John Steinbeck's *The Grapes of Wrath*, about Dust Bowl migrants following the highway to their hoped-for California dreams. In 1946, songwriter Bobby Troupe invited folks to get their kicks on the famous highway, and Nat "King" Cole made the song famous. From 1960 until 1964, Martin Milner and George Maharis drove from one adventure to another in their Corvette convertible in *Route 66*, the TV series. (I always wondered where they put their luggage.)

Today, fans of the historic highway have become something of a cult, and scores of local groups are working to save old soda fountains, service stations and auto courts. All of the states along the route have government-backed Route 66 preservation programs.

And all of this history started in Illinois. Route 66 begins in Chicago, at Lakeshore Drive and Jackson Boulevard. Seven states and 2,400 miles later, it ends at the Pacific Ocean, near the Santa Monica Pier. Illinois has some of the best-preserved and most interesting sections of the highway, and protecting it has become something of a cottage industry. In towns along the route, folks are working to keep it signed and save old landmarks.

Following its 300-mile length from Chicago to St. Louis can be a fun outing. Both the **Illinois Bureau of Tourism** and **Illinois Department of Transportation** have issued folder-maps, available at most visitor bureaus.

The highway takes you through the state's heartland. Along the route, you can enjoy a chocolate malted at an old fashioned drive-in or a drugstore soda fountain, and you can lunch on America's first corn dog. Check out a display of Route 66 "Dream Cars" and visit service stations that have become Route 66 museums.

Navigating the highway is an interesting challenge, since some original sections have vanished and others have been re-aligned and offset to work around new development. You must be alert for brown "Historic Route 66" signs to stay the course. If you get lost, locals will get you back on track.

Buckingham Fountain in Chicago's Grant Park at Jackson Boulevard and Michigan Avenue is the official starting point for the famous highway. However, the *traditional* starting point is at **Lou Mitchell's Café**, which has been serving hefty meals since 1923. It's at 565 W. Jackson Blvd.; (312) 939-3111. With a Lou Mitchell breakfast under your belt, you can begin following those brown "Historic Route 66" signs south.

We don't have space to list all of the sights and diversions along the way, although these are our favorites.

In case you didn't stop at Lou Mitchell's for breakfast, take a break at **Dell Rhea's Chicken Basket** just south of Chicago in *Willowbrook* at 645 Joliet Rd.; (630) 325-0780. The place serves great fried chicken and it's cluttered with Highway 66 memorabilia. The 1926 **Rialto Theatre**, regarded as one of the most elaborate in America, has been meticulously restored and is open to public tours. The Rialto is in downtown *Joliet* at 102 N. Chicago St.; (815) 726-7171; *www.rialtosquare.com.*

The 1956 **Polk-a-Dot Drive In** is a fun stop. Statues of a skirt-blowing Marilyn, sulking James Dean and ditsy Betty Boops are outside, and interior walls are papered with Route 66 and 1950s-60s memorabilia. It's in *Braidwood* at 22 N. Front St.; (815) 458-3377; *www.polk-a-dot.com.* The 1932 **Odell Station**, one of several vintage gas stations along the route, is now a museum, with an old Standard Oil sign hanging out front and lots of memorabilia within. You'll find it in *Odell* at 400 S. West St.; (815) 998-2133. The **Dream Car Museum** displays about two dozen nostalgic American cars on Route 66 in *Williamsville*; (217) 566-3799.

In *Springfield*, seek out the 1946 **Shea's Gas Station** at 2075 Peoria Rd.; (217) 522-0475. It has one of the largest collections of motoring memorabilia along the entire length of the highway, from old gas pumps to antique tow trucks. Also in Springfield is the **Cozy Dog Drive In**, where Ed Waldmire fashioned America's first corn dog in 1949. You'll find it at 2935 S. Sixth St.; (217) 525-1992; *www.cozydogdrivein.com.*

Just south of Springfield, the 1926 **Soulsby Service Station** in *Mount Olive* is being restored by volunteers; (217) 525-2781. Your historic trek across the Illinois midlands ends at **Chain of Rocks Bridge** in *Morrison* at 3900 Reavis Barracks Rd.; (314) 416-9930. It was built in 1929 to carry Route 66 across the Mississippi River to St. Louis. Spanning more than a mile, it's now a pedestrian and cycling bridge offering nice river views.

Where to learn more

Illinois Route 66 Heritage Project, 700 E. Adams St., Springfield, IL 62701; (866) DRV-RT66 or (217) 525-7980; *www.illinoisroute66.org.*

Nauvoo
A peaceful place with a violent past

⚐

We didn't pick Nauvoo for this book because my great-great grandfather Joseph Grafton Hovey followed Brigham Young from there to Salt Lake City in 1845. (And my suppertime glass of wine suggests that I am not a follower of the faith)

We selected it because it's one of the most history-rich small towns in Illinois, and it occupies a pleasing setting, on a wooded bluff overlooking the Mississippi River.

Nauvoo represents one of the most violent chapters in the history of the Church of Jesus Christ of Latter-Day Saints. Founder Joseph Smith led his flock to this site in 1839 after being driven out of Missouri, accused of polygamy and other unsaintly practices. The industrious Mormons soon had a thriving community going, and they began construction on a temple.

However, the old troubles began brewing, worsened by Smith's own dictatorial ways. When a group of Mormon dissidents began publishing a newspaper critical of him in 1844, the church leader-mayor-justice of the peace ordered the printing press destroyed. A complaint was filed and he was jailed. Then an unruly mob of non-Mormons stormed the jail and assassinated Smith and his brother Hyrum. (In his journal, Great-great grandad Hovey reports witnessing the killing.) Brigham Young took over leadership of the church and led many of the Mormons west to establish Salt Lake City. However, some remained behind and created a new faction of the church.

A town of about a thousand souls, Nauvoo is a virtual living history center for this turbulent period of the church's past. It's still predominantly a Mormon town and in 2002, the imposing limestone **Nauvoo Illinois Temple** was completed at the site where the unfinished one had been burned. (In the Mormon faith, a temple has a status similar to a cathedral.) Only Mormons can enter the temple itself, although we heathen can see exhibits relating to their religion and watch a video at the adjacent Visitor Center. It's at Mulholland and Wells streets; (217) 453-6252; *www.lds.org*.

Folks at the **Historic Nauvoo Visitors Center** at Main and Young streets will orient you to the town and its past; (888) 453-6434 or (217) 453-2237; *www.historicnauvoo.net*. You can pick up walking tour maps for more than fifty historic structures, mostly made of sturdy brick. They include restored homes, and businesses such as a bakery, pharmacy, post office and boot and tin shops. You also can learn about Mormon history through exhibits and videos at the center, and arrange for guide service.

Three particularly significant structures in the historic district near the river are the **Brigham Young Home, Heber C. Kimball Home** and **Jonathan Browning Home and Gunshop.** Young resided in this house before leading his followers west and Kimball, his top advisor, became the leader of the church after his death. Both homes are furnished to the period. Browning followed Young west and set up a gun shop in Ogden, near Salt Lake City. Later, his son John Browning became history's greatest gunsmith, developing nearly all the firearms used from the late 1800s through World War I; see Chapter Three, page 146.

The other major attraction in town is the **Joseph Smith Historic Site** overlooking the Mississippi at 149 Water St.; (217) 453-2246; *www.cof-christ.org/js*. It's operated by the church group that stayed behind after Smith's assassination, now called the Community of Christ. Exhibits here include the original 1803 log cabin where Smith and his family first lived and the mansion that was later built for them. It contains some original Smith family furniture. Also on the site is the red brick general mercantile that Smith operated.

Nearby **Nauvoo State Park** preserves a brick home built by a Mormon family, with rooms exhibiting elements of the various stages of Nauvoo's history. It also has typical state park offerings such as a small lake, and picnicking and camping areas. The park is at State Route 96 and Parley Street; (217) 453-2512; *www.dnr.state.il.us*.

You may know that Mormons don't touch tobacco, caffeine or Demon Rum. Yet, the town hosts the **Nauvoo Grape Festival** in the state park over Labor Day weekend. Festivities include wine and cheese tastings, grape stomping, a carnival and arts and crafts exhibits.

Why? After most of the Mormons left town, a group of about 500 French and German immigrants called Icarians settled here in 1849 and set up a commune. Unlike the Latter-Day Saints, they had a taste for the grape, so they planted vineyards. Their communal living experiment didn't work out and most drifted away, leaving a number of wine cellars in their wake.

Folks discovered that old wine vaults made good cheese aging cellars, and this is still a serious cheese and wine producing area. **Baxter's Winery,** a mile east of the state park, welcomes visitors for touring and tasting; (800) 854-1396 or (217) 453-2528; *www.nauvoowinery*. It's the oldest winery in the state, run by descendants of an Icarian family that stayed on.

Where to learn more
Nauvoo Tourism Office, P.O. Box 500 (1295 Mulholland St.), Nauvoo, IL 62354; (877) 628-8661 or (217) 453-6648; *www.beautifulnauvoo.com*.

Oak Park

The home of Wright, Hemingway and—Tarzan?

⚐

Chicago is just too big and famous for inclusion in this book, but we like the grand old city so well that we've chosen one of its most interesting suburbs. Make it a side trip on your next visit to the Windy City.

A trip ten miles west to Oak Park is a journey back a hundred years. Technically administered as a big village and independent of Chicago's government, this town of about 53,000 is a showplace of grand 19th century Victorian, French and early American style homes. They doze contentedly in the shade of ancient oaks and elms, painting the picture of the classic upscale Middle American neighborhood.

Many of Oak Park's fine old structures were designed by Frank Lloyd Wright. The master architect had his home and studio here for twenty years, from 1889 until 1909. Another famous citizen was Ernest Hemingway. He was born and raised here, and graduated from a local high school before setting forth to make his indelible mark on the literary world. Apparently he was glad to leave Oak Park, once referring to it as a town of "broad lawns and narrow minds," which is no longer true. Another famous citizen was Edgar Rice Burroughs, who came up the idea of Tarzan while living here early in the last century.

Twenty-seven Wright-designed homes are scattered about town and thirteen are in the **Frank Lloyd Wright Prairie School of Architecture National Historic District**. Visitors can get maps and rent audio tapes at the **Oak Park Visitors Center** at 158 N. Forest Avenue; (708) 848-1500.

Guided walking tours through the neighborhood can be arranged at the **Frank Lloyd Wright Home and Studio** at 951 Chicago Ave.; (708) 848-1976; *www.wrightplus.org*. It was here that he developed his distinctive architectural style, with sweeping horizontal lines softened by earth tones and the deft use of glass. Wright-designed homes aren't bright and cheery; they're warm and intimate, evoking a sense of calm. An adjacent book and gift shop called Under the Ginko Tree serves as the visitor center and ticket office for historic district walking tours and Wright home and studio tours.

Wright took architecture in a another new direction when he designed the poured-concrete **Unity Temple** at 875 Lake St.; (708) 383-8873; *www.unitytemple-utrf.org*. Completed in 1908, it's still an active Unitarian Universalist church, and tours are conducted for a modest fee.

"This is my contribution to modern architecture," Wright said immodestly at the temple's completion. "And that, to me, *is* modern architecture."

The 1897 **Historic Mount Pleasant Home** is a classic example of Prairie-style architecture, with its geometric shapes and low-slung roof. The thirty-room home was designed by a Wright disciple and is open for tours. It's located at 217 S. Home Ave.; (708) 383-2654. The second floor houses the **Historical Society of Oak Park**, with exhibits focusing on the town's famous citizens including, of course, Wright, Hemingway and Burroughs; (708) 848-6755.

Hemingway is memorialized at two Oak Park sites. The **Ernest Hemingway Museum** at 200 N. Oak Park Avenue has a large collection of the author's memorabilia, including original editions of his books, photos, military fatigues he wore as a war correspondent and one of his diaries. A short video recalls his high school years. The nearby **Hemingway Birthplace** at 339 N. Oak Park Avenue has been restored to the 1890s era when it was owned by his maternal grandparents. The room where the author was born has some of his original playthings, donated by his sister Marcelline. The two sites are operated jointly; (708) 848-2222; *www.ehfop.org.*

A particularly appealing stop is the **Oak Park Conservatory**, a classic old English style greenhouse complex surrounded by landscaped gardens, at 615 Garfield St.; (708) 386-4700. Under glass are the Fern House, the Desert House and the Tropic House with a waterfall and lagoon. Another pleasant retreat is little **Scovill Park** on a low hill with a view of the town. It's near the Unity Temple at Oak Park Avenue and Lake Street. Free concerts are held here on summer Sunday afternoons.

There's more to this picturesque Chicago suburb than homes of the famous. Oak Park offers a diversity of shopping and dining, plus assorted cultural activities. Downtown hasn't suffered the mall flight syndrome of many communities; it's still a vibrant shopping area. Just to the south, several blocks of **Marian Street** have been closed to traffic to create a *shoppingstrauss*, with specialty shops, antique stores and little cafés. Once rundown Harrison Street has been revitalized as the **Harrison East Arts District** with several galleries, studios and home decorator shops.

The professional **Festival Theatre** troupe presents outdoor dramas during the summer in Oak Park's Austin Gardens, on Forest Avenue near Lake Street; (708) 660-0633. The award-winning **Circle Theatre** in next-door Forest Park presents a year-around indoor season of innovative dramas and comedies, at 7300 W. Madison St.; (708) 771-0700; *www.circle-theatre.org.*

Where to learn more

Oak Park Convention & Visitors Bureau, 158 N. Forest Ave., Oak Park, IL 60301; (888) 625-7275 or (708) 848-1500; *www.visit-oakpark.com.*

Springfield
Peaceful politic in Abe's hometown

Ƥ

*N*o one, not in my situation, can appreciate my feeling of sadness at *this parting. To this place, and the kindness of these people, I owe every- thing.*

Abraham Lincoln spent twenty-four years of his life in this genteel town on the southern Illinois prairie, as a young attorney and a state senator. When he left in 1861 as president-elect of the United States, he spoke with great affection for his hometown and the people who had become his friends. When he returned, the nation was in deep mourning, for he was coming home to be buried.

The Illinois state capital, Springfield has changed considerably since Lincoln's day. It's a modern mini-city of 112,000, and when the legislature is in session, it's the lively center of state politics. Yet, it still has a small town atmosphere. Folks strolling about its compact downtown area nod to one another, as earlier citizens would have nodded to Abe as he walked from his modest home to his law office overlooking the old capitol building.

The town's most famous citizen has become one of its most important industries, a situation that would have embarrassed the modest president. His home, his law office and his tomb are major visitor attractions. In 2004, the city opened the largest, most expensive and most high tech presidential library and museum in America. "It tells the entire Lincoln story under one roof," executive director Richard Norton Smith told us. "It's done with imagination and creativity." (After it opened, some critics fussed that it was a bit over the top; more showplace than archive.)

The $115 million **Abraham Lincoln Presidential Library and Museum** is described by Smith as an "immersion space where visitors walk through Lincoln's life." They move from one interactive audio-visual exhibit to another, following Abe from his prairie years through his turbulent Civil War presidency. The museum has 46,000 items and the adjacent Lincoln Presidential Library has more than 12 million documents. The complex is at 112 E. Sixth St.; (217) 785-0348; *www.alincoln-library.com.*

A few blocks away is the **Lincoln Home National Historic Site**, preserving the only house that Abe and Mary Todd Lincoln ever owned. It's part of a four-block area of mid-19th century homes restored to the period, with gravel streets and boardwalks. The site is bounded by Edwards, Seventh, Ninth and Capitol streets; (217) 785-7960; *www.nps.gov/liho.* The **Lincoln-Herndon Law Offices** are downtown at Sixth and Adams, opposite the original Illinois capitol. The restored law office of Lincoln and his partner William Herndon occupies the top floor of this narrow three-story building. A mock-up supreme court chamber is on the second floor and exhibits concerning Abe's legal career are at street level; (217) 785-7960.

The saddest Springfield site is the **Lincoln Tomb** in the almost disturbingly attractive Oak Park Cemetery; (217) 782-2717. Abe, Mary Todd and three of their children are buried in a mausoleum, topped by an imposing obelisk. Just outside the cemetery gate is the **Museum of Funeral Customs** which Betty—a former pharmacist—found intriguing, and I found rather macabre. The focus is funerary practices through the ages, with embalming tools and a horse-drawn hearse, plus a special exhibit on Lincoln's funeral. It's at 1440 Monument Ave.; (217) 544-3480; *www.funeralmuseum.org.*

Back downtown, the 1850s Greek Revival **Old State Capitol** is now a museum of Springfield's political past, with restored legislative chambers and offices; (217) 785-7960. It was here that Lincoln gave his famous "house divided" speech that ultimately led him to the presidency. The "new" 1877 **Illinois State Capitol** at Second and Capitol streets is massive and hulking outside and striking within; (217) 782-2099; *www.illinois.gov.* Check out its marble columns, hand-molded plaster trim and a stunningly ornate dome. Tours take visitors to the senate and house chambers and the governor's reception hall.

Everything in Springfield isn't politic. The **Center for the Arts**, occupying a 1909 Masonic temple building at 420 S. Sixth Street, is the city's cultural hub; (217) 753-3519; *www.springfieldartsco.org.* There are several art galleries and four performing arts venues in town.

The mostly low-rise downtown is an attractive, well-kept district of old brick and new glass and masonry, although the circular thirty-story Hilton Hotel tower sticks out like an outhouse on a hilltop.

While you're in the area, make time for a side trip to **Lincoln's New Salem State Historic Site**, about twenty-five miles northwest of Springfield. It's a reconstruction of the village where Lincoln lived from 1831 to 1837, when he was elected to the state legislature. Costumed docents demonstrate frontier skills such as blacksmithing, barrel-making and spinning. There are several exhibits concerning Abe, including a Lincoln timeline. **Theatre in the Park** is an outdoor summer festival of musicals, plays and historical pageants; (217) 632-4000; *www.lincolnsnewsalem.com.*

Where to learn more

Springfield Convention & Visitors Bureau, 109 N. Seventh St., Springfield, IL 62701; (800) 545-7300; *www.visit-springfieldillinois.com.*

Columbus
A small architectural dream town

⚑

A library plaza designed by I.M. Pei, with a sculpture by Henry Moore. Churches created by renowned Finnish-born architect Eliel Saarinen and his son Eero. A Dale Chihuly glass sculpture outside the visitor center. A golf course fashioned by Robert Trent Jones.

All of this in a south central Indiana town with fewer than 50,000 residents? How could such a thing happen? It happened because the biggest employer in this well-groomed little prairie town is Cummins, Inc., one of the world's largest builders of diesel engines.

Diesel and art? Half a century ago, company officials wanted to spruce up the town, so they offered to pay architectural fees for the design of new schools, as long as they could select the architects. The money came from the non-profit Cummins Engine Foundation, and the program later was expanded to include other public buildings. Excited by what they were seeing, community officials and town leaders started engaging leading-edge architects for other new structures.

The result is a little town with a big list of more than sixty architectural gems, a virtual outdoor museum of creative design. In a poll among American Institute of Architects members, Columbus ranked sixth among U.S. cities for innovative architecture. The other five were the obscure hamlets of Chicago, New York, Washington, D.C., San Francisco and Boston.

To enjoy this treasure trove of design, head for the **Columbus Area Visitor Center** at 506 Fifth Street (look for the Dale Chihuly's "Yellow Neon Chandelier") and sign up for a tour; (812) 378-2622. Or you can buy a map and hoof it or drive the tour route. Exhibits and a short video at the visitor center focus on the town's architectural wonders.

Some of the most striking designs are found in churches. Good examples are the **North Christian Church** at 850 Tipton Lane, with a tall spike thrusting skyward from a flat hexagonal base; **St. Peter's Lutheran Church** at 719 Fifth Street, with a brush-hammered concrete slab exterior and a rounded interior; and the **First Christian Church** at Fifth Street and Lafayette Avenue, sporting a 166-foot tower that's visible for miles.

Not all of Columbus is fashioned of churches that resemble spiked spaceships or other architectural curiosities. Town leaders had the good sense to leave much of its older architecture intact. You'll see late 19th century brick and masonry business blocks and old fashioned storefronts downtown, and the area offers good shopping variety.

Not surprisingly, this city of architectural creativity also is home the **Columbus Museum of Art and Design**, an extension of the Indianapolis Museum of Art, with changing exhibits by regional and national artists. It's downtown on the second floor of The Commons; (812) 376-2597; *www.cmadart.org*. The town's memories, architectural and otherwise, are preserved in the **Bartholomew County Historical Society Museum** at 524 Third St.; (812) 372-3541; *www.barthist.com*.

This small city also has a lively performing arts scene, and the **Columbus Arts Council** can tell you what's happening where; at 302 Washington St.; (812) 376-2535; *www.artsincolumbus.org*. The **Columbus Indiana Philharmonic** presents a series of classic and popular concerts at various venues about town; (812) 376-2638; *www.thecip.org*.

Side trip to Nashville

No, not all the way to Tennessee. Nashville, Indiana, a tiny town in the Cumberlands seventeen miles west of Columbus, is a serious center for both visual and performing arts. This charming village of about 900 folks draws visitors from Indianapolis and well beyond for its lively arts scene.

Like its big brother in Tennessee, the **Little Nashville Opry** offers foot-stompin' country music in its "opry house" on State Road 46 south of town; (812) 988-2235. The **Brown County Playhouse**, run by Indiana University in nearby Bloomington, has been presenting summer stock dramas and comedies since 1948; (812) 988-2123; *www.indiana.edu~thtr*. The **Pine Box Theatre** is a cabaret-style showplace downtown at 168 S. Jefferson St.; (800) 685-9624 or (812) 988-6827. Finally, the outdoor **Melchior Marionette Theatre** on Van Buren Street presents summer shows with cute three-foot puppets; (800) 849-4853; *www.browncounty.org/puppets*.

The arts scene is centered around the **Brown County Art Guild**, with a gallery at 48 S. Van Buren; (812) 988-6185; *www.browncounty.org/artguild*. The **Brown County Art Gallery & Museum** traces the history of the area, with a focus on its artistic development. It's at Main Street and Artist Drive; (812) 988-4609.

Where to learn more

Columbus Area Visitors Center, 506 Fifth St., Columbus, IN 47201; (800) 468-6564 or (812) 378-2622; *www.columbus.in.us*.

Brown County Convention & Visitors Bureau, P.O. Box 840 (Main and Van Buren streets), Nashville, IN 47448; (800) 753-3255 or (812) 988-7303; *www.browncounty.com* or *www.nashville-indiana.com*.

Crawfordsville and Rockville
Writers, weathered barns and covered bridges

⚐

Charming old Crawfordsville and Rockville represent Indiana's heartland, not geographically, but pictorially and esthetically. They're places you envision as you hum "Back home again in Indiana." Think of scenic lanes, sugar maple groves, farmlands and weathered barns, with covered bridges spanning cheerful creeks and Victorian homes in quiet neighborhoods.

Even the write-up on the Crawfordsville visitor's bureau website is folksy: "Crawfordsville has the privilege of having scenic Sugar Creek flow through town." Of course, it would *have* to be called Sugar Creek.

These peaceful towns are near Indiana's western edge, about fifty miles west of—and one world removed from—bustling Indianapolis. Crawfordsville is famed for its writers' legacy, once the home of several noted authors. The Rockville area is noted for its many covered bridges.

Crawfordsville

This coquettish little town of about 15,000 is in the heart of the verdant Sugar Valley. (No, we're not making this stuff up!) Its most prominent citizen was the multi-talented Lew Wallace, who lived here from 1853 until 1905. He wrote portions of *Ben Hur* here, and he also served as a general in the Civil War, as a state senator and the U.S. minister to Turkey. Among other noted authors drawn to this area were Booth Tarkington, Gene Stratton Porter and Theodore Dreiser.

Wallace's large brick studio is now the **Ben Hur Museum**, with exhibits concerning the authors multi-faceted life, including a carriage made for him in Paris. The museum is at Wallace Avenue and Pike Street; (765) 362-5769; *www.crawfordsville.com/benhur.org.*

Another noted citizen is memorialized at the 1845 antebellum mansion called **Lane Place** at 212 S. Water St.; (765) 362-3416; *www.crawfordsville.org/lane.htm.* It was built by former governor and U.S. senator Henry S. Lane, an Abraham Lincoln confidant and a founder of the Republican Party. The mansion's period furnishings include several family originals.

The Lane Mansion is in an old neighborhood called **Elston Grove**, where most of the town's leading citizens built their fancy homes. Tour maps directing you to forty-five historic structures are available at the **visitors bureau** at 218 E. Pike St.; (765) 362-5200.

One of Crawfordsville's oddest attractions is the **Old Jail Museum**, occupying an imposing multi-gabled brick building. One of only seven ever built, it has a rotary cell block with wedge-shaped cells. The jailer cranked a turntable to bring a prisoner's cell to the block's single door. It was kind of like a bad guy dispensing machine. This curious jail is at 225 N. Washington St.; (765) 362-5222; *www.crawfordsville.org/jail.htm.*

Sugar Creek forms a pleasant greenway right through the middle of town. You can rent a canoe for a leisurely paddle, or stroll along the Greenway's 4.5-mile-long Sugar Creek Trail.

Rockville

Twenty-five miles southwest of Crawfordsville, Rockville is the seat of Parke County, famed as the world's covered bridge capital. You can pick up a driving map that directs you to thirty-one them at the visitors bureau at 401 E. Ohio St.; (765) 569-5226.

During their time, they were called "kissing bridges" because a young swain could grab a peck from his sweetie while driving his surrey through the dim passages. Several Amish settlements are in the area, and you might see a sight that will *really* take you back to yesterday—an Amish buggy trundling through one of these venerable structures. Bridges were covered to keep their wooden decks from rotting in damp climates. As farm machinery got larger and traffic became thicker, many of them were bypassed. The Parke County Parks Board has taken over preservation of the remaining thirty-one, which have been declared National Historic Landmarks.

In Rockville, stop by the **Covered Bridge Art Gallery**, with paintings, photos and pottery pieces by more than thirty area artists, including many covered bridge images. It's at 124 W. Ohio St.; (765) 569-9422.

Just east of town on U.S. 36, **Billie Creek Village** is a living history center of the early 1900s; (765) 569-3430. About thirty old buildings have been brought to the site and refurbished, and costumed docents recreate life on the prairie. The complex includes a general store, log cabin homes, an historic inn, sorghum mill, an old sugar maple camp and three covered bridges

West of here in the hamlet of *Dana*, a pair of World War II quonset huts house the **Ernie Pyle State Historic Site**; (812) 665-3633. The Pulitzer Prize winning correspondent, who died in combat in the Pacific, was born on a farm near here, and the house has been moved to this site. The quonsets contain World War II memorabilia, and videos recount the Pyle's life.

Where to learn more

Parke County Convention & Visitors Bureau, P.O. Box 165 (401 E. Ohio St.), Rockville, IN 47872; (765) 569-5226; *www.coveredbridges.com.*

Montgomery County Visitors & Convention Bureau, 218 E. Pike St., Crawfordsville, IN 47933; (800) 866-3973 or (765) 362-5200; *www.crawfordsville.org.*

The Indiana Dunes
A sandy refuge on Lake Michigan

Like hungry livestock pushing to a feed trough, three middle America states crowd in to claim small pieces of Great Lakes shoreline. Pennsylvania, not regarded as a Great Lakes state, takes a nip of Lake Erie at its northwestern tip, and the Illinois lakeshore is limited to a short stretch of Lake Michigan between Chicago and Waukegan.

Most of these lakefront areas are highly urbanized and industrialized. However, Indiana's slice of the Great Lakes pie is an sand dune environment protected by **Indiana Dunes National Lakeshore**. Little known outside the Great Lakes region, it's a sandy sanctuary for hiking, fishing, sunbathing, swimming, picnicking and camping. Winter's mantle of snow turns the dunes into a popular cross-country skiing area.

Although developed visitor facilities are limited within the dunes, they're a-plenty in *Michigan City,* an old resort community on the eastern edge of the preserve.

Indiana Dunes National Lakeshore and the adjacent **Indiana Dunes State Park** cover 15,000 acres and shelter about twenty-five miles of Lake Michigan shoreline. However, there's much more here than windblown sand. Visitors will discover woodlands and boggy wetlands rich with plant and animal life. Indiana Dunes ranks seventh among national parklands in its plant diversity. More than 1,400 different species have been identified.

The dunes, both in the national lakeshore and state park, also are great for bird watching, since this lower end of Lake Michigan is a popular stop on a migration route. Birdwatching is best during the fall migrations, although the area is home to a large year-around shorebird population.

U.S. Highway 12 skims the edge of the dunes, providing a refreshing escape from the adjacent Interstate 94. Two interpretive centers will help visitors acquaint themselves with this distinctive ecological area. The focus of the **Bailly/Chellberg Visitor Center** on Mineral Springs Road is the human history of the region; (219) 926-7561, ext. 225. Living history activities are conducted at Chellberg Farm, a re-created late 19th century Swedish homestead. The remnants of an earlier French trapper's homestead is nearby.

Exhibits at the **Dorothy Buell Visitor Center** on Kemil Road concentrate on the natural science of the dunes, with displays and videos. You'll learn that the dunes were built up over the millennia by persistent northwest winds that have piled sand more than a hundred feet high in places. Inland dunes are anchored by plant life, although the beach dunes still shift.

Several trails take hikers past the preserve's diverse features. For a good cross-section, walk the five-mile **Cowels Bog Trail** from wooded inland dunes through marshlands to the open beach. Rangers conduct interpretive hikes on many of the trails, then in winter, they lead cross-country ski outings. Summer swimming is best at **West Beach**, which offers showers and restrooms. Rangers advise folks to stay out of the water when those northwest winds blow, since waves can be treacherous. **Dunewood Campground** has both drive-up and walk-in sites; there are showers but no hookups.

Facilities at the adjacent **Indiana Dunes State Park** include a nature center, picnic shelters, hiking trails, swimming areas, campsites with electrical hookups and winter cross-country skiing: (219) 926-1952; *www.in.gov/dmr/parklake/properties/park.*

The national lakeshore was created in 1966 to preserve one of the few remaining undeveloped shorelines on Lake Michigan. A leader in the movement to save the dunes was Illinois Senator Paul H. Douglas, who once said:

When I was young, I wanted to save the world. In my middle years, I would have been content to save my country. Now I just want to save the dunes.

Michigan City

This old beach town of 32,000 provides all the essentials for a visit to the dunes. While it doesn't offer opulent beachfront resorts, it has a good assortment of affordable motels and inns, plus a few attractions. Also, several local drama groups entertain folks; check with the visitors bureau for details.

Our favorite attraction is the **Old Lighthouse Museum**, once Indiana's only coastal beacon. A nice collection of nautical artifacts includes shipwreck exhibits. It's on Heisman Harbor Road in Washington Park; (219) 872-6133. The attractive shoreside park also offers the town's best swimming and sunning beach, plus a marina, the **Washington Park Zoo** and an amphitheater where you can catch old fashioned band concerts in summer.

The 1857 Victorian style **Barker Mansion**, built by a railroad baron, exhibits period furnishings and historical artifacts, at 631 Washington St.; (219) 873-1520. The **Great Lakes Museum of Military History** has a remarkably large collection of war memorabilia, from the Revolution to the Iraqi problem; at 360 Dunes Plaza; (800) 726-5912 or (219) 872-2702.

Where to learn more

Indiana Dunes National Lakeshore, 1100 N. Mineral Springs Rd., Porter, IN 46304; (219) 926-7561, ext. 225; *www.nps.gov/indu.*

LaPorte County Convention & Visitors Bureau, 1503 S. Meer Rd., Michigan City, IN 46360; (800) 634-2650; *www.visitlaportcounty.com.*

Kalamazoo
Welcome to Bubbling Waters

Ⓟ

It takes sense of humor to live in a place with a name that was the subject of a silly Swing Era song. Maybe its founders should have named it Bubbling Waters, because that's apparently what *kalamazoo* means. Considering that the area's original residents were called Pottowatomi, we can imagine them coming up with a funny word like that.

However, we come here to praise Kalamazoo, not to poke fun at it. (I still wear my "I gotta gal in Kalamazoo" T-shirt with a steadily diminishing sense of pride.) This handsome town in southwestern Michigan has a surprising number of lures, definitely worth a detour if you're in the vicinity.

The downtown area of this city of 80,000 is well-kept and its century-old business blocks offer good shopping variety. There are three brewpubs here, so you have to like this old town. Civic leaders created America's first downtown pedestrian mall here back in 1959, when they closed four blocks of Burdick Street to traffic. Called the Kalamazoo Mall, it's busy with coffee houses, art galleries, antique shops and cafés. Nearby Burdick Park is a nice place to relax and a popular spot for civic celebrations.

Fine old homes slumber in the shade of ancient elms and maples in tidy neighborhoods. Some have become stylish bed & breakfast inns. Stuart Avenue and South Street west of downtown have been designated as historic districts. **Parkwyn Village** to the southwest is an idealized neighborhood designed by Frank Lloyd Wright in the 1940s.

Southwest Western Michigan University, Kalamazoo Valley Community College and the private Kalamazoo College give the town a cultural lift. The **Kalamazoo Valley Museum** on the campus of the community college offers a busy mix of historic, natural science and high tech exhibits. They range from a 2,500 year-old mummy to an affable robot. The complex also includes a planetarium and the Digistar Theater. It's at 230 N. Rose St.; (269) 373-7990; *www.kalamazoomuseum.org*. Exhibits at the **Kalamazoo Institute of Arts** focus on 20th century American (including Michigan) and European artists. The large facility also has a library, art school and auditorium; near downtown at 314 S. Park St.; (269) 349-7775; *www.kiarts.org*.

Our favorite area attraction is the **Kalamazoo Air Zoo**, whose name suggests that Kalamazooers like to poke fun at themselves. It isn't a large aviary but one of the nation's top aviation museums, with exhibits ranging from a pre-World War II Curtiss P-40 to an SR-71 Blackbird spy plane. Visitors can—urp—ride in flight simulators, watch films about the history of aviation and even take flights in vintage aircraft. This aerial zoo is adjacent to the Kalamazoo/Battle Creek International Airport at 6151 Portage Rd.; (866) 524-7966 or (269) 382-6555; *www.airzoo.org.*

The **Gilmore Car Museum** in nearby *Hickory Corners* is among the nation's best, housed in nine restored old barns on a ninety-acre campus. The collection of more than 200 antique and classic vehicles includes an 1899 Locomobile, a rare Tucker and several 1960s muscle cars. The interpretive center is fashioned as a 1930s-era Shell service station. The auto museum is at 6865 Hickory Rd.; (269) 671-5089; *www.gilmorecarmuseum.org.*

Rivaling some state parks in size, the thousand-acre **Kalamazoo Nature Center** is largest in the Midwest. It has several miles of nature trails, an interactive exhibit on the natural history of the area and an eleven-acre arboretum. The complex also includes a restored 1830s homestead and a farm critter petting zoo. It's north of town at 7000 N. Westnedge Ave.; (269) 381-1574; *www.naturecenter.org.* The **Kellogg Bird Sanctuary** east of town on Wintergreen Lake has several nature trails, and you can scope out local birds of prey and waterfowl. You might spot a rare trumpeter swan, which has been re-introduced here. The preserve is near C Avenue off 40th Street in nearby *Augusta*; (269) 671-2510; *www.kbs.msu.edu/bird-sanctuary.*

Off to see Tony the Tiger

Speaking of Kellogg, the small city of *Battle Creek*, thirty miles southeast of Kalamazoo, is home to the cereal giant. It also was the home of the Seventh-Day Adventist Church, a faith that's strong on health and nutrition. Brothers William Keith and John Harvey Kellogg, working in the sanitarium kitchen, came up with a dry cereal made of corn in 1894, to replace the traditional and unhealthy bacon and egg breakfast. In 1906, William started the company that bears his name.

For a fun look at the history of breakfast food, visit the family-focused **Cereal City USA** at 171 Michigan Ave.; (269) 671-2510; *www.kelloggscerealcity.com.* It offers a mix of trivia, games, old advertising slogans, company artifacts and a mock-up production line. Take home a box of Kellogg's Frosted Flakes with your own picture on the carton. You'll be right up there with Tony the Tiger.

Where to learn more

Kalamazoo County Convention & Visitors Bureau, P.O. Box 1169 (346 W. Michigan Ave.), Kalamazoo, MI 49007; (800) 530-9192 or (269) 381-4003; *www.visitkalamazoo.com.*

The Keweenaw Peninsula
A copper heritage and Isle Royale wilderness

Ⴒ

Hemmed in by the Great Lakes, Michigan is divided into the Upper and Lower peninsulas. Thrusting into Lake Superior from the Upper Peninsula is the dorsal fin-shaped Keweenaw Peninsula, one of the most remote and least populated areas of the entire Midwest.

So why go to such a lonely place? It's a beautiful wilderness with a rich copper mining legacy and it's the gateway to **Isle Royale National Park**. This is the least-visited element of the U.S. park system, receiving about 18,000 folks per annum. Copper was discovered on the peninsula in 1840 more than eleven *billion* pounds of it were mined and processed before operations finally ceased in 1968.

When the boom ended, it left ghost towns, almost-ghost towns, copper king mansions and the aging hulks of copper mills in its wake. The National Park Service is gathering these scattered remnants of history into **Keweenaw National Historic Park**; (906) 337-3186; *www.nps.gov/kewe*. Not a specific place, it's a collection of "Keweenaw Heritage Sites" including some already-established local and state historic units.

This peninsula isn't just a wasteland of tailing dumps, mine shafts and abandoned towns. Nature heals quickly in this wet climate, and in some areas it wasn't even disturbed. This is a pretty region of evergreen and maple forests, fishing lakes, virgin streams and little-visited coastlines.

Following U.S. 41 north onto the peninsula, you'll first encounter rustic old *Houghton*. It's a town of about 7,000 cantilevered into the steep slopes of the Keweenaw Waterway, a channel cut through the isthmus. The copper rush brought folks of many nations, and this heritage is still evident in the town's rich ethnic mix. You can see copper in the raw and other minerals at the excellent **A.E. Seaman Mineral Museum** on the campus of Michigan Technology University; (906) 487-2572; *www.museum.mtu.edu*.

Across the channel, little *Hancock* is home to the **Finnish American Heritage Center**, with exhibits focusing on this large ethnic group, at 601 Quincy St.; (906) 487-7367. Just north of town is the **Quincy Mine**, an element of the national historic park, marked by a towering headframe. Tours take visitors deep underground and through its surface buildings; (906) 482-3101; *www.quincymine.com*. One of the world's richest mines, it produced more than a billion pounds of copper from ninety-two levels of tunnels that probed a mile into the earth.

Just up the highway is *Calumet*, which shrunk from a population of 60,000 to fewer than 900 after its mines closed. Learn all about it at the aptly-named and nicely arranged **Coppertown Mining Museum** at 25815 Red Jacket Rd.; (906) 337-4354; *www.uppermichigan.com/coppertown*.

The town's yesterday wealth is reflected in two beautifully restored buildings. The **Keweenaw County Historical Society** is housed in the former St. Anne's Church at 25880 Red Jacket Rd.; (906) 337-4579; *www. pasty.com/heritage*. It's a striking sandstone structure with stained glass windows and towering vaulted arch ceilings. The 1899 **Calumet Theatre**, with a gorgeous "band shell" style stage, is the town's performing arts center, at 340 Sixth St.; (906) 337-2610; *www.calumettheatre.com*.

Nearby *Larium* is a shabby remnant of its former self, although a few homes of copper barons survive in its old neighborhoods. The 45-room, multi-gabled 1908 **Larium Mansion Inn** offers both lodgings and self-guided tours, at 320 Tamarack St.; (906) 337-2549; *www.larium.info*.

Continuing up the peninsula, you'll hit road's end at *Copper Harbor*, population 30. It's rimmed by a beautiful wilderness coastline that's popular with kayakers. At **Fort Wilkins State Park**, costumed rangers present living history demonstrations; (906) 289-4215; *www.michigandnr.com/parksand-trails*. Twelve miles south of town, owners of the **Delaware Mine** offer tours into its deep shafts; (906) 289-4688; *www.copperharbor.org*.

Isle Royale National Park
Beautiful and thickly-forested Isle Royale on Lake Superior remains the domain of moose, timber wolves, loons and other northland creatures. Ninety-nine percent of the is wilderness, although it has 165 miles of hiking trails and thirty-six campgrounds. It's a great place for boating and fishing.

You can visit the park in comfort by checking into the island's only accommodation, the **Rock Harbor Lodge and Marina**; (906) 337-4993 in summer and (270) 773-2191 in winter; *www.isleroyaleresort.com*. Tucked into a wooded slope, the lodge offers balconied lake-view rooms, a restaurant, boat rentals and guided sightseeing and fishing tours.

The *Isle Royale Queen IV* provides passenger service from *Copper Harbor* to the island; (906) 289-4437; *www.isleroyal.com*. Also, the National Park Service operates its own boat out of Houghton, the *Ranger III*,

Where to learn more
Isle Royale National Park, 800 E. Lakeshore Dr., Houghton, MI 459931-1895; (906) 482-0984; *www.nps.gov.isro*.

Keweenaw Convention & Visitors Bureau, 56638 Calumet Ave., Calumet, MI 49913; (800) 338-7982; *www.keweenaw.info*.

Mackinac Island

A sublime escape into yesterday

⚐

Picture a hilly, low-lying and thickly wooded island with dramatic sea-cliffs, elegant resorts, gleaming white Victorian homes, steepled churches and sailboats in a quaint marina.

Now, picture all of this without the sight or sound of a motor vehicle.

Mackinac Island (pronounced *MACK-in-aw*) is one of the most sublime places we've visited. Automobiles were banned almost as soon as they were invented, back in 1898. This is one of the few places on earth with a village and a roadway system that are virtually vehicle-free. State Route 185 that circles the island has never suffered a traffic accident.

The sounds of the village—folks chatting, the clip-clop of horses' hooves, bike tires crunching on gravel—are the sounds of yesterday, before the infernal combustion engine was developed. The only motorized rigs, rarely seen or heard, are emergency vehicles. Otherwise, this is a 600 horse-power island, for it takes about that many nags to pull the tourists' surreys, stock the riding stables and deliver cargo from the ferries.

No vehicles are needed, for the island measures only two by three miles and covers just 2,200 acres. Even on a lazy day, and most days here should be lazy, you can loop the island on a bicycle, the preferred mode of travel.

Mackinac is easy to love, and its lovers have included early writers, film makers and people who pick favorite places. Alexis de Tocqueville, while researching *Democracy in America* in 1831, said: "This small island is the most picturesque thing I have yet seen in this region." Edward Everett Hale chose this place to write *A Man Without a Country*. It was the setting for the 1979 romantic fantasy *Somewhere in Time* with Christopher Reeve and Jane Seymore. *Conde Nast Traveler* called it one of the world's most beautiful islands, and it's in National Geographic's *Guide to Small Town Escapes*.

This tiny island in time is on Lake Huron, in the Straits of Mackinac, where the five-mile long Mackinac bridge links Michigan's Lower and Upper peninsulas. One of the world's longest suspension bridges, it spans the narrow strait between lakes Huron and Michigan. Towns at its north and south anchorages, *St. Ignace* and *Mackinaw City*, are major tourist draws, although they lack the charm of the island. Both run ferries to Mackinac.

The island gets busy in summer, so for more sublimity, plan a spring or fall vacation. Your experience begins as soon as you step ashore. The first impression may be of just another beach resort, with souvenir shops, cafés, several fudge shops (a local specialty), a small craft harbor and assorted lodgings. However, the four-block village area occupies only a fragment of the island. Most of the rest is comprised of woodlands, meadows and historic sites within **Mackinac State Historic Parks.**

Further, there's more to the village area than fudge shops. The gleaming white 1780 **Fort Mackinac** on a bluff above town was the center of contention among French, British and Americans for more than a century. It has been carefully restored, with excellent exhibits concerning its lively history. Costumed state park rangers offer tours and present historic reenactments; (906) 847-3328; *www.mackinacparks.com.*

Combo tickets will give you admission to the fort and several historic sites in the village, including the **Benjamin Blacksmith Shop**, the **Dr. Beaumont Museum** in a restored 1820 American Fur Company trading post, the 1829 New England style **Mission Church** and two old homes, the English **Biddle House** and the French style **McGulpin House**.

Look to the west and you'll see one of America's grandest resorts on a low hill, inviting you to come up for a visit. The imposing **Grand Hotel** has been pampering the rich and famous since 1887, including five U.S. presidents. Open from May through October, it's the world's largest "summer hotel." Its front porch, with 660 feet of white cane-back rocking chairs, is the world's longest. This AAA Four Diamond hotel has 385 opulently furnished rooms, a dozen restaurants and bars and complete resort amenities. Plan a stay here, even if you can afford only one night. Rates, which start around $500 per couple, include breakfast and a five-course dinner; (800) 33-GRAND; *www.grandhotel.com.*

When you've finished with the village and its attractions, rent a bike and peddle the eight-mile car-free highway that loops the island. You'll rarely be out of sight of water, and the route takes you past several natural and historic attractions, from limestone outcroppings to **British Landing**. Here, British troops put ashore, hiked across the island and captured the fort without a shot during the War of 1812. Several hiking trails lead into woodlands and up to vista points. Despite its small size, the island has nearly 140 miles of trails and roads. The free *Mackinac Island Map* is available from the tourism bureau and from various shops and historic sites in the village.

A fun way to see the island is the old fashioned way. A firm simply called **Carriage Tours** offers two-hour outings to various attractions, plus horse-drawn taxi service; (906) 847-3307.

Where to learn more

Mackinac Island Tourism Bureau, P.O. Box 451, Mackinac Island, MI 49757; (877) 847-0080 or (906) 847-3771; *www.mackinacisland.org.*

Petoskey and Little Traverse Bay
Old Victorian resorts on a woodsy inlet

Little Traverse Bay dips into the thickly wooded shoreline of Michigan's Lower Peninsula, providing an inviting haven for lakefront resorts. Although it's only twenty-five miles from the busy Straits of Mackinac corridor, life moves at a quieter pace here. It has neither the tourist traffic of St. Ignace and Mackinaw City nor the summer crowds of Mackinac Island.

Three picturesque old towns and a new luxury community are tucked against the shorelines. *Petoskey* is the star of the show, an appealing town with brickfront stores and waterfront parks. It's one of the featured places in National Geographic's *A Guide to Small Town Escapes* and David Vokac's *Great Towns of America*. To the south, *Bay Harbor* is rising from one of the country's largest land reclamation projects. Just northeast, *Bay View* has an outstanding collection of Victorian homes. Up around the curve of the bay, *Harbor Springs* is a moneyed old resort village where new generation of the ultra-rich live in multi-million dollar summer mansions.

This is a four-season vacation region, with boating and fishing in Little Traverse Bay, lots of beaches for summer swimming and lolling, several golf courses and a couple of nearby ski areas. Fall colors are gorgeous and the shoreline drive from Bay Harbor to Harbor Springs is awesome any time of the year.

An odd pastime here is seeking "Petoskey stones," Michigan's official rock. They're petrified fragments of a coral reef that formed 300 million years ago when this area was covered by warm seas. These bland coral fragments can be found on beaches all along the bay. A good place to seek them is in **Petoskey State Park** just above Bay View. The small park has a mile of sandy beaches, plus hiking trails and campsites; (231) 347-2311.

A town of about 6,000, *Petoskey* once was a high end summer resort with several luxury hotels, although most of them burned years ago. Folks are still drawn here for its attractive bay setting and its nicely preserved **Gaslight District** with more than sixty boutiques, galleries, antique stores and cafés. Petoskey is growing and locals are trying to keep developers at bay to preserve the charming downtown area. It has been placed on the National Trust for Historic Preservation's endangered species list.

Two city parks, **Bayfront** and **Sunset**, create an attractive green zone along Petoskey's old waterfront, with a marina, picnic areas and walking paths. **Little Traverse History Museum** in Bayfront Park is a busy storehouse of Petoskey's yesterdays; (231) 347-2620. One exhibit focuses on

Ernest Hemingway, who vacationed with his family here when he was a sprout. He returned after being wounded in action during World War I and rented a room downtown to hone his writing skills. The museum occupies the restored 1892 Pere Marquette train depot overlooking the waterfront.

Just south of Petoskey, the planned community of *Bay Harbor* is rising from the site of an old cement plant. Occupying five miles of lakefront, it has a yacht club, extravagant homes, an equestrian center, a shopping and condo complex and twenty-seven holes of golf. Public shoreline parks cap both ends of this multi-zillion dollar development.

The hamlet of *Bay View*, founded as a Methodist Church retreat in 1875, has one of the nation's largest collections Victorian homes. More than 400 houses in this nicely landscaped enclave—many of them gingerbready and multi-colored—are on the National Register of Historic Places.

Bay View is still a Methodist colony and it hosts a variety of concerts, lectures and study groups. There's no commercial district here, although lodgings are available at **Stafford's Bay View Inn**, occupying a restored 1886 Victorian mansion at 2011 Woodland Ave.; (800) 528-1886. The Stafford family also restored Petoskey's only surviving early-day luxury resort, the 1899 **Perry Hotel**. It's at Bay and Lewis streets in the Gaslight District; (800) 737-1899; *www.staffords.com*.

A town of about 1,500, *Harbor Springs* still exudes the old money elegance that made it a Victorian treat for the wealthy. Well-kept buildings in the downtown area offer a mix of trendy boutiques, art galleries and appealing little cafés. The **Andrew Blackbird Museum** is named for a respected Ottawa chief who wrote about his peoples' lives and legends. Occupying Blackbird's former home, it's run by members of his tribe, focusing on their heritage, arts and crafts. It's at 368 E. Main St.; (231) 526-7731.

Luxury yachts and fishing boats loll in the bay, and there's a small swimming beach at the lakefront's west end. **Thorne Swift Nature Preserve** just west of town has a much larger beach, plus a view platform that provides nice vistas of the bay, and interpretive trails through quiet cedar groves.

Harbor Springs' residential areas are centered in two thickly wooded districts—Harbor Point where million-dollar homes huddle behind wrought iron gates, and the less opulent Wequetonsing. Harbor Point is closed to vehicle traffic; you must walk or bike in to envy those gorgeous mansions.

Where to learn more

Petoskey/Harbor Springs/Boyne Country Visitors Bureau, 401 E. Mitchell St., Petoskey, MI 49770; (800) 845-2828 or (231) 348-2755; *www.boynecountry.com*.

Lake Erie loop
Discoveries on and off Marblehead Peninsula

⚑

Much of Ohio's Lake Erie shoreline is industrialized and urbanized, from Toledo to Cleveland. Between them, the ragged Marblehead Peninsula, Sandusky Bay and several offshore islands offer a diversion from the otherwise gently curving and busy lakeshore.

This is the state's coastal vacationland, with lots of beaches, quaint villages, marinas, water-view resorts, winery tasting rooms and a lighthouse or two. The rocky shoreline of the Marblehead Peninsula pokes forty miles into Lake Erie's waters. Vehicle and passenger ferries serve offshore Kelleys Island from Marblehead; and North, Middle and South Bass islands from Port Clinton. You can use ferries to fashion a loop from island to island to shore.

The gateway to the peninsula and its islands is *Port Clinton* an historic lakefront town of about 6,000 residents. It dates from 1824, when one Ezekiel Smith Haines bought 1,212 shoreline acres for about $3.30 an acre. He guessed that the coming Erie Canal linking Lake Erie to the Hudson River would bring prosperity to the area. He named his new town in honor of DeWitt Clinton, who had conceived and fought for the overland canal.

While not a major tourist center, Port Clinton has several motels, inns and restaurants. The old downtown area is undergoing a spruce-up, with new landscaping, pavilions and tree-plantings. The little city has a busy marina and it's known as the Walleye Capital of the World because of excellent offshore fishing. You can learn about Zeke and DeWitt at the small **Ottawa County Historical Museum** at 126 W. Third St.; (419) 732-2237. Having nothing to do with area history or anything else locally is the drive-through **African Safari Wildlife Park** at 267 Lightner Rd.; (800) 521-2660 or (419) 732-3606; *www.africansafariwildlifepark.com.*

The oddly-named village of *Put-In-Bay* on **South Bass Island** is a popular and slightly tacky tourist destination. It has the usual vacation lures—an open air tour tram, a marina with boat rentals, a nine-hole course and mini-golf. Several of its lures are focused around **Perry's Family Fun Center** on Catawba Avenue, including an antique car museum, a small limestone cavern and a butterfly museum; (419) 285-2405; *www.perryscave.com.*

If you like wine or chocolate, stop at the **Heineman Winery Tasting Room**, (419) 285-2811, *www.ohiowine.com*; and the cute **Chocolate Café** with a gift shop and small chocolate museum, (419) 734-7114, *www.choco-*

lateohio.com; both on Catawba Avenue. Other lures are the **Lake Erie Islands Historical Museum** on Town Hall Lane, (419) 285-2804, *www.leihs. org*; **Kimberly's Carousel**, a classic 1917 Herschel round-about on Delaware Avenue, (419) 285-2212; and **Stonehenge**, a restored 1800s-era winery estate on Langram Road, (419) 285-6134, *www.stonehenge-put-in-bay.com.*

Just outside the village is **Perry's Victory and International Peace Memorial**; (419) 285-2184; *www.nps.gov/pevi*. It honors Commondore Oliver Hazard Perry's defeat of a larger British fleet in the Battle of Lake Erie during the War of 1812. He sent these immortal words to General William Henry Harrison: "We have met the enemy and they are ours."

Middle and **North Bass islands** can be reached by sea kayak tours; there are a couple of operators in Put-In-Bay. Middle Bass, also served by ferry, is home to **Middle Bass Island State Park**, with a primitive campground and boat slips; (419) 797-4530; *www.dnr.state.oh.us/parks*. North Bass, also called **Isle St. George**, is mostly vineyards, plus a few private homes.

From Put-In-Bay, you can catch an auto/passenger ferry to charming and quiet little *Kelleys Island*, a low-lying green patch of meadows and vineyards. Part of it is occupied by **Kelleys Island State Park**; (419) 746-2546. Its most noted feature is an area of serrated glacial grooves, gouged out about 25,000 years ago. The park also has campsites, picnic areas, a boat ramp, six miles of trails and a mile-long boardwalk through a wetland.

The tiny Victorian village on Kelley's Island is particularly appealing, with about a dozen family-owned shops and cafés, a few lodgings and a waterfront park. Fewer than 400 people live here year-around. Even though cars are permitted, it's nicer to get around the island with bikes or golf carts; both can be rented in the village. Pause to sip a little wine at **Kelleys Island Wine Company** at 418 Woodford Rd.; (419) 746-2678. Also, check out **Inscription Rock**, a limestone slab etched with 300-year-old petroglyphs.

Complete your Lake Erie loop by catching a ferry back to the mainland at *Marblehead*. It's another quaint resort village, slightly larger and a bit busier than the one on Kelleys Island. At the picturesque marina, you can book a fishing charter to pursue the lake's legendary Walleye and other game fish. Nearby **Marblehead Lighthouse** has been steering ships away from the rocky shoreline since 1822. It's now a state park, with tours and picnic areas. Climb a spiral stairway to the top of the fifty-foot tower for a fine view of Marblehead Peninsula and Sandusky Bay; (419) 734-4424

Where to learn more

Ottawa County Visitors Bureau, 770 S.E. Catawba Rd., Port Clinton, OH 53452; (800) 441-1271 or (419) 734-4386; *www.lake-erie.com.*

Marietta

The way West: Ohio's historic river town

$\bowtie$

Virtually everything about Marietta is attractive, from its pretty name to its woodsy Ohio River locale in the foothills of the Appalachians to its well-tended and old fashioned downtown area.

In *The Great Towns of America*, author David Vokac says this town of about 15,000 souls has "the most appealing mix of history and natural beauty in the Ohio River Valley," and we certainly agree.

Tucked into the state's southeastern corner, across the river from West Virginia, it's Ohio's oldest settlement. It was established by a small band of pioneers in 1788 when this was still part of the Northwest Territory, and that meant everything west of the Ohio River. They named their new town for Queen Marie Antoinette to honor France's role in the recently-ended American Revolution.

Marietta sits at the confluence of the Ohio and Muskingum rivers and its future was assured when Robert Fulton built the first fully operational steamboat in 1811. It cruised the Mississippi and Ohio rivers, and Marietta was one of its ports of call. Still today, steamboats put ashore here. It's one of the stops for the Delta Queen Steamboat Company's riverboats, and the town's own *Valley Gem* sternwheeler offers excursion rides.

Since Marietta was founded when most everything beyond the Ohio was wilderness, it's regarded as the first gateway to the Western movement. The **Memorial to the Start Westward** in Muskingum Park honors the town's frontier role. It was sculpted by Gutzon Borglum before he carved the Mount Rushmore faces. The attractive riverfront park also has a memorial to Civil War veterans and a pavilion for concerts and other activities.

Cruising offshore aboard the *Valley Gem* is a fine way to begin appreciating this historic river town. Moored at the river landing near Washington Street bridge, it offers ninety-minute sightseeing trips, dinner cruises and fall foliage voyages; (740) 373-7862; *www.valleygemsternwheeler.com*. Once back ashore, explore the adjacent **Ohio River Museum** at 801 Front St.; (740) 373-3750; *www.ohiohistory.org/places/ohriver*. Exhibits in three buildings focus on the area's natural history, the golden age of steamboatin' and boat building. Outside is the *W.P. Snyder, Jr.*, America's only operational coal-fed steam-powered sternwheeler towboat.

The river archive is part of **Campus Martius: The Museum of the Northwest Territory**, with exhibits tracing Marietta's development. Within the complex is the log home of town founder Rufus Putnam, the only surviving building from Marietta's earliest days. The museum is at Second and Washington streets; (800) 860-0145 or (740) 373-3750; *ohiohistory.org/ places/campus.*

The town's most imposing structure is **The Castle**, the 1855 Gothic Revival style home of a former Ohio senator. Open for public tours, the mansion has an octagonal tower, stone-capped spires and period furnishings. It's at 418 Fourth St.; (740) 373-4180; *www.mariettacastle.org.*

Most of Marietta's downtown buildings are on the National Register of Historic Places. They now house art galleries, craft shops, antique stores and restaurants. A fun way to see the sights is in one of the rigs operated by the **Hardly Able Carriage Company**, departing from 101 Front St.; (304) 869-3051. Before hopping aboard, check out the adjacent **Lafayette Hotel** overlooking the Ohio River. Built in 1918, it has handsomely refurbished rooms and its **Gun Club Restaurant** is one the town's better dining venues; (800) 331-9336 or (740) 373-5522; *www.lafayettehotel.com.*

The site of a 1785 fort is now a popular visitor stop called **Harmar Village**, with boutiques, specialty shops, cafés and a trio of museums; (740) 374-9995, *harmarvillage.com.* The Marietta Soda Museum traces the history of soft drinks, the Federalist style 1847 Henry Fearing House was the home of a prominent citizen, and the Toy and Doll House has a collection of vintage dolls and other playthings.

For an evening's entertainment, catch one of the comedies or dramas of the **Mid-Ohio Valley Players**, who perform in a former vaudeville house at 229 Putnam St.; (740) 373-9434; *movp.org.* The troupe has dinner-and-show programs linked to local restaurants.

Incidentally, if you want to arrive in Marietta in old fashioned style, book a cruise aboard the **Delta Queen Steamboat Company's** 1927 *Delta Queen* or the newer, built-to-look-old *Mississippi Queen.* The firm operates these sternwheelers out of New Orleans, running cruises throughout middle America's river systems; (800) 543-1919; *www.deltaqueen.com.*

Southeastern Ohio is patched with sections of **Wayne National Forest** whose dogwoods and redbuds display spring blooms and awesome fall foliage. Ohio's **Covered Bridges Scenic Byway** passes through the Marietta section of the national forest, reaching thirty-five miles from Marietta to *Woodsfield.* It passes such bucolic visions as Mail Pouch tobacco signs on old barns, vintage mills, historic inns and—of course—covered bridges.

Where to learn more

Marietta/Washington County Convention & Visitors Bureau, 316 Third St., Marietta, OH 45750; (800) 288-2577; *www.mariettaohio.org.*

Zanesville and about
Pottery central, a cowboy author and more

₽

The east central Ohio town of Zanesville has a couple of completely unrelated claims to fame. Because of the fine sandy soil in the region, it once was America's leading pottery production center, and it still has many potters, ceramists and other artisans. It also is the birthplace of Zane Grey, the leading Western novelist of the last century.

During the 1790s, Revolutionary War veteran Colonel Ebenezer Zane, a paternal ancestor to the famous author, was commissioned by Congress to blaze the first trail through the Northwest Territories wilderness. It became known as Zane's Trace. Zane's brother Jonathan began operating a ferry at the juncture of the Muskingum and Licking Rivers, and one of the Northwest Territory's first communities grew up around it.

Zanesville became Ohio's temporary capital and Zane's Trace became the National Road in 1806, America's first federally funded highway. With pioneer settlements, pottery, an early highway and a Zane Grey historic site, there is much to see in Zanesville and the surrounding hilly, wooded Muskingum County. Zanesville also has an unusual architectural feature, a Y-shaped bridge that spans the junction of the Muskingum and Licking rivers. The original was built in 1814 and the current bridge is the fifth rendition.

A town of about 26,000, Zanesville has an active cultural scene, thanks in part to its pottery past. The **Zanesville Art Center** exhibits American and European art, Ohio pottery and glass, decorative arts and a doll collection. It's all at 620 Military Rd.; (740) 452-07411; *www.zanesvilleartcenter.org*. You can see artists at work in their studios and buy their wares at the **Arts Collective at the Armory**, 814 Elberton Ave.; (740) 450-7285.

More than a dozen pottery factories and many shops keep the region's pottery and ceramic heritage alive. One of the largest factories is **Fioriware Art Pottery**, which uses 19th century techniques and equipment to produce classic pieces; 26 N. Third St.; (740) 454-7400; *www.fioriware.com*. The production facility and showrooms are in a former warehouse, and visitors can take self-guided tours.

The performing arts also are alive in town. The **Zanesville Concert Association** presents a variety of musical events at the Secrest Auditorium at 334 Shinnick St.; (740) 588-0871. The **Zanesville Memorial Concert Band** plays old fashioned concerts in Zane's Landing Park in the summer; (740) 455-3906. The **Zane Trace Players** present comedies and dramas in a former church at 148 N. Seventh St.; (740) 453-8555.

Re-live Zaneville's past by taking a sightseeing or dinner cruise aboard the sternwheeler *Lorena*, moored at Zane's Landing Park; (800) 246-6303. To sample more of the town's yesterdays, explore the **Putnam District** with several old buildings listed on the National Register of Historic Places. The 1805 **Dr. Increase Mathews House** is open for public tours, at 304 Wood-lawn Ave.; (740) 454-9500. The **Putnam Underground Railroad Education Center** occupies an 1838 home where runaway slaves were hidden during the Civil War, 522 Woodlawn Ave.; (740) 450-3100. Exhibits focus on this practice of moving runaways from one community to the next, which was called the "Underground Railroad."

Beyond Zanesville

U.S. Highway 40, paralleling Interstate 70, follows the route of the **National Road**, which extended from Cumberland, Maryland to Vandalia, Illinois. Drive the route east from Zanesville to *Norwich* and the **National Road-Zane Grey Museum** at 8850 E. Pike St.; (800) 752-2602 or (740) 872-3143. This triple-threat museum has extensive exhibits on the historic road, the famous author and Ohio's pottery heritage.

Another famous person—much more contemporary—is honored in *New Concord*, just east of Norwich. The **John & Annie Glenn Historic Site** preserves the boyhood home of an amazing individual. Marine Colonel John Glenn was a World War II and Korean War combat pilot, the holder of a coast-to-coast speed record, the first American to orbit the earth, a U.S. Senator from Ohio and finally, the oldest man to fly in space, at age 77. You'll learn all about John and his wife Annie at his renovated home at 72 W. Main St.; (740) 836-0220; *www.johnglennhome.org.*

If you head south from New Concord on State Route 83 to *Cumberland*, you'll encounter an attraction of quite a different stripe—actually, stripes and horns. **The Wilds** is a 10,000-acre wildlife park occupying a reclaimed strip-mining site. Buses take visitors past assorted critters of Africa, Asia and North America; (866) 444-9453 or (740) 638-5030; *www.thewilds.org.*

A few miles south of Zanesville on State Route 93, between *Roseville* and *Crooksville,* is the **National Ceramic Museum and Heritage Center**. This extensive five-building complex is busy with artists' studios, production facilities and displays of fine ceramics and pottery; (740) 697-7021; *www.ceramiccenter.info.*

Where to learn more

Zanesville-Muskingum County Convention & Visitors Bureau, 205 N. Fifth St., Zanesville, OH 43701; (800) 743-2303 or (740) 4355-8282; *www. visitzanesville.com.*

The Apostle Islands
Returning to the wilderness; wilderness returning

Ƥ

Step aboard a boat at charming little Bayfield in Wisconsin's far north, then cruise out among the Apostle Islands on Lake Superior, the world's largest and most pristine freshwater pond. Out here, you can experience a return to the wilderness. Further, it's an area where the wilderness itself is gradually returning.

The Apostle Islands, scattered like carelessly thrown wood chips off the chubby Bayfield Peninsula, provide a classic example of how man can restore a wilderness destroyed by his predecessors. Too close to shore and thus too vulnerable, the islands were over-trapped, over-hunted, over-fished and most were logged down to their bare bones of Precambrian sandstone. After eighty years of efforts by local conservationists, **Apostle Islands National Lakeshore** was created in 1970, and the healing process began.

Visitors today will see recovering pine, fir, maple, balsam and birch forests. It has generated renewed populations of deer, bald eagles, shorebirds and—to the apprehension of the timid—bears. Visitors also will see a fine landscape of rocky and sandy shores, steep ravines, sea caves and bogs.

The national preserve consists of twenty-one of the twenty-two Apostle islands and a twelve-mile coastal strip on the Bayfield Peninsula's north shore. The islands range in size from a few acres to a few square miles. Some are off limits because they're still recovering from mankind's unkindness. Others have hiking trails and primitive campsites while still others are the realm of kayakers and solitary hikers, often the same people.

There are no developed facilities on the islands in the preserve, although the community of *La Pointe* on **Madeline Island** has essential comforts— places to dine, wine and recline. The **Madeline Island Historical Museum**, surrounded by a log stockade, offers exhibits on native people, white settlement, and the islands' geology, flora and fauna; (715) 747-2051. The largest of the islands, Madeline isn't part of the preserve because it has about 200 residents. The **Madeline Island Ferry** provides service between La Pointe and Bayfield; (715) 747-2051; *www.madferry.com*. And for a really cool winter trip, you can drive across an ice road that's maintained by the state.

Although it's right out there among the Apostles, Madeline Island isn't the gateway to the national lakeshore. That privilege belongs to appealing little *Bayfield*, occupying a wooded upslope of the Lake Superior shoreline.

This once was a popular summer retreat for the idle rich and some of their opulent homes are still here. Most are still occupied, a few pose as bed & breakfast inns, and many are on the National Register of Historic Places.

Although the Depression ended Bayfield's grand era, this town of 600 folks is still a popular tourist stop, since it's the gateway to the Apostles and just because it's so attractive. There are things to do, even if you don't do the islands. The **Lake Superior Big Top Chautauqua** is a large tent theater that presents musicals, plays and assorted other amusements for summer tourists. It's at the foot of the **Mount Ashwabay Ski Area** on Ski Hill Rd.; (888) 244-8368 or (715) 373-5552; *www.bigtop.org*.

Two small museums in town recall the area's yesterdays. The **Bayfield Heritage Museum** has permanent and changing exhibits on regional history at 100 Rittenhouse Ave.; (715) 779-5958; *www.bayfieldheritage.org*. The **Bayfield Maritime Museum** at the ferry dock presents 150 years of the area's nautical history; (715) 779-9919; *www.apostleisland.com*.

The national lakeshore is headquartered in town, with exhibits, films and publication about the islands in its visitor center.

Down at the waterfront, **Apostle Islands Cruise Service** demonstrates that you don't have to be a hiker, camper or Grizzly Adams to have a good look at the isles. The "Grand Tour" takes passengers among all the islands, and passes a couple of the region's many lighthouses. A narration tells you more about the Apostles than you can possibly remember. The company also provides camper drop-offs for Stockton, Oak and Raspberry Islands and water taxi service to all of the isles that aren't off limits; (800) 323-7619 or (715) 779-3925; *www.apostleisland.com*.

The large and busy harbor offers an assortment of fishing charters, "bare-boat" rentals and kayak tours. For landlubbers, there are several trails in and about Bayfield. The **Iron Bridge Trail** starting at the end of Broad Street takes you up to an overlook where you can have the same awesome views of Bayfield and the islands that the occupants of those grand old homes enjoy. The **Railroad Trail** on a former railbed starts at Manypenny and Third streets and follows the shore three miles south to *Port Superior*.

Where to learn more

Apostle Islands National Lakeshore, 415 Washington Ave., Bayfield, WI 54814; (715) 779-3339; *www.nps.gov/apis*.

Bayfield Chamber of Commerce, P.O. Box 138 (42 S. Broad St.), Bayfield, WI 54814; (800) 447-4094 or (715) 779-3355; *www.bayfield.org*.

Madeline Island Chamber of Commerce, P.O. Box 274 (N-806 Main St.), La Pointe, WI 54850; *www.madelineisland.com*.

Baraboo and beyond
Circus lore, cranes and amazing geology

Ⱶ

Baraboo is what you do after you've done the Dells. Or maybe it's what you do instead.

The Wisconsin Dells is the state's post popular visitor attraction, a serpentine section of the Wisconsin River that has carved a 150-foot-deep canyon of fantastic shapes. However, it has disintegrated into Orlando North, with a Believe It or Don't Museum, an auto museum, the Bay of Dreams, Noah's Ark Water Park, Lost Canyon and—well, you get the idea.

We much prefer Baraboo, a little town about a dozen miles south where *real* fantasy was invented without corrupting a beautiful natural landmark. Here, five sons of a German harness maker, recalling a circus riverboat they'd seen, decided to play circus in 1882. They put together a few acts and called it the "Ringling Brothers Classic and Comic Company." The thing just kept growing. In 1907, they bought out P.T. Barnum and James Bailey's show to create the Ringling Brothers Barnum and Bailey Circus. It wintered in Baraboo until 1918, when its winter quarters were moved to Sarasota, Florida, somewhere down there near Orlando.

The Ringlings' former winter quarters is now the **Circus World Museum** on a fifty-one acre site alongside the Baraboo River. It displays thousands of artifacts, from circus wagons and clown costumes to sideshow posters. The collection is *huge* so plan most of a day here if you're a circus fan. And stay for the show. Circus America is performed in summers under an old fashioned big top, with jugglers, trapeze artists, steam calliope concerts, clowns, animal shows and more. It's all at 426 Water St.; (608) 356-0800; *www.circusworldmuseum.com.*

One of the Ringling brothers built the gorgeous **Al Ringling Theatre** as an opera hall for the town. Impeccably restored, it now serves as Baraboo's performing arts center, and tours are given in summer; at 136 Fourth Ave.; (608) 356-8844; *www.alringling.com.* The **Sauk County Historical Museum** has an odd mix of exhibits ranging from native peoples' artifacts to Civil War mementos to old household items. It's housed in a 1903 mansion at 531 Fourth Ave.; (608) 356-9462; *www.saukcounty.com.*

Just west of Baraboo is the **Mid-Continent Railroad Museum** on west Walnut Street in tiny *North Freedom*; (608) 522-4261; *www.mcrwy.com.* It has a refurbished 1894 depot and a fine collection of vintage rolling stock. Visitors can take a 50-minute steam train ride through the scenic Baraboo River Valley.

Baraboo is more than Circusville USA. The town is a real charmer, with an old fashioned business district built around a courthouse square. This tidy little city is located in an exceptionally pretty area on a sharp bend in the Baraboo River, with low wooded hills and mauve quartzite bluffs as backdrops. Nearby are two outstanding preserves.

The **International Crane Foundation** about five miles northeast is a world-respected refuge for Mother Nature's largest flying birds. It's the only place on the globe where you can see all fifteen species of cranes, including the rare whooping crane and hooded Siberian crane. Guided tours are conducted, or you can wander about the foundation's protected prairies and marshlands on your own. It's on Shady Lane Road, off U.S. 12; (608) 356-9462; *www.savingcranes.org*.

Three and a half miles south of town on State Route 123 is **Devil's Lake State Park**, with a deep and mysterious pond that reflects the sparkling colors of its surrounding 500-foot-high quartzite cliffs. The converging forces of glaciers, rivers and erosion have created one of the Midwest's most diverse earth science sites. Ranger programs and exhibits at the visitor center focus on its geological significance. Hiking trails twist among the park's amazingly sculpted quartzite shapes. The most visited park in Wisconsin, Devil's Lake also offers swimming, picnic sites and camping areas; (608) 356-8301; *www.devilslakewisconsin.com*.

The state park's glacial moraine geology marks the southernmost advance of the last Ice Age. If you travel south from here, the dividing line between ice-sculpted, hilly southeastern Wisconsin and the more prairie-like southwestern part is quite evident. And it's an exceptionally scenic drive.

To begin, take State Route 113 south to Highway 78. Then, just for the fun of it, go east briefly to the funky old ten-car ferry that crosses the Wisconsin River between *Merrimack* and *Okee*. Pick up State Route 188 near Okee and continue south alongside the river until you re-join Highway 78.

You'll cross the river again and soon encounter the U.S. 18/151 expressway. Go west briefly to the hamlet of *Blue Mounds* and the adjacent **Blue Mound State Park**; (608) 437-5711; *www.dnr.state.wi.us*. The name comes from two bluish hills where tons of lead were mined in the early 1800s. The park encloses the highest of the two mounds. At 1,716 feet, it's also the highest point in southwestern Wisconsin. Views of the glacial-edge Baraboo Range and Wisconsin River Valley are great from up there.

Where to learn more

Baraboo Area Chamber of Commerce, P.O. Box 442 (600 W. Chestnut St.), Baraboo, WI 53913; (800) BARABOO; *www.baraboo.com*.

Green Bay and the Door Peninsula
It's more than *La Baye Verte* Packers

⚑

Quick sports quiz: What makes the Green Bay Packers different from all other professional sports franchises? No, it's not the rabid fans. Have you ever sat in the Oakland Raiders' Black Hole?

Answer: The Packers are the only team that's owned by a municipality. Thus, when tax-paying Green Bay citizens say it's their team, they're speaking literally. The legal fluke is that if the Packers were ever to move—perish that thought!—they'd have to take the town with them. With a population of just over 100,000, this is the smallest city in America to support a major league franchise.

Lost in the emerald glow of the Packers is the fact that Green Bay is the oldest city in Wisconsin. It dates from 1669 when French missionaries and trappers established *Le Baye Verte* at the base of a deep inlet sheltered from Lake Michigan storms. When it became an American possession in 1816, the Yanks Anglicized the name.

Although the town is famous for its Packers, the waiting time for season tickets is about 200 years. So, why go there before the year 2200? We can give you three good reasons: 1. There's plenty for non-ticketed football fans to see. 2. Green Bay offers lures other than football. 3. It's the gateway to the Door Peninsula, the state's second most popular tourist destination after the Wisconsin Dells.

If you wouldn't know a football from a fooseball and don't care, head for Green Bay's **National Railroad Museum**, which deserves its "national" title. Among more than seventy pieces of equipment are the world's largest steam train called the "Big Boy," the train used by General Dwight D. Eisenhower as his rolling command post in World War II Europe and the super-streamlined 1950s era *Aerotrain*. The large facility also offers multi-media shows, train rides in summer and miniature railroad layouts. It's at 2285 S. Broadway; (920) 437-7623; *www.nationalrrmuseum.org*.

The **Heritage Hill Living History Museum** is a state-run pioneer village with buildings brought in from throughout Wisconsin. Costumed docents re-create the state's early days in four themes: Pioneer, Military Life, Agriculture and Small Towns. The site contains some of the state's oldest buildings; it's at 2640 S. Webster Ave.; (920) 448-5150; *www.heritage-hillgb.org*. The fine **Neville Public Museum** focuses primarily on Green Bay History, although it also hosts traveling exhibits, at 210 Museum Place; (920) 448-4460; *www.nevillepublicmuseum.org*.

If you have kids in tow, or if you're still one yourself, head for the old fashioned **Bay Beach Amusement Park and Wildlife Sanctuary** at the end of Irwin Street; (920) 391-3671; *www.baybeachwildlife.com*. The amusement park offers a dozen rides, mostly for kids (including you big ones). The adjacent 700-acre wildlife refuge has a nature center, a population of regional mammals and birds and seven miles of trails.

And then, there are the Packers. The recently refurbished **Lambeau Field** at 1265 Lombardi Avenue isn't just another place where linemen the size and weight of gorillas butt heads. It's a visitor center and Green Bay Packer shrine. The faithful and the curious can take guided tours of the stadium or dine and shop at the atrium level retail complex.

Also on the atrium level is the **Green Bay Packers Hall of Fame**, a hedonistic museum to past and hopefully future glory days. You'll learn that the Packers are one of the oldest teams in professional sports, established in 1919. They got their odd name because a local meat packing plant offered to furnish their uniforms and give them a place to practice. Fortunately, they eventually changed their team name from the Indian Packing Company Footballers. For all the scoop: (920) 569-7500; *www.packers.com*.

Opening the Door: Life beyond football

The fjord-like Green Bay is sheltered by the skinny, tapered 75-mile-long Door Peninsula. With its charming old fishing villages, state parks, resorts, winery tasting rooms, rocky coastline and offshore islands, it's a favorite summer playground.

It might not be so popular if it still bore the original French name, *Porte des Mortes*. Its rocky shoals and unpredictable storms were Death's Door to many explorers. Today it's busy with lighthouses, which add to its charm.

Begin your exploration at *Sturgeon Bay*, midway up the isthmus. It's the largest town on the peninsula, with a population of nearly 10,000. At the chamber visitor center, you can learn of the area's many lures.

Your "A" list should include Potawatomi State Park on a bluff overlooking Sturgeon Bay, Door County Maritime Museum in the town, Whitefish Dunes State Park with sand dunes and native fauna, the resort village of Ephraim, and Washington Island off the peninsula's far tip. It's reached by a ferry and you can book narrated tram rides around the island.

Where to learn more

Door County Chamber of Commerce, P.O. Box 406 (1015 Green Bay Rd.), Sturgeon Bay, WI 54235; (800) 527-3529; *www.doorcounty.com*.

Green Bay Visitor & Convention Bureau, Box 10596 (1901 S. Oneida St.), Green Bay, WI 54307; (888) 867-3342; *www.packercountry.com*

Madison
A grand place for children of the forest

ꔪ

I first visited Madison many a decade ago when I was a young Marine attending the Naval Journalists School at Great Lakes Naval Training Center in North Chicago. Even then a wanderer, I jumped into my beat-up old car one winter weekend and chugged over the prairie to the Wisconsin state capital, just to see what it was like.

My most vivid recollection was of folks skating on a pond in a tree-covered public park near downtown. It was the most appealing vision I had yet seen, and that Courier & Ives image has stayed with me all these years.

Although it's much larger now, Madison remains the charming, beautiful city that had wowed this kid from Idaho. An urban village of about 210,000, it's gorgeously situated on a narrow isthmus between lakes Mendota and Monona. Two other lakes, Wingra and Waubesa, complete this blue shamrock setting. The site is so imposing that a passing soldier wrote in his journal: "It appears that the Almighty intended it for the children of the forest."

Although politicians can hardly be regarded as children of the forest, Madison was picked as the territorial capital in 1836, even though no town yet existed. The site was just too compelling to resist.

Rich with emerald parklands, richer still with the scholastic influence of the University of Wisconsin, and with a multi-cultural population, Madison often makes "best places" lists. *Money* magazine called it America's most livable city in 1996 and 1998. Recent accolades include "#1 City for Cycling", "Most Romantic U.S. City", "America's Fourth Most Literate City," and it was picked as one of *Outside* magazine's ten "Dream Towns"

Begin exploring where Madison began, at the downtown **Wisconsin State Capitol** that dominates Capitol Square; (608) 266-0382; *www.doa. state.wi.us*. Not the original, this 1917 version rivals the Nation's capitol in size and grandeur. However, at the jealous urging of the Feds, the dome is three feet lower. Tours through its gorgeously marbled interior include the senate and assembly chambers, Wisconsin State Supreme Court, the governor's conference room and the lofty rotunda.

Just to the east is the five-level **Monona Terrace Community and Convention Center** with great arched windows staring across its namesake lake; (608) 261-4000; *www.mononaterrace.com*. It was proposed and designed by Frank Lloyd Wright in 1938. However, due to drawn-out wrangling over its size and cost, it wasn't completed until 1997. Although it's primarily Madison's civic and convention center, the 250,000 square foot complex contains the **Madison Sports Hall of Fame**, a gallery about Wright's architectural works, lots of plazas and a roof garden.

Madison's real crown jewel is neither its oversized capitol nor its sprawling civic terrace. It's the green-clad, lakeside campus of the **University of Wisconsin**; (608) 263-2400; *www.visit.wisc.edu*. Get your bearings at the Visitor Information Center (any student or prof can point it out), then check out its many lures. They include the **Elvehjem Museum of Art** with 16,000 items in its collection, (608) 263-2246; the **Geology Museum** with lots of gems and minerals from this mineral-rich state, plus a dinosaur and mastodon, (608) 262-2399; and the **Washburn Observatory**, where folks can gaze at stellar objects on clear nights, (608) 262-9274.

Madison is home to a pair of outstanding public gardens. The **University of Wisconsin Arboretum** has its own separate 1,260-acre "botanical campus" alongside Lake Wingra, (608) 263-7888. The **Olbrich Botanical Gardens** is in the heart of beautifully landscaped Olbrich Park adjacent to Lake Monona; (608) 246-4550; *www.olbrich.org*

Back downtown, State Street between the capitol and the university campus has been converted into a semi-pedestrian mall, with coffee houses, cafés, boutiques, art galleries, performing arts spaces and six museums.

These cultural occupants are on or near the State Street promenade: The **Wisconsin Veterans Museum** honors the state's war heroes and has exhibits about America's assorted conflicts, at 30 W. Mifflin St.; (608) 267-1799; *www.museum.dva.state.wi.us*. The **Wisconsin Historical Museum** offers extensive collections of the state's memories, at 30 N. Carroll St.; (608) 264-6555; *www.wisconsinhistory.org*. The **Madison Children's Museum** has lots of fun hands-on exhibits at 100 State St., (608) 256-6445, *www.madisonchildrensmuseum.org*. The **Madison Museum of Contemporary Art** features extensive collections of unexplainable blotches and "constructions" at 211 State St., (608) 257-0158, *www.mmoca.org*. An ambitious **Madison Arts District** was under construction in this area at press time, with visual and performing arts venues and artists' studios and galleries.

Since Wisconsin is after all America's dairyland and a major farming state, Madison hosts the **Dane County Farmers Market** every Saturday from April through October on Capitol Square; (608) 455-1999; *www.dcfm.org*. One of the nation's largest, it's also a lively urban fair with food booths, art exhibits and street performers.

Where to learn more

Greater Madison Convention & Visitors Center, 615 E. Washington Ave.; (800) 373-6376 or (608) 255-2537; *www.visitmadison.com*.

COVE POINT LIGHTHOUSE, MD.

Chapter Seven

The Mid-Atlantic

Canandiagua

Saratoga Springs

Cooperstown

New York   Woodstock

Lower Hudson River

North Fork Long Island

Erie

Delaware Water Gap

Pennsylvania   Bucks County

The Pinelands

Laurel Highlands   Lancaster

NJ

Annapolis

Brandywine Valley

Cumberland

MD

DE   Cape May
Southern Beach Towns

Calvert County

WATERWAYS, ROLLING HILLS & HISTORY

The Mid-Atlantic region encompasses two of eastern America's largest states and three of its smallest. New York, the largest, reaches from the Atlantic to the Great Lakes. Big Pennsylvania seems intent on pushing little New Jersey, Maryland and Delaware into the sea. Our Atlantic midland is an area of inland waterways, rolling hills and history.

It's also a region of politics. Our nation began in the Mid-Atlantic, and it remains the seat of our government. The Declaration of Independence was signed in Philadelphia; while Washington, D.C., occupies a Maryland enclave; and Delaware is our oldest state.

DELAWARE says that it's "good to be first" since it was the first state to ratify the U.S. Constitution. We visit a pretty interior valley made famous not by politics but by gunpowder—and maybe that's not too far a stretch. We also visit some of America's nicest and cleanest beaches.

Where to learn more: Delaware Tourism Office, 99 Kings Highway, Dover, DE 19901-7305; (822) 2-VISIT-DE or (302) 672-6857; *www.visit-delaware.com.*

MARYLAND is nearly chopped in half by Chesapeake Bay, home to the state's legendary blue crabs. We visit its nautical capital city on the edge of the bay, plus a rural bayside county and an inland woodland.

Where to learn more: Maryland Office of Tourism Development, 217 E. Redwood St., Baltimore, MD 21202; (877) 209-5883 or (410) 767-6329; *www.mdwelcome.org.*

NEW JERSEY is a surprise to folks who think of it mostly as the home of Atlantic City, and the Big Apple's cross-bay neighbor. Most of its interior is farmlands and woodlands. Our explorations take us from an old resort town into one of eastern America's largest pine forests.

Where to learn more: New Jersey Office of Travel and Tourism, P.O. Box 404, Trenton, NJ 08625; (800) 843-6420; *www.visitnj.org.*

NEW YORK, New York, it's a helluva—state. America's largest city is but a tiny appendage on the bottom of a very big state. Our stops include a "hall of fame town," an historic spa town, America's second largest wine region and an arts district made famous by a raucous concert.

Where to learn more: New York Division of Tourism, 30 S. Pearl St., Albany, NY 12245; (800) 225-5697 or (518) 474-4116; *www.iloveny.com.*

PENNSYLVANIA is another state with much of its population tucked into one corner, and with hills and farmlands beyond. We explore the mis-named Pennsylvania Dutch country, a national battlefield (not Gettysburg), and the home of several famous authors.

Where to learn more: Pennsylvania Tourism Office, 400 North St., Harrisburg, PA 17120-6225; (800) VISIT-PA; *www.visitpa.com.*

The Brandywine Valley
A wealthy corridor that once was a real blast

⚑

The Brandywine Valley is an urban corridor with several pleasing pockets of green. Shaped by the pretty Brandywine River, it reaches from the city of Wilmington through Delaware's curiously curved northern border into Pennsylvania.

One remarkable family is responsible for some of those green areas, for they are elaborate estates now open to the public. The du Ponts probably prefer folks to remember that their labs created such products as Nylon, Lucite, Teflon and Mylar. Yet, the family fortune began with gunpowder.

That's ironic, since Wilmington was founded by Quakers in 1731. Sitting on the banks of the navigable Delaware River, it soon became an important shipping and industrial port. In 1802, Éleuthère Irénée du Pont, son of a wealthy and influential expatriate French family, bought land along the Brandywine River. His intent was to produce black powder, not to promote Quaker pacifism. The du Ponts eventually expanded into chemistry, industry and finance and they're now one of America's wealthiest families.

Many du Pont holdings in the Brandywine Valley have been given or sold to the state, to become public monuments to the family's wealth, status and good taste. The du Ponts built extravagant mansions on extravagantly landscaped grounds. They enjoyed collecting fine furniture, fine art and decorative arts, so these are amazing showplaces.

Another prominent local family was the Wyeths, which has produced three generations of noted American artists. N.C. Wyeth came to the Brandywine Valley in 1902 and some of his descendants still live here.

Begin your exploration with the **Hagley Museum and Eleutherian Mills** where the du Pont fortune began. Head northwest from *Wilmington* on State Route 52 and then go east briefly on State Route 141. The landscaped 235-acre complex includes a lavishly decorated and furnished mansion, plus powder mills, offices and workers' quarters. Tours begin at the Henry Clay Mill, which has interactive exhibits tracing the family history. The complex is at 6 Old Barley Mill Road; (302) 658-2400; *www.hagley.lib.de.us.*

The **Delaware Toy & Miniature Museum** just inside the Hagley gate contains one of America's largest and finest displays of playthings and miniature objects. The collection includes more than 100 furnished doll houses and thousands of vintage toys; (302) 427-8697; *www.thomes.net/toys.*

Another fabulous du Pont estate, just northeast of the Hagley, is the **Nemours Mansion and Gardens**, with a 102-room Louis XVI château. It's a virtual museum of classic art and furniture, and it's surrounded by formal French gardens; (302) 651-6912; *www.nemoursmuseum.org*. **NOTE:** The estate was being refurbished at press time; call for details.

If you return to Route 52 and continue northwest, you'll encounter two more attractions. The small but excellent **Delaware Museum of Natural History** has realistic wildlife dioramas, a large seashell collection and a Great Barrier Reef mockup; (302) 658-9111; *www.delmnh.org*. Across the highway is **Winterthur**, the opulent 979-acre estate of Henry Francis du Pont. The complex includes Henry's mansion with 89,000 examples of early American decorator art, and a sixty-acre horticultural garden; (302) 888-4907; *www.winterthur.org*.

Still another du Pont creation is **Longwood Gardens**, reached by following Route 52 to the town of *Kennett Square, Pennsylvania*; (610) 388-1000; *www.longwoodgardens.org*. Not an estate, it's a gorgeously landscaped 1,050-acre complex of gardens, woodlands and meadows. It has twenty outdoor and twenty indoor gardens, lavish fountains and 11,000 plant varieties.

The Wyeth family is honored at the **Brandywine River Museum** in *Chadds Ford, Pennsylvania*. Occupying a former 19th century gristmill, it features three generations of Wyeth family art, plus works of other noted American artists. Shuttle buses take visitors to the nearby **N.C. Wyeth House and Studio** and the **Kuerner Farm** where Andrew Wyeth did many of his paintings. The complex is north of the Hagley Museum on U.S. 1; (610) 388-2700; *www.brandywinemuseum.org*.

Like many cities, downtown *Wilmington* suffered suburban flight and blight in the 1950s and 1960s. However, it's recovering beautifully. The Wilmington Renaissance Corporation, comprised of business and civic leaders, is working to preserve and redevelop downtown, including the historic **Ships Tavern District** on lower Market Street. It's becoming a trendy shopping and dining area. The once shabby riverfront is being reborn as well, with walkways, shops, restaurants and museums.

Further, Wilmington it demonstrates that all of the region's cultural assets aren't in the Brandywine Valley. The **Delaware History Center** preserves and exhibits the state's past in a converted F.W. Woolworth building at 505 Market Street Mall; (302) 656-0637; *www.hsd.org*.

Where to learn more
Greater Wilmington Convention & Visitors Bureau, 100 W. Tenth St., Wilmington, DE 19801; (800) 489-6664; *www.visitwilmingtonde.com*.

Southern beach towns
Pleasant alternatives to gaudy resorts

⚑

Delaware's southern beaches are its most popular attraction. They stretch for twenty-five miles, with both quiet and upbeat little towns and a pair of state parks. The more popular beaches are busy in summer, although they're rarely as crowded as better known Atlantic Seaboard resort areas.

Once outsiders discover southern Delaware's beaches, they rave about them. The Blue Waves Council—whatever that is—calls them the cleanest beaches in America. *Time* magazine rated the beach towns as the "top nice places to visit, great places to live." *Money* magazine called the region "one of the best places to vacation."

Sections of the southern Delaware beachfront are edged by barrier islands and sandspits. State Route 1 links it all together. It follows a skinny sandspit across the mouth of Rehoboth Bay, skims along the edge of the mainland, then crosses a string of islands and terminates in Maryland.

Lewes (*LOO-is*) and Rehoboth Beach are the area's largest coastal communities, although they're really not that large. The oldest town in Delaware, Lewes has fewer than 3,000 citizens and Rehoboth is half that size. The two towns have completely different personalities. Lewes is quiet and laid back, rich with historic sites. Rehoboth is beach party central, upbeat and busy with bikinis.

Lewes dates from 1631, when it was settled by the Dutch and given an awkward name with a pretty meaning. *Zwaanendael* translates as Valley of the Swans. The settlement was destroyed within the first year by the local Siconese tribe, although another soon rose in the same spot. Sitting at the entrance to Chesapeake Bay, it thrived as a shipping port until engine-powered vessels began bypassing it in favor of Annapolis and Baltimore.

The town's heritage is evident in the multi-tiered Dutch façade of the **Zwaanendael Museum** at Kings Highway and Savannah Road; (302) 645-1148; *www.destatemuseums.org*. Exhibits recall the town's rocky history, from its destruction by the Siconese to a couple of pirate attacks to a British bombardment during the War of 1812. The **Lewes Chamber of Commerce** and a few historical exhibits occupy the 18th century **Fisher-Martin House**, near the museum at 120 Kings Hwy.; (302) 645-8073.

Many of the area's early buildings have been moved to the **Lewes Historical Society Complex**, where they have been restored and dressed with period furnishings. They include a tiny pre-1700s log cabin, the Thompson Country Store and the elegant 1789 Burton Ingraham House. The Ryves

Holt House at Second and Mulberry streets serves as the visitor center; (302) 645-7670; *www.historiclewes.org*. The society also administers the **Cannonball House Marine Museum** with a nice collection of nautical artifacts, at Front and Bank streets. The odd name comes from the fact that it was struck by a cannonball during the War of 1812 bombardment.

The town is set back a bit from its tidy public beach. At the **Anglers Marina**, you can book charter fishing and whale-watching trips. If you'd like to see another old fashioned beach town, hop aboard the **Cape May-Lewes Ferry** for a seventy-minute crossing to *Cape May, New Jersey*; see page 271. Call (800) 64-FERRY for reservations.

Next door to Lewes, **Cape Henlopen State Park** preserves the site of Fort Miles, built in 1941 to protect Chesapeake Bay's entrance. You can explore old weapons batteries, stroll about marshlands and sand dunes, and learn about regional flora and fauna at the **Seaside Nature Center**. The park offers camping, picnicking and lots of swimming beaches; (302) 645-8938.

Just south of the state park, *Rehoboth Beach* and *Dewey Beach* are typical seashore resort towns, and they're often jammed in summer. A boardwalk extends along sixteen blocks of Rehoboth's beachfront, with the requisite fun zone, T-shirt shops, water-play rentals and bikini boutiques. Sun-lovers sprawl on Rehoboth's clean sands during the day, then head for Dewey Beach's clubs and pubs for a little action after dark.

Dewey Beach stands at the entrance to the Rehoboth Bay sandspit, which is mostly occupied by **Delaware Seashore State Park**. Swimmers can chose between the choppy Atlantic side or the calm bayshore. Park facilities include bath houses, water play rentals and food concessions. Also, check out nearby **Indian River Inlet Lifesaving Station Museum** with exhibits about the predecessors to the U.S. Coast Guard; (302) 227-0478.

Continuing south on Highway 1, you'll skim the edge of the mainland, nipping through the hamlets of *Bethany Beach* and *South Bethany*. You'll leave the mainland again as the highway skips across offshore shoals to *Fenwick Island* at the Delaware-Maryland border. These three beach towns are quiet and usually uncrowded little places, popular with families.

In Fenwick, the **Fenwick Island Lighthouse** rises above the old fashioned wood-frame downtown area. The nearby **DiscoverSea Shipwreck Museum**, established by a noted diver, exhibits relics recovered from sunken ships; 708 Ocean Highway; (302) 539-9366; *wwwdiscoversea.com*.

Where to learn more

Southern Delaware Tourism, 103 W. Pine St., Georgetown, DE 19947; (800) 357-1818 or (302) 856-1818; *www.visitsoutherndelaware.com*.

Annapolis
Anchors aweigh and lots of history

⚑

Annapolis is one of my favorite small cities because it's home to United States Naval Academy, which produces America's Navy ensigns and Marine Corps second lieutenants.

I can identify with this town because of my Marine Corps background, although I certainly didn't attend the Naval Academy. I was a buck private grunt, pummeled through boot camp in San Diego.

Annapolis' Naval Academy fame overshadows the fact that it's one of the oldest, most historic and handsome towns in America. There's a Navy-like discipline and order to its Georgian rowhouse buildings and to the square-shouldered, slender-domed Maryland State House. It sits in State Circle, with streets radiating outward, suggestive of a ship's wheel.

The area's roots reach back almost to the beginning of American history. The first settlement hereabouts was Providence, established on the Severn River by a Puritan group in 1649. A second community, Anne Arundel Town, was platted on the opposite bank in 1684. Named for the wife of the second Lord Baltimore, it later was simplified to Annapolis. How appropriate that the future home of the U.S. Naval Academy was named for a woman, since Navymen always refer to their ships as "she."

When Anne Arundel County was formed in 1694, Annapolis became its seat and Providence faded. Annapolis received its charter in 1708, making it one of America's oldest cities. As Maryland's capital, it played a key role at the end of the Revolutionary War. The State House, completed in 1779, served as the U.S. capitol from 1782 until 1784, when a permanent site was chosen at what is now Washington, D.C. The Treaty of Paris ending the Revolutionary War was ratified in the State House on January 14, 1784.

Annapolis is easy to explore because, despite its fame, it's a small town of only about 36,000 residents. If you're a history buff, you'll first head for the Maryland State House. We former Marines and Swabbies like to visit the **Naval Academy**, which was established in 1845 on the banks of the Severn River. Guided tours can be arranged at the **Armel-Leftwich Visitor Center** off King George Street. The **Naval Academy Museum** has thousands of paintings and artifacts tracing Navy and Marine Corps history, and the **Navy Chapel** contains the crypt of John Paul Jones. For tour information: (410) 263-6933; *www.navyonline.com.*

The **Maryland State House** is America's oldest capitol still in use. Exhibits chronicle the history of both Maryland and the new republic. Particularly impressive is a mural of George Washington in the old Senate Chamber, resigning his commission as head of the Continental Army at war's end. For information on tours, call (410) 974-3400.

Annapolis is busy with other historic sites. The Georgian style 1774 **Hammond-Harwood House** at 19 Maryland Avenue is now a museum of decorative art; (410) 263-4683; *www.hammondharwoodhouse.com*. The 1765 **William Paca House**, built by a signatory of the Declaration of Independence, exhibits period furniture and is surrounded by landscaped gardens. It's at 186 Prince George St.; (800) 603-4020 or (410) 267-7619. The **Banneker-Douglass Museum** chronicles the struggle for Black freedom. Named for a noted scientist and the famed Black abolitionist, it's housed in a former church at 84 Franklin St.; (410) 974-2893.

Land and water tours provide opportunities to get acquainted with this fine old town. The Visitor Center at 26 West Street conducts one-hour **Discover Annapolis Tours**; (410) 626-6000. **Three Centuries of Annapolis** tours also depart from the visitor center, and from City Dock. They're conducted by costumed guides; (410) 263-5401; *www.annapolis-tours.com*.

Watermark Cruises leave from City Dock, sailing around the bay and up the Severn River; (410) 268-7600; *www.watermarkcruises.com*. The early 20th century style schooner *Woodwind* cruises Annapolis Harbor and the waterfront, departing from Pusser's Landing at the Annapolis Marriott; (410) 263-7837; *www.schoonerwoodwind.com*. The **Historic Annapolis Foundation** offers do-it-yourself audio walking tours with several different themes; 77 Main St.; (410) 268-5576; *www.annapolis.org*.

Downtown Annapolis is a mix of well-preserved old buildings and spanking new ones, and it offers abundant shopping opportunities. Main Street has a variety of boutiques, clothing stores and little cafés. Other shops, including the usual trinket parlors, are at City Dock. **Market House on City Dock** has several food stalls, bakeries, cafés and takeouts.

While Annapolis is more of an historic archive than a cultural center, it does have several galleries. The **League of Maryland Craftsmen** promotes regional arts and crafts, and its outlet at 216 Main Street offers works of nearly 150 Maryland artists; (410) 626-1277.

Where to learn more

Annapolis and Anne Arundel County Conference & Visitors Bureau, 26 West St., Annapolis, MD 21401; (888) 302-2852 or (410) 280- 0445; *www.visit-annapolis.org*.

Calvert County

Farms and beaches: A quiet side of Maryland

M aryland is a state shaped by waterways. The Potomac River forms its western border and the Susquehanna River fattens into Chesapeake Bay, severing the state in half. Yet another stream, the Patuxent, flows south through western Maryland, forming a stubby peninsula on Chesapeake Bay.

This stub is Calvert County, a rural appendage pleasantly out of pace with much of the rest of the state. A swatch of farmlands, old beach towns and coastal bluffs, it's about seventy miles south of Annapolis and Washington, D.C., and maybe a hundred miles from Baltimore. It's far enough away to escape urban sprawl. This is the kind of region where you can buy turnips from the turnip farmer and follow narrow country lanes to beaches that you might have all to yourselves. Much of the coastline is marked by the Calvert Cliffs, uplifted during the last Ice Age. Inland, the county is relatively level and interlaced with farm lanes, ideal for cycling.

If you're coming from Annapolis, follow State Route 2 to tiny *Owings*, where you'll find the **Fairview Visitor Information Center** at 8120 Southern Maryland Blvd.; (410) 257-5381. For your back-to-the-soil fix, ask for a brochure for direct-to-consumer farm outlets, produced by the Calvert County Agricultural Commission.

From there, go east on State Route 260 to *Chesapeake Beach*. With about 3,100 residents, it's the largest town on the peninsula. Early in the last century, it was one of Maryland's most popular family summer resorts, served by the Chesapeake Beach Railway. A mile-long boardwalk with an old fashioned amusement park ran along the beachfront. Just above town, *North Beach* was a thriving summer cottage community. The Depression put an end to the railroad in 1930, although the amusement park continued to hang on, finally shutting down in 1972.

What remains is the boardwalk with its long public beach and the **Chesapeake Beach Railway Museum**, occupying the old depot at Mears Avenue and C Street; (410) 257-3892; *www.cbrm.org*. It exhibits vintage rolling stock and serves as the area's historical archive. The venerable town hasn't gone to sleep, however; it's still a popular beach retreat. You can crab and shore-fish from **Bay Front Park** and hire fishing charters at the busy marina. You'll find several gift and antique shops in the old fashioned downtown area. Although the fun zone is gone, the **Chesapeake Beach Water Park** on Gordon Stinnett Avenue offers cool summer respite for families, with eight water slides and assorted pools; (410) 257-1404.

Head south along the Chesapeake bayfront, past the hamlet of *Plumb Point*, then swing inland to pick up the State Route 4 expressway above *Prince Frederick.* Although half the size of Chesapeake Beach, it has been the county seat since 1725. Just southwest of here, you'll think you've wound up in Florida when you visit **Battle Creek Cypress Swamp** off State Route 506. There are no 'gators here, although this swamp is home to America's northernmost bald cypress grove. At the visitor center, you can learn about this unusual Maryland ecosystem, then follow a boardwalk over the swamp; (410) 535-5327; *www.calvert.county.com/cypress.htm.*

Continue down the peninsula and go west on State Route 265 at *St. Leonard*, following signs to the **Jefferson Patterson Park and Museum** on the Patuxent River. Once the country estate of National Cash Register's Jeff and Mary Patterson, it's now home to the Maryland Archaeological Conservation Laboratory; (410) 586-8500; *www.jeffpat.org.* Visitors can follow self-guiding trails past several of its more than seventy archeological sites, which range from prehistoric native camps to a Colonial plantation. Exhibits in the visitor center cover "Twelve thousand years in the Chesapeake."

Below St. Leonard, **Calvert Cliffs State Park** provides an opportunity to explore the county's Ice Age bluffs. This day use preserve has thirteen miles of trails, and it's a two-mile hike from the parking area to the beach at the base of the cliffs.

Pressing southward, you'll reach land's end at *Solomons*, which rivals Chesapeake Beach as a popular coastal retreat. This town of about 1,600 has a deep water harbor and it's a major boat-building and boating center. The original town occupies a hook-shaped island, linked to the mainland by an estuary comprised mostly of discarded oyster shells. This once was a major oyster processing center. A walkway takes visitors past the town's string of shops and restaurants along the island's neck. At the busy marina, you can book fishing charters or rent boats to play in the large, sheltered bay.

The **Calvert Marine Museum** is the best archive in the county, with exhibits ranging from the region's pre-history to its maritime history. It's at 14200 Solomons Island Rd.; (410) 326-2042; *www.calvertmarinemuseum. com.* The Drum Point Lighthouse is part of this fine complex. A shuttle takes visitors out to **Cove Point Light**, this chapter's featured illustration.

The county's **Solomons Visitor Information Center** is in town at 14175 Solomons Island Rd.; (410) 326-6027.

Where to learn more

Calvert County Tourism, 175 Main St., Prince Frederick, MD 20678; (410) 535-4583; *www.ecalvert.com/tourism.htm.*

The Cumberland area
Way out west: From canals and coal to tourism

$\boxtimes$

A skinny arm of Maryland extends far to the west, so far that it leaves the state's bays and beaches and winds up in the former coal country of the Allegheny Mountains.

Cumberland, at the midpoint of this peninsula, once was a major coal mining center and transportation crossroad. Beyond Cumberland is Garrett County, Maryland's mountain playground, with woodland hiking trails, lakeside resorts, water sports and fishing streams.

The region's history reaches back to 1755 when 21-year-old George Washington was assigned to British General Edward Braddock at Fort Cumberland during the French and Indian War. America's future leader was given his first command here, and he saw his first combat in that conflict.

The frontier town of Cumberland was founded as an American settlement in 1787, taking its name from the fort. When the National Road was started in 1806, Cumberland was its eastern terminus (page 248). The discovery of coal four years later turned the town into an industrial crossroad, served by the Chesapeake & Ohio Canal and Baltimore & Ohio Railroad. In the early 1900s, as oil replaced coal to power trains and steamships, mining operations began closing down and the town started shrinking.

During the past century, the forest has returned to heal old mining scars and the region has turned to tourism. Cumberland is now an attractive town of about 21,000, and it wears its history well. Much of it is focused in a state historic site called **Canal Place**, where the C&O Canal and B&O Railroad formed the town's transportation hub; (800) 989-9394 or (301) 7114-3655; *www.canalplace.org.* In addition to shops and cafés installed in handsome brick business blocks, Canal Place has several historic sites. Parts of the canal have been restored, and the four-story 1913 **Western Maryland Railway Station** at 13 Canal Street has been refurbished put to several uses.

It serves as the terminal for the **Western Maryland Scenic Railroad** that offers round trips through the Allegheny woodlands to Frostburg; (800) TRAIN-50; *www.wmsr.com.* Passengers ride in old fashioned railcars pulled by vintage steam or diesel engines.

The station also is home to the **Visitor Information Center**; (301) 777-5132; and it's the regional headquarters of the **C&O Canal National Historical Park**; (301) 739-4200; *www.nps.gov/choh.* This linear park follows the canal's Potomac River route from Cumberland to Washington, D.C. Not far from the station, the **Allegany County Museum** at 210 S. Mechanic

Street recalls the town's past, when it rivaled Baltimore as a manufacturing center; (301) 777-7200. Exhibits focus on early settlers and transportation.

For a pleasant stroll, follow the **Trestle Walk** from the railway station to the C&O Canal boat basin, which has historic exhibits and a shopping area called **Crescent Lawn**. The adjacent **Footer Dye Works** has been converted into a theme shopping center. Another interesting path, the **Fort Columbia Walking Trail**, begins in Heritage Park at Canal and Baltimore streets and passes several historic sites. You'll encounter a small one-room log cabin that served as **George Washington's Headquarters** in Riverside Park on Greene Street. It's the only surviving relic of Fort Cumberland.

Shed still more shoe leather by following a walking guide through the **Washington Street Historic District**, with several splendid mansions built by Cumberland's early coal mining and railroad barons. Most have been restored and one, the 1867 **Gordon-Roberts House** at 218 Washington, is open for public tours; (301) 777-8678; *www.historyhouse.allnet.org*.

From Cumberland, head west on Highway 40, which follows the path of the **National Road** into Garrett County and the Allegheny Mountains. Parts of it have been wiped out by Interstate 68, although several sections are intact, with some historical markers along the route.

In *Frostburg*, check out the **Thrasher Carriage Museum** across from the 1891 **Frostburg Depot**, which is the western terminus of the scenic rail trip. The museum has one of America's finer collections of horse-drawn rigs, from surreys and sleighs to milk wagons; (301) 689-3380; *www. thrashercarriage.com*. Next stop is tiny *Grantsville* and **Spruce Forest Artisan Village**. It's a reconstructed log settlement where folks produce Colonial and contemporary crafts; (301) 895-3332; *www.spruceforest.org*.

Grantsville is perched above Garrett County's mountain recreation area, with six state parks, thousands of acres of state forests and some short but lively whitewater streams. More than 80,000 acres of this western Maryland appendage are dedicated to public lands.

The center of its outdoor pursuits is **Deep Creek Lake**, the state's largest pond, covering nearly 4,000 acres. It's popular for boating, fishing, swimming and water skiing. The forest-thatched shores of this reservoir shelter resorts, shopping and dining areas, vacation condos and cabins.

Where to learn more

Allegany County Convention & Visitors Bureau, 13 Canal St., Cumberland, MD 21502; (800) 425-2067; *www.mdmountainside.com*.

Garrett County Chamber of Commerce, 15 Visitors Center Dr., McHenry, MD 215411; (301) 387-4386; *www.garrettchamber.com*.

Cape May County
Lighthouses, fun zones and a Victorian resort

Ƥ

It's about forty miles from Atlantic City to Cape May on New Jersey's southern tip, via the Garden State Parkway. However, it's a different world down there. Atlantic city is second only to Las Vegas—albeit a distant second—as a gaming and party town. Cape May County dances to a different drummer. Here, a party might consist of enjoying drinks with friends on a Victorian veranda while watching the sunset.

We aren't suggesting that the area is dull. The 2.5-mile-long boardwalk in Wildwood is about as lively and upbeat as family beach resorts get. However, much of the peninsula has an old fashioned feel, with none of the glitz and glitter of Atlantic City. If you want the opulence of Trump Plaza or his pretend Taj Mahal, you'll just have to head back north.

The New Jersey coastline is ribbed by barrier islands, and they shelter marshlands and dune forests more suggestive of Georgia and Florida than the Atlantic Seaboard. To reach the Cape May peninsula, avoid the parkway in favor of a little two-lane road that skims down these seaward islands.

Begin your trek at *Ocean City*, a family resort town just south of Atlantic City. It's not really our kind of place because you can't even get a drink in this dry town. However, if you don't require a martini with your sunset, it's a nice family vacation retreat, with a lively boardwalk fun zone. And if you insist in being all that wholesome, you can listen to summer band concerts on **Music Pier**. For more information: (800) BEACH-NJ or (609) 399-1412; *www.oceancityvacation.com.*

Below Ocean City, the coastal road skims past one of several elements of the **Cape May Wetlands Wildlife Area**. They're good places to scope out birds and other critters. South of there, you'll pass a string of hamlets with public beaches and a few places to dine and recline. The town of *Stone Harbor* stands opposite a large chunk of Cape May Wetlands in Jenkins Sound. The fine **Wetlands Institute** focuses on saltwater marsh flora and fauna in its science center, and it has boardwalks out onto the marshes themselves; 1075 Stone Harbor Blvd.; (609) 368-1211; *www.wetlandsinstitute.org.*

Continue south—swinging inland to avoid the entrance to Grassy Sound—and you'll enter beach party country. A string of three towns, *North Wildwood, Wildwood* and *Wildwood Crest* are lively, popular summer destinations, and you can get a sunset martini. The lengthy Wildwood Boardwalk has three fun zones with rides, kid-vid parlors, miniature golf, trinket shops, cafés and a broad sandy beach. It can be something of a hike to get your toes wet because the beach is a thousand feet wide in some areas. Visit the Victorian style 1874 **Hereford Inlet Lighthouse** with five fireplaces and elaborately landscaped grounds; (609) 522-4520; *www.herefordlighthouse. org.*

For a close encounter with New Jersey's inland waterways, book a cruise on the *Delta Lady* paddlewheeler; (609) 522-1919. For more Wildwood information: (888) 729-0033 or (609) 729-4000; *www.gwcoc.com.*

South of here, you'll enter the storied old seaside resort of *Cape May.* Dating from the early 1800s, it was one of the first grand getaways on the Atlantic Coast, rivaling Newport with its opulent oceanfront resorts. Presidents Grant, Harrison, Pierce and Buchanan used to hang out here. Then the Civil War, disastrous fires and changing tastes ended its glory days. Atlantic City and Asbury Park now get most of the area's high end resort traffic.

However, Cape May hasn't faded away. It has become a splendid vision of its past, with beautifully restored 19th century buildings downtown, an old fashioned beach promenade and elegant Victorian homes in the neighborhoods, many of them bed & breakfast inns. The entire downtown area has been declared a National Historic Landmark.

Lest we mislead, Cape May not a living history museum. It offers scores of places to stay, excellent restaurants and good shopping. Ask at the **Cape May Welcome Center** at Lafayette and Elmira streets about carriage tours, trolley tours, historic home tours and guided walks. At the busy marina, you can book charter and excursion trips, rent a variety of boats or catch a ferry across Delaware Bay to the Delaware town of *Lewes* (page 262).

At the restored 1859 **Cape May Lighthouse** in **Cape May Point State Park,** you can climb 199 stairs for rewarding views of the Jersey Cape and Delaware Bay. Learn about the history of the lighthouse at an adjacent visitor center; (800) 275-4278 or (609) 884-5404. The surrounding state park is a good birdwatching area, and you can swim, picnic and explore an old World War II bunker that's said to be haunted; (609) 884-2159; *www. www.state.nj.us/dep/parksandforests/parks.*

To learn about Cape May Peninsula's earlier days, visit the **Historic Cold Spring Village.** It's a living history museum off Highway 9, with twenty-five restored buildings. Costumed docents demonstrate the crafts and rural skills of 19th century New Jersey; (609) 898-2300; *www.hcsv.org.*

Where to learn more

Cape May Chamber of Commerce, 405 Lafayette St., Cape May, NJ 08225; (609) 884-9562; *www.capemaychamber.com.*

The Pinelands
New Jersey's mysterious biosphere wilderness

Although the New Jersey Pinelands National Reserve is the state's largest physical feature, covering twenty-two percent of its land area, it doesn't appear on most maps. It's even a bit difficult to define.

Basically, it's the state's outback, even though it contains fifty-six communities, and is within short drives of population centers such as Camden and Atlantic City. The Pinelands, sometimes called the Pine Barrens, cover 1.1 million acres of pine, oak and cedar forests, with wetlands, remote towns and small family farms. It's the largest open space in the Mid-Atlantic region. The area is interlaced by meandering sandy roads and a few paved ones. Many of its backwoods residents, who call themselves Pineys, "work the woods" by harvesting blueberries, cranberries and other crops. Culturally, the area has changed little through the decades.

However, it wasn't always a sleepy wilderness. A type of ore called "bog iron" was mined here during the 18th and 19th centuries, and several villages operated glassworks. Then late in the 19th century, the last of these industries closed and the Pinelands resumes their sleepy backwater status.

This region where folks lead simple lives, an area rich in wildlife and plant life, was designated as America's first National Reserve in 1978. It's also a United States Biosphere Reserve. This is a "laboratory for fostering a harmonious relationship through a program of research that integrates the social, physical and biological sciences," says the National Park Service. That's a bureaucratic way of saying that society is intrigued with this region where rural folks are at one with their environment of impenetrable forest, meandering rivers and swamps.

So what's this got to do with tourism? It's an intriguing region with several state parks and state forests, and it offers opportunities for hiking, canoeing, kayaking and exploring ghost towns and historic sites.

First, of course, we must find it. The Pinelands are in southern New Jersey, between the Garden State Parkway and New Jersey Turnpike. They cover sections of Ocean, Burlington, Camden and Atlantic counties. Wharton State Forest occupies the heart of the area and the Atlantic City Expressway slices through the lower third of the Pinelands. Look at a map and you'll see little dots of towns with old fashioned names like Friendship, Whitesbog, Dukes Bridge, Sweetwater, Speedwell and Jenkins Neck.

A good starting point for exploring the Pinelands is a place with a great name, **Double Trouble State Park**. It's in Berkeley Township just west of

Garden State Parkway exit 77. Within the park are cranberry bogs managed by a local company and a partially restore historic village. It also has the usual state parkish things such as hiking trails, picnic areas and fishing spots. You can ask rangers about interesting Pinelands sites and drives; (732) 341-6662; *www.state.nj.us/dep/parksandforests*.

Another intriguing site is *Batsto*, a restored village and former iron foundry on the southern edge of Wharton State Forest; (609) 561-0024; *www.batstovillage.org*. It's operated by the New Jersey Department of Parks and Forests. The iron works thrived for nearly a century, then it closed in 1855. Wealthy Philadelphia industrialist Joseph Wharton bought the entire town and 100,000 surrounding acres in 1876. He operated a lumbering and agricultural business here until his death in 1909. Visitors can explore the old iron works and village, tour Wharton's mansion and hike, fish and canoe in the surrounding area. To reach it, take exit 50 from the Garden State Parkway and follow State Route 542 west.

From here, you can explore the Pinelands' forests, bogs and tiny towns by continuing west on State Route 542 or driving north through Wharton State Forest on State Route 563. The Mullica River running through the forest is popular for paddlers; see "Where to learn more" about canoe rentals.

Another interesting historic site is *Whitesbog* on the edge of Brendan T. Byrne State Forest in the northern part of the Pinelands. At this historic village, you can learn more than you ever wanted to know about cranberry and blueberry culture, with tours and interpretive programs conducted by docents. The complex includes an old company town, walking paths and fishing sites; (609) 893-4646; *www.whitesborg.org*.

Incidentally, before you begin exploring this mystical place, you might want to know that it's the home of the New Jersey Devil. He has inhabited the Pinelands for 250 years, after being cursed by his mom for being her thirteenth-born. Hurt by her rejection, he sprouted wings and flew off in a rage. He's has been cruising around the wilderness scaring folks ever since.

Where to learn more

New Jersey Pinelands Commission, P.O. Box 7, New Lisbon, NJ 08064; (609) 894-7300; *www.state.nj.us/pinelands*. This commission, not the National Park Service, administers the pinelands. It can provide, among other things, a list of marinas and boat basins that have canoe and kayak rentals.

Pineypower is a volunteer group that provides lots of information on its website about canoeing, hiking trails and other Pinelands activities; *www.pineypower.com*. You can order a T-shirt that says "Proud to be a Piney from my head down to my hiney."

Skylands and the "Water Gap"
Eclectic lures in northwest New Jersey

⚑

Skylands is the name tourist promoters have assigned to northwestern New Jersey. While not a Rocky Mountain high, this is the loftiest region of the state. The predominate feature here is Delaware Water Gap National Recreation Area, a slender 70,000-acre preserve along the Delaware River, which forms the border between New Jersey and Pennsylvania.

The region's other lures are quite varied, and include a wolf preserve, good fishing lakes and rivers, a national historical park, a Colonial-era village, mining museums and several state parks and forests.

Begin with **Delaware Water Gap National Recreation Area**. It encloses forty miles of riverland scenery, with thick forests, high bluffs, waterfalls and tree-shrouded lanes. Its hardwood forests burst into color in the autumn. The stretch of the Delaware through here has been designated as a Wild and Scenic River and it's popular for rafting.

The Pennsylvania side of the recreation area is in the foothills of the legendary **Pocono Mountains**, long known for their summer and winter resorts. The New Jersey side is more rustic and encloses twenty-five miles of the **Appalachian Trail**. A good place to get oriented is the **Kittanitty Point Visitor Center**. It's just off Interstate 80 at the southern end of the preserve on the New Jersey side; (908) 496-4458; *www.nps.gov/dewa.*

Travel north on either side of the preserve and you'll end up where New Jersey, Pennsylvania and New York collide. The drive along the New Jersey side is more of a meander, with small roads passing through forest-clad hamlets. A required stop is **Millbrook Village**, where costumed rangers portray life in a rural 19th century town; (973) 841-9531. On the Pennsylvania side, U.S. 209 is faster; it offers some nice overlooks and passes two of the states highest and prettiest waterfalls, **Bushkill** and **Dingmans**.

Once you emerge from the national recreation area's north end, go south briefly on State Route 23. That bump you see on the eastern horizon is the highest point in New Jersey—1,803 feet and cleverly named **High Point**. It's surrounded by **High Point State Park**; (973) 875-4800; *www.state.nj.us/dep/parksandforests/parks.* While this probably won't impress folks from Colorado, the view from a monument at the top of High Point is quite nice.

Skylands covers five counties, basically the northwest quarter of New Jersey. Even if you confine yourself to the "Water Gap counties" of Sussex, Warren and Morris, you'll have to gallop off in all directions to see their many attractions. You certainly can spend a full vacation here, and there's an abundance of lodgings available, from Victorian B&Bs to mom and pop motels and the usual national chains. As you gallop through this three-county portion of Skylands, we suggest the following lures for your "A" list:

Sussex County

The **Franklin Mineral Museum** exhibits hundreds of specimens from this former zinc mining region and beyond, including one of the world's largest displays of fluorescent minerals. It's at 32 Evans St., Franklin; (973) 827-3481; *www.franklinmineralmueum.com*. Two miles away, **Sterling Hill Mine and Museum** offers underground tours of its mine shafts and above ground exhibits concerning mining techniques and the lives of miners; at 30 Plant St., Ogdenberg; (973) 209-7292; *www.sterlinghill.org*.

Waterloo Village near *Stanhope* is an outstanding outdoor museum with twenty-six 18th and 19th century buildings. Costumed guides and artisans demonstrate early American chores and skills; (973) 347-0900; *waterloovillage.org*. **Tillman Ravine** in Stokes State Forest near *Branchville* is a gorgeous gorge in a hemlock woodland on the edge of the Water Gap. Several waterfalls cascade down through the narrow chasm toward the Delaware River; (973) 948-3820; *www.state.nj.us/dep/parksandforests/parks*.

Warren County

The **Lakota Wolf Preserve** is the only one of its kind in eastern America, sheltering Arctic, tundra and timber wolves in a wilderness environment. It's near *Columbia* on the lower edge of the Delaware River Gap at 89 Mount Pleasant Rd.; (877) 733-9653; *www.lakotawolf.com*.

Morris County

Morristown has several historic lures, notably **Morristown National Historical Park**, America's first such site. Here, George Washington and his weary Continental Army spent the winter of 1779-80, suffering as miserably as they did at Valley Forge. Units of the park are in various areas of the town; (973) 539-2085; *www.nps.gov/morr*.

The excellent **Morris Museum** has a collection of more than 48,000 objects ranging from decorative arts to paleontology, at 6 Normandy Heights Rd.; (973) 971-3700; *www.morrismuseum.org*. **Fosterfields Historical Farm** is a 19th century living history center at 73 Kahdena Rd.; (973) 326-7645. **Frelinghuysen Arboretum** is a 127-acre horticultural reserve surrounding an elegant Colonial Revival mansion at 53 E. Hanover Ave.; (973) 326-7600.

Where to learn more

New Jersey Skylands, P.O. Box 329, Columbia, NJ 07832; (888) 759-8474; *www.njskylands.com*.

Canandaigua and Palmyra
Wineries and Mormons in the Finger Lakes

⚑

According to Iriquois legend, the Finger Lakes were formed when the Great Spirit put his handprints on the most beautiful terrain in the region. That checks out, because there are ten long, glacial carved lakes extending down from Lake Ontario. Actually, there are more if you count the smaller ones, but that messes up the legend.

Apparently, the Great Spirit returned in 1827 and had the Angel Moroni guide young Joseph Smith to a set of buried golden tablets. This latter-day Moses translated them into the Book of Mormon, the foundation for the Mormon church. This all happened near Palmyra, about fifteen miles north.

New York state is a distant second to California in wine production and most of it is focused in the Finger Lakes region. This fertile land was the nation's leading agricultural area during the early 19th century. It is today a pleasing landscape of orchards, farmlands and vineyards, accented by the slender blue stripes of the Finger Lakes. The region, a favorite weekend retreat for New Yorkers, is dotted with historic sites and wineries.

Of all of God's fingers, our favorite is Canandaigua Lake, which extends south from the town of the same difficult to spell name. The prettiest of the Finger Lakes, it's a popular vacation area, with hundreds of acres of vineyards around its edges. Canandaigua was laid out in 1789 with wide streets that are still its trademark. Main Street in this town of about 11,000 is lined with boutiques, art galleries and antique shops, many in 19th century Greek Revival buildings. The street leads to the City Pier and blends into Lakeshore Drive, the town's tourist focal point. Public beaches are nearby.

To get personal with the lake, book a lunch, dinner or moonlight cruise aboard the paddlewheeler *Canandaigua Lady*, (585) 394-5365, *wwwsteamboatlandingonline.com*.; or a sightseeing cruise with **Captain Gray's Boat Tours**, (585) 394-5270; *www.captaingrays.com*.

Canandaigua's most striking attraction is **Sonnenberg Gardens and Mansion**, a fifty-acre estate overlooking the lake, near downtown at 151 Charlotte St.; (585) 394-4922; *www.sonnenberg.org*. The 1887 Queen Anne style mansion was the summer home of millionaire New York banker Frederic Ferris and his wife Mary Montgomery. She had several beautiful theme gardens created as a memorial after his death. The mansion contains a treasure trove of various styles of Victorian furnishings and decorator art.

Another mansion open to the public is the 1816 Federal style abode at **Granger Homestead,** 295 N. Main St.; (585) 394-1472; *www.granger-homestead.org.* The summer home of former postmaster-general Gideon Granger, it exhibits many original family furnishings. Out back is a fine carriage museum with nearly seventy impeccably restored horse-drawn rigs. The town's memories are exhibited in the **Ontario County Historical Society Museum** at 55 N. Main St.; (585) 394-4975; *www.ochs.org.*

Several small family wineries are in the area and some of them are listed in the *Canandaigua Wine Trail* brochure; (800) 554-7533; *www.canandaigua winetrailonline.com.*

Palmyra preserves its Mormon heritage at three sites. Even if you have no interest in the faith, this old Erie Canal town of about 3,500 is worth a look for its solid brick downtown area. Check out the "four-church intersection" at Main Street and Route 21, featured in *Ripley's Believe It or Not.*

The **Book of Mormon Historic Publication Site** is where Smith's translated tablets were first printed in book form, at 217 E. Main St.; (315) 597-5982. Also in town is the **Alling Coverlet Museum**, exhibiting America's largest collection of hand-woven coverlets, at 122 Williams St.; (315) 597-6737. The **Palmyra Historical Museum** exhibits the town's yesterday memories at 132 Market St.; (315) 597-6981.

Two miles north of town, the modern **Hill Cumorah Visitor Center** is at the site where Joseph Smith supposedly found the golden tablets. It's off I-90 exit 43; (315) 597-5851; *www.hillcumorah.com.* The large center has exhibits and videos concerning the Church of Jesus Christ of Latter-Day Saints. Behind the building, the low hill where he claimed to have unearthed the tablets is topped with a gold-sheathed statue of the Angel Moroni.

The **Joseph Smith Farm** where he spent his teen years is four miles south of town at 29 Stafford Rd.; (315) 597-4383. Smith claims to have received his vision about the new faith from the Angel Moroni behind the white clapboard house when he was fourteen. It's now the Sacred Grove.

Mormons don't drink, smoke or even cuss much, but they know how to party. Each July, they stage the **Hill Cumorah Pageant**, one America's largest and oldest outdoor spectacles. It has a cast of 600 and special effects that would put Las Vegas to shame; (315) 597-5851; *www.hillcumorah.com.*

Where to learn more

Canandaigua Chamber of Commerce, 113 S. Main St., Canandaigua, NY 14424; (585) 394-4400; *canandaigua.com/chamber.*

Finger Lakes Visitors Commission, 25 Gorham St., Canandaigua, NY 14424; (877) FUN-IN-NY or (585) 394-3915; *www.visitfingerlakes.com.*

Cooperstown
Here's to you, Willie Mays

♫

My baseball hero was Willie Mays because I lived in San Francisco during the Giants' golden era, when they nearly beat the dreaded New York Yankees in the 1962 World Series. So it was worth the trip to Cooperstown just to see his magic glove and other baseball memorabilia.

Even if you wouldn't know a slider from a spitball, Cooperstown has much to offer, since it's home to a pair of other excellent museums. It's a classic gem of mid-19th century Americana, with steepled churches, Greek Revival and Federal style homes in old neighborhoods and sturdy brick buildings downtown. Add to this the wooded shorelines of Ostego Lake and the Susquehanna River and you've got the quintessential small town—except that there's a baseball diamond right in the middle of it.

Three famous families are responsible for what Cooperstown has become. It was founded in 1769 by Judge William Cooper. His son James Fenimore, America's first internationally recognized author, used it as the site for *The Pioneers* and other books. The Clark family, which made its fortune with Singer sewing machines, moved here in the late 19th century. A descendant, Stephen C. Clark, established the town's three outstanding museums in the late 1930s and early 1940s. And then there's General Abner Doubleday, the so-called inventor of baseball.

It seems that Cooperstown's most famous attraction is here under false pretenses. There is no historical record that General Doubleday invented baseball, and he himself never made that claim. There's no mention of baseball in his thousands of personal papers, and no verified record that the first ballgame was played here in 1839. In fact, Doubleday was attending West Point at the time, preparing for a long military career. Various stick and ball type games go back centuries. Modern baseball evolved from the "Knickerbocker Rules" drawn up by a Manhattan ball club in 1845. Anyway, Mr. Clark decided to create a baseball hall of fame for his hometown.

But never mind that. For those who enjoy watching America's pastime, the **National Baseball Hall of Fame** is *Valhalla*. Founded in 1939 on the alleged centennial of the game's invention, this huge museum overflows with more than 30,000 items, from the first baseball cards to uniforms of the stars. Now modernized, it has interactive terminals where baseball fanatics can look up the sport's most obscure statistics. And of course, there's Willie's outfielders glove. The hall of fame is at Chestnut and Main streets; (888) 425-5633 or (607) 547-7200; *www.baseballhalloffame.org.*

Another Stephen C. Clark creation is the outstanding **Farmers' Museum**, a mile north of town on Lake Road; (607) 547-1400; *www.farmersmuseum.org*. Occupying land owned by James Fenimore Cooper, this is one of America's finest agricultural archives. It has two elements—a re-created 1845 rural village where costumed docents perform chores and practice crafts of the day, and a working farmyard with appropriate critters. A popular exhibit having nothing to do with farming is the Cardiff Giant, a "petrified" prehistoric goliath that made hucksters William Newell and George Hull a lot of money until it was proven to be a fake in 1870.

Clark's third creation is the **Fenimore House Museum** across from the Farmers' Museum; (607) 547-1400; *www.fenimorehousemuseum.org*. This 1930s Georgian style house was built on the site of the Cooper home, overlooking Ostego Lake. It exhibits works of noted American artists, folk art, Cooper family memorabilia and Americana collectibles. A wing added in 1995 houses a fine collections of native peoples' artifacts.

Is all this working up a thirst? Stop at **Brewery Ommegang** on 656 County Road 33, where hearty Belgian style beers are brewed using Old World methods. You can sip at the end of a tour and take a some six packs with you; (607) 547-8184; *www.ommegang.com*. Eighty percent of America's hops came from Ostego County during the 19th century.

Back downtown, Cooperstown continues it delusional preoccupation with history by touting **Doubleday Field** as the world's first baseball diamond. It's on Main Street, just down from the hall of fame. At the adjacent **Doubleday Batting Range**, you can whack at hardballs (tennis balls for the kids) hurled by a pitching machine; (607) 547-5168. Also downtown, you'll find assorted shops, antique stores and galleries, many in old fashioned storefronts. The **Cooperstown Art Association** offers works of local artists and artisans in its galleries at 22 Main St.; (607) 547-9777.

The **Cooperstown & Charlotte Valley Railroad**, operating out of nearby *Milford*, runs excursion trains between the two towns, using vintage rolling stock and open air gondolas; (607) 432-2429; *www.irhs.com*. The 1869 **Milford Depot** contains a railroading and local history museum.

Ironically, the one thing you can't find in Cooperstown is professional baseball. For that, you must journey to nearby *Oneonta* to watch the Detroit Tigers' class A farm team play; (607) 432-6326. Oneonta also is home to the **National Soccer Hall of Fame** at 18 Stadium Circle; (607) 432-3351.

Where to learn more

Cooperstown Chamber of Commerce, 31 Chestnut St., Cooperstown, NY 13326; (607) 547-9983; *www.cooperstownchamber.org*.

The lower Hudson Valley
A great state's legendary river

⚑

No stream in America more is closely identified with a place than the Hudson River and New York state. Much of the state's—and America's—history was written along its banks.

It was first explored by Giovanni de Verrazano in 1524, in the employ of France. England's Henry Hudson came looking for the Northwest Passage in 1609 and gave it his name. During the 18th century, when rivers were highways, it was an important conduit for early Colonial settlement.

The Hudson River area was the scene of several Revolutionary War battles. During the rise of the powerful industrial and political families of the late 19th century, its banks were graced with grand country estates. Today, even with America's largest city at its mouth, the setting is bucolic and beautiful, with its high river bluffs, wooded hills, fruitful farmlands and vineyards. Its beauty has attracted painters of America's first art school and authors such as Edith Wharton and Washington Irving.

It's a minor stream by river standards—just 315 miles long and with a relatively small flow. In fact, much of the Hudson is a long estuary, subject to the tidal whims of the Atlantic. But it's New York's river, bygawd, from its source in the Adirondacks to its grand entrance into New York Harbor. Because it's calm, it is popular for kayaking, and firms in several towns along the banks offer rentals, tours and lessons.

A drive up the Hudson's east bank provides a fine sampler of what the area has to offer. From Manhattan, take the Henry Hudson Parkway north and at your first good opportunity, exit onto State Route 9, which follows the river's banks. If you pass through the commuter towns of *Dobbs Ferry* and *Irvington*, you're on the right track. Looking more like a lake than a river in this area, the Hudson expands into the Tappan Zee, its widest point.

You'll soon encounter *Tarrytown*, where Washington Irving lived and wrote his *Legend of Sleepy Hollow* and other works. In 1996, *North Tarrytown* changed its name to *Sleepy Hollow* in a successful attempt to attract tourists. The area is busy with historic sites. **Washington Irving's Sunnyside** preserves the seventeen-room fairyland cottage where he lived and wrote from 1835 until 1859; (607) 631-8200. Nearby **Lyndhurst** is a 67-acre estate with a Gothic Revival mansion dating back to 1838. It's now a National Historic Trust site; (914) 631-4481; *www.lyndhurst.org.*

Just above is **Phillipsburg Manor**, a restored 18th century estate with a millpond, gristmill and a small farm; (914) 631-3992; *www.hudsonval-*

ley.org. From here, coaches shuttle visitors to **Kykuit**, the grand 87-acre estate built by John D. Rockefeller in the early 1900s; (914) 631-9491. It served as the country home for four generations of the family, ending with former New York governor and vice president Nelson Rockefeller.

A few miles north is the weathered old town of *Ossining*, noted for an accommodation of quite a different sort, the notorious **Sing Sing State Prison**. Learn about its bad old days at the **Ossining Heritage Area Visitor Center** in the Ossining Community Building at 95 Broadway; (914) 941-3189. The ruins of the original prison, burned in the 1940s, and the solemn walls of the newer version, are visible nearby.

North of here, *Croton-on-Hudson* was a 1930s Bohemian retreat for intellectuals such as poet Edna St. Vincent Millay, writer Max Eastman and feminist Doris Stevens. Their liberal antics shocked the staid populace. The 18th century Dutch-English **Van Cortlandt Manor** is open for public tours at 525 S. Riverside Ave.; (800) 448-4007 or (914) 631-8200.

Moving right along, you'll soon encounter *Peekskill*, an old industrial town that has reinvented itself as a major art center. Galleries and artists lofts occupy vacant factory buildings and its downtown Paramount Theater is an active performing arts center.

Shift to State Route 9-D to stay with the river. This scenic drive will deliver you to *Cold Spring*, the most charming little town on the lower Hudson. Ironically, it bloomed as the site of a federal armory that turned out Union weaponry for the Civil War. It's now a handsomely preserved Victorian village with a town square. Art galleries, antique shops and boutiques occupy 19th century cottages and rowhouses. The town's history is on display at the **Foundry Museum School** at 63 Chestnut St.; (845) 265-4010. A Victorian style riverfront park provides fine views of the Hudson.

That commanding presence on the bluffs across the river is the **United States Military Academy** at West Point. Entry is by guided tour only; (845) 938-2203; *www.usma.edu.* You can sign up for a tour at the large visitor center, and explore the adjacent **West Point Museum**, the official repository for American war memorabilia.

Where to learn more

Cold Spring-Garrison Area Chamber of Commerce, P.O. Box 36, Cold Spring, NY 10516; (845) 265-3200; *www.coldspringchamber.com.*

Historic Hudson Valley, 150 White Plains Rd., Tarrytown, NY 10591; (914) 631-8200; *www.hudsonvalley.org.*

Sleepy Hollow Chamber of Commerce, 54 Main St., Tarrytown, NY 10591; (914) 631-1705; *www.sleepyhollowchamber.com.*

Long Island's North Fork
Escape from New York: villages, farms and wineries

⌐

*A*nd *as the moon rose higher, the inessential houses began to melt away until gradually I became aware of the old island here that had flowered once for Dutch sailors' eyes—a fresh, green breast of the new world.*

— F. Scott Fitzgerald, *The Great Gatsby*

If you've never been to New York City, it may be difficult to grasp a vision of Long Island. A Southern Californian might picture it as an L.A. style sprawl, which is only barely right. The western third of this low-lying island is a suburb of the Big Apple, home to Brooklyn and Queens. If you persist eastward, however, you'll leave the tangle and the traffic.

At its eastern end, the 120-mile-long island separates like a mangled barbecue fork. Just as the island's name isn't very clever, neither are the names of the tongs. They're called the North Fork and the South Fork.

The North Fork is the most peaceful, least populated and most attractive part of Long Island. In fact, considering its proximity to America's largest city, it's surprisingly rural, with family farms, roadside produce stands and vineyards. Villages dot both sides of the peninsula, which has miles of sandy and pebbly beaches. If you're an antiquer, you'll find shops in many of the North Fork towns.

Your exploration can begin at *Riverhead,* just beyond the end of the Long Island Expressway. Dating from the 1720s, it was a commercial center to adjacent farms but as the farms shrank, so did Riverhead's fortunes. It's experiencing a resurgence through tourism, helped by the arrival of the excellent **Atlantis Marine World** aquarium at 431 E. Main St.; (631) 208-9200; *www.atlantismarineworld.com.* It has a lost city of Atlantis theme, and critters from the seven seas swim among the "ruins." The large **Suffolk County Historical Society Museum** tells Long Island's story from the Algonquin people through the Colonial period to the present; (631) 727-2881.

The North Fork is as American as apple pie and you can try some, along with over varieties, at **Briermere Farms** just outside Riverhead at Sound Avenue and State Route 105; (631) 722-3931. From this point on, you'll hit a succession of direct-to-consumer farms, produce stands and winery tasting rooms. In keeping with this rural setting, **Hallockville Museum Farm and Folklife Center** is a restored 1765 homestead at 6038 Second Ave.; (631) 298-5292; *www.hallockville.com.* It has a barn, smokehouse, apple orchard,

The road branches near *Mattituck* and most of the area's wineries and other items of interest are on the south branch (State Route 25). Old *Cutchogue* is a real charmer—a small town gathered around a village green. Several wood frame houses have been assembled here to serve as the **Cutchogue-New Suffolk Historical Council's** outdoor museum; (631) 734-7122. The oldest structure, simply called the Old House, dates back to 1649. Call to learn when the buildings are open, since hours are limited. At other times, you can admire them from the outside.

From here, drop down to *New Suffolk*, once a busy port and now just a tiny old beach town. It's on the edge of a wetlands that's a hangout for ospreys. There's a wide beach here, a few places to eat and not much else.

Beyond Cutchogue, *Southold* is one of the state's oldest settlements, founded in 1640. It has a nice family beach and the North Fork's largest gathering of historic sites. The still-active 1857 **Horton Point Lighthouse** on Lighthouse Road is linked to a nautical museum; (631) 765-5500. The **Southold Historical Society Museum** has assembled a few 18th century houses and a rough-shod old barn, plus a working millinery, blacksmith shop and buttery; on Main Rd.; (631) 765-5500. **Southold Indian Museum** offers a huge collection of native pottery and assorted Algonquin artifacts at 1080 Bayview Rd.; (631) 767-5577; *www.southoldindianmuseum.org.*

Venerable *Greenport* is the North Fork's commercial center and most popular overnight stop, with several B&Bs and other lodgings. Its streets, sloping up from the bay, are busy with boutiques, antique shops and cafés. It's an active boating center and it was a busy port during pre-Revolutionary days. Learn all about it at the **East End Seaport Maritime Museum** at the end of Third Street; (631) 477-0004.

Reached by ferry from Greenport, **Shelter Island** is a wooded retreat speckled with high end vacation homes, some a century or more old. You can tour the 1743 **Havens House** at 16 S. Ferry Rd., (631) 749-0025; and explore **Mashomack Preserve**, operated by the Nature Conservancy, (631) 749-1001, *www.nature.org.*

The North Fork's best beaches are at **Orient Beach State Park** with miles of sand, a bathhouse, snack stand and trails; (631) 313-2440. At the peninsula's tip, you can catch a ferry to New London, Connecticut.

Where to learn more

North Fork Promotion Council, P.O. Box 1865, Southold, NY 11971; (631) 298-5757; *www.northfork.org.*

Riverhead Chamber of Commerce, 542 E. Main Rd., Riverhead, NY 11901; (631) 727-7600; *www.riverheadli.com.*

Saratoga Springs
America's resort?

⚐

Basking in the foothills of upstate New York's Adirondack Mountains, Saratoga Springs just might be America's quintessential summer resort. It's an F. Scott Fitzgerald vision of the beautiful people taking the waters and gambling in the casinos, of cocktails and croquet on the lawn, of concerts under the stars, of spirited polo matches and certainly of a day at the races.

It is all of that, and less. Unfortunately, promoters have dressed down the elegant old resort in recent years. It doesn't really need the National Dance Hall of Fame, the Saratoga Automobile Museum or the Children's Museum. This was a playground for adults; children were left with their nannies. And it's a shame that two of its largest hotels were razed after World War II, ultimately to be replaced by Marriotts and Holidays Inn.

Still, it remains a grand resort, dressed in stately trees, old brick and Victorian architecture. Saratoga Springs' famous race track still draws the touts, the old moneyed, the *nouveau riche* and the flirting young ladies. Unless you're among these, avoid it during the racing season from late July through Labor Day, when this town of 26,000 daily doubles its population—and yes, we liked that play on words.

The Victorian style **Saratoga Race Course** was opened in 1863 and it remains America's oldest racetrack. Book your rooms early if you want to play the ponies, and expect lodging prices to be double. You can get advance race tickets through the New York Racing Association; (518) 641-4700; *www.nyra.com/saratoga.* A newer addition is the **Saratoga Equine Sports Center** where harness races are run the year around; (518) 584-2110; *www.saratogaraceway.com.* Polo matches again are being held in this legendary resort town, organized by **Saratoga Polo**; (518) 584-8108.

There are two horsy halls of fame here, which are more appropriate than museums of dance and automobiles. The **National Museum of Racing** is at 191 Union Ave.; (518) 584-0400; *www.racingmuseum.org.* The **Harness Hall of Fame** is at 352 Jefferson St.; (518) 587-4210.

Mohawk Indians were taking to the area's mineral waters as early as the 14th century. The word got out when tribesmen brought their ill British Indian agent Sir William Johnson here in 1771. In 1802, early pioneer Gideon Putnam bought several acres that included many of the region's more than 122 natural springs, and he built the first of a long line of luxury spa hotels.

The best of old Saratoga is preserved in **Saratoga Spa State Park**, which has to be the most unusual state reserve in the land. It was established by state officials in 1909 when they saw Saratoga's star beginning to fade. Casinos, which had been closed in the previous century, were re-opened. Unfortunately, they eventually came under the control of gentlemen like Lucky Luciano and Dutch Schultz. The casinos where permanently closed during World War II, although the lushly landscaped state park continues to preserve the best part of old Saratoga Springs.

The 2,200-acre complex contains many of the area's mineral springs, plus two European style bath houses, large swimming pools, tennis courts, two golf courses and the grand Georgian style **Gideon Putnam Hotel**, which was built in the 1930s. It also has the sorts of mundane things you'd expect to find in a state park, like picnic areas and hiking trails; (518) 584-2535; *www.saratogaspastatepark.org*.

Summers are culturally rich in Saratoga Springs. The **New York City Ballet, New York City Opera** and **Philadelphia Symphony** perform under the stars in the state park's Saratoga Performing Arts Center; (518) 587-3330; *www.spac.org*. It also presents rock, jazz and popular music concerts. In summer, the Saratoga Spa Little Theatre hosts the highly regarded **Lake George Opera Festival**, whose repertory group works to develop new talent; (518) 587-3330; *www.lakegeorgeopera.org*. This smaller venue also presents chamber music concerts and live theater throughout the year.

One of Saratoga Springs' old gambling parlors, the three-story 1870 **Canfield Casino**, now houses the local historical society museum; (518) 584-6920; *www.saratogahistory.org*. It exhibits a few early gaming relics, but for the most part it's an undisciplined clutter that doesn't do justice to the elegant former gambling den. More appealing is the architecturally striking **Tang Teaching Museum and Art Gallery** on the campus of Skidmore College, which exhibits all disciplines of the visual arts; 815 N. Broadway; (518) 580-8080; *www.tang.skidmore.edu*.

The other Saratoga

Sometimes overlooked in the Saratoga story is the fact that the pivotal battle in the Revolutionary War was fought eight miles south of here. **Saratoga National Historical Park** preserves the site where American general Horatio Gates routed General John Burgoyne's British troops on October 7, 1777. The visitor center on Fraser Hill provides a commanding view of the battlefield, and a 9.5-mile driving tour takes visitors past its historical sites; (518) 664-9821; *www.nps.gov/sara*.

Where to learn more

Saratoga County Chamber of Commerce, 28 Clinton St., Saratoga Springs, NY 12866; (518) 584-3255; *www.saratoga.org*.

Woodstock
Life after the event

౹

The last bedraggled fan sloshed out of Max Yasgur's muddy pasture... That's when the debate began about Woodstock's historical significance. True believers still call Woodstock the capstone of an era devoted to human advancement. Cynics say it was a fitting, ridiculous end to an era of naivete. Then there are those who say it was just a hell of a party.

— Elliot Tiber, *The Times Herald-Record*, Middletown, NY © 1994

Many of the 450,000 free spirits who attended the Woodstock Music and Art Fair in 1969 are probably buttoned-down business men and women by now, or maybe doctors, lawyers, beggermen or long-haul truck drivers.

Looking back, there are three interesting elements to history's largest and wildest outdoor rock concert. First, it happened in a region not known for free love and partying, but for artists and art galleries. Second, it didn't really change the Woodstock art scene; it was just a shock wave that swept through it. And finally, it didn't even happen in Woodstock. It happened in a cow pasture near Bethel, sixty miles to the west.

There are perfectly good reasons for visiting Woodstock and environs. It's in a pleasing setting of wooded hills, rivers and lakes in the Catskills, the legendary resort area in south central New York. More significantly, it's one of eastern America's oldest art colonies, dating back to 1902. It has an extensive selection of galleries and hundreds of working artists.

However, there are no specific visitor attractions in Woodstock, and no "Borscht Belt" resorts for which the Catskills are known elsewhere. The staid AAA *New York TourBook* doesn't even list Woodstock, either in its attractions or lodging sections.

It certainly is featured in John Villani's *The 100 Best Small Art Towns in America*: "This bucolic Catskill Mountain community has become a place where artists of every caliber...decide to settle in and work on their careers."

So, how did Woodstock, The Concert, happen? As the folk music movement gained momentum in the 1950s, singers such as Pete Seeger, Joan Baez, and Peter, Paul and Mary were drawn to this pleasant foothills retreat. Bob Dylan bought a farm here in the 1960s. Recording studios were built in the area, concerts were staged and Woodstock became a popular music scene. The Concert was conceived in Woodstock, although promoters chose Max Yasgur's pasture because there was no space large enough in the area.

This town of 6,000 is threatening to outgrow its charm, since it has become a popular second home retreat for affluent New Yorkers. Still, downtown remains a Currier and Ives page from the past, with a village green and even the old mill stream that inspired that saccharin song by Tell Taylor in 1910. The main drag, cutely called Tinker Street, is busy with art galleries, boutiques, coffee houses and cafés.

Woodstock's charm is blurred on summer weekends when thousands of tourists swarm about, from serious art buyers to art browsers to art curious. Shaggy teenagers hang out on the village green, seeking to pick up vibes from an era that had ended before they were born.

There are two historic sources for local art. The **Woodstock Byrdcliffe Guild** occupies the thirty buildings of the 1902 Byrdcliffe art colony, and several contain studios and galleries; (845) 679-2079; *www.woodstock-guild.org*. The **Woodstock Artists Association** gallery at 28 Tinker Street has been active since 1920; (845) 679-2940. The art of the lens is exhibited at the **Center for Photography**, which has changing shows and classes for photo students at 59 Tinker St.; (845) 679-9957; *www.cpw.org*.

The **Maverick Concerts** summer chamber music series is presented in a rustic auditorium on Maverick Rd.; (845) 679-8217; *www.maverickconcerts.org*. Dating from 1916, it's one of the oldest chamber music series in America. The town also hosts a film fete; *www.woodstockfilmfestival.com*.

Quiet old Saugerties

If you prefer a less crowded version of Woodstock, head seven miles northeast to *Saugerties*, an old port town on the Hudson River. It has become a minor art center in recent years, perhaps catching the overflow from Woodstock. For some, the old town's riverside location is even more appealing. Art galleries, boutiques and a lot of antique shops occupy old brick buildings on its main street.

A one-mile path leads through the woods to the 1869 **Saugerties Lighthouse**. It has a small museum, and the keepers' quarters is a cozy two-unit bed & breakfast; (845) 247-0656; *www.saugertieslighthouse.com*. Guests share a bathroom and have access to a communal kitchen.

Between Saugerties and Woodstock is a strange creation called **Opus 40**, which was thirty-seven years in the making by artist Harvey Fite. Covering six acres in an old bluestone quarry, it's a complex of curving paths, pools, fountains and walkways around the base of a large stone column. A museum is adjacent, busy with 19th century quarryman's tools and household furnishings. It's at 50 Fite Rd.; (845) 246-3400; *www.opus40.org*.

Where to learn more

Woodstock Chamber of Commerce, P.O. Box 36, Woodstock, NY 12498; (845) 679-6234; *www.woodstockchamber.com*.

Bucks County
Colonial towns, historic sites and scenic drives

₪

Although Bucks County is just north of Philadelphia, it has somehow managed to remain charmingly rural. This kelly green region of softly contoured wooded hills and farmlands beside the Delaware River is dotted with small Colonial towns, old stone houses and historic sites.

Bucks County didn't get its name because of deer season. Pennsylvania's founding father William Penn named it because the lush green countryside reminded him of his old home in Buckinghamshire, England. A good base for exploring Bucks County is the attractive and well-groomed county seat of *Doylestown*, an old Colonial village that was settled in 1735. With a population of about 8,300, it's not the county's largest town. However, it has several attractions and a good selection of galleries, boutiques and restaurants in its old fashioned downtown area.

Begin your exploration with the excellent **James A. Michener Art Museum** in the restored 1884 Bucks County Prison building at 138 S. Pine St.; (215) 340-9800; *www.michenerartmuseum.org*. The famous author grew up in Doylestown and he contributed substantially to this museum, which chronicles his life in the exhibit, "James A. Michener: A Living Legacy." Other exhibits feature the works of a variety of artists, mostly American.

A Doylestown citizen who pre-dated Michener was archaeologist, anthropologist and ceramist Henry Chapman Mercer, and he left three historic sites in his wake. The imposing seven-story **Mercer Museum**, built under his supervision in the early 1900s, has a bewildering array of exhibits ranging from native peoples artifacts to early American arts and crafts. It's at Pine and Ashland streets; (215) 345-0210. The **Fonthill Museum** was his castle-like 44-room concrete mansion, at Court Street and Highway 313; (215) 348-946. It now exhibits decorative tiles and prints, although the mansion itself is the main attraction. The **Moravian Pottery and Tile Works**, now a museum, is where Mercer earned his keep, designing and producing mosaics and decorative tiles. It's at 130 W. Swamp Rd.; (215) 345-6722.

Author Pearl S. Buck chose Bucks County as her home after being raised in China by missionary parents. The handsome 1835 stone **Pearl S. Buck House** in *Perkaskie* northwest of Doylestown contains early copies of her books, her Pulitzer and Nobel prizes and an excellent Chinese art collection. It's at 520 Dublin Rd.; (215) 249-0100; *www.psbi.org/site*.

Buck County's most famous historic site is **Washington Crossing State Historic Park**. Every school kid knows that General George Washington won a decisive battle during the Revolution by making a dangerous Christmas night crossing of the ice-infested Delaware River in 1776. His troops marched on Trenton, New Jersey, where they surprised and defeated a contingent of Hessian mercenaries. Elements of the historic park are along the river near the town of *Washington Crossing*. They include McConkey's Ferry, from where Washington and his troops launched; several preserved homes and other buildings of the period, plus the Memorial Building and Visitor Center; P.O. Box 103, Washington Crossing, PA; (215) 493-4076.

A pleasing element of the historic park is **Bowman's Hill Wildflower Preserve**, an 80-acre parcel of woodlands and meadows that bloom profusely in the spring. Several nature trails wind through the complex.

State Route 32, which passes through the Washington crossing site, is an exceptionally scenic drive, following the river and its parallel canal. It runs for several miles in both directions from the historic park. If you drive south along the river, you'll encounter two more Bucks County historic attractions. The **Brandywine River Museum** in *Chadds Ford* features the works of three generations of the Wyeth artist family; see page 261 above. Nearby is **Brandywine Battlefield Park** where General Washington's troops once were routed by the British. Facilities include an exhibit center and the farmhouses where Washington and French ally, the Marquis de Lafayette, were quartered. The site is off U.S. 1 on Creek Road; (610) 459-3342.

Five miles below *Morrisville* on a peninsula of the Delaware River is **Pennsbury Manor**, the 43-acre country estate of William Penn; 400 Pennsbury Memorial Rd.; (215) 946-04001 *www.pennsburymanor.org.* Costumed docents give tours of the reconstructed 1683 manor house and outbuildings, including a worker's house, smokehouse, blacksmithery and stables.

Retrace your route along the Delaware—the scenery's worth repeating—and follow Highway 32 to the village of *New Hope*. An artists and writers colony, this charming Colonial-era town is busy with galleries, antique shops, restaurants—and tourists. The **New Hope Canal Boat Company** offers mule-drawn barge rides on the Delaware River Canal; 149 Main St.; (215) 862-0758; *www.canalboats.com.* A 1925 steam train takes folks on a nine-mile round trip through scenic Bucks County on the **New Hope & Ivyland Railroad**; (215) 862-2332; *www.newhoperailroad.com*

Where to learn more

Bucks County Conference & Visitors Bureau, 3207 Street Rd., Bensalem, PA 19020; (800) 836-BUCKS; *www.visitbuckscounty.com.*

Erie and the northwest
A Great Lake mini-city, oil history and forests

Although we group Pennsylvania with the Mid-Atlantic states because of its geographic location, it doesn't quite touch the ocean. Its only contact with a large body of water is a small strip of Lake Erie shoreline in the extreme northwest. With that link and the state's only national forest, this region is quite diverse. The lakeshore itself provides more diversity—the busy port of Erie and the thickly wooded sandspit of Presque Isle State Park.

Rumpled by the Allegheny Mountains, northwestern Pennsylvania once was covered with nearly impenetrable forest, so most early settlement came via Lake Erie. Its namesake town—the state's first and only open-water port—was established in 1795, although a French military post here dates back to 1753.

There is much of interest in the region, including the place where the world's oil industry started, a primeval forest and the hometown of the world's most famous groundhog. However, **Punxsutawney Phil** only shows up on Groundhog Day, February 2, to determine the start of spring.

Although *Erie* is Pennsylvania's third largest city after Philadelphia and Pittsburgh, it's more of a mini-city, with a population of about 104,000. That's a handy size for exploration. Start with the historic **Bayfront District** on the natural bay formed by Presque Isle. The **Bicentennial Tower**, erected in 1995 to mark the city's 200th birthday, provides a nice overview of the bay, the city and Presque Island State Park. A good selection of shops and restaurants occupy the Bayfront's restored historic buildings, and most of Erie's attractions are within walking distance.

The sleekly modern **Erie Maritime Museum** traces the town's nautical history, with a strong focus on the War of 1812. Local shipwrights built the ships that Commodore Oliver Hazard Perry used to defeat the British fleet and regain control of the lake. The museum is at 159 E. Front St.; (814) 452-2744; *www.www.niagara.org/museum.htm*. A seaworthy replica of Perry's flagship, the *Niagara*, can be toured when it's in port. Regarded as Pennsylvania's flagship, it often takes cruises and participates in tall ship events.

The nearby **Firefighters Historical Museum** displays vintage fire fighting equipment and fire department emblems from all over the world. It occupies a sturdy brick building at 428 Chestnut St.; (814) 456-5969. Also near Bayfront is the **Erie Art Museum** in an 1839 Greek Revival building at 411 State St.; (814) 459-5477; *www.erieartmuseum.org*. Its focus is on folk art, and it hosts a variety of changing exhibits.

The **ExpERIEnce Children's Museum** lets kids have fun while they learn about science and health. It occupies a 1906 department store building at 420 French St.; (814) 453-3743; *www.eriechildrensmuseum.org.* The **Erie Historical Museum** also is just off Bayfront, at 356 W. Sixth St.; (814) 871-5790. It features historical exhibits and period furnished rooms in an 1839 mansion, and an old carriage house contains a small planetarium.

You can reach sandy, tree-covered **Presque Island State Park** via a sandspit road or by water taxi from the Bayfront; (814) 833-7424; *www. dcnr.state.pa.us.* It's a good venue for bird watching and it has picnic sites and swimming bays. A thirteen-mile nature trail circles the island.

Beyond Erie

Other Northwest lures are rather scattered; you can see them by daytripping out of Erie. If you head south on State Route 289, you can check out the **Drake Well Museum** near *Titusville,* where the first commercially successful oil well was drilled in 1859. The complex includes a replica of Col. Edwin Drake's well and exhibits tracing the history of the petroleum industry. It's at the end of Bloss Street; (814) 827-2797; *www.drakewell.org.* The **Oil Creek and Titusville Railroad** offers train rides in 1930s carriages, departing from an 1896 freight station at 409 S. Perry St.; (814) 676-1733.

Southeast of Titusville on State Route 8 is *Franklin*, a former oil boom-town and now a virtual outdoor museum of early American homes. Pick up tour maps at the **Franklin Area Chamber of Commerce** at 1259 Liberty St.; (814) 432-5823. Adjacent **DuBence Antique Music World** exhibits more than a hundred old fashioned music machines; (814) 432-8350.

From Franklin, take a scenic drive northeast on U.S. 62 along the Allegheny River to *Tionesta*, then go southeast on State Route 36 to **Cook Forest State Park**; (814) 744-8407; *www.dcnr.state.pa.us.* It's one of the few old-growth forests in the Mid-Atlantic region, with 350-year-old white pine and hemlock groves. Follow a road north beneath trees so tall and stately that they're called a "Cathedral Forest." Cook Forest is on *National Geographic Traveler's* list of America's fifty best state parks.

Pick up State Route 66 and follow it through the mostly second-growth **Allegheny National Forest**, with hiking trails, picnic areas and campsites. North of the forest, near the town of *Warren* is the 45-mile-long **Allegheny Reservoir.** The **Longhouse National Scenic Byway** around the Kinzua arm of the reservoir is one of the prettiest drives in the state; *www.byways.org.*

Where to learn more

Erie Area Convention & Visitors Bureau, 109 Boston Store Place, Erie, PA 16501; (800) 524-ERIE or (814) 454-1791; *www.visiteriepa.com.*

Lancaster and about
Life among the Pennsylvania *Deutsche*

Although communities of the peaceful, tradition-bound Amish, with their surreys and sunbonnets, are scattered throughout the central states, many people identify them with Pennsylvania. Blame it on the incorrect "Pennsylvania Dutch" label. Or maybe blame it on *Witness,* the 1993 film in which fugitive Harrison Ford hid among the Amish.

"Dutch" is a corruption of *Deutsche,* the German word for their language. Thousands of Germans migrated to America during its Colonial days, to escape religious persecution or simply to seek new opportunities. About ten percent of these were Amish and Mennonites. These fundamentalist religious groups have kept to their simple ways through the decades, avoiding mechanization and modernization, including anything linked to the outside world, such utility lines and phones.

The irony here is that, in avoiding mainstream culture and keeping to their old ways, they have become an attraction. Resigned to the fact that many folks are intrigued by their culture, some Amish have capitalized on it by selling crafts and their traditional German foods to visitors. The so-called Pennsylvania Dutch Country west of Philadelphia is one of the state's most popular tourist areas, with *Lancaster* as its epicenter.

Historic old Lancaster has an odd claim to fame, having nothing to do with the Amish. As members of the Continental Congress fled Philadelphia after General Washington's defeat at Brandywine, they overnighted here, so Lancaster became "capital for a day." This old city also served as the Pennsylvania capital from 1799 until 1812. It is now so tourist-focused that it threatens to become an Amish Orlando, not that the Amish themselves have much to do with it.

Lancaster is busy with tourist gimmicks such as the **American Music Theatre** with fifty "celebrity concerts" a year, (800) 648-4102, *www.amtshows.com*; the **Dutch Wonderland Family Amusement Park**, (717) 291-1888; and—good grief!—even an **Official *Witness* Movie Experience Tour**, (800) PA-DUTCH. There are about twenty attractions in and near this city of 57,000, and many places to buy Amish crafts and foods.

The most interesting places to shop are at Lancaster's two farmers' markets, where you can buy goodies such as *souse,* shoo-fly pie, *schnitz* and Bavarian style pretzels. The **Central Market**, one of America's oldest covered markets, is downtown on Penn Square; and the **Bird-in-Hand Farmer's Market** is on State Route 40.

Since the Amish prefer keeping to themselves in their parallel universe, the best way to learn about their lives is at area cultural centers. The **Mennonite Information Center** shows videotapes about Amish and Mennonite culture, and guides will take visitors on tours of Amish farmlands—in the visitors' own vehicles. A reconstruction of a biblical tabernacle is adjacent to the center, which is 4.5 miles south of Lancaster at 2209 Millstream Road off U.S. 30; (717) 299-0954; *www.mennoniteinfoctr.com.*

While not specifically Amish, the **Landis Valley Museum** is a living history center depicting rural Pennsylvania German life from 1740 to 1940. More than thirty buildings are here, including farm houses, a country store, school, print shop and blacksmith shop. Costumed docents conduct tours and demonstrate rural crafts. It's 2.5 miles north of Lancaster, off State Route 272; (717) 569-0401; *www.landisvalleymuseum.org.*

The **Amish Village** near *Strasburg* southeast of Lancaster is a re-creation of a traditional 19th century farmstead. The complex contains an 1840 farmhouse, a one-room school, blacksmith shop, water wheel and farm critters. Docents chat with visitors about Amish culture and crafts. The village is two miles north of Strasburg on State Route 896; (717) 687-8511.

Strasburg is a picturesque town with several shops selling Amish foods and crafts. It also has its share of visitor attractions; (866) 787-7274; *www.strasburgpa.com.* **Ed's Buggy Rides** offers tours of the countryside in Amish style rigs; (717) 687-0360. The **Strasburg Railroad** takes visitors through Amish and Mennonite farmlands in vintage passenger cars pulled by steam engines; (717) 687-7522; *www.strasburgrailroad.com.* The **Railroad Museum of Pennsylvania** displays a range of rolling stock and locomotives from steam trains to streamliners, at 300 Gap Rd.; (717) 687-8628; *www.rrmuseumpa.org.* Downsized trains are on display at the **National Toy Train Museum**, with five operating model railroad layouts. It's on Paradise Lane off State Route 741; (717) 687-8976; *www.traincollectors.org.*

Another Amish Country attraction having nothing to do with the Amish is the **National Watch and Clock Museum** in *Columbia*, west of Lancaster on the Susquehanna River. This large archive has 12,000 timepieces, a mock-up watch factory and an early 20th century clock shop. Exhibits range from pocket sundials to precisely-time atomic clocks. It's at 514 Poplar St.; (717) 684-8261; *www.nawcc.org.*

Where to learn more

Pennsylvania Dutch Convention & Visitors Bureau, 501 Greenfield Rd., Lancaster, PA 17601; (800) PA-DUTCH or (717) 299-8901; *www.padutchcountry.com.*

The Laurel Highlands
Mountain fun, museums, forts and resorts

⚐

The Laurel Highlands in the Allegheny Mountains might be regarded as the Catskills of Pennsylvania, with outdoor recreation, posh four-season resorts, historic sites and interesting old villages. This southwest corner of Pennsylvania is where Pittsburgh folks and others come to play.

First, it was Pittsburgh's wealthy industrialists. Now, it can be anyone who hops on U.S. 30 and heads for the Highlands. The famed coast-to-coast Lincoln Highway travels through the heart of this heavily wooded region. So does the Pennsylvania Turnpike, although Route 30 passes through some of the area's more interesting towns. We'll begin with the old Lincoln Highway and then proscribe a rough circle through the best of the Highlands.

Your first encounter of interest on U.S. 30 is *Greensburg*, a town of 16,000 in the heart of old Pennsylvania coal mining country. The **Westmoreland Museum of American Art** has an outstanding collection of paintings, sculptures and decorative arts by the likes of Winslow Homer, John Singer Sargent and Louis Comfort Tiffany; 221 N. Main St.; (724) 837-1500. Three miles north on U.S. 119 is **Historic Hanna's Town**. It's a reconstruction of a 1773 English settlement, with a courthouse, log homes, Revolutionary War stockade and jail; (724) 836-1800. Archaeologists continue to unearth thousands of relics from the site.

Back on U.S. 30, you'll pass little *Latrobe*, Arnold Palmer's hometown, and then reach the **Idlewild Amusement Park**. Dating from 1877, it was called "The Most Beautiful Park in America" by the *Amusement Park Guidebook*. It has seven kid-theme areas, from Story Book Forest to the gentle Mr. Rogers' Neighborhood; (724) 238-3666; *www.idlewild.com*.

Just beyond is *Ligonier*, an appealing late 19th century village tucked between forested mountains. It's a good base of operations for exploring the rest of Laurel Highlands. A Victorian bandstand on the town square is its centerpiece, and it has lots of boutiques and galleries to check out, plus an assortment of lodgings, from B&Bs to small resorts.

At the **Laurel Highlands Visitors Bureau** at 120 E. Main Street, you can learn about Ligonier's lures and other attractions in the region; (724) 238-5661. Then head for **Fort Ligonier**, a complete reconstruction of a 1750s-era British bastion. Redcoats at this western outpost successfully fought off an attack during the French and Indian War and gave the British an important forward base during that conflict. It's just off U.S. 30 on State Route 711; (724) 238-9701; *www.fortligonier.org*.

Continue southwest on the Lincoln Highway from Ligonier, then head northeast on U.S. 219 and northwest on State Route 56 to *Johnstown*, which was made famous by disasters. Set in a narrow valley, it has been slammed by three floods in the past 160 years. The worst occurred on May 31, 1889, when a poorly maintained dam gave way upstream, killing 2,200 people and destroying the town. It remains one of America's worst disasters. The excellent **Johnstown Flood Museum** chronicles that fateful event, at 304 Washington St.; (888) 222-1889 or (814) 539-1889; *www.jaha.org.*

Head south on U.S. 219 to *Somerset*, then take State Route 985 four miles north to the **Somerset Historical Center**; (814) 445-6077; *www.somersetcounty.com/historicalcenter*. It's a nicely done sampler of two centuries of Pennsylvania rural life, from 1750 to 1950. The complex includes two farmyards, a maple sugar camp and a covered bridge. Costumed docents demonstrate farm and kitchen skills. Pick up a map at the visitor center for the 60-mile **Somerset Loop** that's quite spectacular in the fall, and really nice any time of the year.

Within that drive, you'll reach the little town of *Ohiopyle*. Between there and *Mill Run*, you can tour what the American Institute of Architects described as "the best all-time work of American architecture." It's Frank Lloyd Wright's **Fallingwater**, a spectacular house of concrete and native stone suspended over a waterfall. Built in 1939 as a weekend retreat for a wealthy retailer, it's now administered by the Western Pennsylvania Conservancy; (724) 329-8501; *www.wpconline.org.*

Nearby **Ohiopyle State Park** preserves a dramatic 1,700-foot gorge cut through the Laurel Ridge Mountains by the Youghiogheny River; (724) 329-8591; *www.dcnr.state.pa.us*. The river also runs through Ohiopyle village, providing a water play area near downtown. Other sections are popular for whitewater rafting, and hikers can follow a 43-mile trail along its banks.

From Ohiopyle, follow State Route 381 south to *Farmington* and **Fort Necessity National Battlefield** of the French and Indian War; (724) 329-5512; *www.nps.gov/fone*. It was built under 22-year-old Colonel George Washington's command. He fought his first battle here and unfortunately lost. Elements of the fort have been reconstructed on their original sites.

Nearby in *Chalk Hill* is **Kentuck Knob**, another Frank Lloyd Wright creation. This angular home of red cypress and rough native fieldstone slabs is on Chalk Hill-Ohiopyle Rd.; (724) 329- 1901; *www.kentuckknob.com.*

Where to learn more

Laurel Highlands Visitors Bureau, 120 E. Main St., Ligonier, PA 15658; (800) 925-7669 or (724) 238-5661; *www.laurelhighlands.org.*

BREAKERS OF NEWPORT, R.I.

Chapter Eight

New England

AMERICA'S COMPACT UPPER CORNER

What surprised us about New England was not its compactness. We'd known since fifth grade geography that any one of our Western states could swallow up the whole shootin' match, with room to spare. What surprised us was finding open swatches of forest and even wilderness areas and whitewater streams. We also found the New England that we had expected—old seaport towns, awesome fall color, maple syrup, historic Colonial villages and mansions of the wealthy.

CONNECTICUT packs a lot of variety in its compactness, including a major maritime center, a famous university town, a prosperous minicity and quiet mountain retreats.

Where to learn more: Department of Economic and Community Development, 505 Hudson St., Hartford, CT 06106; (800) CT-BOUND; *www.ctbound.org.*

MAINE is larger than all the other New England states combined, so it has room for a variety of lures. We explored a mountain and lakes resort area, the hometown of a really scary writer, a remote vacation island and lots of little coastal villages.

Where to learn more: Maine Publicity Bureau, 59 State House Station, Augusta, ME 04333; (888) MAINE-45; *www.visitmaine.com.*

MASSACHUSETTS is a lot about Boston and Cape Cod. We avoided Beantown in favor of other historic communities, and we found a less crowded area of the famous Cape.

Where to learn more: Massachusetts Office of Travel & Tourism, 10 Park Plaza, Suite 4510, Boston, MA 02116; (800) 447-MASS; *www. massvacation.com.*

NEW HAMPSHIRE has its own Canterbury tale, plus a scenic river area and a great mini-city that occupies its only scrap of seacoast.

Where to learn more: Office of Travel & Tourism,. P.O. Box 1856, Concord, NH 03302; (800) FUN-IN-NH; *www.visitnh.gov.*

RHODE ISLAND is tiny in size but not in attractions. We toured summer mansions of the ultra-wealthy, explored its spruced-up old capital city and hid on a hideaway island.

Where to learn more: Rhode Island Tourism Division, 1 W. Exchange St., Providence, RI 02903; (800) 556-2484 or (401) 222-2601; *www.visitrhodeisland.com.*

VERMONT has so few folks that its biggest city is a mini-city and easy to explore—and it's surprisingly upbeat. We also found two woodland resorts, including the one that rings with the Sound of Music.

Where to learn more: Vermont Department of Tourism, 134 State St., Montpelier, VT 05602; (800) VERMONT; *www.1-800-vermont.com.*

The "Maritime Corner"
A seagoing pedigree, past and present

Connecticut has enjoyed a rich seagoing heritage since the mid-17th century and much of it is focused on the southeast coast, in the towns of Groton, New London and Mystic. That heritage continues today, for New London is home of the U.S. Coast Guard Academy and Groton is the nation's largest submarine producer.

The major draw in the area is the old fashioned seacoast town of *Mystic* and its outstanding Mystic Seaport, one of the world's finest maritime museums. The little town of about 2,000 souls is worth a look, for its old fashioned brick and wood frame downtown area. It occupies both banks of the Mystic River and Bay, just inland from the Atlantic.

Upriver on the eastern bank is **Mystic Seaport**, a complete 19th century maritime community; (888) 9-SEAPORT or (860) 572-5315; *www.mystic-seaport.org*. The area once was a leading shipbuilding center, producing fast-sailing clipper ships and America's first ironclad, the *Galena*. In 1929, folks who wanted to preserve this maritime heritage began creating Mystic Seaport in a former shipyard.

It has evolved into a seventeen-acre maritime village with homes, shops and—of course—shipyards, where classic vessels are being restored. Visitors can board America's last surviving wooden whaling ship, the 1841 *Charles W. Morgan;* an 1882 Danish training ship, the *Joseph Conrad;* and the 1921 fishing schooner *L.A. Dunton.* More than 400 other vintage boats are on display. You can dine, shop and see more exhibits in the village, and go on docent-led tours. The *Mystic Whaler* and schooner *Argia* offer cruises on the Mystic River, and you can rent your own craft.

Another major draw is the town's excellent **Mystic Aquarium** at 55 Coogan Blvd.; (860) 572-5955; *www.mysticsquarium.org*. This multi-faceted showplace is home to thousands of sea critters and it has special exhibits on John F. Kennedy's *PT 209* saga during World War II, and the re-discovery of the sunken *Titanic* in 1995.

From Mystic, follow U.S. 1 or Interstate 95 to *Groton* on the Thames River estuary. (Locals pronounce it *'Thaymes.'*) Founded as a trading post in 1649, it's now the home of General Dynamics' electric boat division, America's largest producer of submarines, and the U.S. Navy Submarine Base. At the **U.S. Navy Submarine Force Museum** just outside the base, visitors can board the world's first nuclear submarine, the *U.S.S. Nautilus,* launched in Groton in 1954; (860) 694-3174; *www.ussnautilus.org.* Museum exhibits trace the history of "the silent service" from the Revolutionary War until now. One exhibit concerns Jules Verne's fanciful Nautilus submarine.

You can get a quick study of the world's ocean environments by taking a cruise aboard a research vessel at **Project Oceanography**. It's at the Avery Point campus of the University of Connecticut, 1084 Shenneccosset Rd.; (800) 364-8472 or (860) 445-9007; *www.oceanology.org.* Daily 2.5-hour cruises are offered to the public in the summer.

At the **U.S. Submarine World War II Veterans' Memorial**, names of the 3,600 submariners who died during that conflict are inscribed on a 60-foot black marble wall; (860) 399-8666. Special plaques honor the fifty American submarines lost during that war. The memorial is near downtown at Bridge and Thames streets.

Across the Thames from Groton, *New London* is the largest of the three towns, an industrial mini-city of about 26,000. Founded in 1646, it's still a bit old fashioned, with a seaside amusement park and a well-preserved downtown area. Its sturdy old brick business blocks radiate out from a village green. America's whaling industry was born here and at its peak in the middle of the 19th century, it was home to about seventy-five whalers and lots of hell-raising sailors.

To stay with your maritime theme, head for the **U.S. Coast Guard Academy** at 31 Mohegan Ave.; (860) 444-8501; *www.cga.edu.* The academy began in 1876, with most instruction conducted aboard ships. This campus dates from 1932. Unless conditions change, folks can pick up a map at the visitor center and explore the grounds. Exhibits at the **Coast Guard Museum** in Waesche Hall tells the story of the service; (860) 444-8270.

New London offers several attractions, including the **Lyman Allyn Art Museum** at 625 Willis St., (860) 443-2545; the **Monte Cristo Cottage** that was Eugene O'Neill's boyhood home, at 325 Pequot Ave., (860) 443-0051; and the excellent **Connecticut College Arboretum** off Williams Street, with the **Science Epicenter and DNA Learning Center** on its grounds, at 33 Gallows Lane, (860) 442-0391. If you have kids along, or you're still one yourself, head for **Ocean Beach Park** at the end of Ocean Avenue; (800) 510-SAND or (860) 447-3031; *www.ocean-beach-park.com.* It has an old fashioned boardwalk, a sandy beach and lots of modern water slides.

Where to learn more

Connecticut East Convention & Visitors Bureau, P.O. Box 89, New London, CT 06320; (800) TO-ENJOY; *www.mysticmore.com.*

New Haven
Yale and a lot more

Ⓟ

The cows are gone but the New Haven Green remains where they once grazed. One of the oldest towns in New England, New Haven also has the distinction of being the first planned English-speaking community in America, and that plan included downtown cows.

In 1640, the Reverend John Davenport, a rigid Puritan, purchased land for a townsite from the Quinnipiac tribe for a few trade goods. He platted not just a town core, but a complete community of nine sixteen-acre parcels, with the central one designated as a marketplace and pasture.

Several decades later, a group of Harvard graduates—all clergymen—decided that the growing New England colonies needed a second university, so they established the Collegiate School in Killingworth in 1701. It later was moved to Old Saybrook and then, lured with funds raised by local merchants, it came to New Haven in 1716. It was named in honor of one of the more generous benefactors, Elihu Yale.

Now a town of about 124,000, New Haven is working to regain its identity. It suffered from urban flight, blight and excessive renewal in the years following World War II. Many of the historic structures that weren't demolished are now being renovated and several new buildings have risen downtown, giving old New Haven an interesting architectural mix.

To visit New Haven is to visit Yale because the handsome ivy-clad campus extends into downtown. Begin your exploration where the town began, on the **New Haven Green**. It's occupied by three early 19th century churches—the Gothic Revival Trinity Church, Federal style Congregational Church and Georgian style United Church. The rest of the Green is landscaped parklands, providing an emerald center for the town.

At the nearby **Yale University Visitor Center**, you can pick up a campus map and sign up for a free walking tour; 149 Elm St.; (203) 432-2300; *www.yale.edu*. Stroll over to the Memorial Quadrangle, rimmed by ivy-clad Gothic style buildings and accented by the Harkness and Wrexham towers. Nearby, check out the school's oldest building, the 1753 Connecticut Hall, where patriot Nathan Hale once lived.

Most of New Haven's museums are on the campus. The **Peabody Museum of Natural History** features animal dioramas, fossils and exhibits concerning the world's various indigenous peoples. It's at 170 Whitney Ave.; (203) 432-5099; *www.peabody.yale.edu*. One of the largest natural history museums in America, it supposedly has eleven million specimens in its collections—not all displayed at once, of course. The **Yale University Art Gallery** features broad-based permanent and changing exhibits, ranging from Egyptian and Etruscan relics to paintings by noted American artists. It's at 1111 Chapel St.; (203) 432-0600; *http://artgallery.yale.edu.*

Since New England was settled mostly by the Brits, the **Yale Center for British Art** has one of the best such collections outside the U.K., at 1080 Chapel St.; (203) 432-2800; *www.yale.edu/ycba.* Downtown yet still on campus is the **Beinecke Rare Book Library** with such rarities as a Gutenberg Bible and original Audubon prints, plus a large Eugene O'Neill archive. It's at 121 Wall St.; (203) 432-2977; *www.library.yale.edu/beinecke.*

The **Museum of the New Haven Colony Historical Society** looks back more than 350 years to the town's beginnings, with period furniture, nautical exhibits and paintings, 114 Whitney Ave.; (203) 562-4183; *www.nhshs.org.* Off campus, the **Knights of Columbus Museum** details the history of this Catholic fraternal organization, which was established in New Haven in 1882. It's at One State St.; (203) 864-0400; *www.kofc.org/about/museum.*

Obviously, Yale's presence gives New Haven a strong cultural climate. The 1914 **Shubert Theatre**, which launched some of America's top entertainers, books a variety of programs at 247 College St.; (800) 228-6622 or (203) 562-5666; *www.capa.com/newhaven.* There are several performing arts groups in the area, on and off campus. Students and faculty of the **Yale School of Music** present assorted programs in Sprague Memorial Hall and elsewhere; 470 College St.; (203) 432-4158; *www.yale.edu/schmus.*

Downtown New Haven is predictably busy with student-focused shops, ethnic cafés, galleries, coffee houses and more than a dozen book stores, plus some lively nightspots.

For a pleasant drive, head out to **Lighthouse Point** at the end of Lighthouse Road; (203) 946-8005. The 90-foot-tall candlestick lighthouse was built in 1840. It's closed to the public, although surrounding parklands offer picnicking, boating, fishing and an old fashioned carousel. Views of the region are nice from the point.

Just northwest of downtown, **West Rock Ridge State Park** is a 1,500-acre preserve along a sharp ridgeline, with hiking and mountain biking trails, fishing and picnic areas; (203) 789-7498; *www.dep.state.ct.us/stateparks.* Within the park is **West Rock Nature Center**, a 40-acre woodland with regional critters and interpretive trails; (203) 946-8016.

Where to learn more

Greater New Haven Convention & Visitors Bureau, 59 Elm St., New Haven, CT 06510; (800) 332-STAY; *www. newhavencvb.org.*

The Western edge
Danbury and north to the Litchfield Hills

⚑

Although Connecticut has no large cities, it's one of the most densely populated states in America. However, the western edge offers hills, forests, state parks, scenic drives—and fewer people. Many affluent urbanites have second homes here.

State Highway 7 runs the length of western Connecticut, from Norwalk to the Massachusetts border. Several miles north of *Danbury*, it becomes a designated scenic route, so we'll use that old town as our starting point.

A mini-city of about 75,000, hilly Danbury dates from 1684. It shows its age in irregular street patterns left over from old trails. Never platted, it just grew and eventually became a manufacturing and commercial center. It was the "hat capital of the world" for nearly two centuries until hats went out of fashion in the 1950s and 1960s. At one time, dozens of firms produced millions of fedoras a year, including the "cowboy hat," the famous Stetson.

Occupying wealthy Fairfield County, Danbury today is a mix of blue and white collars, and it provides a more affordable alternative to its ritzy neighboring towns. It also has a few attractions worth a pause.

The **Danbury Railway Museum** occupies the restored 1903 Union Station and railyard, with a nice collection of vintage rolling stock. It's at 120 White St.; (203) 778-8337; *www.danbury.org/drm*. The town's past is preserved in the **Danbury Museum** complex, with three buildings, including a hat shop, at 43 Main St.; (203) 743-5200; *www.danburyhistorical.org*.

Something of a surprise is the **Military Museum of Southern New England**, occupying a drab white building at 125 Park Ave.; (203) 790-9277; *www.usmilitarymuseum.org*. It contains one of the nation's largest collections of armored vehicles, plus combat dioramas and thousands of items of military regalia from World War I to our most recent conflicts.

If you want to play in the water, take State Route 37 and then 39 to **Squantz Pond State Park** on the western shore of **Lake Candlewood**. The state's largest reservoir, it offers boating, fishing, swimming and boat rentals; (203) 797-4165; *www.dep.state.ct.us/stateparks*.

Driving north of Danbury on Highway 7, you'll soon reach *Brookfield*, a pleasant little town dating from Colonial times. The **Brookfield Craft Center** is a leading school for training metalsmiths, potters, weavers, glassblowers and other artisans. It has more than a thousands students, and the works of scores of craftspeople are for sale in the exhibition gallery. The center is at 286 Wisconier Rd.; (203) 775-4526; *www.brookfieldcraftcenter.org*.

You may start wondering, as you continue north of Brookfield past shopping centers and strip malls: When does the scenery begin? It begins as you enter northwestern Connecticut, a region of rivers, ridges and lakes called the **Litchfield Hills**. On its southern edge is *New Milford*, a handsome old town on the Housatonic River, with a brickfront downtown, Victorian gas lamps and a long village green. Browse its shops, stroll its streets and have a bite at one its many interesting restaurants. The town's memories are housed in the **New Milford Historical Museum** at 6 Aspetuck Ave.; (860) 354-3069; *www.nmhistorical.org.* In the works—and maybe completed by the time you arrive—is a riverside greenway.

Continue up Highway 7 along the sometimes tumultuous Housatonic River to the attractive art community of *Kent*. It's another charmer of a town, with renovated brick Colonial and wood frame buildings along its main street. They house several fine art galleries, plus boutiques and cafés.

If you want to say you've done the **Appalachian Trail**—at least a portion of it—you can pick it up on the west side of Kent, where it follows the banks of the Housatonic River.

Two interesting archives are opposite one another on Highway 7 north of town. The **Sloane-Stanley Museum** exhibits early American tools and a pig iron furnace, telling you that this attractive landscape once was torn and ruffled by mining; (860) 927-3849. At the **Connecticut Antique Machinery Association**, docents exhibit and sometimes fire up old steam-driven industrial and agricultural machines; (860) 927-0500; *www.ctamachinery.com.*

North of Kent, you'll enter the state's least populated and most scenic countryside, with that rambling river, ridged hills and thick forests. **Kent Falls State Park** shelters a pair of pretty waterfalls and it offers the usual fishing, hiking, swimming and camping; (860) 927-3238. The town of *Cornwall Bridge* lost its namesake covered bridge during a 1955 storm, although it still occupies a pleasant outdoor setting. Just above, **Housatonic Meadows State Park** has camping, fishing, riverside picnicking and a link to the Appalachian Trail; (860) 927-3238.

What's north of is the more of the foaming river, more quaint old riverside towns and new scenery around each bend of Highway 7. Which of course is why we recommended this route.

Where to learn more

Greater Danbury Chamber of Commerce, 39 West St., Danbury, CT 06810; (203) 743-5565; *www.danburychamber.com.*

Northwest Connecticut Convention & Visitors Bureau, P.O. Box 968, Litchfield, CT 06759; (860) 567-4506; *www.litchfieldhills.com.*

Bangor and north
A handsome old gateway to the north woods

Although the vast mass of Maine is north of Bangor, the town is regarded as the gateway to moose country—the state's remote northern woodlands. In fact, Bangor is only about fifty miles from Maine's southern rockbound coast, up the Penobscot River estuary.

North of there is a huge, mostly uninhabited expanse of glacial lakes, forests and moose marshes—the only large wilderness in northeastern America. However, most of it isn't really a primitive area. Nine million acres are owned by logging companies. Although ninety percent of Maine is covered by woodlands, it has only a small swatch of national forest, dipping in from New Hampshire. However, many state parks have forest preserves.

With a population of just 32,000, *Bangor* is Maine's third largest city. Dating from 1769 and named for an old Welsh hymn, it has a fascinating history. It was twice occupied by the British—during the Revolutionary War and the War of 1812. In the decades that followed, it became the world's leading lumber port. Great rafts of logs from those northern forests were floated down the Penobscot River and cut into lumber at Bangor's 300 sawmills. Lumber barons built Victorian mansions along Broadway, while randy lumberjacks and sailors raised so much hell at the port that it was called the Devil's Half-Acre. (One of those lumber baron's mansions is now occupied by Bangor's best-known citizen, novelist **Stephen King**.)

Although not cutesy and touristy, we like tough old Bangor. Downtown is rather handsome, with sturdy three- and four-story granite and brick business blocks rimming its market square. Nearby, a grinning 31-foot statue of Paul Bunyan honors the town's lumberjack days.

Bangor has several visitor attractions and strong cultural underpinnings, enhanced by the **University of Maine** in *Orno*, fifteen miles upriver. The town's most interesting archive is the **Cole Land Transportation Museum** near a trio of war memorials at 45 Perry Rd.; (207) 990-3600; *www.colemuseum.org* The complex includes a covered bridge, train station and more than 200 vehicles, ranging from wagons to vintage cars and tractors.

You can do a background check on the town's lively past at the **Bangor Historical Society Museum**, occupying an 1836 Greek Revival house at 159 Union St.; (207) 942-5766. The excellent **Maine Discovery Museum** is the largest kids' archive north of Boston; at 74 Main St.; (207) 262-7200.

Two more museums are aboard the university campus. The **University of Maine Museum of Art** at 40 Harlow Street has a small but wide-ranging collection of paintings and sculptures; (207) 561-3350; *www.umma.umaine. edu*. The focus of the **Hudson Museum** in the Maine Center for the Arts building is anthropology and the evolution of world cultures; (207) 581-1901; *www.umaine.edu/hudsonmuseum*. The **Maine Center for the Arts** presents a variety of productions, ranging from dramas to concerts to ballets; (207) 581-1755; *www.ume.maine.edu/~mca*. It's also home field for the **Bangor Symphony**; (207) 942-5555; *www.bangorsymphony.com*.

If you like outdoor activities, Bangor has several in-town forests and parks with walking and cycling trails. The Kenduskeag Stream Trail follows a riparian woodland through the heart of town. Kayakers and canoeists can take to the Penobscot River and paddle all the way to its mouth; there are campsites along the route. Canoes and sea kayaks can be rented from **Epic Sports** at 6 Central St.; (207) 941-5670; *www.epicsportsofmaine.com*.

Bangor has the usual chain motels on its fringes, but for a taste of the town's yesterdays, book a room at the Victorian style 1873 **Charles Inn** at 20 Broad St.; (207) 992-2820. Rates are modest and include breakfast.

North into the woods

Although much of Maine's vast northern woods are privately owned, two areas offer opportunity for hiking, camping, boating, fishing and moose and loon spotting. **Moosehead Lake** is about ninety miles northwest of Bangor via State Route 15. Several outfits in *Greenville* on the lake's edge offer canoe and boat rentals and excursions, including float plane trips and cruises aboard an historic steamship. Contact the **Moosehead Lake Chamber of Commerce;** (207) 695-2702; *www.mooseheadlake.org*.

Baxter State Park protects a 204,000-acre swatch of Maine's boreal forest. It remains as it was before the loggers came, with pristine lakes, marshes and old growth woodlands. There are no developed facilities in the park and roads are dirt or gravel, so come prepared to camp. Or you can day-trip it from *Medway* or *Millinocket*, which have motels and small lodges. Baxter's centerpiece is 5,267-foot Mount Katahdin, the northern terminus of the **Appalachian Trail**. The park is ninety-five miles from Bangor. To get there, take I-95 north to Medway, go northwest on State Route 11/157 to Millinocket and follow signs. The park's visitor center is in Millinocket at 64 Balsam Drive; (207) 723-5140; *www.baxterstateparkauthority.com*.

Where to learn more

Bangor Region Chamber of Commerce, 519 Main St., Bangor, ME 04402; (207) 947-0307; *www.bangorregion.com* or *www.bangorinfo.com*.

The Bethel-Rangeley area
Lakes, mountains and an occasional museum

Maine's western Appalachian Mountains are its most popular inland playground, with lofty peaks, river valleys, lots of lakes and thick forests. Tucked among those peaks and crevices are several appealing little towns. Some are historic villages while others are summer and winter resorts.

The region is noted mostly for its outdoor pursuits of fishing, canoeing, kayaking, hiking and biking. These can be pursued from the comfort of cozy inns, rustic lodges and sporting camps. The area also has miles of scenic highways following winding river courses, quaint shops and an interesting mix of museums. In the fall, the region is ignited by a fine show of autumn colors, and in winter it lures downhill and cross-country skiers.

Our trek starts in one of southwestern Maine's oldest towns and meanders northward to its most popular lakes country. To begin, leave Interstate 95 about midway between *Portland* and *Lewiston* and follow scenic State Route 26 north to *Bethel* on the edge of White Mountain National Forest. Built around a traditional village green, this old resort town sits beside the peaceful Androscoggin River.

The town's yesterdays are preserved in the **Bethel Regional History Center** at 10-14 Broad St.; (800) 824-2910 or (207) 824-2908. Here, you'll learn that it began in 1774 as one of western Maine's first towns. The museum occupies the 1813 Moses Mason House, one of twenty-seven homes in the village's historic district, which rims the Bethel Commons.

With about 2,500 residents, Bethel has a good choice of lodgings, from motels and Victorian inns to fancy resorts, and it has several arts and crafts shops along Main Street. The recent re-emergence of the nearby **Sunday River Ski Resort** has made the area a popular winter destination; (800) 543-2754 or (207) 824-3000; *www.sundayriver.com.*

Short drives south and north of Bethel will deliver you to a pair of interesting spots. Follow state Route 5 and then 35 south to *Waterford*. This cute little town has retained its late 19th century look, with clapboard homes rimming a village green. The town borders on **Keoka Lake**, which has a small public beach. To the north, scenic State Route 26 takes you to **Grafton Notch State Park**, set in a dramatic glacial-carved chasm and rimmed by craggy peaks; (207) 824-2912. It offers swimming, picnicking and hiking. For serious hiking, you can pick up a section of the **Appalachian Trail** here.

After doing Grafton Notch, backtrack to U.S. 2 and follow it east to *Farmington*, a town of about 5,000 in a mountain-rimmed agricultural valley. It's home to a campus of the **University of Maine**, with a small art gallery; (207) 778-7001. Just north of town is the **Nordica Homestead Museum**, birthplace of opera singer Lillian Nordica, the "Yankee Diva" of the late 19th century. Exhibits include her costumes, glittering stage jewelry and other opera mementos. It's at 116 Nordica Lane; (207) 778-2402.

Head north on State Route 4 and then 27 to the attractive town of *Kingfield* and the **Stanley Museum**, which has a dual focus. The Stanley family perfected the dry plate photo process and then sold it to Kodak's George Eastman. Using proceeds from the sale, they developed the famous Stanley Steamer, the first really speedy automobile. Three working "Steamers" and an excellent photo collection of early rural Maine life are on display. The museum is at 40 School St.; (207) 265-2729; *www.stanleymuseum.org.*

North of here, the **Carrabassett Valley** is one of the most scenic regions of the state, with thick woodlands, rushing streams and the lofty peaks of the Bigelow Range. The loftiest is **Sugarloaf,** Maine's second highest mountain (4,237 feet) and home to its best ski resort. **Sugarloaf/USA** also is a popular summer destination, offering lodgings, a golf course, and hiking and mountain biking trails. The **Sugarloaf Outdoor Center** can arrange for fly fishing trips, whitewater rafting, and mountain bike rentals; (207) 237-6830. For lodging, call (800) 843-5623 for condos in the area, and (207) 237-2222 for the **Grand Summit Hotel** at the base of the ski hill; *www.sugarloaf.com.*

Continue northwest for several miles, hang a left onto State Route 16 at *Stratton* and follow it sixteen miles to *Rangeley*. This tree-cloaked resort village is the commercial center for a collection of waterways called the **Rangeley Lakes Region**. With about 1,200 souls, the town has a few motels, lakeside cottages, restaurants and several outfitters and fishing guides. The area is popular for canoeing, and rentals are available. There's a launch ramp in town and at **Rangeley Lakes State Park**; (207) 864-3858.

Just west of Rangeley is the **Wilhelm Reich Museum**, chronicling the life of a really weird student of Sigmund Freud. The museum is on Dodge Pond Road; (207) 864-3443; *www.wilhelmreichmuseum.org.* Reich claimed to have discovered a force field called *orgone* that could cure assorted ills and even change the weather. In 1956, he was imprisoned for taking his treatment gadgets across state lines, and he died in jail just a year later.

Where to learn more

Bethel Area Chamber of Commerce, P.O. Box 1247 (8 Station Place), Bethel, ME 04217; (800) 442-5826; *www.bethelmaine.com.*

Rangeley Lakes Region Chamber of Commerce, P.O. Box 317, Rangeley, ME 04970; (800) 685-2537; *www.rangeleymaine.com.*

Monhegan Island
Maine's tiny, tranquil retreat

⚑

Monhegan Island is where you go to rest your soul and perhaps free up your artistic spirit. It's a tiny sliver of land about a mile and a half long and half a mile wide, lying nine miles off Maine's central coast.

As your ferryboat draws near and you see the island's 160-foot sea-cliffs—the highest in New England—you may think you're approaching a fortress. And it can be that, for once ashore, you can fend off all worldly cares and distractions. There are few cars and no ATMs, and room phones and TV sets are rare in the island's lodgings. Visitors can't bring their cars.

Most tourists day-trip to Monhegan, to explore its quaint rock-bound harbor and tiny village and stroll its gravel paths. However, that doesn't provide an opportunity to absorb the island's slow pace, particularly in summer when it can become quite busy. On weekends, it's often overrun with families. Plan more than a day here, for the island doesn't start working its tranquility until the last ferry has left. It's no longer crowded then, because there are only a few lodgings and just seventy-five residents.

Not surprisingly, the first folks to become enamored with Monhegan Island were artists, who discovered this peaceful enclave in the 1870s. George Bellows, Robert Henri, Rockwell Kent and several generations of Wyeths have come to capture the island's simple beauty. In fact, Jamie Wyeth is a regular visitor and has a cottage here.

There are many ways to spend your days on the island. You can walk its seventeen miles of trails, following them to marshes, beaches, thick woods and vista points atop high seacliffs. Climb up steep **Lighthouse Hill** to admire its 1824 beacon, then visually sort through the eclectic clutter of exhibits in the adjacent **Monhegan Museum**. Unfortunately, it's only open from July through September. A nearby art museum features reproductions of paintings by noted artists who have put the island to canvas.

Birding is excellent, for the island lies in the path of the Atlantic Flyway. More than 200 species pass through or live here the year around. For particularly peaceful moments, walk out to **Cathedral Woods**, a spruce forest where deer hang out.

In the tree-shaded, wood frame village, you have a choice of activities. You can tour artists' studios, browse the few shops and galleries, attend informal concerts and perhaps take an art class or even a yoga class. There is no chamber of commerce or visitor center, so a community bulletin board silently announces upcoming activities.

A swimming cove simply called **Swim Beach** is near the village. However, it's really more of a bundling beach because these north Atlantic waters are cold, even in August. Kids squeal in and out of the surf and then retire to build sand castles or play with beach toys from a communal tub.

After you've exhausted the island's opportunities for amusements, drop into the **Barnacle Café** for a bite or a caffé latte. Late that evening, hike back up Lighthouse Hill and watch the sky go pink; it's a favorite place for sunset-watchers. Or if you've relaxed yourself into a state of laziness, just lounge in an Adirondack chair with a good book, pausing occasionally from your reading to listen to wind and wave.

The only vehicles on the island are golf carts used by residents and seasonal artists, plus a few pickups employed by lobstermen and by the inns to haul guests' luggage up from the dock.

Monhegan Island was first noted in mariners' logs in 1497, then Captain John Smith of the Jamestown colony put ashore in 1614, thinking it would be a fine place to establish a utopian community. However, that plan never developed. In the 1790s, a few fishermen and lobstermen began living here, then the first artists discovered the place in the 1870s.

Theodore Edison, son of the great inventor, became so enamored with the island that he caused it to be what it is today. During the 1950s, he bought up most of the available land and turned it into a nature preserve, confining settlement to the handful of cottages around the village.

Passenger ferries serve the island from *Port Clyde, New Harbor* and *Boothbay Harbor.* Most folks prefer Port Clyde because it's a charming old lobster fishing village, and the ferries pass the Marshall Point Lighthouse and several tree-thatched islands en route to Monhegan. You can choose between the old *Laura B.* and ride with island-bound cargo, or the faster *Elizabeth Ann* with a regular passenger cabin; **Monhegan Boat Line**; (207) 372-8848; *www.monheganboat.com.*

Lodgings can best be described as charmingly rustic. They're available at the old Victorian style **Island Inn,** (207) 596-0371; the **Monhegan House,** a handsome inn dating from 1870, (800) 599-7983 or (207) 594-7983, *www.monheganhouse.com*; and the informal and rather spartan **Trailing Yew,** (800) 592-2520 or (207) 596-0440. All three have restaurants.

Where to learn more

Rockland-Thomaston Area Chamber of Commerce, P.O. Box 508, Rockland, ME 04841; (800) 562-2529; *www.therealmaine.com*. Since Monhegan Island has no visitor center, the Rockland-Thomaston chamber can provide information on ferry services and attractions in the area.

Portland
"The beautiful town seated by the sea"

Ƀ

Surprisingly small, surprisingly interesting and surprisingly cultural. Folks who don't regard Maine's largest city as a serious visitor destination simply haven't been there.

In this thinly-populated state, "largest city" translates to fewer than 65,000 people, so it's a nice size for exploration. Oregon's biggest city, which took Portland's name more than 160 years ago, is eight times larger. The cultural surprise comes from Portland's newly developing role as a major arts center. John Villani's *The 100 Best Small Art Towns in America* ranks it fourth in the nation.

To appreciate Portland's appeal, you must first penetrate an industrial and suburban rim, for the mini-city is on the coastal edge of an urban sprawl of more than 200,000 people. Once you've done this, you'll wind up on a small and very walkable peninsula that's the heart of downtown.

Depending on their interests, most visitors head for the historic waterfront or for Congress Street, the town's cultural core. It's just five blocks up from the harbor. Both areas were transformed in the 1990s as the town recovered from suburban flight and from a 1980s economic downturn.

The **Old Port** has been fashioned into a grand Victorian vision of narrow cobblestone streets, brick sidewalks and gas lamps. Refurbished cargo sheds, merchant exchanges and ships chandleries now contain trendy boutiques, curio shops, restaurants and an amazing concentration of bars and clubs. With the adjacent harbor providing cruises and fishing trips, the Old Port attracts families by day and pub crawlers by night.

Congress Street became a visual arts enclave after the Maine College of Art converted an empty department store into a cultural center. Its centerpiece is the **Institute of Contemporary Art** with five floors of studios, classrooms and exhibit spaces, at 522 Congress St.; (207) 879-5742; *www. meca.edu.* Writes Villani: "Congress Street and its adjoining boulevards shine with new galleries, restaurants, coffee bars...and boutiques..."

Portland also is busy with performing arts. The **Center for Cultural Exchange** hosts various local and international acts, (207) 761-1545, *www.centerforculturalexchange.org;* and the **Portland Stage Company** presents a season of comedies and dramas, (207) 774-0465; *www.portlandstage.com.*

This fine mini-city has too many attractions to fit here, so we'll pick some favorites. The dramatic **Portland Museum of Art**, designed by I.M. Pei, has a versatile collection of classic and contemporary American and

European works and decorative arts, at 7 Congress St.; (207) 775-6148; *www. portlandmuseum.org.* The next-door **Children's Museum of Maine** features a room-sized *camera obscura* and lots of hands-on stuff for the kiddies, at 142 Free St.; (207) 828-1234; *www.kitetails.com.*

Henry Wadsworth Longfellow was born in Portland and the stern brick house built by his father in 1875 is the focal point of the **Wadsworth-Longfellow House & Center for Maine History**. It's just up from the waterfront at 489 Congress St.; (207) 879-0427; *mainehistory.com.* Exhibits at the adjacent **Maine History Gallery** tell the story of the state, from native folks to white settlement. Also near the port is the **Portland Public Market** with produce, meat and fish stalls, a coffee shop, wine shop and seafood café; 25 Preble St.; (207) 228-2000; *www.portlandmarket.com.*

Ferries, sightseeing boats and charter boats cruise off in all directions from the waterfront. The sleek **CAT** auto and passenger ferry offers high-speed runs to *Yarmouth, Nova Scotia*; (888) 249-7245; *www.catferry.com.* **Casco Bay Lines** takes folks out to the six offshore Calendar Islands in Casco Bay; (207) 774-7871; *www.cascobaylines.com.* The **Olde Port Mariner Fleet** offers harbor cruises, lighthouse tours and whale-watching trips, plus deep-sea fishing charters; (207) 775-0727; *www.marinerfleet.com.*

Portland has several restored 19th century homes, most notably the **Victoria Mansion** at 109 Danforth St.; (207) 772-4841; *www.victoriamansion. org.* This gorgeous Italianate, built between 1858 and 1863, is regarded as one of America's finest Victorian era brownstones.

Out at the entrance to the harbor, check out the 1794 **Portland Head Light & Museum**, one of the most photogenic lighthouses on any coast; (207) 799-2661. Surrounding parklands offer picnic sites, a pebbly beach and nice views of the harbor. The light is now automated and the lightkeeper's house contains a small museum, tracing the town's nautical history.

In the beginning, it wasn't easy being Portland, Maine. The town was established on this natural harbor in 1632, then in 1676 native tribes sacked and burned it, sending residents in panicked flight. They gradually returned, then the British destroyed the town in 1775. An accidental fire ravaged poor old Portland one more time, in 1866. This time it was rebuilt for keeps, with grand Victorian architecture that's still evident in many areas.

Portland has become, in the words of native son Longfellow: "The beautiful town that is seated by the sea."

Where to learn more

Greater Portland Convention & Visitor's Bureau, 245 Commercial St., Portland, ME 04101; (207) 772-5800; *www.visitportland.com.*

Cape Cod's outer reach
Chatham and the national seashore

♫

If you're fond of sand dunes and salty air,
Quaint little villages here and there,
You're sure to fall in love with old Cape Cod.
— By Claire Rothrock, Milt Yankus and Allan Jeffrey, © 1957

The problem is, many areas of Cape Cod don't seem that old anymore. Not with the growth of time share condos, T-shirt shops, "Victorians" built in this century and big box stores sitting on bigger parking lots.

To discover the "Old Cape Cod" that Patti Page warbled about in 1957, head for Chatham, and then continue on Cape Cod National Seashore. Chatham is one of the Cape's wealthiest communities and its old money residents can afford to focus more on preserving their village than promoting tourism. And of course, rangers at the national seashore try to keep the Cape as it was when the Pilgrims first saw it.

The shape of Cape Cod has always reminded us of the skinny 98-pound weakling trying to flex his muscles. Chatham is at elbow and the national seashore occupies the forearm. Within the flex is sheltered Cape Cod Bay.

Since Cape Cod is New England's most famous tourist destination, try to avoid it in summer when cars jam the roadways and families crowd the beaches and fill the resorts, inns and motels. Fall is a grand time for Chatham and any other part of the Cape, when the air is clear and crisp and the rug rats are back in school. The downside is that many lodgings and shops close, often because their summer help also has gone back to school.

The good news is that once you reserve fall lodging in Chatham—check well ahead—the nearby national seashore doesn't shut down. You can enjoy its interpretive centers, beaches and nature trails the year around, although some ranger programs may be curtailed.

The Outer Cape was one of the last areas of this skinny arm to be settled, although it was one of the first to be encountered by outsiders. Pilgrims of the good ship *Mayflower* spent their first five weeks near present-day Provincetown at the Cape's tip. Then they left to establish their Plymouth colony on the mainland because it had more reliable water sources.

Unlike the more popular Provincetown with its T-shirt shops, sightseeing cruises and multiple tourist sites, Chatham is quieter and more conservative. Much of the flavor of old Cape Cod survives here. Commercial fishermen still unload their daily catches at Chatham Harbor and summer concerts are still held in Kate Gould Park's old bandstand. Art galleries and high end boutiques outnumber T-shirt shops in the wood frame downtown area.

Chatham does have a couple of specific attractions. At the **Atwood House Museum** you can see how one of the early sea captains lived. Built in 1752, the shingle-sided house has several period furnished rooms, plus exhibits recalling Chatham's earlier days. It's seven miles south of town at 347 Stage Harbor Rd.; (508) 945-2493; *www.chathamhistoricalsociety.org.* Back in town, the 1887 **Chatham Railroad Museum** houses vintage train lore in a former passenger station on Depot Road; (508) 945-5199; *www. chathamrailroadmuseum.org.*

The waters around Chatham are noted for their bluefish, bass and snapper catches, and you can hire a charter fishing boat at the harbor. And for a good view of those waters, head for the **Chatham Light** on a coastal moor.

Just south of town is **Monomoy National Wildlife Refuge** on a couple of offshore islands. They're noted for their bird populations and seal colonies. Refuge headquarters is on Morris Island south of the lighthouse, reached by Morris Island Road; (508) 945-0594; *www.fws.gov/northeast/ monomoy.* Here, you can learn about trips to the refuge.

Cape Cod National Seashore

The 43,608-acre national seashore was established in 1961 to arrest Cape Cod's development and protect a swatch of its landforms. It rambles for some thirty miles along the Cape's forearm, extending down a barrier island across the face of Chatham. It preserves coastal bluffs and beaches, sand dunes, pine forests, fresh water kettle ponds and salt water marshes. The national seashore also contains some old cottages, former cranberry bogs and other signs of earlier human habitation.

The preserve has eleven self-guiding nature trails, some mountain biking trails and four picnic areas. If you're here in summer when it's warm enough to swim—barely—six beaches are staffed with lifeguards.

The **Salt Pond Visitor Center** on U.S. 6 near *Orleans* has exhibits and lots of publications about the preserve. At either location, you can get schedules of ranger programs. Some of these programs continue through October, so this still works for a fall vacation.

Where to learn more

Cape Cod National Seashore, 99 Marconi Site Rd., Wellfleet, MA 02667; (508) 349-3785; *www.nps.gov/caco.*

Chatham Chamber of Commerce, P.O. Box 793, Chatham, MA 026333; (800) 715-5567 or (508) 945-5199; *www.chathaminfo.com.*

Lexington and Concord
Those shots heard 'round the world

Ʒ

As much as we're tempted to head for Boston and spend these two pages on its wonderful Freedom Trail, that is hardly an undiscovered city. Lesser known, except in grade school history books, are Lexington and Concord, a few miles apart in the tree-thatched Merrimack Valley

About twenty miles northwest of Boston, these are the towns where the sparks of the Revolutionary War were ignited. Although Lexington and Concord are small, with just a few thousand residents each, sprawling Boston suburbs threaten to engulf them. However, both towns have managed to preserve their historic downtown areas, giving them more of a village feel.

In case you've forgotten your grade school history, the American Revolution began on April 19, 1775. The British sent troops from Boston to intimidate the Massachusetts militia and seize its arms and powder supplies. Silversmith Paul Revere made his famous midnight ride to Lexington the night before to warn the colonists that the Redcoats were coming.

The next day, a militia of about seventy-seven men, confronted by 700 British regulars on the Lexington Green, thought it wise to retreat. However, someone fired a shot and the British sent a volley into their ranks, killing eight colonists, six as they fled. Later that same day, a larger group of better organized militia met the Redcoats at Concord's North Bridge, where they inflicted heavy casualties and sent the Brits in retreat. They were harassed and fired upon by militiamen and armed civilians all the way back to Boston, suffering 250 killed, wounded or missing.

Start your exploration where the first shots were fired, in *Lexington* on the village green, since re-named the **Battle Green**. It has a statue of minute man Capt. John Parker, who told his troops: "Stand your ground. Don't fire unless fired upon, but if they mean to have a war, let it start here."

Three nearby structures that figured in that first day of the conflict are now museums run by the Lexington Historical Society; *www.lexingtonhistory.org*. The 1709 **Buckman Tavern** was the headquarters of the Lexington minute men, and the two couriers, Revere and William Dawes, supposedly quaffed a couple here; it's at One Bedford St.; (781) 862-5598. The 1698 **Hancock-Clarke House** is where Revere awakened patriots John Hancock and Samuel Adams with the news that those bloody British were coming. It's at 36 Hancock St.; (781) 862-1703. The 1695 **Munroe Tavern** served as temporary British headquarters, where they treated their wounded after the battle; at 1332 Massachusetts Ave.; (781) 862-1703.

State Route 2A, which links Lexington and Concord and is now called the "Battle Road," has been designated as **Minute Man National Historical Park**; (978) 369-6993; *www.nps.gov/mima*. Several sites along the five-mile route mark that bloody opening day of the war, and the countryside has been restored to its Colonial look.

There are visitor centers at both ends. The **Minute Man Visitor Center** is just outside Lexington at Route 2A and Airport Road; (781) 862-7753. A 25-minute audio-video show recreates the events of that fateful day. The **North Bridge Visitor Center** in Concord at 174 Liberty Street displays uniformed mannequins and artifacts of the war; (978) 369-6993. Nearby is the famous bridge and the Minute Man of Concord, Daniel Chester French's statue. Its base is engraved with Ralph Waldo Emerson's immortal verse:

> *By the rude bridge that arched the flood*
> *Their flag to April's breeze unfurled.*
> *Here once the embattled farmers stood*
> *And fired the shot heard 'round the world.*

While the North Bridge is the most famous landmark in *Concord,* the town has a goodly number of other lures. And it isn't just about the Revolution. Some of America's most famous early writers are associated with Concord. The honor roll includes Emerson, Henry David Thoreau of nearby Waldon Pond fame, and Louisa May Alcott. Sculptor French later created the seated statue for the Lincoln Memorial in Washington, D.C.

Learn about the town's cultural and revolutionary history at the excellent and extensive **Concord Museum**, with five period-furnished rooms and thirteen galleries at 200 Lexington Rd.; (978) 369-9609; *www.concordmuseum.org*. The extensive collections include Paul Revere's lantern, Emerson memorabilia and a reconstruction of Thoreau's study at Waldon Pond.

Across from the museum, the **Emerson House** preserves the place where the gifted author lived and wrote from 1835 until 1882; (978) 369-2236. It displays Emerson mementos and some original family furniture.

Thoreau's nearby hideaway is now **Walden Pond State Reservation**, with a replica of his cabin, where ranger talks are given; (978) 360-3254. A popular swimming hole, this deep kettle pond becomes extremely crowded in summer, and the parking lot often fills up, particularly on weekends.

Where to learn more

Concord Chamber of Commerce, 100 Main St., Suite 310-2, Concord, MA 01742; (978) 369-3120; *www.concordchamberofcommerce.org*.

Lexington Visitors Center, 1875 Massachusetts Ave., Lexington, MA 02421; (781) 862-1450; *www.lexingtonchamber.org/visitor.html*.

The Mohawk Trail
A scenic ramble through the northwest corner

♫

Since Massachusetts is America's third most densely populated state, it's difficult to escape crowds and traffic. If you feel the need to get away, head for the northwestern corner and follow the Mohawk Trail.

The scenically busy 63-mile route—State Highway 2—twists, climbs and crawls through some of the state's roughest and least settled terrain. You'll encounter whitewater rivers, state park woodlands, country inns and a string of small towns of diverse personalities.

Following the Deerfield River for much of its length, the trail began as a native path, once used by the Mohawks to raid early Dutch and English settlements. As the native people were subdued, settlers improved the trail as a wagon route. In 1775, patriot Ethan Allen took his troops—including still-loyal Benedict Arnold—over the trail from Boston to capture New York's British-held Fort Ticonderoga.

The historic route was paved in 1914 and designated as one of America's first scenic highways. Nearly a century later, the *National Geographic Traveler* listed the trail among its top fifty scenic routes. Tourism along the trail is something of a cottage industry. Except for North Adams and Williamstown on the western end, you'll encounter lots of mom and pop motels, family-owned cafés, souvenir shops and little roadside attractions.

To get to the Mohawk Trail, shoot across Massachusetts on Interstate 90 then go north on I-91 to the old market town of *Greenfield.* Dating from 1753, it's the seat of Franklin County and it serves as the area's commercial center. Other than being charmingly old fashion, it offers no specific attractions except the interesting brick **Poet's Seat Tower** atop Greenfield Mountain, which offers a nice panorama of the surrounding hills.

A section of the Mohawk Trail goes east from Greenfield, but we'll follow the main route west. This exceptionally pretty drive along the Deerfield River soon will deliver you to *Shelburne Falls*, a charming little Victorian town of galleries and craft shops. It's locally famous for its **Bridge of Flowers** across the Deerfield River. Locals have turned this former trolley crossing into a pedestrian bridge festooned with flower boxes. At the **Historical Society Museum** in the Arms Academy building, you'll learn that the first Yale locks were made in Shelburne Falls by Linus Yale. East of town and below **Salmon Falls**, note a series of potholes gouged out by glaciers.

If you're tempted by the river's rushing rapids, you can sign up for a whitewater rafting trip in *Charlemont* a few miles west of Shelburne Falls.

A couple of outfitters offering short trips are **Zoar Outdoor**, (800) 532-7483, *www.zoaroutdoor.com*; and **Crab Apple Whitewater**, (800) 553-7238, *www.crabappleinc.com*. Charlemont dates from 1749 and its story is told in the **Historical Society Museum** in the town hall.

Route 8A leads north of Charlemont to the little art colony and farm community of *Heath,* where you can pick your own blueberries or—if you're here in August—attend the old fashioned **Heath Fair**. South of Charlemont, the same highway leads to *Hawley* and **Kenneth M. Dubuque Memorial State Forest**, with an historic charcoal kiln and a mineral spring. Back on Highway 2, **Mohawk Trail State Forest** just west of Charlemont shelters a preserved section of the original trail as it looked before the asphalt crews arrived. The park also has a good network of hiking trails.

Just beyond the oddly-named hamlet of *Florida*, the highway climbs to Western Summit pass and spirals down into *North Adams*, a town of 16,000 set against the lofty Berkshires. In 1875, the Hoosac rail tunnel was completed through the mountains after a 25-year effort, and North Adams became a major manufacturing center. It has since lost its industries and is reinventing itself as an art colony. The community's boldest effort is the **Massachusetts Museum of Contemporary Art**, a visual and performing arts facility occupying a huge complex of twenty-seven former factory buildings; (413) 662-2111; *www.massmoca.org*. If it manages to fill the 150,000 square feet of space, it will be one of America's largest art centers.

Nearby **Western Gateway Heritage Park** recalls North Adams' heyday as an industrial center. Its collection of six restored buildings contain exhibits, shops and a restaurant; at 9 Furnace St.; (413) 663-6312.

The last stop on the Mohawk Trail is *Williamstown*, an attractive community in the northern part of the Berkshires resort area and a worthy destination in its own right. Rich in Georgian architecture, this handsome Colonial style town of 5,000 people is home to **Williams College**, an eminent liberal arts school; *www.williams.edu*. On campus is the **Williams College Museum of Art**, (413) 597-2429; and the **Chapin Library of Rare Books**, (413) 597-2462.

The superb **Sterling and Francine Clark Art Institute** occupies a 130-acre complex of trails, lily ponds and gardens at 225 South St.; (413) 458-2303; *www.clarkart.edu*. The art collection includes works of Robert Sterling Clark and other Americans, plus French impressionists and old masters.

Where to learn more

Mohawk Trail Association, P.O. Box 1044, North Adams, MA 01247; *www.mohawktrail.com*.

Connecticut River Valley ramble
Exploring the western borderland

Ɗ

New Hampshire and Vermont viewed together resemble a rectangular block with a seam running corner to corner, northeast to southwest. That seam is the Connecticut River and by declaration of King George III, the river lies entirely within New Hampshire. He granted the New Hampshire Colony title to the stream, and the border between the two states is still on the west bank, not in the middle of the river.

However both states have cooperated to create the Connecticut River Scenic Byway, with pretty drives on both sides of the stream. The Connecticut River Valley is idealized New England, with Colonial towns built around village greens, steepled churches and old town halls, green hills thatched with oaks and maples, country lanes lined with stone walls, and pasturelands presided over by contented cows.

Our ramble covers the central portion of the Connecticut River Valley. It begins in the market town Lebanon where Interstate 89 crosses into Vermont and continues north to Woodsville on the edge of the White Mountains. State Highway 10 stays close to the river's edge for most of the route.

Before starting north, pause to explore the **Shaker Village Museum** in *Enfield* on U.S. 4 northeast of the interstate; (603) 632-4346. The Shakers were a fundamentalist, self-contained religious group from England, similar to the German Amish. They got their odd name from their practice of writhing on the ground to rid themselves of sin. At the village, artisans demonstrate folk crafts—a Shaker specialty—and a museum displays artifacts and furniture. Self-guided walking tours take visitors to a church, a stone dwelling, cemetery, grist mill, dairy barn and gardens.

Lebanon, a town of about 13,000, is more of a provisioning center than a visitor destination. However, if you're artistically inclined, its **Alliance for Visual Arts Center**, located in a converted factory at 11 Bank Street, is a major focal point of regional artists; (603) 03766; *www.avagallery.org*.

Immediately north of town, on a plateau above the river, *Hanover* is cloaked with the sophistication of **Dartmouth College**. The community and its college merge around a huge green and both offer fine studies in neoclassic brick ivy-clad architecture. Dartmouth was founded in 1769 to give both Indian kids and whites a good Christian education, although it evolved into the blue blood institution it is today.

Stroll the huge green along Dartmouth Row, and check out murals created by Mexican artist José Orozco in the **Baker Library** in 1932. He spent two years here as a guest instructor. The nearby **Hood Museum of Art** has a small but broad-based collection ranging from Asian art to Picasso; (603) 646-2808; *www.hoodmuseum.dartmouth.org*. The **Hopkins Center** is the performing arts venue for the college and the college town; (603) 646-2422; *www.hop.dartmouth.edu*.

As you explore well-groomed Hanover, you'll note that this ain't no Berkeley. There are no head shops or beer pubs festooned with collegiate banners. You'll find instead smart little cafés, book stores and a few galleries and boutiques. **Webster Cottage Museum** stores Hanover's past in a 1780s home built for the daughter of Dartmouth founder Eleazar Wheelock. It's at 32 N. Main St.; (603) 646-3371. If you want to enjoy a peaceful walk, head for **Pine Park** at the north end of town. Its birch and hemlock woodlands reach down to the banks of the Connecticut River.

North of Hanover, Highway 10 unrolls a beautiful river valley panorama of bluffs, low hills, dairylands and woodlands. *Lyme* is a tiny town of 1,500, with clapboard 19th century buildings rimming a village oval. North of here, watch for the River Road that keeps you closer to the stream, and keep an eye out for a covered bridge. In *Orford*, a rural village of barely a thousand folks, note seven stylish 18th and 19th century homes all in a row, crowning a low bluff over the highway.

Farther along, you'll pass tiny *Pierpont*, dating from 1764, and then a collection of villages that were settled in the 1760s and clumped together as *Haverhill*. Between Haverhill and North Haverhill, the small **Bendell Bridge State Park** preserves the site of a covered bridge that once spanned the river. Although a storm wrecked the last version in 1979, you'll find a pleasant little green and picnic area at the old anchorage. Continue on to *North Haverhill*, which has a striking collection of federal, Georgian and Colonial style homes around the town oval.

About ten miles beyond North Haverhill, our tour ends at *Woodsville*, a gateway to the **White Mountains** which are now dominating the northeastern horizon. The town has no specific lures, although it offers a few restaurants and lodgings if you want to overnight before starting back. Or you may be tempted to play in the White Mountains, New Hampshire's most popular outdoor recreation area.

Where to learn more

Hanover Area Chamber of Commerce, P.O. Box 5105 (216 Nugget Bldg.), Hanover, NH 03755; (603) 643-3115; *www.hanoverchamber.org*.

Keene and Petersborough
Culture, covered bridges and a big mountain

The towns of Keene and Peterborough in southwestern New Hampshire's Monadnock region are decidedly different, although they have one thing in common—the arts.

Keane is a busy and lively crossroads town of about 23,000 and much of its artistic patina comes from Keene State College. Peterborough is a quiet tucked-away village of fewer than 3,000 residents. Artists at its world-respected MacDowell Colony have earned Pulitzer prizes, Guggenheim Fellowships and other significant awards.

The two communities are separated by the imposing mass of 3,165-foot Mount Monadnock and by twenty miles of winding road. They're both popular weekend retreats, although Keane is an easier reach and it has more overnight facilities. Folks are drawn the surrounding countryside for its covered bridges, wooded hills, pasturelands, lakes and trout streams.

The largest town in southwestern New Hampshire, *Keene* dates from Colonial times. It became an important milling and weaving center in the 1800s when folks built mills on the Ashuelot River. For more than a century, the Faulkner and Colony Woolen Mill spun military uniforms for the troops of several wars and a line of civilian goods, until it finally closed in 1953.

Built around a city center with a gazebo, town hall and steepled church, Keene thrives today on light industry and the tourist lures of the region. The old Colony Mill at 222 West Street now houses a shopping complex called the **Colony Mill Marketplace**; (603) 357-1240; *www.colonymill.com.*

Keene's history is served up at the **Horatio Colony House Museum** at 199 Main St.; (603) 352-0460; *www.horatiocolonymuseum.org.* The 1806 house exhibits international art and artifacts collected by a much-traveled owner of the Colony Mill. The **Wyman Tavern** now an historic site, had two moments of fame. Trustees of Dartmouth College first met here in 1770, and the local militia gathered here in 1775 to quaff a few and then march off to war. It's at 399 Main St., (603) 357-3855.

The historic downtown area has several galleries, boutiques and antique shops. The **Thorne-Sagendorph Art Gallery** at Keene State College features student, regional and traveling art exhibits; (603) 358-2720; *www. keene.edu.* Keene State's **Redfern Arts Center** on Brickyard Pond presents a varied season of plays, recitals and concerts; (603) 358-2168. The recently renovated **Colonial Theater** downtown at 95 Main Street hosts plays, musicales and films; (603) 352-2033; *www.thecolonial.org.*

The state's largest concentration of covered bridges spans streams around *Swanzey*, south of Keene. You can get a driving map for them at the **Swanzey Historical Museum** on State Route 10; (603) 352-6639.

Like Keene, *Peterborough* initially thrived as a water-driven milling town. It also became a major brick-making center, drawing from nearby ferrous clay deposits. That red brick heritage is still evident in its handsome downtown buildings.

This pretty village in a narrow wooded valley gained international fame after composer Edward MacDowell created the **MacDowell Colony** summer artists' retreat in 1907. It's now the oldest such colony in the United States and it was awarded the National Medal of Arts in 1997. Its resident artists include sculptors, painters, film makers, composers and writers. Colony Hall, the library and MacDowell's grave site are open to the public. The colony is at 100 High St.; (603) 924-3886; *www.macdowellcolony.org.*

Incidentally, Peterborough was Thornton Wilder's model for his play, *Our Town*, written while he was in residence at the colony.

Another longtime cultural institution is the **Peterborough Players**, a professional summer stock company that began in a barn in 1933. The highly regarded troupe still performs in a barn, albeit a completely renovated one, on Hadley Road; (603) 924-7585; *www.peterboroughplayers.org.*

Downtown, **Sharon Art Center** features a variety of permanent and changing exhibits at its two galleries at 30 Grove St.; (603) 924-7676; *www.sharonarts.org.* A mockup Colonial kitchen and a mill worker's house are focal points of the **Peterborough Historical Society Museum** at 19 Grove St.; (603) 924-3236; *www.peterboroughhistory.org.*

Mount Monadnock, the dominant geological feature of this region, also is its most popular attraction. It's supposedly the world's second most frequently climbed peak, after Japan's Fujiyama. And like Fuji, it stands alone in a region of low hills and valleys, making it appear higher than it is. At **Mount Monadnock State Park**, rangers can point you to the several trails leading to the top; (603) 532-8862; *www.nhstateparks.org/parkspages.*

En route to the mountain, take a break in *Dublin*, home to Yankee Publishing Company. You can pick up a copy of its famous *Old Farmer's Almanac* or the latest issue of *Yankee Magazine*, well known in the northeast.

Where to learn more

Greater Keene Chamber of Commerce, 48 Central Square, Keene, NH 03431; (603) 352-1303; *www.keenechamber.com*

Greater Peterborough Chamber of Commerce, P.O. Box 401, Peterborough, NH 03458; (603) 924-7234; *www.peterboroughchamber.com*

Portsmouth
New Hampshire's lively window on the world

ᛈ

When colonial boundaries were drawn in pre-revolutionary America, New Hampshire was granted a tiny eighteen-mile strip of Atlantic shoreline between Massachusetts and Maine. Since then, folks have certainly made the most of it. Within this strip are an historic seacoast town, quaint Colonial villages, rocky and sandy beaches, fun zones and three state parks.

The most appealing community on this shortened coastline is Portsmouth, a handsomely preserved mini-city of about 25,000 residents. It can serve as your base for exploring the rest of the New Hampshire shoreline.

Despite is small size, Portsmouth is quite urbane, with a fine selection of restaurants, upscale boutiques and import shops, and a vibrant cultural scene. And unlike much of New Hampshire, it's a rather liberal community.

Th focal point for Portsmouth's appeal is the **Old Harbor** area. During an economic downturn in the 1970s, community leaders wisely preserved empty cargo sheds and ships' chandleries instead of urbanly renewing them. Thus, the area retains its rustic seaport look, and its venerable structures are abrim with specialty shops, cafés and galleries.

Portsmouth recently was ranked among *Money* magazine's ten best places to live in America, and the town earned a spot in *The 100 Best Small Art Towns in America.*

During its early years, Portsmouth was one of the largest and most prosperous towns in the colonies, and it was a major shipbuilding center. John Paul Jones came here to during the Revolutionary War to oversee construction of America's first two warships, the *Ranger* and the *America*. Portsmouth was—and remains—New Hampshire's window on the world. International cargo ships still call at its busy harbor.

The oldest town in New Hampshire, it was founded in 1630 by a group of Puritans from the Massachusetts Bay Colony. As settlers aboard the *Pied Cow* sailed up the Piscataqua River, they noted that its shores were covered with wild strawberries. And so they named their new settlement Strawberry Banke—presumably while pigging out on the fresh berries.

This is a fine place to begin your exploration. The site of the original settlement, **Strawberry Banke** is both a museum and an historic waterfront neighborhood; (603) 433-1100; *strawberrybanke.org*. Within the ten-acre museum complex are forty-five small homes and businesses—mostly wooden—spanning 350 years in age and architecture. Some have been restored and furnished to their various periods, and costumed docents present living history demonstrations. Other buildings are still being refurbished. The area is bounded by Marcy, Court, Washington and Hancock streets.

The next logical stop should be the Portsmouth Historical Society's 1758 **John Paul Jones House** at Middle and State streets; (603) 436-8420. America's first naval commander stayed at this former boarding house in 1777 and 1781 while supervising ship construction. Exhibits include a model of the *Ranger* and costumes and artifacts of the era. Attractive **Prescott Park** between the Banke Museum and the waterfront preserves the 1705 Sheafe Warehouse where Jones outfitted the *Ranger*. It now houses an art gallery with changing exhibits; (603) 431-8748.

The **Port of Portsmouth Maritime Museum** in Albacore Park offers a more contemporary view of the Navy that Jones established. Its star attraction is the *U.S.S. Albacore*, the sleek American sub that predated today's nuclear craft. Guided tours are conducted through the sub's innards, or you can go on your own. An adjacent visitor center exhibits submariner memorabilia, at 600 Market St.; (603) 436-3680; *www.ussalbacore.org*.

Return to the past at the 1766 **William Pitt Tavern** on Court Street, part of the Banke Museum complex. Revolutionary notables who gathered here to sip suds and discuss the latest antics of the British included George Washington, Thomas Jefferson and John Hancock. The local suds-sipping tradition continues, for little Portsmouth has no less than three microbreweries.

If you want to see the town from the sea, harbor cruises are offered by the **Isles of Shoals Steamship Company**, (800) 441-4620, *wwwisleofshoals.com*; and **Portsmouth Harbor Cruises**, (800) 776-0915, *www.portsmouthharbor.com*.

The local chamber of commerce has put together a **Portsmouth Harbour Trail** that hits historic sites on the waterfront. You can sign up for guided tours at the visitor center at 500 Market Street or buy an inexpensive guidebook and go at your own pace.

Portsmouth's lively cultural scene comes in several forms. The **Music Hall** at 28 Chestnut Street presents amusements ranging from rock and folk concerts to foreign films; (603) 436-2400; *www.themusichall.com*. The 1892 Bow Theatre at 125 Bow Street hosts a variety of live shows by the professional **Seacoast Repertory Theatre** and the **Portsmouth Academy of Performing Arts**; (800) 639-7650; *www.seacoastrep.org*. The town also has a good selection of art galleries and several artists' studios.

Where to learn more

Greater Portsmouth Chamber of Commerce, 500 Market St., Portsmouth, NH 03802-0239; (603) 436-1118; *www.portsmouthchamber.org*.

Block Island

Eleven square miles of yesterday

♭

There is a charm about Block Island that is indescribable--that is particularly its own. There are green hills and beautiful valleys; ponds innumerable, their bosoms white with the beautiful water lily; cozy cottages; and grand cliffs, with the mighty waves of the Atlantic beating at their feet.

— Hygeia Hotel brochure, 1916

Although the writer of that old hotel brochure called Block Island "indescribable," he or she did a thorough if rather flowery job of describing it. And in the ninety years since that gushy copy was written, this island twelve miles off Rhode Islands' coast hasn't really changed that much.

Despite its unglamorous name, it's a very appealing getaway. It strikes a happy medium between luxurious and history-busy Mackinac Island (page 240) and the rather spartan Monhegan Island (page 308). Owned mostly by a few solitude-loving families and by the Nature Conservancy, it exists in a pleasant state of arrested development. The island's only town is an old New England vision of white clapboard and saltbox cottages, shingle-sided houses and Victorian hotels. The island's only town is called *Shoreham* although locals mostly refer to it as the Old Harbor Village.

More than half the island's 900 or so residents live in the village, while a few of the wealthy occupy gorgeous ocean-view homes built out on the moors. The island has a three-man police force, an all-volunteer fire department and no mail delivery. Folks come to the post office to pick up mail and gossip. There are no street addresses, although "fire numbers" have been assigned to buildings for emergency crews.

Summer weekend visitors almost love the island to death, although there are no tacky fun zones or video parlors to generate racket. Things can get lively at a couple of pubs that offer live entertainment. Mostly the visitors— as many as 15,000 on a summer weekend—poke about the shops and galleries, dine on lobster and other seafoods at quaint old cafés, hike the island's many trails or cycle its uncrowded roads. Cars are permitted on the island although they are few and visitors needn't bring them, since they can rent bikes or mopeds when they get off the ferry.

Because Block Island resists change, its buildings often are recycled instead of being replaced. The original post office is now the Post Office Bagel Shop and a former bakery serves as the Bakery Inn. And you've got to like the multipurpose Twin Maples Apartments, Bait and Tackle Shop, where you can rent a room or fishing tackle, or buy a fresh lobster.

There are few trees on the island, except in some Nature Conservancy preserves. The landscape is mostly green moors, with sandy beaches at the base of seacliffs, and it's dotted with a remarkable number of small ponds. The Great Salt Pond occupies the upper middle of this gourd-shaped island and its calm waters are nice for kayaking. Despite the name, this "pond" is open to the sea, with a marina and a ferry terminal at **New Harbor**.

The original terminal is at **Old Harbor**. If you arrive there, your first vision will be of a gleaming white rank of Victorian hotels, standing invitingly just up from the ferry slip. Block Island offers a good choice of lodgings, from older hotel rooms to cushy and luxurious Victorian inns. The Hygeia Hotel from that old brochure is now the **Hygeia House B&B**, offering nice harbor-view rooms; (401) 466-9616; *www.hygeiahouse.com.*

The island's "attractions" consist mostly of Nature Conservancy preserves, a pair of old lighthouses and an extensive network of hiking trails. The Nature Conservancy holdings are checkerboarded throughout the island and most are open to the public. Check with the conservancy office at Fire Number 352 on High Street; (401) 466-2129; *www.nature.org.*

More than twenty-five miles of trails shoelace the island, many in the Greenway Trail System. Some are Nature Conservancy holdings while others travel through private property. However, most landholdings are embedded with perpetual rights-of-way. We never saw any "keep out" or "no trespassing" signs.

The 1875 **Southeast Light**, perched atop the lofty Monhegan Bluffs, has a museum in the former lightkeepers house; (401) 466-3200. The tower is open for tours in summer. The tower of the 1829 **North Light** is closed, although it, too, has museum in the keeper's house; (401) 466-5009. The bluffs offer nice views of the Rhode Island mainland, twelve miles distant.The lighthouse is reached by a half-mile walk from Corn Neck Road.

Block Island got its name from Dutch navigator Adrian Block, who sailed around it in 1614. It's a pity that later residents didn't keep the name used by the Manissean tribe that once lived here. They called it *Manisses* or the "Island of the Little God."

Where to learn more

Block Island Chamber of Commerce, Drawer D, Block Island, RI 02807; (800) 383-2474; *www.blockislandchamber.com.* The *Block Island Ferry* serves the isle from Judith Point and Newport; (866) 783-7996 or (401) 783-7996; *www.blockislandferry.com.*

Newport
Of mansions, museums and mariners

⚐

Newport is best seen from the sea, for it is a city of the sea. Take a harbor cruise or rent a boat, get out on Newport Harbor and look back to one of the most appealing maritime settings in all of America:

Sailboats at rest, wharfingers reaching into the harbor, and a New England backdrop of old brick and masonry, of church steeples and shingle-sided homes, cloaked in ancient trees.

Newport is simply the most appealing small city in America—charming, walkable and clean-swept, with a picturesque waterfront, gorgeous mansions, stately old churches, excellent museums and over all of this, a pleasantly weathered patina of history.

If you love to walk, as we do, this is your town. Follow the oceanfront Cliff Walk past the ranks of famous Newport Mansions, then return on Bellevue Avenue's sidewalk to see their grand façades. Walk along the waterfront and poke about the shops on cobblestone Bowen's Wharf and Bannister's Wharf, then return along Thames Street, lined with cafés, curio shops, galleries and boutiques. Get out to Fort Adams and walk its irregular shoreline along Rhode Island Sound and Newport Harbor.

Newport certainly isn't "undiscovered" for it gets about two million visitors a year. However, we never realized until we spent five days there just what a discovery it was! And we still didn't see it all. Even with its tourist popularity, nothing is really contrived here. Although Newport has its share of fudge and T-shirt shops, there are no gimmicks such as fun zones or wax museums or Ripley's Believe It or Don't. The downtown and wharf areas don't even have fast food parlors.

The city's most amazing attractions are its nine **Newport Mansions**, built mostly in the mid to late 19th century as summer "cottages" for the Astors, Vanderbilts, Winthrops and other ultra-wealthy families. These are palatial homes with dozens of rooms, where the spoiled rich entertained one another, pampered by their servants. They aren't beach houses; most stand on sea bluffs, surrounded by lavish landscaping. The wealthy owners usually spent only their summers here, and left their mansions in the care of their servants for the rest of the year.

What's amazing is that most of these grand dames of architecture and their lavish furnishings are beautifully preserved and open to the public. Five of them are under the auspices of the Preservation Society of Newport; (401) 847-1000; *www.newportmansions.org.*

One of our favorites, managed by the Beechwood Foundation, is **Astors' Beechwood Mansion** at 580 Bellevue Ave.; (401) 846-3772; *www.astors-beechwood.com*. While docents give tours at the other mansions, costumed performers at Beechwood—many of them theater arts majors—conduct living history encounters, performing as characters from the past. Beechwood is where society was born, for it was Lady Caroline Webster Schermerhorn Astor who compiled America's first social register.

As if the mansions weren't sufficient, Newport offers many other visitor lures. Get your historic bearings at the **Museum of Newport History** housed in an old brick market building at 127 Thames St.; (401) 846-0843; *www.newporthistoric.org*. Here, you'll learn that Newport was founded in 1639 and—with its protected deep harbor—soon became an important seaport. By the 1700s, it was one of the five leading ports in the country.

The **International Tennis Hall of Fame** occupies the buildings and spacious grounds of the former Newport Casino at 194 Bellevue Ave.; (401) 849-3990; *www.tennisfame.com*. It once a popular playground for Newport's high society. Exhibits trace the history of tennis and focus on its stars.

Two houses of worship are worth a look. Still an active parish, **Trinity Church** was built in 1726, with an imposing triple-tiered steeple and old fashioned box pews; (401) 846-0660. The 1763 **Touro Synagogue** at 85 Touro Street, now a National Historic Landmark, is the oldest Jewish synagogue in America; (401) 847-4794; *www.tourosynagogue.org*.

For more attractions, head for **Fort Adams State Park** on a thumb-shaped peninsula west of downtown; (401) 841-0707; *www.riparks.com/fort adams.htm*. It once was America's largest coastal fortification, and you can join guided tours of its sturdy brick and masonry buildings. Also on the fort's expansive grounds is the **Museum of Yachting**, which is full of photos, nautical artifacts and trophies, not yachts; (401) 847-1018; *www.moy. org*. Exhibits focus on Newport's rich history as a maritime and yachting center, with special emphasis on the America' Cup race.

We began by urging you to get out on the water. The *M.V. Spirit of Newport* offers cruises around Newport Harbor and Narragansett Bay; (401) 849-3575; *www.bowenswharf.com*. Try to ignore the narration and the jabbering tourists and pretend you're returning home from a long sea voyage. Is that old Robert Louis Stevenson requiem running through your head?

Home is the sailor, home from the sea

Where to learn more

Newport County Convention & Visitors Bureau, 23 America's Cup Ave., Newport, RI 02840; (401) 845-9123; *www.gonewport.com*.

Providence
An old city in renaissance

⚐

Packaged in a convenient size of about 180,000 residents and nicely arrayed along the Providence River, Rhode Island's capital city is one of America's most underrated destinations. It's an interesting blend of university town, historic center, art community and multi-cultural culinary haven.

This former factory town has made a dramatic recovery after a manufacturing downturn in the 1970s and 1980s sent it into a tailspin. Officials began rehabilitating Providence by uncovering and cleaning up the river and its tributaries, which had been buried under streets and factory parking lots. Several million dollars later, they had created the handsomely landscaped Providence Riverwalk. It became a magnet that drew people and businesses back to the city center, reversing the typical suburban flight of the last half of the last century.

People are literally drawn downtown by a spectacle conceived by local artist Barnaby Evans called **WaterFire**; (401) 372-2111; *www.waterfire. org.* He had a hundred braziers installed in the waterways. Every other Saturday night from May to November, they're filled with wood and set ablaze, creating an awesome spectacle of fire flickering on water. The cauldrons are ignited by black-clad men in black boats, to the percussive sounds of international music, creating a kind of voodoo effect. While thousands of spectators watch and sometimes dance to the music, the boatmen cruise silently about, keeping the fires refueled and burning until after midnight.

Providence was founded by independent-thinking Roger Williams, who was booted out of the Massachusetts Colony in 1636 for insisting that people should be free to worship as they please. Fleeing south, he wintered among the native folks, who later gave him a tract of land. The town he founded is still a bastion of creative and independent thought.

The old city looks positively pleasing these days. The river walk really dresses up downtown, with its plazas, lawns and Venetian-style arched bridges. Glass and steel office towers share the skyline with yesterday's weathered brick buildings. Add to this fine museums, a vital arts scene and interesting cuisine, and you've got a great visitor destination.

A good place to begin your exploration is **Prospect Terrace** at Cogdon and Cushing Streets, a grassy knoll among fashionable old homes. It provides a nice view of downtown. A fourteen-foot statue of old Roger stands here, looking pleased at what he created. The vista is particularly striking on a "WaterFire night."

To learn about Providence's past, head for the **John Brown House Museum** at 52 Power St.; (401) 273-7507; *www.rhs.org/museums.html*. After admiring the furnishings and exhibits in this 1788 Georgian style house, you can sign up for walking tours of the city's various historic sites. At the **Rhode Island State House**, you can join a guided tour or explore on your own; (401) 222-3983; *www.sec.state.ri.us/pubinfo/tours*. The capitol is a handsome space of brass, marble, carved woods and coffered ceilings.

Providence is home to eight colleges and universities and their presence influences much of what you see. The city's best attraction is the **Rhode Island School of Design Museum** at 244 Benefit St.; (401) 454-6500; *www.risd.edu/museum.cfm*. This huge archive has more than 80,000 items in its collections. Its forty-five galleries exhibit everything from Greco-Roman and Chinese sculpture to French impressionist paintings, plus decorative arts of every conceivable media. The Rhode Island School of Design is one of the most respected institutions of its type in the country.

If your taste runs to culinary design, head for the **Culinary Archives & Museum** at 315 Harborside Blvd.; (401) 598-2805; *www.culinary.org*. On the campus of Johnson & Wales University, this "Smithsonian of the commercial food industry" focuses on the history of dining and hospitality. It has more than half a million items, ranging from 50,000 cookbooks and White House dining ware to antique kitchen appliances and an Art Deco diner. Tours of the Johnson & Wales culinary academy can be arranged.

Brown University is one of New England's prestigious Ivy League schools, and its handsome brick campus shelters a couple of outstanding libraries; (401) 863-1000; *www.brown.edu*. The **John Hay Library** contains a collection of Abraham Lincoln writings, plus American poetry and plays, and military memorabilia; (401) 863-2146. The **John Carter Brown Library**, in a handsome 1904 Beaux-Arts building, houses some of the earliest maps and books printed in the Western Hemisphere; (401) 863-2725.

We were impressed with the city's dining and shopping variety, particularly in its older neighborhoods. **Atwell's Avenue**, an old Italian enclave in the Federal Hills area, has a variety of American and ethnic restaurants, along with traditional Italian delis. **Wickenden Street** is busy with specialty shops and sidewalk cafés, quartered in old wood frame buildings. The town's "collegiate row" is **Thayer Street** near the Brown University campus, with a variety of ethnic restaurants, book shops and boutiques.

Where to learn more

Providence Warwick Convention & Visitors Bureau, One Exchange St., Providence, RI 02903; (800) 233-1636 or (401) 274-1636; *www.pwcvb.com*.

Burlington
The Green Mountain State's upbeat urban corner

T o most folks, Vermont is a rural vision of green-clad hills, fall color and Colonial villages with white steepled churches. They would be right until they visited Burlington and the state's only urban region.

The fall color and steepled churches are here, although this mini-city is no sleepy village. The town is old but life here is upbeat and contemporary, with a lively theater and nightclub scene and an ample supply of brewpubs and coffee houses. The more than 10,000 students from its three area colleges help fuel this animated scene.

Burlington is beautifully situated on the shores of Lake Champlain, in the wooded foothills of the Adirondack Mountains. The 136-mile-long lake—the largest in eastern America—reaches north into Canada, so boat owners can cruise up to Montreal. Burlington's population is about 40,000, although more than 150,000 live in the urban area. That's about a quarter of the population of this predominately rural state.

Residents and visitors enjoy the good life along Burlington's waterfront. Shops, galleries and restaurants occupy renovated brick and masonry Federal style buildings that were saved from urban renewal. At the **King Street Dock** and the nearby Victorian style **Community Boathouse**, you can book lake cruises, rent boats or just sit and enjoy the scene. The **Lake Champlain Transportation Company** offers car and passenger service across the pond to *Port Kent, New York*; (802) 864-9804; *www.ferries.com*.

The 7.5-mile **Burlington Bikepath** passes through Waterfront Park and follows the shoreline to several other parks and swimming beaches. Bike rentals are available from waterfront vendors. Uphill from here, four blocks of Church Street have been converted into the **Church Street Marketplace**, a brick pedestrian mall that has become the city's major shopping, dining and night life area.

A free trolley runs from the waterfront along College Street to the **University of Vermont** campus; *www.uvm.edu*. The **Fleming Museum** at 61 Colchester Avenue on the campus offers a mix of American, European and Middle Eastern art, plus works by local artists; (802) 656-0750.

Burlington was chartered in 1763 and among its early landholders was patriot Ethan Allen. You can learn all about it at the **Ethan Allen Homestead** just north of town at the end of College Street; (802) 865-4556;

www.ethanallenhomestead.org. A restored whipsaw board farmhouse contains exhibits about his life and the founding of Burlington.

To enjoy the city from a Lake Champlain perspective, book a cruise with the *Spirit of Ethan Allen III*, (802) 862-8300, *www.soea.com*; or **Lake Champlain Cruise & Charter**, (802) 864-9804, *www.lakechamplain-cruises.com.* Both offer sightseeing, dining and specialty cruises.

Burlington's visual arts scene revolves around the **Firehouse Center for the Arts** at 135 Church St.; (802) 865-7165. It features works of Vermont artists and it sponsors a free Art Trolley Tour of local galleries on the first Friday of each month. You also can pick up a gallery guide here.

Performing arts action is focused at the **Flynn Center** at 153 Main St.; (802) 86-FLYNN; *www.flynncenter.org.* It books a variety of regional, national and international performers and shows, and it's home field for the professional **Vermont Stage Company;** (802) 862-1497; *www.vtstage.org.* Two other area drama groups are the professional **St. Michael's Playhouse**, (802) 654-2281; *www.smcut.edu*; and **UVM Theatre** at the University of Vermont's Royall Tyler Theatre, (802) 656-2094; *www.umvtheatre.org.*

South to Shelburne

Some of the area's best visitor attractions are in *Shelburne*, six miles south of Burlington. The outstanding **Shelburne Museum** is a forty-five acre complex containing one of America's finest collections of folk art; (802) 985-3344; *www.shelburnemuseum.org.* Its extensive exhibits include a railroad depot with rolling stock, the sidewheeler *Ticonderoga*, a covered bridge and a vintage inn, plus coaches and carriages, a carousel, paintings by noted American artists and heirloom quilts.

Shelburne Farms at Bay and Harbor Roads is a still-active 1,400-acre dairy farm; (802) 985-8686; *www.shelburnefarms.org.* The facility includes an 1880s lakeside estate, a massive brick Norman style barn, a farm store and visitor center. Watch docents make cheese and perform farm chores, then head for the Childrens Farmyard to meet domestic critters and take a hayride. The complex has eight miles of trails. The main estate was designed by Frederick Law Olmsted, creator of New York's Central Park.

While in Shelburne, you've just gotta stop at the **Vermont Teddy Bear Company** at 6655 Shelburne Rd.; (800) 829-BEAR or (802) 985-3001; *www.vtbearcompany.com.* You can learn about their history in the teddy bear museum, watch them being made and even make one yourself.

Where to learn more

Lake Champlain Regional Chamber of Commerce, 60 Main St., Suite 100, Burlington, VT 05401; (877) 686-5253; *www.vermont.org/visiting.*

Stowe
Summer-winter play and Trapp family memories

One could almost picture Julie Andrews cresting a hill and singing the title song from *The Sound of Music*. The mountainous area around Stowe could easily pass for the hills and valleys of Austria. When the von Trapp family fled Austria in 1938 after the German occupation, they settled on a farm near Stowe since it reminded them of their homeland.

They re-established their career as a family singing group, then built a lodge in 1950. The current version is still owned by family members. Of course, the von Trapps didn't leave Austria by hiking hand-in-hand into the hills to the refrain of *Climb Every Mountain*. They simply took a train to Italy, then continued on to America. But then, Rogers and Hammerstein always took ridiculous liberties with their material.

Never mind all that. Stowe is Vermont's most popular summer and winter resort. Since this isn't a book about winter sports, we can report that it gets most of its visitors in summer. And despite the growth of resort facilities and condos, the keepers of Stowe have done an effective job of preserving the original 200-year-old mountain village. It's still much the way it was when the Trapp Family Singers arrived, give or take a few curio shops and coffee houses. This is no Orlando of the Green Mountains. Virtually all of the area's shops, restaurants and lodgings are family-owned.

Winter or summer, Stowe is mostly about having fun outdoors. If you want museums and night life, refer to our previous listing. *Burlington* is just thirty miles west. Much of Stowe's outdoor activity is centered around broad-shouldered **Mount Mansfield** which, at 4,395 feet, is Vermont's highest peak. Activities include hiking, biking, fishing, gondola rides, golf and a "mountain slide." The scenic 5.5-mile **Stowe Recreation Path** rims the mountain's base. There are several bicycle rental shops in the village and a couple of outfits offer mountain bike tours.

The mountain itself can be the high point of your outdoor recreation and yes, that was a play on words. If you're up to it, hike the Toll Road (free for walkers) to the **Mount Mansfield Summit Station** at just over 4,000 feet. Or you can take the gondola to the **Cliff House Restaurant**. From either point, well-marked trails lead to the summit. You also can drive the toll road for a fee, then hike to the top. On a clear day, you can see for seventy miles, beyond Vermont to New Hampshire, New York state and Quebéc.

The eight-passenger **gondola** runs from mid-June through mid-October, from Midway Lodge; (802) 253-7311. If you don't want to hike to the summit, you'll still get nice views from the Cliff House. If you prefer downhill to uphill, the **Stowe Alpine Slide** is a snowless sled skid down the mountain from the top of the Spruce Peak chairlift; (802) 253-3500. Don't fret; the sleds are easy to control.

Stowe Village retains much of its early 19th century charm, anchored by a steepled meeting house and an old brick stagecoach inn. The little town, which is busy with shops, boutiques and cafés, is easily walkable. The **Helen Day Art Center** on School Street occupies a former Greek Revival style high school; (802) 253-8358. Its changing exhibits range from local and regional to national art works. The **Bloody Brook Schoolhouse**—not a pleasant name—recalls the inkwell desk and chalkboard schools of yesteryear. It's usually open in summer; ask at the art center.

The Stowe area has about a hundred restaurants and sixty lodgings that range from luxurious to relatively inexpensive. Our choice is the **Stoweflake Mountain Resort & Spa** on sixty acres of landscaped grounds; (800) 253-2232; *www.stoweflake.com*. It's Stowe's only AAA Four Diamond lodging. Stowflake has complete resort amenities—several restaurants, a full-service spa, indoor and outdoor pools, tennis courts and hiking trails.

If you seek more historic digs, head for the large Austrian-style **Trapp Family Lodge** at 700 Trapp Hill Rd.; (800) 826-7000; *www.trappfamily. com*. It has a charmingly rustic look, yet with resort amenities such as indoor and outdoor pools, tennis courts and a sauna. Views of the mountains are impressive, and the resort opens onto 2,700 acres of woodlands.

Although the village of Stowe is two centuries old, skiing didn't enter the picture until the early 1900s, when several Swedish families moved to the area. It remained informal until 1937, when a rope tow was set up, powered by a Cadillac car engine. In 1951, various winter sports operations merged into the Mount Mansfield Company, which still runs the ski resort.

Take time from your Stowe vacation to slip down the hill for an ice cream break. The little town of *Waterbury* is home to **Ben & Jerry's Ice Cream Factory**; (802) 882-1260; *www.benandjerrys.com*. Take the tour and you'll understand how Burlington high school buddies Ben Cohen and Jerry Greenfield managed to make enough ice cream to peddle across the whole country. And of course, you get samples. Surprisingly, this is Vermont's number one visitor attraction; Shelburne Museum is in second place. Incidentally, Ben & Jerry no longer own the company.

Where to learn more

Stowe Area Association, P.O. Box 1320 (51 Main St.), Stowe, VT 05672; (877) 669-8693; *www.gostowe.com*.

Woodstock
An ideal village with an environmental message

฿

*I fear that man has brought the face of the earth to a devastation al-
most as complete as that of the moon.*
— George Perkins Marsh in *Man and Nature*, 1864

Because George Perkins Marsh believed that the earth was worth saving,
he set in motion a chain of circumstances that helped preserve an ideal village in south central Vermont. This eventually led to the creation of the
state's only national park.

A town of about a thousand souls, Woodstock isn't a typical Vermont
village; it's beyond typical. Aristocratic Colonial, Victorian and Greek Revival homes stand along a manicured green; many are now elegant inns.
Sturdy 18th and 19th century buildings in the town's nearby business district
shelter art galleries, boutiques and cafés. The large **F.H. Gillingham &
Sons** emporium sells everything from hammers to Vermont folk crafts to
paté. The Romanesque library and the Windsor County Courthouse are little
changed from yesterday. The Ottauquechee River cuts a riparian swath
through town, and all of this is cradled in green-clad hills.

The village achieved its elegant form in the 1790s when wealthy professionals, merchants and bankers were drawn to this pretty river valley. They
built elegant homes on the green and fine commercial buildings downtown.
Then came the chain of events that helped preserve Woodstock as a model
Vermont village and an environmental showplace.

Woodstock native Marsh, a U.S. Congressman and diplomat, was ap-
palled at the clear-cutting in his state and of man's devastation he had seen
in his world travels. In 1864, he wrote *Man and Nature,* one of the first
books about human impact on the environment. Another area native, Frederick Billings, made a fortune in land speculation during the California Gold
Rush, and later became president of the Northwest Railroad. Inspired by
Man and Nature, he returned to Woodstock in 1871 and bought Marsh's old
farm. He created a model farming operation and had more than 100,000
trees planted in the region.

The scene moves to the last century. In 1934, Billings' granddaughter
Mary French married Laurance Rockefeller, environmentalist and resort
builder. They lived part time on their Billings estate, and created the Woodstock Foundation for local historic preservation. In 1983, they established
the Billings Farm & Museum on the Marsh-Billings property. Upon Mary's
death, Rockefeller donated the Billings family estate to the National Park

Service. It became the Marsh-Billings-Rockefeller National Historic Park in 1992. The park and farm museum are opposite one another, north of town on State Route 12, and they share a common visitor center.

Marsh-Billings-Rockefeller National Historic Park is the first federal preserve to focus on man's stewardship of the land; (802) 457-3368; *www. nps/gov/mabi*. Facilities include the Billings-Rockefeller mansion, a carriage barn exhibit center and the surrounding 550-acre farm and forest. A timeline in the exhibit center focuses on the people responsible for the park, and displays concern conservation and land stewardship around the world.

The **Billings Farm & Museum** is a living history center of life on a "gentleman's farm" of the late 1800s; (802) 457-2355; *www.billingsfarm. org*. Farm chores through the seasons are portrayed in four renovated old barns. The complex also has a modern dairy where visitors can watch day-to-day operations.

Conservation and preservation also are the focus of the **Vermont Institute of Natural Science & Raptor Center**, southwest of Woodstock at 27023 Church Hill Rd.; (802) 457-2779; *www.vinsweb.org*. The folks at this 78-acre nature preserve operate a rehab and exhibit center for eagles, falcons, owls and other birds of prey. The facility also has native plant gardens, an ornithological library, a gift shop and nature trails.

The Woodstock Historical Society has preserved the 1807 **Dana House**, which has period furnished rooms and history exhibits, at 26 Elm St.; (802) 457-1822; *www.woodstockhistorical.org*. Joseph Cotton Dana was a museum director and librarian of the early 20th century.

Three **covered bridges** are in or near Woodstock and you can get driving directions at the **Chamber of Commerce** at 18 Central St.; (802) 457-3555. Also, ask about several other scenic drives in the area.

One of the state's more interesting natural wonders is **Quechee Gorge**, a 163-foot chasm carved by the Ottauquechee River just east of town. State Route 4 provides a dizzying look down into the chasm. The gorge is within **Quechee State Park**, with picnic areas and hiking trails down to the river; (802) 295-2990; *www.vtstateparks.com/htm/quechee*.

Just beyond, *Quechee* is a former mill town with a large condo and resort home complex tucked into nearby forests. Its old Dewey Mill is now a theme shopping complex. Other curio and antique shops are on Highway 4 near the chasm in **Quechee Gorge Village**.

Where to learn more

Woodstock Area Chamber of Commerce, P.O. Box 486 (18 Central St.), Woodstock, VT 05091; (888) 496-6378; *www.woodstockvt.com*.

FREDERICKSBURG, VA.

Chapter Nine

The
Mid-South

CIVIL WAR SITES AND SIPPIN' WHISKEY

One of the interesting things about the Civil War is that most of it was fought not in the deep South but more to the north. In fact the Confederate capital of Richmond was just 110 miles from Washington, D.C. In exploring the mid-South, we visited some of the sites where the war's last great battles were fought. We also discovered what most folks identify with the Mid-South—the Blue Ridge Mountains, Cumberland Gap area, little country music towns, folk craft centers and Bourbon.

KENTUCKY is about bluegrass and bourbon and we encountered both, plus a fascinating art and folk craft center, Abe Lincoln's birthplace and a scenic recreation area.

Where to learn more: Kentucky Travel Department, 500 Metro St., Frankfort, KY 40601; (800) 225-8747; *www.kentuckytourism.com.*

NORTH CAROLINA, the genteel state, offered us a cultural coastal resort, an appealing university town and of course, the Blue Ridge Parkway.

Where to learn more: Travel & Tourism Division, 301 N. Wilmington St., Raleigh, NC 27601; (800) VISIT-NC; *www.visitnc.com.*

SOUTH CAROLINA introduced us to pair of picturesque port towns, a Thoroughbred country that isn't in Kentucky and an appealing old town in the mountainous Upcountry.

Where to learn more: South Carolina Department of Parks, Recreation & Tourism, 1205 Pendleton St., Columbia, SC 29201; (800) 617-6200; *www.discoversouthcarolina.com.*

TENNESSEE provided us with sippin' whiskey, a rustically attractive hill country town and what may be America's finest aquarium. We also visited a mini-city famous for the blues, Elvis and civil rights.

Where to learn more: Tennessee Tourist Development, 212 Eighth Ave. N., 25th Floor, Nashville, TN 37243; (800) GO-2-TENN; *www.tnvacation.com.*

VIRGINIA is for lovers, they say, although it was a major Civil War battleground and we visited several sites. Seeking contrast, we also found a famous small town theater and a "country music road."

Where to learn more: Virginia Tourism Corporation, 901 E. Byrd St., Richmond, VA 23219; (800) VISIT-VA; *www.virginia.org.*

WEST VIRGINIA was the Mid-South's only "northern state" during the Civil War and we visited the site of John Brown's raid, plus a village noted for its folk crafts and a former industrial town turned interesting.

Where to learn more: West Virginia Division of Tourism, 90 MacCorkle Ave. SW, Charleston, WV 25303; (800) CALL-WVA; *www.wvtourism.com.*

Bardstown and beyond
"My Old Kentucky Home" and Abe's birthplace

Although it's not fashionable to use the original lyrics, Kentucky's state song was written by Stephen Collins Foster supposedly while he was visiting his cousin in Bardstown in 1852. Thirty-two miles southwest is the birthplace of a man who may or may not have ever used the term "darkie."

Kentucky's second oldest community, antebellum Bardstown was established around 1780. Rich with Georgian style architecture, this town of about 12,000 souls is in the heart of the Kentucky Bluegrass Country. This is grass of choice for the state's famous Thoroughbreds. It's an attractive region of gently rolling pasturelands, horse paddocks with white board fences and country lanes marked by old stone walls. U.S. 60 from Bardstown to Lexington has been designated as the Bluegrass Parkway.

Less than an hour's drive southwest on scenic U.S. 31E is the **Abraham Lincoln Birthplace National Historic Site**. Yes, he was born in Kentucky, although he mostly grew up in southern Illinois.

There is strong evidence that *My Old Kentucky Home* was not written while Foster visited his cousin, Judge John Rowan. He spent most of his life in Pittsburgh and never lived in Kentucky, according to scholars at the University of Pittsburgh. But never mind that. It was adopted as Kentucky's state song in 1928. Rowan's mansion is the centerpiece of My Old Kentucky Home State Park, and *Stephen Foster—the Musical* is presented there in the summer. Not bad for a little ditty penned by some guy from Pittsburgh.

More important—at least to this observer—is that Bardstown is known as the "Bourbon Capital of the World" because Jim Beam, Maker's Mark and several other notable whiskies are distilled hereabouts.

Bardstown exhibits its history with pride if not always with dignity. There's that musical (*'tis summer, the—uh—people are gay...*), plus My Old Kentucky Dinner Train. And I believe we saw Old Kentucky Home Motel on Stephen Foster Avenue. Maybe we'll skip the show and the dinner train and head for the place where they enshrine booze.

The **Oscar Getz Museum of Whiskey History** tells the story of bourbon, America's contribution to sipping ;(502) 348-2999. Exhibits include old advertising posters, copper stills, antique bottles, jugs and barrels, an old bottling line and even a Carrie Nation display. If you visit the museum, you'll learn how the term "booze" originated .

The museum is in the old brick Spaulding Hall behind the 1823 **Basilica of St. Joseph** on Stephen Foster Avenue; (502) 348-7300. It's worth a look for its collection of 17th century paintings donated by Louis Philippe, future king of France, who briefly lived in exile here. Nearby in the Spaulding Hall Chapel is the **Bardstown Historical Museum**; (502) 348-2999. It exhibits frontier artifacts, Civil War weapons and more gifts from Msr. Philippe.

For more whiskey lore, hop aboard the **Heaven Hill Distilleries Trolley**; (502) 337-6490; *www.bourbonheritagecenter.com*. It provides a one-hour tour through old Bardstown and winds up at Heaven Hill Distillery's Heritage Center, where you can tour and taste. **My Old Kentucky Dinner Train** offers trips through the bluegrass countryside and serves meals in 1940s era dining cars. The depot is at 602 N. Third St.; (502) 348-7300.

My Old Kentucky Home State Park is just outside of town on U.S. 150; (502) 323-7803; *www.myoldkentuckyhome.com*. Docents in antebellum costumes conduct tours through Judge Rowan's sturdy brick 1795 Federal style home. *Stephen Foster—the Musical* is performed at the park's outdoor amphitheater from June through August; (800) 626-1563 or (502) 348-5971; *www. stephenfoster.com*.

To Abe Lincoln's birthplace

Head southwest through bluegrass country on Route 31E. After a few miles, fork left onto State Route 247 and follow it four miles to the rustic European style **Abbey of Gethsemani**; (502) 549-4129. You can tour the beautiful and silent sanctuary and pick some fruitcake and cheese made by the Trappist monks. Back on Highway 31E, pause in *New Haven* for the **Kentucky Railway Museum** at 136 S. Main St.; (502) 549-5470. It exhibits railroad memorabilia and offers vintage train rides through the countryside.

North of *Hodgenville* you'll reach the first of two units of **Abraham Lincoln Birthplace National Historic Site**; (270) 358-3137; *www.nps.gov/abli*. It's a reconstructed cabin where he and his family lived for five years. In Hodgenville, the **Lincoln Museum** at 66 Lincoln Square has—good grief!—waxen figures representing stages of his life; (502) 358-3163.

Continue nine miles on State Route 84 to the **main historic site**. Lincoln was born in a one-room cabin here in 1809, then the family moved to the site above Hodgenville. The memorial seems rather odd—a stately Grecian style marble and granite structure with a grand stairway, sheltering a simple log cabin. It isn't the original cabin; there's no record of where that went.

Where to learn more

Bardstown Tourist & Convention Commission, P.O. Box 867 (200 Court Square), Bardstown, KY 40004; (800) 638-4877; *visitbardstown.com*.

Berea
Kentucky's folk arts and crafts capital

⚑

The town and the college of Berea have been woven together for more than a century as one of America's finest folk art and craft centers. They share a town square in the attractive Cumberland foothills of east central Kentucky.

More than fifty artists and crafts people live and work in this woodsy town of about 10,000 souls. They produce finely carved woodwork, ceramics, basketry, wrought iron, hand-woven goods, Shaker style furniture, cornhusk dolls and more. Many of their studios are open to visitors. You can watch them work and then buy their results.

What sets Berea (*buh-REE-uh*) apart from other American folk craft centers is the marriage of town and college. Berea was founded in 1853 when wealthy landowner and abolitionist Cassius Marcellus Clay gave a tract of land to the Reverend John G. Fee. Their goal was to establish a utopian community where all races and classes could live and work in harmony—a rare concept in the pre-Civil War South.

Fee created a village and an interracial school, which he called Berea, after the Macedonian town where the Bible says St. Paul was converted to Christianity. Berea became an abolitionist center during the Civil War until the Confederacy chased Fee out of the state. At war's end, he returned and reopened his school as Berea Literary Institute. Kentucky banned interracial education in 1904, so college president William Frost focused on educating poor whites from the surrounding hills. He started a policy of letting students pay their tuition with their handmade crafts, so anyone could afford an education. He got such a response that he established the Berea Fireside Industries to market the students' handicrafts nationally.

From this evolved a work program in which students could earn their keep by producing crafts for sale or performing assorted college chores. By the 1920s, the college was in the forefront of reviving traditional Southern folks crafts. As word spread, artisans and crafts people were drawn to this area from all over the South. The college still charges no tuition; it accepts only low income students and allows them to work for their keep.

A good starting point for your Berea exploration is the Southern plantation style **Boone Tavern Hotel** at 100 Main St.; (800) 366-9358 or (859) 986-9358; *www.berea.edu/boonetavern*. Built in 1909 as a guest house for school visitors, it's operated as one of the student work programs. You can book a room here and pick up a walking guide to the small, attractive campus. Tours of the school's craft shops, where students are busily learning their skills, are conducted several times a day.

Arts and crafts shops, sales rooms and studios are located in three areas of town: **College Square** adjacent to the hotel and campus, **Old Town** and **Chestnut Street**. For a good selection of local and regional crafts, stop at the large state-sponsored **Kentucky Artisan Center** at 975 Walnut Meadow Rd.; (859) 985-5448; *www.kentuckyaritsancenter.ky.gov*. It will immerse you into a Kentucky-fried infusion of arts, crafts, music and food.

Another good venue is the college's **Log House Craft Gallery** on College Square at Estill and Center streets; (800) 347-3892 or (859) 985-3226; *www.berea.edu/studentcrafts.com*. You can buy crafts such as classic handmade brooms with carved handles, cornhusk dolls and hand-turned ceramics. Several students are usually in the gallery working on their creations.

Among other studios and galleries that should go on your A-list are **Weaver's Bottom Craft Studio** at 140 N. Broadway, (859) 986-8661; **Churchill Weavers** at U.S. 25 and Lorraine Court, (859) 986-3127, *www.churchillweavers.com*; and **Warren May's Woodworking Shop** for handcrafted furniture at 110 Center St., (859) 986-9293.

The college's **Appalachian Center** is one of America's leading research institutes on this southern culture. You can see a variety of exhibits on Appalachian society and folk crafts at the center's **Artifacts & Exhibits Studio**; (859) 985-3140; *www.berea.edu/appalachiancenter*.

There's music in these hills as well as art, and we mean mostly folk and bluegrass. Live music is presented periodically at the **Acton Folk Center** at 212 W. Jefferson St.; (859) 986-8033; and Berea College's **Appalachian Center**. Both music and arts are celebrated during several annual festivals, including the Mountain Folk Festival in April, Kentucky Guild of Artists & Craftsmen shows the third weekend of May and the second weekend of October, and the Big Hill Mountain Bluegrass Festival in August.

If you'd like to literally immerse yourself in the local cultural scene, several artists conduct summer workshops. For details, contact the Berea Arts Council at (859) 985-9317; *bereaartscouncil.org*.

To learn about the men who started this all, head north twenty miles on I-75 to **White Hall State Historic Site**; (859) 623-9178. It preserves the 1798 home of abolitionist Cassias Clay, who donated the land for Berea.

Where to learn more

Berea Welcome Center, 201 N. Broadway, Berea, KY 40403; (800) 598-5363 or (859) 986-2540; *www.berea.com*.

The Cumberland Gap and beyond
Exploring the Wilderness Road

ⵣ

In the settlement of America, "west" was a relative term, at least until folks reached the Pacific Ocean. During the 1700s, "west" meant anything beyond the Appalachians, and that rugged mountain range kept most people from going there.

There was a natural gap in the mountains, although no one knew about it except migrating buffalo, deer and native people. Then in April of 1750, Dr. Thomas Walker, a surveyor seeking a way into the "Kentuckee" unknown, found this rough passage and named it Cumberland Gap. He and his group penetrated several miles into the wilderness, and he built Kentucky's first cabin to mark his claim.

Only a few hundred settlers braved these wilds until Daniel Boone blazed a trail through the rough-hewn gorge in 1769. He spent two years exploring the area, and was twice capture by and escaped from the native folks. In 1775, in the employ of the Translylvania Company, he took a party of settlers farther into the frontier. They hacked out the Wilderness Road and built Fort Boonesborough near present-day Lexington.

During the next thirty-five years, as many as 300,000 people passed through the Cumberland Gap, settling the Kentucky and Tennessee wilds and—as usual—displacing the original residents. Recognizing the significance of this first road west, the National Park Service established Cumberland Gap National Historical Park in 1940.

We have fashioned a driving trip through the gap and then north along the Wilderness Road. It passes little towns with folk craft shops, scenic woodlands, old coal mining areas and some interesting state parks.

Cumberland Gap National Historical Park encloses about 20,500 acres of thick pine and hardwood forest along the Kentucky-Tennessee-Virginia border. Its centerpiece is the 800-foot-wide gap with rough cliffs rising above. U.S. 25E follows the route of the old Wilderness Road blazed by Boone. After completion of a double-bore highway tunnel in 1996, the winding road through the gap was restored to its late 1700s appearance.

Stop by the visitor center to learn about the gap's historical significance and check on interpretive programs and hikes. You can stroll several nature paths or tackle some of the more than fifty miles of serious hiking trails. Several of the park's features can be reached only by trail. A four-mile paved road leads from the visitor center to **Pinnacle Overlook** which provides an awesome view of these mountainous wilds.

For a comprehensive exploration of the area, sign up for a **Wilderness Road Tour** through the gap, up to the overlook and past some old Civil War fortifications; (606) 248-2626; *www.wilderness-road.com.*

The tour company is based in *Middlesboro*, immediately outside the historical park. It's evident that this is coal mining country, for the Bell County Chamber of Commerce is housed in the **Coal House Museum**, built in 1926 from blocks of bituminous; (606) 248-1075; *www.bellcountychamber.com.* Perhaps more fascinating is the **Lost Squadron Museum** at the Bell County Airport; (606) 248-1149; *www.thelostsquadron.com.* The star of the museum is "Glacier Girl," a restored and flyable World War II P-38 that had been freed from a Greenland glacier where it had crash-landed in 1942.

Five miles north of Middlesboro, watch on your right for **Miracle Mountain Crafts**; (606) 248-2971. The James Miracle (pronounced *MY-racle*) family has been making fine woodcrafts for generations, including dulcimers, furniture, carved animals and classic folk puppets called Limberjacks. The family was written up in a 1967 edition of the *Smithsonian.*

Continue north on Highway 25E—the Wilderness Road—to the small town of *Pineville*, with basic services and a few folk craft shops. Nearby is **Pine Mountain Resort State Park**; (800) 325-1712 or (606) 337-3066; *http://.parks.ky.gov/resortparks.* Kentucky has seventeen of these resort parks with amenities such as lodges, dining rooms and recreational facilities. Pine Mountain is the oldest, dating from 1924. It has a golf course, nature center, amphitheater and hiking trails to some beautiful natural areas.

Next stop on Boone's road is *Barbourville*, an old commercial center surrounded by coal mines, tobacco and timber. It was one of the first towns along the Wilderness Road. Nearby, **Dr. Thomas Walker State Historic Site** has a replica of the cabin built by the man who found the gap; (606) 546-4400. The park has been cluttered up with a playground, basketball court and even a mini-golf course, but the cabin is interesting.

Final stop on this historic route is **Levi Jackson Wilderness Road State Park**; (606) 878-8000. To reach it, go briefly north on Highway 25E and then shift to State Route 229 at a town with a fun name, *Baileys Switch*. Follow the highway eighteen miles through scenic mountain meadows. This is an appealing park, with a meandering river and a restored 1812 gristmill. Its Mountain Life Museum focuses on Wilderness Road settlement. Just beyond here is civilization in the form of *London* and Interstate 75.

Where to learn more

Cumberland Gap National Historical Park, P.O. Box 1848, Middlesboro, KY 40965; (606) 248-2817; *www.nps.gov/cuga.*

Versailles
Bluebloods and bourbon

ꗭ

Here's to old Kentucky, the state where I was born, where the corn is full of kernels and the colonels are full of corn. — a traditional Kentucky toast

Versailles is the penultimate picture of the Old South. Stroll tree-shaded streets in its vintage neighborhoods and admire its antebellum mansions with their colonnaded front porches. It's easy to imagine gentlemen in white linens and fine Panama hats, sipping their bourbon and speculating on who is going to win the next Kentucky Derby.

This town of about 7,500 sits in the heart of Bluegrass Country and Bourbon Country, a perfect fit for the sport of kings. Called by some the "Horse capital of the world," Versailles is rimmed by several stud farms with their baronial barns, white-fenced paddocks and well-groomed steeds on well-groomed estates. Classic American horse racing began in nearby *Lexington* in the early 1800s and the Lexington Jockey Club's *American Stud Book* is both the Bible and the almanac of Thoroughbred racing.

Bourbon production in Kentucky dates from the late 1700s and one of the earliest producers was Elijah Pepper, who began distilling near Versailles in 1797. He moved his operation to nearby Glenn's Creek in 1812, and that's now the site of Woodford Reserve Distillery. Should you wonder, the difference between this and other whiskies is that bourbon must be distilled primarily from corn. Kentucky produces more than half of America's output. It's considered top quality because it uses naturally filtered water from the region's limestone aquifers.

Versailles occupies an ideal location, away from the urban congestion of Lexington and the urban politics of the state capital at Frankfort. Yet it's within an hour's drive of either. It was founded in 1792 and named for the French city in appreciation of France's aid during the Revolutionary War. However, Kentucky folks pronounced it Ver-SALES.

Downtown and the neighborhoods are dressed in Victorian, Beaux Arts and Federal architecture. Along well-tended Main Street, you'll find a mix of good restaurants, specialty shops and particularly antique stores.

Begin your visit with a background check on Versailles at the **Woodford County Historical Society Museum** in an 1819 church building at 121 Rose Hill; (859) 873-6786; *www.woodfordkyhistory.org*. It has the usual regional history exhibits, plus a major genealogical library, in case you ever wondered if you had moonshining ancestors. The **Nostalgia Station Toy**

Train Museum has a fun collection of Lionel trains, plus railroading memorabilia and old toys. Appropriately, it's housed in a restored 1911 railroad station at 279 Depot St.; (859) 873-2497; *www.bgrm.org/nostalgiastation.*

For a full-sized train experience, head for the **Bluegrass Railroad Museum** two miles west of town. It's off U.S. 62 in Woodford County Park; (800) 755-2476 or (859) 873-2476; *www.bgrm.org.* Browse through railroading exhibits in a vintage train car and then catch a one-hour excursion through Bluegrass Country on the old Louisville Southern Mainline. You'll pass—among other sites—the Wild Turkey bourbon distillery.

Which prompts us to head six miles south of town on U.S. 60 to the **Woodford Reserve Distillery** on McCracken Pike; (859) 879-1812. Small batches are produced in this old limestone building along Glenn's Creek, using the classic pot still method that Elijah may have used. Its reserve bourbon won a double gold at the 2005 World Spirits Competition. Guides take visitors on tour and then offer them a taste of—shucks—bourbon candy.

From here, continue past the distillery on State Route 1659, then turn left onto Route 1964 and follow signs to the **Clyde E. Buckley Wildlife Sanctuary**; (859) 873-5711; *www.audubon.org.* Operated by the Audubon Society, this 374-acre preserve along the wooded banks of the Kentucky River has hiking trails, and bird blinds for close-up peeps and photos of various peepers. There's also a nature center and gift shop.

Another out-of-town attraction is the 1797 **Jack Jouett House**; (859) 873-7902. To reach it, follow McCowans Ferry Road five miles west of Versailles and turn onto Craig Creek Pike. This modest three-room home was owned by a Revolutionary War hero who rode all night through Virginia to warn then-governor Thomas Jefferson of a pending British attack. It probably saved the future president's life. Exhibits include period furnishings, and paintings by Jouett's son Matthew, an accomplished artist.

If you're headed either to Lexington or Frankfort from Versailles, split the difference by taking U.S. 62 north to *Midway.* A former railroad company town, it's now a small community with a few cafés, antique shops and some interesting old homes. Check out the still-operating 1818 **Weisenberger Flour Mill** on South Elkhorn Creek, where you can buy whole earth stone-ground flour; (859) 254-5282. Present owners use the water power to generate electricity, which runs things. Also, take a tour and sip some wine at the **Equus Run Vineyards** at 1280 Moores Mill Rd.; (859) 846-9463.

Where to learn more

Woodford County Chamber of Commerce, P.O. Box 442 (141 N. Main St.), Versailles, KY 40383; (859) 873-5122; *www.woodfordchamberky.com.*

Asheville
Art Deco hip and mountain cool

⚑

Describing North Carolina's most upbeat city involves some verbal contradictions. Asheville is a grand showplace of Art Deco design, yet with Haight-Ashbury overtones. It's old money and new art and—in this rather conservative state—it's as liberal as Berkeley. This is the kind of city where you can catch bluegrass, hard rock and Bach, probably on the same day.

The lively town of about seventy thousand offers the multi-ethnic, artistic, culinary and shopping diversity of a large city, without the crowds and congestion. Add to this the surrounding beauty of the Blue Ridge Mountains traversed by the Blue Ridge Parkway and you've got one of the South's most appealing vacation destinations.

However, it's little known outside the region, except perhaps for its Vanderbilt mansion, the incredible 250-room Biltmore House. Obviously, it's the city's most popular tourist draw. However, the mansion is just the icing. There's lots of cake underneath. Asheville has several museums and parks, and an historic and vibrant downtown area where you can get everything from sushi and caffé latte to fine art and folk crafts.

A good way to feel the pulse of this diverse community is to follow the 1.7-mile **Urban Trail** that loops through the downtown area. It's marked by pink granite plaques embedded in the sidewalk, and twenty-seven works of art have been installed along the way. Urban trail maps are available from several sources, including the visitor center, hotels and art galleries. You can get a map and rent an audio-tape from the **Asheville Art Museum** in Pack Place; see below. If you'd rather not hoof it, hop aboard the **Asheville Historic Trolley** that hits may of the same sites; (888) 667-3600; *www.ashevilletrolleytours.com*. You can catch a trolley at one location, hop off to explore the area and then board a later one.

Pack Place is a downtown focal point—a cultural, shopping and entertainment complex at 2 S. Pack Square; (828) 257-4500. The **Asheville Art Museum** specializes in American art of the last century, and it hosts a variety of changing exhibits; (828) 253-3227; *www.ashevilleart.org*. The **Colburn Gem & Mineral Museum** has a large collection of specimens from North Carolina plus items from around the globe; (828) 254-7162; *www.colburnmuseum.org*. **The Health Adventure** teaches about family health, with some fun hands-on exhibits; (828) 254-6373; *www.thehealthadventure.org*.

The **YMI Cultural Center** focuses on African-American culture, with a large collection of African artifacts; (828) 252-4614; *www.ymicc.org*.

Asheville also has visitor lures elsewhere. The **Grovewood Gallery** exhibits American folk arts and crafts at 111 Grovewood Rd.; (828) 253-7651; *www.grovewood.com*. The complex also includes the **Estes-Winn Memorial Automobile Museum**, with more than twenty vintage vehicles.

The **Smith-McDowell House Museum**, occupying an 1840 brick mansion, has furnished rooms from different periods, and displays of early American artifacts, at 283 Victoria Rd.; (828) 253-9231. The **Thomas Wolfe Memorial State Historic Site** preserves the famous author's childhood home at 52 N. Market St.; (828) 253-8304; *www.wolfememorial.com*.

And now for the icing. The **Biltmore Estate**, sitting on 8,000 landscaped and wooded acres, is a huge superlative to the almost obscene wealth of late 19th century industrialists. The largest private home ever constructed, this 250-room sprawl was built for George Washington Vanderbilt, grandson of railroad and shipping magnate Cornelius Vanderbilt. Employing a thousand workers and craftsmen, George started his little country home in 1889 when he was just twenty-six years old. It took five years to complete, and he traveled the world to fill it with fine international furnishings and art.

You can see this grand monument to excess on one of several house and gardens tours; (800) 922-0036 or (828) 225-1333; *www.biltmore.com*. Plan most of a day here. The complex also includes a plant nursery, several shops and restaurants, and a winery tasting room that's said to be the most-visited in the United States. You can book plush lodgings at the **Inn on Biltmore Estate**; (828) 225-1660. Just outside the gates is **Biltmore Village**, an old English-style complex with shops, cafés and a public market.

Asheville was established in the late 18th century and named for North Carolina governor Samuel Ashe. With several sulfur springs in the area and its clean mountain air, it became a popular spa. Then after young George arrived, it evolved into a major resort center. For decades, it was both a playground for the rich and a haven for tuberculosis suffers, who came for treatment in the area's many sanitariums.

However, Asheville was so highly leveraged by disposable wealth that the stock market crash kicked the props out from under it. The city was burdened with debt until 1976. It has taken decades for it to recover as a popular resort destination—this time catering to a more liberal and upbeat crowd.

Where to learn more

Asheville Convention & Visitors Bureau, 151 Haywood St., Asheville, NC 28801; (800) 257-1300 or (828) 258-6101; *www.exploreasheville.com*.

Beaufort
Pirates, artists and coastal charm

꒰

No one has swashed a buckle off the North Carolina coast for three hundred years, yet folks in this handsome old coastal town still talk of the days when Blackbeard roamed offshore aboard the *Queen Anne's Revenge*. His exhibit at the large maritime museum is one of its most popular attractions. Kids seem fascinated with this almost mythical figure.

Legends of Edward Teach—dba Blackbeard—fit the fabric of this almost painfully picturesque seaport village on the state's central coast. Citizens of Beaufort (*BOW-fert*) work hard to preserve its heritage, with its charming old waterfront, its dozens of Victorian, Greek Revival and Federal buildings, and its modest neighborhoods with little white clapboard homes behind picket fences.

The town is so appealing that it has to fight off suitors like a beautiful southern belle at her debut. It has drawn numerous artists, which is fine. And many of its weathered old captains' homes have been refurnished as inns, which may be fine as long as they retain their old charm. However, Beaufort also is luring wealthy retirees and second home buyers who may change the character of the old village. And it's becoming so crowded on summer weekends that you should consider a weekday or off-season visit.

Still, when the time and weather are right, Beaufort can offer a charmer of a low-key vacation. Stroll its clean-swept old streets and poke into art galleries and curio shops. Read the fading headstones in the Old Burying Ground where—according to locals—graves are pointed east so the dead will face the sunrise on judgment morning. Loaf at the waterfront, listening to the wind clacking rigging against masts. Head for one of the sandy swimming beaches, protected by the barrier reefs of the Outer Banks.

There are specific lures of course, although not so many as to become a nuisance. At the excellent **North Carolina Maritime Museum**, you'll learn that Blackbeard terrorized offshore shipping, probably kept a woman in town and wound up with his head on a spike. Other exhibits include fish fossils, aquariums, assorted boats, ship models and various kinds of nautical gear. The museum is at 315 Front St.; (252) 728-7317.

At the **Beaufort Historic Site and Welcome Center** on Turner Street, costumed docents lead tours to six period furnished buildings; (800) 575-7483 or (252) 728-5225; *www.beauforthistoricsite.org*. Stops include the ancient Hammond House, once an inn and a Blackbeard haunt. A twelve-block area of Beaufort has been declared an historic site.

There are more than a dozen art galleries in town. The **Mattie King Davis Gallery** in the Rustell House at the Beaufort Historic Site exhibits the works of several local and regional artists; (252) 728-5255.

Getting on the water

Beaufort is part of a popular water recreation area called the Crystal Coast, which includes some of the last undeveloped coastal islands in America. **Cape Lookout National Seashore** occupies a 55-mile-long strip of barrier islands on the Outer Banks; (252) 728-2250; *www.nps.gov/calo.* The preserve can be reached only by boat. Spring through fall passenger and vehicle ferries depart from *Harkers Island, Atlantic* and *Davis.*

Just across the water from Beaufort is the **Rachel Carson National Estuarian Preserve,** a fine place for exploring saltwater marshes and mudflats and for scoping out birds. The office is in town at 216 Front St.; (252) 728-2170; *http://nerrs.noaa.gov/northcarolina* Ask about volunteer-led guided tours to the preserve. Rachel Carson, the author of *Silent Spring,* performed some of her environmental research in this area.

You can arrange trips out to the islands and the preserve at the Beaufort waterfront. **Outer Island Kayak Adventures** books a variety of guided sea kayak tours; (877) 786-1051 or (252) 504-1001; *www.outerislandkayak. com.* **AB Kayaks** has kayaking tours, and rentals if you have the skills to go it on your own; (252) 728-6330; *www.abkayaks.com.* How about sleeping on the water? **Outer Banks Houseboats** has floating home rentals in various sizes; (252) 728-4129; *www.outerbankshouseboats.com.*

Or you can book an offshore "Mystery Cruise" with **Mystery Tours, Inc.**; (866) 230-BOAT or (252) 728-2527; *www.mysteryboattours.com.* Why Mystery Tours? You might get boarded by pirates, matey. The company also offers longer trips out to Cape Lookout and other areas of the Crystal Coast.

Beaufort is one of North Carolina's oldest towns, established by a group of English settlers in 1709. They initially called it Fish Town, a literal translation of the Coree Indian word *Cwarioc.* Fortunately, they later decided to name their settlement after Henry Somerset, the Duke of Beaufort.

Things got mighty unsettled in 1747 when Spanish pirates pillaged the town and sent the residents in flight. The citizens later armed themselves and re-took their village. With its idyllic setting and warm weather, Beaufort has been a popular leisure retreat since the late 19th century.

Where to learn more

Beaufort Welcome Center, 130 Turner St., Beaufort, NC 28516; (252) 728-5225; *www.historicbeaufort.com.* Also check *www.crystalcoast.org* and *www.blackbeardthepirate.com.*

Blue Ridge Parkway
The Southern Highlands' picturesque promenade

⚑

The Blue Ridge Parkway is *not* undiscovered. It's one of the most visited elements of the National Park Service. We're including it because many people don't realize what a rich cultural and outdoor experience it offers. And we're listing it in the North Carolina section because of the National Park Service's own admission: "Generally, the Parkway sections of North Carolina are higher in elevation and more rugged in their beauty."

This is much more than just a pretty drive. It passes through recreation areas with campgrounds and picnic sites, and hiking trails to natural attractions. There are restaurants and rustic lodges along the route, and historic sites ranging from old cabins to old mansions. Visitor centers focus on the history, geology and folk cultures of the region. The scenery's just grand, from rocky spires and wooded hills to rivers and waterfalls. The highway was designed to compliment the scenery, with fine stonework bridges and viaducts gracefully cantilevered into steep, curving slopes.

America's longest scenic route, the Blue Ridge Parkway stretches 469 miles from Shenandoah National Park in Virginia to Great Smoky Mountains National Park on the North Carolina-Tennessee border. It was started as a Civilian Conservation Corps project in 1935, although it wasn't fully linked until 1987. For most of its length, it follows the ridges and valleys of the Blue Ridge Mountains, offering fine vistas of America's Southern Highlands. This is no expressway. It's a lazily winding two-lane road and the speed limit is generally 45 mph.

Summer is peak season and crowded, and "leaf peepers" throng the road to admire fall foliage. Spring is nice, although some visitor activities will be curtailed. The road is open in winter but snowstorms can cause closures.

Begin your parkway experience just across the Virginia border, at exit 8 off Interstate 77. We're starting you in Virginia so you can check out the **Blue Ridge Music Center** on the parkway's Milepost 213 near *Galax*; (276) 236-5309; *www.blueridgemusiccenter*. Rotating exhibits focus on traditional and contemporary mountain music, and concerts are held at an outdoor amphitheater during the summer.

Heading south from here, you'll soon cross into North Carolina and encounter **Cumberland Knob Visitor Center**; (336) 657-8161. This is the site where parkway construction began in 1935, and exhibits focus on its history. There's a picnic area adjacent, and hiking trails lead to Cumberland Knob and Gully Creek Gorge. **Doughton Park** at Milepost 238 offers camping and picnicking and it's a good wildlife spotting area. Just below is **Bluffs Lodge and Restaurant** with rooms and good old Southern Highlands cooking; (336) 372-4499. At the rustic chink log Brinegar cabin nearby, folkcraft demonstrations are presented in the summer.

The next major stop of interest is the combined **Moses H. Cone** and **Julian Price Memorial Parks** at Milepost 294. The restored century-old Flat Top Manor House contains the **Parkway Crafts Center**, where you can watch artisans at work and buy their products; (828) 295-7938. The combined parks offer hiking trails, camping, picnicking, boating and fishing.

Just below is the **Linn Cove Viaduct**, the most dramatic section of the parkway. The highway hugs the steep, curving slopes of Grandfather Mountain, and you can learn about this engineering marvel at the Linn Cove Visitor Center; (828) 733-1354. If you need a break, *Blowing Rock* is a popular mountain vacation village built around a pretty town center.

Pressing onward, pause at Milepost 316.4, where **Linville Falls** crashes into a deep, craggy ravine. Nearby is a handsome stone arch bridge, and there's a picnic area alongside the Linville River. Hop off the parkway at Milepost 331 to check out the **Museum of North Carolina Minerals** near *Spruce Pine*; (704) 765-2761. At **Crabtree Meadows** eight miles below, you can hike to Crabtree Falls, cascading down a rocky slope.

Craggy Gardens at Milepost 364.6; (888) 667-3600; *www.ashevilletrolleytours.com* earns its name from the spectacular display of rhododendrons and other summer wildflowers on the rough slopes of Craggy Mountains. Fifteen miles below is the excellent **Southern Highland Folk Art Center**, with sales, demonstrations and folk craft exhibits; (828) 298-7928. And suddenly, you're in *Asheville* and Blue Ridge Parkway headquarters; see below.

Continuing on, you'll reach a **Mount Pisgah** stop at Milepost 408.6, with camping, picnicking and hiking trails. One leads to the 5,721-foot summit. Recover from your hike at the **Pisgah Inn** on a scenery-rich perch at the mountain's 5,000-foot level; (828) 235- 8228; *www.pisgahinn.com*.

As you near Great Smoky Mountains National Park, Milepost 431 marks the highest point on the parkway—6,015 feet. **Waterbrock Knob** at Milepost 451.2 offers a splendid 360-degree view of the surrounding sea of mountains. A visitor center here has parkway exhibits; (828) 298-0398.

Where to learn more

Blue Ridge Parkway, 199 Hemphill Knob Rd., Asheville, NC 28803; (828) 271-4779; *www.nps.gov/blri*.

Blue Ridge Parkway Association, P.O. Box 2136, Asheville, NV 28802-2136; *www.blueridgeparkway.org*.

Chapel Hill
A cute town somewhere left of liberalism

Þ

Universities and colleges seem to do this to communities, and in our way of thinking, it's a good thing. Education opens minds and generally nurtures liberal thought, unless you're talking about Bob Jones University. For the most part, Chapel Hill and the University of North Carolina, are one. They're joined at the hip physically and the *cerebral cortex* mentally. This is where you come if you think Asheville is Newt Gingrich country.

Some Southern rednecks refer to the town as the "Peoples Republic of Chapel Hill." However, it nurtures a genteel kind of liberalism, responsible and open minded. Chapel Hill is the Sierra Club, not the Earth Liberation Front. This is where my daughter-in-law Sonja came to get her masters degree in physical education for the handicapped. While free-spirited, this is still a goodie two-shoes kind of place.

What this means for visitors of any political bias is that it's a melting pot of cultures, of good ideas, good food and good art. It's on John Villani's list as one of *The Ten Best Small Art Towns in America*. It's on our list as an extremely attractive and pleasant place to visit.

The town is probably growing faster than most locals want, since it has become a magnet for nor'easter families and retirees who have discovered that they can have warm weather, art, good entertainment and liberalism, too. With prices on the rise, families and even some shops and galleries are spilling over into adjacent *Charrboro*, a former blue-collar mill town.

The old university town is in the state's central region called Piedmont, where the mountains soften into hills and rivers slow their flow. It's North Carolina's most populated area, home to Winston-Salem, Greensboro, Durham and Raleigh. Chapel Hill is a well-manicured community of about 55,000, with another 24,000 at the university. The two literally grew up together. One of America's oldest state-supported universities, UNC was chartered in 1789 and Chapel Hill was created as a community support center.

Town and campus merge at Franklin Street, whose old brick buildings are occupied by ethnic cafés, art galleries, coffee houses and book stores. The attractions and performance venues of the handsome old campus are but a short stroll. Surrounding neighborhoods are pleasing visions of winding streets, with old homes set back on green lawns and shaded by mature trees. This is a health-conscious community as well as an attractive one. The Chapel Hill Greenways Commission is developing a network of twenty-eight miles of in-town bike and pedestrian trails.

Start your Chapel Hill exploration at the university. It occupies a 729-acre campus of brick walkways and Federal and Greco-Roman style buildings with column-supported porticoes. The campus is shaded by hardwoods that go Technicolor in the fall. Its centerpiece is the brick **Morehead-Patterson Bell Tower** that chimes the time and periodically plays music. You can arrange for a campus tour by contacting the **Visitors' Center**; (919) 962-1630; *www.unc.edu/visitors.*

UNC's **Ackland Art Museum** covers a broad range of disciplines and media, and it exhibits works of masters such as Degas and Rubens; (919) 966-5736; *www.ackland.org.* Tar Heel fans will want to check out the **Carolina Athletic Memorabilia Room** at the Smith Center; (919) 962-6000. The **Morehead Planetarium** features science exhibits and it presents a variety of shows in its Star Theater; (919) 549-6863; *www.morehead.unc.edu.*

Elaborately furnished Elizabethan and early Colonial rooms are the high point of the **North Carolina Collection** in the Winston Library; (919) 962-1172. Off campus but run by UNC, the **North Carolina Botanical Garden** on Old Mason Farm Road displays plants native to the American South, including some carnivores; (919) 962-0522; *www.unc.edu/depts/ncbg.* Nature trails wind through its 600 acres.

Incidentally, the list of University of North Carolina graduates includes President James K. Polk, actors Jack Palance and Andy Griffith, TV newsmen Roger Mudd and Charles Kuralt, writer Thomas Wolfe, Motley Fool founder David Gardner and some tall black guy named Michael Jordan.

Downtown, the **Chapel Hill Museum** is the region's history center, exhibiting the "character and characters" of the region. It's at 523 E. Franklin St.; (919) 967-1400; *www.chapelhillmuseum.org.* For a glimpse of old Southern yesterday, stop by **Patterson's Mill Country Store** off I-40 at 5109 Farmington Rd.; (919) 493-8149. It displays a wonderful clutter of "mercantile Americana," from drygoods to pharmaceuticals to old tobacco products. The complex also includes an early 20th century doctor's office.

Chapel Hill's performing arts scene is particularly active, with theater and music groups both on and off campus. The university's recently refurbished 1885 **Memorial Hall** is the area's performing arts center, hosting a variety of entertainments; (919) 843-3333; *www.unc.edu/performing arts.* The **UNC Department of Music** presents concerts from jazz to pop to classic at various venues; (919) 962-1039; *www.unc.edu/depts/music.*

Where to learn more

Chapel Hill/Orange County Visitors Bureau, 501 W. Franklin St.; (888) 968-2060 or (919) 968-2060; *www.chocvb.org.*

Aiken

A handsome town in the Carolina horse country

Ⱶ

Thoroughbred racing may have developed around Lexington, Kentucky, but it's certainly alive and thriving in this upscale community in the Lowcountry of southwestern South Carolina.

Even if you're thoroughly bored by thoroughbreds, there are other attractions in Aiken. A recipient of several "most livable city" awards, the handsome old town itself is the main attraction. It's a well-heeled and carefully groomed community of about 26,000, with dozens of historic buildings. One of America's largest urban forests sits right in its middle.

Unless you're a horse lover, we wouldn't classify Aiken as a major tourist destination. However, the community is so attractive that it's worth a side trip if you're in the neighborhood.

What's really fun about Aiken as that you can explore historic buildings in its well-tended central core and its residential areas, and then take a hike in the 2,000-acre **Hitchcock Woods** without leaving town. This is an appealing urban woodland with sandy carriage roads and hiking and equestrian trails. Incidentally, you can hike or ride a horse or a carriage in this downtown forest but bicycles aren't allowed.

The town's most popular attraction is the **Thoroughbred Racing Hall of Fame** in Hopeland Gardens at 135 Dupree Place; (803) 642-7630; *www. aikenracinghalloffame.com*. Exhibits are in a former carriage house and they honor the many Aiken-trained horses that have had successful racing careers. The hall of fame sits amidst the lushly landscaped fourteen-acre **Hopeland Gardens**. Outdoor concerts are held Monday evenings here from May through August.

This town has an interesting and monied history, and it's told at the **Aiken County Historical Museum**, a complex of several structures at 4343 Newberry St. SW; (803) 642-2015; *www.aikenhistoricalmuseum.aiken.net*. The main museum occupies a 14,000-square-foot 1930 mansion called Banksia. It's one of several grand "cottages" built by the horsey set. The chamber of commerce pamphlet, *Presenting the Charm and Elegance of Aiken's Past*, can steer you to several other imposing old structures.

Most of Aiken's mansions are still private residence. However, you can dine and recline in the town's historic inn, which was revived a few years ago after a forty-year sleep. The Colonial style **Willcox Inn** offers luxurious lodging and fine dining at 100 Colleton Ave.; (803) 648-1898; *www.thewillcox.com*. This opulent "Queen of Aiken" was built in 1898 to host the wealthy and powerful, and its guest list included Franklin D. Roosevelt and Winston Churchill.

To check out the artistic side of this community, visit the **Aiken Center for the Arts** at 255 Laurens St. SW; (803) 641-9094; *www.aikencenterforthearts.org*. It exhibits the works of local and regional artists and helps coordinate the area's art scene. The town has several other galleries, and it's serious turf for antique collectors, with four large malls.

Aiken was established in 1820 as a farming community. Then it just sort of evolved into a resort area. Coastal dwellers came in summer to escape humidity and mosquitoes, and northeastern industrial barons came in winter to escape the bitter cold. Some of these refugees noted that the sandy soil and temperate climate were ideal for training and racing horses. By the late 19th century, the region was the "Carolina Thoroughbred Country."

It remains so today. Aiken's equine culture thrives, with many upscale horse stables in the countryside and several equestrian facilities in town. Local equine enthusiasts pursue all facets of the Sport of King: Thoroughbred racing, polo, the steeple chase and—good grief!—even fox hunting. This is a humane version, however.

Most horsey activities are clustered on the southern edge of town. Races are held at the **Aiken Training Track** off Two Notch Road and the **Aiken Mile Track** at Banks Mill Road and Lyons Drive. For polo action, it's the **Whitney Polo Field and Track** at Knox Avenue and Magnolia Street. The jumpers perform at the **Steeplechase Track** on Audubon Road. A club called the Aiken Hounds sponsors fox hunts in the Hitchcock Woods. The Aiken Chamber of Commerce can provide schedules and contact information, and admission fees for these equine activities are very modest. Most of the racing action is from fall through spring, climaxed by the **Aiken Triple Crown** in March.

The chamber and the Aiken Parks and Recreation Department sponsor a 90-minute bus tour on Sundays, hitting the Thoroughbred Racing Hall of Fame, several of the equestrian facilities and town historic sites.

If you want to do a little wine sipping, stop by the **Montmorenci Winery**. It's a few miles southeast of town on Highway 78 in the hamlet of *Montmorenci*; (803) 649-4870; *www.montmorencivineyards.com*.

Where to learn more

Greater Aiken Chamber of Commerce, P.O. Box 892 (121 Richard Ave. E), Aiken, SC 29802; (803) 641-1111; *www.aikenchamber.net*.

Beaufort
A charming antebellum beach town

If you have read Pat Conroy's *The Great Santini, The Prince of Tide* or *Beach Music,* you have experienced this graceful old Lowcountry beach town. And if you saw the film version of *The Great Santini* or *The Prince of Tides*, you've been here.

The author, who once taught English in Beaufort, captured the town in several of his books and exposed it to public examination. During the peak of Conroy's popularity from the 1970s to the 1990s, if people didn't know they were reading about Beaufort, they know it now. And because it's a wonderful old town, they hopefully see it without Conroy's cynicism. I think he liked Beaufort; he just didn't care much for some of its residents.

This excessively charming antebellum community amidst South Carolina's Sea Islands is becoming too popular. We're sure that many of its citizens wish all those visitors would go instead to nearby Hilton Head, a place designed for tourism. And go quickly, before somebody starts selling Tom Conroy T-shirts. (The author lives on nearby Fripp Island.)

Despite its numerous tourists, it remains an elegant old town, where the plantation south meets the Sea Islands. In fact, many of these islands once grew some of the finest cotton in the land and Beaufort grew up as a well-heeled plantation town. The cotton-meets-the-sea duality is evident in its white frame antebellum mansions with typical Southern porches and verandas, and traditional seacoast widows' walks on the roofs. Climbing wisteria and live oaks wearing shawls of Spanish moss complete a pleasing picture.

Established in 1711, Beaufort is South Carolina's second oldest town, after Charleston. This genteel old village suffered a not so gentle history. The first settlement was wiped out by the Yamassee Indians. During a long period of peace, it became a wealthy planters town and those grand mansions began rising above the waterfront. Then three wars took their toll. Beaufort was captured by the British during the Revolutionary War, and townsfolk had to fight them off again during the War of 1812. Union troops came a-calling during the Civil War and the planters' families fled, leaving thousands of abandoned slaves in the care of their befuddled liberators.

At least, the current invaders only leave money behind, after they've visited the shops and galleries, cafés and fine seafood restaurants along Bay Street. There are lots of ways to spend—carriage rides through Beaufort's old brick and false front downtown and its magnolia-scented neighborhoods, coastal cruises and fishing charters, van and bus tours and even air tours.

If you'd just like to relax and watch others play tourist, stroll over to the **Henry C. Chambers Waterfront Park**. You can have a picnic and turn the kids loose—if any—on a Victorian-theme jungle gym. Frequent free concerts on an outdoor stage will take you back to an old Southern yesterday.

To get a sense of the semitropical Sea Islands that Conroy wrote about, drive the back roads past swamps, marshlands and estuaries, and follow lanes canopied by gnarled oaks. Then just for the fun of it, return to town and drive past the antebellum 1856 **Tidal Home** mansion. It's just off the water near the end of Hancock Street. Look familiar? It was the home of Bull Meachum and his family in the film version of *The Great Santini*. It's a private residence, so look but please don't touch.

For an historic site you can touch, head for the **Beaufort Arsenal Museum** in a 1798 bastion at 713 Craven St.; (843) 525-7077. This small archive traces the town's lively history, with tribal relics and memorabilia from plantation days, the Revolutionary War and Civil War. The Federal style **John Mark Verdier House** has been restored as it was when the wealthy planter entertained the Marquis de Lafayette in 1825. During the Civil War, it was Union headquarters. It's at 801 Bay St.; (843) 379-6335.

The 1724 **St. Helena's Episcopal Church** is one of the oldest buildings in town and a survivor of the Yamassee raids. During the Civil War, tombstones in the graveyard were toppled and used as operating tables. It's at 501 Church St.; (843) 522-1712. Out on Highway 21 is the **Beaufort National Cemetery**, established by Abraham Lincoln in 1863; (843) 524-3925.

It may seem a bit ironic that these idyllic sea islands also are home to one of the toughest military installations in the land, the **Parris Island Marine Corps Recruit Depot**. With proper ID, you can go aboard and explore this historic post. Sign up for a base tour at the Douglas Visitors Center; (843) 228-3650. Come during a graduation week, when you can watch the precision drill of the newly-minted Marines. You can learn about the Corps' history and heroism at the **Parris Island Museum**; (843) 228-2951; *www.mcrdpi.usmc.mil/visitors*.

The ironic juxtaposition of beautiful, genteel Beaufort and tough as nails Parris Island wasn't lost on Conroy. His abusive father, a Marine Corps officer, was the subject of many of his writings, including *The Great Santini,* a virtual autobiography.

Where to learn more

Greater Beaufort Visitors Center, P.O. Box 910 (121 Richland Ave. E), Beaufort, SC 29901-0901; (800) 638-3525 or (843) 524-3163; *www.beaufortsc.org*. Also check out *www.beaufortusa.com*.

Georgetown
A slower pace on the Grand Strand

ꖶ

South Carolina's most popular playground, the Grand Strand is a curving sixty-mile strip of beach along the state's northernmost edge. The seaside resort of Myrtle Beach is the state's best known resort and for that reason it's a lot of things that seaside resorts shouldn't be but often are—congested, commercialized, and littered with tacky tourist shops, gimmick attractions and fast food parlors.

Georgetown is where you go to avoid all that tourism excess and still enjoy the white sand beaches, calm surf and balmy weather of the Grand Strand. Myrtle Beach *does* have a lot of lures, such as scores of golf courses, very good shopping, fine restaurants and live entertainment—mostly country music.

By staying in Georgetown, less than forty miles south, you can sample Myrtle Beach's lures and then retreat to this quieter and less expensive haven. However, avoid the commute on weekends since the highway between the two communities, U.S. 17, can become an impromptu and very long parking lot. As a comparison between the relatively quiet and the extremely busy communities, the AAA *TourBook* for the region lists nine lodgings in Georgetown and 122 in Myrtle Beach!

Georgetown has a few things in common with Beaufort. It's a very old town—number three in South Carolina seniority after Beaufort and Charleston. It's on an inland waterway and thus more sheltered than the Grand Strand beach communities. And it's an attractive old town whose citizens are working to preserve its yesterday look.

There are differences, however. With a deep water harbor, Georgetown is a busy seaport, although it has a population of fewer than 9,000. And it's not quite as antebellum picturesque as the slightly larger Beaufort. The look here is more old brick, particularly downtown. However, it does have a large historic district covering thirty-two blocks, with sixty buildings listed on the National Register of Historic Places.

While Beaufort thrived on cotton, Georgetown's crop of choice was rice and you can learn all about it in the **Rice Museum**. It occupies the 1842 Old Market building topped by a clocktower, at Front and Screven streets; (843) 546-7423. Exhibits are centered on the local history of rice growing and rice cultivation in general. At the nearby **Chamber of Commerce** office at 1001 Front Street, you can pick up a walking tour map of the downtown area's old brick and iron-front buildings; (843) 546-8436.

Kaminski House Museum in a 1769 antebellum home on the waterfront at has an outstanding collection of antiques in its furnished rooms; it's at 1003 Front Street, (888) 233-0383 or (843) 546-7706. Nearby is the **Prince George Winyah Church** at 301 Broad St.; (843) 546-4358. The oldest building downtown, it served as both a government facility and a church, and it's still an active Episcopal parish.

Downtown Georgetown is an appealing place. Stroll its 1,500-foot **Harbor Walk** along the Sampit River. Enjoy southern cookin' at a river-view restaurant and browse its specialty shops, book stores and antique stores. Many are housed in pastel colored storefronts.

Sitting on Winyah Bay at the confluence of five rivers, Georgetown is popular for water sports. **Black River Expeditions** has kayak and canoe rentals, and the firm offers tours of the waterways, from blackwater swamps and tidal marshes to former rice plantations; (843) 546-4840; *www.black-riveroutdoors.com*. The *Jolly Rover* offers historic cruises along the waterfront and in nearby streams; (843) 546-8822; *www.rovertours.com*.

For a look at two former rice plantations, head south of town on U.S. 17. After twelve miles, you'll reach the **Hopsewee Plantation**; (843) 546-7891; *www.hopsewee.org*. Sitting on a landscaped rise above the Santee River, its antebellum mansion is one of the oldest in the South. It was built in the 1740s by Thomas Lynch, a delegate to the Continental Congress. His son Thomas, Jr., who was born at the plantation, was a signer of the Declaration of Independence. In nearby *McClellanville* is the **Hampton Plantation State Historic Site** at 1950 Rutledge Rd.; (843) 546-9361. Its 1730s era two-story mansion contains period furnishings and interpretive exhibits. The surrounding parkland has a picnic area.

The British Colonial government granted a charter for Georgetown Parish in 1721, although the Yamassee uprising delayed settlement for eight years. Early planters first focused on indigo as a cash crop. After the Revolutionary War, the Georgetown area became the new nation's "rice basket," producing nearly half the country's supply.

Following the Civil War, the economic focus shifted to lumber, then a paper mill was built in 1936. It's now owned by International Paper Company and it has swelled into the world's largest. The sight of this and a nearby steel mill may be disconcerting, until you reach the old waterfront and realize that Georgetown is indeed an attractive visitor destination.

Where to learn more

Georgetown County Visitors Bureau, P.O. Box 2068, Pawleys Island, SC 29585; (866)368-8687; *www.visitgeorgetowncountysc.com*.

Greenville
From textile mills to music in the mountains

ᛒ

Tucked into the green-clad hills of South Carolina's Upcountry, Greenville is another of those former industrial city surprises. Once the world's leading textile mill center, it's now a popular vacation retreat for Carolinians fleeing summer's coastal humidity.

This mini-city of about 56,000 supports a remarkably diverse cultural scene, with two major performance centers, a symphony orchestra, a ballet theater and four drama groups. The city and next-door Bob Jones University each has an excellent art museum.

For its work in preserving its old downtown area, Greenville won the 2003 Great American Main Street Award from the National Trust for Historic Preservation. Surrounding this appealing town, the Blue Ridge Mountains offer whitewater rafting, fishing, hiking and other outdoor lures. Two national forests are within short drives. And Greenville itself is certainly green, with sixty public parks. (However, it was named for early settler Isaac Green, not for chlorophyll.)

We'll first deal with an irony and then get on with exploring the town. Greenville is the birthplace of civil rights advocate Jesse Jackson. It's also home to Bob Jones University which—as of this writing—was so conservative that it prohibited interracial dating and forbade women students from wearing slacks or shorts. The guys had to be in ties.

However, we didn't get the sense that the university dominates the culture of the town. While this ain't Berkeley, Greenville's theater group productions aren't necessarily that conservative, and downtown is busy with brewpubs, sports bars and coffee houses.

A particularly appealing attraction is the newly renovated **Falls Park** green space on the Reedy River. Its centerpiece is the gracefully curving **Liberty Bridge**, a 380-foot walkway cantilevered off a sixty-foot waterfall. It was here that Richard Pearis built a grist mill and trading post in 1776 to start the town. In the following years, the river's cascades powered the mills that made this the "textile center of the world."

Greenville's Civil War history is portrayed at the **Confederate Museum** at 15 Boyce Ave.; (864) 421-9039; *www.confederatemuseum.org*. Although the town saw no direct action, it served as a treatment center for wounded Confederate soldiers and as a haven for lowlanders fleeing the advancing Union army. Museum exhibits include Confederate uniforms, weapons and other artifacts.

As we noted, the community has two outstanding art museums. The **Greenville County Museum of Art** focuses on American artists, with one of the country's finest collections of works by Andrew Wyeth, plus pieces by Georgia O'Keeffe and several Southern artists. It's at 420 College St.; (864) 271-7570; *www.greenvillemuseum.org.* The **Bob Jones University Museum & Gallery** exhibits several rare religious works by the masters, from Rembrandt to Rubins. Overall, it has one of the world's best collections of religious art. The museum is on campus at 1700 Wade Hampton Blvd.; (864) 770-1331; *www.bjum.org.*

Greenville's hometown hero is Joseph Jefferson "Shoeless" Jackson, the son of a mill worker who went on to become a top baseball star early in the last century. He is honored at **Shoeless Joe Jackson Memorial Park** at West Avenue and Osteen St.; (864) 288-6470. The park's baseball diamond is on the site where Jackson first played the game as a child.

The town's lively performing arts scene happens mostly in two venues. The sleekly rounded **Bi Lo Center** books top world performers, local groups and sporting events, at 650 N. Academy St.; (864) 241-3300; *www.bilocenter.com.* The large **Peace Center for the Performing Arts** hosts entertainments ranging from Broadway shows to concerts, at 300 S. Main St.; (800) 888-7768 or (864) 467-3000; *www.peacecenter.org.*

The area's newest attraction is the **BMW Zentrum**, off Interstate 85 exit 60 between Greenville and *Spartanburg*; (864) 989-5537; *www.bmwzentrum.com.* Housed in a dramatic crescent shaped building, the Zentrum is a leading-edge museum that focuses on the history of this famous driving machine and research on new ultra-safe, non-polluting models. Several past and futuristic vehicles are on display. Tours of the adjacent BMW assembly plant—the only one in North America—begin from here.

For a postcard sampler of South Carolina's Upcountry, take a ride on the **Cherokee Foothills Scenic Byway** (State Route 11). Once the pathway of native folks and early fur traders, it meanders for 130 miles through low woodland hills and valleys at the base of the Blue Ridge escarpment. The highway passes several state parks and two national battlefields. It's quite gorgeous during fall color season. For details: *www.byways.org.*

Depending on where you're going next, start your byway drive at the west end in *Fairplay* or at the east end in *Gaffney*. Both are just off I-85.

Where to learn more

Greenville Convention & Visitors Bureau, 631 S. Main St., Suite 301, Greenville, SC 29601; (800) 351-7180 or (864) 421-0000; *www.greatergreenville.com/visitors.* Also check out *www.greenvilleonline.com.*

Chattanooga
Won't you choo choo us home?

₧

We've included this historic and upbeat Tennessee River town because it will surprise you. Thanks to Glenn Miller's 1941 ditty, everyone on the planet has heard of Chattanooga, so this is no new discovery. However, Tennessee-bound travelers faced with the temptations of Nashville, Memphis and Great Smoky Mountains National Park may debate whether Chattanooga is worth a special trip.

It definitely is.

Old Chatts has one of the finest aquariums in the United States, a very attractive and walkable downtown area and some attractions that are just plain fun. We aren't talking about wax museums or amusement parks. We mean really fun stuff, like the International Towing and Recovery Hall of Fame and the Battles for Chattanooga Electric Map and Museum. We don't mind corny tourist lures as long as they're *creative*ly corny.

Chattanooga faced the same urban crisis that hit most towns and cities in the latter half of the last century—suburban flight, job loss and downtown deterioration. In recent decades, officials have done an outstanding job of fixing the problem here, with a major rehabilitation of the central core and riverfront. Key elements are the multi-million-dollar Tennessee Aquarium and the adjacent Ross's Landing, which is a combined open space and historical park, completed in 1992.

Although Chattanooga is a mini-city of about 156,000, its downtown area is compact and walkable. Many of its major attractions are within a tight radius of the riverfront. If you book lodgings in the city center—and there are several choices—you can leave your car parked most of the time. Start with the **Chattanooga Visitors Center** just off Ross's Landing at 2 Broad St.; (423) 756-8687. And then head for the city's stellar attraction.

The **Tennessee Aquarium** takes visitors on an environmental journey down the Tennessee River, from its source high in the Appalachians to its mouth on the Gulf of Mexico; (800) 262-0695 or (423) 265-0695; *www.tennesseeaquarium.org*. It rivals Denver's Ocean Journey as the best and largest river-to-the-sea aquarium in the United States. More that 7,000 kinds of critters swim, fly, slither and walk in its four realistically replicated ecological zones, from mountain cascades to tidal flats. This outstanding facility also examines life on the mighty Amazon, the Yenisey River of Siberia, Japan's Shimanto and the Zaire river of Africa. An **IMAX Theater** is adjacent to the aquarium, showing a variety of ultra-wide screen spectacles.

Once you've seen the best, you lots of other choices. Of course, there's the **International Towing and Recovery Hall of Fame and Museum** with antique tow trucks and toys, at 3315 Broad St.; (423) 276-3132. Push buttons and watch 5,000 miniature soldiers and cannons do combat at the **Battles for Chattanooga Electric Map and Museum**, 1110 E. Brow St.; (423) 821-2812; *www.battlesforchattanooga.org*. The **Houston Antique Museum** in an 1892 Victorian exhibits three centuries of antiques and decorative arts, at 201 High St.; (423) 267-7176; *www.thehoustonmuseum.com*.

The **Chattanooga African-American Museum** in Bessie Smith Hall focuses on black culture in the city and elsewhere, with a special exhibit on Chattanooga's legendary blues singer, at 200 E. Martin Luther King Blvd.; (423) 266-8658; *www.caamhistory.com*.

You certainly can't leave downtown without checking out the **Chattanooga Choo Choo** at 1400 Market St.; (800) 872-2529 or (423) 266-5000; *www.choochoo.com*. Actually, it's the 1909 train terminal for the Southern Railway that linked Chattanooga to northern cities. (*You leave Pennsylvania Station 'bout a quarter to four...*) This massive complex now houses a replica of the legendary train that inspired the Glenn Miller song, a model railroad museum, shops, restaurants and a Holiday Inn with rooms built into old railroad cars; (800) 872-2529 or (423) 266-5000.

Take a stroll across the Tennessee River on the **Walnut Street Bridge**, a former automobile and trolley crossing turned into a recreation path. At the far side, you can relax in **Coolidge Park** and take a ride on an old fashioned carousel. The 22-mile-long **Tennessee River Walk** passes through the park.

There's more to see in and about this lively old town, but save time for the **Chicamauga and Chattanooga National Military Park** on the Tennessee-Georgia border southwest of town; (706) 866-9241; *www.nps.gov/chch*. America's first national military park, it preserves the sites of several vicious Civil War battles. More than 1,600 markers help visitors trace the ebb and flow of the clashes that cost thousands of lives on both sides.

Also in this area is **Lookout Mountain**, where one of the world's steepest incline railways has been hauling passengers up for great views for more than a century; (706) 820-4030; *www.carta-bus.org*. Incidentally, lookout mountain is not a wilderness; it's an upscale residential area.

Where to learn more

Chattanooga Area Convention & Visitor's Bureau, 2 Broad St., Chattanooga, TN 37402; (800) 322-3344; *www.chattanoogafun.net*.

Franklin to Lynchburg
Heritage, horses and whiskey in the heartland

⚑

Tennessee's heartland is a gently rolling swatch of emerald green countryside south of Nashville. It's home to scores of stately antebellum mansions, the famous Tennessee walking horse and whiskey.

When we toured the area, two comments helped paint a picture of gossipy Southern charm and country humor. This is one of the wealthiest areas of the state, and owners of some of the grand antebellum mansions occasionally open them to public tours. After we'd been escorted through one of them, we commented to our tour guide how gracious it was of the homeowner—a wealthy widow—to show us her fine home.

"Why, yes," our guide said in her soft Southern drawl. "She is such a grand lady. It's a shame that she has a drinkin' problem."

The other comment came from our Jack Daniel's Distillery guide in Lynchburg. He pointed out the irony that Lynchburg was in a dry county, so folks couldn't consume its most famous product here. When we asked where one could get a legal drink, the guide grinned and said: "Well, the nearest place is in Tullahoma, twelve and three-quarter miles northeast of here, and then eighteen paces from the parking lot."

You can spend a pleasant day or few exploring this area as a side trip from Nashville. We'll point out some of the region's highlights.

Franklin, south of Nashville off Interstate 65, is one of the best preserved antebellum towns in the entire South. Walking its shady, clean-swept streets and admiring its grand mansions, you may find it hard to believe that a brief yet bloody Civil War battle was fought here. Confederate General John Bell Hood, hoping to march on Nashville, clashed with Union General John Schofield's dug-in troops on the southern edge of Franklin on November 30, 1864. Hood's forces charged the entrenched Union troops thirteen times and suffered 6,000 casualties and the loss of five generals.

In one of the war's most poignant moments, young Confederate Lieutenant Tod Carter led a charge to try and retake his family home, which was now serving as Union headquarters. He was mortally wounded and his family, who had been cowering in the basement, found him lying on the battlefield. They carried him back into the house, where he died in his own bed.

The **Carter House** is now an historic site, with period furnishings and exhibits concerning the Battle of Franklin. It's at 1140 Columbia Ave.; (615) 791-1861; *www.carter-house.org*. Another historic site farther south, the 1826 **Carnton Plantation** served as a temporary Confederate hospital during the Battle of Franklin. Grim reminders of this role are floorboards still showing bloodstains from hasty amputations. **McGavock Cemetery**, America's largest Confederate burial grounds, is behind the house. The complex is at 1345 Carnton Lane; (615) 794-0393; *www.carnton.org.*

In *Spring Hill*, about fifteen miles south of Franklin on U.S. 31, you can tour the 1850s era **Rippavilla Plantation** at 5700 Main St.; (931) 486-9037. Here, Hood had breakfast with his other generals on the morning they marched into battle. By day's end, five of them were dead. Behind the house, the **Mule Museum** displays not mules but old farm equipment. A nearby attraction of quite a different sort is the huge General Motors Saturn plant. Visitors can arrange for tours by contacting the **Saturn Welcome Center** at 100 Saturn Parkway; (931) 486-5440; *www.saturn.com.*

Columbia, fifteen miles south of Spring Hill, has a fine collection of historic mansions, including the **James K. Polk Home** at 301 W. Seventh St.; (931) 388-2354; *www.jameskpolk.com.* It was during his presidency—1845 to 1849—that the United States annexed Texas and snatched the entire Southwest as a Mexican War prize. Near the Polk home, the 1835 **Athenaeum Rectory** is a curious blend of Moorish, Gothic and Italianate architecture, at 808 Athenaeum Way; (931) 381-4822; *www.athenaeumrectory. com.* It was the rectory for the former Columbia Athenaeum School for girls.

From Columbia, follow U.S. 50 about twenty miles southeast—crossing I-65—to *Lewisberg* in the heart of Tennessee walking horse country. The **Tennessee Walking Horse Breeders and Exhibitors' Association** in town welcomes visitors to its Hall of Fame and nearby stables; (800) 359-1574; *www.twhbea.com.* In *Shelbyville*, fifteen miles east on State Route 64, you can visit the 900-acre **Waterfall Farms** where walking horses are bred. It's at 2395 Hwy. 64 E; (931) 684-7894; *www.waterfallfarms.com.*

Thirsty? Too bad. In *Lynchburg,* southeast of Shelbyville, you can look but you can't taste samples at **Jack Daniel's Distillery**. Tours are conduced daily through the famous facility that Mr. Daniel established in 1866. It's the dominant feature of the downtown area. A few curio and gift shop occupy old fashioned storefronts on the nearby town square.

Where to learn more

Lynchburg-Moore County Chamber of Commerce, Box 421, Lynchburg, TN 37352; (931) 759-4111; *www.lynchburgtenn.com.*

Middle Tennessee Visitors Bureau, Hunter Mathews Building, 8 Public Square, Columbia, TN 38401; (888) 852-1860; *www.antebellum.com.*

Williamson County Convention & Visitors Bureau, P.O. Box 156, Franklin, TN 37065; (800) 356-3445; *www.visitwilliamston.com.*

Jonesborough and Greeneville
Two historic towns in the Appalachians

Ⱡ

Tennessee began in this mountainous far eastern corner of the state when Jonesborough was established in 1779, followed by Greeneville in 1783. They were both in North Carolina at the time, but in 1784 Carolinians ceded this region to the newly established federal government.

However, the Feds didn't respond, so local folks decided to form their own state, with Greeneville as its capital. They called their state Franklin, in honor of everybody's favorite kite flyer. After North Carolina officials heard about this brash move, they decided they wanted their territory back. Confusion and occasional fist fights ensued. Finally, when Tennessee was formed from a piece of the Southwest Territory in 1796, Jonesborough wound up as the oldest town in the new state, with Greeneville in number two spot.

The *Jonesborough* you see today is the work of town officials who set about restoring old brick storefronts in the 1970s. The move was as much about tourism as it was about preservation. Thousands of visitors were drawn to this part of the Appalachian Mountains and particularly to Great Smoky Mountains National Park thirty miles west. Folks in Jonesborough decided they might as well grab part of the action.

Then someone came up with the idea of creating a National Storytelling Festival, since no other community had one. By the time this was all accomplished, downtown Jonesborough had become Tennessee's first designated National Historic District and the National Storytelling Festival became a major event, drawing noted folk yarn spinners and thousands of visitors.

The festival is the first full weekend of October. If you can't make it then, stop by the impressive 14,000-square-foot **International Storytelling Center** at 116 W. Main St.; (800) 952-8392 or (423) 753-2171; *www.story-tellingcenter.com*. It offers live story sessions daily from May through October, and it has a large gift shop with storytelling books, tapes and CDs. The center has become one of the world's leading folk story archives.

The main street of this little town of about 4,200 is so attractive that it looks almost artificial. Sidewalks are bricked, street lights resemble gas lamps and flower planters brighten its clean-scrubbed two and three-story brick buildings. This isn't antebellum Tennessee; it's tourist Appalachia, all washed and neatly hung out to dry in the sun to be admired.

Folks at the **Historic Jonesborough Visitor Center** at 117 Boone Street can give you a self-guiding tour map to significant structures, many of which are now bed & breakfast inns. The building also houses the **Jones-**

borough-Washington County History Museum, where you can learn all about that State of Franklin business; (423) 753-1015.

Downtown shops offer good selections of regional folk crafts, such as homespun woolens, quilts, preserves, and wooden toys. There are also a few boutiques and art galleries and several antique stores here. The **Jonesborough Antique Mart** is the largest, at 115 E. Main St.; (423) 753-8301.

Thirty miles southwest, *Greeneville* also is a nicely preserved old town, although not as deliberately so as Jonesborough, and it is thrice the size. Its focus seems more on attracting growth and light industry.

Andrew Johnson was born in North Carolina and finished growing up in Greeneville, apprenticing as a tailor. The **Andrew Johnson National Historic Site** has four elements in town; (423) 638-3551; *www.nps.gov/anjo.* The visitor center and Andrew Johnson's tailor shop are at College and Depot streets. Across College is his parents' home, with two rooms open to visitors. Three blocks away at McKee and Main streets is the square-shouldered brick Andrew Johnson homestead, where he lived from 1851 until his death in 1875. He and several family members are buried in the **Andrew Johnson National Cemetery** south of downtown.

The town was named for Revolutionary War hero Nathanael Greene, who never lived here and probably never even visited. Despite its name, the **Nathanael Greene Museum** is mostly about Andrew Johnson and other aspects of the town's history. It's at 101 W. McKee St.; (423) 636-1558.

Across from the town hall near College and Church streets is the site of capitol for the **"lost state of Franklin."** The original log structure is gone, so a new building has been erected, with appropriate historical markers.

Greeneville is one of the world's largest tobacco centers. If you want to hear the machine-gun chatter of a classic Southern auctioneer, attend one of the auctions for the evil weed. Get details at the Chamber of Commerce

Between here and Jonesborough is the birthplace of frontiersman Davy Crockett of the Alamo and Fess Parker fame. **Davy Crockett Birthplace State Park** just off Highway 11 contains a replica of his family's rude squared-log cabin; (423) 257-2167; *www.state.tn.us/environment/parks.* The attractive sixty-acre park on the banks of the Nolichucky River also has a small Davy Crockett museum, camping and picnic sites and a pool.

Where to learn more

Greeneville County Chamber, 115 Academy St., Greeneville, TN 37743; (423) 638-4111; www.*greenevillecountypartnership.com.*

Historic Jonesborough Visitor Center, 117 Boone St., Jonesborough, TN 37659; (866) 401-4223 or (423) 753-1010; *historicjonesborough.com.*

Memphis
Different kinds of Kings

♪

When we visited Memphis several years ago, it was for the purpose of checking out Elvis Presley's Graceland and hearing some good blues on Beale Street. We weren't even aware that the motel where Dr. Martin Luther King, Jr., was assassinated had been converted into a civil rights museum.

Sitting in Tennessee's southwestern corner, Memphis is the largest city we've included in this book, with a population of more than 650,000. However, after the emotional experience of visiting the National Civil Rights Museum, we wanted to spread the word about that facility and the city which it occupies. If you're concerned about civil rights, being at the place where the great leader was killed will grip your soul. If you aren't concerned, maybe the experience will change you.

There are other reasons for visiting this big, bustling city on the Big Muddy. It's no San Francisco or Chicago or New York, but it has a startling number of attractions. Dramatic new architecture rises from its once shabby downtown area and Beale Street, home of the blues, has been revitalized. The city is on a roll. Like Dallas, it seems that Memphis has finally shed the guilt of being a place where a national leader was assassinated.

Plan on visiting the town's two most famous attractions on the same day. If the civil rights museum leaves you with a heavy heart, the wonderful tackiness of Graceland should cheer you up—particularly if you lived during the era when Elvis was The King. What's interesting, however, is that you often see people weeping at both places.

The **National Civil Rights Museum** occupies the former Lorraine Motel in an older section of Memphis at 450 Mulberry St.; (901) 521-9699; *www.civilrightsmuseum.org*. Leading-edge technology and vivid black and white murals tell the story of America's struggle for equality. Some exhibits get right to the point. There's a life-sized model of a lunch counter sit-in, with mannequins patiently holding their seats. If you step aboard a mockup bus and start to sit up front, an angry voice orders you to the back. If you sit anyway, an object—like someone's cane—starts banging on the back of your seat. I'm a Scottish-American honkey, yet the experience was still unnerving. After you've looked out onto the balcony where Dr. King was killed, you'll need cheering up, so head for the archive of the other King.

After Elvis Presley hit the big time, the 14-acre **Graceland** estate in southwest Memphis was his home until he died in 1977; (800) 238-2000 or (901) 332-3322; *www.elvis.com/graceland*. This place makes the Liberace

Museum in Las Vegas seem rather restrained. We need to remind ourselves, after gawking at this monument to excess, that we're the ones who bought all those records and concert tickets. The kid from Tupelo, Mississippi, could do whatever he wanted with our money. There are several versions of tours, plus the total package that includes a car collection, his two private planes, the shrine-like grave site, the overly decorated mansion and a museum of Elvis memorabilia. All of this wonderful excess has so impressed historians that Graceland became our newest National Historic Landmark in 2006.

You will learn, as you continue your exploration of Memphis that this big old city is no longer a blue collar town, and maybe it never was. It rightfully calls itself the "Home of the Blues and the Birthplace of Rock and Roll." In addition to this rich popular music legacy, it has world class art and history museums, a striking sports arena, several professional drama groups and dance companies, and the Cannon Center for Performing Arts, where the Memphis Symphony does it thing.

Of course, the soul of Memphis is still gaudy Beale Street, where established artists and unknown performers looking for a break work the many small clubs. The great B.B. King has his own club at 143 Beale Street and he often drops by to perform; (901) 524-KING; *www.bbkingclubs.com*. Unfortunately, some T-shirt and curio shops besmirch the look of the old street, although you can still find lots of good live entertainment.

A short walk away is a bit of high class whimsy—the legendary **Peabody Memphis Hotel**, a posh AAA Four Diamond digs where ducks paddle about an elaborate lobby fountain. It's at 149 Union Ave.; (901) 529-4000; *www.peabodymemphis.com*. Nearby is the huge, circular **Peabody Place Retail and Entertainment Center** with shops, restaurants and a 22-screen theater. Within the complex, the **Center for Southern Folklore** preserves and exhibits the South's culture, folk art and music; (901) 525-3655; *www.southernfolklore.com*. The **Peabody Place Museum** has a fine collection Asian and European art; (901) 523-8603; *www.belz.com/museum*.

Obviously, we've just scratched the surface of Memphis, and hopefully its back. Your "A" list also must include the **Memphis Rock 'n' Soul Museum**, a combined museum and music academy called **Soulsville**, the massive **Pyramid** multi-event sports arena that's larger than all but two of Egypt's pyramids, the **Memphis Brooks Museum of Art** and the **Mud Island River Park** recreation area in the middle of the Mississippi River.

Where to learn more

Memphis/Shelby County Visitors Center, 12036 Arlington Trail, Arlington, TN 38002; (901) 543-3333; *www.memphistravel.com*.

Abingdon
Theater, art and friendly ghosts

⚐

*W*hen I heard that door snick shut, the little tiny hairs on the back of
my neck started creepin' all the way up to the top of my head.

Donnamarie Emmert, one of the costumed docents who conducts historical walking tours of downtown Abingdon, recalled—in her soft Southern accent—a night many years ago when she had been confronted by a ghost in
the Barter Theater. She was alone in the town's famous playhouse when a
door mysteriously closed behind her, then an apparition appeared.

"It had a man's face, but a wiggly Casper-ish tail," she said, her eyes
wide with the recollection. "To this day, I never go into that theater alone."

If this little tree-cloaked town in the hills of rural western Virginia is
haunted—and many insist that it is—those spirits must be relatives of Cas-
per, the friendly ghost. There is no record of them ever harming anyone;
they just like to have a little fun. Who can blame them for hanging around?
Once you experience Abingdon's charm, you may not want to leave either.

Spirits of the town's lively past abound, and ghost stories are part of free
historic walking tours that can be booked at the convention and visitors bureau. In addition to the Barter Theatre, hauntings have been reported at the
historic Colonial style Martha Washington Inn; the back shop of the *Abingdon Virginian,* the town newspaper that was founded in 1844; and behind
the bar at the 1879 Abingdon Tavern.

Incidentally, in addition to these guided tours, you can pick up a walking
tour map to forty buildings in Abingdon's historic district. And if you *really*
like to walk, the **Virginia Creeper Trail** that follows an old rail line
through the surrounding Appalachian countryside passes through town.

Abingdon is one of America's most captivating small communities. Although its edges are rimmed by the usual service stations and strip malls, the
gently hilly downtown area has been carefully preserved. Ancient maples
and dogwoods cast leafy canopies over Colonial era brick and clapboard
buildings; flower baskets hang from lampposts. There are no fast food outlets and no chain stores downtown. Small shops, inns, galleries and cafés occupy weathered and well-tended storefronts.

Although its population is less than 8,000, Abingdon is one of Virginia's
leading cultural centers. Its legendary **Barter Theatre** at west Main and
College streets is one of America's oldest professional drama groups, dating

from 1933; (276) 628-3991; *www.bartertheare.com*. The pitched-roofed red brick structure that it occupies is even older, built in 1830 as a church.

Tourism is Abingdon's major industry, generating more revenue than local property taxes. And tourism's primary machine is the Barter Theatre. Its two stages draw more than 150,000 patrons a year. The Barter is a professional Equity group, and its distinguished alumni include Kevin Spacey, Hume Cronyn, Patricia Neal, Gregory Peck and Ernest Borgnine.

The theater's odd name comes from founder Robert Porterfield's willingness to trade "ham for Hamlet" to feed his performers during the Depression. Early playbills advertised live dramas for "thirty-five cents or the equivalent in victuals." The troupe still performs for victuals at least three times a year and donates the proceeds to a local food bank.

Abingdon also is home to a pair of major art venues. The **William King Regional Art Center**, housed in a former high school building at 415 Academy Drive, offers a variety of changing exhibits, featuring national and international artists; (276) 628-5005; *www.wkrac.org*. The **Arts Depot**, in a former railroad station at Main and Fuller streets, is home to several artists in residence. Visitors can see them at work, and buy their creations; (276) 628-9091; *www.abingdonartsdepot.org*.

If history's more to your liking, visit the 1860 **Fields-Penn House** at 208 W. Main St.; (276) 676-0216. It's Abingdon's historical museum, with exhibits and period furnished rooms. The nearby **Martha Washington Inn** is both an historic site and a luxury lodging, at 150 W. Main St.; (888) 888-5252 or (276) 628-3161; *www.marthawashingtoninn.com*. It was built as a private residence in 1832, then it was expanded to become Martha Washington College in 1860. It later served as a Civil War hospital and it has been an inn since 1935.

The name is significant, since Abingdon was named in honor of Martha Washington's ancestral English home of Abington Parish in Oxfordshire. Abingdon's predecessor was Black's Fort, established in 1774 as the first English-speaking settlement west of the Appalachians. It literally was a fort; settlers often fled to the safety of its log stockade during Cherokee raids.

It was incorporated as Abingdon in 1778, and it became an important outpost and trading center along the Wilderness Road. Far from the lights of Broadway and the movie cameras of Hollywood, it's now an outpost of theater arts—and a few friendly ghosts.

Where to learn more

Abington Convention & Visitors Bureau, 335 Cummings St., Abingdon, VA 24210; (800) 435-3440 or (276) 676-2282; *www.abingdon.com/tourism*.

Charlottesville
The essence of Virginia

Charlottesville is "Virginia central," both geographically and spiritually. It occupies the state's rolling midlands, close to the Blue Ridge Mountains, and not far from the sea and the capital of Richmond. This small city reflects the best of the state, with its cultural diversity, sense of tolerance and pride of history. In fact, its slogan is "So very Virginia."

It's home to America's first secular university, founded by Thomas Jefferson, and it was home to Jefferson himself. He noted in 1822 that its citizens "all mix in society in perfect harmony." People who were born near here, lived here or passed through here comprise an honor roll of great Americans—Jefferson, Lewis and Clark (both born nearby), James Monroe and James Madison.

This community of about 45,000 occupies a pleasing setting of farmlands, country estates, horse paddocks and glistening rivers. It topped the list of Frommer's *Cities Ranked and Rated* as the best place to live in America. Although the usual big box stores and strip malls sit on its outskirts, downtown is an attractive study in old architecture and green space. Perhaps the greenest is the large University of Virginia complex, whose huge commons is simply called "The Lawn."

Charlottesville is a very bookish community, a condition that residents note with pride. Despite its relatively small size, it has more than twenty book stores. It's home to authors John Grisham, Ann Bettie and Rita Mae Brown. The University of Virginia offers one of the nation's leading creative writing programs.

Charlottesville comes in two sections, linked by a strung-out business district along West Main Street. An area called "The Corner" is tucked up against the university on the west side. The school's influence on this corner is obvious, with its book stores, coffee houses and places with names like the Buddhist Biker Bar & Grill. To the east is historic downtown, wrapped around a seven-block-long pedestrian mall on Main Street.

The Downtown Mall is an appealing space of shade trees, benches, fountains and statues. Cafés, specialty shops and galleries rim the mall's edges. As you explore the area, you will be reminded of the political irony that was Virginia: It was home to several leaders of the American Revolution and it was the bastion of the Confederacy during the Civil War. Statues here honor Robert E. Lee and Stonewall Jackson. However, a third memorial is non-political, depicting Lewis and Clark and Sacajawea.

The **University of Virginia** is one of America's most architecturally rich schools; (434) 924-7969; *www.virginia.edu*. When Jefferson began its construction in 1819, he wanted to create an "academical village" with ten pavilions around a great lawn, each with a different style of architecture. Its centerpiece is the Rotunda, a Roman style domed library. Tours are offered daily during the academic year, September through April. Specific lures include the **Kluge-Ruhe Aboriginal Art Collection** on Peter Jefferson Place, (434) 244-0234; and the **University of Virginia Art Museum** in the Bayly Building, (434) 924-3592.

Charlottesville's premiere historic site, which you see every time you spend a nickel, is Jefferson's country estate of **Monticello** just southeast of town. The distinctive domed mansion that Jefferson designed can be visited on guided tours; (434) 984-9822; *www.monticello.org*. What's significant that nearly everything here is original. During your ten-room tour, you will see Jefferson's furniture, personal possessions, books, scientific instruments and some souvenirs that Lewis and Clark brought back from their western vacation trip. The adjacent **Monticello Visitors Center** exhibits more personal items, plus artifacts found during excavations of the grounds. A movie chronicles the great statesman's life.

Near Monticello is the 1784 **Michie Tavern** on Thomas Jefferson Parkway; (434) 977-1234; *www.michietavern.com*. It's a restoration of a typical 18th century roadhouse, with ladies' and gents' parlors and the "Ordinary," where you can have a hefty Colonial style buffet lunch. Living history programs are presented from April through October—your chance to dance a tavern reel.

Another former presidential estate is **Ash Lawn-Highland** southeast of Monticello; (434) 293-9539; *www.ashlawnhighland.org*. The country home of James Monroe, it occupies a tract of land that Jefferson had recommended. It's now a working 19th century plantation operated by the College of William and Mary. Visitors will see Monroe family furniture and possessions in the main house, plus slave quarters and the overseer's cottage.

It's no surprise that culturally rich Charlottesville nurtures a lively performing arts scene. Among several endeavors are a drama group called **Live Arts**, (434) 977-4177, *www.livearts.org*; and the **Charlottesville and University Symphony Orchestra**, (434) 924-3984; *www.virginia.edu/music*.

Where to learn more

Charlottesville-Albemarle County Convention & Visitors Bureau, P.O. Box 178 (600 Cottage Dr.), Charlottesville, VA 22902; (877) 386-1102 or (434) 977-1783; *www.soveryvirginia.com*.

The Crooked Road
Virginia's heritage music trail

I can't remember the gentleman's name but the music he plucked from that banjo still sings in my ears.

The Crooked Road is a 227-mile-long meander through Virginia's mountainous western tip, where America's music—bluegrass and country—was born. The route passes through several hill towns rich with the heritage of these old time sittin' and pickin' front porch mountain melodies.

A few years ago, we stopped by Barr's Fiddle Shop in Galax, where Tom Barr hand-crafts fine fiddles, banjos and dulcimers. We were chatting with one of his assistants and I asked to see a banjo. I can't play anything except a radio but I've always liked the banjo's rich twangy sound.

"Lemme see if it's in tune," he said and started plinking at the strings. Then Betty asked if he could play a little something. He kind of shrugged and grinned and then that banjo suddenly came to life. It was as if the theme from *Deliverance* had exploded into the room. And then he stopped.

"I reckon it's in tune," he said.

The Crooked Road begins in *Ferrum* south of *Roanoke*, heads west through *Bristol* and then curls north to *Clintwood*. There's more than music in them thar hills. Along the way, you'll enjoy the rough-hewn scenery of the Blue Ridge and Appalachian mountains. On the return leg, you can shift down to the famous **Blue Ridge Parkway** by following U.S. 421 southeast from *Bristol* through the tip of Tennessee to *Boone, North Carolina.*

SCHEDULING NOTE: There's a live radio show in Galax on Friday night and the Carter Family Fold concert is on Saturday night. You can start your Crooked Road tour on Friday morning, then stay overnight in Bristol, the largest town on the route. It's twenty miles from the Carter place.

You'll get a good preview of mountain music heritage in tiny *Ferrum* at the **Blue Ridge Institute & Museum** at Ferrum College; (540) 365-4416; *www.blueridgeinstitute.org.* It features changing exhibits about regional music, arts and crafts and it sponsors concerts and other folkloric events. If you're here in late October, you can catch the Blue Ridge Folklife Festival.

The next stop is little *Floyd* and the big surprise is that it's home to the world's largest distributor of country, bluegrass and folk music. **County Records & Sales** stocks more than 3,500 CDs and cassettes and it does most of its business by mail order and the internet. It's at 117 W. Main; (540) 745-2001; *www.countysales.com.* Nearby, the **Floyd Country Store** has a Flatfoot Jamboree every Friday night, with stompin' and dancin', and it often hosts top mountain music performers on Saturday night. The store is at 206 S. Locust; (540) 745-4563; *www.floydcountrystore.com.*

Galax is another major mountain music center. You can catch a free live radio show every Friday night at the old Art Deco **Rex Theater** at 111 E. Grayson St.; (276) 276-5773; *www.rextheatergalax.org.* Area folks—from kids to grandads to families—perform country, bluegrass and gospel music. And this is really a down-home show: Between performers, the announcer reads commercials from local merchants. At **Barr's Fiddle Shop**, you can admire Tom Barr's fine handcrafted instruments, and take one home if you have music in your soul. It's at 105 Main St.; (276) 236-2411.

Follow signs from Galax to the **Blue Ridge Parkway** and the excellent Blue Ridge Music Center; (276) 236-5301; *www.blueridgemusiccenter.org.* This fine museum has exhibits on folk music traditions and the parkway, and concerts are held at an outdoor amphitheater in the summer.

Continuing westward, you'll pass *Abingdon* (page 370), then you'll soon encounter *Bristol*, a mid-size town that straddles the Virginia-Tennessee border. You're now in the birthplace of country music. Talent scout Ralph Peer from the Victor Talking Machine Company came to town in 1927 to make the first commercial recordings of regional performers, and a new industry was born. Learn all about it at the **Birthplace of Country Music Alliance**, housed in Bristol Mall; (276) 645-0035; *www.birthplaceofcountry music.org.* Construction is underway on a much larger facility, to be called the **Birthplace of Country Music Heritage Center**.

Twenty miles west of Bristol, tiny *Hiltons* is the home town of mountain music's most famous family, the Carters. The **Carter Family Fold** is a heritage museum and performance hall in the former grocery store operated by family patriarch A.P. Carter. It was created in 1976 with the help of the late Johnny Cash and his wife June Carter Cash. Come on a Saturday night—the only time it's open—to tour the museum and A.P.'s cabin birthplace, and then attend a mountain music concert; (276) 386-6054 (recording) or (276) 645-0035; *carterfamilyfold.org.*

The last stop on the Crooked Road is *Clintwood*, home to the **Ralph Stanley Museum and Traditional Mountain Music Center** in an antebellum mansion on Main Street; (276) 926-5591; *www.ralphstanleymuseum. com.* Opened in late 2004, in features permanent and changing exhibits and it honors Ralph Stanley, the Grammy Award winning country musician.

Where to learn more

The Crooked Road, P.O. Box 268, Big Stone Gap, VA 24219; (866) MTN-MUSIC; *www.thecrookedroad.org.*

Fredericksburg
Colonial calm and a Civil War storm

ᛰ

$\mathbf{W}$e strolled along Caroline Street, nodding to early morning joggers, listening to birds chirping in the thick canopy of trees and admiring Colonial storefronts. We found it difficult to imagine that Fredericksburg once was the scene of one of the Civil War's bloodiest battles.

Blame it on geography and politics. This prosperous marketing town stood in the path of history's anger. Union General Ambrose E. Burnside, marching south from Washington in late 1863 with 115,000 troops, intended to reach the Confederate capital of Richmond by blasting through Fredericksburg. Robert E. Lee's 78,000 Confederates, entrenched on high ground south of town, was determined to stop them. Lee prevailed, but the town did not. It was bombarded, invaded and then pillaged by Union troops.

"Had all the imps of hell been called together and turned loose upon the city, it could scarcely have been more blasted, ruined and desecrated than when left by the Yankee Army," wrote a *Charleston Courier* correspondent.

At battle's end, however, it was the Union army that was desecrated. Eight thousand federal troops had been slaughtered trying to storm Lee's hilltop fortifications. It was the worst Federal defeat of the war.

Despite its Civil War role, today's Fredericksburg seems more a Colonial town than a Southern city, both physically and historically. Many of its slab-sided homes and rows of narrow brickfront stores survive from its early days as a British colonial village. It was founded in 1728 during the reign of King George II and named for his son, Prince Frederick. Sitting at the head of navigation on the Rappahannock River, it became an important inland seaport for the Virginia colony.

The town served as a major supply center during the Revolutionary War, although no battles were fought here. However, when Virginia chose to side with the South during the Civil War, conflict was inevitable, since the town stood midway between Washington and Richmond. After the vicious Battle of Fredericksburg, three more major conflicts were fought nearby—Chancellorsville, the Wilderness and Spotsylvania Courthouse; see below. These four engagements accounted for one in five Civil War casualties.

Although it's surrounded by suburban sprawl, Fredericksburg is a quiet tree-shaded enclave, tilting gently down to the banks of the Rappahannock. Its core is a Colonial gem; 900 homes and businesses are preserved within a forty-block National Historic District. The centerpiece is Caroline Street, a tree-shaded avenue of shops, antique stores, art galleries, restaurants and sidewalk cafés. This is no contrived living history center like nearby Williamsburg. It's a busy working community whose citizens have chosen to preserve elements of its past. Supporters immodestly call Fredericksburg "America's most historic city."

Combination tickets to eight of the town's historic sites are available for a thirty-percent discount at the Fredericksburg Visitor Center, 706 Caroline St.; (540) 373-1776. There are too many attractions in the area to list in our limited space, so we'll offer our favorites.

Fredericksburg National Military Park above town preserves the site of the Union troops' bloody and fruitless assault on Lee's entrenched Rebels; (540) 373-6122; *www.nps.gov/frsp.* A tour map guides you to the Confederate fortifications and Union killing fields. The park also is the site of Fredericksburg National Cemetery, where 15,000 Union soldiers are buried.

The **Fredericksburg Area Museum** preserves the town's history in the 1816 red brick former town hall, at 907 Princess Anne St.; (540) 371-3037; *www.famcc.org.* James Monroe started his law practice in town and his former office is now the **James Monroe Museum** at 908 Charles St.; (540) 654-1043. Exhibits chronicle his long and illustrious public service career.

In the **Rising Sun Tavern** at 1304 Caroline Street, "tavern wenches" play living history roles in a restored 1760s era inn; (540) 371-1494. You'll learn that gentlemen slept five to a bed, head to toe, for a penny a night.

Across the Rappahannock in *Falmouth*, the 18th century Georgian-style **Chatham Manor** served as Union headquarters during the bombardment of Fredericksburg. It's now headquarters for the **Fredericksburg and Spotsylvania National Military Park**; (540) 654-5121; *www.nps. gov/frsp.* Just beyond the Chatham Manor turnoff on King's Highway, **Ferry Farm** marks the site of George Washington's boyhood home; (540) 370-0732; *www. kenmore.org.* The original house is gone, although signs show what once was. It was here that the legend of the chopped-down cherry tree began.

Several art galleries in Fredericksburg provide fuel for the culture-conscious. The largest complex is the **Liberty Town Arts Workshop,** a few blocks off Caroline at 916 Liberty Street; (540) 371-7255. It has twenty studio galleries for more than forty artists and crafts people. Another major cultural venue is the non-profit **Fredericksburg Center for the Creative Arts** at 813 Sophia St.; (540) 373-5646. It displays the works of local artists and sponsors art workshops, lectures, films and poetry readings.

To learn more

Fredericksburg Visitor Center, 706 Caroline St., Fredericksburg, VA 22401; (800) 678-4748; *www.fredericksburgvirginia.net.*

Virginia's Civil War battlegrounds
"The great opera of death"

Ϸ

When Virginia's political leaders decided—after much debate—to side with Confederacy during the build-up to the Civil War, they brought the furies of hell down on their heads. The Confederate capitol of Richmond was virtually a northern outpost for the South. It was within a few days' march of Washington, D.C., and a lot of angry Union troops.

Some of the war's bloodiest battles were fought on Virginia soil. Three of them occurred just west of Fredericksburg and tens of thousands of lives were lost on both sides. In one of these clashes, the Battle of the Wilderness, commanding generals Ulysses S. Grant and Robert E. Lee faced one another in combat for the first time.

The Union didn't win any of these engagements. The South won the Battle of Chancellorsville, and the clashes at the Wilderness and Spotsylvania Courthouse were fought to a draw. However, they so depleted Confederate forces that the dogged Grant was able to keep pressing until he forced Lee's surrender at Appomattox.

The battle sites are part of the **Fredericksburg and Spotsylvania National Military Park**. Trails through each of the sites will put you up close and personal with those violent days. Although nature has healed the combat wounds, the areas have changed little in the past century and a half, since they occupy woodlands, meadows and farmlands. Markers, diagrams and occasional ranks of cannons will help you reconstruct the battle scenes. However, these combat zones are now so green, quiet and disarmingly peaceful that it's difficult to imagine they were savage killing fields.

The three sites are within seventeen miles of *Fredericksburg*, so it's an easy day's outing. Pick up a driving map at the **Fredericksburg National Military Park** at 1013 Lafayette Blvd.; (540) 373-6122. To begin your tour, head west out of town on Highway 3, crossing over Interstate 95. You'll pass through several miles of thick suburban commercialism, and eventually roll into the attractive green Virginia countryside.

The first part of the route is a fast expressway, leading directly to the **Chancellorsville Visitor Center**; (540) 786-2880. It's the only visitor facility for the three battle sites. The others have "interpretive shelters" and lots of signs and markers. Exhibits at the center cover all three area campaigns, and a well-done 25-minute film paints a rather vivid picture of the conflicts. Incidentally, if you bypassed Fredericksburg to get here, you can pick up a driving guide at the center's small book store.

The battles of Chancellorsville and the Wilderness were fought close to-gether but nearly a year apart. The Chancellorsville fight—named for an inn that was destroyed during the conflict—began in late April of 1863, and the Wilderness clash was the following March. Both conflicts occurred in a 70-square-mile region of tangled undergrowth that local farmers had named "The Wilderness" decades earlier. These tangles had been pretty much left to nature until fate chose them as battlegrounds. And they were among the most violent and terrifying conflicts of the war. Many men died when they were trapped by forest fires started by muzzle blasts and shell explosions.

The **Chancellorsville** campaign consisted of a series of complex and dif-ficult maneuvers as the opponents shifted their troops about in the clawing thickets. The South eventually gained the upper hand and the Union Army withdrew across the Rappahannock River near Fredericksburg. In what one general described as a "great opera of death," 3,000 men had been killed and 20,000 were wounded.

From Chancellorsville, narrow country lanes lead through pretty mead-ows and farmlands to the other two sites. The **Battle of the Wilderness**, pit-ting Grant against Lee for the first time, lasted only a few days and ended in a stalemate. Again, the troops had to fight in a Gothic tangle of thickets. In the smoke and confusion, many men died from forest fires and from friendly fire. The Wilderness Interpretive Shelter on State Route 20 outlines the con-fused course of the conflict, in which the North suffered more than 17,000 casualties and the South lost 12,000.

The **Spotsylvania Courthouse** battle was a two-week war of attrition. Fifty thousand Southern troops dug in behind long trenches and breastworks and Grant's forces tried to uproot them. The name refers to a small hamlet near the battle site, although the armies never clashed in the town. A trail leads from the interpretive shelter on Route 613 to a site called the Bloody Angle. Here, the armies clashed in savage hand-to-hand combat for twenty hours. Both sides lost a third of their troops and withdrew. With its trails and many markers, this is the best place on the tour to get a grasp of the conflict.

The great Stonewall Jackson was accidentally wounded by his own men during a calm in the Battle of Chancellorsville. The national park's driving map will direct you to the **Jackson Shrine**, a plantation office where he later died; (804) 633-6076. The bed in which he expired is still here, along with a few exhibits concerning the war.

Where to learn more

Fredericksburg and Spotsylvania National Military Park, 120 Chatham Lane, Fredericksburg VA 22405-2508; (540) 654-5121; *www.nps.gov/frsp.*

Harpers Ferry and Charles Town
John Brown, gorgeous scenery and The Trail

♭

*J*ohn Brown died that the slaves might be free,
John Brown died that the slaves might be free,
His soul goes marching on.

— William Steffe, 1855

As we all learned in school, Harpers Ferry is the site of John Brown's reckless raid on a federal arsenal to arm his followers and free the slaves. The site, which is both a tiny town and a national historic park, occupies one of the most striking settings in all of the south. Tucked into a steep and thickly wooded slope above the Shenandoah River, Harpers Ferry's ancient buildings seem to be peeking almost shyly out on today's world.

Nearby Charles Town, where John Brown was tried and hanged, also is a charmer of an old village. Both communities are in an incredibly pretty region of the Shenandoah Valley, where the Shenandoah and Potomac rivers join. They occupy a spur of West Virginia called the Eastern Panhandle, which looks on a map like a tilted cap. Thomas Jefferson said of this region: "The passage of the Patowmac through the Blue Ridge is perhaps one of the most stupendous scenes in Nature." Some say that the late John Denver was inspired to write *Country Roads* after passing through this area.

Almost heaven, indeed.

However, it was hell for John Brown. A fanatical abolitionist, he led his 21-man "army of liberation" in a raid on Harpers Ferry Arsenal and Armory on October 16, 1859. Unfortunately, it became dog day afternoon instead of a liberation movement. Most of his men were killed or wounded and he was captured after the arsenal was stormed by a squad of Marines led by Colonel Robert E. Lee. He was tried in Charleston and strung up on December 2. However, his dramatic action galvanized America's abolitionist movement.

William Steffe's *John Brown's Body* was a popular Union marching song, and several verses were added as it was marched along. One line was: "They'll hang Jeff Davis from a sour apple tree." Later, that same rhythmic melody was attached to *The Battle Hymn of the Republic.*

When you visit Harper's Ferry, you'll learn some surprising facts about this place, which are overshadowed by Brown's raid. John H. Hall developed interchangeable parts for weapons at the arsenal, which revolutionized manufacturing. America's first successful railroad ran through here and, appropriate to the memory of abolitionist John Brown, one of America's first integrated colleges was opened here in 1867.

The arsenal is gone, although twenty-five old buildings have been restored and now have period furnishings or historical exhibits. Guided tours are conducted in the summer. A hiking trail leads to Maryland Heights, where you can explore remnants of Civil War batteries while enjoying a fine view of the Shenandoah Valley and its two rivers. For information: **Harpers Ferry National Historical Park**; (304) 535-6029; *www.nps/gov/hafe*.

The town of Harpers Ferry, with only about ninety residents, retains most of its yesterday charm, with the unfortunate exception of the **John Brown Wax Museum**. What's more significant than waxen images is that the non-profit **Appalachian Trail Conservancy**, which maintains that famous hiking route, is based here, at 799 Washington St.; (304) 545-6331; *www. appalachiantrail.org*. The ATC's visitor center has maps, hiking gear and lots of information about the trek. Obviously, the 2,144-mile-long route from Georgia to Maine passes through this area.

Check out the **Harpers Ferry Toy Train Museum** two miles west of here on Bakertown Road off U.S. 340; (304) 545-2291. It has lots of model trains and you can be a kid again, riding the Joy Line Railroad's miniature passenger cars pulled by a steam locomotive. The Potomac and Shenandoah rivers present fine rafting and floating opportunities, and several firms offer whitewater trips and tube, kayak and canoe rentals. For a list, contact the Jefferson County Chamber of Commerce; see below.

Five miles west of Harpers Ferry, *Charles Town* is a pleasant community of about 3,000 that's threatening to get larger as Washington, D.C. 'burbs continue to spread. Head for the 1893 **Jefferson County Courthouse** at Washington and George streets; (304) 725-9761. Here, you can visit the courtroom where John Brown was tried. The **Jefferson County Museum** at Samuel and Washington streets has a fun clutter of exhibits, including the wagon that carried Mr. Brown to the gallows; (304) 725-8628.

Racing fans of two sorts can be entertained in Charles Town. Auto racing happens at the **Summit Point Motorsports Park**; (304) 725-8444; *www.summitpoint-racing.com*. Thoroughbreds gallop at the **Charles Town Races**; (800) 795-7001 or (304) 725-7001; *www.ctownraces.com*. Parimutuel betting is permitted, and the facility has a year-around casino.

Where to learn more

Jefferson County Chamber of Commerce, P.O. Box 426 (29 Keyes Ferry Rd., Suite 200), Charles Town, WV 25414; (800) 624-0577 or (304) 725-2055; *www.jeffersoncounty.com*.

Lewisburg and about
A cultural and historic haven in the Alleghenies

⚑

The New River-Greenbrier Valley of southern West Virginia offers both scenic and cultural lures. Charming villages, thriving art centers and luxury resorts are tucked into the hilly, wooded folds of the Allegheny Mountains. Our focus is Greenbrier County, on the eastern side of the valley. It's home to the art and architectural enclave of Lewisburg and the old resort community of White Sulfur Springs.

Lewisburg has the finest collection of well-preserved Colonial, Federal and Victorian architecture in the state, and it's West Virginia's leading art colony. Everyone, it seems, likes this little tree-canopied town of about 3,700 contented souls. It's featured in National Geographic's *Guide to Small Town Escapes* and *The 100 Best Small Art Towns in America*. The National Trust for Historic Preservation selected it as one of its "Dozen Distinctive Destinations."

The community's centerpiece is classic Grecian style **Carnegie Hall** on the town square at 105 Church St.; (304) 645-7917; *www.carnegiehallwv.com*. Like the one in New York City, it was funded by philanthropist Andrew Carnegie. In 1902, he contributed funds to the Lewisburg Female Institute for the hall's construction. The school later became Greenbrier College and the hall today is the region's performing arts and visual arts center, with classrooms, artists' studios and a 500-seat auditorium.

Lewisburg's other major cultural lure is the professional **Greenbrier Valley Theatre** troupe, which has been presenting musicals, comedies and dramas for nearly half a century, at 113 E. Washington Street; (304) 645-3838; *www.gvtheatre.org*.

Colonists began settling the Greenbrier Valley in the 1740s, although they were frequently attacked by native folks who objected to their intrusion. Colonel Andrew Lewis of the Virginia militia was dispatched to do battle with them in 1774, and the community that grew up around his encampment was named in his honor. You can learn about this and a couple of local Civil War battles at the **North House Museum**. It occupies a gabled 1820 structure at 301 W. Washington St.; (304) 645-3398.

Stop by the Lewisburg Visitor Center at 540 N. Jefferson Street and pick up a walking guide to the town's many historic buildings. Check out the 1796 **Old Stone Presbyterian Church** at 200 Church Street. It's the oldest church west of the Alleghenies in continuous use—unless you count some Spanish mission churches in the American Southwest. Another handsome structure is the red brick 1837 **Greenbrier County Courthouse** at 200 N. Court Street. Visit **Andrew Lewis Park** and check out the old stone spring house that encloses the spring discovered by the town's benefactor.

A couple miles north of Lewisburg on Fairview Road is **Lost World Caverns**; (866) 228-3778 or (304) 645-6677; *www.lostworldcaverns.com.* Several large limestone caves sport goodly collections of stalagmites, stalactites and flowstone, plus some rare pure calcite formations.

Three miles east of Lewisburg on U.S. 60, near the town of *Caldwell,* you can pick up the **Greenbrier River Trail**. This hiking and biking path follows the old Chesapeake & Ohio railbed for seventy-six miles north to *Cass.* The adjacent river is popular for canoeing and fishing.

Just beyond Caldwell is the resort village of *White Sulfur Springs,* whose mineral spas have drawn well-heeled health seekers since the late 1700s. Its most famous resort—indeed, one of the most famous in America—is **The Greenbrier**; (800) 624-6070 or (304) 536-1110; *www.greenbrier.com.* The recipient of a rare AAA Five Diamond Award, it occupies a 6,500-acre woodland in the Allegheny foothills. This opulent Colonial style resort hosts assorted members of the rich and famous, and many of the power brokers of nearby Washington, D.C. In fact, as revealed by the *Washington Post* a few years ago, it even has an elaborate network of underground bunkers where our national leaders can duck incoming a-bombs.

Because of a new "gate policy," we ordinary folks can't just drop by and nose around. Only registered guests and people who book a round of golf or have dinner reservations for the main dining room are admitted to the grounds. It may be worth your while to pay the high green fees or have dinner, so you can check out the resort's flamboyant decor and lushly landscaped grounds. Or book a room; rates begin at a mere $500 a night.

Easier on your wallet or purse is a visit to **Oakhurst Links** at One Montague Drive in White Sulfur Springs; (866) OAK-1884; *www.oakhurst links.com.* It's the nation's oldest golf club, established in 1884. Check out its interesting display of ancient golf gear in a small museum.

The village of *Alderson* southwest of Lewisburg on State Route 12 has an impressive collection of Greek Revival, Federal and Colonial buildings. It's also home to the federal woman's prison that hosted Martha Stewart from October 2004 to March 2005. The town enjoyed a mini-tourist boom as the Stewart faithful came to view the prison and buy souvenir T-shirts.

Where to learn more

Greenbrier County Visitors Center, 540 N. Jefferson St., Lewisburg, WV 24901; (800) 833-2068 or (304) 645-1000; *www.greenbrierwv.com.*

Wheeling
A surprisingly diverse mini-city

W heeling is what happens when preservationists take the remnants of a once busy industrial city and fashion them into an appealing, history-rich and vibrant new community. Sitting on the banks of the Ohio River, reached by railroads and by the National Road, Wheeling was a thriving industrial and trade center in the mid-19th century.

As Civil War clouds gathered, the State of Virginia was on the border between the North and the South, both geographically and politically. Its leaders ultimately decided to join the Confederacy. However, several north-western counties that related more to Union industrialism than Southern slavery broke away. They established the "Restored Government of Virginia," with Wheeling as its capital. Then in 1863, the new entity was admitted to Union as West Virginia. The capital was shifted to Charleston, although Wheeling continued to thrive as an industrial crossroad.

If you look at a map, you'll see that Wheeling and its skinny Northern Panhandle are indeed thrust into Northern turf, bordering Ohio and Pennsylvania. West Virginia probably should be in the Mid-Atlantic chapter.

The town went into its predicable decline as America lost manufacturing jobs in the last century. Officials and residents turned this problem into an opportunity. They restored Victorian mansions, reworked the riverfront into a park, and fashioned downtown into a Victorian style shopping area.

Your family can build an entire vacation around this surprisingly diverse and appealing mini-city of about 32,000. All of the essentials are here— plenty of places shop, dine and recline, a variety of attractions and a pleasingly mixed bag of cultural offerings. As local tourist promoters like to say, you can get that "Wheeling feeling."

In fact, you can spend a lot of your time in Wheeling's huge municipal park, called **Oglebay Resort**; (800) 624-6988 or (304) 243-4000; *www.oglebay-resort.com*. This broad-based 1,650-acre complex has lodging, dining, museums, golf and miniature golf, tennis courts, landscaped gardens, hiking and riding trails and water play. A sound and light show is presented nightly during the summer.

The resort's best attraction—and it has a great name—is **Oglebay's Good Zoo** with eighty-five kinds of North American critters, a science discovery lab, planetarium, zoo train and kids' petting farm; (304) 243-4030. The Resort's **Mansion Museum** is the region's historical archive, with exhibits focused on in this part of the Ohio Valley; (304) 243-4058. The **Car-**

riage House Glass Museum features Wheeling's role as a major glass-pro-
ducing area, with a large glassware collection; (304) 243-4058. The **Henry
Stifel Schrader Environmental Education Center** has five miles of nature
trails, waterfalls and butterfly-busy flower gardens; (304) 242-6855.

One of the few local attractions that isn't in Oglebay Resort is the de-
lightful **Kruger Street Toy and Train Museum** at 144 Kruger St.; (877)
242-8133 or (304) 242-8133; *www.toyandtrain.com*. Housed in a 1906 Victorian style school building, it's busy with toy trains, doll houses and all
sorts of other playthings, plus exhibits about toy manufacturing.

Downtown Wheeling is a handsome study in bay-windowed Victorian
splendor, looking—we think—a bit like San Francisco. **Wheeling's Historic Centre Market** between Market and Main streets has lots of boutiques, specialty shops, art galleries, antique stores and cafés. Adjacent to
downtown is the handsomely landscaped **Wheeling Heritage Port** along the
riverfront. In summer, free "Waterfront Wednesday" concerts are presented
here. Walkers and cyclists can follow the **Heritage Trail** that starts here and
extends thirteen miles along the Ohio River.

Wheeling's "capitol" history began and ended at the **West Virginia Independence Hall Museum** at 1528 Market St.; (304) 238-1300; *www.
wvculture.org*. Built as a customs house, it served as the state capitol until
the new government was shifted to Charleston. Exhibits focus on West Virginia's complex role in the Civil War.

To explore the town's neighborhoods, sign up for the **Victorian Homes
Tour** that departs from the historic Eckhart House at 823-R Main St.; (888)
700-0118 or (304) 233-1600; *www.eckharthouse.com*.

This mini-city's most cherished landmark is the gracefully old fashioned
900-foot-long **Wheeling Suspension Bridge**, with its stone towers and large
globe lights. Built in 1849 to carry the National Road west, it's still in use.

Wheeling plays second fiddle only to Nashville as a major country entertainment center. In fact, Nashville stars come regularly to perform at **Jamboree USA**. Started in 1933, it's second only to the Grand Old Opry as the
oldest live radio show in the country. The Jamboree happens every Saturday
night in the posh **Capitol Music Hall** at 1015 Main St.; (800) 624-5456;
www.jamboreeusa.com. The Oglebay Institute's **Stifel Fine Arts Center**
presents a mix of jazz concerts, art exhibitions and performing arts classes;
at 1330 National Rd.; (304) 242-7700; *www.oionline.com*.

Where to learn more

Wheeling Convention & Visitors Bureau, 1401 Main St., Wheeling,
WV 26003; (800) 823-3097 or (304) 233-7709; *www.wheelingcvb.com*.

FORT MEYERS PIER, FL.

Chapter Ten

The
Deep South

MANSIONS, MAGNOLIAS & BEACHES

The Deep South conjures images of antebellum mansions, gardens scented with magnolia blossoms and of course sandy beaches. However, America's subtropical vacationland can't be stereotyped. It also has major cities, which we don't visit, and fascinating Colonial towns, which we do. Further, the South is about the space age and we visit an often over-looked rocket site while avoiding the obvious one.

ALABAMA is about cotton plantations and space flight and we sampled both. We also found a grand old city in the only area where Alabamans can stick their toes into saltwater.

Where to learn more: Bureau of Tourism & Travel, P.O. Box 4927, Montgomery, AL 36103-4927; (800) ALABAMA; *www.touralabama.org.*

ARKANSAS is a border state, partly South and partly Midwest, so we sampled its extremes, from a popular northern mountain resort to a southern folkcraft center to an historic town in between.

Where to learn more: Arkansas Department of Tourism, One Capitol Mall, Little Rock, AR 72201; (800) NATURAL; *www.arkansas.com.*

FLORIDA is one of our most popular tourist states, so we offer lots of choices, including an old Spanish town on the Panhandle, a traditional beach community and an off-the-beach art colony. We steered clear of Orlando, although we get you within commuting distance. **CLIMATE NOTE**: Because of its length, Florida has two vacation seasons. Summer is high season in the Panhandle and southern Florida is a winter retreat.

Where to learn more: Visit Florida, Inc., P.O. Box 1100, Tallahassee, FL 32302; (888) 735-2872; *www.visitflorida.com.*

GEORGIA on your mind? We're mindful of several interesting places to explore, including a great college town, the ultimate southern belle of a city, and coastal getaway and a surprise—a gold rush town.

Where to learn more: Georgia Tourism Division, 75 Fifth St. NW, Suite 1200, Atlanta, GA 30308; (800) VISIT-GA; *www.georgia.org/travel.*

LOUISIANA is recovering from its hurricane trauma and it offers much to explore, including its famous Cajun Country, a "plantation row" and one of the oldest settlements in the Deep South.

Where to learn more: Louisiana Department of Tourism, Box 94291, Baton Rogue, LA 70804-9291; (800) 677-4082; *www.louisianatravel.com.*

MISSISSIPPI is classic Old South, and we provide a Southern sampler that includes a weathered seaport, a genteel mini-city, the famous Nachez Trace and Elvis' birthplace—but not because of Elvis.

Where to learn more: Mississippi Division of Tourism, P.O. Box 849, Jackson, MS 39205; (866) SEE-MISS; *www.visitmississippi.org.*

Eufaula to Tuskegee
Stately homes, a top university and famous airmen

ꔫ

The oddly named Eufaula *is* the deep South, with one of the finest collections of 19th Civil War era mansions in the state. About fifty-five miles northwest, Tuskegee is noted for its university, its great scientist Dr. George Washington Carver and for the Tuskegee Airmen, the all-black fighter pilots of World War II.

Both communities are in a low lying area of southeastern Alabama that was covered with forests until settlers came in the 1830s and felled the trees to create large cotton plantations.

With a population of about 14,000 and named for a local Creek Indian tribe, *Eufaula* sits beside the Chattahoochee River. At this location, however, it's a long and skinny lake, trapped behind Walter F. George Dam. Lakepoint Resort State Park just to the north offers access; see below.

When you get to town, head for the **Chamber of Commerce** at 333 E. Broad Street and pick up the **Historic Eufaula Walking-Driving Tour** map. Although they're not all on the map, more than 500 structures are registered as local, state or national historic landmarks. In addition to its fine collection of antebellum mansions, Eufaula's yesterday look is further enhanced by well-preserved 19th century buildings in the downtown area.

The town's most striking abode is the neo-classic **Shorter Mansion** at 340 N. Eufaula Ave.; (888) 383-2852 or (334) 687-3793. Not antebellum, it's a post-Civil War mansion, built by a wealthy planter in 1884 and expanded to its present size in 1906. The main floor contains period furnished rooms, and a regional history museum occupies the second level. Another impressive mansion is the Italianate style **Fendall Hall** at 917 W. Barbour St.; (334) 687-8469. Although it was built just prior to the Civil War, its decor reflects the late 19th to early 20th century era.

If you want to play on Eufaula Lake, head for **Lakepoint Resort State Park**, seven miles north of town on U.S. 431; (800) 544-LAKE or (334) 687-8011; *www.alapark.com/parks*. It's a full-service resort with lake-view rooms, and you can rent boats and other water play equipment at the adjacent marina. The lake is noted for its bass fishing. The state park also has a golf course, playground, hiking trails, campsites and picnic areas.

Nearby is **Eufaula National Wildlife Refuge**, where local and migratory waterfowl hang out; (334) 687-4065; *www.fws.gov/eufaula*. More than 280 species have been sighted in this reserve on the Chattahoochee River. You can see regional wildlife exhibits and pick up a driving tour map of the refuge at the visitor center.

From here, pick your way northwest through farmlands and woodlands of the low lying Alabama countryside to *Tuskegee*. Much older than Eufaula, it occupies the site of a Creek village and a later French fort built in the early 1700s. The British gained control of the territory in 1763, and Andrew Jackson used the fort to launch his successful campaign against the Creek Confederation.

Today, Tuskegee is one of the most famous African-American history sites in the South. Booker T. Washington founded the all-black **Tuskegee Institute** in 1881. It was primarily a teachers' college, then Washington invited young George Washington Carver aboard to create an agriculture and science department. Carver spent the next half century creating amazing byproducts from peanuts and other vegetables.

Early in World War II, the institute was selected by the U.S. Army Air Corps to train a squadron of all-black fighter pilots at nearby Moton Field. Flying fighter escorts for American bomber missions over Europe and North Africa, these **Tuskegee Airmen** of the 332nd Fighter Group didn't lose a single bomber to attacking German aircraft.

Now called **Tuskegee University,** the school is both an active liberal arts college and a national historic site; (334) 727-6930; *www.tuskegee.edu* and *nps.gov/tuin*. At the **George Washington Carver Museum** near the campus entrance, you can see his preserved laboratory and learn about the hundreds of products that he developed; (334) 727-3200.

Also on campus, you can visit **The Oaks,** the home where Booker T. Washington lived from 1900 until his death in 1915; (334) 727-3200. The restored Queen Anne style house contains period furnishings, including a desk and personal items in Washington's study.

Moton Field is now home to the **Tuskegee Airmen National Historic Site**; (334) 727-6390; *www.nps.gov/tuai*. The hanger, control tower and other facilities are being restored to the era when the young black pilots trained here. Photos and other exhibits in the hanger tell their story.

Where to learn more

Eufaula-Barbour County Chamber of Commerce, P.O. Box 697 (333 E. Broad St.), Eufaula, AL 36017; (800) 524-7529 or (334) 687-6664; *www.eufaula-barbourchamber.com*.

Tuskegee Area Chamber of Commerce, 212 S. Main St., Tuskegee, AL 36083; (334) 727-6619; *www.tuskegeeareachamber.com*.

Huntsville
From the Alabama frontier to the moon

Ƿ

Although the NASA facilities at Cape Kennedy and Houston get most of the attention these days, America's space program actually started at the Redstone Arsenal in Huntsville in 1950. It was here that German scientist Dr. Werner von Braun and his team developed the Saturn V moon rocket.

NASA's Marshall Space Flight Center adjacent to the arsenal has the world's largest space museum. That's just one of several good reasons to plan a visit to this northern Alabama mini-city of about 160,000. The state's oldest English-speaking settlement, Huntsville is busy with historic sites. Nearby Wheeler Reservoir on the Tennessee River is a serious source of water recreation, and there's a national forest just to the south.

It's a wonderful irony of history that Alabama's oldest English-speaking settlement, founded in 1805, would be the site of the development of the first moon rocket. Begin at the beginning, at **Big Spring International Park** west of Courthouse Square, where John Hunt founded his namesake town. The Fearn Canal, used to transport cotton to the Tennessee River, runs through the park. A good mix of gift shops, galleries, antique stores and cafés occupy old storefronts around the square.

Invaded by the Yanks but not burned, Huntsville has one of the largest collections of antebellum homes in Alabama. Many of these are in the **Twickenham Historic District** northeast of the square, and some are occupied by descendants of the original owners. The convention and visitors bureau conducts periodic walking tours; call (256) 551-2230.

Alabama was admitted to the Union in 1819, and the **Alabama Constitution Village** marks the site of the its constitutional convention. Costumed docents provide slices of life of the early 1800s, and visitors can help them dip candles and perform other pioneer skills. The reconstructed village is at 109 Gates Avenue; (256) 564-8100.

The big yellow train station at 320 Church Street, where conquering Union soldiers rode into town, is now the **Huntsville Depot Transportation Museum**; (256) 564-8100. Built in 1860, its the oldest train station in Alabama. After being greeted by a robotic stationmaster, telegrapher and engineer, you can view railroad exhibits, locomotives and assorted rolling stock.

The 1819 Federal style **Weeden House Museum** was the birthplace of artist-poet Maria Howard Weeden; 300 Gates Ave.; (256) 536-7718. Docents read her poetry as they guide visitors through period furnished rooms. Just out of town, **Burritt on the Mountain** sits atop Round Top Mountain at

3101 Burritt Dr.; (256) 536-2882; *www.burrittmuseum.com.* The complex includes a 14-room mansion and a restored early 18th century farm with living history demonstrations.

And now, back to the future.

The **George C. Marshall Space Flight Center** is just southwest of town off Interstate 565, with a great address—One Tranquility Base; (800) 637-7223 or (256) 837-3400; *www.nasa.gov/centers/marshal.* It displays a literal forest of rockets and other space gear, and its museum has leading edge interactive exhibits that will keep you occupied for hours. You can take a "space shower" where water doesn't know which way is up, visit a space station and hitch a rocket ride to Jupiter.

The center goes beyond scientific exhibits by offering several fun family amusement attractions with space age themes. In the Spacedome IMAX theater, you can tilt back and get dizzy as the ultra-wide screen takes you somewhere out there. Experience tummy-lurching G-forces and a couple of seconds of weightlessness at the Space Shot. Take a simulated space walk and try to scramble up the Mars Climbing Wall.

Incidentally, if you have kids and want to steer them toward careers in science, ship them off to the center's Space Camp; (800) 637-7223; *www.spacecamp.com.* During this multi-day outing, participants sleep in space capsules and go on simulated space flights. All the while, they learn lots of neat stuff about science. There's an adult version called Aviation Challenge.

From the great beyond, you can return to earth and explore the great outdoors. About twelve miles southwest of Huntsville, you'll reach the town of *Decatur* and **Wheeler Lake**, a long reservoir backed up by Wheeler Dam. At marinas around Decatur and *Florence* further west, you can rent boats and play on the water.

The adjacent **Wheeler National Wildlife Refuge** encloses woodlands, swamps and bottomlands that lure lots of birds; (256) 350-6639; *www.fws.gov/wheeler.* The preserve has trails, picnic sites and boating and fishing areas. Midway between Decatur and Florence is the waters-edge **Joe Wheeler State Park**; (800) 544-4639 or (256) 247-5461; *www.alapark.com/parks.* Its extensive facilities include a lodge, cabins, a marina, golf course, tennis courts, trails and picnic sites. Finally, if you want to take a walk in the woods, **William B. Bankhead National Forest** is just to the south, with hiking trails, fishing streams and camping and picnic sites; (256) 489-5111.

Where to learn more

Huntsville/Madison County Convention & Visitors Bureau, 500 Church St., Huntsville, AL 35801; (800) 772-2348; *www.huntsville.org.*

Mobile
An old city grand, near lots of sand

⚐

The venerable city of Mobile and its surrounding beach towns are popular with Alabamans because this is their only outlet to the Gulf Coast; their opportunity to bask on wave-caressed sand. However, few folks outside the Deep South regard it as a vacation destination. That makes it undiscovered in our book, both literally and figuratively.

With a population around 200,000, Mobile offers full visitor amenities without overwhelming visitors, because it's not part of a megalopolis. It sits at the head of Mobile Bay, within a short drive of several beach towns.

Since Mobile and its beach communities are on the Gulf of Mexico, this is subtropic country. It's warm enough for beach play from spring through fall. Summers can get crowded and fall is hurricane season, so we'd vote for spring. The town's **Festival of Flowers** happens in late March, and you can follow a 47-mile **Azalea Trail** through the region. Summer isn't too crowded in Mobile itself, since most visitors are headed for those nearby beaches. In any case, book your summer lodgings early.

We prefer Mobile to its beach towns because many have a carny atmosphere, with amusement rides, miniature golf, lots of T-shirt shops and the like. However, *Fairhope* and *Daphne* have some nice resorts. If you want things quiet, **Dauphin Island** is appealing, since most of it is a bird refuge.

Mobile is about as handsome as towns get, with ancient buildings shaded by giant Spanish moss-draped oaks. It spring, its gardens and parklands burst with azaleas, magnolias and other blooms. **Bienville Square** in the heart of downtown is particularly appealing, decorated with its centuries-old live oaks and flowering shrubs.

Begin your visit at **Fort Conde**, built by the French in 1711 to protect the settlement they had established nine years earlier. You'll learn at this partially reconstructed bastion that Mobile is Alabama's oldest city. It was Mobile, not New Orleans, that served as first seat of the Louisiana Territory. And Mobile, not New Orleans, celebrates America's oldest Mardi Gras, dating from 1703. During the town's rollercoaster history, it served under the flags of France, England, Spain and of course the Confederacy. One of the Civil War's major sea battles raged in Mobile Bay in 1864, and the old city fell to the Yanks in 1865 after a long siege.

At the **Fort Conde Welcome Center**, you can pick up walking tour maps to Mobile's historic districts and its oak-and-flower bedecked parklands; 150 S. Royal St.; (251) 208-7658.

Mobile's best attractions are its historic districts. **De Tonti Square** several blocks north of the business core has the city's best collection of elegant Federal, Queen Anne and Greek Revival mansions. They were built when the city was a major cotton shipping port. The square is dressed with lacy wrought iron, flagstone sidewalks and gas lamps. The **downtown commercial district** features a mix of 19th century European style brick rowhouse commercial buildings and modest skyscrapers of the early 20th century.

Homes in the **Oakleigh Garden District** range from 18th century Creole cottages to late 19th century mansions. At the **Oakleigh Historic Complex**, you can tour three types of these old homes. It's at 350 Oakleigh Place; (251) 432-1281; *www.historicmobile.org*. The Oakleigh Period House Museum occupies an 1833 Greek Revival home, with furnished rooms and regional history exhibits. The Cox-Deasy Cottage is a typical Gulf Coast Creole style home, elevated to let the breezes blow underneath. The modest middle class Mardi Gras Cottage has exhibits about that colorful celebration.

For an attraction of quite a different sort, head for **USS Alabama Memorial Park** at 2703 Battleship Parkway; (251) 433-2703; *ussalabama.com*. You can go aboard the battleship *USS Alabama* and scramble through the innards of the *USS Drum* submarine. Both saw action during World War II. Other exhibits include military aircraft, tanks and artillery pieces. The 175-acre military park complex is dedicated to Alabama's veterans.

The **Mobile Museum of Art** is one of the best on the Gulf Coast, with more than 6,000 items, including American, European, Asian and African art and a large display of decorative arts. It's off Springhill Avenue in Langan Park; (251) 208-5300; *www.mobilemuseumofart.com*. The nearby **Mobile Medical Museum** displays three centuries of medical instruments and artifacts, at 1664 Springhill Ave.; (251) 434-5055; *www.mobilemedicalmuseum.com*. The **Gulf Coast Exploreum** has an interactive science center and an IMAX theater that shows science-focused films, at 65 Government St.; (877) 625-4386 or (251) 208-6873; *www.exploreum.net*.

In *Theodore* just south of town off I-10 is the **Bellingrath Gardens and Home**, an elaborate 900-acre estate and mansion built by Coca-Cola founder Walter Bellingrath; (800) 247-8420 or (251) 973-2217; *www.bellingrath.org*. The brick and wrought iron mansion is busy with museum quality furniture, plus crystal, china and silver collected by his wife, Bessie Morse Bellingrath. It includes an outstanding display of Boehm porcelain.

Where to learn more

Mobile Bay Convention & Visitors Bureau, One S. Water St., Mobile, AL 36602; (800) 5-MOBILE or (251) 208-2000; *www.mobilebay.org*.

Eureka Springs
The town where they took to the waters

The alleged curative powers of mineral waters created health resorts throughout America during the great medical quackery era of the 1800s, and Arkansas has two of them. Hot Springs is much better known, so of course we picked lesser-known and more charming Eureka Springs.

When science figured out that "taking the waters" offered no medical benefits other than relaxation and cleaning out one's pores, most of those old spas faded from the scene. Hot Springs had next-door Hot Springs National Park to keep it going. The city continued thriving as a tourist center, eventually suffering the arrival of the Josephine Tussaud Wax Museum. Eureka Springs had no such luck, so it seemed destined to fade away.

However, folks began discovering this sleepy little town in recent decades, with its wonderful if weathered collection of 19th century buildings. They've been spruced up and many are now occupied by B&Bs, boutiques, art galleries and cafés. Eureka Springs is back in the tourist business, thankfully without a wax museum.

Tucked into a narrow valley of the Ozarks in far northwestern Arkansas, this old town is an absolute charmer. And perhaps it's bit of a liberal shock to neighboring communities. In addition to its lively music and arts scenes, it has an active gay and lesbian culture and a harmless sub-community of spiritualists and over-the-hill hippies. What would Sam Walton of nearby Bentonville have thought of all this?

Perhaps the old town redeems itself with its summer-long Great Passion Play, and a seven-story statue of Christ towering from a nearby hill. ("What? This isn't Buenos Aires?")

Everything's cool here, J.C. This is just a happy, fun-loving place. For instance, folks gather in the evening at their version of an outdoor theater, watching movies projected onto the white-painted wall of an old building. Patrons are encouraged to dress in the type of clothing worn by performers in the film, and prizes are awarded. It must have been a blast during the showing of *Shakespeare In Love*.

With fewer than 2,500 souls, this forest-shrouded town is easily walkable. You can spend hours exploring its galleries, crystal shops, boutiques, antique shops, folk craft stores and—well, yes, there are a few fudge and T-shirt shops. Most businesses are tucked into brick and rough-cut stone buildings. The most striking of these is the four-story gingerbready **Flatiron Flats** building that looks to have somehow been transported here from San Francisco. It's about the tallest thing in town and the whole downtown shootin' match has been declared a National Historic District.

The **Eureka Springs Historical Museum** will get you started on local lore, at 95 S. Main St.; (479) 253-9417; *www.eshm.org.* You'll learn that the town was founded in the 1850s, although native folks took the waters long before that. It reached its peak in the late 1800s, when it had more than thirty resort hotels. Then came the truth about this funny tasting water—soak in it, don't drink it—and the town went to sleep for a few decades.

When we suggest that Eureka Springs is less touristy than Hot Springs, we aren't saying it lacks tourist hype. It's just more hip here. There's fun stuff, like **Frog Fantasies** at 151 Spring St.; (479) 253-7227; *www.frogfantasies.com.* It has so many kinds and shapes of frogs that Kermit would turn green with envy. And check out **Dinosaur World** on State Route 187, with ninety life-sized dinosaur replicas and a forty-foot-high King Kong; (479) 253-8113; *dinosaurworld.info.* (King Kong was a dinosaur?)

For cool Christian kitsch, head for the **Great Passion Play** complex three miles east of town off U.S. 62; (800) 882-7529 or (479) 253-9200; *www. greatpassionplay.com.* Catch the show itself, which is quite well done. Then check out the **Bible Museum** with more than 6,000 editions of the Good Book in assorted languages, and the **Sacred Arts Center** with more than a thousand pieces of Christian art and artifacts. Take the **New Holy Land Tour** past recreated biblical-historical scenes on a fifty-acre plot. And above it all—as he should be—is that imposing statue of Christ.

There are many more visitor attractions in and about Eureka Springs but we've got to save room for a side trip to *Bentonville.* It's about thirty-five miles west via twisting Highway 62. No, we're not Wal-Mart fans; don't even shop there. But curiosity maked us want to see the hometown of the man who launched the world's largest retail chain.

At the **Wal-Mart Visitors Center**, you'll learn how Walton built his empire and—dang!—you can even see his desk. It's at 105 N. Main St.; (479) 273-1329; *www.walmartstores.com.* Also in the area are the **Peel House Museum and Historical Gardens**, an 1875 Italianate villa at 400 S. Walton Blvd., (479) 273-9664, *www.peelmansion.org*; and the **Fusion Fine Arts Gallery** and art shop at 109 N. Main St., (479) 273-9278.

Where to learn more

Eureka Springs Chamber of Commerce, Box 551 (81 Kings Hwy.), Eureka Springs, AR 72632; (800) 638-7352; *www.eurekasprings.org.*

Mountain View and about
Arkansas' Ozark folk heritage center

Most every evening in summer, they come in from the hills and from their homes, with their fiddles and banjos and dulcimers and their shy grins.They settle on Mountain View's Courtsquare or on nearby porches and benches, and they begin playing and singing. Visitors wander from one group of performers to the next, listening to this mountain music that is at once sad and cheerful. It's music that wails from the fiddle and chuckles from the banjo and sighs from the dulcimer.

This little town in the hills of the north central Ozarks is the heart of Arkansas' folk music and craft culture. It's the culture of the Scottish-Irish hill people who settled here in the 1800s and remained isolated for decades until it occurred to someone to build roads. And now it's the crossroads—literally—of that heritage. It sits at the junction of five meandering two-laners that wander in from other Ozark villages. Mountain View is like Virginia's Crooked Road, except that it's all in one convenient location.

Arkansas has taken steps to preserve this heritage with the creation of the **Ozark Folk Center**, perhaps the only state park in America devoted to rural music and cultural preservation; (870) 269-3851; *www.ozarkfolkcenter.com.* The center supports the entire spectrum of Ozark culture—music, dance, folk crafts and oral histories. There are live concerts almost daily during the summer. Artisans demonstrate weaving, candle-dipping, quilting and the more esoteric skills, making bent-wood rocking chairs and apple-face dolls and practicing tintype photography. More than twenty-five different "cabin crafts" are practiced, from coopering to blacksmithing. The folk center also has a country style restaurant and a lodge; (870) 269-3871.

Special heritage events are held throughout the year at the park and in town. The Annual Arkansas Folk Festival and Southern Mountain and Hammer Dulcimer Workshop are in April. In mid-September, it's the Arkansas Old-Timer Fiddlers State Competition, followed by the Fall Harvest Festival in October. And then there are festivities with an Ozark mountain twist—outhouse races, tall tale contests and baked bean competitions.

Life is pretty laid back here. Many buildings and homes don't have street numbers, and some of the streets themselves lack names. However, names and numbers aren't necessary in a town this small and compact. Courtsquare, with the old fashioned Stone County Courthouse as its centerpiece, is rimmed with folkcraft, specialty, gift and antique shops and country style restaurants. Downtown also has several B&Bs and old hotels.

Mountain View is noted for its "pickin' barns" and other entertainment venues. Among them are **Cash's White River Hoedown** featuring country, blues and gospel music, (800) 759-6474, *www.auntminniesonline.com*; **Jimmy Driftwood's Barn** with folk and bluegrass music, (870) 269-8042; **John Taylor's**, offering mountain music and square dancing, (870) 269-9597; and **Brickshy's Backstreet Theater** with country corn variety and comedy shows; (870) 269-6200.

Check out **Mellon's Country Store** on State Route 9 North, an old fashioned mercantile that sells antiques, gifts and grub, (870) 269-3354; and the **Old Mill**, a restored grist mill on Main Street that once ground corn and wheat for the town; (870) 269-5337. The **Arkansas Craft Guild Gallery**, one of the oldest in the South, shows and sells the works of 300 crafts people, at 104 E. Main St.; (870) 269-3897; *arkansascraftguild.com*.

Nature has crafted the area's other major attraction. Spelukers rate **Blanchard Springs Caverns** as one of the best limestone cave complexes in America; (888) 757-2246 or (870) 757-2211; *www.fs.fed.us/oonf/ozark*. It's fifteen miles northwest of town on State Route 14, in Ozark National Forest. Visitors can choose from three different tours, from an easy stroll to a four-hour spelunking scramble. The national forest also has several miles of hiking and mountain biking trails.

Pressing northward through the Ozarks on State Route 5, you'll encounter the hamlet of *Mountain Home*, with several antique stores and crafts shops. **Rapps Barren Settlement** here is a restored pioneer village in Cooper City Park on Spring Street; (870) 424-9311.

To the Northwest on Bull Shoals Reservoir is the town of *Bull Shoals,* with several small lakeside resorts and another pioneer village and limestone cavern. **Mountain Village 1890** contains ten old structures moved here from elsewhere; (800) 445-7177 or (800) 445-7177; *www.1890village.com*. Docents demonstrate folk crafts and conduct tours of the furnished buildings. Admission to the village also includes entry into **Bull Shoals Cavern**, a small limestone cave complex.

If you head south from Mountain View on Highway 5, you'll reach **Greers Ferry Lake** reservoir near *Heber Springs*. You can visit a trout hatchery and aquarium, and view area history exhibits at the **Greers Ferry Dam Visitor Center**. The nearby Little Red River is noted for trout fishing.

Where to learn more

Mountain View Area Chamber of Commerce, P.O. Box 133, Mountain View, AR 72560; (870) 269-8068; *www.ozarkgetaways.com*. The chamber visitor center is on Courtsquare.

Pine Bluff
A woodsy town with a curious mix of lures

This mini-city in the Arkansas pinelands is as pleasant as its name, with comfy old homes on wide tree-shaded streets and a downtown area embellished with historic murals. With a population of about 56,000, it's one of those "just my size" communities with a surprising number of attractions.

Founded as a trading post in 1819 by Joseph Bonne of French-Indian descent, it's the second oldest town in the state. Bonne built his log cabin outpost on a pine tree bluff overlooking the Arkansas River, so he didn't have to think too hard to come up with a name. This is one of the few Arkansas communities with pre-Civil War homes and you'll find several of them along West Barraque Street.

Local historians say the first skirmish of the Civil War occurred near Pine Bluff when a home guard seized some Federal supply boats on the Arkansas River in April of 1861. This was before the first shots were fired at Fort Sumter. Later, the city wound up in Federal hands and Union troops fought off a Rebel attack in 1863, saving its fine old homes and business blocks from a destructive invasion.

The town's history is painted on a series of thirteen murals in its well-kept business district. Pine Bluff has an interesting array of visitor attractions, from historic sights to a band museum to a multi-million dollar art and science center.

Exhibits at the **Pine Bluff/Jefferson County Historical Museum** range from native folks, early settlement and the Civil War to the area's black heritage. The museum also has a large antique doll and miniature home collection. It's at 201 E. Fourth St.; (870) 541-5402. The **Arkansas Railroad Museum** has a 1940s theme, with locomotives and rolling stock at its Cotton Belt Railway Shops at 1700 Port Rd.; (870) 535-8819.

The town's most versatile attraction is the **Arts and Science Center for Southeast Arkansas** at 701 Main St.; (870) 536-3375; *www.artssiencecenter.org*. This modern complex has three large art galleries, a hands-on science center and a theater that hosts local and traveling shows.

Pine Bluff's kitschiest attraction is the **Arkansas Entertainers Hall of Fame** at One Convention Center Plaza; (800) 536-7660 or (870) 536-7660. Push buttons on an animatronic Johnny Cash and he'll welcome you to the center and sing a choice of songs. Enshrined in the hall of fame are entertainers with Arkansas roots, including Glenn Campbell, Alan Ladd, Charley Rich, Dick Powell, Billy Bob Thornton and Conway Twitty.

The community's most fun attraction is the **Band Museum** at 423 Main St.; (870) 534-4676; *www.bandmuseum.org*. You can learn all about good old American band music with its large display of vintage instruments, then enjoy a lime phosphate at a 1950s style soda fountain.

If you're a tree-hugger, head for the fine **Delta Rivers Nature Center** in Jefferson County Regional Park off U.S. 65-B; (870) 534-0011; *www.delta rivers.com*. The large complex preserves river, wetland and woodland habitats, with live and stuffed critters, nature films, a 20,000-gallon aquarium and a trail to wildlife observation posts. The regional park has a boat launch on the Arkansas River, picnic areas, an RV park and even an eighteen-hole golf course; (870) 536-0920.

Pine Bluff has a lively cultural base, fostered in part by the presence of the **University of Arkansas**; *www.uapd.edu*. It was established in 1873 as Branch Normal College, the state's first black university. African-American history is preserved in the **Keepers of the Spirit** exhibit in R.C. Childress Hall. The nearby **University Fine Arts Gallery** hangs a variety of rotating exhibits. The phone number for both is (870) 575-8236.

Pine Bluff Convention Center, the largest in Arkansas, has a multi-purpose performing arts facility and sports arena at One Convention Center Plaza; (800) 536-7660 or (870) 536-7660; *www.pinebluffonline.com*. One of its clients is the professional **Pine Bluff Symphony**; (870) 536-7666.

A pair of pioneer villages

About twenty miles south of Pine Bluff off U.S. 79 in the town of *Rison* is the **Rison Pioneer Village**, offering a look at Arkansas life in the late 19th century; (870) 325-7289. The complex has an old fashioned mercantile where you can buy lemonade, hoop cheese and crackers, plus an 1867 church, a cottage, smokehouse and blacksmith shop.

Follow State Route 190 about twenty miles west of Pine Bluff to *Sheridan* and its **Grant County Museum and Heritage Village**; (870) 942-4496; *www.grantcountymuseum.org*. It's a curiously mixed complex, with history displays, an exhibit on the Jenkens' Ferry Civil War battle (below), World War II vehicles, several log buildings and a restored Depression era café.

Just below Sheridan on State route 46 is the **Jenkens' Ferry Battlefield** site, where retreating Union troops clashed with Confederates on the Saline River on April 20, 1864. It's an Arkansas State Landmark; (501) 682-1191.

Where to learn more

Greater Pine Bluff Chamber of Commerce, P.O. Box 5069 (612 W. Fifth St.), Pine Bluff, AR 71611; (870) 535-0110; *www.pinebluffchamber. com*. Also check *www.pinebluffonline.com*.

Amelia Island
The state's first beach resort

Ⱶ

Since Florida is one of the most visited states in America, finding undiscovered places was a bit of a challenge. What we have found are several areas that are appealing yet aren't mainstream tourist destinations. We begin where the state's tourism began. Amelia Island is off Florida's far northern Atlantic Coast, a Frisbee toss from Georgia and about forty-five minutes from *Jacksonville*.

This appealing retreat is eighteen miles long and three miles wide. It's a most picturesque island, with the feminine curves of sand dunes, groves of moss-laden live oaks and thirteen miles of sparkling quartz sand beach. The island has none of the tourist gimmickry of Orlando or the night life fervor of South Beach. It does have some of the state's most upscale resort areas. The island's southern area is strictly high end, with opulent retreats where you check your wallet at the door.

Still, Amelia is a place where mere mortals can afford to play. The island offers reasonably priced lodgings in its only town of *Fernandina Beach* near the northern end, on the bay side. There are miles of public beach on the island, even in the pricey resort areas, and both the northern and southern ends are capped by state parks.

Start your visit in Fernandina Beach, a town of about 10,000 folks that dates back to Civil War Days. That heritage is reflected in a 30-square block area of 19th century homes and businesses known as **Centre Street Fernandina**. Head for the chamber of commerce **welcome center** in a vintage train station at 102 Centre Street, where you can pick up walking and driving tour maps of the town and the rest of the island; (904) 261-3248.

You can learn about the island's lively and sometimes wicked past at the **Amelia Island Museum of History**, occupying the 1878 brick Nassau County jail building at 233 S. Third St.; (904) 261-7378; *www.ameliamuseum.org*. Docent-led tours of this fine museum take you through Amelia Island's pages of history.

That history began in with French colonizing attempts as far back as the 1560s. The island later became a haven for smugglers and pirates and was described by President James Monroe as a "festering fleshpot." The first permanent facility, Fort Clinch, was started in 1847, but it was never completed. It was occupied by Union troops during the Civil War, and many of them, warmed by the idea of year-around toasty climate, returned after the conflict ended. This began the island's role as Florida's first resort.

Hours can be spent prowling among the vintage storefronts of Centre Street. They house a good selection of antique stores, specialty shops, book stores and cafés. Stop for lunch or a brew at the classic brick **Palace Saloon** at Centre and Second streets; (904) 491-3332. The **Island Art Association Gallery** sells works of regional artists, at 18 N. Second St.; (904) 261-7020.

The **Amelia Island Charter Boat Association** can arrange for deep sea fishing charters and sightseeing cruises; (800) 229-1682. You can rent kayaks and assorted other boats at the waterfront at the end of Centre Street.

When you've done with Fernandina Beach, head for **Fort Clinch State Park** on the island's extreme northeastern tip—in fact, it's the northeastern tip of Florida; (904) 277-7274; *www.floridastateparks.org/fortclinch.* Georgia's Cumberland Island is just across the water. Rangers in period uniforms reenact the fort's daily military routines. They also lead nature walks out to Willow Pond where 170 kinds of birds—and occasional alligators—have been seen. The fort has campsites and a large public beach area.

Most of Amelia Island's beaches are on the Atlantic side and you can take your pick, since there's public access even in the resort areas. If you take Centre Street east from town, you'll merge onto Atlantic Avenue and hit **Main Beach**. It has all the essentials—restrooms, picnic shelters, a food stand, a playground and sand. Farther down the Atlantic side, you'll encounter **Peters Point Beach Front Park**, with picnic tables and restrooms.

Just below is the **Ritz-Carlton**, one of the Island's two most luxurious resorts. Stop by for a look and perhaps a meal in one of its many restaurants; (800) 241-3333 or (904) 277-1111; *www.ritzcarlton.com.* Continuing south, you'll reach the even more expansive **Amelia Island Plantation**, a resort sprawled over 1,350 acres; (888) 261-6161 or (904) 261-6161; *www.aipfl. com.* The complex is so large that tram service is provided so folks can commute to its three golf courses and its many other facilities.

At the island's southern tip, **Amelia Island State Park** covers more than 200 unspoiled acres of beaches, marshlands and forests; (904) 251-2320; *www.floridastateparks.org/ameliaisland.* There are no facilities other than trails and restrooms. Activities consist of swimming, sunning, seashell hunting, fishing and wildlife watching. You can book beach horseback rides at the Kelly Seahorse Ranch; (904) 491-5166; *www.kellyranchinc.com.*

Where to learn more

Amelia Island Chamber of Commerce, 961687 Gateway Blvd., Amelia Island, FL 32034; (866) 4-AMELIA; *www.ameliaisland.org.*

The Coastal Byway
Skimming the scenic and historic north shore

⚐

If you're planning to wind up in Orlando or maybe Daytona Beach, take the scenic route down northern Florida's Atlantic Coast. And if Amelia Island also is in your plans, just head south from there.

This 105-mile drive combines three Florida state scenic routes and has been designated a National Scenic Byway. It's formally called the A1A Scenic and Historic Coastal Byway, running from Amelia Island to Daytona Beach. The route hugs the shoreline most of the way, often skimming between the beach and intracoastal waterways. It passes seemingly endless miles of inviting white sand, plus woodlands and jungled estuaries busy with wildlife. With luck, you might even spot a manatee. The historic star of this linear show is America's oldest city.

As you head south from Amelia Island, you'll skim the edge of the bustling city of *Jacksonville* and pass near **Big Talbot Island** and **Little Talbot Island**. They're two of the last unspoiled barrier reef islands in the state and both are state parks; (904) 251-2320; *www.floridastateparksorg*.

Then in quick succession, you'll encounter the coastal communities of *Atlantic Beach*, *Neptune Beach* and *Jacksonville Beach*. These are basically Jacksonville's shoreside playgrounds with the usual beach concessions, fishing piers, restaurants, lodgings and lots of bikini-clad bodies.

Continuing south, you'll soon shed Jacksonville sprawl and hit the other extreme—the protected waters of the **Guana-Tolomato-Matansas National Estuarine Research Reserve**. If you have a kayak or other floating device aboard, you can explore the lushly vegetated channels of the estuary.

Just below the reserve is splendid old *St. Augustine*, one of America's most historic cities. It's the oldest continually inhabited settlement in the land, beating out Santa Fe, New Mexico, and Jamestown, Virginia, both settled in 1607. St. Augustine dates from 1565.

Despite the intrusion of wax and believe it or don't museums, alligator farms and similar gimmicks on the fringes of the town, the heart of old St. Augustine remains remarkably intact and unblemished. Although nothing here dates from the 1500s, its old fort, the iron city gates and Spanish quarter reach back to the 17th and 18th centuries.

St. Augustine's focal point is the 17th century Spanish fortress at **Castillo de San Marcos National Monument**; (904) 829-6506; *www.nps. gov/ casa*. At the **Visitor Information Center** in front of the fortress at 10 Castillo Drive, you can pick up a walking tour map of the old town area; (904)

825-1000. St. Augustine's many "must-sees" include the reconstructed **Colonial Spanish Quarter**, now a living history museum; the **Government House Museum**, the ancient city's main archive; and the **Lightner Museum**, with a huge collection of Victorian memorabilia.

Pressing southward—if you can pull yourself away—you'll pass several beach towns and then reach **Fort Matanzas National Monument**; (904) 471-0116; *www.nps.gov/foma.* It was built on an offshore island to warn St. Augustine of attacks from the south. Just below there is **Marineland**, established in 1938 as the world's first oceanarium. It was modernized in 1994, with a new Dolphin Conservation Center and a 450,000-gallon aquarium; (888) 279-9194; *www.marineland.net.*

The **River to the Sea Preserve** near Marineland is a 90-acre ecological site between the Matansas River and the Atlantic, with sand dunes, wetlands and scrub oak groves. Just below Marineland is **Washington Oaks Gardens State Park**, a picturesque 400-acre swatch of formal gardens, tidal marshes and unusual rock outcroppings; (386) 446-6780; *www.floridastateparks.org.* Once part of a large plantation, it's a good shorebird and wildlife spotting area. Next comes the attractive little community of *Palm Coast*, a resort area set among trees between the ocean and the intracoastal waterway, with several places to dine and recline, plus golf, tennis, fishing and boating.

Farther along is the village of *Flagler Beach*, named for railroad baron Henry Flagler. It's an old fashioned shoreside town with a boardwalk and fishing pier. With a population of 4,000, it's large enough to offer complete services, yet it has escaped the sprawl of nearby *Daytona Beach*. The town and its six miles of strand are called the "Peaceful Beach" by the Flagler Beach Chamber of commerce; (800) 298-0995; *www.flaglercounty.com.*

Pressing onward, you'll pass two more state reserves. **Gamble Rogers Memorial State Recreation Area** has lots of beachfront, with camping, picnicking, hiking trails and a boat ramp; (386) 517-2086; *www.floridastateparks.org.* The inshore **Bulow Plantation State Park** preserves the ruins of an old sugar plantation, with a sugar mill, spring house and slave quarters; (386) 517-2084; *www.floridastateparks.org.* It offers hiking trails, a picnic site and boating in the estuary.

Just below here, as traffic and commercialism begin to thicken, you'll know you're on the edge of busy of *Daytona Beach*.

Where to learn more

St. Augustine Visitors & Convention Bureau, 88 Riberia St., Suite 400, St. Augustine, FL 32084; (800) 653-2489; *www.visitoldcity.com.* Also check *www.byways.org/brows/byways/2477.*

Fort Meyers
Following the famous

⚐

Fans follow famous people, even if they're inventors and industrialists instead of movie queens and rock stars. When Thomas Edison and Henry Ford chose Fort Meyers as their winter retreats, they unintentionally put this quiet community on the map.

One gets the impression that, like a good hostess expecting company, the citizens of Fort Meyers have kept their community attractive for their visitors. This town of about 50,000 is a pleasing vision of palm-lined streets and lush flowering tropical plants. Thankfully, its citizens have left the tourist gimmickry to Orlando and Tampa Bay. Actually, Edison had a hand in the city's present look, by importing many of those palms from Cuba.

Overworked and exhausted, he came to Fort Meyers on the advise of his doctors in 1885, and he wintered here until his death fifty years later. However, he didn't lie on the beach. An avid botanist as well as an inventor, he became fascinated with tropical flora and turned his estate into a virtual botanical jungle. He also continued tinkering with some of his 1,000-plus inventions, calling his Florida stays "working vacations." It was here that he perfected the incandescent light bulb, phonograph and movie camera.

The Edisons and Fords were good friends and in 1916, the wealthy automaker and his wife built a home next door so the two families could winter together. Today, the two homes are a joint historical landmark and the most popular visitor attraction in southwest Florida.

The **Edison-Ford Winter Estates** are in a lush tropical setting at 2350 McGregor Blvd.; (239) 334-7419; *www.edison-ford-estate.com*. Entry is by guided tour only and the tours harmlessly hokey, since costumed performers portray the Edisons, Fords and their friends. (It's certainly a cut above a push-button Johnny Cash; see page 398.)

Although it's called Seminole Lodge, the Edison home is a Victorian style edifice and it remains the way it was when the great inventor puttered about. You'll see some of his early light bulbs in his cluttered lab, and a museum exhibits several of his inventions. The home is shaded by Florida's largest banyan tree, presented to Edison by his friend Harvey Firestone in 1925. The smaller cottage style Ford home, called the Mangos, is furnished to the 1920 era. An adjacent garage contains a collection of vintage Ford automobiles. Both homes have elaborate gardens. While you're here, take a cruise on the Caloosahatchee River aboard the *Reliance*, a replica of an electric launch invented by Edison.

Handsome old Fort Meyers offers several other attractions. Also, you can canoe or kayak on the calm Caloosahatchee River estuary, or book a river cruise. If you're here in winter, get acquainted with the town by taking a two-hour walking tour conducted by the **Fort Myers Historical Museum** at 2300 Peck St.; (239) 332-5955; *www.cityftmyers.com*. The museum itself is located in a Spanish style 1924 train depot. Among its historic exhibits is the Esperanza, the longest private Pullman rail car ever built.

For more history, visit the 1901 Georgian Revival **Murphy-Burroughs Home** on the Caloosahatchee River at 2505 First St.; (239) 332-6125. Built by Montana cattle baron John T. Murphy and later bought by the Burroughs family, it contains many original furnishings. For something more contemporary, the **Imaginarium Hands-On Museum** is a science and nature center with sixty interactive exhibits, at 2000 Crawford Ave.; (239) 337-3332. Displays range from Florida's environment to the weather to prehistory.

The **Seminole Gulf Railway** offers sightseeing and dinner/murder mystery excursions in vintage coaches, departing Fort Meyers' Colonial Station at Colonial Boulevard and Metro Parkway; (800) 736-4853 or (239) 275-8487; *www.semgulf.com*. It crosses a Caloosahatchee River trestle and travels south to *Bonita Springs* and back.

If you'd like to see Florida's famous manatees, head for **Lee County Manatee Park** east of town off State Road 80; (239) 694-3537. You might spot some of the pale, shy critters from observation platforms on a canal. The park also has walking trails through native habitats, and a butterfly garden. Two boat tours on local waterways also offer manatee-spotting potential—**Manatee World Boat Tours**, (239) 693-1434; and **J.C. Cruises**; (239) 334-7474; *www.floridatravel.com/jccruises*.

If you'd like to paddle yourself, you can rent kayaks and canoes from **Estero River Tackle & Canoe Outfitters** in nearby *Estero* at 20991 S. Tamiami Trail; (239) 992-4050; *www.www.all-florida.com/swestero.htm*. The firm also conducts nature trips and historic tours.

Finally, are you ready for some baseball? Two major league teams conduct spring training here in February and March. The **Boston Red Sox** play in City of Palms Park at Edison Avenue and Broadway; (877) 733-7699 or (239) 334-4799; *www.redsox.mlb.com*. The **Minnesota Twins** perform at William Hammond Stadium in the Lee County Sports complex off Six Mile Cypress Parkway; (800) 338-9467 or (239) 768-4200; *www.twins.mlb.com*.

Where to learn more

Greater Fort Meyers Chamber of Commerce, P.O. Box 9289, Fort Meyers, FL 33902; (800) 366-3622 or (239) 332-3624; *www.fortmeyers.org*.

Pensacola
The ancient city of five flags

⚑

T he queen of the Florida Panhandle, Pensacola is a kindred sister of St. Augustine—a fine old Spanish-French style city that has seen many flags flutter in its skies.

History is written all over this venerable brick and wrought iron town. It was established as a Spanish colony in 1698 and through the decades was occupied by the French, English and two renditions of Americans—Yankee and Confederate. That adds up to Pensacola's motto of "The City of Five Flags." Another interesting historical statistic: Its government has changed hands thirteen times. ("Who's in charge this week?")

This vital deep water port was occupied by the British during the War of 1812 until General Andrew Jackson drove them out. It was here that Jackson negotiated Spain's sale of Florida to the United States in 1821 and it became the territorial capital, with Jackson as its governor. The old port city was alternately occupied by Yanks and Rebs three times during the Civil War.

Downtown Pensacola is completing a major renovation to restore its yesterday look. Most of this is focused around the Seville Square Historic District between Government and Alcaniz streets. Buildings of assorted architectural heritage have been refurbished and fitted with galleries, boutiques, cafés and museums. This old city of about 57,000 also is as modern as tomorrow, with the presence of the Pensacola Naval Air Station, home to the famous Corps Blue Angels.

The city and the panhandle relate more to the mainland South than to the rest of Florida, and the region gets many of its visitors from Alabama and Georgia. You'll detect a soft Southern twang, probably sent over from Mobile, and you'll see greens 'n' grits on some restaurant menus. Wrought iron grillwork on old homes give it the genteel look of New Orleans or Savannah. Needless to say—and this is why we like it so much—life moves at a much slower pace here than in glittery Miami and Disneyesque Orlando.

Another thing that the mainland South contributed to Pensacola and its panhandle is powdery white quartz sand beaches, washed down from the Appalachians. This results in a turquoise blue ocean as clear as tinted Lucite.

You can get a sense of the way things were at the **Historic Pensacola Village** in the heart of downtown; (850) 595-5985; *www.historicpensacola.org*. Several restored buildings tell of the city's 250-year history, with the help of costumed docents. Homes here reflect several architectural styles, from the elegant Greek Revival Door House and the humble Julee

Cottage to the Lavalle House, a rare example of surviving French Creole architecture. Also within the village are the **Museum of Commerce** with printing presses, a mockup store and a buggy collection; the **Museum of Industry** with exhibits concerning Florida's role in the industrial revolution; and the **Florida State Museum** in the 1907 Renaissance Revival former city hall, with broad-based exhibits covering the state's history.

Outside the village complex, the **Pensacola Historical Museum** targets the town's military and maritime past, with artifacts and photos. The museum occupies the 1882 Arbona Building at 115 E. Zaragoza St.; (850) 434-5455; *www.pensacolahistory.org*. The **Civil War Soldiers Museum** at 108 S. Palafox Street has full-sized field camp dioramas and various artifacts of that sad conflict; (850) 469-1900; *www.cwmuseum.org*.

Now, head straight for Naval Air Station Pensacola for the outstanding **National Museum of Naval Aviation**; (800) 327-5002 or (850) 453-NAVY; *www.naval-air.org*. As a former member of the First Marine Aircraft Wing, I think it should have been called the "National Museum of Naval *and* Marine Corps Aviation," although it does give the Corps its due. Navy and Marine Corps pilots have been training at Pensacola since Naval air began early in the last century and this huge museum tells the entire story. More than 170 Naval and Marine Corps aircraft are on display, from the 1920s to the present. A close-formation flight of Blue Angels A-4 Skyhawks is suspended from a ceiling. Special exhibits include a mockup of a World War II Marine forward air base on a Pacific Island, a Skylab command module and a prisoner of war exhibit. Get dizzy watching the Blue Angels perform in the *Magic of Flight* film, shown at the big-screen IMAX Theater, then catch a bus tour of the museum's restoration area.

The region's resort complex is *Pensacola Beach* on Santa Rosa Island, which it shares with Gulf Islands National Seashore. It has a concert pavilion, mini-golf, walk-up beach bars, a boardwalk and that sugary white sand.

Gulf Islands National Seashore preserves 150 miles of the region's finest and most pristine beaches on a string of offshore islands. Its most visited element is **Fort Pickins** at the western end of Santa Rosa Island, seven miles from Pensacola Beach. This imposing brick fort was built in the 1830s to guard the entrance to Pensacola's harbor, and it saw a lot of action during the Civil War. The national seashore headquarters is at 1801 Gulf Breeze Parkway; (850) 934-2600; *nps.gov/guis*.

Where to learn more

Pensacola Convention and Visitors Center, 1401 E. Gregory St., Pensacola, FL 32501; (800) 874-1234; *www.visitpensacola.com*.

The Keys
Memories of the perfect Key lime pie

⚐

When Betty and I explored the Florida Keys several years ago, we found the perfect Key lime pie at a little seafood place called Denny's Dolphin on Key Largo. We've searched in vain and not tasted its equal, although we'll keep trying.

This is another instance in which we break our own rules, probably as an excuse to go on a Key lime pie search. The Florida Keys are about as discovered as a tourist destination can get, receiving a million or more visitors a year. We'll focus on the Keys' many natural areas and its historic sites, not tourist attractions.

The Keys *are* special, for they contain the only living coral reefs in the United States and thus provide mainland America's best snorkeling and diving. The best part of the Florida Keys is simply the experience of driving them—following the 128-mile-long Overseas Highway that skips from island to island. On longer bridge stretches, you seem to be traveling across open water; your car has become a boat. When the highway does touch land, it touches a changing panorama of funky towns, tourist towns, palm and pine groves and mangrove swamps, and around all of this—the deep blue sea. The horizon is the sea and it draws you onward until you reach Key West. You are now closer to Cuba than you are to Miami. Hi, there, Fidel!

The Overseas Highway begins in *Florida City*, although there's a better approach. We stole this idea from our friends Bill and Diana Gleasner, authors of *Off the Beaten Path Florida*. Buy their book; it does a much better job of discovering undiscovered Florida than we can do in our limited space. Anyway, pick up Card Sound Road in Florida City. It takes you toward the northern end of **Key Largo Island**, away from the often heavy traffic of the Upper Keys. Your diversionary route takes you across marshlands, then blends into the Overseas Highway just above the town of *Key Largo*.

Made too popular by the 1948 Humphrey Bogart movie—which was filmed elsewhere—Key Largo is the most commercialized and tourisy of the Key towns. We'd breeze right on by except this is where you gain access to the outstanding **John Pennekamp Coral Reef State Park**, the country's first undersea preserve; (305) 451-1202; *www.pennekamppark.com*. It protects a 188-square-mile section of mainland America's only living reef. Of course, when we say you can gain access to the park, we mean you have to get wet. Outfitters in Key Largo run diving and snorkeling trips. With its clear, shallow water and white sand, vision is usually excellent.

Pressing on past the tourist lures of Key Largo, you'll soon reach *Islamorada*, where you can catch boat tours to a pair of pristine keys—that's what islands are called out here. **Indian Key Historic State Park** is the site of a former settlement destroyed in 1840 during a Seminole raid, and **Lignumvitae Key** is a state botanical park. Both are undisturbed by man—at least, since that 1840 raid—and Lignumvitae is noted for its particularly lush tropical vegetation; (305) 664-2540; *www.floridastateparks.org.*

Fifteen miles beyond Islamorada is **Long Key State Recreation Area**, perhaps the best place to play in the keys; (305) 664-4815. This tropical reef isle offers swimming, hiking, canoeing, snorkeling and camping.

The Keys' longest open water stretch, where you can really get that feeling of driving over the ocean, is the **Seven Mile Bridge** just beyond *Marathon*. In fact it's America's longest over-water bridge. A new span was built in 1985 and you can stroll on the original bridge and enjoy fine views.

Almost under the bridge is **Pigeon Key**, a former construction camp on a four-acre island that's now an historic site. At *Knight's Key* on the bridge's eastern end, you can catch a shuttle across the old span and visit the site's buildings and a history museum; (305) 743-5999; *www.pigeonkey.org.*

After passing and hopefully pausing at several more natural areas, you'll reach *Key West*. This once funky old town has been seriously compromised, with the arrival of the Hard Rock Cafe and the like. However, it still has its rustic and historic lures. Push past the tourist crowds on Mallory Square and head into the older neighborhoods. First stop is the **Ernest Hemingway Home and Museum** at 907 Whitehead St.; (305) 294-1136; *www.hemingwayhome.com.* Although he often roamed elsewhere, the great author owned this jungle-shrouded Spanish Colonial house from 1931 until his death in Idaho in 1961. Obviously, it's abrim with Hemingway memorabilia.

Another worthy stop is the **Audubon House and Tropical Gardens** at 205 Whitehead St.; (305) 294-2116; *www.audubonhouse.com.* John James Audubon stayed here while he was painting the Keys' abundant varieties of birds. It's furnished with museum quality antiques and it contains many Audubon engravings and prints. The surrounding flora is quite lavish.

Spend some time wandering about this older section of Key West. You'll find quiet places where you'd almost expect to encounter Jimmy Buffet lounging on his hammock—although he now lives in Palm Beach.

Where to learn more

The Florida Keys & Key West (Monroe County Tourist Development Council), 106000 Overseas Hwy., Key Largo, FL 33037; (800) FLA-KEYS or (305) 451-1414; *www.fla-keys.com.*

Mount Dora and surrounds
Staying on the fringes of Orlando

♭♩

In a state where the highest elevation is just 345 feet above sea level, calling anything a "mount" is being rather optimistic. In fact, Mount Dora's elevation is only half that much. But never mind technicalities. It's one of Florida's most appealing and peaceful inland communities and it's only about forty-five miles northwest of all that commotion around Orlando.

This is your place if you plan to spend some time at Walt Disney World and surrounds and you don't really need a monorail running through your hotel lobby. Further, it's a perfectly nice place to spend a vacation even if you don't intend to visit Mickey and his bunch.

Mount Dora isn't on a mountain; it sits contentedly on the shores of Lake Dora in a gently hilly area of north central Florida, surrounded by citrus groves and pine forests. Sometimes called the "New England of the South," it was established in 1874 as a winter retreat for wealthy northerners. It has a Victorian-tropical look, with New England style homes graced by Florida flora, sycamores and old live oaks bearded with Spanish moss.

Although it has a population of about 10,000, it has a country village look, with lakeside parks and quiet downtown streets shaded by palms and old hardwoods. The small, tidy business district is busy with antique shops, boutiques, cafés and art galleries. Mount Dora is one of Florida's leading antique centers, attracting both dealers and collectors. There are some remarkably good restaurants downtown, and no fast food parlors.

Unfortunately, this charming lakeside community has become too popular. Although its visitor traffic is a tiny fraction of Orlando's, many who come are so charmed that they decide to stay. It's population increased by more than thirty percent between 1990 and 2000 and it's still growing.

Despite its growth, the central core retains its yesterday appearance. About thirty structures date from the late 19th and early 20th centuries. The **Chamber of Commerce** occupies a 1914 former train depot at 341 Alexander Street. Several of the town's fine old homes have been converted into bed and breakfast inns. Mount Dora's classic lodging is the 1893 Victorian style **Lakeside Inn**, with lake-view rooms in the main lodge and several cottages. The historic inn is at 100 N. Alexander St.; (800) 556-5016 or (352) 383-4101; *www.lakeside-inn.com.*

In vivid contrast to the garish glitter of Orlando theme parks, the pace in Mount Dora is quite serene. You can take a carriage or trolley ride along tree-shaded streets, where Victorian and New England style homes doze behind carefully manicured lawns. The **Mount Dora Road Trolley** offers narrated tours of the town, departing from the Lakeside Inn; (352) 357-9123.

Much of the town's charm comes from its lush green waterfront parks. In Palm Park, the longest lakeside boardwalk in Florida extends 1,700 feet into a cypress swamp. It's rich with wildlife and with luck, you might spot a grinning 'gator. Gilbert Park has an old fashioned croquet court, boat dock and—just for appearances—the Grantham Point Lighthouse. Florida's only inland beacon was built with local donations in 1980.

Lake Dora is part of a chain of lakes linked by the Dora Canal, which literally opens up many avenues of water exploration. It extends to the St. Johns River, providing a water route all the way to the Atlantic. There are more than a thousand lakes in this appropriately named Lake County. Several firms in town offer scenic lake cruises. **InuTrax Outdoor Adventures** at 171 S. Clayton Street books a variety of guided kayak tours; (352) 455-9892; *www.inutrax.com.*

The citizens of Mount Dora support a lively cultural scene. The **Mount Dora Theatre Company** has been presenting comedies, musicals and dramas in a former ice house for more than half a century; (352) 383-4616; *www.icehousetheatre.com.* The local visual arts scene is focused around the **Mount Dora Center for the Arts** at 138 E. Fifth Ave.; (352) 383-0880; *www.mountdoracenterforthearts.org.*The town's history is told at the small **Royellou Museum** in the old city jail 450 Royellou Lane; (352) 352-0006.

If you're looking for more reasons not to go to Walt Disney World or the Holy Land Experience or Gatorland or the Orlando Odditorium, there are three natural amusement parks nearby.

Ocala National Forest is a flatland woodland ten miles north of Mount Dora on State Road 19; (352) 625-2520. It offers warm water springs that are great for a dip, plus several streams, hiking trails, and camping and picnic areas. In **Seminole State Forest**, ten miles east off State Road 46, you can play in cool Blackwater Creek and hike or mountain bike along several miles of trails; (352) 360-6675; *www.fl-dot.com.*

The scenic Wekiva River is the centerpiece of **Wekiwa Springs State Park**, a few miles east of town off state roads 434 or 436; (407) 884-2008; *www.floridastateparks.org.* The stream is popular for canoeing, swimming and fishing. Park facilities include camping and picnic areas, hiking and cycling trails, boat rentals and a food concession.

Where to learn more

Mount Dora Area Chamber of Commerce, P.O. Box 196 (341 Alexander St.), Mount Dora, FL 32756; (352) 383-2165; *www.mountdora.com.*

Vero Beach and Sebastian
Florida the way it was

ᗺ

Sitting on the northernmost nub of a vacation area called the Treasure Coast, Vero Beach and Sebastian are yesterday Florida. This was the Florida before Mickey came to Orlando, and when South Beach was just a beach, not a nightspot and a diet plan. Vero Beach is an old money coastal resort and Sebastian is one of the state's last remaining small fishing villages.

Their location is a blessing. They are so far from Orlando, Fort Lauderdale and Miami that those vacation centers siphon off most of the inbound tourist traffic. Vero Beach and Sebastian are primarily retirement communities. However, the Sebastian Inlet is Florida's top surfing spot, giving the old fishing village something of a youthful streak.

With a population of about 22,000, Vero Beach is large enough to provide all of one's vacation essentials, yet it's relatively uncrowded. However, its beaches can get busy on weekends. The two communities are anchored to the mainland. However, Vero Beach has reached across the Indian River estuary to plant most of its resorts, shops, galleries and restaurants on a long, skinny barrier reef.

Many baseball fans have heard of Vero Beach—perhaps without knowing where it is—because it's the spring training camp of the Los Angeles Dodgers. The team abandoned Brooklyn way back in the sixties but they've kept their facility here, although there's talk of it being moved west.

Surrounding Indian River County has been known for its excellent citrus crops since the late 19th century. Vero Beach also has been around that long, although it didn't evolve as a resort center until the 1950s. This was a rather a slow evolution, funded mostly by old money from up north.

Some of the region's first visitors didn't come willingly; they were washed ashore. A vicious storm in 1715 smashed a fleet of Spanish galleons in Sebastian Inlet, sending cargoes of gold and silver to the bottom.

This misfortune has created a cottage industry, as two museums exhibit relics and treasure from that disaster. **Mel Fisher's Museum** on U.S. 1 in Sebastian displays a multi-million dollar collection of gold coins, ingots and artifacts; (772) 589-9874; *www.melfisher.com.* The **McLarty Treasure Museum** occupies the site of a salvaging camp from that shipwreck, on Route A1A near Sebastian Inlet; (772) 589-2147. It doesn't have the treasure trove of the Fisher museum, although it displays a good number of artifacts salvaged from the wrecks. A video describes the challenging and dangerous work of deep-sea treasure hunting.

Near the shipwreck museums, **Sebastian Inlet State Recreation Area** is one of the Florida coast's best-equipped state parks; (321) 984-4852; *www.florida stateparks.org.* The facility offers lots of sandy beaches, plus kayak, paddleboat and canoe rentals, a surf shop, snack shop, picnic tables and campsites.

One of the region's best attractions is the **Environmental Learning Center**, occupying 51-acre Wabasso Island in the Indian River lagoon. Although the brackish waters look rather uninviting, this estuarian reserve is home to thousands of kinds of plants, animals, birds and fish. It's one of the most diverse ecosystems in America. The facility has a 600-foot boardwalk through a mangrove swamp and a nature center with lots of hands-on exhibits, and microscopes for peering at bugs and things. The complex is at 255 Live Oak Drive, off the 510 Causeway; (772) 589-5050; *www.elcweb.org.*

Vero Beach has lots of strand, and its most popular swimming area is **South Beach State Park**, with the usual essentials of potties, picnic areas and showers to wash off the salt. If you want to avoid its weekend crowds, there are plenty of less developed beaches along the barrier island.

Riverside Park on the Indian River at 3001 Riverside Park Drive offers walking and cycling trails, picnic areas and tennis and racquetball courts. It's also home to the **Center for the Arts**, exhibiting works by Florida, national and international artists; (772) 231-0707. The park's **Riverside Theatre** presents live entertainment; (772) 231-6990.

Dodgertown is worth a visit even if the Dodgers (or their Vero Beach Dodger farm team) aren't in town. More than a spring training camp, it's an extensive 450-acre complex that includes two golf courses and a country club, a movie theater, rec room and even a small residential community. It's at 3901 26th St.; (772) 569-4900; *www.dodgertownverobeach.com.*

McKee Botanical Garden is one of the oldest in Florida, established in 1932. It was abandoned for years, then it was placed on the National Register of Historic Places in 1998, inspiring a complete cleanup. It's now one of the South's finest gardens, with royal palms, live oaks and a lush jungle of native plants; 350 U.S. 1, Vero Beach; (772) 794-0601; *mckeegarden.org.*

The history of the local citrus industry is told at the small **Indian River Citrus Museum** at 2140 14th Ave., Vero Beach; (772) 770-2263. You can compare different varieties of trees at a demonstration grove. At a gift shop, you can buy citrus-theme items and arrange to have fruit shipped home.

Where to learn more

Indian River County Tourist Council, 1216 21st St., Vero Beach, FL 32961; (772) 567-3491; *www.vero-beach.fl.us/chamber.*

Athens
Cool sounds from an old university town

Like many university towns, Athens and the University of Georgia are fused together. Beginning at College Square in the heart of downtown, the large campus extends southward and downhill like a long appendage. On the map, it dwarfs Athens' compact town center, like a very fat tail wagging a little square dog.

The university wags the town in other ways, too—intellectually, politically and culturally. It provides Athens with the predictable underpinnings of political liberalism, and both town and school share a dynamic cultural scene, with major performing arts venues and many art galleries.

All of the above is predictable for a university town. What's surprising, unless you're really hip to the current music scene—and we aren't—is that this is considered one of the hottest rock venues in the country. The university's art school and its partnering community have spawned the likes of REM, the B-52's and other top bands that we've never heard of. More than a hundred other local bands are waiting in the wings to go national.

Of course, they're not really waiting. Dozens of clubs keep downtown Athens jumping, and several recording studios are located here. If you're in town in June, you can hear scores of local bands perform free during the annual Artfest.

A city of about 100,000, Athens occupies rolling wooded hill country in northeastern Georgia. Both the downtown area and the university offer a fine collection of late 19th and early 20th century Federalist and—appropriate to the town's name—Greek Revival architecture. The district near the campus at Broad Street and College avenue has the usual collection of book stores, coffee houses, cafés and art galleries, plus those many nightclubs and music halls that jump when the sun sets.

Stop by the downtown **Athens Welcome Center** at 280 E. Dougherty Street to get your bearings and pick up maps to the town's many historic structures; (706) 353-1820. The welcome center itself is housed in an historic building—an 1820 Federalist style structure.

The **Taylor-Grady House**, an 1840s Greek Revival mansion, is dressed in beautiful period furnishings, at 634 Prince Ave.; (706) 549-8688. The antebellum Italianate **Lyndon House** is an annex to the Municipal Arts Center at 293 Hoyt St.; (706) 613-3623; *www.itown.com/athens/lyndonhouse.*

The **State Botanical Garden of Georgia** occupies 313 acres alongside the Middle Oconee River at 2450 Milledge Ave.; (706) 542-1244; *www.uga. edu/botgarden*. It has a conservatory, an International Garden and five miles of nature trails where little critters roam and birds flit about. The conservatory houses a visitor center, gift shop and a café that serves lunch.

The University of Georgia is supposedly America's oldest state chartered school of higher learning, established in 1785. (The University of North Carolina at Chapel Hill makes that same claim, but unless someone's fudging on dates, it's in second place; see page 352.) Athens was but a pioneer settlement at the time the university was chartered, so they grew up together. In fact, university founders suggested the name Athens because a nearby hill reminded one of them of the site of the Acropolis.

The handsome thickly-wooded 40,000-acre campus is fine place to explore, since it holds many of the town's attractions. Also, it's just a nice place for strolling about. Pick up a walking map and maybe sign up for a campus tour at the **UGA Visitor Center** at College Station and River roads; (706) 353-1820; *www.uga.edu*. Some worthy campus stops are the **University Chapel** and nearby **Founders Memorial Garden**, which is beautifully landscaped, with fountains, patios and an arbor; and the **Butts-Mehre Sports Hall of Fame** near the Stegman Coliseum, with sports memorabilia, including an Olympics exhibit about that other Athens: (706) 542-4662.

The excellent **Georgia Museum of Art** on campus at 90 Carlton Street has an impressive collection of 8,000 items, with a focus on 19th century and 20th century art; (706) 542-4662; *www.uga.edu/gamuseum*. The nearby **UGA Performing Arts Center** is the major performance venue for both the university and the town; (706) 542-4400; *www.uga.edu/pac*.

Live entertainment venues off campus include the **Classic Center**, booking everything from local entertainers to traveling shows, at 300 N. Thomas St.; (706) 357-4555; the **Georgia Theater**, a former movie palace turned showplace at 215 N. Lumpkin St.; (706) 549-9918; and the elegant 1910 **Morton Theater**, the town's community performance venue at 195 W. Washington St.; (706) 613-3770; *www.mortontheater.com*.

Two miles east of Athens is an attraction of a different sort—the **Naval Supply Corps Museum** at the Naval Supply Corps School campus, 1425 Prince Ave.; (706) 354-7349. (Call before you go.) The museum displays old mess gear, military uniforms and ships models; *www.nscs.navy.mil*.

Where to learn more

Athens Convention & Visitors Bureau, 300 N. Thomas St., Athens, GA 30601; (800) 653-0603 or (706) 357-4430; *www.visitathensga.com*.

Dahlonega
Gold in them thar Georgia hills

It seemed, within a few days, as if the whole world must have heard of it... They came afoot, on horseback, and in wagons, acting more like crazy men than anything else. — Benjamin Parks, 1828

Everyone has heard of the great California gold rush. But the great Georgia gold rush? Folks in the north central mountain town of Dahlonega (*dah-LON-a-gah*) have heard of it. In 1828, Benjamin Parks found a nugget while hunting in the forest, and the first gold rush in American history was on.

When gold was discovered in California twenty years later, many of Dahlonega's argonauts were lured west. However, mining continued here until the 1920s, when the price of gold was fixed at $35 an ounce, making further efforts unprofitable. Before the party was over, $36 million in bullion had been pulled from the earth and a branch of U.S. mint was stamping gold coins here. They're now among the rarest of numismatic collector items.

About the only ones who didn't fare well were the local Cherokees, who were driven out by greedy whites. They'd found some of the stuff but didn't have much use for it. *Dahlonega* was their word for "yellow metal."

As a nice bonus for the visitor, this old town of about 3,800 is surrounded by the exceptionally scenic Blue Ridge section of the Appalachian Mountains. Since we live part of the year in an old California mining town, we felt right at home here. With its mining tours and museums and gold panning, it could have been part of the California Gold Country.

As in California, the town grew up almost overnight, and it became the Lumpkin County Seat in 1835. It still is, although the Grecian style 1836 county courthouse on Town Square is now the **Dahlonega Gold Museum State Historic Site**; (706) 864-2257; *www.georgiastateparks.org*. It displays a few nuggets, gold dust, mining gear and mining photos. A film, *Gold Fever*, recalls the town's glory days. The former courthouse was built of local bricks and if you squint carefully, you might see some shiny flecks in them.

You can't take a brick home as a souvenir, but you can pan for gold. The **Consolidated Gold Mine** has tours into its deep underground shafts, where guides point out hard rock mining techniques and explain the functions of the mining gear on display. The mine operated into the last century, so it had electric-powered equipment. Back on the surface, "miners" in period dress show you how to pan for gold. The mine is at 185 Consolidated Gold Mine Rd.; (706) 864-8473; *www.consolidatedmine.com*.

At the **Crisson Gold Mine**, you can watch mining machinery in motion in Georgia's only working stamp mill (ore crusher). Try your hand at gold panning and results are guaranteed, which suggests the gravel in the pans is salted. The Crisson mine is two miles beyond the Consolidated, at 2736 Morrison Moore Parkway E.; (706) 864-6363; *www.crissongoldmine.com.*

Radiating out from Town Square, downtown Dahlonega is a National Historic District, with several restored 19th century buildings. They house an assortment of specialty and antique shops, galleries and cafés. The **Historic Holly Theatre** offers community drama productions, dinner theater and movies, at 69 W. Main St.; (706) 864-3759; *www.hollytheatre.org.* The multipurpose **Buisson Arts Center** has art galleries, a dinner theater and a music hall, 199 Choice St.; (706) 867-0050.

Gold City Corral and Carriage Company offers carriage rides, horseback rides and Western style chuck wagon dinners; at 49 Forrest Hills Dr.; (706) 867-9395; *www.goldcitycorral.com.*

If you'd like to get out there, **Appalachian Outfitters** offers guided canoe and kayak trips on the Etowah and Chestatee rivers, our you can rent boats from the firm and paddle on your own. The company is on State Route 60 at 2084 S. Chestatee; (800) 426-7117 or (706) 864-7117; *www.canoe georgia.com.* If you prefer sipping to paddling, there are three wineries in the area, with tours and tasting rooms.

Amicalola Falls State Park is eighteen miles west of Dahlonega off State Route 52; (706) 265-4703; *www.georgiastateparks.org.* The prime attraction is its namesake waterfall, spilling 729 feet down a rough rock face. It's the highest cataract east of the Mississippi River. The park has several hiking trails, picnic areas, and camping and RV sites. Enjoy the area's attractions in comfort at the modern **Amicalola Falls Lodge and Restaurant**, perched atop a ridge with spectacular views of this mountain wilderness; (800) 864-7275 or (706) 265-8888.

The world's most famous path, the 2,144-mile-long **Appalachian Trail**, begins just outside the park boundary at Springer Mountain. If you don't feel up to the entire trek, you can follow the **A.T. Approach Trail** from the park to the Appalachian trailhead. However, that's still a good workout of 8.5 miles each way. As a compromise, hike 4.6 miles to the **Len Foote Hike Inn**, where you can have dinner, sleep in a comfortable bed and hike back to the park the next day; (800) 573-9656; *www.hike-inn.com.*

Where to learn more

Dahlonega-Lumpkin County Chamber of Commerce, 13 S. Park St., Dahlonega, GA 30533; (800) 231-5543; *www.dahlonega.org.*

The Golden Isles
Georgia's scenic slice of the Atlantic

The Spaniards have a romantic way of saying things. When they discovered a cluster of subtropical barrier islands on Georgia's southern coast in the 16th century, they called them the "Golden Isles of Guale."

They certainly offer golden opportunities for visitors, since they're among the most versatile collection islands along the coastline. St. Simons is a laid back resort island, state-owned Jekyll Island is Georgia's most popular offshore playground, Little Simons Island is an exclusive hideaway and Cumberland Island is a national seashore.

The Golden Isles complex contains fifteen islands and most are uninhabited. If you look at a map, you'll see that they're only just barely islands. They're actually delta tidal flats cut off from the mainland by narrow water channels. St. Simons and Jekyll islands are linked to the mainland by bridges and Little St. Simons can be reached by boat from big St. Simons. Cumberland Island National Seashore is served by a passenger ferry.

Perhaps the most charming of the Golden Isles is *St. Simons*. Many of its roads, walking trails and bike paths are canopied by moss-bearded live oaks, and saltwater marshes draw wildlife watchers. The village on the island's southern end offers a mix of Victorian and modern buildings that contain a mix of art galleries, specialty shops, restaurants and tacky souvenir shops.

Neptune Park is the island's main activity center, with a playground, picnic areas, visitor center and public swimming pool. The **Castro Theatre** hosts local drama productions; (912) 638-4722. From Neptune Park, you can catch the **St. Simons Trolley** for a jolly tour of the island; (912) 638-8954; *www.stsimonstours.com*. The adjacent **St. Simons Island Lighthouse Museum** preserves the area's history in an 1872 lightkeeper's quarters; (912) 638-4666; *www.saintsimonslighthouse.org*. A 129-step climb to the top of the light will reward you with a stellar view. **SouthEast Adventure Outfitters** provides a variety of sea kayak and canoe trips among the Golden Isles; (912) 638-6732; *www.southeastadventure.com*.

Fort Frederica National Monument preserves the remnants of a fortification built in 1736 to protect a British colonial settlement from Spanish raids; (912) 638-3639; *www.nps.gov/fofr*. Only fragments of the bastion remains and a museum exhibits a few artifacts. Nearby **Bloody Marsh** marks the site where the British defeated an attacking Spanish troupe in 1742.

Little St. Simons Island is a lush private retreat with diverse wildlife habitats. The entire isle is yours to explore if you book a room at the **Lodge**;

(888) 733-5774; *www.littlesimonsisland.com*. Rates include all meals, and the island is never crowded because the lodge sleeps only thirty guests.

Jekyll Island, once one of the most exclusive private resort clubs in America, is now accessible to the rest of us. The island was purchased in 1886 by a group of millionaires that included J.P. Morgan, Joseph Pulitzer and William Rockefeller. They created the exclusive Jekyll Island Club, with a lavish clubhouse and "cottage" mansions that hosted some of the world's most powerful figures for generations.

It's now an active family resort center, with ten miles of public beach, bicycle trails, golf and mini-golf, tennis, nature walks, camping, a water park—the works. You can book sightseeing cruises or charter fishing trips and rent boats at the **Jekyll Island Marina**; (912) 635-3152; and the **Jekyll Island Wharf**; (912) 635-3152. Several resorts and hotels offer affordable lodgings. The island also is a fine wildlife preserve, with the typical coastal ecosystems. It's regarded as one of Georgia's top bird-spotting areas.

Its best attraction is what those millionaires left behind. The **Jekyll Island Historic Landmark Tour** takes visitors through the main clubhouse, cottage mansions and other surviving buildings of that magnificent Jekyll Island Club; (912) 635-2762; *www.jekyllisland.com*.

Like Jekyll, *Cumberland Island* once was a retreat of the rich. Andrew Carnegie's brother Thomas bought most of it in 1881 and built a grand mansion. His heirs added other homes as family retreats, and several survive. In 1972, the National Park Service bought much of the isle and created **Cumberland Island National Seashore**; (912) 882-4336; *www.nps.gov/cuis*.

The island's northern end has been set aside as a wilderness preserve. It's one of the finest on the entire Southern coast—an blend of sand dunes, saltwater marshes, mudflats and coastal forests. The preserve is busy with hundreds of shorebirds, armadillos, wild turkeys and even wild horses, which are descended from herds brought by the Spanish centuries ago.

Only 300 people a day are permitted on the island, so make reservations early as possible by calling the island's ferry service at (877) 860-6787. Park headquarters is on the mainland in *St. Marys* at 101 Wheeler Street. You can camp on the island or book a room at the oceanfront 1901 **Greyfield Inn**, once a Carnegie family mansion; (800) 292-6480; *www.greyufieldinn.com*.

Where to learn more

Jekyll Island Welcome Center, P.O. Box 13186, Jekyll Island, GA 31527; (877) 453-6955 or (912) 635-3636; *www.jekyllisland.com*

The St. Simons Island Experience, P.O. Box 22044, St. Simons Island, GA 31522; (888) 945-7992; *www.stsimonislandexperience.com*.

Savannah
America's ideal city?

༄

Savannah is more than the South's most attractive city. It is the only city of its kind in the country. It was conceived as a model community nearly three centuries ago and miraculously, that concept survives today.

When England's General James Oglethorpe decided to create Georgia's first town on the Savannah River in 1733, he had a vision. He fashioned it as a grid-like collection of twenty-four villages of homes and businesses, each built around a public square. Despite war, recession and the awful hand of 1950s urban renewal, all but three of those squares survive today.

Each is its own nucleus, most with European style row houses facing onto little plazas. They're landscaped with magnolias, oaks, flowering shrubs, fountains and statues. Think of a grid-like city with twenty-one little public parks, each a bit different from the next, then stir in a generous portion of wrought iron lace, cobblestone and Corinthian columns.

Savannah gets nearly six million visitors a year, so this is not an undiscovered destination. However, it may be a new discovery if you've never visited this part of America—for instance, if you're from Wilder, Idaho, and your picture of the South is some vague Uncle Remus vision.

This is not small town. Savannah has about 132,000 residents, and an equal number live in the suburbs. To avoid having to wade through that sprawl, we recommend staying downtown. You'll have a good choice of hotels and several B&Bs tucked into handsome antebellum mansions. Expect to pay $150 a night and beyond. Your reward is that you'll be staying in a relatively compact and easily walkable area—all of it a National Historic District. Downtown Savannah's twenty-one "villages" occupy only about 2.5 square miles.

Since this is a grid, it's difficult to become misplaced. You can get oriented and learn about the city's past with one stop—the **Savannah Visitors Center** and the **History Museum**; (912) 238-1779; *www.chsgeorgia.org*. They're side-by-side at 301 and 303 Martin Luther King Boulevard. The museum occupies a 19th century train shed. A fine multimedia presentation tells the story of the city, and you'll find exhibits ranging from an 1890 locomotive to the park bench on which Tom Hanks sat in *Forrest Gump*.

There are many ways to see the town. You can simply pick up a walking tour map at the visitor center, or sign up for one of several tours. They include carriage rides—the classic way to go, Gray Line Tours and a "Ghosts and Legends of Savannah" tour. We like **Old Town Trolley Tours** because you can step off one trolley, explore a particular area and then catch the next one; (912) 233-0083; *www.trolleytours.com.*

For a river's eye view, hop aboard one of the **Riverstreet Riverboat Company** cruises that depart from a dock at 9 E. River St.; (800) 786-6404 or (912) 232-6404; *www.savannahriverboat.com.* Two replica 19th century sternwheelers offer sightseeing, lunch, brunch and dinner cruises.

Stroll past the old rowhouse businesses buildings of **Factors Walk** along a bluff above the river. This is where factors—merchants and brokers—conducted their trade. Architectural highlights here include the 1887 **Cotton Exchange** and the golden-domed 1906 **City Hall**. Iron bridges link sections of the walk; and its cobblestone pavers came from merchant ships' ballast.

For a look at old Savannah, stop at **Telfair's Owens-Thomas House**, on Oglethorpe Square at 124 Abercorn St.; (912) 233-9743; *www.telfair.org.* Built between 1816 and 1819, it's furnished with antiques and decorative arts, and the carriage house contains reconstructed slave quarters. The **Telfair Museum of Art** occupies an ornate Regency style former governor's mansion on Telfair Square at 121 Barnard St.; (912) 232-1177; *www.telfair. org.* Its focus is American and European impressionists.

The **Ships of the Sea Maritime Museum** traces the area's nautical history, with a focus on the *Savannah*, the first steamship to cross the Atlantic. The museum building itself a relic—an 1819 Regency style mansion at 41 Martin Luther King Blvd.; (912) 232-1511; *www.shipsofthesea.org.* Another point of interest is the **Birthplace of Juliette Gordon Low** at 10 E. Oglethorpe Ave.; (912) 233-4501; *www.girlscouts.org.* The web address is your first and only clue; Ms. Low founded the Girl Scouts in 1912. The home is furnished in the 1880s period.

If you're a rail nut, visit the outstanding **Roundhouse Railroad Museum** at 602 W. Harris St.; (912) 651-6823; *www.chsgeorgia.org.* It's supposedly the largest and oldest vintage railroad manufacturing and repair facility in the Western Hemisphere. Dating from 1833, the complex has a huge roundhouse, antique machinery and several restored locomotives.

For shopping and entertainment, head for the large **City Market** complex at Congress and Jefferson streets. Replacing a market built in 1775, it's an upbeat gathering of specialty shops, art galleries, cafés, nightclubs and bistros. The original mart on adjacent Ellis Square is being restored and will feature a farmer' market.

Where to learn more

Savannah Visitor Information Center, 301 Martin Luther King Blvd., Savannah, GA; 31402; (877) SAVANNAH; *www.savannahvisit.com.*

Lake Charles and Eunice
Southwest Louisiana's Cajun country

Ᵽ

Forget your antebellum mansions, New Orleans jazz and Creole cooking for the moment. Cajun Country in southwestern Louisiana is where many folks from the Deep South come to play, and to sample Acadian culture. It's the state's second most popular visitor area after New Orleans. Lake Charles, with a recreational lake and three casinos, is primarily a vacation area. Eunice is a small town rich in Cajun culture and music.

You probably know that Cajuns are French-speaking Acadians from Canada's Maritime Provinces who were kicked out when the British gained control of the country. Refusing to bow to British rule, they were rounded up by the boatload and set to sea in the mid to late 1700s. Newly developing Louisiana, under Spanish rule at the time, welcomed thousands of them because they were Catholic and they were willing to work the soil and build settlements in the western Louisiana wilderness.

Cajun and Creole cultures are quite different, although both have French ethnic roots. Many Creoles were refugees from Haiti who settled mostly in New Orleans, so their culture is a blend of French, Caribbean and African.

A city of about 75,000, *Lake Charles* is the center of a diverse vacation region, with casinos, swimming, boating and nearby wildlife refuges. This part of the Gulf Coast was slammed by Hurricane Rita on September 24, 2005, although it had been downgraded from a Category 5 to a Category 3 by the time in made landfall. Damage was severe but not nearly as devastating as Hurricane Katrina's, and most of it has been repaired.

Three large casinos are the area's most popular lures. They weren't sunk by hurricanes because two are anchored to the Lake Charles shoreline and the third is part of a racetrack. If you want to squander your quarters, check out **L'Auberge du Lak** off I-210 exit 4, (866) 580-7414, *www.idlcasino. com*; **Isle of Capri Casino** off I-10 exit 27, (800) THE-ISLE, *www.isleof-capricasino.com* and the **Delta Downs Racetrack & Casino** off I-10 exit 4 in *Vinton*, (800) 589-7441; *www.deltadowns.com*. (A fourth, Harrah's Casino Hotel, was wrecked by Hurricane Rita.)

NOTE: Most of Louisiana was spared the savagery of hurricanes Katrina and Rita. This great state—including the three areas we present in this section—is still very much in the visitor business.

The city's centerpiece is its namesake lake, which lures sunbathers, boaters and windsurfers. The lake, which is virtually surrounded by the city, has the only inland white sand beaches in the Gulf Coast area. It's is linked to the coast by a waterway and several local outfitters offer fishing trips.

Like many other Louisiana towns, Lake Charles stages a Mardi Gras celebration, and it exhibits the South's largest collection of costumes at the **Mardi Gras Museum of Imperial Calasieu**. It's in the old town Calasieu historic district, in the Central School Arts & Humanities Center at 809 Kirby Street; (337) 430-0043. The **Imperial Calasieu Museum** at 204 W. Sallier Street presents the history of the Lake Charles area with period furnished rooms, artifacts and photos. The museum's Gibson-Barnam Gallery features changing art exhibits; (337) 439-3797.

The best place to sample rural Cajun music, food and culture is in *Eunice*. It's in the prairie country sixty miles northeast of Lake Charles on U.S. 190. In fact, this town of about 11,000 calls itself the "Louisiana's Prairie Cajun Capital." Larger *Lafayette* also is a major Cajun center, although we prefer the homespun charm of Eunice.

The **Prairie Acadian Cultural Center**, part of the Jean Lafitte National Historical Park, preserves the Acadian culture with nicely-done exhibits, artifacts and living history presentations. Costumed docents demonstrate traditional crafts and they prepare typical foods in an Acadian style kitchen. The complex is at 250 W. Park Ave.; (337) 457-8499; *www.nps.gov/jela/prairie acadianculturalcenter.htm*.

Local groups present a live radio show of Cajun culture and music on Saturday nights at the adjacent **Liberty Theater**; (337) 457-7389. The small **Eunice Museum** is busy with artifacts relating to rural Cajun culture, at 220 S. CC Duson Dr.; (337) 457-6540. The **Cajun Music Hall of Fame**, which honors notable contributors to the music, exhibits traditional instruments, recorded music and photos, at 240 S. CC Duson Dr.; (337) 457-6534.

For more live Cajun music, along with some contemporary sounds, check out the famous **Purple Peacock** at 3284 U.S. 190; (337) 546-0975. There are several Cajun restaurants in Lake Charles and Eunice; contact the tourist information centers below for details.

Where to learn more

Eunice Chamber of Commerce, P.O. Box 508, Eunice, LA 70535; (337) 457-7389; *www.eunice-la.com*.

Southwest Louisiana/Lake Charles Convention & Visitors Bureau, 1205 N. Lakeshore Dr., Lake Charles, LA 70601; (800) 456-7952 or (337) 436-9588; *www.visitlakecharles.org*.

St. Francisville
A grand little town in "English Louisiana"

⚑

Your first impression of this splendid village on the Great River Road may be that it's on the wrong side of the border. Located above Baton Rouge near the Mississippi state line, St. Francisville is the quintessential Mississippi antebellum town, with splendid plantation homes shaded by moss-draped live oaks and magnolias, and with a definite English accent.

There's an interesting story behind this English settlement in predominately French Louisiana. Late in the 1700s, Spain gave land grants along the Mississippi River to several English and Scottish families to encourage settlement. With the Louisiana Purchase in 1803, their descendants assumed they would become part of the United States. However, this strip of land was still considered to be within the colony of Spanish West Florida.

After waiting seven years for a resolution, impatient planters kidnapped the Spanish governor in Baton Rouge in 1810 and set up the Free and Independent Republic of West Florida, with St. Francisville as its capital. The new nation lasted exactly seventy-four days. Forced to make a decision, the federal government sent troops to the town and officially claimed the land for the United States.

A pristine village of fewer than 2,000 residents, St. Francisville is the second oldest town in Louisiana, established on high ground above the Mississippi River in 1785. At one time, it was one of the richest towns in the South. It had vast areas planted in cotton, plenty of slaves to pick it, and the river for shipping it to market. Some historians claim that, during the 1850s, as many as two thirds of America's millionaires lived along the banks of the river between New Orleans and Natchez, Mississippi.

In St. Francisville, planters built grand mansions on bluffs overlooking the river and many survive as splendid relics of the South's golden age. So that everyone who could afford it had a view, the town was strung along the river bluff for two miles. Downtown is a fine study in 19th century homes and churches, although those plantation mansions are the area's greatest visitor attraction. They form one of most splendid corridors of wealth in the country, comparable to Rhode Island's Newport mansions.

The finest is **Rosedown Plantation Historic Site** near U.S. 61 and State Route 10; (888) 376-1867 or (225) 635-3332; *www.crt.state.la.us/rosedown/rosedown.htm*. The extensive complex includes the immaculately kept 1835 mansion, a 28-acre formal garden and a dozen other buildings. The plantation house contains many original furnishings imported from Europe.

The 1806 Oakley Plantation off U.S. 61 on State Route 965 is better known as the **Audubon State Historic Site**. John James Audubon was a live-in art teacher here in 1821, and he painted the local birds between classes. A collection of his first edition *Birds of America* prints are on display; (888) 677-2838 or (225) 637-3739; *www.stfrancisville.us.*

Four other plantations mansions are open to the public and you can learn about them—and about St. Francisville—at the **West Feliciana Historical Society Museum** at 11757 Ferdinand St.; (225) 635-6330; *www.audubonpilgrimage.info.* The museum also is the town's tourist information center. You'll learn that nearly 150 structures in this small community are listed in the National Register of Historic Places. You can pick up a walking tour map and see many of them.

Some structures worthy of pause include the 1858 Gothic **Grace Episcopal Church** at 1621 Ferdinand Street; the 1893 **Our Lady of Mt. Carmel Catholic Church** at Ferdinand and Sewell; and the 1810 Creole-cum-Georgian **Seabrook** house at 8998 Royal Street. The splendid gingerbready Victorian Gothic **St. Francisville Inn** at 5720 Commerce Street is now a B&B and restaurant; 488-6502 or (225) 635-6502; *www.stfrancisvilleinn.com.*

Carefully groomed downtown St. Francisville has a nice selection of specialty shops, galleries, antique stores and restaurants. Many of its older neighborhoods are simply gorgeous, with a mix of grand old homes and simple cottages on streets lined with flowering trees and shrubs.

In addition to the plantations, there are other attractions in the area. The Nature Conservancy's **Mary Ann Brown Preserve** is a 105-acre swatch of upland forest in the Tunica Hills, with hiking trails and picnic sites. It's off State Route 965; (225) 338-1040; *www.nature.org.* The **Port Hudson State Commemorative Area** marks the site of a 48-day siege that ended in a bloody but little known Civil War battle. The site, which contains remnants of the fort and a museum, is about ten miles south at 236 Hwy. 61; (888) 677-3400 or (225) 654-3775; *www.lastateparks.com.*

Audubon seems to have stirred up a lot attention wherever he went. St. Francisville's major annual event is the **Audubon Pilgrimage** the third weekend of March. It's not a birder outing but an opportunity to tour several area homes and mansions; (800) 879-4221.

Where to learn more

West Feciliana Parish Tourism Commission, P.O. Box 1548 (11757 Ferdinand St.), St. Francisville, LA 70775; (800) 789-4221 or (225) 635-6797; *www.stfrancisville.us.* Also check *www.stfrancisville.com;* and *www.audubonpilgrimage.info.*

Natchitoches
Louisiana's historical French charmer

ſ

If you've seen the 1989 film *Steel Magnolias*, you've already seenone of the most charming and historic towns in Louisiana. Natchitoches was both the setting of the story and the location for the film.

Situated in the state's north central Creole region, Natchitoches (*NACK-uh-tish*) is the oldest town in the entire Louisiana Purchase. It was established as a French trading settlement in 1714, and that even pre-dates New Orleans. You will note some similarities between Natchitoches and St. Francisville, with their fine collections of 18th and 19th century buildings. Both are in National Historic Landmark districts. However, the Natchitoches look is classic Louisiana French, with lacework iron, and Creole cottages and cooking. It's fun to compare the pair.

Because of the film, raves in national publications and the town's own promotional efforts, Natchitoches is almost too popular. (When Oprah Winfrey calls it "the best small town in the U.S.A.," you know it's going to attract crowds.) Try to avoid it on weekends, when droves come in from nearby areas. It's the most popular visitor destination in northern Louisiana.

Not a village like St. Francisville, it's a midsize town of more than 20,000 and its fringes are busy with big box stores, shopping centers, chain motels and service stations. Locals do protect their downtown area with a fervor, and once you've slipped through the commercial rim, you're in an old French village—albeit one with tour buses and souvenir shops.

The town was established at the end of navigation on the Red River. A massive 100-mile-long log jam prevented further upstream travel. It became an important transfer point for cargo going downriver to New Orleans and overland to new settlements to the west. Both El Camino Real from Mexico and the Natchez Trace passed through here. However, the river rerouted itself in the 1820s, leaving Natchitoches without water access; the stream was now five miles away. Even though the log jam later was broken, Natchitoches had lost its port. It dozed for decades and many of its fine old buildings just sat there, awaiting discovery by entrepreneurs and tourists.

The former riverfront is now Cane River Lake, which has become the town's centerpiece. Brick-paved Front Street parallels the lake, shaded by live oaks and magnolias, and lined with antebellum homes, galleries and shops, many trimmed with wrought iron lace.

Although you can check into an ordinary chain motel on the outskirts, opt for one of the town's more than forty bed & Breakfast inns, where you can sleep with history. Once settled, pick up a walking tour map of the 33-block historic district at the **Natchitoches Tourist Information Center** at 781 Front St.; (318) 352-8072. One of the tours is the **St. Denis Walk of Honor**. Like the Hollywood Walk of Fame, it honors folks who have brought recognition to Natchitoches, with plaques on the sidewalks. Among honorees are—good grief!—Julia Roberts, who starred in *Steel Magnolias*.

Several companies offer historic tours of the area. Despite the name, we passed up Buzzin' With Betty Tours in favor of **Natchitoches Transit Company**, which offers both carriage and trolley tours; (318) 356-8687. And yes, tour guides do point out *Steel Magnolias* sites. The movie, incidentally, was based on a play written by local boy Robert Harling, Jr.

The **Old Courthouse Museum** offers exhibits on area history and the Louisiana Purchase. It occupies an 1896 structure at 600 Second St.; (800) 568-6968 or (318) 357-2270. Check out the **Kaffie-Frederick Mercantile** at 758 Front St.; (318) 252-2525. Shelves of this 1862 drygoods store are stocked with fun gift items and old style housewares.

To see Natchitoches as it was, head for **Fort Jean Baptiste State Historic Site** at 130 Moreau St.; (888) 677-7853 or (318) 357-3101; *www.crt. state.la.us*. This five-acre site contains a faithful reconstruction of a 1732 French trading post and fort. The complex includes a warehouse, barracks, chapel and the commandant's quarters. Call ahead for tours—at least two weeks ahead in summer.

Part and parcel to Natchitoches is **Cane River Creole National Historical Park**, which encompasses sixty-seven structures, including several nearby plantations; (318) 356-8441; *www.nps.gov/cari*. Its Cane River National Heritage Area stretches from Highway 49 to the Red River, taking in just about all of Natchitoches. The park's best attraction is the 1796 **Melrose Plantation** at highways 119 and 493; (318) 379-0055. Many notables, including Erskine Caldwell, spent time in this gorgeous antebellum mansion. **NOTE:** At press time, several of the park's properties were being renovated and were closed to visitors, so call to see what's open.

If you don't mind crowds, come for one of Natchitoches' annual celebrations—the **Jazz & R&B Festival** the first Saturday in April, the **Pilgrimage of Historic Homes and Plantations** the second weekend of October and the gaily decorated **Christmas Festival** the first Saturday in December. After the Saturday festivities, the lavish decorations stay up through the holidays.

Where to learn more

Natchitoches Convention & Visitors Bureau, 781 Front St., Natchitoches, LA 71457; (800) 259-1714 or (318) 352-8072; *www.natchitoches.net*.

The Gulf Coast
Shrimp boats, scenery, casinos and T-shirt shops

Mississippi's slice of the Gulf Coast is a contradictory mix of history and schlock, of scenic offshore islands and garish casinos, of sugar sand beaches and tourism excess. With the proper sense of indulgence, you can have a lot of fun here, particularly since the natives are notorious for their friendliness.

Legalized gambling on the Mississippi Gulf Coast is a mixed blessing, generating visitor dollars but turning charming old towns into tourist hot-spots. The region's two largest cities, *Biloxi* and *Gulfport*, offer several interesting attractions once you get past their tacky tourist lures. They're both large enough to provide good lodging variety and they have some fine seafood restaurants that prepare the famous gulf shrimp anyway you'd like.

If you prefer quieter retreats, seek out the quaint art colony of *Bay St. Louis* on the western end of the Gulf Coast, or *Ocean Springs* just east of Biloxi, which is featured in *The 100 Best Small Art Towns in America*.

The coast itself can be absolutely beautiful, with its idyllic waterscapes, cloud-painted sunsets and offshore shrimp boats crowned with halos of seagulls. A good part of the shoreline is graced with tidal reefs and alligator swamps. Most of its barrier islands are wildlife sanctuaries under the protection of Gulf Islands National Seashore. And these aren't coastal deltas; they're true offshore islands, about ten miles out to sea.

For the most part, the Gulf Coast's white sand beaches are more playgrounds than swimming areas. Trapped between the shoreline's sediment-bearing streams and the offshore islands, the water in many areas is tea-colored and quite shallow. At some beaches, it takes a good hike just to get water up to your knobby little knees. Amazingly, the 26-mile stretch of beach from Biloxi west to Gulfport and beyond is man-made, courtesy of a six million cubic yard effort by the Army Corps of Engineers in the 1950s. It's the world's longest man-made beach.

Incidentally, the Mississippi Gulf Coast is hurricane country, so keep that in mind if you plan a late summer-to-fall visit. The area was hit by Hurricane Katrina in 2005, although damage was less severe here than in New Orleans. Hurricane Camille slammed into this area in 1969 with 205-mile-an-hour winds, causing more extensive damage than Katrina. But don't worry; there are good hurricane watchers out there.

Biloxi, a town of about 53,000, manages to be charming and garish at the same time. Its busy beachfront has the usual tourist lures, T-shirt shops and pretend beach shack bars. Almost dwarfing the town is the most stylish casino outside of Las Vegas and in fact built by the legendary Steve Wynn— **Beau Rivage**. It's as elegant as gambling parlors get, winning raves from the likes of *Conde Nast Traveler*. The casino is at 875 Beach Blvd., (800) 567-6667, *www.beaurivage.com*. Despite this and other casinos in the area, this venerable town—one of the oldest in the South—has an interesting historic district, and there several worthwhile non-touristy attractions hereabouts.

The most noteworthy is **Beauvoir**, the Jefferson Davis Home and Presidential Library. It's between Biloxi and Gulfport off U.S. 90; (800) 570-3818 or (228) 388-1313; *www.beauvoir.org*. The deposed Confederate president lived on this 51-acre estate from 1879 until his death ten years later. Tours begin in the Presidential Library, where mementos and films tell the story of his troubled life. The adjacent **Confederate Museum** contains a large collection of Civil War weapons and mementos.

Back in Biloxi, the **Mardi Gras Museum** exhibits three hundred years of this festive event's history, in the historic Magnolia theater at 119 Rue Magnolia; (228) 435-6245. Our favorite outing here is the **Biloxi Shrimping Trip**, departing from the small craft harbor; (800) 289-7908; *www.gcww. com/sailfish*.The captain shows his "crew" how a shrimp net is set, then it's hauled in and he discusses the various sea critters they've caught.

Nearby *Gulfport*, a town of about 71,000, is a little less garish than Biloxi, with an old fashioned working waterfront. The **Mississippi Sound Maritime Museum** preserves the nautical history of the Gulf Coast, at 1300 24th Ave.; (228) 863-8765. Aboard the nearby Navy Construction Battalion base, interesting displays at the **Seabee Museum** focus on the accomplishments of Seabees and the Navy's Civil Engineering Corps through assorted wars; (228) 871-3164.

Gulfport is the gateway to the Mississippi portion of **Gulf Islands National Seashore**, which stretches for 150 miles; (228) 875-9507; *www.nps. gov/guis*. Mississippi's share contains three barrier islands—Ship, Horn and Petit Bois. Scheduled excursion boats leave the Gulfport Small Craft Harbor for Ship Island, said to have some of the finest beaches on all of the coast; (866) 466-7386. Horn Island, a wildlife preserve, can be reached by chartered boat from the marina, and it offers primitive overnight camping.

Where to learn more

Mississippi Gulf Coast Convention & Visitors Bureau, P.O. Box 6128, Gulfport, MS 39506; (888) 467-4853; *www.gulfcoast.org*.

The Natchez Trace
Mississippi's "Ribbon of Time"

Ꝥ

Although it nips a corner of Alabama and stops just short of Nashville, the 444-mile-long Natchez Trace Parkway is mostly about Mississippi—its history and its landforms.

The route of the legendary roadway, which cuts a diagonal across the state from Natchez, isn't as geologically dramatic as the Blue Ridge Parkway, with its mountains and valleys and cliffs. Mississippi is a rather flat state, and the Natchez Trace is more of a scenic meander past lush green forests, farmlands, meadows, split-rail fences and streams.

"The twists and turns do not arise so much from the pavement as from the overlay of lives of those to whom the Trace has meant so many different things," writes F. Lynn Bachleda in *Guide to the Natchez Trace Parkway*.

With a speed limit of fifty miles an hour along most of its route, it provides a leisurely opportunity to relax and enjoy the gently rolling Mississippi countryside while passing many points of interest.

Natchez is a fascinating antebellum town on the Mississippi River and *Jackson* is the state capitol, with its attendant attractions. A side trip will take you to **Vicksburg National Military Park**, site of a pivotal Civil War battle. The Trace's headquarters is in *Tupelo*, the birthplace of Elvis Presley; see below. For the most part, however, this slim two-lane highway manages to miss civilization, keeping to the quiet side of Mississippi.

As you travel, you'll encounter interpretive signs and wayside exhibits, and places where you can enjoy a lazy picnic or follow a nature trail into the woods. The Trace passes state parks where you can hike, picnic and camp. Sections of the route will take you into Mississippi's past, with paleo-Indian mounds, Civil War battle sites and almost ghost towns. In several sections, you can see ruts and shallow ravines of the original trace.

Like most early American roads, the Trace started as a game trail, in this case leading to salt springs in present day Nashville. Native people followed the game as they always did, then came trappers and finally settlers. French maps traced the Trace as early as 1773. As settlement continued, the federal government roughed out a post road in 1800, and started an overland stage mail service that continued for about twenty years. Then riverboats put the mail service out of business and the old trail was left to the weeds.

After nearly a century of neglect, the Trace was about to disappear without a trace. Then in 1905, members the Mississippi chapter of the Daughters of the American Revolution proposed marking the route and restoring it. After decades of effort, they finally convinced Congress to take action. Restoration of the Trace became a National Recovery Act project in 1937. The next year, the Natchez Trace Parkway was created as a unit of the National Park Service. Although much of it was completed during the years that followed, the final link—a bypass around Jackson—wasn't finished until 2005.

The National Park Service is currently working on the **Natchez Trace National Scenic Trail**, a hiking and biking route that parallels the roadway. At this writing, sixty-three miles of the recreational path had been completed in four different areas.

One of the first significant stops on the Natchez Trace Parkway is the **Mount Locust Inn** at Milepost 15.5. One of the few surviving way stations on the route, it's now a National Park interpretive center. Just beyond at Milepost 20 is the **Grand Village of the Natchez Indians**. It's an ancient ceremonial site with an interpretive museum containing artifacts unearthed here, and a few reconstructions of the original village; (601) 446-6502.

You'll next encounter two plantations, one still active and another abandoned. Open for public tours, **Springfield Plantation** at Milepost 20 was built in the 1780s. It was one of the first to use the classic colonnades that came to define antebellum mansions; (601) 786-3802. Near Milepost 30, you can explore what's left of **Windsor Mansion**, an abandoned plantation house with still-standing columns that suggest a Roman ruin.

Near the town of *Raymond* just south of *Jackson* is the **Battle of Raymond** site at Milepost 78.3. Here, Union and Confederate armies clashed on May 12, 1863, during General William T. Sherman's famous march to the sea. You can see a more peaceful side of the Old South at the **Mississippi Crafts Center** at Milepost 104.2, where folk crafts and Choctaw tribal crafts are sold; (601) 856-7546.

Just short of the Alabama state line at Milepost 304.5, the parkway passes through scenic **Tishomingo State Park** in the Appalachian foothills. It's one of the most interesting parks along the route, with swimming, boating, hiking trails, and picnicking and camping areas: (662) 438-69124.

Where to learn more

Natchez Trace Parkway, 2680 Natchez Trace Parkway, Tupelo, MS 38807-9715; (800) 305-1714; *www.nps.gov/natr*; and *www.nps.gov/natt* for the Natchez Trace National Scenic Trail.

Guide to the Natchez Trace Parkway by F. Lynne Bachleda (© 2005) is the most comprehensive book about the trail, with milepost-by-milepost details and lots of historic background. It's published by Menasha Ridge Press, P.O. Box 43673, Birmingham, AL 35243; *www.menasharidge.com*.

Oxford and Tupelo
From Faulkner to Elvis

⌐¬

About the only things that Oxford and Tupelo have in common are proximity and famous people. One is a dignified old university town and art center, and the home of Nobel Prize winning author William Faulkner. The other is a quiet mid-sized community that was catapulted to fame as the birthplace of Elvis Presley.

Since these two towns in Mississippi's rolling northern hill country are only about fifty miles apart, you can package them into an interesting side trip. The dignified old Southern atmosphere of Oxford and the Elvis sites of Tupelo provide a fun contrast.

A picturesque town of about 12,000, *Oxford* is Mississippi's most appealing community. National Geographic's *Guide to Small Town Escapes* calls it "friendly, yet sophisticated; historic, yet hip." Much of the sophistication and the hip come from the University of Mississippi, whose student population nearly equals that of the town.

William Faulkner used Oxford as a setting for some of his powerful novels about dysfunctional old Southern families. In his writings, the town became Jefferson, and Lafayette County was his fictitious Yoknapatawpha County. Faulkner was born in *New Albany* about thirty miles northeast and grew up in Oxford. He attended classes for a year and a half at Ole Miss, where his father was business manager. The young Faulkner also served as the university's postmaster. He soon quit the job, not caring to "be at the beck and call of any fool who could afford a postage stamp."

Other noteworthy writers, lured either by the Faulkner mystique or the town's cultural charm, have spent time here, including William Morris, Barry Hanna and Larry Brown. Top-selling author John Grisham has a large estate near Oxford.

Visitors generally head first for **Rowan Oak** on **Old** Taylor Road, the two-story antebellum home where Faulkner wrote most of his books; (662) 234-3284; *www.olemiss.edu/depts_museum/rowan*. It's preserved as it was when lived here, with original furnishings, and his old manual typewriter in his study. Although Faulkner traveled some, this white clapboard Greek Revival structure was his home from 1930 until his death in 1962. It's now an extension of the University of Mississippi Museum.

You'll find more Faulkner lore on the handsome tree-canopied campus of the **University of Mississippi**; (662) 915-7211; *www.olemiss.edu*. It can be reached by a walking trail from Rowan Oak. His Nobel Prize and National Book Award are displayed in the **J.D. Williams Library**. The fine **University Museum** has a versatile collection of more than 16,000 objects, ranging from Greek and Roman antiquities and old scientific instruments to Southern folk art; (662) 915-7073; *www.olemiss.edu/depts_museum.*

Downtown Oxford is built around **Courthouse Square** with the Grecian style 1873 Lafayette County Courthouse as its focal point. If you're old enough, you'll recognize it from the 1959 movie version of *The Sound and the Fury* with Yul Brynner and Joanne Woodward. Surrounding the square are the places you would expect to find in a university town—good book stores, coffee houses, intimate cafés and a couple of bistros. A bronze of Faulkner sits on a bench here, frozen in contemplation of all this.

And now, back to populist reality. Thrice as large as Oxford, Tupelo is a two-industry town as far as tourism goes. The National Park headquarters of the **Natchez Trace** is located here (page 430), and of course this is where Elvis Aaron Presley joined the world on January 8, 1935.

He was "born into humble circumstances," as biographers like to say, in a tiny wood frame cottage. Humble indeed; the family was evicted two years later because they couldn't meet their mortgage payments.

The **Elvis Presley Birthplace** is at 306 Elvis Presley Drive; (662) 841-1245; *www.elvispresleybirthplace.com.* A surrounding park was created when he staged a benefit concert to raise funds for a playground for under-privileged children. The park happened to contain the old shanty that his parents had lost to lenders. The 450-square-foot cottage is overshadowed by a large museum containing the predictable Presley memorabilia. A bronze of a thirteen-year-old Elvis carrying his first guitar stands nearby.

The story of young Presley in Tupelo begins here, and just keeps going. At the convention and visitors bureau, you can pick up a driving tour map to several "Elvis sites." They include his elementary and junior high schools and the drive-in where he hung out with his buddies.

The most popular stop is **Tupelo Hardware** at 114 W. Main St.; (662) 842-4637; *www.tupelohardware.com.* Here, Elvis' mom Gladys bought him his first guitar for $7.75. Dating from 1941, it's still just an old fashioned hardware store, selling paint and cabinet pulls. Of course, you also can buy a T-shirt imprinted with: "Where Gladys bought her son his first guitar."

Where to learn more

Oxford Tourism Council, P.O. Box 965, Oxford, MS 38655; (662) 234-4680; *www.touroxfordms.com.*

Tupelo Convention & Visitors Bureau, P.O. Drawer 47 (399 E. Main St.), Tupelo, MS 38802; *www.tupelo.net.*

Chapter Eleven

The Very Best Of America

Our favorites from sea to shining sea

After discovering America's best 201 overlooked vacation destinations, we'll have a little harmless fun by selecting the "Ten Best of the Best" in several different categories. Our favorite choice tops the list in each category, followed by the other nine in alphabetical order. Thus, we have no losers, only winners and runners-up.

The Ten Best overall vacation destinations

This list represents the ultimate best—our favorite undiscovered vacation spots in all of America. These are places with enough attractions to keep a family or a couple occupied for a week or more.

1. **Mackinac Island** in Michigan is truly a one-of-a-kind place—America's only getaway where peace, quiet and a slow pace are assured, because motor vehicles are prohibited. Chapter Six, page 240.

5. The "Maritime Corner," Connecticut—Chapter Eight, page 298.

6. Mendocino-Fort Bragg, California—Chapter Two, page 74.

7. Pensacola, Florida—Chapter Ten, page 406.

8. Portland, Oregon—Chapter One, page 40.

9. Valley County, Idaho—Chapter Three, page 124.

10. Wheeling, West Virginia—Chapter Nine, page 384.

The Ten Best midsize towns and mini-cities

1. **Newport**, Rhode Island, is the most attractive, best preserved midsize town in America. It's busy with historic mansions and museums, with a picture perfect waterfront and no highrises. Chapter Eight, page 326.

2. Boise, Idaho—Chapter Three, page 118.

3. Asheville, North Carolina—Chapter Nine, page 346.

4. Annapolis, Maryland—Chapter Seven, page 264.

5. Boulder, Colorado—Chapter Three, page 106.

6. Madison, Wisconsin—Chapter Six, page 256.

7. Mobile, Alabama—Chapter Ten, page 392.

8. Savannah, Georgia—Chapter Ten, page 420.

9. Sioux Falls, South Dakota—Chapter Four, page 186.

10. Tacoma, Washington—Chapter One, page 52.

The Ten Best small towns

1. **Ashland**, Oregon, achieves small-town perfection, with its famous Shakespearean Festival, its tidy downtown area and beautiful Lithia Park, plus access to southern Oregon's outdoor lures. Chapter One, page 30.

2. Columbus, Indiana—Chapter Six, page 230.

3. Eureka Springs, Arkansas—Chapter Ten, page 394.

4. Grand Marais, Minnesota—Chapter Four, page 170.

5. Haines, Alaska—Chapter One, page 16.

6. Oxford, Mississippi—Chapter Ten, page 432.

7. Portsmouth, New Hampshire—Chapter Eight, page 322.

8. Ste. Genevieve, Missouri—Chapter Five, Page 202.

9. Taos, New Mexico—Chapter Three, page 100.

10. Versailles, Kentucky—Chapter Nine, Page 344.

The Ten Best towns for arts and culture

1. **Berea**, Kentucky, is both a town and a college, interwoven to create America's finest center for the preservation and creation of folk art. Students earn their tuition by creating crafts to sell. Chapter Nine, page 340.

The Ten Best historic towns or sites

1. **Columbia State Historic Park** tells the full story of the great California Gold Rush with its historic buildings and docent tours. Visitors can pan for gold, ride stagecoaches, stay in historic hotels and pretend they're part of yesterday. Chapter Two, page 68.

The Ten Best national parks & monuments

1. **Hawai'i Volcanoes National Park** on the Big Island offers a rare opportunity to see a volcano in action, since Kilauea has been burping and venting continuously since the 1980s. This is probably the only place on earth where you have a good chance—with a flyover—of seeing molten lava. Chapter One, page 23.

The Ten Best museums and attractions

1. **Mystic Seaport**, Connecticut, is simply the best maritime museum in America and one of the best historical museum of any kind. With nautical exhibits, hundreds of old ships, docent tours and cruises, it offers the total maritime experience. Chapter Eight, page 298.

2. Buffalo Bill Historical Center, Cody, Wyoming—Chapter Three, page 152.

3. Chattanooga Aquarium, Chattanooga, Tennessee—Chapter Nine, page 362.

4. Circus World Museum, Baraboo, Wisconsin—Chapter Six, page 252.

5. High Desert, Bend, Oregon—Chapter One, page 34.

6. Hubbard Museum of the American West, Ruidoso, New Mexico—Chapter Two, page 99.

7. Kalamazoo Air Zoo, Kalamazoo, Michigan—Chapter Six, page 236.

8. National Baseball Hall of Fame, Cooperstown, New York—Chapter Seven, page 278.

9. National Civil Rights Museum, Memphis, Tennessee—Chapter Nine, page 368.

10. U.S. Space & Rocket Center Museum, Huntsville, Alabama—Chapter Ten, page 391.

index

LAS VEGAS: THE BEST OF GLITTER CITY

This impertinent insiders' guide explores the world's greatest party town, with expanded Ten Best lists of casino resorts, restaurants, attractions, buffets, shows, pubs, clubs and more! — *312 pages; $16.95*

NEVADA IN YOUR FUTURE

It's a complete relocation guide to the Silver State, with useful information for job-seekers, businesses, retirees and winter "Snowbirds." A special section discusses incorporating in Nevada. — *292 pages; $16.95*

SAN DIEGO: THE BEST OF SUNSHINE CITY

Winner of a Lowell Thomas gold medal for best travel guide, this lively and whimsical book features the finest of sunny San Diego, featuring its Ten Best attractions, restaurants and much more. —*248 pages; $16.95*

SEATTLE: THE BEST OF EMERALD CITY

This upbeat and opinionated book directs visitors to the very best of Emerald City's attractions, activities, restaurants and lodgings, with interesting side trips to the rest of Western Washington. —*236 pages; $15.95*

THE ULTIMATE WINE BOOK

This handy little pocket-sized book takes the mystique out of wine. It covers the subject in three major areas—Wine and Heath, Wine Appreciation and Wine with Food. And it does so with good humor, poking harmless fun at wine critics. —*194 pages; $10.95*

UNDISCOVERED AMERICA

Don't say you've been there and done that until you've read this fascinating guide to 201 of America's best undiscovered places. The authors have found intriguing attractions in all fifty states. They're a mix of cool towns and cities, overlooked national parks and monuments, intriguing vacation regions, scenic driving tours and more. — *448 pages; $18.95*